From the blazing North African desert
to the secret nerve-centers of
the Reich...

## THE SEARCH FOR THE TRUE
## FIELD MARSHAL ROMMEL

"The real Erwin Rommel, as British biographer David
Irving presents him to us, is even more interesting
than the legendary one. . . . A brilliant biography."
*The Christian Science Monitor*

"The most thrilling war book I have ever read. It yanks
Rommel out of the hazy aureole of legend and flings
him down before us: hungering for medals, escaping
unscathed while a shell blows his comrade's back off,
restaging whole battles for propagandists. I could no
more stop reading this book than the French could
stop Rommel's panzers."
David Kahn (author of *The Codebreakers*)

"Perhaps the most charismatic figure to have come out
of World War II. . . . Rich in detail, handsomely
illustrated: a treat."
*Business Week*

"A major achievement in the study of a complex yet
compelling man."
*King Features Syndicate*

**MAIN SELECTION OF
THE HISTORY BOOK CLUB**

*32 PAGES OF PHOTOGRAPHS*

# THE TRAIL OF THE FOX

## DAVID IRVING

AVON
PUBLISHERS OF BARD, CAMELOT AND DISCUS BOOKS

AVON BOOKS
A division of
The Hearst Corporation
959 Eighth Avenue
New York, New York 10019

First Avon Printing, November, 1978

AVON TRADEMARK REG. U.S. PAT. OFF. AND IN
OTHER COUNTRIES, MARCA REGISTRADA, HECHO EN
U.S.A.

Printed in the U.S.A.

# Contents

What will history say
in passing its verdict on me?
If I am successful here,
then everybody else
will claim all the glory. . . .
But if I fail,
then everybody
will be after my blood.

*—From the unpublished
Rommel diary,
April 16, 1944*

# On the Trail of
# the Fox

IT is May 18, 1944. At Hitler's war conference he is told that the enemy has carried out two spy operations during the night on the heavily defended French coastline. At one place, near Calais, German troops have found shovels and a flashlight lying on the beach after a shootout. At another, in the estuary of the river Somme, two British officers have been captured. "They came ashore by rubber dinghy," General Alfred Jodl, chief of Wehrmacht operations, tells Hitler. "Their interrogations so far have revealed that they were set down by a British motor launch."

The scene changes to a French château built against a steep rock face overlooking the Seine valley. It is two days later. A small German army staff car swerves into the driveway to the château and comes to a halt. Two soldiers climb out, stiff from their 150-mile drive from the coast of the English Channel. They lead two other men, blindfolded and handcuffed, from the car. These two men wear no insignia, but the empty stitching on their khaki battle dress shows all too clearly where the purple Combined Operations badge and the narrow Special Service shoulder flash have been removed; they are British commandos. Their blindfolds are untied, and they blink in the sunlight.

1

Their expressions are grim; they know that Hitler has given standing orders that all commandos are to be turned over to the Gestapo and shot.

When they are pushed into their cells, they find tea and sandwiches waiting for them. One of them, Lieutenant Roy Woodridge, curtly refuses to talk. The other, Lieutenant George Lane, is less tight-lipped and is taken to see Colonel Hans-Georg von Tempelhoff. A suave and handsome blond, Tempelhoff stands up and holds out his hand. "It must be very beautiful in England just now," he says pleasantly.

Lane's face betrays his surprise at the colonel's flawless English. Tempelhoff explains: "My wife is English." For a moment he stands eyeing Lane, then briskly directs him to wash his face and hands, clean his fingernails and smarten himself up. "You're going to meet somebody very important. Very important indeed. Field Marshal Rommel!"

The Allied invasion of Nazi-occupied France is just seventeen days away. In English harbors a mighty invasion fleet is assembling for the operation. Here in France, Hitler has put one man in command, his favorite field marshal, Erwin Rommel, the celebrated Desert Fox. Rommel is a veteran of campaigns against the British and Americans. He knows what makes them tick. He believes he can anticipate their every move. Luftwaffe reconnaissance planes have sighted landing craft massing across the Channel from the Somme estuary. This latest commando spy operation on that very coastline confirms to him that this is where the Allied invasion will come. How is Rommel to know that the landing craft are dummies and that these commandos have been deliberately played into Nazi hands to feed misleading information to him? It is all part of a deception plan code-named Fortitude, master-minded by British intelligence.

Rommel has chosen this château as his tactical headquarters because it is honeycombed with cellars. He has blasted more bombproof tunnels deep into the cliffs behind it. For the last five months he has been preparing the German army for the coming battle and devising ingenious and deadly anti-invasion defenses—spiked staves, barbs, submerged booby traps, minefields and entanglements. He is not surprised that the British are willing to take risks to find out what he is up to.

As Lane is brought into Rommel's study, the field marshal is seated at his desk in the far corner, gazing out of his window. It is a long room, hung with four priceless tapestries; rare carpets lie upon the highly polished floor; vases and lamps of ancient porcelain stand along the walls. Rommel himself is a short, stocky man with receding, close-cropped hair, a set jawline and penetrating gray-blue mastiff eyes. He is tanned from weeks of touring the new coastal fortifications. At his throat glitters the rare blue and gold cross of the Pour le Mérite, the highest medal in Prussia's power to give, awarded him in 1917.

Rommel rises, walks around his desk and courteously greets the British officer. Then he motions Lane over to a low round table, surrounded by antique chairs, on which orderlies have laid a rather incongruous collection of cheap metal teapots and exquisite bone china.

"So you're one of those commando gangsters?" Rommel asks the prisoner.

"I'm a commando and proud of it. But not a gangster. None of us are."

"Perhaps you aren't a gangster, but we've had some nasty experiences with you commandos. They haven't always behaved as impeccably as they should." Rommel smiles distantly. "You're in a bit of a spot. You know what we do with saboteurs . . ."

Lane turns to the interpreter and comments, "If your field marshal thinks I'm a saboteur he wouldn't have invited me here."

"So you regard this as an invitation?" asks Rommel, grinning.

Lane bows slightly. "I do, and I must say I'm highly honored."

At this everybody chuckles. Rommel casually inquires, "How's my old friend General Montgomery?"

"Very well, thank you," replies Lane. "I hear he's planning some sort of invasion . . ."

Rommel feigns surprise. "You mean there really is going to be one?"

"So the *Times* tells us," the prisoner answers, "and it's usually reliable enough."

"You realize this is going to be the first time that the British have had to put up a proper fight?"

"What about Africa, then?"

"That was child's play," scoffed Rommel. "The only reason I had to retreat there was that no more supplies were getting through to me."

For twenty minutes Rommel reminisces about the war and lectures Lane on Britain and its fading empire and on the great future of Hitler's Third Reich. Lane listens spellbound and finally asks permission to put a question himself: "Would your Excellency tell me whether you regard military occupation as an ideal situation for a vanquished country?"

Rommel argues that by their very upbringing soldiers make ideal dictators. Soldiers are accustomed to crisis, they know how to master even the direst emergency. "If you travel around occupied France today and keep your eyes open, you'll see everywhere just how happy and contented the French people are. For the first time they know just what they have to do—because we are telling them. And that's the way the man in the street likes it!"

After a time the blindfold is replaced on Lieutenant Lane. In this brief interview something of Rommel's magnetism has electrified him, and as he is led out to the car to resume his journey to a prison camp and safety—as the field marshal has personally guaranteed—Lane grasps the arm of Colonel Anton Staubwasser, Rommel's intelligence officer.

"Do me one favor," he says. "Tell me—where am I now?"

Staubwasser politely refuses, for security reasons. Lane tightens his grip and pleads with him: "I swear I'll never tell anyone. But when this war's over I want to come back here with my wife and children—I want to show them where I met Rommel!"

*The records that relate Erwin Rommel's illustrious career are now widely scattered in archives throughout the Western world. This story of the commandos, for example, is documented in the German army's interrogations of the two British prisoners, and these interrogations are among the papers of a former German intelligence officer, stored*

4

*in the Black Forest. The incident is referred to also in the shorthand notes taken on Hitler's daily war conferences, deposited in an American university. It is recounted in the private diaries of German officers close to Rommel, and in the recollections of George Lane himself, which he wrote when he returned to England.*

*To get beyond the myth-marshal of historiography and discover the true Rommel, one must search in sources such as these. The trail of the fox leads from vaults in West Germany to government files in Washington, from a military museum in South Carolina to presidential libraries in Kansas and Missouri, from the drawing rooms of Rommel's surviving comrades to the musty attics with their tantalizing boxes and files of papers as yet unopened by the widows and families of the comrades who died. These records conduct us through the hills of Rommel's native Swabia, up Alpine gorges, across the sand-swept tableland of Cyrenaica, to the tangled bocage of Normandy. Sometimes the trail grows faint, or vanishes. There are gaps in the evidence that none of the documents, memoirs or interviews can fill. Those aspects of Rommel must remain a mystery. But the trail leads eventually to a fuller understanding of this extraordinary man, and to the final mystery: why he chose to die as he did.*

In 1944 Rommel was already a living legend. He was known as a great commander in the field, distinguished by that rare quality, a feeling for the battle. Bold, dashing and handsome, he was relentless in combat, magnanimous in victory and gracious to his vanquished enemies. He seemed invincible. Where he was, there was victory: he attacked like a tornado, and even when he withdrew, his enemies followed very gingerly indeed.

What were the principal elements of the Rommel myth in 1944? The first was his romantic image—a general, small in stature, with a vulpine cunning and a foxy grin, time and time again confounding a vastly superior enemy. He was regarded as a modern Hannibal, running rings around his foes, bewildering them, demoralizing them and snatching victory after victory until force majeure obliged even Rommel to cut his losses and retreat.

He was young for his rank, a born leader, adored by his troops. He was said to have revived a long-forgotten style of chivalrous warfare. In a war brutalized by the Nazi extermination camp and the Allied strategic bomber, Rommel's soldiers were ordered to fight clean. Prisoners were taken and then treated well—he ignored Hitler's order to execute captured members of the Jewish brigade. Private property was respected. In his files, dated October 15, 1943, is his secret instruction to all his commanders in Italy forbidding arbitrary looting, "to preserve the discipline and respect of the German Wehrmacht." He rejected the use of forced labor in France—workers were to be recruited and paid in the normal way. He disregarded Hitler's notorious "Commando Order" of October 1942, which made the execution of captured enemy commandos mandatory. When destitute Arabs were hired by the enemy to sabotage Axis installations, Rommel refused to encourage reprisals or the shooting of hostages. "It is better to allow such incidents to go unavenged than to hit back at the innocent," he said later.

He took no delight in the death of an enemy soldier. A Montgomery would order: "Kill the Germans wherever you find them!" An Eisenhower would proclaim: "As far as I am concerned, any soldier that is killing a German is somebody for whom I have a tremendous affection, and if I can give him something so he can kill two instead of one, by golly I am going to do it." Rommel never descended to such remarks. He outwitted, bluffed, deceived, cheated the enemy. It was said that his greatest pleasure was to trick his opponents into premature and often quite needless surrender.

He was, most spectacularly, a battlefield general, eagerly flinging himself into the fray, oblivious to danger. No enemy shell could cut him down, though men to his right and left were shot away; no mine could shatter his body, no bomb would fall near enough to kill him. He seemed immortal.

So powerful was Rommel's myth that it captivated even his enemies. The Allies unwittingly and then later deliberately publicized his invincibility—at first to explain away their own misfortunes in battle against him, then to make their victories over him seem worth that much more, and finally to conjure up a kind of anti-villain, a benign Nazi in contrast with whom the regular run of Nazis would seem all the more despicable. The time came when Rommel's name alone was worth entire divisions. When he fell ill, his name was left on the battlefield to fight on in absentia. When the enemy realized that he was indeed gone, they anxiously speculated where the Fox could now be. The OSS files in Washington bulged with reports that "Rommel" was now commanding a secret army in Greece, in Rumania, or Yugoslavia. Or was he really in Italy, or France? Twice he received the ultimate accolade, unprecedented in Allied military history: assassins were sent to gun him down. (Each time they missed. Like Hitler himself, Rommel seemed indestructible, and believed it himself.)

The mesmerization of the Allies was so extensive that in March of 1942 General Sir Claude Auchinleck, the British commander in North Africa, felt it necessary to warn his top officers in a memo: "There is a real danger that our friend Rommel will turn into a bogey-man for our troops just because they talk so much about him. He is not superhuman—energetic and capable though he is. And even if he were a superhuman, it would be most undesirable for our soldiers to attribute supernatural powers to him." Four months later a copy of this admonition came into Rommel's hands after a battle on the Egyptian frontier, and he smiled at Auchinleck's unconvincing postscript: "I am *not* jealous of Rommel." Still later, Rommel learned that Auchinleck's successor, Bernard Montgomery, had a framed portrait of Rommel hanging in his battle trailer. Rommel, however, was never bewitched by any of his enemies. In the thousands of pages of the Rommel diaries there is not one reference to an adversary by name.

If the enemy was enthralled by Rommel, how much more were his own people. As early as 1941, Rommel was the name on every German's lips. No film star was ever so lionized. Generals writing to other generals kept referring to this Rommel phenomenon, in lines tinged with both admiration and rue. He won battles that other good generals would probably have lost, they granted him that. But he had learned his tactics and strategy on the battlefield, an imperfect school; for a general, combat experience was not enough. Rommel disdained the war academies and their trained and elegant products, the officers of the General Staff, and he tried to do without the skills they set such store by—intelligence, logistics, signals, personnel, operations. General Enno von Rintelen later said, scoffing, "Rommel was just not a great strategist. He lacked the General Staff training for that, and this put him at a large disadvantage." General Gerhard von Schwerin, who fought under Rommel, said sardonically that Rommel "learned a lot by his own mistakes." Field Marshal Gerd von Rundstedt spoke of him contemptuously as "just a good division commander, but no more than that."

Some of these criticisms were well founded; even so, they revealed underlying hostilities. Unlike many of the older General Staff officers, Rommel was for most of his career a hardy supporter of Adolf Hitler and the New Germany, and this dedication repelled them. And there was envy. Much of it was fixed upon the publicity lavished upon Rommel as Hitler's favorite field marshal. It is true that Rommel quickly mastered the art of combat propaganda and appreciated its psychological effect on his own troops and also the enemy. "A kind of Rommel cult emerged," a general later wrote. "He seldom went anywhere without a posse of personal photographers." Many of the dramatic pictures of Rommel are as carefully posed as the famous Raising the Flag on Mount Suribachi. The various tactical headquarters in Africa soon learned that one way to attract his good humor was to station men with cameras at his arrival point—even if they had no film in their cameras. This attention-seeking struck many generals as "unprofessional" and they found it galling. Among the private papers of tank expert General Heinz Guderian is a letter written from the Moscow battlefront in which he instructed his wife: "Under no circumstances will I allow any propaganda ballyhoo over me à la Rommel, and I can only strengthen you in your determination to prevent it."

The envy of Rommel was expressed in many forms. "Every week he used to talk on the telephone with Hitler in person," said one general, repeating the popular allegation about Rommel, "and eagerly went over all his technical ideas with him." In fact, Rommel phoned Hitler only once during the entire war—and was so pleased to speak with his Führer that he mentioned it in many letters afterward. Thus the envy was to some degree a product of the myth. We shall find that the jealousy of his fellow generals played a significant part in Rommel's own tragic end. When he needed friends among his peers, there were none.

Since Rommel's death, his legend has grown. For many reasons, men have kept alive the fantasy image of the Fox. In postwar West Germany, the reputations of other field marshals have been allowed to lapse, as if in embarrassment or even antipathy, but Rommel's name has been burnished. It has been given to a warship by the navy, and the army has "Rommel barracks" in many a German town. There are Rommel streets, a unique distinction for any World War II German general, and there is even an alley named after his adjutant. His former enemies the Americans produced an adulatory film, *The Desert Fox,* and it was exceedingly popular. There has been little effort, however, to get behind the legend and come to terms with Rommel himself: was he a Nazi, to be despised, or a hero of the anti-Hitler resistance? This is one section of the trail we must pursue.

There is a moment in the Rommel story where he is in command of a panzer corps and has been advancing along an established, well-paved road. Suddenly he must take his entire reputation in both hands, abandon that road and plunge across a desert wilderness, uncharted and forbidding. It is like that with the trail on which we now set out. After a while we find that the legend is not enough. There follows an unknown land, into which we must now plunge.

9

# The Useful Soldier

*I*N *a mid-Victorian building just off St. James's Park in London a safe is opened and a thick, brown pasteboard folder tied with string is pulled out. The cover label was printed by the presses of the Prussian War Department long before the days of Hitler. It exudes the familiar stale paper smell that excites the senses of every trained historian—not that any other outside historian has been allowed to set eyes on this folder before. A notation in English has been written on it: "Top Secret. Personal File of Field Marshal Rommel and a copy of his Wehrpass." The Wehrpass, his service record book, is missing, no doubt removed by souvenir hunters. But the rest is there intact. The first documents date all the way back to March 1910; an eighteen-year-old youth, full name Johannes Erwin Eugen Rommel, a sixth-former at the secondary school in the Swabian township of Gmünd, is trying to get into the army.*

Erwin Rommel was a pale and often sickly youth. He had not set his heart on an army career. He had a mechanical bent and a vague hankering to be an aeronautical engineer. As a fourteen-year-old he, with a friend, had built a full-scale box-type glider in a field in nearby

Aalen—there is a tiny, faded brown photograph of it among family papers. He proudly boasted in later years that the glider did fly, although not far. It was still a triumph, considering that this was 1906, the year of the first powered flight in Europe.

His mother, Helene Rommel, was the daughter of a senior local dignitary, Regierungs-Präsident von Luz. Erwin took his looks from her, and adored her. His father was a schoolmaster, like his father's father before him. Headmaster of the secondary school at Aalen, Erwin Rommel, Sr. was strict and pedantic. His short hair was slicked down to either side of a fashionable middle part and his stern pince-nez eyeglasses rode tightly on the dominating nose. The face was characterless, which even a bushy walrus moustache failed to conceal. After his death in 1913, Erwin would mainly remember that his father constantly pestered him with educational questions: "What's the name of this building? What's the species of that flower?" He was harsh and overbearing and once provoked Erwin's older brother, Karl, into attacking him with a chair.

The family diverged in their careers. Brother Karl volunteered for the army—but only so as to avoid taking his final examinations. He became an army reconnaissance pilot, and his fine photographs of the Pyramids and the Suez Canal are in the family papers. Gerhard, youngest of the Rommel brothers—and still alive today—became a struggling opera singer. All three brothers and their sister, Helene, were closer to their mother than to their father, and his early death was little loss to them.

It was Rommel's father, however, who prodded the reluctant Erwin into the career for which he proved so splendidly suited. In a letter he recommended his schoolboy son to the Württemberg army as "thrifty, reliable and a good gymnast." Both the artillery and the engineers rejected young Rommel's application, but in March 1910 the 124th Württemberg Infantry Regiment ordered him to report for a medical examination. The doctors found that he had an inguinal hernia but was otherwise acceptable. His father arranged for the necessary operation and signed the papers promising to pay for his son's upkeep and to buy him a uniform as a Fahnenjunker, an officer cadet. On July 19, six days after leaving the hospital, eighteen-year-old Erwin joined his regiment. Soon afterward he was posted to the Royal Officer Cadet School in Danzig.

In his personnel file are two faded sheets in Rommel's own handwriting—at that time a regular, spiky copperplate—setting out the brief story of his own young life in so far as he believed it would interest the army:

*Aalen, March 1910.*—I was born on November 15, 1891, at Heidenheim on the Brenz as the second son of the schoolmaster Erwin Rommel and his wife Helene, née Luz, both of the Protestant faith. As far as I can recall my early years passed very pleasantly as I was able to romp around our yard and big garden all day long. . . .

I was supposed to start primary school in the fall when I was seven; but as my father was promoted to headmaster at Aalen that year and there is no primary school there, I had to acquire the necessary knowledge by private tuition in order to be able to get into the elementary school at Aalen. Two years later I entered the Latin School, and stayed there five years.

At about this time occurred the deaths of my dear maternal grandmother and my grandfather on my father's side as well. . . . In the fall vacation of 1907 I had the misfortune to break my right ankle jumping over a stream. But the foot was well set and it has healed satisfactorily, so that despite even the most strenuous activities I have never noticed any aftereffects. In the fall of 1908 I started in the fifth grade of the Royal Secondary Modern school at Gmünd and a year later the sixth grade, to which I still belong. The subjects that have most attracted me of late are mathematics and science.

I have occupied my spare time with homework and reading, and apart from that with physical exercises like cycling, tennis, skating, rowing, skiing, etc.
—ERWIN ROMMEL

When Rommel finished cadet school, in November 1911, the commandant wrote an evaluation of the earnest young man. In rifle and drill work, said the commandant, Rommel was "quite good." At gymnastics, fencing and riding he was "adequate." But, said the commandant somewhat anxiously, "he is of medium height, thin and physically rather awkward and delicate." Still the lad was "firm in character, with immense willpower and a keen enthusiasm. . . . Orderly, punctual, conscientious and comradely. Mentally well endowed, a strict sense of duty." Cadet Rommel was, said the commandant in prescient summary, "a useful soldier."

At Danzig, one of Germany's most beautiful Hanseatic ports, the cadets were obliged to attend regular formal balls in the officers' mess—functions of stifling propriety, at which the daughters of the good Danzig citizens were invited to present themselves. Young Erwin's attention was captured by a particularly graceful dancer, Lucie Mollin, a slender beauty whose father, like Rommel's, had been headmaster of a secondary school, but was now dead; she had come to Danzig to study languages. At first she found Erwin overly serious, but soon they fell deeply in love. She was tickled by the way he sported a monocle in the Prussian fashion. (He always tucked it out of sight when a superior officer met them in the city—cadets were forbidden to wear monocles!) When Erwin received his lieutenant's commission in January 1912, he had still not proposed to Lucie. Upon his return to Württemberg he began a daily correspondence with her—writing secretively to her in care of her local post office so that her mother could not intercept the letters. One photographic postcard to her pictures him in a straw hat at a period fashion ball. It is dated March 28, 1912. "I received your nice card from your hometown," wrote Erwin. "I'm still waiting for the photos. I'm going to get mad at you soon if you make me wait much longer. I'm looking forward hugely to your long letter. I hope you're going to make it really intimate."

The photo that Lucie sent him was a stunner. She had just won a tango competition, and her looks certainly had not let her down. All her ancestors' Italian and Polish blood was to be seen in her finely drawn features, and one sees in the family photo album that as Lucie matured, her beauty grew as well. There is a conventional portrait of Lucie and Erwin—she in a dark, wide-brimmed hat, he in the ferocious spiked helmet of the Württemberg army. There is a later picture of them, Lucie by now a Red Cross nurse and Erwin with an Iron Cross pinned to his uniform. And there is the most charming picture of them all, of Lucie—by now his wife—sitting with her head demurely inclined while Lieutenant Erwin Rommel stands proudly behind her, with the suggestion of a moustache upon his lip and a rare medal for valor on a ribbon at his throat.

The 124th Infantry was garrisoned in the ancient monastery at Weingarten, near Stuttgart. For the next two years Rommel drilled recruits. He had little in common with the other lieutenants. Virtually a nondrinker and a nonsmoker, he was serious beyond his age, dedicating himself with monastic devotion to his career. Nor did Rommel and the local women of Weingarten have time for each other. Later, in the years of his fame, he received many inviting letters from women, and he then said jokingly to Lucie, "If only I had got all these offers when I was a young Lieutenant!"

On March 1, 1914, Rommel was attached to the Forty-ninth Field Artillery Regiment at Ulm, not far from his hometown, and he was commanding a battery in this unit as the darkness of the First World War enveloped his fatherland. The original manuscript of his memoirs, later published as a book, vividly describes what he saw and felt at the time:

*Ulm, July 31, 1914*—Uneasy lies the German countryside beneath the sinister threat of war. Grave and troubled faces are everywhere. Fantastic rumors are running wild and spreading with lightning speed. Since dawn the kiosks have been besieged by people, as one extra follows another.

About 7:00 A.M. the Fourth Battery of the Forty-ninth Field Artillery clatters across the city's ancient cobblestones, with the regimental band in front. The strains of "The Watch on the Rhine" echo through the narrow streets. Every window is flung open; old and young join in the lusty singing.

I am riding as platoon leader of the neat horse-drawn battery I have been attached to since March 1. We trot out into the morning sun, exercise as we have done on other days and then ride back to barracks again accompanied by thousands of cheering people.

For me this is the last exercise with the artillery. . . . As things are now growing very serious indeed, I must get back to my own parent regiment, the 124th Infantry, at all costs. I must get back to the riflemen of Number Seven Company, whose last two years' recruits I have trained.

Helped by my orderly, Hanle, I hastily pack my worldly possessions. After I reach Ravensburg late in the evening, I walk to our garrison town—Weingarten—with my pal Lietuenant Bayer who has come to meet me. We talk about the grave times ahead of us in war, particularly for us young infantry officers.

In August 1914 the regimental barracks in the massive monastery at Weingarten is a beehive of activity. Outfitting in field gray! I report back from my posting and greet the men of Seven Company whom I'll probably be leading into battle. How all their young faces glow with joy, anticipation and fervor—surely there can be nothing finer than to lead such soldiers against an enemy!

At 6:00 P.M. the whole regiment is on parade. After Colonel Haas has inspected his riflemen in field gray for the first time, he delivers a fiery speech. As we fall out, the mobilization order itself arrives. So this is it! An exultant shout of militant German youth echoes around the time-honored walls of the monastery. Our Supreme Commander is calling us to arms! What we have only just promised to our regimental commander we can and shall now prove by our deeds as well: Faithful—unto death.

As darkness fell next evening, Rommel watched his regiment leave Ravensburg station for the western frontier, bands playing and crowds cheering. He himself followed three days later. The journey through Swabia's pretty valleys and meadows was unforgettable. The troops sang, and at each station they were welcomed with fruit, chocolates and bread.

"At Kornwestheim," wrote Rommel, "I see my mother and two brothers and sister for a few moments, then the locomotive whistles that it is time for farewells. One last look, a clasp of hands! We cross the Rhine at night, as searchlights finger the skies for enemy fliers and airships. The singing dies away. The riflemen fall asleep on seats and floors. I myself am standing on the loco's footplate, staring into the open firebox or out into the rustling and whispering of the oppressive summer night. Will I ever see my mother and family again? We arrive late on the afternoon of August 6, and we are happy to get out of the cramped transport train. We march through Diedenhofen to Ruxweiler. Diedenhofen itself is not a pretty place. The streets and houses are dirty, the people hostile. It is all so different from our Swabian homeland. We march briskly onward. As night falls, it begins to pour. Soon we are soaked to the skin. Our packs weigh us down. A fine start this is. We can hear sporadic shooting from the French frontier a few miles away."

The captured Rommel personnel files exhaustively document his subsequent campaigns and battles. For more than two years he stayed on the slaughterhouse battlefields of France. In September at Varennes he was wounded by a ricocheting rifle bullet in his left thigh—characteristically for him, he was confronting three French soldiers alone and with an empty rifle. He was awarded the Iron Cross, Second Class. When he returned to the 124th Infantry from the hospital on January 13, 1915, it was fighting in grueling trench warfare in the Argonnes forest. Two weeks later he crawled with his riflemen through 100 yards of barbed wire into the main French positions, captured four bunkers, held them against a counterattack by a French battalion and then withdrew before a new attack could develop, having lost less than a dozen men. This bravery won Rommel the Iron Cross, First Class—the first for a lieutenant in the entire regiment. In July he was again injured, this time by shrapnel in one shin. He hoped to be sent to the new Turkish war theater, and even began learning Turkish. But in October he was posted, as a company commander, to the new Württemberg Mountain Battalion. After a year of training, the battalion's six rifle companies and six mountain machine gun platoons were transferred to Rumania, where the Germans were fighting the Russians.

Even this early there was something that marked Rommel out from the rest. Theodor Werner, one of his platoon leaders, recalled: "When I first saw him [in 1915] he was slightly built, almost schoolboyish, inspired by a holy zeal, always eager and anxious to act. In some curious way his spirit permeated the entire regiment right from the start, at first barely perceptibly to most but then increasingly dramatically until everybody was inspired by his initiative, his courage, his dazzling acts of gallantry." Later, Werner became Rommel's aide. "Anybody who once came under the spell of his personality," Werner wrote, "turned into a real soldier. However tough the strain he seemed inexhaustible. He seemed to know just what the enemy were like and how they would probably react. His plans were often startling, instinctive, spontaneous and not infrequently obscure. He had an exceptional imagination, and it enabled him to hit on the most unexpected solutions to tough situations. When there was danger, he was always out in front calling on us to follow. He seemed to know no fear whatever. His men idolized him and had boundless faith in him."

January 1917 found Rommel commanding an Abteilung—an ad hoc detachment varying in strength from three to seven mountain companies. Until July the battalion was again stationed in France, then it returned to the Rumanian front. On August 10, only two days after his arrival there, Rommel was again wounded. A bullet fired from far in the rear passed through his left arm, but despite this injury Rommel fought on for two weeks. On September 26 his battalion was transferred to a far more demanding theater—northern Italy.

Since entering the war in 1915, the Italians had been fighting Austria with the hope of winning back the Adriatic port of Trieste. By the time Rommel arrived, eleven battles had already been fought on the frontier river, the Isonzo. A year later the Italians staged their twelfth attempt: fifty infantry divisions supported by thousands of guns had crossed the middle reaches of the river. Heavily outnumbered, the Austrians appealed for help. In response, the German supreme command created a Fourteenth Army, under General Otto von Below, to go to the Isonzo front. This was why in October 1917 Rommel again found himself marching toward the sound of gunfire.

The battlefield here was very different from France—it was a breathtaking backdrop of towering mountains, bottomless ravines, treacherous precipices, swirling mists and rushing rivers. Every enemy shell burst threatened to bury General von Below's troops under avalanches of rocks; every shot filled the air with razor-sharp rock splinters that killed or maimed any man they hit. It rained heavily, which helped conceal Below's coming offensive from the Italian defenders. But the rain had turned mountain streams into raging torrents that swept officers, men and pack animals to their deaths.

General von Below's aim was to penetrate the main defense line south of the Isonzo River. The high points of the line were the towering Monte Mataiur, Monte Kuk, Kolovrat Ridge and Hill 1114. Tens of thousands of Italian troops and well-constructed gun sites commanded each of these high points, and the German unit commanders scrambled to take them, knowing that honors would be the reward. The rivalry among these young officers—leading proud units from the German provinces of Bavaria, Silesia and Rommel's Swabia—was ferocious.

Lieutenant Ferdinand Schoerner, a Bavarian commander, set the pace, driving his coughing, staggering volunteers so ruthlessly forward—despite their heavy loads of machine guns and ammunition—that one of his men dropped dead from exhaustion before the unit reached the objective: Hill 1114, key to the whole Kolovrat Ridge. For taking Hill 1114, Schoerner was awarded Prussia's highest medal, the Pour le Mérite. That outraged Rommel. He considered that the credit was due him.

Rommel's part in breaching the Kolovrat position was indeed great. As night fell on that first day of the offensive, Schoerner's promising position had seemed thwarted by Italian fortifications. Rommel's superior, Major Theodor Sproesser, commander of the Swabians, wrote a battle report, a faded copy of which still survives, which describes the emplacements. "Like fortresses," he wrote, "the strongly built concrete gun positions . . . look out over us. They are manned by hard-bitten machine gunners, and bar our further advance to south and west." During the night Rommel reconnoitered the enemy defenses and found a gap, and shortly after dawn his Abteilung penetrated the Italian lines. Three hours later he stormed Monte Kuk itself. Finding Rommel in their rear, the Italians panicked, their line began to crumble and German infantry poured through the breach.

But Schoerner, the Bavarian, got the Pour le Mérite! Rommel was stung by this injustice, and after the war he asked the official army historian to make petty corrections to the record; he even arranged for future editions to read "Leutnant," not "Oberleutnant," in referring to Schoerner, and he persuaded the Reich government to print a fourteen-page supplement which in part set out his own role in more vivid detail—describing how forty Italian officers and 1,500 men had surrendered to Oberleutnant Rommel, how he had pressed on ahead of his unit with only two officers and a few riflemen, how the Italians had surrounded and embraced him and chaired him on their shoulders and rejoiced that the war was over for them. This sort of prideful revisionism would become part of the Rommel style.

But Rommel still had a chance for a Pour le Mérite. General von Below had specifically promised one to the first officer to stand atop the loftiest Italian high point, the 5,400-foot Monte Mataiur. Rommel intended to be that officer. His own fourteen-page supplement to the official army history tells the story: "Before the prisoners from the Hill 1114 engagement were removed, some German-speaking Italians betrayed to Lieutenant Rommel that there was another regiment of the Salerno brigade on Monte Mataiur that definitely would put up a fight. . . . Heavy machine gun fire did indeed open up as the [Swabians] reached the western slopes." By nightfall, after hours of hard fighting, Rommel was at the base of the last rise of Mataiur. He and his men were dog-tired, but he drove them on. The report of his superior, Major Sproesser, takes up the account: "There is an Italian with a machine gun sitting behind virtually every rock, and all the appearances are that the enemy has no intention of giving up Monte Mataiur so easily. Although their strength is almost at an end after fifty-three hours of continual full-pack march and battle, Rommel's Abteilung crawls in to close quarters. After a hail of machine gun fire, which has a murderous splinter effect among the rocks, the enemy tries to escape into a ravine."

Hesitantly, one Italian after another came out into the open and surrendered. At 11:30 A.M. the last 120 men on the actual summit surrendered to Rommel. Ten minutes later he stood there himself. He ordered one white and three green flares fired to announce his triumph. Rommel had reached the top first and victory was his—all the sweeter, too, for having cost the life of only one of his men.

The victory soon turned sour. Next day General Erich von Ludendorff, chief of the General Staff, announced the capture of Monte Mataiur—by the gallant Lieutenant Walther Schnieber, a Silesian company commander. Schnieber accordingly carried off the prize promised by General von Below for the feat, the coveted Pour le Mérite.

It was obvious to Rommel that Schnieber had captured the wrong summit. Choking with anger, he complained to his battalion commander, Major Sproesser. Sproesser advised him to forget the matter, but Sproesser did mention in his dispatch of November 1 that during the hour that Rommel's Abteilung had rested on the Mataiur's summit they never saw any signs of the Silesian regiment. Rommel was not satisfied, and—according to his own account many years later—he sent a formal complaint all the way to the commander of the Alpine Corps, claiming that the medal belonged by rights to him. Silence was the only reply.

This disappointment did not effect Rommel's fighting zeal. He stayed hard on the heels of the retreating Italians. His Abteilung was at the head of Sproesser's battalion of Swabians, and that battalion was the spearhead of the whole Fourteenth Army. On November 4 the river Tagliamento was reached. Now Rommel began a relentless pursuit of the demoralized Italians, using the same tactics of bluff, bravado, surprise attack and rapid pursuit that were to distinguish him later as a tank commander.

He had found his métier. He had learned how to exploit sudden situations—even when it meant disobeying orders from superiors. He led his troops to the limits of human endurance so as to take the enemy by surprise—climbing through fresh snowfalls that were murder to the heavily laden men, scaling sheer rock faces that would give pause even to skilled mountaineers, risking everything to work his handful of intrepid riflemen and machine gunners around behind the unsuspecting Italian defenders. He suddenly attacked the enemy—however greatly he was himself outnumbered—from the rear with devastating machine gun fire on the assumption that this was bound to shatter the morale of even the finest troops.

His little force's victories were remarkable. On November 7, Rommel's companies stormed a 4,700-foot mountain and captured a pass. Two days later he launched a frontal attack on some seemingly invincible Italian defenses and captured another pass. Then followed an action of the purest Wild West, one that wonderfully illustrates Rommel's physical courage and endurance.

He was following an extremely narrow and deep ravine toward the town of Longarone—the kingpin of the entire Italian mountain defensive system. What Rommel found ahead of him was a road blasted into the vertical rock face soaring 600 feet above. The road first clung to one side of the ravine, then crossed to the other side by a long bridge precariously suspended some 500 feet above the ravine floor.

"Relentlessly the pursuit goes on toward Longarone," Major Sproesser wrote. "Now the big bridge spanning the Vajont ravine lies ahead. Not a moment to lose! . . . Lieutenant Rommel and his men dash across, tearing out every demolition fuse they can see."

The Swabians took the next stretch of road at a trot. But when they emerged from the valley, they came under heavy rifle and machine gun fire from the direction of Longarone, about a half mile away. Between them and the town lay the river Piave. Almost at once a loud explosion signaled the demolition of the only bridge across the river. Through field glasses Rommel could see endless columns

21

of Italians fleeing south on the far side of the river. The town itself was jam-packed with troops and war paraphernalia. He ordered one of his companies and a machine gun platoon to advance downstream. He himself went with them, then watched as eighteen of his men successfully braved the Piave's fast-flowing waters under violent enemy machine gun fire. More men followed, and by 4:00 P.M. they had established a position on the other shore, a short distance south of Longarone. From there they could block the road and railway line leading out of town. Over the next two hours this small force disarmed 800 Italian soldiers who ran into their trap.

As dusk fell, Rommel himself forded the river, followed by five companies of troops. Taking a small party, he began to advance on Longarone. Stumbling into a street barricade manned by Italian machine gunners, Rommel ordered a temporary retreat, and now the Italians began running after him. It was a tricky situation: there were some 10,000 Italian troops in Longarone, so Rommel was vastly outnumbered. In fact, he had only twenty-five men with him at that moment, and when the Italian officers saw how puny Rommel's force was, they confidently ordered their men to open fire. All Rommel's force here was wounded or captured, but he himself managed to slip away into the shadows.

He reassembled his Abteilung just south of Longarone in the darkness. Six more times the Italian mob tried to overrun him, but six times Rommel's machine gunners sent them running for cover back into the town. To prevent the enemy from outflanking him in the darkness, Rommel set fire to the houses along the road, illuminating the battlefield. By midnight, reinforcements began arriving from Major Sproesser and from an Austrian division.

Rommel decided to renew the attack at dawn. His official account concludes: "There is, however, no more fighting to be done. South of Rivalta, Rommel's Abteilung meets Lieutenant Schoeffel, who was taken prisoner during the night's skirmish, coming toward them. Behind him follow hundreds of Italians, waving all manner of flags. Lieutenant Schoeffel brings the glad tidings of the surrender of all enemy forces around Longarone, written by the

Italian commander. An entire enemy division has been captured! . . . Exhausted and soaking wet, the warriors . . . fall into well-earned beds in fine billets and sleep the sleep of dead men."

In his later published account of the battle of Longarone, Rommel romanticized. There he described how he himself had swum the icy Piave at the head of his Abteilung. Yet there can be no doubt of his own physical courage in battle, even if these 1917 victories over the Italians were purchased relatively cheaply. In the ten-day battle ending in the Italians' humiliating defeat at Longarone, Sproesser's entire battalion lost only thirteen enlisted men and one officer (he fell off a mountain). At Longarone, Rommel captured 8,000 Italians in one day. Not for another quarter century would Rommel really meet his match.

One month later, the Kaiser gave him the tribute he ached for, the matchless Pour le Mérite. The citation said it was for breaching the Kolovrat line, storming Mataiur and capturing Longarone. Rommel preferred to attribute it to Mataiur alone—unless he was in Italian company; then he took a certain sly pleasure in saying he won it at Longarone. Rommel was never diplomatic.

After that he always wore the distinctive cross on a ribbon around his neck. But he sensed the envy that his fellow officers felt about it. He told his old school friend Hans Seitz years later, "You can't imagine how jealous the officers are of my Pour le Mérite. There's no spirit of comradeship at all."

There weren't many men entitled to wear the medal—a Maltese Cross of dazzling electric-blue enamel trimmed in gold, on a black and silver ribbon. Most of them—men like air heroes Ernst Udet, Werner Mölders and Baron von Richthofen—became legends in their own lifetime.

*Where is Rommel's medal now? In a little village office in Swabia is a cheap metal cupboard, pretentiously described as the Rommel Archives. The archives are opened only one day a year, October 14. The day I visited, it was October 16. But they opened it for me all the same, showed me the contents and asked me to lock up before*

*I left. I found a few letters, photograph albums and other memorabilia.*

*On the cupboard floor was a dusty cardboard box. In it was the Pour le Mérite, its enamel slightly chipped where once it struck an asphalt road. In the same box was a high-peaked cap. A pair of yellowing Perspex goggles. Three glass bottles filled with desert sands of different colors. And a khaki sleeve brassard, with a silver palm tree motif and one word: "Afrika."*

# The Instructor

ERWIN Rommel had gone briefly on leave to Danzig late in 1916, and there he had married his Lucie. She was twenty-two, dark-eyed and lithe. He had just turned twenty-five, was upright, fair-haired and jerky. After his return to the battlefield their correspondence resumed—in fact, they kept up a daily correspondence throughout their marriage, whenever they were apart. He was deeply dependent on her emotionally, and he yearned for home life with her.

When he returned from the First World War, Lucie was no longer a girl but already a woman of resolute character, with a direct gaze and handsome features. Gone was the delicate ballroom bloom of Danzig. She still liked to laugh, long and loud, but she was not easygoing. She completely dominated Erwin. He adored her. "It was wonderful to see how much Erwin fussed around her," one of her women friends recalls. "His favorite phrase seemed to be, 'Whatever you say, Lucie!'" Toward the end Lucie became something of a virago. If she cast out a friend, all her other friends had to ostracize that woman, too. Rommel indulged her, but in 1944, as we shall see later, it had the most unforeseen consequence for him when Lucie picked a row with the wife of Rommel's chief of staff.

The First World War ended with Rommel twenty-seven and an army captain. He had been posted early in 1918 to the staff of an army corps, and this brief experience of paper work had cured him of any desire to become a staff officer. The rigors of war had made a tough and wiry man of him. He was stocky now and no longer a weakling. He offset his shortness by a harsh parade-ground voice and a rough manner, reverting to the lisping Swabian dialect only when among friends.

Germany in 1918, after its collapse, was in the throes of upheaval—political, social and economic. Bands of Communists and revolutionaries roamed the streets. The armies had marched back into Germany following the armistice in good order, and the new republic turned to the army officers to restore stability. In March 1919, Rommel found himself sent to Friedrichshafen on Lake Constance to command Number Thirty-two Internal Security Company, a truculent bunch of Red sailors who jeered at his medals and refused to drill. He soon licked them into shape. His file shows that in the spring of 1920 he was also involved in "operations against rebels in Münsterland and Westphalia," and his adjutant Ernst Streicher has described one episode in which Rommel used fire hoses like machines guns against revolutionaries storming the town hall of Gmünd, dampening their violent ardor.

He was in fact very lucky to be able to stay in the army; many officers were being let go. A civilian existence would have been unthinkable for Rommel. The army was his life. The few existing photographs of him in plain clothes show him an awkward, shambling misfit, a figure somewhat reminiscent of a small-time hoodlum. Without that uniform, helmet and, above all, the blue enamel medal, he was not one tenth the man.

In these last years before Hitler, the Germany army was in the doldrums, but Rommel was busy. On October 1, 1920 he went to Stuttgart to command a rifle company in an infantry regiment—part of the tiny army permitted to Germany by the Treaty of Versailles. He stayed a company commander in Stuttgart for the next nine years, expanding his knowledge of the art of war. He studied the heavy machine gun, becoming proficient at firing and dismantling it. He learned all there was to know about the internal combustion engine. He also found time to teach his riflemen the social graces, even organizing dances. He acquired a dog, started a stamp collection, resumed his painful attempts to learn the violin and pulled a motorcycle apart and put it together again. He showed his men how to build a ski hut in the mountains and how to make a collapsible boat. Rommel put a lot of emphasis on sports.

Lucie, too, was forced to join in some of these arduous endeavors with him. She lamely protested, "I swim just about as well as a lead duck!" He nearly lost her when she capsized a boat. On one occasion he took her skiing, but she sat down stubbornly in the snow and moaned about the cold. Erwin called back to her, "You'd better get up—I don't recommend death by freezing." But she stayed put, so he had to give in and let her ride back down the mountain.

And so went the early years of the marriage and Rommel's early career—the uneventful 1920s. In 1927 he sat Lucie on the pillion seat of his motorcycle and took her around the scenes of his war exploits in Italy. But German officers were not popular there; his camera aroused hostility in Longarone and he was asked to leave. After that trip Lucie was allowed a respite, because she was expecting a child. The baby was born in December 1928, a boy. Rommel called him Manfred and had great hopes for him.

In Rommel's confidential personnel file are several of the annual evaluations of him written by his superiors with ponderous Teutonic thoroughness. How different his personality at this time seems from that of his later years. In September 1929 his battalion commander described him as "a quiet, sterling character, always tactful and modest in his manner." He went on to laud Rommel's "very great military gifts," particularly his sure eye for terrain. "He has already demonstrated in the war that he is an exemplary combat commander. He has shown very good results training and drilling his company. . . . There is more to this officer than meets the eye." The officer suggested that Rommel might make a good military instructor. This advice was heeded. On October 1, 1929, Rommel was posted to Dresden's School of Infantry.

A junior instructor, he concentrated on turning out

lieutenants who would make good company commanders. "I want to teach them first how to save lives," he would say. This was one lesson Rommel had learned from the war: he wanted different kinds of commanders from those who had so callously sent good men to their slaughter. "Shed sweat—not blood," was another of his maxims; he wanted the lieutenants to realize the value of proper digging in.

Here at Dresden he ran into Ferdinand Schoerner, his old rival from the Italian campaign, who had infuriated Rommel by winning the Pour le Mérite for the capture of Hill 1114. Schoerner was also an instructor now, and a favorite of the school's commandant, who, like Schoerner, was a Bavarian. Schoerner often played practical jokes on Rommel, who did not always know how to reply. One of Schoerner's frequent pranks was to plant silver cutlery from the mess in the pockets of guests at formal banquets and watch their embarrassment when the spoons and forks fell out. Rommel, when it happened to him, was not amused. Their rivalry persisted to the end. It was generally friendly, and once, after Schoerner had made a name for ruthlessness bordering on brutality in the Crimea in 1944, Rommel solicitously took him aside and candidly urged him to try a different method. Schoerner won Hitler's last major victory against the Russians, in 1945, and to him went an unusual posthumous "distinction." On his death as a field marshal in 1974 the West German government secretly circularized all offices, *forbidding* any tokens of respect. How different from the case of Rommel, as we shall see.

Rommel was one of the most popular instructors at Dresden. As a virtuoso at small-scale wars in difficult terrain, he lectured on the system he had used to beat the bunkers in the Argonne forest and his cunning employment of machine guns in the mountain warfare in Rumania and Italy. He never spoke more than ten minutes without sketching an illustration and projecting it onto a screen for the cadets to see. When other lecturers tried it, the cadets dozed off in the darkness. One instructor complained at having been allotted the difficult Monday morning slot. Rommel volunteered to fill it—"I can guarantee they won't fall asleep on me!"

Most popular of all was his talk on Mataiur—the battle around which his whole young life revolved. Another instructor wrote years later, "You can understand Rommel only by taking his storming of Mount Mataiur into account. Basically he always stayed that lieutenant, making snap decisions and acting on the spur of the moment." In a confidential report in September 1931 the school commandant wrote on Rommel: "His tactical battle lectures, in which he describes his own war experiences, offer the cadets not only tactical but also a lot of ideological food for thought. They are always a delight to hear." A year later the senior instructor added: "He is a towering personality even in a milieu of hand-picked officers. . . . A genuine leader, inspiring and arousing cheerful confidence in others. A first-rate infantry and combat instructor, constantly making suggestions and above all building up the cadets' characters. . . . Respected by his colleagues, worshiped by his cadets."

In October 1933 he moved up to a battalion command in Goslar, in the Hartz mountains of central Germany. The Third Battalion of the Seventeenth Infantry Regiment was a Jäger battalion—literally "hunters," but in fact a rifle battalion distinguished merely by a traditional service color of green instead of white. Rommel, however, insisted that all his officers should learn to hunt and shoot, until stalking and killing became second nature to them. Here, in the forests with horse and gun, he spent two of his happiest years since the war. From the start he outclassed all his men in toughness. On the day he had arrived at his new command, his officers had tried to deflate him by inviting him to climb and ski down a local mountain. He did so, three times; when he invited them to a fourth ascent, they blanched and declined. "Head and shoulders above the average battalion commander in every respect," was how the regiment's commander appraised him in September 1934. A year later his successor wrote of Rommel, now a lieutenant colonel: "His Jäger battalion is in fact the 'Rommel battalion.' He is preeminently qualified to be a regional commander or senior instructor."

It was at Goslar in 1934 that Rommel had his first incidental meeting with the man who was to be his destiny, Adolf Hitler. The Nazis had swept to power in January 1933 on a rising tide of unemployment and militant unrest. Within a year, by radical reforms and revolutionary economic measures, Hitler had cured most of the economic troubles and restored the country's lost national pride. He secretly assured his generals that the German army's famed strength would be restored and that a campaign of imperial conquest in the east would be launched when he was ready. Thus he won the generals' support. Just how he captured the colonels', too, is evident from Rommel's case.

Rommel was virtually nonpolitical. If anything, he leaned toward the socialists, the typical reaction of a combat soldier to the callous upper classes whom he blamed for the horrors of the battlefield. (At home once, his son, Manfred, asked what war was like. By way of answer Rommel deftly sketched a surrealist scene of ruined horses, broken trees, mud and slaughter.) As he was also a patriot, the appeal of the Nazis was strong. Most of their radical slogans left him unmoved. When Manfred once pointed to the hooked nose of the Goslar battalion's medic, one Doctor Zechlin, and innocently asked, "Papa, is *he* a Jew?" Rommel was highly indignant. Like most of his brother officers, he loathed the brownshirted bullies of Ernst Röhm's Sturmabteilung, the SA—the private army of 2 million men who had strutted and persecuted as they policed the Nazi rise to power. The regular army, of only 100,000 professional soldiers, had good cause to fear the SA now that Hitler was in power: there were signs everywhere by early 1934 that Röhm was preparing a take-over. Rommel could see the SA's preparations right under his nose in Goslar. Then—in the notorious Night of the Long Knives in June 1934—Hitler struck: he massacred Ernst Röhm and many of his unsavory cronies. The entire army hailed Hitler's strike with relief, and Rommel was relieved, too, although to his adjutant he privately expressed criticism of the actual massacre. "The Führer did not have to do that," he said. "He doesn't realize how powerful he is, otherwise he could have exercised his strength in a more generous and legitimate way."

Still, according to Manfred his father's tolerant attitude

toward the Nazis—to put it no higher—can be traced back to that date. Manfred was only six at the time, but his father obviously discussed it quite openly with him in later years. Lucie's letters show that she came to admire Hitler with an almost religious fervor, while Erwin's stolid prose betrays at most an initial gratitude for the esteem in which Hitler held the army, followed by admiration for his incisive leadership—as shown against the SA—and his military "genius."

*I tried hard to establish the date of their first meeting— Hitler and Rommel. In his early biography of Rommel, Brigadier Desmond Young ascribed it to September 1935, but all the sources, including Young, agree that the occasion was when Hitler came to Goslar to meet a farmer's delegation before the annual Harvest Festival, a huge open-air rally of a million farm workers from all over Germany. My researches indicated that they in fact met on September 30, 1934—from Martin Bormann's diary we know that there was no other date when Hitler visited Goslar at a time when Rommel still commanded the Jäger battalion. I put the question to Manfred the next time I visited him. Manfred said, "I think I can settle that right away." He went upstairs and returned with a framed photograph of the event. It bore the pencil inscription: "1934." It shows Hitler inspecting the battalion's guard of honor at the Kaiserpfalz castle, with Rommel's surprisingly small figure at his side. Rommel is wearing a steel helmet that looks as large as a coal scuttle, and polished riding boots. Their meeting was in fact only formal, and we have no evidence of Rommel's impressions that day.*

One year later, in 1935, he was posted to Potsdam, the cradle of Prussian militarism. "I have been earmarked as a full-blown instructor at the new Potsdam school of infantry," he wrote delightedly to Lucie. "Top secret! So make tracks for Potsdam! But keep it under your hat!"

The Kriegsschule was alive with activity. In March of 1935 Hitler had defiantly proclaimed the expansion of the Wehrmacht and the reintroduction of conscription. Thousands of new army officers were undergoing training. Two hundred and fifty at a time, the cadets marched into the academy's Hall of Field Marshals and listened spellbound to Rommel's lectures, while the oil paintings of forty German and Prussian field marshals looked down approvingly from the walls.

Rommel emphasized the need for physical fitness. When Cadet Hellmuth Freyer—asked for his views in 1937—respectfully submitted: "Two hours' early morning PT is too much, we are too tired afterward to follow the lectures properly," Rommel barked at him to be about his business. Most of the cadets liked his style and individuality. They adored his disrespectful attitude toward the red-trousered General Staff officers. "Those men are like marble," he told Kurt Hesse, who lectured on the history of Prussia. "They are smooth, cold and black at heart." When his cadets quoted Clausewitz at him— Clausewitz was the staff officers' military gospel—Rommel would snap back: "Never mind what Clausewitz thought, what do *you* think?" In fact his idol was Napoleon, also a man of action. As a young lieutenant he had bought an engraving of Napoleon on Saint Helena, gazing out to sea, and hung it on the wall. It took Lucie to bring a portrait of a German military hero, Frederick the Great, into their matrimonial home.

Erwin and Lucie lived very quietly near the Potsdam academy and did not mingle with Berlin society or the new elite. Unlike other war heroes, Rommel did not frequent the luxurious restaurants such as the leather-paneled Horcher's. He kept fit, went riding, practiced his hobbies. He memorized the table of logarithms, no small feat as mathematicians well know, and could thus perform astounding mental calculations like extracting the seventeenth root of any given number. He tried to interest Manfred in mathematics too; indeed, he spent the last days of his life vainly trying to explain differential calculus to his willfully uncomprehending son. "My father," says Manfred now, "had three ambitions for me: he wanted me to become a fine sportsman, a great hero and a good mathematician. He failed on all three counts."

Rommel naturally tried out his own dogmas on Manfred. "Courage is easy," was one of them. "You just have to overcome fear for the first time." Manfred still winces when he recalls how his father tried that idea on him when he was eight. "I found myself marching gamely at his side to the Potsdam swimming pool," Manfred said, "clutching his hand, with a big rubber swimming ring under my other arm. He made me go up to the top diving board and told me to jump. That's when I discovered there's a big difference between theory and practice. My father had collected all his cadets to watch. I said, 'I'm not going to jump.' He asked why not, and I shouted back down to him, 'Because I value my life. I can't swim.' My father reminded me that I was wearing the ring. 'What if the ring bursts,' said I, and my father reddened and shouted back that then he would jump in and save me. 'You're wearing riding boots!' I pointed out, and he replied that he would take them off if the need arose. 'Take them off *now*,' I challenged him. My father looked around at all the cadets, and refused. So I climbed back down the ladder."

One might say that Manfred had inherited and employed the strategy of the indirect approach many years before his father first used it to brilliant effect in his own campaigns.

When Manfred was seven, his father took him to the academy for his first ride on a horse; it was done in secret, for Lucie believed the child was too young to ride. His feet were tucked into the stirrup straps, since his legs were too short to reach the stirrups. The horse bolted and dragged the boy for 100 yards by one leg. Manfred's head was gashed, and Rommel was horrified. He pressed a coin into the boy's hand. "If you tell your mother you fell downstairs, when you get home, you can keep this!" At home the wound was bathed in iodine. Manfred howled with pain. Rommel furiously demanded his money back—but Manfred was a good Swabian and had already tucked the coin away. Colonel Rommel did not let him ride again.

*Very early in my researches, I turned to the thousands of letters exchanged between Rommel and Lucie during their years together. The letters had been taken from the family by the Americans in 1945 but were eventually returned intact—except for a few written early in 1943, in which Rommel, somewhat prematurely, questioned the ability of certain U.S. generals. I learned that the letters are now in an archive in Germany—but closed until the coming century. Then I discovered that the Americans had made a microfilm copy, and that it was in the National Archives in Washington. But this copy was locked away too. No one was allowed to see it. I appealed to Lucie. She gave me a hand-written letter of access, and the officials in Washington finally produced the film from their safe.*

*Erwin's letters display what had by now become large, flourishing penmanship. He dashed them off once and sometimes twice a day on whatever paper came to hand in his office or battle headquarters. Lucie's are carefully composed in a tight and regular hand. Her later letters were typewritten; her former manservant Rudolf Loistl told me, "She was a real night bird. I used to hear her typing until two or three in the morning, letters to him." Her letters show shrewdness and perception unusual for a soldier's wife. Although she was initially a rather more uncritical admirer of Adolf Hitler than her husband, some of her letters after 1939 show that nonetheless she was concerned about Germany's future.*

*Erwin's letters sometimes disappoint. Their language is often dull, their grammar is unsteady, they are repetitive and even philistine. His only cultural reference in them is to a visit to the ballet (it had bored him). He was in fact a single-minded army officer, wrapped up in army life. Theodor Werner, his aide in the First World War, writes: "There wasn't much talk on his staff. I can't recall that there was ever any discussion of religion or philosophy." Yet their value as biographical documents is undeniable. There are indiscreet snap judgments on contemporaries, there are lines written with casual disregard for secrecy. Above all, they are reliable as source material where, for instance, war diaries are not. Diaries can always be back-dated or altered to their authors' advantage, but letters once consigned to the mailbox are beyond the correcting hand guided by hindsight.*

*To read everything that a man writes over thirty years to his wife is to gain some insight into that man's soul— his inner torments and ambitions, his moods and intimate beliefs. The sheer frequency with which certain ideas re-cur in Rommel's letters is a guide to his inner imperatives. The letters show him well endowed with all the traditional Swabian characteristics—thrift, frugality, homesickness, loyalty, industry. They show him hungry for responsibility and greedy for medals and acclaim. Rommel relished rivalry and made no attempt to set aside old feuds or restore broken friendships. He bore a fashionable contempt for the privileged classes and the nobility. When he learned in 1939 of an embezzlement scandal involving an aristocratic cavalry captain, Rommel triumphantly wrote to Lucie: "And he had married a countess too! C——now agrees that my views on the aristocracy have proved more accurate than his own."*

It was September 1936 before Hitler really noticed Rommel. He had been attached to Hitler's escort for the Nazi Party rally in Nuremberg, a fairly routine job which made Rommel responsible for the little more than security arrangements. One day Hitler decided to go for a drive, and instructed Rommel to ensure that no more than half a dozen cars followed. At the appointed hour Rommel found the road outside Hitler's quarters seething with ministers, generals, gauleiters and their cars, all jostling for a place in Hitler's excursion. Rommel let the first six pass, then stepped into the road and halted the rest. The party notables loudly swore at him. "This is monstrous, colonel, I intend to report this to the Führer." Rommel replied that he had stationed two tanks farther down the road to block it. Hitler sent for Rommel that evening and congratulated him on executing his orders so well.

Another matter soon brought Rommel to Hitler's attention again. While senior instructor of the A Course at Potsdam, Rommel had taken his lecture notes, dramatically rewritten them in the present tense, edited them into a taut, exciting book and submitted it to a local publisher, Voggenreiter's. It appeared early in 1937 as *Infanterie Greift an* [The Infantry Attacks]. Hitler certainly read it, and it was probably one of the best infantry manuals ever written. It attracted wide acclaim and went into one edition after another. Rommel confessed to his fellow instructor, Kurt Hesse, "It's astounding, the money there is to be made from such books. I just don't know what to do with all the cash that's flooding in. I can't possibly use it all, I'm happy enough with what I've got already. And I don't like the idea of making money out of writing up how other good men lost their lives."

For tax reasons too, the royalties were an embarrassment. In 1976 the Stuttgart revenue office returned his old tax files to the family—and these indicate just how he contrived to conceal his considerable literary income from the Reich fiscal authorities. Perhaps it was sheer innocence, but more probably it was the foxy cunning that marked Rommel out even among Swabians: he simply directed Voggenreiter's to pay him each year only 15,000 Reichsmarks from the accumulating fortune and to keep the rest on account for him, gathering interest. On his tax returns, Rommel declared only the 15,000 Reichsmarks.

As Rommel's book became a best seller, Germany's youth came to worship him, and he liked it. "Working with the lads here is a *real* joy," he had written to his adjutant from Dresden in 1931. His views about youth were conservative. Once he told an army officer he met skiing in the mountains, "I regard it as my job to combat the mood of modern youth—against authority, against their parents, against the church and against us too." This sort of attitude won favor with the Inspector of War Schools, Lieutenant General Georg von Küchler, who wrote a report noting that Lieutenant Colonel Erwin Rommel was "a senior instructor with a particularly powerful influence on youth." Somebody's ears evidently pricked up at this last sentence, because in February 1937 Rommel was assigned an unusual new job—the War Ministry's special liaison officer to Baldur von Schirach, leader of the Hitler Youth.

At twenty-nine, Schirach was leader of 5,400,000 boys. His organization gave them sport, culture and the Nazi philosophy. The War Ministry had decided that they must receive paramilitary training too. Had not the battle of Königgrätz been won in the classrooms of Prussia's elementary schools? The Führer himself had written in *Mein Kampf,* "The army is to be the ultimate school for patriotic education," and had stated, "In this school the youth shall turn into a man."

The liaison was doomed to failure. Schirach was eleven years younger than Rommel, handsome and westernized (his mother was American). Rommel was so Prussian that Schirach was astounded to hear him talk in the Swabian tongue when they first met in April in the Youth leader's lakeside home. "Rommel stayed to supper," Schirach recalled. "My wife drew his attention to the beautiful view onto the Bavarian mountains from our window. This cut no ice with him. 'Thank you, but I'm very familiar with *mountains*,' he said, without even so much as glancing out of the window. Henriette had unintentionally given our guest his cue, because Rommel had received the Pour le Mérite in 1917 for storming some mountain or other in the Julian Alps. He now held forth on this for two hours. I found his story quite interesting, but to Henriette all such military matters were anathema and she nearly fell asleep." A month later Schirach reluctantly introduced Rommel to 3,000 Hitler Youth leaders during a camp at Weimar.

At about this time Rommel produced a startling plan: the Wehrmacht's young bachelor lieutenants should be brought in to train the Hitler Youth. Schirach said he strongly doubted that young army officers had nothing better to do with their free weekends than drilling hordes of boys in how to stand at attention. Rommel replied, "They will just be ordered to." Schirach fobbed him off. "Rommel was put out by this," said Schirach. "He then journeyed up and down the country a lot, speaking to my Hitler Youth leaders. The content of his speeches was always the same, how he had stormed Monte Mataiur. . . . Willing to hero worship though they were, my more intelligent leaders took umbrage and protested to me. Rommel, moreover, was propagating some kind of premilitary education, which would have transformed my Hitler Youth into some kind of junior Wehrmacht."

Rommel himself virtually admitted as much in a private letter to a general in August 1938: "In my view postenlistment training should be left mostly to those SA [Brownshirt] leaders whose own service record shows they are well prepared for the nation's greatest testing time—by which I mean war."

Schirach's bitterness toward Rommel did not lessen. At

a gala theater performance he sat in the first row and put Rommel in the second. Rommel pointedly moved forward into an empty seat next to him, loudly announcing: "I represent the Wehrmacht, and in this country the Wehrmacht comes first." The chief of the Wehrmacht's national defense branch, Alfred Jodl, sadly noted in his diary that Schirach was "trying to break up the close cooperation initiated between the Wehrmacht and the Hitler Youth by Colonel Rommel."

Eventually, Schirach succeeded. But the clash with Hitler's favorite, Schirach, did not blight Rommel's career. On the contrary, he was suddenly selected to act as temporary commandant of the Führer's headquarters. At Munich on September 30 the Great Powers had forced Czechoslovakia to cede to Germany the disputed Sudeten border territories, and Hitler had decided to tour the ancient German cities there. Rommel's job would be to command the military escort. For an ambitious officer, the posting was a godsend—it catapulted him into the very highest company overnight. In Washington, D.C., in the captured albums of Hitler's personal photographer, are prints showing Rommel and SS chief Heinrich Himmler sharing a table in Hitler's special train, laughing uproariously.

These bloodless Nazi victories impressed Rommel as they did millions of other Germans. He saw for himself the liberated German communities of Asch, Eger and Carlsbad turning out in their thousands to cheer the Führer. Twice—in Austria in March and now here in September—the "man of action" had been proved right and the General Staff pessimists confounded. It is a certainty that by 1938 Hitler was a man greatly to Rommel's own liking. While many of his brother officers still hesitated to commit themselves to the Nazi philosophy, Rommel's conversion was undoubtedly complete. Even in private postcards to his friends, he now signed off: *"Heil Hitler!* Yours, E. Rommel."

In January 1937 and again one year later he had attended nine-day Nazi indoctrination courses for the Wehrmacht. After listening to Hitler speak in secret in the Big Hall of the War Ministry on December 1, 1938, Rommel approvingly noted down two sentences that had particularly struck him: "Today's soldier must be political, because he must always be ready to fight for our new policies"; and, "The German Wehrmacht is the sword wielded by the new German Weltanschauung [philosophy of life]." The extent of his dedication to Nazi ideals is evident, for instance, from the report he submitted to Berlin a few days later, after lecturing in various Swiss cities on his war exploits at the invitation of Swiss army officers. "Although Swiss army officers emphasized in conversation with me their desire for independence and the need for a national defense," Rommel wrote, "they show that they are strongly impressed by the momentous events in Germany. The younger officers, particularly, expressed their sympathies with our New Germany. Individuals among them also spoke with remarkable understanding of our Jewish problem."

A new posting awaited him now that Hitler had annexed Austria: commandant of the officer cadet school at Wiener Neustadt, near Vienna. He arrived on November 10, 1938—the day after an orgy of anti-Jewish looting and destruction in the Reich. He, Lucie and Manfred lived in a charming bungalow in a large garden not far from the Maria-Theresia Academy, the mighty castlelike structure that housed the school. Rommel's ambition was to make this the most modern Kriegsschule in the Reich.

Distant though he was from Berlin, he could not escape the pull exerted from Hitler's chancellery. Twice during March 1939 the Führer again sent for him to command his mobile headquarters—during the occupation of Prague on the fifteenth, and once again on the twenty-third when Hitler sailed into the Baltic port of Memel to supervise its "voluntary return" by Lithuania to Germany.

The invasion of Prague in mid-March showed Rommel that Hitler had physical courage, and that impressed him. The elderly Czech president Emil Hacha—who, under threat of air bombardment, had signed the invitation to the Wehrmacht to invade—was still in Berlin when Hitler left for the frontier. Rommel met him in a blizzard at the Czech border. The SS escort was late, but the panzer corps commander, General Erich Hoepner, proposed nonetheless that Hitler drive on into Prague to show who was now the boss. Himmler and the other generals were horrified at the idea. Rommel later bragged to his friend Kurt Hesse, "I am the one who persuaded Hitler to drive on—right to Hradcany Castle—under my personal protection. I told him he had no real choice but to take that road right into the very heart of the country, the very capital, to the citadel of Prague. To a certain extent I made him come with me. He put himself in my hands, and he never forgot me for giving him that advice."

That night Rommel wrote to Lucie from Prague, "All's well that ends well. Our bigger neighbors are putting a very sour face on things." This was a reference to Poland and France, who had both lost Czechoslovakia as an ally. Rommel added: "Thank goodness you packed enough warm underwear for me."

Hitler now raised claims on Poland, too, for the return of former German territories. At first Rommel was confident that Hitler would get his own way. But as he followed in the Nazi newspapers the growing clamor against Poland—the reports of border "incidents"—and saw Poland's intransigence, he realized that Hitler was going to have to invade. It would be idle to pretend that Rommel did not share the relish with which virtually every red-blooded German army officer looked forward to attacking Poland. His own affection for the disputed city of Danzig was as strong as Lucie's. It had been German when they met there and fell in love and for centuries before, becoming a "free city" only after World War I. Rommel did not expect it to be a long war.

Early in August 1939 he was given a typhus vaccination, which confirmed his expectations. On August 22 he was summoned to Berlin and briefed about the new job awaiting him. "My guess was right," he tersely informed Lucie on a postcard postmarked Berlin. He was to command the Führer's war headquarters during the attack on Poland.

# Hitler's General

**"I** left the Reich Chancellery as a brand new general, wearing a brand new general's uniform," Erwin Rommel proudly wrote to Lucie.

He had formally reported to Hitler as commander of the Führer's headquarters at 3:45 P.M. on August 25, 1939. Berlin sweltered in a heat wave. Just forty-three minutes earlier, Hitler had stepped out of a conference with foreign minister Joachim von Ribbentrop and announced that he was going to attack Poland at dawn.

At 4:45 P.M. on Hitler's orders, Rommel started his escort battalion moving toward Bad Polzin, a little railroad town in Pomerania, not far from the Polish frontier, where Nazi troops were massing for the attack. The battalion had a total of sixteen officers, ninety-three noncommissioned officers and 274 enlisted men. It was equipped with four 37-millimeter antitank guns, twelve 20-millimeter flak (antiaircraft) guns and other weapons.

He wrote ingenuously that day to Manfred, now eleven: "What do you make of the situation?" His next letters laid bare his own robust optimism: he believed that the war would last only fourteen days; that Hitler was doing what was best for Germany; that Britian and France would keep out—and that even if they did not, Germany could easily deal with them too. Perhaps he was dazzled by his own promotion; in fact, Hitler had instructed that Rommel's promotion should be back-dated to June 1, a great sign of his favor. "I find that very decent," Rommel wrote, and displayed a sneaking pleasure that Schoerner, his rival from the Italian campaign, had been promoted only to "honorary" colonel. A proud letter composed two weeks later tells much about his character: "I'm together with the F[ührer] very often, even in the most intimate discussions. It means so much to me that he confides in me—far more than being promoted to general."

When Rommel arrived at Bad Polzin that evening, he learned that the Reich Chancellery had phoned an hour before: the invasion of Poland had been suddenly postponed. Rommel was baffled. We now know that during the afternoon all Hitler's political assumptions had proved wrong. Britain had firmly ratified its treaty with Poland, and Italy had refused to declare war at Germany's side. For a week there was an extraordinary stalemate, while Hitler hedged and hesitated. Rommel's troops helped local farmers with the harvest while he and many other generals chafed at the bit. He flew to Berlin on the twenty-seventh to find out what was happening.

"Apart from the privilege of lunching at the Führer's table, there was little new," he confided to Lucie. "The troops are waiting impatiently for the order to advance, but we soldiers must just be patient. There are some snags, and they'll take some time to straighten out. The Führer will obviously reach whatever decision is proper." Four days later Rommel went farther than that: "I'm inclined to believe it will all blow over and we'll end up getting back the [disputed Polish] Corridor just as we did the Sudeten territory last year. If the Poles, British and French really had the guts to act, then these last few days were far and away the best time for them to do so." Later that day, August 31, 1939, he added, "Waiting is a bore, but it can't be helped. The Führer knows what's right for us."

Almost at once the telephone call came, ordering him to stand by. That evening, the phone rang again in the railroad station waiting room where he had set up his office. "The invasion begins tomorrow, 4:50 A.M."

Thus the Second World War began. Nobody, least of

all Erwin Rommel, could foresee that the military operations that began on September 1, heralded by a ranting and self-justificatory Reichstag speech by the Führer, would inexorably involve one country after another; would last six years; would leave 40 million dead and all Europe and half Asia ravaged by fire and explosives; would destroy Hitler's Reich, ruin the British Empire and end with the creation of new weapons, new world powers and a new lawlessness in international affairs.

Rommel wrote excitedly next day, "What do you make of the events of September 1—Hitler's speech? Isn't it wonderful that we have such a man?" But Lucie's feelings were mixed—part those of a woman, wife and mother, part those of a fanatical follower of Hitler who now asked her friends and visitors, "Do you too say a prayer for the Führer every night?" "Despite everything," she wrote to Erwin on September 4 from Wiener Neustadt, "we were all hoping to the very end that a second world war could be avoided—we all hoped that reason would prevail in Britain and France. . . . Now the Führer has left last night for the Polish front. May the dear Lord protect him, and you too, my beloved Erwin." She mentioned that she had discussed Hitler's speech with all her friends and shopkeepers, and all agreed that he had done the only proper thing. "All of them beg me to ask you to plead with him not to expose himself to unnecessary dangers. Our nation can not possibly afford to lose him. One shudders at the very thought!"

At 1:56 A.M. on September 4, Hitler's special train—it was incongruously code-named *Amerika;* nobody knows why—pulled into the railroad station. Fifteen minutes later *Heinrich,* the headquarters train of Himmler and the senior Nazi ministers, also arrived. Rommel's troops put on their "Führer's HQ" brassards. A security cordon was thrown around the station, and the antiaircraft guns were manned.

Rommel had expected Hitler to pay only a formal courtesy visit to the front. But the Nazi dictator stayed for three weeks. Almost every day he climbed into an armored half-track and drove forward—through forests still infested with Polish snipers, along roads blazing with the wreckage of Poland's antiquated army, to the very banks of the San to watch his storm troops force the river crossing. Rommel's eyes also were everywhere, watching, assessing, absorbing—learning the paraphernalia and techniques of a kind of warfare unknown to him during his own exploits, such as the employment of fast-moving tank units and assault troops and the use of dive bombers in close support.

One after the other, Hitler's secret predictions to his staff were dramatically fulfilled. Britain and France had so far not fired one shot for Poland, just as he had maintained.

"I think the whole war will peter out, once Poland is done for—and that won't be long now," wrote Rommel on the sixth. Three days later he stuck his neck out further: "I think I'll be home before winter. The war's going just the way we planned, in fact it's exceeding even our boldest expectations. . . . The Russians will probably attack Poland soon. Two million men! . . . Every evening there's a long war conference here. I'm allowed to attend it and even chip in from time to time. It's wonderful to see the firmness in the way [Hitler] deals with problems." "The Führer's in the best possible mood," he wrote just after they had visited the Warsaw front. "I have quite frequent chats with him now, we are on quite close terms."

By September 19 it was virtually all over. Hitler ceremonially entered Danzig and broadcast to the Reich—and to the world—from the port's Artushof Guildhall building, erected by German craftsmen in the fourteenth century. "Today sees our entry into magnificent Danzig," Rommel jotted down. "The Führer will be speaking to the entire world. I was able to talk with him about two hours yesterday evening, on military problems. He's extraordinarily friendly toward me . . . I very much doubt that I will still be at the Kriegsschule much longer, when the war is over."

When Hitler visited the Polish port of Gdynia, there was an incident that knocked the first nail into Rommel's coffin. After a desperate battle, the last Polish stronghold had just fallen and Hitler's party decided to drive down to the water's edge. The street was narrow, and the descent was steep. Again playing the role of traffic controller, Rommel brusquely ordered: "Only the Führer's car

and one escort car will drive down. The rest wait here!"
As at Nuremberg he stepped into the road to make sure
his order was obeyed. The third car moved forward, then
halted. Rommel could see in it the burly Nazi Party Chief,
Martin Bormann. Bormann gesticulated and shouted but
Rommel refused to budge. "I am headquarters commandant," he announced. "This is not a kindergarten outing,
and you will do as I say!" Bormann purpled under the
snub and waited five years to take his revenge.

In his exuberance over victory, Rommel turned a blind
eye to the grimmer aspects of Poland's defeat. On the
eleventh, he blandly observed that there were masses of
Poles everywhere in plain clothes: "Most are probably
soldiers who have managed to organize civilian clothes
after the tide of battle turned against them. They're already being rounded up by our police and deported." A
few days later he amplified this observation: "Guerrilla
warfare won't last much longer in Poland. All able-bodied
men are being rounded up and put to hard labor under
our supervision." The fate of the Poles once deported did
not occur to him.

Once Lucie wrote asking him to trace a particular Pole
who had vanished. Erwin replied that the inquiry must
go through proper Party channels. "I'm getting similar requests every day." On September 14, he did visit her
uncle, a Polish Catholic priest, Edmund Roszczynialski,
somewhere in the "liberated" Corridor. After that the
priest vanished without a trace. This time Rommel did
write, on May 1, 1940, to Himmler's adjutant for information. Months later an SS letter informed "General
Frommel" in cold terms that all inquiries about the priest
had drawn a blank. "The possibility must be faced that
he has fallen victim to the vagaries of war or to the cruel
winter." In fact the priest was probably liquidated like
thousands of other Polish intellectuals by the SS "task
forces," a horror of which Rommel learned only four
years later.

By September 23, 1939, Poland was nearly finished.
Only Warsaw was still holding out, under terrific Luftwaffe and artillery bombardment. "The Führer's in a relaxed mood," Rommel contentedly informed Lucie. "We
eat at his table twice a day now—yesterday evening I

45

was allowed to sit next to him. Soldiers are worth something again." But his rise in Hitler's esteem attracted the envy of the dictator's staff, and Colonel Rudolf Schmundt —three years Rommel's junior and Hitler's chief Wehrmacht adjutant—made no secret of it. Rommel returned with Hitler to Berlin on the twenty-sixth and confided to Lucie next morning: "At present, relations with Schmundt are strained. Don't know why: apparently my position with F[ührer] is getting too strong. Not impossible that a change will be insisted on from that quarter. . . . Of course I want to know just where I stand. I've no desire to be pushed around by younger men."

He went on leave to Wiener Neustadt for a few days with his family. On October 2 he flew to Warsaw to prepare Hitler's victory parade. After the brief respite with Lucie, the Polish capital was a horrifying, stinking nightmare. He returned to Berlin and dined that evening with Hitler at the Chancellery. "Warsaw has been badly damaged," Rommel wrote to Lucie. "One house in ten is burst to a shell. There are no shops left. Their showcases are smashed, the shopkeepers have boarded them up. There has been no water, power, gas or food for two days. . . . The main streets were blocked off by barricades, but these stopped all civilian movement too and often exposed the public to a bombardment from which they then couldn't escape. The mayor puts the dead and injured at 40,000. . . . The people are probably relieved we've come and put an end to it all."

After the army's two-hour victory parade on the fifth —the newsreels show General Rommel standing right in front of Hitler's tribune—he returned to the boredom of barracks life in Berlin. Next day Hitler again made a "fabulous speech" to the Reichstag, this time formally offering peace to Britain and France (now that Poland no longer existed). Rommel was confident that he would soon be back with Lucie. "I'm glad to say that H[itler]'s speech is being openly discussed in Paris and London," he wrote on the eighth. "The neutrals are in favor. I attended Hitler's conference for an hour and a half yesterday. The Führer's in good spirits and quite confident." That was the conference where Hitler announced that— if he attacked the West—he would invade Belgium too, to keep the war well away from his vital Ruhr factories. Rommel began to feel the cold, but hesitated to ask Lucie to send his winter coat to Berlin in case he was suddenly moved elsewhere. On the ninth he wrote, "Apart from the Führer's war conference, which is always highly interesting and lasts anything up to two hours, there's nothing doing here. We're still waiting for the other side to decide, in the light of Hitler's speech."

All Hitler's hopes of a peaceful settlement with Britain and France had gone. When a time bomb—planted by an eccentric clockmaker, Georg Elser—exploded in November a few feet from where Hitler had only just delivered a speech, he blamed the perfidious British. "That Munich bomb attempt has only redoubled his resolve," Rommel wrote his wife. "It is a wonderful thing to see." He was aghast that Hitler's security staff had not protected the dictator better. "Five feet of rubble covers the spot where the Führer spoke last night. That's how violent the explosion was. If the bomb attempt had really succeeded—it just doesn't bear thinking about."

By late November 1939, the General Staff were dragging their feet over Hitler's idea of attacking the Western powers at such a numerical disadvantage. Rommel had no doubt that Hitler was right, but other generals lacked this confidence. On November 23, Hitler summoned his senior generals to the Chancellery and gave them the rough edge of his tongue. He was highly critical of the generals and downright abusive about the General Staff. Rommel relished every word. Afterward he related it all to Lucie: "I witnessed yesterday's big speech to the military commanders and their chiefs of staff. The Führer didn't mince his language. But it seemed to me to have been highly necessary, because when I speak with my fellow generals I rarely find one who supports him body and soul."

This mutual admiration between Hitler and Rommel explains how Rommel now got the new posting that he did. In October he had hinted that he would like to command a division. The chief of army personnel suggested that a mountain division at Innsbruck or Munich would be appropriate, in view of Rommel's famed exploits. Rommel, however, asked Hitler for something better—

indeed, the best: a real panzer division. The army personnel chief refused. Rommel, he pointed out, was only an infantry officer and knew nothing about tanks. Hitler overruled him, and on February 6, 1940, Rommel received a telegram telling him to report four days later to Bad Godesberg on the Rhine, where he was to take over the Seventh Panzer Division.

At 7:00 A.M. on the tenth Rommel was looking from his train window at the fast-flowing Rhine. A few hours later his new officers were parading before him. Unlike any other general they knew, Rommel had greeted them with *"Heil Hitler!"* But that was just the beginning. He announced that he would tour their sector next morning —ignoring their protests that it was Sunday.

He found that instead of the usual two tank regiments, the division had only one, the Twenty-fifth Panzer. To his surprise he also learned that of this regiment's 218 tanks, over half were lightly armored and of Czech manufacture. The men of the division were largely from Thuringia, a province not noted for producing soldiers of great promise. Rommel would have until the spring to lick them into shape.

He briefly reported back to Hitler at midday on February 17, and later he wrote to Lucie: "Jodl [Hitler's chief strategic adviser] was flabbergasted at my new posting." Hitler had handed him a farewell gift, a copy of *Mein Kampf* inscribed, "To General Rommel with pleasant memories." Then they had gone in to luncheon with four other generals, all newly appointed corps commanders. Hitler began to talk about the notorious *Altmark* incident, in which a British destroyer party had just raided an unarmed German vessel in Norwegian waters, knowing it to be carrying hundreds of British captives. The Nazi press was shrieking vengeance for this violation of neutral waters, but within the Chancellery walls, Hitler now praised Britain's bold act. "History judges you by your success or failure," he pontificated. "That's what counts. Nobody asks the victor whether he was in the right or wrong."

Before Rommel returned that evening to his new division, he called on his publisher in Potsdam and collected ten copies of *Infanterie Greift an,* for his subordinates to read. This was one clue to how he proposed to use his tanks in the coming battles—adventurously, like an infantry commander on a storm troop operation. Years later one corps commander, Leo Geyr von Schweppenburg, recalled a second clue—a snatch of playful conversation he had overheard while waiting in line in the Chancellery for Hitler to appear that forenoon. Rommel had asked Rudolf Schmidt—who had been his commanding officer in the Thirteenth Infantry Regiment—in a loud stage whisper, "Tell me, general, what's the best way to command a panzer division?"

Schmidt growled back: "You'll find there are always two possible decisions open to you. Take the bolder one —it's always best."

# Spook Division

SIX o'clock on a blustery February morning in 1940. It is still dark, but the solitary stocky figure of a man nearly fifty is jogging methodically along a narrow woodland path near Godesberg. His clenched fists are held close to his chest, in the manner of a long-distance runner. From the Rhine comes the distant hooting of passing barges.

This is General Erwin Rommel, the new commander of the Seventh Panzer Division, determined to regain his physical fitness after six fat and lazy months as a member of Hitler's entourage. During the Polish campaign he noticed the first heart complaints, and once he felt distinctly faint. He has told nobody but Lucie. She has sent him a big packet of Lecithin medicine—but jogging is his tonic: ten minutes every morning he runs a mile like this, as shock treatment for his slumbering frame, or as he himself puts it, "To fight back the inner Schweinehund in me that pleads, 'Stay in bed—just another fifteen minutes!' "

As he trots back through the barracks gates it is ten past six. "I don't suppose I'll find many men anxious to follow my example," he writes to Lucie later this day. "Most of my officers are very comfortably inclined. And some are downright flabby."

50

Rommel's arrival had electrified the division. His first act as commanding officer was to send his regimental commanders on leave. "I won't be needing you until I've learned the ropes myself." At five to seven each morning his Mercedes rolled out of the barracks, taking him to his troops. He listened to the German and foreign newscasts on the car radio at seven, and again at twelve-thirty, when he returned for lunch. He felt fit and on top of his job, and he began to throw his weight around. On February 27 a battalion commander displeased him. Rommel dismissed him and had him on his way within ninety minutes. "Word of this rapid firing will soon get around," he wrote, "and some of the others will pull their socks up."

Politically, too, the division's officers did not come up to scratch. When a top Nazi was attached to his staff, Rommel observed: "It's no skin off my nose. I won't need to watch my tongue, but some of the others will have to be on guard. Seems that National Socialism is still a bit of a stranger to the folks around here." The Nazi official was Karl-August Hanke, thirty-six, one of the senior aides of Propaganda Minister Joseph Goebbels. He was assigned as a lieutenant to Rommel's staff. Rommel put him in a Panzer IV tank, the most modern he had. A number of other Nazis were also sent to him, including Corporal Karl Holz, chief editor of the anti-Jewish tabloid *Der Stürmer*. The arrival of these men, all in their mid-forties, raised eyebrows at Godesberg.

His main striking force was the Twenty-fifth Panzer Regiment, for which Berlin had given him Colonel Karl Rothenburg, a tough ex-police colonel who had, like Rommel, won the Pour le Mérite as a company commander in 1918. At forty-four, he was one of Germany's finest tank regiment commanders. Like Rommel, he figured that he had escaped death so many times that he was already living on an overdraft of life. He was the kind of man who knows no fear because death holds no terrors for him. He met his death the next year on the Russian front.

Day after day Rommel watched the tanks exercise at Wahn, marveling at the feats performed by these monsters —veritable fortresses that clanked and creaked their way up even the steepest inclines. It was no secret that the Western powers heavily outnumbered Germany in tanks and aircraft, but the German tanks were better. The best tanks in Rommel's force were Panzer IIIs and IVs—twenty-ton behemoths, nearly nine feet tall, each with a five-man crew, a 320-horsepower Maybach gasoline engine and a top speed of about twenty-five miles per hour. Half of Rommel's tanks were Czech-built 38Ts: the 38T weighed less than nine tons, because it had even less armor plate than the relatively thin-skinned Panzer III and IV, but it was faster, and its gun packed a bigger punch.

By April 1940, Rommel had steeped himself in the theory and practice of tank warfare and developed a few ideas of his own to surprise the enemy. He began taking his units cross-country in large and small formations, fast, and practicing radio procedures and gunnery. Evenings, he briefed all his officers, right down to platoon level, then did his paper work until 11:00 P.M. At 6:00 A.M. he was already up again, jogging through the woods along the Rhine. His stamina and condition were phenomenal.

Rommel's Seventh Panzer Division and another, the Fifth, would be controlled by General Herman Hoth's Fifteenth Corps; Hoth had already won the Knight's Cross in Poland, and Rommel liked him. Hoth's corps was the armored spearhead of General Günther Hans von Kluge's Fourth Army, which would advance into Belgium when Hitler gave the code word. After the main British and French forces had thus been lured forward to meet them, the real German breakthrough would follow across the Meuse—to Rommel's left. This major thrust would, Hitler hoped, end in the rapid encirclement of the enemy. Such was the strategy underlying Hitler's western campaign: the plan was his, and not the General Staff's. It was top secret.

From the Seventh Panzer Division's rest area on the Rhine, all the way forward to the Belgian frontier, Rommel had signposted his designated route of advance with the symbol DG7, for Durchgangsstrasse [Throughway] 7. This violated all the rules of the General Staff; but Rommel meant to push that DG7 right through to the Channel coast ahead of his rivals.

On May 5, a rainy Sunday, he wrote his "last letters" to Lucie and Manfred, to be delivered to them if he did not return from the coming battle. On May 9, Rommel was with Colonel Rothenburg watching his tanks and artillery maneuvering on the firing range at Wahn. At 1:45 P.M. the code word—"Dortmund"—reached Rommel. It meant that the attack in the west would begin at 5:35 A.M. the next day. He drove frantically back to the barracks in Godesberg, and seized a pad to write to Lucie: "We're leaving in half an hour. Don't worry. Things have always gone well so far, and it's going to be all right. We jump off at dusk—how long we've been waiting for this moment!"

As dusk fell, he drove off down Throughway 7 in an armored command vehicle. The road was jammed with elements of the Second Corps, inexplicably crossing Rommel's throughway. The chaos was awful—it was like a bad start to a horse race, with all the contestants fouling each other's lanes. Rommel was enraged. Not until twenty minutes before zero hour did the last of his riflemen reach their allotted positions.

The air filled with German planes. As dawn came he could see that his engineers had crossed the Belgian frontier according to plan. He could hear no gunfire at all, just distant thumps as the retreating Belgians demolished bridges or blew up roads. In the first villages he drove through, followed by his radio truck and two dispatch riders, the response was quite unexpected: "We were greeted everywhere with shouts of *Heil Hitler,* and delighted faces," he wrote in the first draft of his history of the campaign.

In Belgium, and then in France, Rommel renewed his fame. Over the next nineteen days his panzer division blazed its Throughway 7 across the countryside at breakneck speed. Rommel's technique was to push forward boldly, ignoring the risk to flanks and rear, calculating that—as at Mataiur in 1917—the shock to enemy morale would more than offset the risk. His division poked like a long forefinger straight through the enemy line, sometimes advancing so fast that it became detached from the main fist of Kluge's Fourth Army—and continued to race along its throughway on its own, with only the most tenuous connection in the rear to its logistical support. Rapid and determined enemy actions could have sheared this finger off, but as Rommel had calculated, the enemy was too confused and alarmed to move decisively.

Always, Rommel rode at the very tip of his panzer division. His command vehicle was a specially adapted Panzer III. Sometimes he would ride in Colonel Rothenburg's Panzer IV command vehicle; sometimes he flew over the battlefield in the army's light Storch observation plane and landed among the leading tanks. After two days, by late May 12, his division had reached the Meuse River. Rommel's assault troops forced a crossing in rubber boats at 4:30 A.M. the next day, but took heavy casualties. Rommel himself, already hoarse from shouting orders, crossed that afternoon, oblivious of enemy small arms fire, in time to restore his troops' dwindling morale. That night he ordered a pontoon ferry to be rigged up, and had his anti-tank guns and tanks hauled across the 120-yard stretch of water. The attack was resumed.

Onward through the Belgian towns of Flavion and Philippeville swept the panzer division. Rommel's new tactics were paying off. His inventiveness never failed him. To provide a smoke screen for the Meuse crossing, he had simply ordered houses set on fire—just as at Longarone. To maintain security when radioing orders to his tank commanders, he had devised the Stosslinie system—a "line of thrust" penciled by all officers between two prearranged points on their maps; any point could be described by giving its distance along and from this line. To find out which enemy villages were defended, he devised his famous fireworks displays—the entire panzer regiment opened fire, thus provoking any defenders to betray their positions. If the enemy was holding, say, a wood, then Rommel just drove in, with every barrel shooting indiscriminately into it.

"The day goes to the side that is the first to plaster its opponent," he later said. And in a private letter that he wrote to Rudolf Schmundt, Hitler's adjutant, begging for a second panzer regiment ("There's no hope through proper channels—too much red tape!"), Rommel stated: "The method that I have ordered, of driving into the enemy with all guns firing and not holding fire until they are already knocking out my tanks, has worked magnificently. It costs us a lot of ammunition, but it saves tanks and lives. The enemy have not found any answer to this method yet. When we come up on them like this, their nerves fail and even the big tanks surrender. If only they knew just how thin our armor is compared with theirs!"

His method did, of course, cause mishaps. One of his tank commanders, Ulrich Schroeder, described it in a private manuscript: "On the way we met a column of trucks coming toward us. They evidently mistook us for British and drove sedately on. Our front company let them come within a few yards, then let the truck drivers have it with machine gun fire. With horrible regularity they slumped over to the right in their driving seats, one after another, all dead. The trucks swerved off the road into the ditch, eight or ten of them, all ending up there in the same convoy spacing. Unfortunately, as we passed them we found out they were ambulances. So the front company was ordered to cease fire."

On balance, however, Rommel's rough tactics saved lives on both sides. His dramatic breaching of the Maginot Line extension was an example. Between this main bunker line and the French frontier were woods in which the French had dug forward fortifications. Rommel reached the wood at Cerfontaine on May 16, 1940. He wanted to get through it fast, so as to reach the bunkers themselves before dark—but how, without alerting the bunkers that he was coming? Rommel took the microphone and quietly ordered all tank commanders to drive through the woods, this time without firing a single shot. Their crews—gunner, radio operator, loader and commander—were to ride outside the tanks and wave white flags. He himself rode Colonel Rothenburg's Panzer IV. Ulrich Schroeder recalled: "The enemy was in fact so startled by this carnivallike procession that instead of shooting at us they just stood back to either side and gaped."

With the woods now safely behind them, Rommel ordered the last battalion to about-face and cover them in case the troops there decided to fight after all. His tanks were arrayed behind a long hedgerow. At a signal from him, they fired smoke shells at the bunker ahead, while assault engineers crawled forward and burned out the closest bunkers with flamethrowers. At midnight, with the way ahead lit by the glare of fires, the Seventh Panzer Division began to roll through a gap blasted in the bunker line. The leading tanks fired into the darkness ahead; all the rest fired broadside to keep the enemy's heads down. It was a fantastic spectacle. As they gathered speed westward, an inferno of gunfire began. The tanks roared through French hamlets with names like Solre-le-Château, Sars-Poteries and Semousies. Sleeping villagers were wakened by the thunderous sound and flung open their windows. Terrified civilians and French troops huddled in the ditches. Refugee carts laden with household goods, abandoned by their fleeing owners, were smashed under tracks or overturned.

None of the French had expected the bunker line to be breached so fast. "Immediately behind the bunker line," wrote Schroeder, "we came upon astonished French troop columns—some fleeing inland, others pushing toward us." After a while Rommel stuck his head out of the tank's hatch. "Ahead of us," he wrote, "the flat countryside unfurled in the moon's wan light. We were through—through the Maginot Line."

In that one night he and Colonel Rothenburg advanced thirty-five miles. His right-hand neighbor, the Fifth Panzer Division—far better equipped with tanks than was Rommel—was lagging about thirty miles behind.

Rommel did not pause until he reached Avesnes, his tactical objective. Even then he drove right through the town and waited in the hills to the west for the rest of his panzer division to catch up. Impatiently he sent his aide, Lieutenant Hanke, back down the road in a Panzer IV to hurry on the stragglers. "We waited with mounting impatience," recalled Schroeder, "as we wanted to get moving again. . . . After about an hour we heard tank engines and tracks approaching from the rear. Rommel assumed this was the rest of our division, and ordered the advance resumed."

In fact the sounds came from a French heavy tank unit, which had counterattacked in Rommel's rear and already destroyed several tanks. All alone Hanke's Panzer IV drove these attackers back—an act of bravery for which a grateful Rommel recommended him for the Knight's Cross.

Rommel's repeated radio calls for further orders for the

division went unanswered. So he resolved that at dawn he would rush the bridge across the Sambre at Landrecies, eleven miles farther on. At 5:15 A.M the panzer regiment moved off, followed by the motorcycle battalion belonging to Rommel's division.

It was all so like the early victories over the Italians in 1917. There was no firing. Every French unit he met meekly surrendered and, at Rommel's suggestion, began plodding eastward into captivity, the enemy evidently believing that their position was more precarious than Rommel's, which was not so. That day he took 3,500 prisoners, according to his panzer division files.

One brave French lieutenant colonel tried to defy Rommel. "He looked like a fanatical officer," recalled Rommel in his history. "His eyes burned with hatred and impotent fury. . . . I decided to take him with us. He had already gone on about fifty yards farther east, but he was brought back to Colonel Rothenburg. Rothenburg ordered him up onto our command panzer. But as the French officer curtly refused—three times, in fact—to come with us, there was nothing to do but to shoot him down." Rommel often discussed this disturbing episode with Manfred. He took no pleasure in killing, but for a soldier it was sometimes necessary.

"A thousand yards east of Marbais," he wrote, "a French car emerged from a side road on the left and crossed our armored car's path. It was flagged down, and a French officer got out and gave himself up. A whole convoy of trucks had been following him, raising a lot of dust. I quickly decided to divert the convoy to Avesnes. Lieutenant Hanke swung aboard the leading truck. I myself stayed briefly at the crossroads, indicating by sign language and shouts that the war was all over for them and that they were to throw down their arms. There were machine gunners on some of the trucks, manning machine guns against air attack. I couldn't see how long the convoy was because of the dust. After ten or fifteen had driven past, I went to the front of the convoy and drove to Avesnes. . . . At length we reached the southwest entrance to the town. Without halting, Lieutenant Hanke swiftly led the truck convoy following us onto a parking lot and disarmed them. Only now did we realize that no fewer than forty French trucks, many carrying troops, had tagged along behind us."

It would have taken only one trigger-happy Frenchman to end Rommel's career there and then. He made no attempt to conceal his rank or person: his natty army uniform, his high-peaked cap, his medals and loud voice marked him out above his tank commanders. But he continued to lead this charmed existence, as countless episodes revealed. Here is Rommel, standing defiantly on top of a railway embankment, directing the battle while his men are being picked off one by one by Scottish snipers; or walking up to a motionless German tank, through a hail of fire, and rapping on the turret to know why it is not firing. And here is his new aide, Lieutenant Most, suddenly sinking to the ground at Rommel's side, mortally wounded, with blood gushing from his mouth. Rommel reports laconically to Lucie, "Major Schraepler has come back already: his successor was killed just a yard away from me." And here are Rommel and Major Erdmann, who commands his reconnaissance battalion, running for cover under heavy gunfire as a 150-millimeter howitzer shell lands between them; Erdmann's back is torn open and he perishes instantly—Rommel is shocked but unscathed. It is incidents like these that give a man a dangerous belief in his own immortality.

Once Lieutenant Hanke saved his life, near Sivry on the Belgian frontier. They had suddenly driven smack into a large force of French bicycle troops. Hanke mowed them down with his machine gun, "thereby extricating me as division commander from a very tricky situation," Rommel admitted in his commendation of Hanke for bravery.

*During this campaign and in all those that followed, there was a camera slung around Rommel's neck. It had been given to him by Goebbels, and with it he took countless photographs. His captured albums are in a London museum, and they tell us as much about him as about the subjects themselves—we find ourselves seeing the war through Rommel's eyes. As I turned the album pages, I saw the dramatic spectacle of Rommel's division in formation drive across the French cornfields, the columns of*

*trudging prisoners, French black troops, ducks in village
ponds and fine horses gamboling with their newborn foals,
oblivious to the onrush of war around them. Here too are
bewildered refugees sitting near cart horses, disarmed
troops in kilts at Rouen and the French war memorial at
Fécamp.*

*A year later the weekly* Frankfurt Illustrated *published some of Rommel's photographs. "Manfred got it
out of the shopping basket," Lucie wrote to Rommel on
the day the magazine appeared, "and after a few seconds
suddenly whooped with excitement and shouted, 'Mama—
look, it's Papa!' At first I thought you might be paying us
one of your favorite surprise visits; but then he showed me
the magazine with your picture on the front page, snapping pictures from your tank turret."*

For a while, Rommel was so far up front that the press
could not keep pace with him. His friend Colonel Kurt
Hesse, the former Potsdam lecturer—now touring the
battlefield with a group of German war correspondents—
found it almost impossible to catch him: "He was always
ten miles ahead of us. Once French forces, including
tanks, had already pushed in between the little advance
party with which he spearheaded his attack and the main
force of his division. Even this did not stop him from just
driving ahead. 'They will just have to battle through as
best they can,' was his only comment."

Hesse wrote a description of Throughway 7: "I have
never seen anything like the scenes along Rommel's route
of advance. His tanks had run into a French division coming down the same road, and they had just kept advancing
right on past it. For the next five or six miles there were
hundreds of trucks and tanks, some driven into the
ditches, others burned out, many still carrying dead and
injured. More and more Frenchmen came out of the fields
and woods with abject fear written on their faces and
their hands in the air. From up front came the short, sharp
crack of the guns of our tanks, which Rommel was personally directing—standing upright in his ACV with two
staff officers, his cap pushed back, urging everybody
ahead. A *feu sacre* inflamed him: he brooked no opposition, from friend or foe. If somebody could not keep up,

then let him stand back if only he, Rommel, and two or three tanks could reach the river Somme!"

Rommel caught sight of Hesse and barked at him: "In this war the commander's place is here, right out in front! I don't believe in armchair strategy. Let's leave that to the gentlemen of the General Staff." Hesse wrote that down, and Rommel's next remark as well: "This is the age of Seydlitz and Ziethen all over again. We've got to look at this war like a cavalry action—we've got to throw in tank divisions like cavalry squadrons, and that means issuing orders from a moving tank just as generals once used to from the saddle."

These tactics appalled the General Staff and aroused apprehension at the Führer's headquarters. But on Rommel rolled. On May 18, he found that beyond Landrecies he had to pass through a sprawling forest concealing a big, well-guarded enemy ammunition dump. To avoid a time-consuming pitched battle, he used the same trick of waving white flags and having the crews ride outside their tanks. Again the gaping Frenchmen stood aside and willingly obeyed the tank commanders' shouts of *"A bas les armes!"*

At the other end of the forest was the village of Pommereuil. Rommel's tanks formed up in a defensive "hedgehog" on top of the hill beyond the village, tails in, guns pointing outward. On the far horizon they could see Le Cateau, their next objective. He collected the commanders. "Your route now will be Le Cateau—Arras—Amiens—Rouen—Le Havre," he bellowed. "Fuel up! Advance!"

They were stunned at Rommel's words. Le Havre was on the English Channel, and they had barely slept for a whole week. Soon, however, he and his tank commanders were fighting off determined attempts by the French to wipe out their "hedgehog." To make matters worse, the tanks were nearly out of gasoline and after a while Rommel learned why. The rest of his division was still back in Belgium, and his chief staff officer, Major Otto Heidkämper, having heard nothing from him and having written off both him and Colonel Rothenburg as lost, had made no attempt to send them fuel. Heidkämper's conclusion shocked Hitler's staff. The Führer himself later sent word to Rommel: "Your raid cost me a sleepless night. I couldn't see any way of extricating you from that snare."

Somehow, in the confused way of battles, the French relaxed their grip on Rommel and he escaped again. But weeks later he still fumed at Heidkämper's feebleness. "I'm going to get rid of him as soon as I can," he snarled in one letter. "This young General Staff major stood back some twenty miles behind the front, terrified that something might happen to him and the operations staff, and naturally lost contact with the combat group I was commanding at Cambrai. Then, instead of rushing everybody forward to me, he drove back to Corps Headquarters and got them all worked up into believing that my division was slipping out of their control. To this day he still thinks he was a hero."

Rommel had taken Cambrai with little opposition, capturing 650 enemy troops there on the nineteenth and 500 more the next day. But on May 20, he felt as though he had butted his head into three feet of solid masonry: for the first time he came up against British professional soldiers, the enemy he learned to respect, fear and admire every time they crossed his path over the next four years. By the twenty-first, Rommel was in a jam. The enemy were regrouping for a desperate attempt to break out of the Flanders pocket, and Rommel's infantry and guns were now confronted by a tank they could not stop—the slow, cumbersome but heavily armored Matilda Mark II. The standard 37-millimeter shell was useless against it.

Rommel must have been dog-tired, but he did not show it in this crisis at Arras on May 21. He personally directed the fire on the approaching Matildas. He found by harsh experience that only the heavy flak, the big 88-millimeter guns, had sufficient muzzle velocity to stop these brutes. "With the enemy tanks so dangerously close," he wrote in his manuscript, "only rapid fire from every gun could save the situation. We ran from gun to gun. I brushed aside the gun commanders' objections that the range was too great." It was here that his adjutant Lieutenant Most was killed one yard away from him. Moments like these distinguished the true-born battlefield commander, and Rommel's example inspired his troops to stand their ground that day.

After the bloody fighting at Arras, the Seventh Panzer Division briefly rested. Equipment was repaired, tanks were refueled, letters written. Hitler had ordered all the panzer forces to halt anyway on reaching this canal line, running westward from La Bassée. On May 26 Hitler lifted the order. Rommel immediately threw a bridgehead across the canal. A rifle regiment got across, but a machine gun battalion to its right was prevented by heavy sniper fire. This unit's history relates that Rommel himself now appeared: "He complained that we weren't doing enough to combat the British snipers and climbed up on top of the railroad embankment, then, standing upright amid the enemy fire, proceeded to dictate targets to the antitank gun crews of Numbers Four and Seven companies. One after another their leading gunners and gun commanders were shot dead, clean through the head, but the general himself seemed totally immune to the enemy sniping."

By the afternoon of May 27, Rommel's troops had established two makeshift bridges. To the chagrin of Lieutenant General Max von Hartlieb, who was senior to Rommel, the corps commander, Hoth, now placed the Fifth Panzer Division's two tank regiments under Rommel's temporary command for the coming attack on Lille. This was a powerful reinforcement indeed, and Rommel was very impressed by the large numbers of brand new tanks in the regiments. He called a conference of both divisions' tank commanders—and had a blazing row with Colonel Johannes Streich, of the Fifteenth Panzer Regiment, who pointed out that Rommel was not reading the maps right.

At the end of the conference there was a ceremony that surprised Rommel and staggered the others present. His aide Karl Hanke appeared, wearing his steel helmet and "full warpaint," saluted him and announced: "On the Führer's orders I herewith bestow on Herr General the Knight's Cross." (This made Rommel the first divisional commander to get the award in France—and the obvious Nazi Party string-pulling caused wry faces among the other officers.) At 6:00 P.M. Rommel began his push northeastward from the canal.

Lille was one of France's biggest industrial cities, and Rommel was determined to get there first. When his panzers reached the day's interim objective, he heard that his rivals' divisions were bivouacking for the night. Jubilantly, he decided to press on—"Mount up! Start engines! Advance!"—and he alone continued the attack.

This action blocked the enemy's escape to Dunkirk, where the evacuation of the British and French armies across the English Channel had already begun. Now far in front of the main German forces, Rommel found he was taking fire from both enemy and German guns. He was exhausted, but he badly wanted to be the first German in Lille. "After one and a half hours' sleep, I took fresh troops forward to the front line, and fuel and ammunition for the tanks," he wrote to Lucie. That was the night that Major Erdmann was killed a few feet away from Rommel.

The next morning he himself drove into Lille, out of sheer eagerness. The war nearly ended for Erwin Rommel there and then, because the streets were still swarming with enemy soldiers. He rapidly reversed his car and escaped unharmed.

By his coup he had trapped half the French First Army. Infantry divisions moved up to occupy Lille and allow Rommel's troops a few days' rest. "I've been in action for days on end," he wrote, "constantly on the move in a tank, armored car or staff car. There's just no time to sleep at all. In a mechanized division you've got to be damned fast. So far I have been, hence the Seventh Panzer Division's huge successes—about which the public still knows absolutely nothing."

In the rest area, Rommel rapidly composed an interim dispatch on his campaign. He had taken 6,849 prisoners, captured forty-eight light tanks and knocked out eighteen heavy and 295 light tanks. ("Not bad for Thuringians!" he observed triumphantly to Lucie.) He proudly sent copies of the dispatch to Hitler and to Schmundt. His ulterior purpose in doing so was quite clear from a candid remark to Lucie: "I've got to act fast, or the same thing will happen as happened after [Hill

1114]." The memory of that Pour le Mérite awarded to the wrong officer in 1917 still rankled him. When Rommel was in a philosophical mood in later years, he liked to quote: "Victory in battle can boast of many fathers; but defeat is an orphan."

Hitler was impressed by the dispatch. The upshot was that Rommel, alone of all the division commanders, was invited to meet Hitler on June 2, 1940, when the Führer called his commanders to Charleville in the Ardennes to discuss the last acts in the defeat of France. Hitler put on his familiar avuncular act. "Rommel," he cried, "we were all very worried for your safety during those days you were on the attack!" At the secret conference that followed, Hitler told his generals that the new offensive would begin on June 5. France would be given the coup de grâce. General Wilhelm von Leeb noted in his private diary these words of Hitler's: "It will be easy to find a basis of peace with Britain. But France must be smashed into the ground, and then she must pay the bill."

Back in action, Rommel forced his panzer division across the Somme—which he found to be a wretched little stream rather than a river—early on June 5, using two railroad bridges that the enemy had failed to demolish. For a few hours, enemy artillery pinned him into a small bridgehead. His men took large numbers of black prisoners—French colonials fighting for a fatherland they were seeing only now for the first time.

At 4:00 P.M. he began his dramatic thrust southward. He had thought up another brilliant new idea, the Flächenmarsch or "formation drive" in which the entire panzer division steamrolled across the open, undulating countryside in a box formation. A tank battalion formed the front and sides, while the rear was brought up by antitank and reconnaissance battalions. The rifle regiments filled the center of the box, their wheeled transport following the tracks flattened through the waist-high corn crops by the tanks. Up hill and down dale they rolled, around the villages, through the hedgerows—spewing fire and leaving behind pillars of smoke and wrecked enemy equipment, while herds of riderless horses stampeded along in the wake like the end of a disastrous steeplechase. On some farms the carts were already harnessed and laden with furniture. Petrified women and children cowered beneath them as this deadly monster engulfed their farmsteads. Rommel's officers shouted to them to stay where they were.

Never before had a panzer division moved so fast. It was averaging forty or fifty miles each day. The enemy was never ready for him. At Thieulloy a British truck convoy was overrun and looted; it was rich in cigarettes, chocolates, canned sardines and Libby's canned fruit. There were tennis rackets and golf clubs too—Rommel guffawed, observing that the British had clearly not been expecting the war to take its present nasty turn. His approach caused chaos behind the French lines. At Elbeuf, a woman rushed up and caught him by the arm: *"Vous êtes anglais?"* Rommel shook his head. *"Oh, les barbares!"* she screamed, and vanished back into her house.

With a bit more luck, he would even have been able to rush the Seine bridges at Elbeuf, but a handful of determined men there managed to blow them up before Rommel arrived. He reached the river at Sotteville toward midnight on June 8. Rommel's was the first German unit to arrive at the Seine.

The adjutant of a tank battalion described the arrival: "Our battalion HQ was billeted on Anthieux [near Elbeuf]. I found a château there, but its heavy oak gates were closed and didn't open even after much ringing. So I forced it open with my tank. The château was well furnished, but abandoned by its owners. We inspected the various rooms and decided on who should sleep where. We had just finished upstairs when we heard voices downstairs: General Rommel and the division's adjutant, Major Schraepler, were also looking for a billet. Rommel asked me which room he could have—'I just want to sleep a couple of hours, then get moving again.' He then really did sleep only two hours, lying fully dressed on a sofa, and drove on again before the rest of my battalion even arrived. While he was sleeping I picked some strawberries in the garden. When he awoke I served them to him on a rhubarb leaf, to his evident delight."

On June 10 Rommel's troops saw the sea at last. It was near Dieppe. At his order, the Twenty-fifth Panzer Regiment drove flat out toward the coast. When it arrived, Rothenburg smashed his sturdy Panzer IV right through the seawall and drove the tank down the beach until the waves of the Channel were lapping around its gray-painted hull. Rommel, riding with him, clambered on top, to be photographed for the press back home. Then they backed out and rolled on toward Fécamp, through wildly cheering crowds who tossed flowers into their path— again mistaking them for Englishmen.

Twenty-four hours later Rommel was on the cliffs south of Saint-Valéry. On the narrow path below the brow of the cliffs they found thousands of British troops cowering, waiting for the flotilla of small boats lying off-shore to come and rescue them. They waited in vain. The French admiral in authority had until now refused permission for the evacuation; the French High Command was still hoping to launch a counterattack toward the Somme. Now Rommel had come, and his guns drove off the rescue flotilla. Grenades were dropped onto the cliff path, forcing a steady stream of prisoners to the top.

Rommel called on Saint-Valéry to surrender by 9:00 P.M. The French troops wanted to accept, but not the British. They built barricades with their bare hands and fought like wildcats all day. So at 9:00 P.M. Rommel called down heavy artillery and a terrifying dive bomber attack on the town. That did it. When he drove in the next morning, through narrow streets full of trucks, tanks and equipment that the enemy had hoped to salvage and take back to England, there was little fight left in the defenders. The commander of the French Ninth Corps surrendered to him in the market square, followed by eleven more British and French generals. Newsreel cameras filmed the scene.

The British were rather annoyed at the way things had turned out. Major General Victor Fortune, who had commanded the Fifty-First (Highlands) Division, eminently disliked having to surrender to such a youthful general. The French smoked cigarettes and accepted their defeat with more aplomb. One gray-haired general, old enough to be Rommel's father, clapped him in typical Gallic manner on the shoulder and advised him: "You are far too fast, young man." Another Frenchman asked with morbid curiosity which was Rommel's division. Rommel told him. *"Sacre bleu!"* exploded the Frenchman. "The Spook Division again. First in Belgium, then at Arras and on the Somme and now here, again and again our paths have crossed. We call you the Spook Division."

For four days the Spook Division enjoyed the Channel sun, beaches and hotel wine cellars. At 5:30 A.M. on June 16 this idyll ended. The division crossed the Seine over a Wehrmacht bridge at Rouen and raced south. The next day Rommel heard on the car radio that the French were appealing for an armistice. Hitler ordered his army to occupy the French Atlantic coastline fast, clear down to the Spanish frontier; and Rommel covered the distance at an incredible speed. On June 16, 100 miles. On the seventeenth, 200. It was a wonder that the tanks survived.

He met no resistance until June 18, at Cherbourg, France's most important deepwater port. Hitler had ordered its immediate capture. Although his division was outnumbered twenty times or more, and the fortress guns were still powerfully intact, Rommel took Cherbourg in his stride—that day the stride was over 220 miles. "I don't know if the date's right," he wrote to Lucie on June 20, "as I've rather lost touch, what with the combat actions of the last few days and hours." He added, "Only by striking fast were we able to execute the Führer's specific order that Cherbourg was to be captured as rapidly as possible." Later he wrote, "I've slept seven hours now, and I'm going out to look over my troops, the immense booty and our prisoners—there are twenty or thirty thousand in and around Cherbourg."

Thus ended Rommel's blitzkrieg through France. He and the Spook Division had taken 97,000 prisoners, at a loss of only forty-two tanks.

Despite the brilliant success, tongues began to wag in the German officer camps. Many generals were frankly envious of the glory that Rommel had earned. Others, like General Georg Stumme, who had commanded the Seventh Panzer Division before him, were quietly impressed. Rommel's corps commander, Hoth, praised him in public —for instance, at the division staff dinner later that summer. (Rommel proudly noted, "He says that my predecessor, Stumme—who was regarded as a real dynamo in Poland—is a lame old cart horse compared with me, and much else. Of course all this was said under the influence of much alcohol, but it does my commanders a lot of good to hear how highly their corps commander rates our division's achievements.") But in private Hoth expressed interesting reservations. In a confidential report on Rommel in July, he warned that the general was too prone to act on impulse. Rommel would be eligible for a corps command, said Hoth, only if he gained "greater experience and a better sense of judgment." Hoth also accused Rommel of being ungenerous about the contributions others had made in the battles Rommel won.

Kluge, the Fourth Army commander, echoed this criticism. When Rommel invited Kluge to contribute a foreword to a manuscript on the campaign, Kluge agreed—but gently pointed out to him that several of the book's diagrams and references had been falsified to the Seventh Panzer Division's advantage. The part played by the Luftwaffe, he said, and particularly the dive bombers, was virtually ignored. Rommel's left-hand neighbor, the Thirty-second Infantry Division, was shown making much slower progress than it really had. Nor would Kluge accept Rommel's caustic references to his right-hand neighbor, Lieutenant General Hartlieb's Fifth Panzer Division. Hartlieb, in fact, had formally complained to Berlin about Rommel. It seems that Rommel had used up all his own bridging tackle on the first day, and so on May 14, when he wanted to bridge the Meuse, he had helped himself to Hartlieb's tackle. Hartlieb insisted on its return, but Rommel refused, saying that his own division was going to cross first. This delayed Hartlieb's movements for hours on end. Rommel then had the gall to complain that the Fifth Panzer Division was falling too far behind! (Colonel Streich later added a sidelight. "Rommel seized this opportunity to filch my own heavy tanks for use in his division's advance as well," he wrote. "When my general, Hartlieb, protested, he was told that General Hoth had sanctioned it; I myself don't believe for a minute that Rommel asked his permission. Our infantry took very heavy casualties as a consequence.") At the river Scarpe on May 25, the same thing happened again, and there was a furious scene. Later Rommel piously claimed in a letter to Bodewin Keitel, the army's chief of personnel: "No coarseness resulted that I am aware of."

Johannes Streich later commented in a manuscript: "During the war a book titled *The Spook Division* was published. In it, various operations successfully executed by our Fifth Panzer Division were cynically claimed by the Seventh Panzer. That the Seventh Panzer took far heavier casualties than any other division in the west, including even infantry divisions, shows how ruthlessly Rommel treated it."

Another factor in the growing controversy over Rommel was his favoritism toward the Nazi bigwigs in his division. Thus for the final assault on Saint-Valéry he had given Karl Hanke command of a tank company, although even Hanke protested that he was not qualified. A shell fragment soom jammed the turret of Hanke's Panzer IV, whereupon Hanke panicked and halted, thus blocking the entire regiment's advance. Rothenburg had to send his own adjutant in person to get him to move over. Hanke was also at the center of one of Rommel's most scandalous acts. He had recommended Hanke for the Knight's Cross, and—again a sign of blatant favoritism—sent the citation up by special courier to the Führer's headquarters, bypassing all regular channels. Almost at once, however, Hanke offended Rommel. He happened to mention that as a state secretary in the propaganda ministry he held a rank that technically was greater than Rommel's as major general. Rommel immediately sent an adjutant to the Führer's headquarters to intercept his own citation for Hanke's medal. It was viewed as an unusually spiteful step. "This action," wrote one tank commander, "became common knowledge in the division. It badly tarnished the image that all of his troops had gained of him on account of his courage and genius as a leader."

# Not a Penny for
# Africa

TO the Nazi propaganda writers, Rommel's exploits that summer of 1940 were a gift. "Like one of the Horsemen of the Apocalypse," they called him. His panzer division was "like a ghost fleet."

"His magic word is speed, boldness is his stock in trade. He shocks the enemy, takes them unawares, outflanks them, suddenly appears far in their rear, attacks them, outflanks them, encircles them, uses his genius and everything he's got, taking night and fog and river and obstacle in his stride. Thus his tanks carve long bloodstained trails across the map of Europe like the scalpel of a surgeon." So wrote one glorifier, an officer who had served with Rommel in the First World War and now met him again. "Like a film, his story goes on: isolated acts of bravery shine briefly, there are the individual tragedies, crises and death. I look into his eyes. There is still the intrepid look I saw all those years ago, but something of it is overshadowed by the sheer grandiose scale of today's events."

Another propagandist produced these words: "Yes, they know him now in France—they know his face, with its blue eyes and their hint of hidden cunning, the straight nose, the firm jaw with its lips tightly compressed when he is thinking, and the chin that says all there is to be said about these noble features—their energy, their will-power, uniformly modeled, strong and masculine to look at, but of a severity softened by the twinkling eyes and the two small wrinkles at the corners of his mouth, that show he is not averse to irony and wit."

The Wehrmacht troops settled into occupied France and prepared for the next operation—the invasion of England. Rommel may not have been aroused by the buxom French girls promenading in only their bras and panties, because of the heat—but he noticed them; he ingenuously mentioned them in a letter to Lucie that August. In fact he had little time for women and did not take them seriously. His friend Kurt Hesse wrote, "I only recall him talking about them once. He had been to visit a town in East Prussia, and told me he had noticed that it was full of pretty girls. What he liked were horses and dogs, but he never spent money on them either." Rommel, added Hesse, always dressed correctly, but never with great style. "He felt most at home in riding boots, an old army tunic, with his cap slightly cocked and a riding whip in his hand. He rarely carried a pistol, but he was an expert shot and if he ran into the enemy, then he grabbed the first rifle or machine gun he could lay his hands on."

He spent his off-duty hours shooting with French land-owners, who tended to be pro-German out of staunch anticommunism, or at his farmhouse headquarters writing up his own campaign history. "Do you want to see how I write?" he asked Hesse, and pointed to a row of boxes under his bed. "Here—let's take the twenty-third of May. First folder, orders received and reports sent up to my superiors. Second folder, orders to the troops and their reports to me. Third folder, maps and sketches of May twenty-third. Fourth folder, my photographs. Fifth folder, other items of historical interest like letters found on the dead, captured enemy orders and home news items about my division and myself." He explained, "All this is going to occupy me on my retirement. I'm going to write a sequel to *Infanterie Greift an*."

The Nazi propaganda minister, Goebbels, asked him to collaborate on a big army film about the campaign,

*Victory in the West.* Rommel spent part of August re-enacting for the movie cameras the Spook Division's crossing of the Somme. He had a great time playing movie director, and he schooled his troops in acting techniques. A battalion of French black troops was hauled out of the prison camps to stage the surrender of a village. Again, this time for the cameras, Rommel's tanks charged, guns blazing. He told the blacks to come out toward the tanks with their hands up and looking scared; but the men overacted, rolled the whites of their eyes and screamed with terror. Rommel cut the cameras, and patiently explained through interpreters that actors had to show their emotions more subtly than that. The battle scenes were finally filmed on such an epic and reckless scale that several more lives were lost, though through no fault of Rommel's. "No expense has been spared to show it as it really was," he wrote on the last day of shooting. "There were blacks in it again today. The fellows had a whale of a time and thoroughly enjoyed putting up their hands all over again."

During this period his following among the younger army officers grew phenomenally. They came from far and wide to see Rommel. He got on well with the troops, too, asked about their wives and families and inquired about their furloughs and medals. The Nazi press was filled with his exploits. But the publicity brought him more enemies in the OKW—the German High Command—and among the army's General Staff. Hesse, by now the army's press chief, wrote privately to him, warning of the ill feeling being stirred up. Rommel dismissed it as the old General Staff resentment against any up-and-coming outsider.

The summer of 1940 passed, with Rommel's division practicing relentlessly for the invasion of England. He continued to thirst for new distinctions, but the thirst went unquenched. In Hitler's Reichstag speech of July 19 many promotions were announced, but none for anyone below the rank of corps commander. In August, Rommel again felt slighted when Friedrich Paulus and Karl Kriebel—two of his prewar friends—moved up to lieutenant general: to be leapfrogged by two General Staff officers particularly stung him. "It seems that as usual we combat soldiers are only good for cannon fodder," he muttered in one letter. "As long as this clique is at the top level, things will never change."

Rommel's heart leaped one evening when he was ordered by telegram to present himself at Hitler's Chancellery on September 9. So certain was he that he was about to be awarded the Oak Leaves cluster for bravery that he purchased a new medal bar for his uniform. But Hitler had planned just a polite meeting with his generals. Rommel sat on his left at the luncheon and stood on his right at the subsequent war conference. "Just official business, so a fresh medal wasn't in the offing," he wrote to Lucie. "Not that I care," he added unconvincingly.

The air battle over southern England was reaching its height that September and the meeting in the Chancellery took place only a few days after Hitler's famous speech threatening to "wipe out" Britain's cities if Winston Churchill would not desist from his night air raids on Berlin. "The Führer showed me the results we have obtained already—it's quite astonishing how many military objectives we have already knocked out in London. And all this is probably only just a beginning."

Afterward he called on his friend Kurt Hesse, a mild, thoughtful man, in a suburb of Berlin. Hesse told him that rumors in the General Staff had it that Hitler intended involving Germany in Italy's adventures in North Africa. Rommel reassured him: "Not one man and not one penny for Africa—that's what the Führer has just told me in person." Hesse then asked how Hitler intended to defeat England. Rommel sprang up, his eyes blazing: "He says he's going to smash Britain to smithereens and wrap the country in a shroud of death!" His voice echoed Hitler's harsh, guttural tones.

Rommel returned to the Channel coast. At Rouen on September 14 his divison practiced embarking tanks and trucks onto invasion barges—concrete-lined river barges, primitively converted for their new function with improvised landing ramps instead of sterns. The idea was that tugs would tow strings of these unwieldy craft across the Channel when Hitler gave the order. What Rommel did not know was that the whole show was one enormous bluff. Hitler had secretly abandoned his invasion plans long before and was turning to other, indirect ways of influencing Britain.

More weeks passed. Manfred Rommel, nearly twelve now, wrote to him proudly that he had won good marks in Latin—but only a "satisfactory" in math—and that he had had difficulty getting lettuce for his rabbits. It was a shame, the boy wrote, that his father was so seldom home. "Do you still go hunting?" he inquired wistfully in November. Rommel sent him shapshots from a recent hunt. Manfred replied, "I'm green with envy after seeing those hunting photos. The only good thing about it all is that you'll soon be here again, and *surely* you'll take me hunting in the forest with you!" But only one week after Rommel had ventured home to Wiener Neustadt on leave he was suddenly recalled to his division; it was being transferred to Bordeaux. So he missed sharing Christmas with his family.

*On my second visit to Manfred Rommel at his home in Stuttgart, of which he is the mayor, he brought out an oversized albumlike book, bound in red leather and tooled in gold. This was his father's idea of how a war diary should look. Rommel had worked it up into a continuous narrative—at his friend Rudolf Schmundt's suggestion—and sent it to Hitler. As I turned the heavy cartridge paper and looked at the meticulous maps facing each page, I could imagine how pleased the Führer must have been by the general's thoughtfulness. Hitler's response, a letter dated December 20, 1940, was in a file I studied afterward in Washington. "You can be proud of your achievements," he wrote to Rommel. Rommel reported this ecstatically to Lucie: "For the Führer to have found time, despite his burden of work, to look at my history of the division and to write to me—that makes me enormously proud."*

*There is no doubt that it was a smart and timely move on Rommel's part, as events soon showed.*

It was early in February of 1941. In Berlin, crowds were thronging the movie theater showing the new film *Victory in the West*. Rommel went home to Austria again, hoping to resume his interrupted furlough. But on the evening after his arrival at Wiener Neustadt, one of Hitler's adjutants appeared with a message ordering him to fly immediately to Berlin for a meeting with the commander in chief of the army and with Hitler himself. Obviously something was in the wind.

He left Lucie next morning, the sixth of February. Some days later the postman brought her a letter from him: "Plane landed at Staaken airport at noon forty-five. . . . Drove first to commander in chief who briefed me on my new job; then to F[ührer]. Almighty hurry. My kit's coming here. I can only take barest essentials with me. You can imagine how my head is swimming with it all. . . . So our furlough was once again cut short. Don't be upset, either of you, that's just the way it has to be. The new job is very big and important."

But where was he going? Next day there was another letter from Berlin. "Slept on the new job last night. It'll be one way of getting my rheumatism treatment. . . ."

Lucie remembered that the doctor treating Erwin's rheumatism in France had once advised him, "You need sunshine, general. You ought to be in Africa." She guessed where destiny was about to take her husband.


After the last British soldier embarked at Dunkirk in June 1940, there was no point of contact between the British and German armies. Two weeks later, Italy's proud dictator, Benito Mussolini, greedily declared war on France and Britain, hoping for a share of the spoils. Since 1890 Italy had had colonial possessions in Africa, and there were now 220,000 Italians under arms in Libya, the closest colony to Italy itself. Mussolini ordered his army to attack the British in Egypt, and capture the Suez Canal.

In September 1940, Marshal Rodolfo Graziani launched a ponderous offensive into Egypt. It was halted at Sidi Barrani, not far inside the frontier. Hitler offered Mussolini, his new ally, a German panzer division in support. Mussolini's generals were too arrogant to accept, and Hitler's representative in Rome—General Enno von Rintelen—was informed in October that Italian forces were considered sufficient for the offensive and that it would be resumed late in December. "Thereafter," the

Italians conceded, "perhaps one or two German divisions might like to join in the attack on the Nile Delta, where there are about 200,000 British."

Nothing came of all this. On October 28 Mussolini invaded Greece from Albania. This was a severe shock to Hitler, who had secret plans of his own. He was furious and piqued by Italy's act. "Nothing for Libya and nothing for Albania," he said to the General Staff on November 1. Two days later he spelled it out to the army's tank warfare expert, General Wilhelm von Thoma; he had decided against sending over that panzer division, at any rate "for the time being." He would send only air force units to the Mediterranean, to help prevent a complete Italian fiasco, which would have side effects on Germany's own strategy.

Italy's pride took severe knocks in North Africa during December 1940. The British army opposing them at Sidi Barrani, just inside Egypt, had assembled motorized forces from all over the Empire and staged a counterattack under Lieutenant General Sir Richard O'Connor's local command. It gained ground so fast that in ten days the British were besieging the Libyan fortress at Bardia, where Marshal Graziani's September offensive had begun. Now Mussolini appealed for German aid—he wanted that panzer division after all and also materials and equipment for his own forces.

Hitler let him stew in his own juice until January 9, 1941. By then Bardia had fallen and the heavily fortified port of Tobruk, farther to the west, was under British siege. Only now did Hitler decide that a small armored force should begin moving to Libya, in February. At a meeting in Berchtesgaden, Mussolini accepted. Meanwhile the rate of Italian collapse in Libya quickened. On January 22, before the Germans left for Africa, Tobruk surrendered to the British. This was a real calamity. Also alarming was the report that came three days later from the commander of the Fifth Light Division, the blocking force chosen to help the Italians defend Tripoli. This officer, Major General Hans Baron von Funck, a splendid aristocrat of the old school, had gone to Libya to assess the situation for the German General Staff. He found that the proposed blocking force would be too small to save

Libya. A week later he stated this to Hitler in person. According to one of Hitler's adjutants, the Führer was shocked. "The lunacy about it all," he said, "is that on the one hand the Italians are screaming blue murder and painting their shortages of arms and equipment in the blackest terms, and on the other hand they are so jealous and infantile that they find the idea of using German soldiers and German materials quite repugnant. Mussolini would probably like it most if the German troops would fight in Italian uniforms!"

Hitler's first reaction was that a bigger German force would have to go. "The British must be exhausted both in personnel and materiel terms after their long advance," he explained to field marshals Keitel and Brauchitsch on February 3. "If they come up against fresh and well-equipped German forces, it will be a very different kettle of fish." He ordered the General Staff to prepare a complete panzer division for the transfer to North Africa on the heels of the original blocking force, the Fifth Light.

The Führer's second reaction was instinctive: General Funck was too gloomy about North Africa—he was evidently tainted by the Italian debacle. Another general must be found to command the Fifth Light. The choice fell on Johannes Streich, forty-nine. It was pointed out that a corps staff would also be needed for the overall command of the expedition. Hitler selected Rommel. (In 1942 he told an Italian diplomat he had also considered Erich von Manstein for the job. "But I picked Rommel because he knows how to *inspire* his troops, just like Dietl up in Narvik. This is absolutely essential for the commander of a force that has to fight under particularly arduous climatic conditions as in North Africa or the Arctic.")

Thus Rommel was called to the Chancellery on February 6, 1941. Hitler showed him British and American illustrated magazines with photographs of Sir Richard O'Connor's victorious drive into Libya. Rommel gleaned several ideas from these photographs. When he left, he had in his pocket written guidelines from Keitel—the chief of the High Command—for any dealings he might have with the Italians in Rome and Libya. The document reflected Hitler's uncompromising mood: "German troops will not be committed to a pointless battle." By this he meant the Italians' current intention of defending only Tripoli itself. This area was too small to allow the Luftwaffe an air base. If the Italians would not agree to hold a line far to the east of Tripoli, then Rommel was to express regrets to Marshal Graziani that there was "no point" in sending Germans over.

With the formal title of Commander in Chief, German Troops in Libya, Rommel left the Reich capital tingling with anticipation. Characteristically—for his ambitions were undimmed—he clung to that designation even when his command was formally designated the German Afrika Korps a few days later: Commander in Chief (Befehlshaber) was one rung higher in the military jargon than Kommandierender General, the commander of a corps.

His mission was ostensibly to explore the military situation, but Rommel intended to take absolute command the moment his own troops arrived. "I hinted to General von Rintelen, our military attaché in Rome, that such was my intention," he later wrote. "He advised me to drop the idea, saying that that way I only stood to loose my name and reputation."

When his plane brought him onto North African soil for the first time, at noon on February 12, 1941, the Italians were still in full retreat toward Tripoli. Rommel found them busy packing to catch what ships they could back to Italy before the British came. Graziani had been replaced by General Italo Gariboldi as field commander. Gariboldi was a burly North Italian with a white moustache and not much more tact than the average noncommissioned officer. When Rommel now talked of manning a forward defense line at Sirte, far to the east of Tripoli, he just shrugged and retorted that Rommel should go take a look out there for himself. Rommel climbed into a Heinkel bomber that afternoon and did just that.

From the Heinkel's cockpit, Rommel could not see much sign of any field defenses around the port of Tripoli. East of it, he noticed a belt of sandy country that would probably be useful as a natural obstacle to enemy vehicles. He still had to find out the most elementary facts. For example, could heavy tanks drive in the desert at all? Italian generals said that they could not. A few days earlier, Rommel had asked Lieutenant Hans-Otto Behrendt, a lanky, mild-mannered Egyptologist assigned to him as an Arabic interpreter, whether even wheeled trucks could drive in sand. Behrendt was the author of a pamphlet entitled *Tips for Desert Drivers in Egypt*. He replied that the secret was to drive on slightly soft tires.

As Rommel flew east, he saw the Sirte desert himself—shimmering hot and inhospitable. He wondered how well his troops would survive the heat, assuming that the British allowed them time to acclimatize. Along the Mediterranean coastline he could see the highway built by Marshal Balbo—the Via Balbia, extending from Tripoli right to the Egyptian frontier. He wondered what cooperation he could get from the Italians: his first impressions of both the generals and their men had been uniformly favorable.

Back in Tripoli he found General Gariboldi waiting with the Italian Chief of General Staff, Mario Roatta. After talking bluntly with them, Rommel sent this radio message to Germany: "First talks with Generals Gariboldi and Roatta have passed off satisfactorily. Our suggestions are being put into effect. Foremost fighting units are at Sirte. Personally flew reconnaissance mission out there myself."

That evening he dined with the Italian generals at a Tripoli hotel. One inquired where he had won his Pour le Mérite. Rommel retorted without thinking: "Longarone!" That killed all further small talk that evening.

Two days later his first combat troops sailed into Tripoli—the vanguard of the Afrika Korps.

# The Elite Corps

ON the fourteenth of February, 1941 a troopship sails past the wrecked hospital ship at the entrance to the port of Tripoli, richest jewel in Italy's colonial empire. Rommel's soldiers line the decks for their first glimpse of Africa. They see glistening white modern buildings, palm trees, broad boulevards, cool shadows. Some of the men even begin to think they are going to like it here. They belong to the Third Reconnaissance and Thirty-ninth Antitank battalions—the vanguard of Rommel's force. Despite the risk of air attack, Rommel orders the ship to be unloaded by floodlight that same night. Six thousand tons of war equipment are put onto the dockside between dusk and dawn, breaking all records for the port: trucks, guns, ammunition, armored cars, tents, mosquito netting.

At eleven the next morning a military parade is held in front of Government House. Watched by curious Italians and Arabs, the German troops march past smartly in their new tropical uniforms and pith helmets under the baking African sun. Rommel, the Italian generals standing pompously at his side, takes the salute himself. He is stocky, fit and sharp-featured. One of his staff war correspondents, Hanns-Gert von Esebeck, wrote of him at this time:

"He has a high, symmetrical forehead, a forceful nose, prominent cheekbones, a narrow mouth with tight lips and a chin that juts defiance. There are hard lines from his nostrils to the corners of his mouth, but they are softened by something often akin to an artful smile. And in his clear blue eyes, too, cold and appraising, penetrating and keen, there is something of a cunning that brings real warmth to this man's features when it breaks through."

Rommel delivers a brisk speech, the German and Italian national anthems are played and the men drive off directly to the east. This is only the first of many such parades, as the units of Rommel's Afrika Korps begin to flow into Tripoli. They are small in number, but they become dedicated and professional elite which Rommel will lead with such skill and unorthodox methods that eighteen months later Winston Churchill will declaim: "Rommel! Rommel! Rommel!—What else matters but beating him!"

Colonel Rudolf Schmundt, Hitler's jug-eared chief adjutant, had been attached to Rommel's party. Rommel sent him back to Germany with a report on Rommel's initial impressions. "If the British advance on Tripoli immediately without regard for casualties," Rommel wrote, "our general situation will be very grave indeed." Schmundt gave the document to Hitler two days later and wrote afterward to Rommel: "I reached the Berghof on Sunday and found the Führer already waiting feverishly for news! I briefed him just as you said, and the Führer was obviously delighted with the initiative you have shown in tackling the job, Herr General. He is deeply apprehensive about the Libyan war zone, and dreads the next two weeks."

Hitler, said Schmundt, granted all Rommel's requests. He agreed to ship antitank weapons, mines and the Fifth Light Division's main armored fist—the Fifth Panzer Regiment—to Libya at once. Moreover, the Fifteenth Panzer division would follow in a few weeks' time. Schmundt also touched on the prestige issue, so dear to Rommel's heart. "On this much you can rest assured," he informed Rommel. "The Führer will take care this time that there won't be any historical distortion of where the credit goes."

For Rommel, this initial buildup went agonizingly

slowly. In a letter to Lucie on February 26, he described the first minor skirmish with a British tank, 470 miles east of Tripoli, and added: "The next two or three weeks are going to be crucial. After that things will even up. . . . The enemy know now that we're here, and they have begun digging in."

Two days later Hitler assured Mussolini: "If we get just fourteen more days, then any fresh British advance on Tripoli is bound to fail. . . . When our first panzer regiment arrives, I think it will tilt the balance very dramatically in our favor."

Some days later the Fifth Light Division's panzer regiment disembarked at Tripoli. Now Rommel was really in business. There was the usual propaganda parade. The sight of the squat, powerful German tanks rattling through the Libyan capital brought an awed silence, then gasps and cheers from the crowds. There seemed in fact no end to the number of tanks, partly because Rommel had cleverly ordered them to drive several times around the block, like a stage "army," before rolling off to the east. "We've got to keep the enemy guessing about our strength —that is, about our *weakness*—until the rest of the Fifth Light Division gets here"—so he told the panzer regiment's officers.

He had another trick up his sleeve. To fool the enemy's air reconnaissance, he ordered his troops to manufacture hundreds of dummy tanks of wood and cardboard. Some were stationary, others were mounted on ordinary Volkswagen cars. Trucks and motorcyclists drove around between them, and real tanks methodically churned tracks across the sand for the enemy planes to photograph. According to the Fifth Light's war diary, "Intercepted enemy radio messages report having sighted medium tanks. This shows that our deception has worked."

Rommel's information about the British early in March 1941 was sketchy. He reported one rather puzzling aspect about Tobruk, a port far behind the enemy lines. "Tobruk harbor is full of shipping, and there are big troop concentrations around Tobruk." Were the British bringing in reinforcements by sea—or were troops being pulled right out of North Africa for some other campaign? Unknown to Rommel, the British were withdrawing their best units from Libya, to launch what was to prove a highly unprofitable expedition in Greece. Too late the enemy would learn from radio intercepts of Luftwaffe signals that Hitler had actually sent a German expeditionary force to North Africa.

For the enemy to withdraw troops on the very eve of victory in Tripolitania, however, was so patently absurd that Rommel did not dwell on it. Instead he ordered General Johannes Streich—who had arrived a week later —to explore eastward along the coast from Sirte with advance units of his Fifth Light Division. Streich easily reached El Mugtaa, on March 4, without even seeing the enemy. From here a salt marsh—virtually impassable to vehicles—extended inland from the Via Balbia, creating a defensive position which materially strengthened Rommel's hand. He wrote a buoyant letter home: "The front is now 480 miles east [of Tripoli]. . . . My troops are coming over. It's the tempo that matters now."

From the surviving documents, it is clear that this easy advance dazzled even Rommel. He began to daydream of great conquests. On March 5, at a gala showing of *Victory in the West* in Tripoli, he proclaimed to his audience that one day they would be seeing a film called *Victory in Africa*. When a young lieutenant—just driven out of Eritrea by the British army—reported to him as a staff officer, Rommel bragged: "We're going to advance to the Nile. Then we'll make a right turn, and win it all back again!" And on March 9 he boldly predicted in a draft letter to Berlin that he would resume his drive early in May, and keep going eastward along the coast until the summer heat stifled all further operations. "My first objective," he declared, "will be the reconquest of Cyrenaica; my second, northern Egypt and the Suez Canal." The canal was 1,500 miles east of Tripoli, but Rommel meant every word of what he said.

Of course, he was far outnumbered by the British. He had altogether only one panzer regiment, two machine gun battalions, two reconnaissance battalions, three batteries of artillery and a flak battalion—only about the same force as he had commanded in France. But he had big ambitions. In his draft letter to Berlin he airily dismissed the most obvious drawback: "Organizing supplies for such operations will be extremely difficult—but the brunt of the fighting will come in Cyrenaica, and there is water in abundance there." He hopefully mailed to Berlin this ambitious plan for conquest.

He himself flew to Berlin on March 19 and saw Hitler in person next day. Hitler began the audience by pinning on Rommel's chest the Oak Leaves medal that he had been coveting ever since France. It was the only pleasant moment. The General Staff threw cold water on Rommel's plans. General Franz Halder, the acid and professional Chief of General Staff, firmly advised Hitler not to accept them. It is clear from remarks made by Halder in prison camp in August 1945—recorded by a concealed British microphone—that he hated Rommel:

"At the time I was constantly telling Field Marshal von Brauchitsch that with the enemy dominating the Mediterranean the very most we could send over and keep supplied were three or four divisions. . . . Sooner or later things were bound to go against the Italians, but the longer we could stave it off, perhaps even for several years, the better. . . . Rommel explained that he would soon conquer Egypt and the Suez Canal, and then he talked about German East Africa. I couldn't restrain a somewhat impolite smile, and asked him what he would be needing for the purpose. He thought he would need another two panzer corps. I asked him, 'Even if we had them, how are you going to supply them and feed them?' To this I received the classic reply, 'That's quite immaterial to me. That's your pigeon.' "

There was a momentous secret Rommel could not be told. Hitler was going to invade Russia, and he would need every available division for that. So Rommel was instructed merely to hold his present line and prepare a strictly limited attack. These verbal orders were reinforced by written instructions the next day, March 21. He flew back to North Africa disgruntled, disappointed and determined to disobey.

In the desert, the tank is the capital weapon of the war and the tank man is the chosen warrior. To the infantryman falls the exhausting, debilitating fighting in the open, naked to his enemies, digging for cover where the ground is too hard to dig, thirsting where there is no water, trudging to the fight and trudging back again. But the tank crewman has the exhilaration, even arrogance that comes from commanding twenty tons of snorting armor plate and steel, a fire-spewing monster that can rumble clean through brick walls or copses of trees, and here in the open desert can thrust die-straight across the wilderness as long as the going is reasonably firm and the gasoline last —110 miles in a Panzer III.

"Mount up!" Five men climb through the round entry hatch atop the thick steel turret, and thread their bodies into their assigned places. Driver, radio operator and commander cannot see each other's faces, but all are connected to the tank's radio receiver, and the gunner manning the high-velocity fifty-millimeter gun and his loader can also talk by intercom. The outside world is visible only through slits in the armor, narrow enough to keep out bullets. There is the stench of raw fuel and gun oil and sweat. The heat is stifling when the turret hatch is bolted down, the metal already baking in the African sun, and the temperature climbs impossibly as the heat from the engine and the guns is added. The men wear black and work in shirt sleeves.

Their machine is a citadel unto itself, with two and a half inches of armor plate in front, a gun by Krupp's of Essen that can throw a high-explosive or armor-piercing shot a mile or more, and two machine guns that can scythe away the enemy's naked opposing infantry. But God help the five men if their machine should founder—trapped in a treacherous slough of sand or its track blown off by a mine or shell. They are inside a mechanized bomb, with hundreds of gallons of gasoline stowed behind them, 100 shells in the racks beside them, and 3,750 machine gun bullets in belts, all waiting to erupt and engulf them if one enemy projectile should explode inside this space. Only in front is their armor thick—to either side and in the rear it is only half as strong, and on top and below it is even thinner.

The tank surges across the battlefield. Its tracks churn up dense and choking plumes of sand. The noise inside is deafening. The 320-horsepower Maybach engine roars and races as the driver shifts up and down through the manual gears. The hot spent-shell cases clatter around the metal deck. The tank stops, the gun barks, and then again, continuing until the enemy is destroyed or the target is lost. Here in the open desert the rules are the same for both sides. Every tank commander instinctively dreads the sight of enemy tanks appearing on his flank. He and his opponent both try to come up behind low rises, "hull down," so that they can open fire while exposing nothing of their bulk. Both know the penalty of error—entombment in a blazing tank, with the hatch jammed and flames licking toward the ammunition racks.

A tank crew thirsts for battle but is immensely relieved when delivered from it. Then they can lever themselves up into the open air, emerging from their oven into the relative cool of the desert heat; they can stretch out in the tank's shadow and brew coffee. They are an elite, men of high esprit, like submarine men—their comradeship forged by shared hazards and the shared intoxication of manning intricate, almost invincible machines.

In Libya, Rommel found on his return, the tantalizing British retreat had continued. El Agheila, a dirty fort and watering point twenty miles east of El Mugtaa, had just fallen to Streich's light forces with hardly a fight on March 24. The British withdrew thirty miles to Mersa Brega, an Arab village straddling sand hills near the coast; it was a tactical bottleneck relatively easy to defend. The speed of Streich's advance put Rommel in a dilemma. As he explained in a letter to Lucie, "I've got to hold my troops back now to stop them from galloping on ahead."

According to his directives from Berlin—and from General Gariboldi—he was not allowed to attack Mersa Brega until the end of May, when he would have the Fifteenth Panzer Division too. But his radio intercept company had arrived, with skilled English-speaking operators listening in to the enemy's signals; and from these signals and Luftwaffe reconnaissance Rommel knew that the enemy were digging in and bringing up reinforcements. By May, the enemy defenses might be impregnable. On March 31 he ordered Streich to attack Mersa Brega, regardless of the directives from Berlin. The British abandoned their positions, and Rommel ordered a strong belt of mines and antiaircraft guns installed to prevent them from coming back.

In a good humor, he drove forward to Streich's command post at noon next day. "Na, when are we going to meet in Agedabia?" he called out. Agedabia was the next big town, fifty miles farther up the Via Balbia—far beyond the stop line ordered by Halder. Streich could not tell whether Rommel was serious or not, and purposely did not ask. "We'll have to see about that," he replied, matching his superior's bantering tone as close as he could. After Rommel had gone, Streich ordered his division to resume the advance next morning, April 2. He did not inform Rommel, and Rommel—most unusually—avoided contact with him until 1:00 P.M., when he caught up with the Fifth Light's foremost troops, feigned surprise, and exclaimed: "What's going on here?"

Streich evenly replied, "I thought we ought not to give a retreating enemy any chance of digging in all over again. So I have moved my whole division forward to here, and I'm about to attack Agedabia."

Rommel replied without a trace of anger, "Those weren't my orders—but I approve."

Thus Agedabia also fell at 4:00 P.M. that afternoon. Rommel reappeared in time to hear the great news. In his memoirs, *War without Hate*, he subsequently took full credit.

*Several times afterward, Streich got a raw deal from Rommel, but he is not a man to bear grudges. When I ran him to ground for an interview, in an old peoples' home outside Hamburg in northern Germany in 1976, he was a spry, slightly built, soldierly figure of eighty-five—neatly dressed, going deaf, eating dainty cakes in a circle of elderly ladies who cannot have asked him very often to recite these dramatic weeks with Rommel. The conversation was not very productive, but it did bear fruit later. Out of the blue came a lengthy sheaf of close typescript, written by Johannes Streich many years before but never published, entitled "Memoirs of Africa." The war diary of his Fifth Light Division has also turned up in private hands, and bears out Streich's version in every detail.*

Now Rommel realized that the British had begun a general withdrawal from the bulbous peninsula of Cyrenaica;

evidently they were desperate to keep their remaining forces intact. Agedabia was the starting point of half a dozen desert tracks cutting across the peninsula. Rommel determined to exploit them to the east. On April 2 a stern veto came from Gariboldi: "This is in contradiction to what I ordered. You are to wait for me before continuing with any advance."

Rommel did not wait. On April 3 he decided on a dramatic three-pronged thrust across the peninsula. If he moved fast enough he might destroy the entire enemy force right there. The southernmost prong of his thrust would cut clean across the desert, following an ancient caravan trail known as the Trigh el Abd; the trail led from Agedabia onward through Ben Gania, Bir Tengeder, Bir Hacheim and Bir el Gubi to the Egyptian frontier. A "Bir" was a waterhole—in theory. Rommel put Count Gerhard von Schwerin, a spiky but experienced half colonel, in charge of a mixed German-Italian force for this prong. Streich would lead another task force on a parallel track and—since a passing Italian priest had just tipped him off that even Benghazi, capital of Cyrenaica, was being abandoned—Rommel sent a reconnaissance battalion straight up the coast road to the big port. They drove in through cheering crowds at 10:00 P.M. that evening, just as a furious General Gariboldi was confronting Rommel about this disobedience of his veto.

An orgy of destruction and murder had marked Benghazi's second change of owners in three months. The British had detonated 4,000 tons of Italian ammunition and fires were still raging everywhere. A German navy commander sent next day to investigate this port's capacity for supply ships reported: "Australian troops and Arabs looted the buildings and robbed the Italian civilians of all their valuables at pistol point." One of his officers wrote of a building he took over, "In the rooms where the young girls had been slaughtered I arranged for photos to be taken of the pools of blood before they were mopped up." But now General Sir Philip Neame's motley "Cyrenaica Command" was being hustled straight out of the peninsula by Rommel's unexpected advance.

Rommel unquestionably knew that he was disobeying. He boasted about it to Lucie that day: "My superiors in

Tripoli, Rome and perhaps Berlin, too, must be clutching their heads in dismay. I took the risk, against all orders and instructions, because the opportunity was there for the taking. Probably it will all be pronounced okay later. They'll all say they would have done just the same in my shoes."

In Berlin there was indeed consternation. How was the impetuous general to know that his exploits were unbalancing months of meticulous secret planning for the Nazi intervention in the Balkans and Russia? The German High Command gave him a sharp rap across the knuckles. Keitel radioed him—using the so-called "Enigma" code—on April 3 that Hitler had firmly specified that Rommel's job was to stand fast and tie down British forces. "Any limited offensive moves that this necessitates are not to exceed the capabilities of your small force. . . . Above all, you are to avoid any risk to your open right flank, such as is bound to be entailed in turning north to attack Benghazi." If the British armor pulled out of Cyrenaica, of course, then a new situation would arise—but even then Rommel was still to await fresh orders.

Now history received a taste of Erwin Rommel, the master of deception, the headstrong adventurer who always got his way. At 9:00 P.M. that same day the fat Italian commander Gariboldi confronted Rommel in his trailer headquarters at Agedabia, his white gloves twitching with fury, and demanded absolute obedience. Rommel merely grinned. "There's no cause whatever for concern about our supply situation," he declared at one stage. They nearly came to blows. After three hours they were interrupted by the radio signal from Keitel ordering Rommel to stay put. Rommel read it, then announced to Gariboldi that it stated that the Führer had given him "complete freedom of action." This was very far from the truth, but Gariboldi was too slow-witted to spot it. Rommel even persuaded himself, it seems, because he told Lucie, "From the Führer have come congratulations for our unexpected successes, plus a directive for further operations that entirely fits in with my own ideas."

His own commanders were appalled at the prospect of striking out immediately across the desert peninsula. Streich objected that he needed at least four days to replenish the Fifth Light's supplies—all their dumps were way back at the Arco dei Fileni, "Marble Arch," the towering white trumphal arch built by Mussolini in 1937 on the frontier between Tripolitania and Cyrenaica. Rommel curtly ordered him to unload all the division's trucks in the open desert immediately and send them back empty, each carrying a spare crew (provided by the tank crews) for a round-the-clock trip to collect gasoline and ammunition from those dumps. Streich warned lugubriously, "Then my division will be stranded for at least a day." Rommel insisted: "This is the way to save bloodshed and to conquer Cyrenaica!" (The words are in the Afrika Korps diary.) He made a mental note to get rid of this quarrelsome general. The crossing of Cyrenaica then began.

A Luftwaffe general wrote at this time:

Cyrenaica is an almost treeless and therefore shadowless lunar landscape. The Jebel el Akdar is a wildly fissured mountain range broken only by a few valleys in which sand, usually white or reddish yellow, stunts the growth of any vegetation. Mobility is restricted almost entirely to the desert road, so it is startling in the midst of this barren waste of sand and stone to fly across the tents, flocks of sheep and camels of Arabs of whom no European knows: what caravan trails do they use, what is their living, what laws and customs do they obey? The farther east you go along the desert road, the more inhospitable the landscape becomes: while for about thirty miles east of Benghazi the colonizing work of the Italians is evident, around Derna and Tobruk there are no signs of human habitation. Even the pitiful stunted pines fall off. The thorny shrubs barely struggle up to knee height.

For one week, that April of 1941, Rommel's little force trekked across this desert, through the shimmering heat of a high noon sun that raised the arid air to 120° F. and more, and the cold of nights that dropped in one hour to freezing point. There were sand vipers and scorpions and armies of loathsome flies. The worst enemy of all, after their cruel thirst, was the sudden sandstorm. It would start as a curious little dust devil whirling between the bushes and develop into a torment of seventy-mile-an-hour winds whipping billions of tons of hot, fine red sand across the desert. The storm might last for days on end. The fine sand penetrated everything—even the watches the troops wore. It choked the engine filters; it got into tents, eyes and noses; it ran off car windshields like rain; it cut visibility. "Can't see more than three yards," wrote one of Rommel's company commanders in a diary. "In the afternoon, thank God, the storm subsides. We all crawl out, like moles from our holes, and begin the job of digging everything out again."

Rommel's great gamble began on April 4. Schwerin's little force was already moving east, with orders to cut straight across the peninsula to the other coast at Tmimi —Rommel could never get his tongue around that word, and stammered "Tmimini" instead—and block the coast road there against the withdrawing British troops. At 2:00 P.M. Colonel Gustav Ponath's Eighth Machine Gun Battalion also plunged eastward into the raw desert, with trucks carrying enough gasoline, food and water for 300 miles; their target was Derna, also on the other coast. Rommel had assured Schwerin that supplies would be airlifted to him. Since the Fifth Light Division's trucks had not yet returned from the dumps, Rommel looked for Streich, found him sleeping fitfully in his Kübel car, and announced: "You are to empty all the gas tanks of your remaining transport into your combat vehicles and tanks, and advance at once through Ben Gania to the coast, between Derna and Tobruk. The rest of your division can catch up when the trucks get back from the fuel dumps." An Italian general anxiously interrupted Rommel: "But that trail is a death track! We saturated it with Thermos mines two months ago during our retreat!" Rommel brushed his objections aside.

By fading light, one driver after another, accustomed only to the easy motoring of Europe's asphalt highways, turned off the firm Via Balbia and plowed into the desert sand and gravel. Streich's tanks were crewed by stand-ins, since the tank drivers were away trucking gasoline back from the dumps. Soon the wheeled equipment was up to its axles in sand drifts. The trucks that followed tried to skirt around them and bogged down too. Tractors went forward in the darkness to haul them out. Within hours, Streich's whole force was crippled and spread over a wide area; he was not pleased at all, and he ordered all headlights switched on and the trucks to winch each other out and keep together as well as they could. They soon lost sight of the desert trails, and the maps provided by the Italians proved useless. Guided by compass or stars alone, some elements managed to make some headway, but others were stranded and left behind to face thirst and hunger in the desert. Hefty explosions suddenly lit the sky as the first Thermos mines were hit. An ammunition truck erupted in a ball of fire, illuminating the desert for miles around. By dawn most of Streich's force was again immobilized and out of gasoline.

The heat of the sun brought new problems. At Ben Gania the tanks halted as the engine oil overheated and ran thin. Virtually all radio communication failed. Rommel could not raise his base headquarters, and they could not reach him. Days of unremitting chaos were beginning —how many of his drivers would ever reach the other coast after 200 miles of this? Rommel ranged across the desert in a Junkers 52 transport or light Storch plane, trying to control the movements. Twice he blundered into enemy units he had mistaken for his own. He landed to berate generals and colonels for their slowness, and cursed them because the enemy was slipping eastward out of their grasp. Once Schwerin saw the Storch flitting past overhead and swore: "That must be Rommel!" Another time a struggling motor column dared to pause for breath. The Storch zoomed in at shoulder height and a piece of paper fluttered to the ground: "If you don't move off again at once, I'll come down!—Rommel." Those who were lost, he found and pointed in the right direction again. But which direction was right? There was one solitary signpost, in mid-desert—but not a trail or track to be seen.

The key to the desert seemed to be the ancient Turkish-built fort at Mechili, a crumbling white stone pile rising above the desert mirages—the hub from which seven desert trails radiated like spokes to the coasts and the distant interior. Rommel believed it would be only lightly garrisoned. He rose at 4:00 A.M. on the fifth and wrote to Lucie: "Big things are happening in Africa. Let's hope we can pull off the coup we've now launched."

Air reconnaissance that day detected that the fort at Mechili was occupied by quite strong enemy forces after all, but Rommel decided to concentrate first on Mechili anyway. His base staff back at Agedabia disagreed: "We would prefer," they noted, "to see Tobruk as the objective, to interrupt the coast road there and stop the enemy escaping, and to leave just a masking force at Mechili." Rommel was of two minds. Twice on the sixth he gave different orders to Ponath's machine gun battalion. First, "Attack Mechili!" and then "Forward to Derna!" after all. Then a plane was sent to head off Count von Schwerin and an officer ran over with a message: "Rommel orders you to turn north and attack Mechili!"

Six-thirty A.M. on April 6 found Rommel only fifteen miles south of the fort—but he was virtually alone. His Afrika Korps was still stranded across the desert. After a while his aide Lieutenant Behrendt, the Egyptologist, arrived with a few trucks, the first of Schwerin's party. Rommel sent him skirting around Mechili to block its exits to the east. Another aide found Streich at seven-thirty, halted at a dried salt lake some miles away. Rommel called Streich and Schwerin to a furious conference. They were lightly clad in khaki shorts; he was in full uniform, with riding boots, breeches and thick gray tunic. In the broiling heat his temper snapped, and he ordered them to attack the fort at 3:00 P.M. Streich refused, and pointed out that his tanks and vehicles were still scattered back across the desert for 100 miles, with broken frames, overheated engines, no gasoline. Rommel screamed at him that he was a coward. Streich unhooked his Knight's Cross—won for gallantry in 1940—and snapped: "Nobody has dared tell me that before. Withdraw that remark, or I'll throw this at your feet." Rommel muttered a withdrawal, but showed he did not mean it.

Later that afternoon, Rommel returned, pulled out a watch and barked at Streich: "It is now five P.M. You will attack Mechili at six with Schwerin's group, and capture it. I will order the Italian artillery to support you." At that moment Streich had only two trucks armed, with light antiaircraft guns, and no other weapons at all. Schwerin had little more and perhaps a few machine guns. How were they to move the fifteen miles to Mechili before the sun set, with its usual abruptness, at seven? And where was Schwerin now, and the Italian artillery? Streich set out with his few trucks, looking for Schwerin. He failed, lost his way, returned long after dark and reported to Rommel. The latter said nothing (he had in the meantime tried to find the Italians and failed). That night Rommel tried to capture the fort himself with the few platoons he had. "This operation miscarried," Streich's war diary drily observes. Rommel's own memoirs do not mention it.

Twice during the seventh he sent a lieutenant into the fort with an ultimatum to bluff the British. On both occasions the officer was sent back blindfolded, the second time with a scribbled message: "No intention of surrendering." Several times next day Rommel took off in his Storch to look for his main task force, Colonel Olbrich's Fifth Panzer Regiment. Not until the sun had set did he find it, picking its way around a boulder-strewn region that not even tanks could cross. He flew off the handle, and privately decided that Olbrich too would have to go. After dark he landed near Streich's command post. Eight tanks had now arrived from the company commanded by Major Ernst Bolbrinker. Rommel tersely ordered yet again, "You will capture Mechili tomorrow!"

Before dawn he climbed wearily out of bed and wrote dutifully to Lucie: "Don't know if the date's right. We've been advancing across an endless desert for days on end, and we've lost all notion of time and space. . . . Today's going to be another decisive day. After a 220-mile march across the desert sand and stones, our main forces are arriving and are going into action. . . . Now there's going to be another Cannae, modern style." Cannae was Hannibal's most famous victory.

At about six he again left in his Storch to tour the battle area. His aide, Lieutenant Hermann Aldinger, wrote a few days later:

The Storch lifts off for a quick look over the front lines and battle dispositions. The pilot gets a sign:

"Go lower!" but no sooner is he down than the Italian troops (in error) are letting fly at it with all they've got. Bullets begin hitting his wings, and with a burst of aerobatics the pilot just manages to get the hell out of there. Far to the west are dust clouds: they must be our troops. On the run in, the general gets a real shock—they are British troops heading west. Stragglers? Or a British counterattack? He's got to warn our troops moving up from the west about this danger. Eight miles later the general sees our own leading troops, and goes in to land. The pilot doesn't see a big rock, the Storch loses half its undercart. "Desert pileup."

Our troops have an eighty-eight-millimeter gun with them, but they tell the general that it was disabled last night in a shoot-out with the British. They're heading north now to try to contact the rest. The general asks, "What transport have you got?" "A truck." "Then let's get the hell out of here. The British will be here within five minutes, they mustn't find us. We'll make a detour through the desert. I know the way."

Everything is loaded aboard, and a crazy drive begins. On the way we pick up three or four more trucks that have lost their way. Despite all these adventures, the general gets back to our command staff safely. Meanwhile we can see a sandstorm brewing— a Ghibli. His command staff are ready to move off. We haven't gone 800 yards before we are suddenly engulfed in the violent storm. All our staff are scattered and we find ourselves alone. We can only guess which way we are going by compass and speedometer. We zigzag, we strain our eyes ahead, sometimes the sky lightens, sometimes it turns dark red. We see three dispatch riders in the sandstorm, their heads bent, their motorcycles covered; we take them with us and grope our way toward the airfield. There we find more stragglers. We ask them how the attack is going. Nobody knows. Slowly we feel our way along the telephone line, and suddenly we find that we are just outside the fort of Mechili. There are weapons and equipment lying around, and hundreds of prisoners cowering on the ground while the sandstorm rages and covers everything—like a blizzard in dense fog.

In the fort's yard the division commander [General Streich] reports to the general: "Mechili has fallen. We have taken 1,700 prisoners, including seventy officers and a general, and we have captured quantities of guns, trucks and food."

Thus Rommel missed the party at Mechili. So did Colonel Olbrich's main tank force; it did not arrive until noon. His tank turrets were jammed tight by the sandstorm anyway. Rommel approved the suggestion that the turrets should be dismantled and cleaned, and he sent Schwerin's force and a pursuit group along the desert track to Derna on the coast. Lieutenant Behrendt had taken the same desert trail to Derna on the day before in an eight-wheeler, and had driven right into the beautiful, well-laid-out port. The British had already passed through, and Arabs flocked in brightly colored cloaks around the Wehrmacht trucks, offering eggs, oranges, dates and other delicacies for sale. Gustav Ponath's machine gunners had followed in Behrendt's tracks, and after a heavy fire fight had established a foothold at Derna airfield. When Rommel drove onto the airfield at six-thirty that evening, April 8, Colonel Ponath proudly announced the capture of 900 prisoners, including four more generals—one of them Sir Richard O'Connor himself. Ponath added that his machine guns were down to literally their last belt of ammunition each. His troops were worn out, but Rommel was relentless. He ordered Ponath to continue eastward at once along the highway, toward Tmimi and Tobruk.

Disenchanted with both the colorless General Streich and Colonel Olbrich, Rommel handed over command of the leading units reaching the highway from the desert to Major General Heinrich von Prittwitz, who had only just arrived in Libya in advance of his division, the Fifteenth Panzer. This was a slap in the face for Streich; but the successes that Rommel had achieved so easily against a startled and fumbling enemy had dangerously inflated his estimate of his own ability. Speed was all that mattered. His intention for April 9 was that an Italian infantry division should kick up dust west of Tobruk, while the Fifth

Light Division circled around it inland and attacked unexpectedly from the southeast quarter. "I had imagined that the Fifth Light was already on the move," he later wrote—forgetting that he himself had sanctioned the dismantling of the turrets for cleaning. When at 6:30 P.M. he found the panzer regiment still doing this at Mechili, way back, he again lost his temper at the inoffensive General Streich.

By his unexpected strike across the peninsula, Rommel had certainly caught the British on the wrong foot—for a reason that he never dreamed of. All his secret communications with the German High Command were being encoded by the Enigma machine, rather like a small, wooden-boxed electric typewriter. The Nazi code experts had pronounced this machine absolutely safe from enemy code breakers. The messages were radioed in this code to Rome, and transmitted by wire to Hitler's headquarters. Deep in the English countryside, however, the enemy had constructed a far superior machine, as big as a house, capable of decoding the secret Enigma signals. Radio listening posts fed the German signals to the machine, a large multi-service organization translated and interpreted the fantastic results and they were transmitted back, marked "Ultra Secret," to the enemy commanders facing Rommel. It was the biggest secret of the war.

However, more than once Rommel disobeyed the orders issued to him in Enigma code. For example, on this occasion, in April 1941, the British knew only of the orders issued to Rommel to stand fast at Benghazi; not yet knowing Rommel, they had assumed he would obey. This explains the surprised collapse of the British defense of Cyrenaica when he advanced. But now Winston Churchill had signaled from London that Tobruk was "to be held to the death without thought of retirement." On the night of the eighth the main Australian force, retiring from Cyrenaica, had reached Tobruk and began manning its Italian-built fortifications, in pursuance of Churchill's order.

Rommel did not realize this. Early on the tenth he was still confident, and he predicted: "The enemy is definitely retreating. We must pursue them with all we've got. Our objective is the Suez Canal, and every man is to be informed of this."

As he was dictating these words into the Afrika Korps war diary, the machine gunners of Ponath's battalion reached Kilometer Stone 18 on the Via Balbia, eleven miles short of Tobruk. Heavy artillery fire began to drop around them. By a supreme effort, Ponath managed to take his storm troops 2,000 yards closer, but here murderous antitank and machine gun fire swept the road. The German troops dived for what little cover there was and waited for heavy artillery support. Farther back down the asphalt highway, Prittwitz arrive at Schwerin's command post in some perplexity. "Rommel has sent me to take command of the attack. But I've only just arrived in Africa—I don't know the first thing about the troops or the terrain." Schwerin briefed him and the general snatched some sleep.

At sunrise, Rommel stood at the new general's tent flap, bawling to know why the attack on Tobruk was stagnating. "The British are escaping," he bellowed. Prittwitz flushed pink with confusion. Schwerin loaned him his car and driver, and saw them drive off at high speed down the highway toward Tobruk. They were driving into the unknown. Rommel had no maps or air photos of the fortress. He had no notion of its defenses. He might have survived the next few minutes, but Prittwitz did not have Rommel's nine lives. The astonished machine gunners, now at Kilometer 16, saw the car with the general's pennant racing through them from the rear. A gun crew nearest to the highway screamed a warning: "Halt! Halt!" Prittwitz stood up in his speeding car and shouted back: "Come on! Forward! The enemy is getting away!" At that instant a British antitank shell slammed into his car and tore clean through him. He and his driver were killed outright.

Schwerin found out at once. "I saw red," he said in 1976. "I marched straight over to the famous white house where Rommel had set up his headquarters. Rommel drove up, and I informed him that the general that he had just sent up front was already dead. That was the first time I saw him crack. He went pale, turned on his heel and drove off again without another word."

Rommel drove south of Tobruk to inspect the lie of the land there. A number of trucks and a twenty-millimeter gun were in his party. A lookout spotted two small vehicles speeding and bumping along their wheel tracks, catching up from the rear. Through his telescope, Rommel saw that one was a British command car—the other looked like its German equivalent. He was a brave man, but also prudent. "Get the gun ready," he ordered, and all the trucks halted. In no time the two strange cars were upon them and skidded to a halt. Out of one jumped General Streich, red-faced and angry, shouting the news of Prittwitz's death. Rommel coldly interrupted him: "How dare you drive after me in a British car? I was about to have the gun open fire on you."

Streich did not flinch. "In that case, " he retorted, "you would have managed to kill both your panzer division commanders in one day, Herr General."

# Kilometer 31

R OMMEL needed Tobruk for two good reasons. This grubby port was still the best harbor in Cyrenaica —in fact, in all North Africa. And it blocked out a twenty-two-mile stretch of the coastal highway, forcing his supply convoys moving forward to the Egyptian frontier onto a fifty-mile inland detour along a desert trail of indescribable condition. With Tobruk in enemy hands, even Rommel dared not resume his offensive toward Egypt and the Nile valley, because the Tobruk garrison could lance down across his supply lines at any time.

At first it did not dawn on him that the enemy intended to fight there to the death. Until far into April 1941 he eagerly believed every morsel of radio or photographic intelligence that indicated that the British were pulling out—that they had only escaped from Cyrenaica into this port to stage a second Dunkirk-style evacuation. Rommel wasted many lives and much ammunition before he realized his mistake. In fact, this situation raised the most disturbing problems for Rommel, and at first he refused to address himself to them—above all, the problem of how to supply his own forces during the siege.

Initially this snag was easily overlooked by the German public. He was the hero of the press. The public liked to measure a general's triumphs in simple terms, and as the Afrika Korps swept eastward toward Egypt the sheer distances he covered seemed to testify to his greatness. They had raced southward past Tobruk and captured Bardia on April 12, and next day Fort Capuzzo, barring the frontier road into Egypt itself, fell and the frontier wire was breached. Sollum, the first town on Egyptian soil, was captured too. But in the desert, as in war at sea, distances count for little; not even the capture of prisoners counts for much. What matters most is the destruction of the enemy's hardware—their tanks and guns. Without them, in the desert, an army cannot fight.

The enemy's material strength, particularly in the fortress of Tobruk, was intact. Before Rommel could permit his main forces to follow east along the "Rommelbahn," as his staff sometimes dubbed the Via Balbia, he had to secure his lines of supply. "The prerequisite for this," he said on April 13, "is the capture of Tobruk." By that date his first attempts had failed, disastrously—the first rebuffs that any of Hitler's commanders had ever suffered. Rommel blamed his generals, writing in his memoirs later: "Remarkably, some of my commanders kept wanting to pause so as to take on ammunition, fill up with gasoline and overhaul their vehicles, even when an immediate thrust by us would have had superb chances." Years later, reading the book, General Streich scornfully scribbled in the margin: "Disgraceful nonsense!" and "What about fuel?" As Streich pointed out: "That was always the salient point, that there just wasn't any gasoline for Rommel's pipedreams. And that wasn't the fault of 'some of' his commanders, but of Rommel himself."

Standing on a high plain above the Mediterranean, facing toward Egypt, Rommel surveyed the landscape features that would dictate his battle tactics. To his left, a sheer cliff face fell away to the rim of the sea; the coast was like this virtually all the way to the Egyptian frontier. To his right the land rose in one-hundred-foot steps, until a maximum height above the sea level of 500 feet was reached about twenty miles inland. These steps, or escarpments, would become important battle objectives. Diagonally across this rising plain ran gentle riblike undulations, like waves in the sand, up to three miles apart and fifteen feet high. These would aid Rommel—he could advance between them, conceal his tanks "hull down" behind them. But there were also wadis—dry gulches or riverbeds where battle vehicles could negotiate crossings only in few places.

In the morning and late evening, visibility was unlimited; but by day the hot air shimmered and reflected and would play hell with the gunners' aim. All around them appeared great lakes of water as mirages; but the real water had shriveled down into the bowels of this continent millennia before, and now there were only dried-up or poisoned cisterns built by the Arabs to capture the winter's brief rainfalls. All day long the sun grilled the soldier's bodies—dehydrating, blackening, peeling. The hot wind cracked lips, tangled hair, veined eyes with red. The whole nervous system was under excruciating strain, which exacerbated the depression and loneliness of the men who fought in Africa.

Rommel now lived in a small Italian-built trailer—protection against the sub-zero nights. He moved it, along with his battle headquarters, to a shallow stony gully just south of the Tobruk front line, where the increasingly troublesome enemy planes could not so easily find him. Every waking hour was taken up with preparing the assault on Tobruk. He did not even find time to write Lucie and detailed his batman to write to her instead. ("This morning Herr General has ordered me to write to you," Corporal Günther began his compulsory letter to her on the eleventh; Lucie cannot have been much flattered.)

With his legs spread out beneath his stocky figure, his face blistering in the African sun, Rommel gripped his Zeiss binoculars and peered at Tobruk. He wondered just what and where its defenses were. He pushed his cap back to a jaunty angle so that the sun glinted on the big Perspex goggles that were to become a famous part of his image; he had seen them in the booty at Mechili and taken them for himself. Then he climbed back into his command vehicle, "Mammut," and drove on to another vantage point.

Mammut (which means mammoth in German) was his name for the British ACV given him by Streich, who had captured three of these enormous conveyances at

Mechili. A black and white Wehrmacht cross painted on its sides marked its change of owners. War reporter Fritz Lucke described it in a soldiers' newspaper a few days later: "An armored box as big as a bus, on giant balloon tires as big and fat as the undercarriage wheels of a Junkers plane. A spent machine gun bullet is still embedded in it. The walls are windowless and painted in blue-gray camouflage tints. Only the driver and his co-driver have windshields, protected behind armored visors." Rommel's Mammut became a familiar sight to his troops in Libya.

What happened next, in this second week of April 1941, rattled Rommel and shook his soldiers' faith in him. Tobruk defeated him. He learned the hard way—by bloody tactical biopsies—just how strong its defenses were.

He ordered Streich to make the first attack on the eleventh. Streich sent in Ponath's weary Machine Gun Battalion Eight from the south, and all Olbrich's available tanks—about twenty—on a parallel approach just to the right. Air reconnaissance somehow suggested that the British were evacuating Tobruk by sea. "You'll have to move fast!" Rommel had ordered. "Raise a lot of dust!" At 4:45 P.M. the tanks began to roll. The machine gunners' war diary tells the rest: "Close behind the last tanks our battalion leaps out and runs behind them and the advancing wall of fire. But to our horror the tanks suddenly turn around and come back to speed through our lines still accompanied by heavy shelling. One of their officers screams to our commander [Ponath]. 'There's a very deep and wide antitank trench four hundred yards farther on! We can't get over it!' " An hour later Colonel Ponath, a tall, handsome, now haggard man, was reporting this in person to Rommel and Streich. Behind the tank trap he had also seen an extensive barbed wire barrier. The attack was halted; his men were pinned down, unable to withdraw. His battalion had lost eleven dead, just to find out this most elementary information.

Next day, April 12, a furious sandstorm began. Rommel ordered a new assault, using the sandstorm as cover, to begin at 3:30 P.M. Just before then, however, the storm abated. Streich asked, "Are we still to attack?"

Rommel ordered, "That attack must be carried out at all costs." Streich ordered Rommel's words recorded in his division's diary, and sent in sappers to try to blow up the tank obstacles. A hail of artillery fire met them, at point-blank range. British bombers joined in. Nevertheless, later that day Rommel again decreed: "Your division is to take Tobruk!"

The result was the same. At 6:00 P.M. Olbrich, the tank regiment commander, reported back. Again his tanks had failed to breach the defenses, and the attempt had been costly, too. The Fifth Panzer Regiment had started these battles with 161 tanks. Now it was down to less than forty. Of the seventy-one best tanks, the Panzer IIIs, only nine were left. Streich accordingly refused Rommel's demand for a new assault until it could be properly prepared: he wanted proper air photos, dive bomber attacks on the enemy guns, air cover and spotter planes for his own artillery. The war diary does not record Rommel's reply.

However, the plight of Ponath's machine gunners—only a few hundred yards from the enemy lines—left Rommel no option but to renew the attack; they had to be rescued soon. By night they froze; by day they had to lie motionless beneath the baking sun—the slightest movement attracted a hail of rifle fire. The ground was too hard to scoop out foxholes. The defenders seemed to be concealed in some kind of bunkers. "Our division cannot even inform us where the enemy positions are," the machine gun battalion complained in its diary.

At midday on the thirteenth, Easter Sunday, Ponath was called back to Rommel's headquarters. When Ponath crawled forward again to his machine gunners at 5:00 P.M., he dictated this order to his adjutant, lying full-length in the dust and sand next to him. "The general [Rommel] has ordered a new attack on Tobruk. Before that, from 6:00 to 6:05, six artillery battalions will pour concentrated shellfire onto the wire barrier ahead of us." Sappers would then move forward and blow in the tank ditch, and Ponath's battalion would infiltrate to the far side and establish a bridgehead for the tank regiment to exploit just before dawn. In effect, Rommel would be pitting 500 machine gunners and about twenty tanks against a fortress defended by 34,000 of the British Empire's toughest troops.

That evening, as Ponath's operation began, Rommel called all his assault commanders to his Mammut and set out his plan for the dawn attack. He told them that radio reconnaissance had again indicated that the enemy were pulling out of Tobruk by sea. "If the enemy do pull out," he told General Streich, "then we'll follow through with our tank regiments at once, tonight." He put Streich in command of the attack, and disappeared from the vehicle. Toward midnight Ponath's adjutant appeared, hot and disheveled, and told Streich that his machine gun battalion had breached the tank ditch and wire without any enemy resistance at all—should they press on? Streich smelled an ambush and forbade any further move until first light. The German bridgehead was about 500 yards wide. But as the assault troops quietly dug in—and how easy that sounds! —disturbing things began to happen. Shadows flitted against the moonlight and then vanished, leaving soldiers with their throats slit or stabbed by bayonets. Were there enemy defenders hidden just nearby? An hour passed, then a mass of enemy troops suddenly rose out of the blackness, singing "It's a Long Way to Tipperary"; forty more Germans were cut down—then the enemy vanished back into their hidden bunkers. In fact, without realizing it, the Germans had penetrated right into the midst of the first line of enemy bunkers—they were built flush with ground level —and the Australian defenders were only waiting for the dawn to come to mow them down.

As yet it was still dark. At 3:30 A.M., an hour before the tank regiment was due to go into the breach, Rommel was still confident. "The battle for Tobruk will probably come to its conclusion today," he informed Lucie. "The British are fighting stubbornly with a lot of artillery, but we're still going to pull it off."

An hour later Olbrich's tanks roared into the breach. Rommel had given Streich the use of an Italian artillery regiment and a flak battery for close support. At first light, Rommel drove up the road from El Adem toward Tobruk: from the light signals and gunfire in the north he could see that Ponath's machine gunners were well inside the tank ditch. But something alarmed Rommel. He now drove off to the Italian Armored Division Ariete and ordered it to follow Olbrich's tanks through the breach. Ariete, however, had only just arrived and could not help.

The story of the next three bloody hours can be briefly told. At dawn the British troops pinched off the breach behind the machine gunners, preventing their escape. At 7:45 A.M. Olbrich's tanks were forced to turn back by the enemy guns; the enemy also threw aircraft and superior Matilda tanks into the battle. Olbrich drove to Rommel and spelled out the failure of his attack. He had seen the liquidation of virtually the entire machine gun battalion with his own eyes. Of 500 men only 116 were left to escape during the following night. The rest were dead or in enemy captivity. The flak battery had fought heroically but had lost most of its equipment. Olbrich himself had lost half his tanks, and the turrets of most of the others were jammed.

Rommel was angry and perplexed. In a rage he ordered Streich to attack again at 4:00 P.M.—if not to capture Tobruk, at least to help Ponath's hapless surviving machine gunners to escape. Streich did not refuse, he merely declined to accept responsibility. Earlier he had told Rommel's operations officer, Major Ehlers, "Herr General Rommel may not like to hear it, but it is my duty as next senior officer to point it out: if the British had had the least daring, they could have pushed out of their fortress through the breach and not only overrun the rest of my division, but captured the Afrika Korps headquarters and mine as well. That would have been the end of the German presence in Libya, and the end of Herr General's reputation. Be so good as to tell your general that." Ehlers returned with this message for Streich: "Rommel has instructed you to revert to an 'offensive defense.'" Streich walked out, shaking his head.

Olbrich supported Streich's refusal to attack again. Count von Schwerin said: "Over my dead body." All considered that any further slaughter incurred in attacking defenses of which they knew nothing would be a crime. Rommel's headquarters diary limply concludes, "A second attack was scheduled . . . but did not take place."

He masked this ghastly defeat in his evening report to

the General Staff ("casualties cannot yet be assessed"). But it could not be entirely concealed. The brave commander of the machine gun battalion, Gustav Ponath, was dead; so were most of his men. A crisis of confidence began: for the first time an anti-Rommel faction emerged among the troops. He had "burned" good men rather than prepare the assault properly, they said. Major Bolbrinker, Olbrich's successor, subsequently criticized Rommel for ignoring his tank commander's advice.

Rommel would not admit his own fault and continued to put the defeat down to other reasons. "During the offensive in Cyrenaica," he explained to the War Office in July, "and particularly during the early part of the siege of Tobruk, there were numerous instances when my clear and specific orders were not obeyed by my commanders, or not promptly; there were instances bordering on disobedience, and some commanders broke down in face of the enemy."

To Berlin he telegraphed an appeal for more troops. He lamented that he was now so preoccupied by Tobruk that "despite unique opportunities offered by the overall situation," he could not resume his offensive to the east. The plaintive tone brought peals of unsympathetic laughter from the General Staff. At last Rommel had been taken down a peg or two! Franz Halder, chief of the General Staff, quoted Rommel's words mockingly in his diary and added: "Now at last he is compelled to admit that his forces are just not strong enough. . . . We have had that impression here for quite some time."

Over the next days, Rommel continued to salvage his self-esteem by finding scapegoats for the disaster. He blamed Streich and Olbrich for the slaughter of the machine gun battalion. "I don't get the support I need from all my commanders," he confided to Lucie in one letter. "I've put in for some of them to be changed." He fell out with his own chief of staff, Colonel von dem Borne—a calm, circumspect officer. He sent his operations officer Major Ehlers home and engineered his dismissal from the General Staff. (Ehlers had suggested in the corps diary that if Rommel had not gone gallivanting across the desert to Mechili on April 5, it might have been possible to reach Tobruk before the enemy instead of getting bogged down.)

Rommel even regained some of his lost confidence. On the sixteenth he assured Lucie, "The battle for Tobruk has calmed down a bit. The enemy are embarking. So we can expect to be taking over the fortress ourselves very shortly." Visiting the shattered remnants of the machine gun battalion that day, he encouraged them: "We'll be in Cairo eight days from now—pass the word around." He made no attempt to call on the nearby headquarters of General Streich, although it was Streich's fiftieth birthday. So Streich guessed his days there were numbered.

"Herr Lieutenant General Rommel regretted the casualties our battalion took," a machine gun officer reported to Streich, "and told us: 'You mustn't let it get you down. It's the soldier's lot. Sacrifices have to be made.'" Rommel blamed the battalion's faulty leadership for not having first opened up a wider breach in the defenses. "He explained it to us on his map with short pencil marks. When Lieutenant Prahl pointed out that the battalion just did not have the means available to widen the breach, he replied: 'Then the division should have taken care of it.'"

Already Rommel was planning new exploits. He exuded fresh optimism when two top Luftwaffe generals flew in two days later—General Hoffmann von Waldau, the deputy chief of Air Staff, and Field Marshal Milch, Hermann Göring's deputy. While Waldau shivered in a bitterly cold tent, Milch shared Rommel's warm trailer and later wrote this account—it is among his private papers:

"The time I spent with him was short but sweet, as we both got on well with each other. He was very happy about the increase in fighter plane strength"—elements of the Twenty-seventh Fighter Wing had just arrived at nearby Gazala—"as he was one of our more air-minded generals. He was quite starry-eyed about his prospects. Bending very close to his maps—he was desperately shortsighted—he exclaimed, "Look Milch, there's Tobruk. I'm going to take it. There's the Halfaya Pass. I'll take that too. There's Cairo. I'll take that. And there—there is the Suez Canal: I'm taking that as well.' What else," wrote Milch, "could I say to that except: 'And here am I. Take me too!'"

Roars of laughter came from the trailer. But other, less

congenial visitors were already on their way from Berlin to Rommel. On April 23 General Halder recorded sharply in his diary: "Rommel has not sent us a single clear-cut report all these days, and I have a feeling that things are in a mess. Reports from officers coming from his theater, as well as a personal letter, show that Rommel is in no way equal to his task. He rushes about the whole day between his widely scattered units, stages reconnaissance raids and fritters away his forces."

Thus it came about that as Count von Schwerin lay prostrate in the desert, scanning Tobruk's defenses through field glasses while enemy shells and machine gun bullets pierced the shimmering air above him, he felt a tugging at his sleeve and found Halder's deputy, Paulus, lying next to him. Paulus had flown from Berlin, driven and finally crawled to this battlefield to try to find out what was happening. (Paulus and Rommel, both army captains at the time, had both been company commanders in the same regiment in 1927–29 in Stuttgart.) "He's probably the only man," reflected Halder, "with sufficient personal influence to head off this soldier gone raving mad."

It was April 27 when Paulus arrived at Tobruk to see things for himself. Rommel's nerve was already tattered. The terrible heat and the backbiting on all sides did not help. Twice in the last week he had missed death only by inches: an enemy salvo had dropped right on them as he stopped to talk to infantry officers digging in west of El Adem; one lieutenant was killed outright, another lost an arm. And on the twentieth, as he was returning from a visit to Bardia, Hurricane fighter planes had suddenly swooped out of the dying sun and machine-gunned his Mammut at zero altitude. His driver was hit before he could close the steel door. A truck driver and a dispatch rider were killed outright. The radio truck was destroyed. Rommel himself bandaged his driver's bad head wound and climbed into the Mammut's driving seat.

Rommel now had only puny forces left to hold Bardia and the Egyptian frontier, and they reeled under the blows of enemy tanks, bombers and even ships' guns. On April 24, Rommel had sent renewed appeals for help to Berlin: "Situation at Bardia, Tobruk graver from day to day as

British forces increase." He demanded an airlift of the promised Fifteenth Panzer Division, the early expansion of the Fifth Light to a full-bodied panzer division, powerful Luftwaffe reinforcements and U-boat operations along the coast. He added briefly: "Italian troops unreliable." When Hitler heard of Rommel's plight next day, one of his staff jotted in a private diary: "Führer uses very strong language." Two days later, the leading elements of the Fifteenth Panzer Division began to arrive by air in Benghazi.

Hitler's language about the General Staff was mild compared with the oaths that rang out from Rommel's officers now, as they at long last received from the Italian High Command detailed plans of the defenses of Tobruk: now they could see what they had been up against. Italian engineers had designed and built 128 interconnected strongpoints all along the thirty-mile-long perimeter. Like the tank ditch guarding each strongpoint, the gangways were all covered with wood and a thin layer of sand to conceal them; they housed antitank gun and machine gun positions and were all finished off flush with ground level to make them invisible to attackers until they were right on top of them. There were heavy barbed wire entanglements around them. Little wonder that Rommel's last attempt to rush Tobruk had been repulsed so bloodily. Besides, as Paulus commented privately to Streich: "Can you give me one instance in history where a penetration of enemy lines that was begun in the evening was ever successfully exploited on the following morning?" As Streich had pointed out, the evening move gave the enemy all the advance warning they needed to be on guard when the main push began.

It was about this time that Rommel called the Italian commanders and Streich for a joint conference on his new battle plans. Streich interrupted. "A few days ago," he said, "some of my officers and I had a look over the ground *southeast* of Tobruk. It's level and offers us a good chance of moving our troops forward at night, right up to their fortifications, without being noticed; they can then attack at dawn." Rommel scornfully rebuked him: "I don't want to hear any ideas from you—I just want to hear how you intend to put my plan into effect." (After all else had failed, it was Streich's plan that he was to adopt successfully later on—once the general had left Africa.)

Rommel was still incredibly optimistic. He admitted privately to Lucie on April 25, "I've rarely had such military anxieties as over the last few days. But things will probably look very different soon. Probably Greece will be finished soon, and then I'll get more help." He repeated this hope some days later, so it is quite clear that even his old associate General Paulus had not revealed to him Hitler's "Operation Barbarossa," the plan to hurl 200 divisions against Russia in June.

The relationship between Paulus and Rommel was an awkward one now. They were both lieutenant generals, but Paulus had a few months' edge on him, and since he was Halder's deputy he could pull both rank and station on Rommel. Rommel had no choice but to obey. He suspected that the general's surprise visit was an intrigue by the General Staff. Probably he was right. He sent Paulus around the perimeter of the siege ring and told him he was planning a big new attack on Tobruk's southwestern sector on the last day of April. Paulus was skeptical.

Dissatisfied with Streich, Rommel put General Heinrich Kirchheim in command. Kirchheim was a War Office tropical warfare expert who just happened to be in Libya at the time. (This appointment would have fateful consequences for Rommel, in October 1944.) The attack would be by night, focused at first on the shallow Hill 209, known to the long vanished local Arabs as Ras el Mdauuar. From 209, the enemy was harassing Rommel's rear lines of communication. Again he had great expectations: "We've got high hopes," he wrote to Lucie that morning. "The enemy artillery has fallen very silent, although we're giving them hell ourselves." Surprise was complete, thanks to Rommel's well-planned deception tactics. But again the attack failed, and again it was because of German ignorance of Tobruk's fortifications.

Rommel drove through to the first line to observe the battle from his Mammut. At one stage he crawled the last few hundred yards forward to where Kirchheim's shock troops were pinned down near one bunker. By 9:00 A.M. a machine gun battalion had taken Hill 209 from the rear, and the main attempt to drive northeastward toward

Tobruk itself began; but the penetration was too narrow, and as the troops advanced they stumbled on yet more well-concealed strongpoints. On May 1 Baron Hans-Karl von Esebeck—Prittwitz's successor in the Fifteenth Panzer Division—informed Rommel: "Our troops and particularly officers have suffered heavy casualties from infantry and antitank fire coming from numerous undetected bunkers and from saturation artillery fire. Most units have 50 percent casualties, some even more. Morale is still absolutely magnificent, both among our shock troops, who went in as planned to attack the objectives, and among the infantry companies, who followed them eastward in heavy close combat with the reviving bunker crews and held out despite artillery fire."

A stinging sandstorm sprang up and stifled the rest of the battle. Rommel hung on to Hill 209, and to several hundred prisoners—including Australian troops, some of the largest, most muscular Australian troops he had ever seen. But Paulus ordered him peremptorily to call off the rest of the attack. Rommel's soldiers had suffered further appalling casualties—over 1,200 men killed, injured and missing. More significant, his ammunition dumps had been so depleted by warding off enemy counterattacks that he found himself facing his first real crisis of supplies.

Rommel first hinted at these "supply difficulties" in a letter home on May 9. Paulus had rubbed it in: the fact was that Rommel's brilliant but undisciplined advance to Tobruk had failed to bring decisive victory but had added another 700 miles to his already extended lines of supply. Tobruk harbor was denied to him by the Australians. Benghazi was closer than Tripoli, but the Italians were refusing to send supply ships there for reasons of which Paulus thoroughly approved: the port had only limited capacity, the sea route was longer and the danger of British interference that much greater. German navy officers sent to organize Rommel's supply routes had returned to Italy having been unable to speak to him. ("General Rommel had flown off to the front with his chief of staff and had been out of contact with his operations staff for twenty-four hours.") This left only the long road from Tripoli harbor to Tobruk. It was 1,100 miles long—the distance from Hamburg to Rome; and this introduced another serious bottleneck, the truck transport itself.

The mathematics of his situation were plain enough. For bare survival, the Afrika Korps at this time needed 24,000 tons of supplies each month. To stockpile for a future offensive, it needed another 20,000 tons a month. The Luftwaffe needed 9,000 tons of supplies. Add to this the 63,000 tons needed by the Italian troops and Italian civilian population in Libya, and a staggering monthly requirement of *116,000 tons* arose. But the facilities at Tripoli could handle only 45,000 tons a month. Juggle as they might with these hard facts, the German representatives in Rome could not find any way of providing Rommel with more than about 20,000 tons a month—less than bare survival.

It was a problem of Rommel's own making, and the knowledge of this only angered him the more. How easy it had been to make that retort to Halder in March: "That's your pigeon!" As the supply crisis worsened, his venom turned on the Italians—responsible for supply shipments across the Mediterranean—and he even suggested that Italy's troops should withdraw, leaving the fighting to the Afrika Korps, as the Italians were "useless mouths" to be fed.

His injustices toward the Italians derived from the frustration of his hand-to-mouth existence. A temporary crisis in shipping occurred because the nearby British-held island of Malta, with its naval and air bases, had not been effectively neutralized. But over the whole period of the war in Africa, the Italian navy performed its convoy duties well. The figures show that, on average, each transport ship had more than one naval escort—a ratio never reached by the Allies. Of 206,402 men shipped to Africa, 189,162 arrived safely (over 91 percent); of 599,338 tons of fuel, 476,703 tons arrived (80 percent); of trucks and tanks, 243,633 tons arrived of 275,310 tons sent (85 percent); 149,462 tons of arms and ammunition, of 171,060 tons sent. As far as the German forces alone were concerned, Rommel got 82 percent of the fuel and 86 percent of the other supplies that were sent to him. This hardly justified the words he used with increasing amplitude to explain his supply crisis: "Italian treachery."

For Rommel's troops besieging Tobruk, stifling, static war began. More than once, in the scribbled pencil notes of his staff on the anxious talks with other commanders, explicit comparisons with Verdun crop up. But where were the trenches? Here there was just dirt, and hard rock, and ferocious sun and flies. His men were ill and strained. The least graze—unavoidable when digging holes in this barren ground—and the slightest scratch from the camel thorn bushes stayed unhealed for months as a permanent running sore on arm or leg. Noses peeled, lips cracked and blistered. The tough commander of the forces holding the Egyptian frontier at Sollum, Colonel Maximilian von Herff, a man of ludicrous affectations, but a brave one, wrote in a letter to Berlin: "Gastric disorders—a kind of chill—are rife here. They occur about once a month and leave you very weak for a while. After three days of it recently I felt so bad that I fainted three times in one day . . . but I got over it without reporting sick. At any rate all of us Africa warriors, officers and men alike, will be glad to see the back of it. We say, Never again Africa!" Herff earned his ticket back to Berlin some weeks later and became chief of personnel in Himmler's Waffen SS. Erwin Rommel had to endure Africa for two more years.

Even men half his age found the going tough. The food was monotonous, the diet lopsided. His troops had to survive on biscuits, olive oil (because butter would go rancid), canned sardines, coffee, jam, soft cheese in "toothpaste" tubes and unidentifiable meat in Italian government cans embossed "AM"—the soldiers suspected it stood for Alter Mann [old man]. Of course there were no eggs, ham or milk, let alone fresh fruit or vegetables. All the greater was their envy of the British. "How pitiful our equipment is in every respect, compared with the British," wrote Herff. "Just look at the supplies they get—mineral water, canned preserves and fruit, things that we sorely lack. This lack is becoming increasingly evident from the damage to our youngsters' health as the days get hotter. Even our twenty-five-year-olds are already losing their teeth and their gums just won't stop bleeding. It's not going to be an easy summer."

It was by now so hot that Rommel drove around in shorts, a real concession in a general so stiff and formal.

Every day began at six, as he began the intensive training of all ranks in the unfamiliar infantry tactics they would need to eliminate Tobruk's defenses bunker by bunker. The knowledge that he had failed, and at such cost, oppressed him and he could guess the tone of Paulus's report to Berlin. Everywhere he sensed the murmur of rising criticism. Even Herff had written to Berlin about the losses his regiment had suffered so far in the war: "In the west we had already lost over 1,000 men, then the sinking of a convoy cost me 250 more and my gun company, and Tobruk alone has already cost me nearly 450 men. Nobody here understood these first attacks on Tobruk: although the strength and garrison of the fortress were well known, each newly arrived battalion was sent in to attack and naturally enough didn't get through. The upshot is that there isn't a unit at Tobruk that hasn't taken a mauling. . . . A lot of the more impulsive commands issued by the Afrika Korps we junior officers just don't make head or tail of." Herff's telling letter was placed in Rommel's personnel file, like a permanent black mark.

There was a German army cemetery near Tobruk, beside the Via Balbia. Many times Rommel paused there to read the names on the newest graves.

"I remember," said one of the war correspondents assigned to him, "seeing General Rommel stand there one day, at Kilometer thirty-one outside Tobruk—the last kilometer in so many brave soldiers' lives—and I watched him meditating. That long summer of 1941 the war cemetery here swelled to quite a size, and in the eerie twilight of a sandstorm it seemed to us, in all its cruel loneliness, something of a symbol of man's transience. We were looking at the grave of an officer. For a while he stood there, absolutely motionless. Then he turned away without a word and left. But in his eyes I believe I saw what moved him—there was deep sorrow in them. It was the sorrow of a man saying farewell to an old friend and comrade."

The high African summer was upon them. Tanks standing in the open—and in the desert there was nowhere else for tanks to stand—heated up to 160° F. Too hot to touch. Rommel ordered his movie cameraman to take pictures of eggs being fried on the tanks, to impress the public in Germany. The eggs refused to fry, so Rommel sparked an acetylene burner and applied the flame to the metal. His old genius had not left him yet.

# The Commanders'
# Revolt

TAKE the road that Marshal Balbo built, as Rommel does so often now—from Tobruk eastward along the Via Balbia to the next big town, Bardia. It is an hour's fast drive, with the sea never far away to the left and the tall escarpment to the right. After Bardia the road climbs ten miles until it meets the Trigh Capuzzo, the old camel route across the high plateau. Here the Italians have built a stone fort, Ridotta Capuzzo, to guard the frontier with Egypt just two miles farther on. The frontier is a broad barbed wire entanglement orginally built to keep the rebellious Sanusi warriors out of Libya. It stretches into the desert, as far as the eye can see.

A few hundred yards beyond the frontier, into Egypt, the road begins a steep, tortuous descent of the escarpment toward the town of Sollum. Its untidy quays are silhouetted against the deep blue of the Mediterranean. Left of the coast road that runs on from here are dazzling white sand and sea. To the right the escarpment again rises, steep and uneven, to heights of 600 feet and more. This road goes on to Cairo, but a few miles after Sollum another road forks off to the right and scales the escarpment in a series of hairpin bends—serpentines, the Germans call them. This is the Halfaya Pass, which Rommel's troops under

Colonel von Herff have captured late in April 1941. Only at Sollum and Halfaya can tanks easily climb the escarpment to the desert plateau and thus gain access to Libya. This is the importance of the Sollum front: if it caves in, Rommel is vulnerable to a British attack from Egypt; he will have to abandon the siege of Tobruk, and fall back on a line at El Gazala or retreat even farther west. Obeying Paulus, he has issued blueprints early in May for the fortification of the Sollum front—he has sketched the designs himself, based on Tobruk bunkers that he himself inspected under fire some days before.

On May 22, he takes this road in his Mammut to visit Herff and his troops. Hermann Aldinger, his aide, writes that day a portrait of life in the Afrika Korps:

After days of tough fighting on the Sollum/Capuzzo front the general has today paid a visit to this sector and called on the troops. We leave his headquarters at dawn and set out over forty-five miles of roadless, pathless desert across boulders and camel thorn shrubs. The ACV rolls about as though we are on the high seas, and we are thrown about inside however tight we hold on. The general and I climb up and sit on the roof—there are three exit hatches on top—and keep a lookout on all sides, because enemy aircraft can be a real menace. Convoys of trucks, swathed in clouds of dust, are moving hither and thither. Day and night the drivers have to go about their arduous and not unrisky duty, because the front is by no means closed and the enemy's armored cars and sabotage units are also moving about.

The troops stand to attention and salute, and are delighted when the general speaks to them. We reach the Via Balbia and have to go on more miles to the east. The road is badly worn and there are potholes big enough to swallow half a car. Soon we reach the Sollum front and we have one conference after another. But then the general feels the urge to meet the men actually face to face with the enemy, he has to speak with them, crawl right forward to them in their foxholes and have a chat with them. You can see the real pleasure on their faces, when these ordinary soldiers are allowed to speak in person to their general and tell him about the hard fighting here over the last few days. The ground is hard rock, impossible to dig in; cover can only be made by heaping up rocks, and a canvas sheet is stretched out over them to provide some shelter from the scorching sun. This is why the soldiers don't wear much either—often just a pair of shorts. The lads are as brown as Negroes. And so we move from position to position—infantry, artillery, tanks, observers, etc. Our victories over the last few days, and defensive successes, give them all great hope.

When Rommel saw this front on May 22, Colonel von Herff had just inflicted a crushing rebuff to the British. ("Rommel told me when he visited us," wrote Herff, "that he was scared stiff for us as there wasn't anything he could have done to help us.") Rommel had ordered Herff one month earlier to adopt an aggressive and fluid defense, sending raiding parties far behind the enemy lines. The colonel showed great initiative. He exploited the first sandstorm to attack the British and steal their trucks. He dug position. He trained his joint German/Italian force of some 6,000 men. For the Italians he had high praise: "With patience and energy," he recorded some weeks later, "I succeeded in making useful and brave soldiers out of them; they held out to the end against the enemy and knew how to die without fear."

This was just as well, because the British decided to strike here with fifty-five tanks of the Seventh Armored Division and the Twenty-second Guards Brigade before Rommel's new panzer division, the Fifteenth, could arrive. The blow fell at dawn on May 15. At least ten of the enemy's tanks were dreaded Matildas, all but impervious to the German antitank guns. It was obvious to Rommel from the radio intercepts obtained by his intelligence staff that this was a major enemy attempt at relieving Tobruk from the rear. He admitted a few days later: "It hung by a thread."

However, Herff made the right decision, to roll with the enemy's initial punch—although this meant abandoning ground—and then sidestep after dark to strike unexpectedly on the enemy flank the next morning. Herff's narrative continues: "By afternoon [May 15] I had things under control again. I withdrew that night with all the German troops and early on the sixteenth I struck back with eight tanks into the enemy's flank. By evening I had recaptured all the lost ground except the Halfaya Pass."

This first battle of Sollum had given Rommel a nasty fight, and he sent a string of jumpy signals to Berlin at two- or three-hour intervals as it ebbed and flowed, cajoling, beseeching, reassuring, warning, appealing and then triumphing as Herff—aided by a battalion of the Eighth Panzer Regiment—restored the situation. Rommel's nervousness nearly brought an abrupt end to his African career, already under a cloud because of protest letters reaching Berlin over the slaughter in Tobruk. Field Marshal von Brauchitsch himself sent a six-page signal to him on May 25, demanding that in the future the general's signals be "sober" and show a "certain continuity": he was not to get rattled when the enemy threw surprises at him. "You are to avoid reporting too optimistically or too pessimistically under the immediate influence of events," Brauchitsch directed. Rommel petulantly dismissed the commander in chief's telegram as "a colossal rocket, the reason for which is completely beyond me."

Fortunately for his prestige, Rommel's Sollum front commander now launched a counterattack that proved a stinging blow to the enemy. The British had left the Twenty-second Guards Brigade to garrison the Halfaya Pass. Late on May 26 Herff, again supported by the Eighth Panzer Regiment, decided to spring a surprise attack on this garrison next morning. "We rolled into action at 4:30 A.M. [first light] on May 27," Herff said, "and by 6:15 the pass was in our hands. The British took to their heels along the coastal plain toward Sidi Barrani. We picked up a lot of booty, above all artillery [nine guns], tanks [seven Matildas, including three in working order] and the trucks we so badly need."

This was a useful boost to Rommel's reputation. He wrote a jaunty and aggressive reply to Brauchitsch's telegram—the reply is not in the files but it was clearly a threat to shake the dust of Africa off his feet. He wrote

Lucie ironically on May 29: "I had a big rocket from the Army High Command—to my mind quite unjustified—in gratitude for all we have achieved so far. I'm not going to take it lying down, and a letter is already on its way to von B." A few days later he amplified on this: "My affair with the High Command is still extant. Either they do have confidence in me, or they don't. And if they don't, then I have asked them to draw the appropriate conclusions. I'm curious to see what will come of that . . . . Bellyaching is so easy if you're not having to sweat things out here."

In the Reich, Rommel's fame was spreading—assiduously fanned by the corps of news- and cameramen he had attached to his staff. It was no coincidence that his chief aide was, like his predecessor Karl Hanke, one of the senior officials of the Nazi propaganda ministry: the thirty-six-year-old Lieutenant Alfred Berndt. Burly, wavy-haired and dark-skinned, Berndt had the lumbering gait of a bear and a physiological oddity—six toes on one foot. He was literate and personable, poked his nose in everywhere, and was put in charge of keeping the Rommel diary. Before joining Rommel's staff as a kind of Party "commissar," he was already a tough, ambitious Nazi zealot. Berndt had a brash frankness that Rommel readily accepted, fearing otherwise to slight his feelings. In April, for instance, Berndt had advised him with a cheeky grin: *"Mein Lieber,* I would not advance too far if I were you!" In return, Berndt skillfully nourished the Rommel legend. And when anything unpleasant needed saying to Adolf Hitler, then Rommel sent Alfred Berndt, because he was a brave man. Berndt died proving it in Hungary in 1945.

An avalanche of letters descended on Rommel. The Nazi women's organization sent him parcels of chocolate —though how it fared in the desert heat defies imagination. A ten-year-old girl saw her idol in a newsreel and wrote to him from Augsburg: ". . . I don't have to be frightened of getting a cold reply from you like from the others. To you, General Rommel, I can speak from the bottom of my heart. I admire you and your Afrika Korps so much, and dearly hope you will win through to victory." Rommel, the People's General, replied to the child with equal warmth.

He knew, however, that victory was a long way off. The air force was doing what it could to destroy Tobruk's water supply and prevent British supply ships from coming in. But he acknowledged that the Afrika Korps had met its match: "The Australian troops are fighting magnificently and their training is far superior to ours," he privately told Lucie. "Tobruk can't be taken by force, given our present means." So he settled down for a long, exhausting siege and began to retain his troops in the "old-fashioned" infantry tactics that had succeeded in similar situations in World War I. He taught his men how to dig in, and how to prevent unnecessary bloodshed.

"He's a master of deception and disguises," said Lieutenant Berndt in a propaganda broadcast, "and always does what one least expects. If the enemy believe we are particularly strong at one place, then you can be sure we are weak. If they think we are weak, and venture close to us, then we are definitely strong. 'With your general we just didn't know where we were!'—that's what one British prisoner complained. If he stages attacks coupled with feint attacks, then the enemy virtually always think the wrong one is the real one, and lay down their entire artillery fire on that. If the enemy act on what they regard as the typical signs of feint attacks, then next time it is different and then they are wrong again. If they think they are dummies and ignore them, then they're the real ones!

"For a time," Berndt continued, "the enemy at Tobruk were annoying us by shelling our observation posts. So Rommel orders the erection of observation *towers:* whole streets of telegraph poles are sawed down and thirty such towers are erected during the night around Tobruk, complete with uniformed dummy soldiers intently keeping watch on the enemy and now and again climbing up and down the ladders—on ropes operated from a dugout. The enemy are puzzled and open up a murderous bombardment on them. For days on end they give these towers every shell they've got. Some are knocked down, others remain. After a while they give up the effort—and that is when we replace the dummy soldiers with real flesh-and-blood observers."

What was the secret of Rommel's success in North Africa? He was a born desert warrior, discovering talents that not even he had previously suspected. In terrain often devoid of landmarks he developed an uncanny sense of location. His memory seemed to have registered every empty oil drum, broken cairn or burned-out tank littering the sands. He had acquired the desert dweller's sixth sense, too. Driving far out in the desert one day with his chief of staff, he suddenly cried, "Let's pull out! In half an hour the enemy will be here!" Soon a dust cloud appeared on the distant horizon, betraying the approach of enemy armored cars.

In this new environment he developed a new style of battle command. He liked to leave a fixed operations staff in the rear, in permanent contact with his Italian superiors and with the lower echelons, and then drive off himself with a small command staff in a few open cars, followed by mobile radio trucks to keep him in touch with the operations staff and combat units. This did produce problems, because radio sets often failed under the extraordinary climatic conditions, and batteries rapidly ran down. With its black, white and red command flag on its fender, his own Volkswagen "Kübel" car was clearly visible. From it, he set the angle and tempo of the attack. If his car was shot up or ran over a mine, he simply commandeered another. Thus he could appear in the thick of any battle and take personal command, without the time-consuming waiting for messages that bedeviled other—and particularly the enemy—commanders.

When battle began, Rommel rarely slept and seldom ate. He could survive for days on a few pieces of bread or a quick cold snack served up by his orderly, Corporal Herbert Günther. Uncompromising, hard and realistic with himself, he demanded endurance and courage from his commanders. Once he found a general still breakfasting at 6:30 A.M.: "You will return to Germany!" he barked at him. The number of commanders who failed to meet his standards was, at the beginning, very high, and their turnover was great. Italian troops who fought under him came to worship him. They had rarely seen an *Italian* general on the battlefield. They relished the brusqueness with which he treated those of the porky and indifferent Italian generals who fell foul of him. Above all, he humanely recognized that the Italians had their limitations, and that it was callous and foolish to dictate impossible battle tasks to them. "There are more virtues in life than just being a soldier," he reminded his aide Lieutenant Berndt that summer. In October 1943 a German intelligence report noted the astounding fact that Italian soldiers were expressing the view that Italy should be governed by a leading German "like Göring or Rommel."

The first half of June 1941 saw Rommel reshuffling his commanders and preparing for even harder challenges. The rest of the Fifteenth Panzer Division had arrived. Under the youthful Colonel Walter Neumann-Silkow's command, it was sent to the Sollum front. In the other panzer division, the Fifth Light, Rommel had taken harsh steps to eliminate what he termed "the crisis in the officer corps." He had court-martialed a tank battalion commander for bursting into tears during the last vain attack on Tobruk—on May 1—and refusing to attack the "impregnable" Matilda tanks. He had made Major Ernst Bolbrinker the panzer regiment's new commander after Colonel Olbrich reported sick to avoid what he described as "further flattery" from Rommel. And he had got rid of Streich. One day at the end of May he telephoned Streich's command truck.

"Streich," he said, "I have asked for you to be replaced. You will continue in command, however, until your replacement arrives."

"Does Herr General have any further orders?" Streich coldly inquired, and hung up before Rommel could reply.

The reason Rommel gave for sacking him was that he had questioned Rommel's orders and embarked on "long-winded discussions." His successor was Major General Johannes von Ravenstein, who arrived on May 31. Aristocratic, lean and good-looking, he was a bit of a dandy, but like Rommel he wore the Pour le Mérite. The sauna temperatures of Libya were too much for his fragile constitution, and he spent his first few days lying exhausted on a camp bed.

Streich left Africa a few days later, his career permanently blighted by his differences with Rommel. As they parted, Rommel gruffly rebuked him: "You were far too concerned with the well-being of your troops."

Streich saluted stiffly. "I can imagine no greater words of praise for a division commander," he replied.

As his Mammut bucked and jolted around the desert, Rommel developed a gut feeling that the British were about to launch a big offensive. He told the Italians that he had had "a premonition"—in fact, his radio monitors had intercepted enough evidence. On June 6 they warned him of a change in the enemy dispositions. A week later they identified messages from British armored red units at Habata calling for ammunition. Habata was the only place, apart from Sollum and Halfaya, where tanks could climb up to the Libyan desert plateau. Rommel wrote to Lucie: "The British have moved off forty miles into the desert. The trouble is, I don't know if they're falling back or preparing a new attack. We're ready for them."

This was the enemy's operation "Battleaxe." On Churchill's orders that Rommel was to be destroyed, a convoy had sailed the Mediterranean to deliver 238 new tanks to Alexandria. It was a colossal increase in strength. Sir Noel Beresford-Peirse, Commander of the British Western Desert Force, decided to attack promptly.

On June 14 Rommel's monitors heard every British unit being warned by radio that "Peter" would be next day. (A name like that had also preceded the attack in mid-May.) That evening, therefore, he alerted the Sollum front and ordered his mobile reserves to stand by.

At 4:30 A.M. the next day a two-pronged British attack developed there, both down on the coastal plain and on the high plateau. By nine it was clear that this was a major enemy offensive. It was the first time that Rommel, the Afrika Korps,—indeed, the entire modern Nazi Wehrmacht—was confronted by such an offensive, the first time it had to fight a major defensive action. The eyes of the world were on him, and he was acutely conscious of the fact.

Throughout the first day, June 15, 1941, violent and bloody tank and infantry battles raged under the scorching heat and choking dust clouds. Rommel's prospects did not look good. He had fewer tanks than the enemy— about 150 to their 190—and only 95 of his were real battle tanks, Panzer IIIs and IVs. Of the enemy's force, about 100 were the fierce Matildas—twice as heavily armored as the Germans', and invulnerable to the thirty-seven-millimeter Pak (antitank) gun. The diary of Machine Gun Battalion Eight that day describes how eight Matildas came in to attack:

Again our thirty-seven-millimeter Pak is powerless. Its shells just bounce off the tank's thick armor; only a lucky shot in its tracks or turret bearings has any effect. So they rumble on to within 100 yards of our position, halt and then knock out our Paks one by one. We watch bitterly as one gun after another stops firing. Even individual acts of gallantry cannot help in this situation. Gunner Blank of Seven Company is still firing on a Matilda at five yards' range: no good. The steel colossus rolls on over him and his gun. His comrades bring the brave young lad back to us, our surgeon has to amputate both legs on the battlefield because they are just pulp. Later he died of his injuries.

An incident like this told a lot about the spirit that Rommel had already inculcated into the Afrika Korps. But spirit was not all. He had not been idle since the fighting at Tobruk. Knowing that only the eighty-eight-millimeter flak gun was a match for the Matilda, he had dug in five of these scarce weapons at Halfaya and four on the Hafid Ridge, and he had given his other four eighty-eights to the Fifteenth Panzer Division which was standing guard behind the Sollum front. In the other strongpoints along the Sollum line he installed the new Pak 38, a fifty-millimeter gun that was an improvement on the thirty-seven-millimeter. By the time of this battle, the line was admittedly only half completed and poorly provisioned with ammunition, food and water. But it was held by one of the most indomitable characters in North Africa, Captain Wilhelm Bach, the gangling, cigar-smoking commanding officer of the first battalion of the 104th Rifle Regiment. Bach was a former pastor, gentle and soft-spoken. He inspired a unique affection from his men.

The fighting on June 15 was inconclusive, but that evening Rommel was optimistic. Not only had the Halfaya Pass held, but of the twelve big Matildas that had lumbered toward its upper (plateau) end, eleven had been picked off by Bach's well-hidden eighty-eights, and four of the six Matildas that had approached from the coastal end were lying knocked out in the minefields Rommel had laid. That night Colonel Neumann-Silkow reported that the Fifteenth Panzer had destroyed sixty enemy tanks. He was now planning a counterattack. Rommel—who resisted the urge to rush to the Sollum battlefield, staying instead at his corps headquarters 100 miles away—radioed his approval and then spent a sleepless night. "The battle will be decided in a hard contest today," he wrote to Lucie at 2:30 A.M.

Neumann-Silkow's tanks opened their counterattack at dawn, April 16. His plan had been to sweep past the crumbling ruins of Fort Capuzzo—which the British had captured the evening before—cross the frontier wire and then attack the enemy's long flank. But he made little headway. At 7:45 A.M. Rommel's radio monitors told him that a big tank battle was raging. Later that morning the Fifteenth Panzer Division had to disengage. Only thirty-five of its eighty tanks were still running. Shortly after noon the other panzer division, the Fifth Light, was also stalled by strong enemy armor near Sidi Omar on the frontier.

Without doubt, as Rommel later wrote, this was the turning point of the battle. If the British now concentrated their forces and pressed on regardless, he would have to abandon the siege of Tobruk. So he made a decision—one of the great decisions of his career. Gambling on the evident British nervousness about their flanks, he radioed the Fifteenth Panzer at 12:35 P.M. to disengage at Capuzzo and advance south, paralleling the Fifth Light's line of advance. Before dawn, these two divisions would cut right into the enemy's flank and strike toward the coast at Halfaya, thus lifting the siege on Captain Bach and cutting off the entire British expedition. Meanwhile he sent a fighter plane to drop a thrilling message to the Halfaya defenders: "Our counterattack now making fine progress from the west. Enemy forced onto the defensive.

Victory depends on your holding the Halfaya Pass and the coastal plain."

The Fifth Light set off on time, at 4:30 A.M. By six it had reached its first objective, Sidi Suleiman. The Fifteenth Panzer Division also arrived at its objective. Intercepted radio messages told Rommel—still at his headquarters 100 miles away—of the enemy's frustration, surprise and then panic. At 7:45 A.M. the enemy's Seventh Armored Brigade was monitored reporting that it had no ammunition left: "The situation's desperate." A British tank commander was heard calling for Sir Noel Beresford-Peirse to come from Cairo to the battlefield. Rommel repeated this great news to his panzer division commanders and urged them to act fast. They thundered into the Halfaya Pass in midafternoon, ending Bach's heroic ordeal. Thus Rommel had won his first pitched tank battle.

The next day, June 18, Rommel drove over from his headquarters to see his exhausted German and Italian troops and thank them. Their beaming faces were reward enough—and he found their new adulation exhilarating. Having rationed himself this time to only one terse message to Berlin each day of the battle, now he announced triumphantly his impressive victory. He claimed to have destroyed 180 to 200 enemy tanks and a few days later revised the figure to 250. The real number was somewhat less than either figure, but as he had lost only twelve tanks there was no minimizing his own achievement. "The British," he boasted to Lucie, "thought they could overwhelm us with their 400 superheavy tanks. We had nothing like that weight of armor to pit against them. But our dispositions and the stubborn resistance of German and Italian troops—although cut off for days on end—enabled me to mount the crucial operation with every combat group I still had mobile. Let the enemy come again—they'll get an even sounder thrashing!"

Rommel had won by his superior tactics and better training. He had lured the enemy armor onto his anti-tank guns; he had ambushed them; he had made moves by night and taken them in the flank. He had laid the bogey of the Matilda, too. (A captured British major asked to see the gun that had destroyed his tank. Shown the flak eighty-eight, he said, "That's not fair, to use an antiaircraft gun against a tank!") The enemy, who did not know the secret, assumed that the Panzer III and IV had delivered the knockout punches. Thus both Rommel and his tanks were now talked of with awe abroad.

At home too his reputation was sky-high. Three times now—in April, May and June 1941—it had hung on a slender thread in the desert. Each time his nerves had proved stronger than his enemy's. And as the fanfares announcing Rommel's Sollum victory still blared from the Reich's radio stations, several writers decided that Rommel now merited a full biography. "I want to create a work of lasting value," a colonel wrote him. "It will show the typical young general of our times, offer him to coming generations as an example and thus provide something of a starting point for waves of military enthusiasm and exaltation."

Hitler proposed that Rommel should be promoted to full panzer general. But the General Staff rebelled at this. They were outraged at the prospect of Rommel's being raised from lieutenant colonel to full general in less than two years. Their resentment of Rommel had by no means abated over the previous months. Halder was continuing his vendetta. In May he had commented in his diary, "Rommel cannot cope," and he had secretly proposed to Brauchitsch that strong reins be put on Rommel. A second Chief of Staff, Halder suggested, Lieutenant General Alfred Gause, should be attached to the Italian High Command in Libya. There had also been talk of setting up a full army headquarters in Libya under Field Marshal Wilhelm List, the victor in Greece and a former superior of Rommel's, at Dresden.

Whatever the designs, fate again played into Rommel's hands. The full army headquarters was not authorized. General Gause was, in fact, sent to Africa, but he was a quiet, polite soul and anything but an intriguer. He chanced to arrive at Rommel's trailer on June 15—the first day of the Sollum fighting. He marveled at Rommel's grasp of the battle, decided that the Afrika Korps commander could "cope" very well and promptly placed his entire and impressive staff at Rommel's disposal— forty-three officers, twenty civilians, 150 enlisted ranks and forty-six vehicles. Halder recalled Gause for consultations in Berlin, then wrote his own summary of Gause's report. "Personal relationships are complicated by General Rommel's peculiarities and his pathological ambition," Halder claimed Gause had said. "Rommel's faults make him appear a particularly unattractive character, but nobody dares to cross swords with him because of his brutal methods and the backing he has at the highest level." How the generals envied Rommel's easy access to Hitler!

The upshot was that the Army High Command decided to set up a "Panzer Group Rommel." A Panzergruppe was rather less than an Armee, but its establishment left no alternative but to promote Rommel to full general after all. He would command his old Afrika Korps and the Italian Twenty-first Corps of infantry divisions. A few days later he learned that it was his influential aide who had helped push the promotion through—to "the highest level." He wrote Lucie: "As I have just found out from Lieutenant B[erndt], who visited the Führer and Goebbels, I have only the Führer to thank for my recent promotion. . . . You can imagine how pleased I am—to win his recognition for what I do and the way I do it is beyond my wildest dreams."

A full general at only forty-nine! That meant Rommel had really come up smelling like a rose despite the ugly disputes during the weeks of Tobruk. "It's very nice to rise so high while still so young," he reflected just after the promotion became effective. "But I'm stocking up with even more stars, just in case."

Meanwhile Rommel learned that Hitler had invaded the Soviet Union. His commanders were astounded. Schwerin told his staff privately, "That's that. Now we have lost the war!" Rommel as usual was optimistic. He expected a rapid victory and rejoiced at this blow to Churchill's hopes. Of course, he conceded to Lucie, it would mean delaying his own proposed journey to Germany: "I can't very well appear at the Führer's headquarters with my own problems at present."

Now at last it dawned on him why Hitler and the General Staff had refused to flood panzer divisions, heavy artillery and supplies into North Africa. The truth was that

Hitler, the Wehrmacht High Command and the General Staff were looking ahead to the "post-Barbarossa" era—the time when, with Russia defeated, Hitler's invincible Wehrmacht would begin a campaign of conquest along the roads that Alexander the Great and his *hoplites* had marched more than 2,000 years before. On a rainy day in early June at the Berghof, the Führer's fortified Bavarian mountain home, he had confided to his intimates: "The Russians have massed their entire strength on their western frontier, the biggest concentration in history. If Barbarossa goes wrong, we are all lost anyway. As soon as that is all over, Iraq and Syria will take care of themselves. Then I'll have a free hand, and I'll be able to push on down through Turkey as well."

These dreams took concrete shape in a draft High Command directive secretly circulated three days later. It put Rommel's job in Libya firmly into perspective. He would capture Tobruk first, then investigate ways of invading Egypt from the west; the Wehrmacht, after conquering the Caucasus, would come down and invade Egypt from the east. On June 28 Halder instructed Rommel to submit a draft plan for this. "We are making mighty progress in Russia," Rommel commented to Lucie on the thirtieth, "probably much faster than we expected. This is most important to us here, as we're going to have to hold on tight until the Russian campaign is over." Was Rommel betraying a trace of anxiety, now that he realized that many of his assumptions that spring had been groundless, because of the campaign against the USSR?

By this time Rommel's personnel dossier in Berlin was bulging with angry letters and complaints from other officers. Many had been privately interviewed by the General Staff on their return from Africa: there was the mild-mannered General Streich, Kirchheim, Olbrich, Rommel's chief of staff Colonel von dem Borne, a panzer battalion commander, Major Koehn, and Count von Schwerin. Schwerin warned that Tobruk was degenerating into "a mini-Verdun" and appealed for an active regiment elsewhere. "The wastage rate of generals and commanders out here is such that I can compute just when my turn will come," he sardonically wrote. Colonel von Herff criticized Rommel's "erratic leadership" and "grotesque decisions" and characterized as unacceptable Rommel's habit of court-martialing any officer who in his view failed in action: "This has not been the way in the German army before. We are all horrified about it." Streich called the habit "downright proletarian." When army Commander in Chief Brauchitsch asked him, at Hitler's headquarters, "Was it so hot down there that you all just got on each other's nerves?" the general replied: "No, Herr Feldmarschall: But one thing's got to be said—there's a big difference between being a brave and adventurous company leader and a field commander of great genius."

General Bodewin Keitel, chief of army personnel, was generous enough to blame this rash of backbiting on the grueling African climate and the battle strains that all panzer commanders are subjected to. "But," he said in a confidential memorandum in June, "in the Afrika Korps there is quite another burden too: that is the general's personality, and his way of expressing it and of giving orders." Indeed, Rommel frequently issued impossible orders—which nobody could take seriously—and then revoked them immediately. He thought nothing of insulting senior commanders like Kirchheim. Courts-martial ordered by Rommel mostly acquitted the officers he charged. "It is remarkable that in the case of one officer, a battalion commander in the Fifth Panzer Regiment," Bodewin Keitel commented, "a recommendation for the Knight's Cross, a cowardice charge and his dismissal followed one another in the briefest interval. While in another instance a senior general who had won the Pour le Mérite was wholly incomprehensibly threatened on the telephone with dismissal while the very next morning [Rommel] denied to his face ever having used such language to him." (This must have been General Kirchheim.)

Full general now or not, Rommel was sent a severely worded reprimand by Field Marshal von Brauchitsch on July 9. The commander in chief lectured him: "I think it my duty to tell you all this not only in the interest of the Afrika Korps, but in your own personal interest too." Rommel's reply showed no humility whatever.

He probably relished this kind of controversy. "Through

my new promotion I've leapfrogged over enormous numbers of my comrades," he bragged in a letter on July 12. "And this is bound to attract a lot of envy—a lot." And it did. The end of the year was to find Goebbels complaining at a secret staff conference that, while the birthday of a minor Luftwaffe civil servant had been fêted in the Nazi press, the Wehrmacht censorship authorities had forbidden any mention of Rommel's fiftieth birthday.

The General Staff's activation of his panzer group, now called Panzergruppe Afrika—effective from August 15—caused anomalies. Just what was a panzer group? And what would Rommel's pay and entitlements as its commander be? "I don't rightly know whether this makes me an *Oberbefehlshaber* [commander in chief] or not," he puzzled on August 11. "Normally that only goes for a full army commander." Being Rommel, he adopted both styles and waited for reactions. On his headed notepaper he was content with a mere "Befehlshaber," but the very first order issued on August 15 went out with the pretentious headline: "Army Order No. 1."

As usual, he got away with it. Six days later, he drew the obvious corollary: "All my colleagues in equivalent positions are colonel [four-star] generals. If all goes according to plan here, I'll probably be one too by the time the war's over." Studying his first pay slip late in September, he found that he was getting an army commander's expense allowance. "Sometimes I think I'm dreaming," he exulted to Lucie. Rommel's "smash and grab" tactics worked because by now everybody knew that he had Hitler's backing. Besides, Libya was far away and the leaders of the Wehrmacht were hypnotized by the pace of their advance into Russia.

Among the Italian generals, however, Rommel's rapid advancement struck raw nerves. Somehow this officer, who had arrived with one light division in February to tide them over their misfortunes, was now virtually Axis Land Commander, North Africa, and vested with considerable territorial and administrative powers as well. The consequence was an undisguised hostility between Rommel and the Italian High Command, which was presently based in a marble-pillared palace far to the rear in ancient Cyrene. On July 12 Gariboldi, the Italian field commander, whom Rommel had come to like for the affable, pliable and avuncular old duffer that he was, was suddenly replaced by General Ettore Bastico, a trim, moustached man, a personal friend of Mussolini. Bastico was described by one German as difficult, autocratic and violent"—so it was clear that there was no room for both him and Rommel in the same desert theater. Formally Rommel's superior, he summoned the dusty and disheveled Desert Fox to his palace at Cyrene later in July and made it plain he proposed to muzzle him. "A journey to Berlin is becoming imperative," said Rommel, fuming, in his next letter home.

He flew back to the Reich on July 28. For two days he stayed with Lucie at the war academy in Wiener Neustadt. Lucie thought he looked unwell and urged him to go see a doctor. Rommel knew she was right but refused to go. "I don't trust doctors," he said, chuckling. "In 1915 they wanted to amputate my leg!" So he flew on to Hitler's headquarters, the Wolf's Lair in East Prussia, on the thirty-first.

Hitler's handshake was itself a tonic. The Führer congratulated him on the Sollum victory and showed him the battle maps of the Russian front, where huge encirclement operations were breaking the back of Stalin's army. This set Rommel's own mind thinking along these lines: How could he trap and encircle the British army in North Africa?

Before Rommel left, Hitler granted all his demands for special measures against Tobruk—except one: German scientists had developed a "hollow charge" shell of immense penetrating power. It was code-named "Redhead," and stocks were already in Libya. However, it was still top secret and Hitler refused permission to Rommel to use it yet. But he did order the Luftwaffe to throw the first of its new two-and-a-half-ton bombs at Tobruk when Rommel's big attack began. He instructed the navy to move half a dozen U-boats and some motor torpedo boats to the Mediterranean to help blockade Tobruk. He asked the Foreign Ministry to explore ways of using Bizerta and other ports in Tunisia—still controlled by Vichy France —and he proposed that the vanishing Axis shipping tonnage in the Mediterranean should be replenished by the construction of hundreds of simple war transports of 400 to 600 tons displacement—although Hitler admitted to Rommel that he saw no prospect whatever of persuading Italian shipyards to build them.

After that, he sent Rommel to see Mussolini and General Ugo Cavallero, the pompous, ineffectual chief of the Italian High Command in Rome. Cavallero always looked more like a poor family lawyer than a general. Rintelen, the German attaché, wrote this account:

> General Rommel spoke in my presence with General Cavallero and the Duce on the morning of August 6. Evidently going on a report from General Bastico, they took the view that no attack on Tobruk will be possible in the foreseeable future because of transport difficulties and our exclusion from Bizerta. They examined the possibility of abandoning Sollum and the Tobruk front instead, and falling back onto a reserve line west of Tobruk.
>
> But the Duce was very impressed by General Rommel's confident description of the Sollum front, and of our prospects of holding it even against superior forces, provided he is assured of adequate supplies. The Duce believes that Britain's next moves will depend on how the situation develops on the Russian front.

As usual, Rommel had got his way: his big set-piece attack on Tobruk was to go ahead when he was ready. Mussolini instructed Cavallero and Rintelen to fly to Libya at once to make the necessary plans.

Before he left Rome, Rommel noticed in the mirror that his eyes and skin were turning yellow. He spoke of this to no one, fearing that the General Staff or his Italian friends would use it as a pretext to stop him from flying back to Libya.

On the return flight his Luftwaffe plane developed engine trouble, and it had to land at Athens for repairs. An enemy air raid kept him awake all night at his hotel. He was still complaining about the "bugs" in the plane's engines when it finally touched down safely on Bardia airfield, near his new stone-built headquarters, on August 8. Next day—as Rommel was thrashing out with Cavallero and Bastico their common strategy in Libya—he heard that the same Luftwaffe plane had just crashed in flames, killing everybody aboard.

He was sorry about the crew, of course, but shrugged off the accident philosophically. "Just goes to show how quickly it can come to you," he told Lucie.

# The Coming of
# Crusader

IT is a rainy night three months later—in mid-
November 1941. Libya is having one of the worst
rainstorms in years. Long, dry wadis have become torrential rivers that roll boulders onto the troops bivouacking in them and wash away tanks and trucks; airfields are
flooded and telephone lines torn down.

At thirty minutes past midnight, half a dozen shadowy figures run toward the squat two-story Prefettura
building at Beda Littoria, built on the coast near Cyrene,
in a cypress grove. They jump the German sentry guarding the entrance and force their way in. They are British
commandos. A British officer living in the town in the dis-
guise of an Arab has identified the building to them as the
headquarters of Rommel's Panzergruppe Afrika. The sentry tries to raise the alarm. A salvo of shots spreadeagles
him in the corridor, but the shots wake the men in the
ground floor office of the chief armorer's section.

Technical Sergeant Kurt Lentzen looks out with a
flashlight—a burst of Sten gun fire hits him. Lieutenant
Kaufholz draws his revolver, but the Sten gun splatters
him in the chest and arms. Hand grenades are tossed into
the room and explode with a shattering roar. The lights
of the whole building go out—its electricity generator has
also been blow up.

The noise has alerted the Panzer Group's chief engineer, Major Barthel, and Rommel's assistant quartermaster, Captain Weiz, both in conference upstairs. They sound the alarm, lock away their secret files and grab revolvers. By flashlight they can see a body lying outside the office downstairs—so they both report later in writing to Rommel—and firing is still going on around the building. They wait awhile, until the firing and shouting cease.

By the time they get downstairs, the body has gone, leaving a trail of blood. The chief armorer's office is a shambles—water from a shattered radiator is already an inch deep on the floor, mingling with the blood of the other men. Here is Private Kovacic, his stomach torn open by the blast. There is Kaufholz, moaning barely audibly: "I'm bleeding—bleeding to death." Both men die soon after. Outside, patrols find Lieutenant Jäger—shot dead as he jumped out of the window. Farther away is the body of a British major. The blood trail evidently came from him. Nearby is an injured British army captain, dressed, like the dead major, in khaki overalls and crepe-soled shoes. Of the other intruders there is no trace.

Rommel's staff examine the contents of the two men's knapsacks—more explosives, fuses, detonators, grenades. On the major's body they also find Egyptian and Italian money, a girl's photograph, a leather diary—which identifies him as Major Geoffrey Keyes, leader of a twelve-man commando killer squad—and other trappings of his trade. Both he and the prisoner have several days' growth of beard. The Panzer Group's investigations establish that they and their companions were landed some days back from British submarines, with orders to eliminate Rommel and Bastico and to blow up an important telegraph mast on the eve of a major British offensive. Keyes was killed by one of his own men in the confusion, and the daring raid collapsed.

Rommel scanned the reports and shook his head in puzzlement. Why Beda Littoria, of all places? Did the enemy really believe that he, Rommel, would lead his troops from a safe headquarters 200 miles to the rear? The Italians had, admittedly, given him the austere Prefettura building, and he had dutifully set up his Panzer Group headquarters there on August 14, 1941, but he had instantly disliked it. The food was too good—he remarked that he felt like a real "military plutocrat"—and the scenery, 2,000 feet above sea level, was too lush. Beda Littoria was "well out of danger—well out," he impatiently told Lucie. After just ten days there he handed the Prefettura over to his quartermaster's staff, and loaded his own grumbling officers onto trucks to take them to a new headquarters much closer to the battlefields, in the square, white-painted *cantoniera*—roadhouse—at Gazala. "From there I'll have more influence on the course of events," he wrote.

Major Keyes was buried with full military honors a few days after the fiasco, side by side with the four men from Rommel's quartermaster staff who also died. The joint military funeral was symbolic of the chivalry that Rommel encouraged in his men.

*Rommel's own manuscripts fall silent after Sollum and do not resume their narrative until the spring of 1942. But I shortly chanced on a fascinating, very useful document. In an archive guide I saw a reference to a "notebook of an adjutant at an African headquarters" and asked to see it. An hour later it was lying before me, still dusty and unopened these last thirty years or more—a grubby, Italian-made notebook with a black calico cover. Its 270 pages were covered with shorthand writing, but isolated words stood out—Tobruk, commander in chief, the names of Rommel's generals.*

*It proved impossible to find anybody conversant with both this shorthand system (in Germany there are half a dozen systems) and Second World War terminology. A sample transcript of two pages, done by a specialist firm in Bavaria, proved unacceptable. The heap of shorthand pages tantalized me for many months, until my own secretary, a woman born in Düsseldorf, caught sight of them and announced: "I think I can transcribe them!" It's not easy to interpret a stranger's shorthand, but for 200 hours she worked at it, dictating her transcript to me while I typed it. Over the next year we kept going back to the more stubborn portions, until we had cracked the whole document. It turned out to be the long-lost Rommel diary. It had been dictated by Rommel and his staff each day*

*and taken down by his secretary, Corporal Albert Bött-*
*cher. This was a find of considerable significance, and it*
*yielded many surprises.*

On Rommel's return to Bardia from Rome in August, his
doctors had diagnosed jaundice and prescribed a bland
diet and much rest. He adopted the diet but ignored the
other advice. Remarkably he survived his own obstinacy
—but he was not well, and he knew it, suffering particularly from the gastric disorders that plagued both friend
and foe. (In September he wrote to Lucie with a forced
humor that he had been stricken again: "It's going to be
the usual three-day race," he said.) His troops heard that
he was ill and sent him gifts of fruit, eggs, potatoes and
live chickens, bought after hard bargaining with haggling
Arabs.

His commanders might grumble, but his troops loved
him. They were not a hand-picked elite, but somehow he
gave them the feeling that they were. Major Friedrich Wilhelm von Mellenthin, the amiable cavalry officer who was
his new intelligence officer, put it like this: "Between
Rommel and his troops there was that mutual understanding that cannot be explained and analyzed, but which is
the gift of the gods. . . . The men knew that 'Rommel' was
the last man Rommel spared; they saw him in their midst,
and they felt, 'This is our leader.' " He knew how to make
them feel somehow immortal. Take this spontaneous remark by Rommel to the cameramen of a propaganda
company, recorded by his interpreter Wilfried Armbruster
in his diary: "Tell your men to shave off their beards. We
want *young* soldiers—we're never going to grow old!"

But Libya attacked the young men's health too, and the
mounting sick rate caused Rommel permanent alarm. One
division suffered a serious epidemic of diphtheria and
jaundice that September. The health of the officers seemed
particularly fragile. General Ferdinand Schaal, Rommel's
successor at Afrika Korps headquarters, was too ill to take
over. Rommel put the next senior general in Africa, Philip
Müller-Gebhard, in temporary command, but dysentery
forced this general to léave Libya in mid-September. And
since Lieutenant General Ludwig Crüwell did not finally
arrive to take command of the Afrika Korps until October

—having been first on furlough and then in the hospital—the corps was effectively "orphaned" for two months.

That summer the Libyan stage gradually filled with the cast for the winter battles. Troops were arriving in large numbers—in late August a new division, Special Service Afrika, had begun to arrive (it became the Ninetieth Light). And the big names who were to dominate Rommel's career came too—he had appropriated most of them with Alfred Gause's staff. "My new staff is much better than the old one," he said of them in one letter.

At Panzer Group headquarters his new operations officer was a tall, elegant lieutenant colonel of thirty-nine—the aristocratic, arrogant Siegfried Westphal. U.S. officers examining him in 1945 defined him as a typical militarist, highly intelligent and conceited. "War is his métier." Westphal would probably have liked the description. "He was brilliant and he knew the chief of staff, Gause, who won Rommel's favor." Like a small boy who has found a new friend, Rommel kept telling Lucie how much Gause was to his liking. He was an engineer general, a good, dry staff officer from East Prussia. Gause confided in him—telling him for instance that Streich had tipped him off, "You won't stand Rommel for long!"

Finally, in early October, a forty-two-year-old colonel arrived to act as new chief of staff to Rommel's beloved Afrika Korps, which was still the main striking force in his Panzer Army. He was Fritz Bayerlein, a private and noncommissioned officer in the First World War who in this war would become one of Rommel's best-known commanders. Bayerlein had an obsequious manner, but he was good. He had garnered his tank warfare experience under Heinz Guderian on the shell-scarred road to Moscow. He also apparently confided in Rommel immediately. The day he arrived, Rommel wrote: "Guderian and he had the same trouble with Streich as I did." He took an instant liking to Bayerlein.

Rommel moved out of Beda Littoria and set up his forward headquarters at Gambut—bug-infested, flyblown and unclean, but midway between the two places where the coming great battles would be fought—Tobruk and the frontier. Here at Gambut the Germans and Italians painstakingly built up their supply dumps and repair work-shops—large, well-camouflaged factories excellently provided with machine tools, heavy lifting tackle and vast stocks of spare tank parts. Even badly damaged trucks could be hauled off the field in mid-battle and returned, fighting fit, within days. Meanwhile Rommel waged war on the insects in his bed. The war was ruthless, and went on until he exterminated the "Last of the Mohicans"—as he called these tenacious vermin—by drenching his iron bedframe in gasoline and cremating them alive. "Now only their bites on my body are left to remind me of these loathsome pests," he wrote to his son Manfred at the end of August.

At Gambut, his headquarters was well within range of the enemy's guns at Tobruk. But every day that summer Rommel rode forth in his Mammut, jolting across the desert from outpost to outpost, following ancient camel trails to where German and Italian gangs armed with jackhammers and explosives were building the Tobruk bypass road. Then he would drive back again to the Sollum front to watch the work on the new strongpoints; he ensured that each position was provisioned with enough food and ammunition for eight days' battle, and he put extra muscle into the line with reconditioned Italian guns that had been lying rusting and derelict about the desert ever since the winter retreat. Everywhere the troops were training and drilling—with live ammunition, because there was no other in Libya—for the big set-piece attack that he was going to mount against Tobruk as soon as all his artillery and ammunition had arrived from Germany.

Not that he took only a parochial view of the war. He devoured intelligence reports on the navy's fighting in the Atlantic. He marveled at the victories in the USSR. "On my walls hang all kinds of maps, above all one of Russia," he wrote to young Manfred, now twelve. "And on that map every advance we make is immediately drawn in." He was torn between remorse—that it was the panzer divisions of his rivals that were encircling Kiev or besieging Leningrad ("A shame that I can't be there, and have to mark time down here")—and admiration: *"Four* Russian armies encircled," he wrote jubilantly on September 20. "I bet that wipes the grins off the Russians' faces!" For

reasons of prestige alone, he now had to take Tobruk—
and soon.

His plan remained essentially unchanged from July
1941, when he submitted it to the General Staff, through
October, when it was issued (as an "army order") to his
commanders, to the following June, when he was finally
able to try it out. Days of heavy bombing would soften
Tobruk's defenses. After a heavy artillery bombardment
the Afrika infantry division would open a breach in the
southeastern perimeter for the Fifteenth Panzer Division
—just where General Streich had suggested. The left
flank of this German assault force would be secured by the
Italian infantry divisions commanded by General Enea
Navarini's Twenty-First Corps. The German push would
go straight up to the port, and Tobruk would then have to
surrender or starve. Rommel privately reckoned with a
two-day battle.

The snag was, as the shrewd little General Bastico—
Rommel called him "Bombastico"—pointed out, that the
British were not going to stand idly by and let Rommel
get away with it. They would strike from Egypt into his
rear, after he attacked, or even try and scoop him altogether by launching a major offensive *before* he was ready
to go into Tobruk. Rommel's strategic answer was twofold.
He would locate a mobile reserve in the desert, well
placed to scotch any such move by the British. And by
lengthening the Sollum line of fortifications into the
desert, he hoped to force the enemy to make such a
lengthy detour that they could not arrive in his rear for
at least three days—by which time he would already have
dealt with Tobruk. In fact, he was convinced that the
British were too heavily committed elsewhere in the Middle East to launch any such offensive here.

His prestige enhanced by the great June 1941 victory,
he got on well with all his lesser Italian commanders.
"They try their hardest to get everything right," commented Rommel, "and they are extraordinarily polite."
But this politeness was absent in Bastico and Bastico's
superiors. "The Italian High Command here is annoyed
that it has so little say," Rommel observed with satisfaction. "We are always being spited in petty ways. But

we're not going to stand for it. Perhaps they're casting around for some way of getting rid of me."

The truth was that Bastico still regarded Rommel's interest in Tobruk as an unhealthy obsession. In an exchange of letters on September 6 he recommended attacking Egypt without bothering about Tobruk. Rommel sent Gause—behind Bastico's back—directly to Rome, where it was quite simply ruled that since Hitler and Mussolini had both decided that Tobruk was to be captured first, the matter was settled. It was an "absolute necessity," Rome said, before any advance by Rommel on the Nile. Rome promised to send supplies to Rommel so that he could attack in early November. He was to draft a suitable plan, and Bastico would then authorize it and fix the date. Weeks later Rommel was still gloating over this rebuff to Bastico. "His letters are getting downright insulting," he chuckled. "Evidently he's trying to provoke a row. Okay by me. He'll come off worse."

To consolidate his position, however, Rommel did take some precaution. He invited a close friend of Mussolini, a Major Melchiori, to visit Panzergruppe Afrika. "I have high hopes of this visit, as feelings against us are running high at present," Rommel wrote. "Well, nobody's going to pull any fast ones on me." He took the major—a dapper figure, in neat, tailor-made uniform—hunting in the desert. Rommel's shooting was done with a machine gun from fast-moving open cars. The targets were fleet-footed gazelles; their livers, Rommel told Lucie, tasted delicious. Then he arranged a real spectacular for Melchiori—a day trip into Egypt at the head of a panzer division.

This was the operation code-named "Midsummer Night's Dream." Rommel wanted to boost morale after months of idleness. His target was a "huge British supply dump" believed to be just fifteen miles beyond the frontier wire. There is a German saying, "Your appetite comes with eating," and the entire Afrika Korps had developed a healthy appetite for items of British-made uniforms (minus insignia); for Dodge, Ford and Rover cars and trucks; for Argentine corned beef, Canadian canned butter, American canned milk and English bacon. So the Twenty-first Panzer Division—the old Fifth Light— rolled through the barbed wire into Egypt at dawn on

September 14, to envelop the enemy supply dump and meet at Deir el Hamra many miles beyond. Sixty empty trucks followed to pick up the choicest booty. To his aide, Lieutenant Schmidt, Rommel looked more like a U-boat commander as he gave the signal from his tank turret to get moving and shouted: "We're off to Egypt."

General von Ravenstein's tanks and trucks dragged brushwood with them to simulate a huge tank force. A reconnaissance battalion cruised up and down the frontier and raised bogus radio traffic to simulate an attack by the entire Afrika Korps. But there was no enemy to be blinded by these deceits. Probably forewarned by code breaking, the enemy had simply ordered their forces here to fall back across the plateau, far enough for the Germans to run out of gasoline. Müller-Gebhard later wrote, "Our three battle groups pushed about sixty miles into enemy territory and then rendezvoused, without any combat at all. I was stunned to find General Rommel waiting for us at the rendezvous—he had driven on ahead of us all." For nearly three hours they milled around in hungry disappointment; the tanks refueled as best they could. Rommel was puzzled. Then, at 12:55 P.M.—like the moment in Hitchcock's *North by Northwest* when the lone cropspraying plane turns nasty—the RAF bombers suddenly arrived.

Even the newly found war diary of the Twenty-first Panzer Division does not disclose how many tanks were hit. Two trucks laden with gasoline blew up at once; the panzer regiment had six men killed, and a flak gunner died too. Rommel's Mammut was hit, his boot heel was blown off by a bomb blast and his driver badly injured. It was a thoroughly unsettling experience. He ordered the pursuit abandoned, and the whole force beat an undignified retreat back into Libya. The enemy lost only two prisoners and one disabled armored car—apparently the Orderly Room truck of a South African armored car regiment. In the truck were secret documents. "Herr General," said the Twenty-first Panzer's commander, Ravenstein, "the capture of these documents alone is enough to justify the outlay." The documents included an Eighth Army order of battle which—together with the emptiness of the desert he had just invaded—led Rommel to a fateful conclusion: that the enemy was not currently planning any offensive against him. There is evidence that the British had arranged to have Rommel capture these documents.

"It all went very smoothly," he lied to Lucie.

Later in September, warnings began reaching Rommel from both Berlin and Rome that a major British offensive was in the cards. He disregarded them. The almost illegible pencil notes his aide took of a speech Rommel made to his commanders contain the sentences: "One thing our sortie of the fourteenth has shown is that the enemy has *no* offensive intentions. It is to be presumed that he will not be able to launch any attack over the next few weeks, or months."

Of all his problems, obtaining the supplies needed for the attack on Tobruk caused most difficulties. British air attacks from Malta presented a renewed risk to the convoy route, because many of the German planes that would have fended them off had been sent in June to Russia. The port of Benghazi was now being used as well as Tripoli, but its capacity was low. October brought little improvement. The same shipping losses were suffered as in September, 23 percent. Once again it was Hitler who came to Rommel's rescue. Warned by his generals that Britain's only chance of reversing its declining fortunes quickly would be to attack Rommel soon, Hitler decided to transfer an entire Luftflotte—air force—to the Mediterranean. He put one of the Luftwaffe's best field marshals, Albert Kesselring, in command and designated him "Commander in Chief, South." On October 27 he went even further, instructing the navy to move two dozen U-boats from the Atlantic into the Mediterranean—stifling navy protests by saying this was necessary to stave off "a catastrophe" in Africa. So the independent strategy Rommel had pushed since April was beginning to have far-reaching consequences on other theaters.

All this wild talk of a "British offensive" annoyed Rommel. It conflicted with his own wishes—therefore he ignored it. One is reminded of a famous verse by the German humorist Christian Morgenstern:

And thus, in his considered view,
What did not suit—could not be true.

He was timetabling three important events for November. He would fly to Lucie in Rome in the first week, celebrate his fiftieth birthday in the second week, destroy Tobruk in the third. There was no room for any British offensive in this timetable. Since early September no letter had passed between Erwin and Lucie without his making some mention of these plans.

Several times during October, German and Italian intelligence nonetheless warned that Britain was reinforcing its army in Egypt. Rommel refused to panic. He reassured Lucie: "The British have other worries just right now." When General Max Sümmermann (of the new Afrika infantry division) suggested an armed reconnaissance behind enemy lines, Rommel's headquarters retorted that Midsummer Night's Dream had already established that the British had no intention of attacking.

Probably this willful disregard of the accumulating evidence derived from Rommel's fixation on Tobruk—the first objective that had so far defeated him. An artillery commander, Major General Karl Boettcher, had just arrived to direct the German firepower against Tobruk. By mid-November Rommel would have altogether 461 German and Italian big guns ready to rain shells on the city. He directed minor operations to improve the Bologna and Pavia divisional sectors, and, well schooled now in Rommel's tactics, the Italian infantry moved effectively and suffered no casualties. "All quiet," he reported to Lucie on October 19. "The British barely reacted to our latest gain in ground. Either they are too weak to, or they're shamming. . . . Anyway—rendezvous at Hotel Eden in Rome, November 1!"

Bastico had lapsed into a sullen silence. But not his chief of staff, General Gastone Gambara, who also commanded Italy's independent motorized force, the Twentieth Corps. Rommel badly wanted his corps too, but Gambara put him firmly in his place. Rommel flared out in his next letter home: "I never did think much of these fine gentlemen. Shits they are and shits they always have been."

Censure of this ferocity was reserved by Rommel only for the Italian *officer* caste. He blamed the Italian army's misfortunes solely on their officers and their poor weapons; their enlisted men he described frequently—for example, to Milch—as "magnificent soldier material." His interpreter Ernst Franz recalls how, after even an elite Bersaglieri position was overrun, their commander tearfully pleaded with Rommel: "Believe me, my men are not cowards." And Rommel replied, "Who said anything about cowards? It's your superiors in Rome who are to blame—sending you into action with such miserable weapons." (Some units in the Sollum line were equipped with artillery captured from the Austrians in the First World War: quite useless against modern armor.)

Still Rommel ignored the clamor of warning voices. On October 20 the Italian High Command sent an explicit warning to Bastico about a possible British offensive. But six days later Rommel issued his "army order" for the attack on Tobruk. "In my opinion," he told a resigned Gambara on the twenty-ninth, "The attack can begin on November 20 without our running any risk."

His own High Command made one last attempt to change Rommel's mind. Given Britain's growing air supremacy in Africa, they asked, would it not be better to wait until 1942? Rommel's headquarters replied that it would not: the Axis land superiority was so great that Tobruk would probably surrender within two days. Having sent this reply to Berlin, Rommel flew to Rome.

He was waiting for Lucie at the railroad station there next morning as her sleeping car pulled in. They spent two happy weeks sightseeing in the autumn sun and rain. General von Ravenstein was also there on furlough with his wife. Like typical tourists, they visited Saint Peter's. Rommel was not impressed by the architecture—he gripped Ravenstein's arm and said, "That reminds me: we've got to insert another battalion on Hill 209."

Their rooms at the Hotel Eden were ice-cold, but he did not notice. His mind was with his troops and on Tobruk. The maps of the fortifications were already being printed and corrected. Air photographs of each bunker to be stormed were being obtained. Several times he called on the attaché and on the Italian High Command: the conferences revolved around the knotty problem of supplies. As if to rub it in, late on November 8 an entire Axis convoy with 40,000 tons of supplies was sunk. The

Italians halted further convoy operations, and no more ships reached Libya until mid-December. (None had arrived there since October 16.)

Cavallero, chief of the Italian High Command, became even more apprehensive. Rommel assured him that Tobruk would fall after forty-eight hours at most, and that the British would never dare to attack if they risked having their retreat cut off. Cavallero acquiesced, but there were level-headed Italians in Libya who were not so easily fobbed off. Bastico's intelligence officer, a Major Revetria, was one. On November 11 Rommel's intelligence officer, Mellenthin, accosted the Italians' liaison officer. "Tell your Major Revetria he's much too nervous," he said. "Tell him not to worry—because the British aren't going to attack." Nonetheless, that same day Bastico urgently warned Cavellero that an enemy attack *was* looming up. He had photographs of the desert railroad, of new supply dumps and airfields, and reports of radio traffic showing that the British were about to launch "a heavy offensive aimed at forcing a final decision."

Similar data definitely reached Rommel's headquarters. There was an aerial photograph of a new British airfield south of the Qattara Depression, packed with over 100 planes: dated November 11, it was forwarded to headquarters by the chief Luftwaffe reconnaissance officer, Colonel Augustin. Other photographs showed the military railroad being built across the desert from Mersa Matruh toward the frontier wire. Some of these photos were even shown to Rommel in Rome, and Ravenstein saw him snatch the photographs away and irritably dash them to the floor, exclaiming: "I refuse even to look at them!"

Rommel visited Cavallero on November 13 and again persuasively argued that his attack on Tobruk must get the green light, despite the supply snags. Two days later —his fiftieth birthday—Rommel had an audience with Mussolini. The Fascist dictator confirmed that Tobruk must be attacked as soon as possible. Afterward his hosts showed him their new film, *Onward from Benghazi*. Rommel particularly liked the scenes showing Italian troops storming the city. (In fact, one of Rommel's smaller units had captured it.) "Very interesting and informative," he told the Italians sardonically. "I often wondered what happened in that battle."

Outside Tobruk, his storm troops had now moved forward to their starting points. His radio intercept company reported to headquarters on November 17 that a South African division had been identified moving off from Mersa Matruh into the desert. Intoxicated with their coming victory, Rommel's headquarters staff paid no heed to this report.

Where was Rommel now? He had left Rome early on November 16, but a thunderstorm forced his plane to land for the night at the devastated city of Belgrade. Next day engine trouble necessitated a further overnight stop at Athens. Not until the eighteenth did he land back in Libya. The news there was that a band of commandos had raided his former headquarters at Beda Littoria. The airfields—indeed, the whole countryside—were awash with rain. Apparently for this reason no reconnaissance sorties were being flown.

Rommel believed that he still had several days to prepare his great attack on Tobruk. But he did not, for the enemy's army—now reorganized as the Eighth Army—had that very morning forced the frontier wire, unseen, and was many miles inside Libya. Over 100,000 troops and more than 700 tanks were about to teach Rommel a lesson.

Rommel's headquarters staff, in his absence, had not tipped off the lower echelons about the gathering evidence of a coming enemy offensive. Thus, when on the eighteenth the enemy suddenly commenced radio silence, nobody had inquired why. Behind this veil of silence, the enemy's infantry had advanced to the Sollum line, while a powerful armored force had *already* outflanked the Sollum line on the desert plateau and was approaching Rommel's domain from the southeast.

Here, along the Trigh el Abd—a desert track—the Twenty-first Panzer Division had thrown out only a thin screen of armored cars, the Third and Thirty-third Reconnaissance battalions, united under Lieutenant Colonel Irnfried von Wechmar. At 5:30 P.M. on the eighteenth Wechmar informed Afrika Korps headquarters that seven hours earlier the Thirty-third had run into an "enemy reconnaissance in force" and that earlier, at 5:00 P.M., the Third had been attacked by "200 armored vehicles." Vague rumors flew. During the afternoon the Fifteenth Panzer Division informed the nearby Afrika division: "British attack intentions are possible in the south."

In consequence of all this, Ravenstein proposed sending his panzer regiment down toward Gabr Saleh that night, to meet the developing threat. Gabr Saleh was just a mark on the map, on the Trigh el Abd, forty miles south of Gambut. Crüwell, the Afrika Korps's solemn, ponderous Rhinelander commander, found himself in an awkward dilemma and discussed it with his chief of staff, Bayerlein. On the one hand, he said, Rommel had always dismissed any idea of an enemy offensive as "absolutely impossible." On the other, aircraft had now sighted 1,650 enemy vehicles massing along the frontier wire, from Sidi Omar south toward Fort Maddalena. At 7:00 P.M. Bayerlein privately oriented his divisions. "We cannot exclude the possibility of an operation to outflank us from the south." Together, Crüwell and Bayerlein decided to alert the Fifteenth Panzer, and to send Ravenstein's panzer regiment south to Gabr Saleh as proposed.

First, however, at 8:00 P.M. they phoned Rommel for permission. Rommel snapped at Crüwell, "We mustn't lose our nerve." He added that Ravenstein was not to send his panzer regiment south: "We must not show our hand to the enemy too soon." He invited Crüwell to meet him—at noon the next day.

This was a display of coolness which the Italians refused to emulate. Although reassured by the Germans at 10:00 P.M. that there was "no cause for anxiety," Gambara knew better and issued orders before midnight alerting both his divisions on the Bir el Gubi end of the Trigh el Abd (the Ariete and Trieste divisions).

There followed an even more glaring example of Rommel's obstinacy. At 11:00 P.M. Afrika Korps headquarters telephoned that an Italian patrol had picked up a British soldier near Sidi Omar, and the man was claiming convincingly that a large part of the enemy's Eighth Army was already on the move into Libya. Rommel's staff dismissed this prisoner as "untrustworthy." Despite this, Crüwell rushed a full interrogation report by dispatch rider overnight to Rommel. The prisoner was Driver A. J. Hayes, chauffeur of the commander of one of the crack field batteries attached to the Fourth Indian Division. "He says Hitler has on several occasions offered Britain good peace terms. But Churchill, inspired by malice and ruthlessness, is leading the British people toward the abyss. The prisoner's manner of speaking makes his testimony seem trustworthy."

Rommel read it contemptuously at 9:00 A.M. next day. His staff formally discounted it as "lies and exaggerations." At noon Crüwell arrived and bluntly disagreed, but he was met with a chorus of jeers from Gause, Mellenthin and even Rommel. Over twenty-four hours had passed since the great British offensive, code-named "Crusader," had begun. But not for another twenty-four hours would Rommel actually believe it.

# The Desperate Foray

THE operating tent is a lean-to, set up behind a three-ton army truck. The surgeon, in his white coat and cap, is Major Ian Aird, a British officer. His field hospital near Sidi Omar, on the Egyptian frontier, has been over-run by German troops, but his surgery on the battle cas-ualties—primarily Italians from the Sollum line and members of the Fourth Indian Division attacking it—must go on. He has explored a dozen abdominal wounds during the night, he is weary enough to drop, but still the casual-ties are being carried in.

It is November 25, 1941—a week since the British offensive, Crusader, began. Already the Libyan desert is littered with the blackened hulks of tanks. Once more the war has spilled over onto Egyptian soil, and Aird and all his hospital staff are prisoners of the Germans.

Toward noon there is a flurry of excitement. A stretcher party hurries in with a bloodstained, groaning air attack victim. It is Fritz Stephan, commander of Rommel's Fifth Panzer Regiment. Aird examines him rapidly—he notes in his diary that the panzer colonel has a large sucking wound in the chest. He has been hit by shrapnel and the right lung is all but severed from the heart. The Germans have applied a shell dressing to cut the bleeding, and they

153

ask Aird to apply a pressure dressing so they can fly him back to base.

Stephan is conscious, stalwart, but in deep shock. To Aird's trained eye it is obvious that the colonel will not survive without immediate surgery. The German doctor accompanying Stephan hesitates, and hurries out to consult with the panzer officers waiting with their armor close by. Aird starts a transfusion and has the surgical equipment prepared for an immediate operation.

Shells attracted by the German column are beginning to drop near the field hospital, making the sand under Aird's feet shudder. The German doctor hurries back to Aird: "The Herr General asks you to be so good as to proceed with surgery."

The shells are getting closer. An anesthetist points out that the explosions are disturbing the other injured men. Aird, however, does not heed the shell bursts. The surgery already seems a hopeless task. During the operation Aird looks up once briefly and sees that a dozen panzer officers have slipped into the tent and are quietly watching him operate on their comrade. Among them is a general with the blue Pour le Mérite displayed at his throat—Erwin Rommel himself.

A particularly near miss brings another appeal from the anesthetist. Without a word, the Germans return to their armored vehicles and pull back a safe distance from the hospital. Rommel's doctor pauses to thank Aird and say, "We'll return again tomorrow on our way back into Egypt."

But none of them met again. Nor did any of them forget this extraordinary desert encounter. Aird, impressed by Rommel's humanity, later traced Stephan's widow— the colonel died a few hours after the operation—and described it to her. And Rommel, asked by Goebbels in a broadcast a year later whether he did not perhaps take unnecessary risks, hesitated and gave a quite unexpected answer. The British fought fairly in the desert, he began. "I once paid a visit to a British field hospital . . ."

Then he pulled himself together and said, "Uh, you don't have to worry about my safety. I know how to look after myself."

Stephan died on the seventh day of the extended Crusader offensive. It was a long series of interlocking battles launched by the British to destroy Rommel before he could knock out the Tobruk garrison. The enemy were fielding 724 tanks against him, with 200 more in reserve, while he had only 260 (and the Italians 154). For three weeks the battles ebbed and flowed, pausing each day at dusk and resuming at dawn. They began on November 18 and had still not really ended by December 8, when Rommel angrily announced the retreat. The skies were low and overcast, the melee churned up turbid clouds of dust and smoke. Tanks dueled with tanks or guns over an area some fifty miles square, from the Egyptian frontier wire in the east to the road south out of Tobruk in the west. The tanks ranged across the high coastal plain, laboring up the escarpments and spilling down them like rodents running amok over a flight of stairs.

It was not an easy battle for even the commanders themselves to follow. The Rommel diary records him cursing on November 22: "Our signals networks could hardly be worse. This is war the way the ancient Teutons used to fight it. I don't even know at this moment whether the Afrika Korps is on the attack or not."

Crusader conformed to no pattern, but proved Rommel's own favorite dictum: "It is not possible to make any battle plan that holds good longer than the first day." His opponents' plan did not last even as long as that. Lieutenant General Sir Alan Cunningham, commander of the Eighth Army, had intended to plant his armored brigades on the points of a triangle around a battleground of his own choosing—whereupon, he hoped, the Afrika Korps would duly oblige and present itself there for obliteration. For no particular reason, the site he chose was Gabr Saleh, a meaningless desert location sixty miles southeast of Tobruk. Cunningham hoped to deduce Rommel's strategy from his reaction to the approach of the British Thirtieth Corps as it rounded Rommel's Sollum line and headed for Gabr Saleh. But Rommel had not even noticed the British movement, and when Ravenstein finally proposed moving his Fifth Panzer Regiment—Colonel Stephan's regiment—to Gabr Saleh, Rommel had instinctively stopped him. "We must not show our hand to the enemy too soon," he explained: an astute decision that had the hallmark of the master.

His failure to act on the earlier days had stupefied the enemy. The commander of the British Thirtieth Corps, Major General Willoughby Norrie, took matters partly into his own hands. He decided to thrust well beyond Gabr Saleh—indeed, to attack Sidi Rezegh, just south of Tobruk: Rommel *would* be forced to defend that. So Norrie fatefully varied the Cunningham plan. On November 19 he sent an armored brigade to Sidi Rezegh and two others to attack the intervening points of Gabr Saleh and Bir el Gubi. Merely by not reacting, therefore, Rommel had split his enemy's main armored force into three diverging bodies.

The events of the first four days of Crusader are quickly told. Rommel, perplexed and infuriated by this interference with his plans to take Tobruk, virtually abdicated all initiative to Crüwell, the Afrika Korps commander. For three days Rommel continued plotting the Tobruk attack —even though a British armored brigade seized Sidi Rezegh, a vital tableland only ten miles in his rear.

On the afternoon of the nineteenth, the Germans bestirred themselves at last. Colonel Stephan's panzer regiment probed southward to Gabr Saleh, bumped into another armored brigade there, and destroyed twenty-three American-built Stuart tanks for the loss of two of his own. This first mobile action of the campaign revealed strengths that augured well for Rommel. First, the panzer regiment dared to remain on the battlefield as dusk fell, while the British withdrew into defensive formation called a "night-leaguer." This allowed the Germans to recover the disabled German tanks left about the field. Secondly, the Germans had developed the process of recovering tanks in mid-battle to a fine art. And above all they showed new skill at coordinating heavy mobile guns and tanks; as a result they had inflicted great slaughter on the enemy.

The fighting of the next weeks revealed a curious relationship between Rommel and the new Afrika Korps commander, Crüwell. Technically, Crüwell was required to obey Rommel's orders without question. But events often showed him acting with an independence bordering on disobedience, and in retrospect it is remarkable that the field marshal put up with it. His own hidden complexes partly explain his reticence. Crüwell was a real cavalier type, the son of a wealthy Dortmund family of printers whose fortunes rested on a church monopoly of hymnbook publishing. Intellectually he was head and shoulders above Rommel; and this fact, coupled with the burning ambitions of his new chief of staff, Fritz Bayerlein—who had a powerful influence on him—put the Panzer Group commander at a psychological disadvantage.

Initially, their differences concerned the enemy's intentions. Rommel still believed on November 20 that the enemy thrusts were not a serious attempt to lift the siege of Tobruk. Crüwell was not deceived, however, and decided to concentrate his Afrika Korps forces to deal with each of the three enemy brigades in turn. He briefed his two panzer division commanders, the aristocratic General von Ravenstein and the dashing General Neumann-Silkow, at 2:35 P.M. They were to concentrate on Gabr Saleh. "I refuse," said Crüwell, "to stand idly by and watch the enemy advance unmolested on Tobruk."

What opened Rommel's eyes to the ugly truth was not the arguments of his generals or the air reconnaissance reports, but an open broadcast by the BBC in Cairo. "The Eighth Army," said its evening news bulletin, "with about 75,000 men excellently armed and equipped, have started a general offensive in the Western Desert with the aim of destroying the German-Italian forces in Africa."

This stung Rommel into action. During the night he telephoned Crüwell about the "critical situation" and ordered the Afrika Korps's two panzer divisions to begin rolling northward from Gabr Saleh toward Tobruk at the first light, following in the tracks churned up by the enemy armor. "Your objective," rasped Rommel into the telephone, "will be the center of the airfield at Sidi Rezegh." The enemy infantry, tanks and gun crews had already installed themselves on this airfield, and were winding up for a last heave to break through Rommel's siege ring into Tobruk.

At six-thirty—still before dawn—Rommel climbed out of his Kübel car at Belhamed hill, where General Boettcher's artillery was dug in. This was about three miles north of the airfield. He ordered Boettcher to turn the guns around to bombard the airfield. Looking south through his binoculars at 7:45 A.M. as the light improved, Rommel could see the enemy infantry and tanks forming up on the airfield for their last push on Tobruk. They began to move soon after. Almost simultaneously, the enemy garrison in Tobruk itself, behind Rommel's back, began a fierce tank assault on the siege ring, planning to break out and link up with the airfield force near El Duda, a hill weakly held by Rommel's infantry. This really made Rommel's force here the "meat in the sandwich." But as he raised his binoculars over the airfield's horizon to the south, he saw what he was looking for—the towering dust clouds raised by the fast approach of the entire Afrika Korps coming to the rescue.

Twice that morning Rommel himself took command of the counterattacks between Belhamed and El Duda, thwarting the enemy's attempts to hammer a corridor through to the Tobruk fortress. He drove about the battlefield, took temporary command of the armored cars of Baron Irnfried von Wechmar's reconnaissance battalion, added four of the magnificent flak eighty-eights to this improvised task force and saw them shoot down tank after tank in flames.

Meanwhile a holocaust had begun on the enemy-held airfield at Sidi Rezegh, on the desert side of the "sandwich." Boettcher's heavy guns were pounding and cratering the airfield. Rommel could see the dust and blaze as the Afrika Korps tanks charged to the airfield perimeter and opened fire at a range of 2,000 yards. By the morning's end the British Seventh Armored Brigade had only ten tanks left. But another enemy armored brigade was believed to be coming north to join battle the next day— thus sandwiching the Afrika Korps in from the rear too.

That night Rommel was unable to sleep. One slip, he knew, might cost him the battle and perhaps lose him the campaign too. At 7:00 A.M. he was already back on Belhamed hill to check that Boettcher's guns knew what they had to do. The hill was a good vantage point for the coming battle. Twice that morning he changed his battle plan, finally—at midday—ordering the Twenty-first Panzer's rather jumpy commander, General von Ravenstein, to launch an immediate direct attack on the airfield. It began at 2:20 P.M., with the fifty-seven tanks of Colonel Stephan's panzer regiment slamming the field from the west and the infantry trucking in from the north.

This was the battle's turning point. The British gunners put up a terrific fire as Stephan's tanks charged them—most of the stalwart gunners fell where they fought. The photographs show their corpses draped unromantically across the wreckage of their twenty-five-pounders. Too late, the British Twenty-second Armored Brigade now arrived on the airfield from the south—about 107 tanks in all. How the surviving British gunners cheered—until Rommel's powerful screen of antitank weapons began to bark. The enemy tanks were outgunned; the end was inevitable.

By dusk the airfield at Sidi Rezegh was again in Rommel's hands. His two panzer divisions still had 173 tanks in working order. The enemy's Seventh Armored Division, the only force confronting him, had only 144. By superior tactics and with a lot of luck, he had more than turned the tables on the Eighth Army.

Through field glasses that evening Rommel watched the battle end, and counted the charred and blackened enemy tanks until they disappeared into the darkness. The Germans used the phrase "shot down" to describe what happened when a shell pierced a tank and ignited all that it contained. The British phrase "brew up" was more descriptive. Long tongues of flame would curl out of every orifice. The shells and machine gun bullets inside would begin exploding until the whole hull seemed to bulge and convulse. Glistening rivulets of molten aluminum would run from the dead engine like tears, congealing on the desert sand in hard mirrors of spent metal. Then the rubber and oil would catch fire, and a spiral of funereal smoke would rise from the awesome pyre. Around the burned-out tank would lie the corpses of its crewmen, sometimes seeming just asleep, sometimes headless or limbless or scorched black. These were the men who preyed on every tank commander's conscience. Rommel himself had no fear that one day this might happen to him—it always happened to "the other man"; but he had the burden of responsibility, and no man could take it from his shoulders.

That evening, November 22, he congratulated Ravenstein at his command post. "Today's victories have greatly eased our situation," he said. But even now a further disaster awaited the enemy. Crüwell—out of contact with Rommel most of that day—had independently sent the Fifteenth Panzer marauding westward late that afternoon. By chance it rolled right into the night-leaguer of the enemy's Fourth Armored Brigade. In the following melee, lit by headlights, blazing tanks, machine gun and cannon fire, Crüwell captured fifty armored fighting vehicles and the headquarters of the British brigade as well. Thus the enemy's last coherent armored force was rendered leaderless.

The next day saw the greatest of the tank battles so far. This, the last Sunday in November, was the day on which Germany's war dead traditionally were remembered. It was called the "Sunday of the Dead"—Totensonntag—and by this forbidding name the battle of November 23 came to be known.

It was very much General Crüwell's battle. He and his chief of staff, Colonel Bayerlein, had not seen Rommel for four days. The battle provided another example of a victory obtained in defiance of Rommel's orders. As the Panzer Group commander, Rommel had sent Crüwell a long-winded command directive at 10:30 P.M. on the twenty-second, planning the coming battle. It boiled down to a southward push by Afrika Korps's two panzer divisions, meeting a northward advance by the Italian armored division Ariete from Bir el Gubi: the enemy would be caught and destroyed between these two moving fists. Crüwell ignored this directive. At 3:00 A.M. he issued his own—for what was to be basically an encirclement. When Rommel's overlong directive arrived, evidently around 4:30 A.M., Crüwell caustically noted that it contained a surfeit of "totally irrelevant" detail and tossed it aside. He left with Bayerlein about an hour later to fight the battle *his* way. He drove through the gathering morning mist to join the Fifteenth Panzer Division: they would move off to the southwest.

Rommel spent most of the day at the Twenty-first Panzer's fixed command post. Again he told General Boettcher that he expected the artillery to decide the day's battle. His diary shows most interestingly that he was already thinking far beyond that day's events: "His aim is to annihilate the armored forces encircled south of Sidi Rezegh today and tomorrow. After that he intends to strike fast toward Sidi Omar and then to prepare to attack Tobruk." General Boettcher warned him that they would run into ammunition difficulties if they renewed their attack on Tobruk.

By about 11:00 A.M., under leaden skies and icy winds, Crüwell had already massacred the thin-skinned supply echelons of the enemy. Then he began to concentrate his forces in a methodical, determined way until by 2:30 P.M. he had all three of his armored formations—Ariete, the Eighth and the Fifth Panzer regiments—parading abreast in a line near Bir el Gubi, facing north and ready to bully the enemy back toward Sidi Rezegh. Artillery and mobile eighty-eights would travel with them. What was unorthodox about Crüwell's plan was his order that the two regiments of infantry were to be trucked close behind the tanks, and were not to dismount "until they come under heavy infantry fire." It seemed like a recipe for mass suicide, almost, but his officers and men accepted it without question.

Of all this Rommel had little or no inkling. At about 2:00 P.M. his diary had lamented, "Contact with Afrika Korps cannot be established." Neither he nor Crüwell yet knew that at dawn that day the Afrika Korps's mobile headquarters, complete with its irreplaceable radio trucks, had been overrun by an enemy force advancing undetected toward Sidi Rezegh.

At 3:00 P.M. tank turret hatches clanged shut. A thin drizzle was falling. The trucks were loaded with crouching infantrymen; clips were snapped into rifles, ammunition belts were fed into machine guns, and Crüwell's triple-headed hammer began swinging northward toward Rommel's anvil—the fixed artillery and infantry holding the escarpments at Sidi Rezegh. Between them was the enemy, by now well dug in and waiting for them. Crüwell's tanks rolled north, gathering speed, spewing armor-piercing and machine gun fire. A company commander looked back and saw an unforgettable scene: "There were armored troop carriers, cars of various kinds, caterpillars hauling mobile guns, heavy trucks with infantry, motorized flak units." A hail of enemy fire met them—shells and bullets whining horizontally past them. The smoke from shells and burning vehicles darkened this infernal scene. The tanks were heavily hit, but most still rolled on, converging on the enemy. As the infantry trucks bumped and jounced over the hard, wet gravel, intense fire greeted them. The German officers stood erect in their cars and trucks, to encourage their men. Lieutenant Colonel Zintel, commander of a rifle regiment, twisted sideways, a bullet having passed through his brain, and toppled from his car. Moments later his battalion commander, Major von Grolmann, was killed by a direct hit on his truck. Officer after officer was mortally wounded. The regiment's adjutant, a mere lieutenant, took command.

By now they were squarely among the enemy positions. At 6:00 P.M., the hammer reached the anvil and the enemy's morale cracked. Crüwell's costly brute-force tactics had resulted in the annihilation of the rest of the British Seventh Armored Division and most of the First South African Division. The news of this great victory was passed to Rommel, at Ravenstein's headquarters, at 6:50 P.M. He turned a blind eye on Crüwell's defiance of his own battle directive. He broke his three-day silence in a letter to Lucie: "The battle seems to be the worst crisis. I'm okay, in fine spirits and good heart. Over 200 tanks shot down so far. Our fronts have held."

At dusk, as fires from blazing tanks flung fantastic shadows across the desert south of Tobruk and medics moved from wreck to wreck to tend the injured and ease the pain of the dying, Rommel returned to his own headquarters. His diary relates that he had "briefly discussed" the order he intended issuing to Crüwell next day. Rommel had decided on a raid so audacious and spectacular that even now he kept half of it to himself: Beginning at 10:00 A.M. the next day he was going to hurl his two panzer divisions down the Trigh el Abd—the desert track running parallel to the coast, forty miles inland—to the frontier wire at Sidi Omar—the desert end of the Sollum front. He would destroy the enemy believed to be massing there, and he would then stand astride the supply lines of the British units that had invaded Libya to relieve Tobruk. This would give him total victory—the Eighth Army would be done for.

He issued the first orders in the hour before midnight. He informed Colonel Westphal and his apprehensive staff, "I will put myself at the head of the Africa Korps, and begin the pursuit. I'll probably be away from here until tomorrow evening—or the morning after at the latest." There is no doubt that Rommel ignored the presence of a large New Zealand force advancing on Bardia from Tobruk. (His own hand-colored sketches indicate that he was obviously uncertain that such a force even existed.) He also overestimated the enemy's disorganization—and overlooked his own.

Crüwell, fresh from the battlefield, did not. His Afrika Korps had lost its own headquarters unit and seventy-two of his 162 tanks that day. The Fifteenth Panzer Division had also lost its radio trucks, and many of Rommel's most outstanding officers had been butchered in the frontal assault on the enemy's guns that afternoon. Crüwell was a forceful and thoughtful commander. He first heard of Rommel's desperate plan at sunup on November 24, when he gate-crashed a meeting called by Rommel on the Tobruk bypass road. He objected and suggested to Rommel a routine mopping-up operation first. "We have got to clean up the battlefield and salvage the immense booty before the enemy has time to come and fetch it himself," he said emphatically.

Rommel disagreed. He told Ravenstein, "You have the chance of ending this campaign tonight!"

At 10:30 that morning the spectacular operation, Rommel's dash for the frontier wire, began. Rommel stood straight up in his open car, the raw wind biting his face, as he piloted the Twenty-first Panzer Division from the Sidi Rezegh airfield. Crüwell was some way behind with all that was left of his headquarters unit—his own Mammut, one radio truck, two dispatch riders and two cars. Neumann-Silkow's Fifteenth Panzer spent the morning patching its injuries, refueling and ammunitioning; at noon it followed in Ravenstein's tracks, heading for the frontier. The sun was breaking through the wet clouds as this, the most erratic act in Rommel's African campaign, began.

"I'll be back this evening!"—with Rommel's cheery words ringing in their ears, the appalled Panzer Group staff watched him go. He meant it, too: he didn't even take his toothbrush. His chief of staff, Gause, went with him, and so the Panzer Group responsibilities devolved on Siegfried Westphal, his youthful operations officer. For many days afterward Westphal tried frantically to contact Rommel for instructions. Nobody knew where Rommel was, sometimes Rommel least of all. Westphal's intelligence officer, Mellenthin, remembers: "Huddled in our greatcoats, in the wooden bus that served as our headquarters at El Adem, Westphal and I viewed the situation with increasing apprehension." Because now, with Rommel gone, the real effort of the British to break the siege ring around Tobruk was about to begin.

For Rommel the dash to the wire was a grand adventure. Faster and faster he drove toward the frontier, looking neither left nor right as he charged down the very axis of the enemy's Thirtieth Corps. Like picnickers before an angry swarm of bees, the enemy began to flee eastward and southeastward as the Afrika Korps made its unannounced and desperate foray. Near Gabr Saleh, halfway to the wire, tanks, armored cars, trucks and guns were caught in the rush, while the German armor charged among them and blasted them at will. Brigadiers, corporals, black drivers, typists, cipher clerks, mechanics, war correspondents—panic gripped them all regardless of rank. The enemy air force scrambled from its landing grounds—the sky was full of Hurricanes and Tomahawks retreating east. The Eighth Army commander, Cunningham himself, just barely escaped in a Blenheim bomber, taking off through herds of trucks stampeding across the rough Gabr Saleh airstrip.

At 4:00 P.M. Rommel and Ravenstein reached the frontier, at Bir Sheferzen, twenty-five miles in from the sea. Like a monster caterpillar, the barbed wire entanglement rolled north and south as far as they could gaze. Thus far the gamble had paid off. Recklessly, Rommel dispatched Ravenstein northeast into Egypt with orders to establish himself southeast of Halfaya, the pass through the Mediterranean escarpment overlooking Sollum, before dusk. This would expose Ravenstein to great danger. He had only the truck he stood in—he had neither tanks nor artillery as yet, for his division's 2,000 vehicles were still strung out behind him along the Trigh el Abd, striving to catch up. But gamely Ravenstein obeyed.

An hour later, at five, Crüwell's Mammut jolted to a halt near the wire. Rommel boisterously announced: "I've just sent Ravenstein on up to Halfaya."

Crüwell was appalled. His proud Afrika Korps, yesterday's awesome victor, was now sprinkled across the sixty miles of desert from Gabr Saleh to Halfaya. Rommel told him that the Afrika Korps and the Italian Twentieth Corps were going to "encircle and destroy" the enemy. He had not troubled to ask the Italian division here—Savona—just where the enemy was. He assumed, wrongly as it turned out, that they were all in the outer zone of the frontier fortifications. "The panzer divisions will drive the enemy onto the minefields of our Sollum front and will force them to surrender," he announced. Crüwell dutifully drove on into Egypt.

For a while Rommel stayed at the wire, waiting for his striking forces to catch up. Colonel Stephan's Fifth Panzer Regiment, however, with only thirty tanks still running, was stranded in Libya, temporarily out of gasoline and ammunition. Ariete was being held up by opposition from a South African brigade. Nor had the Fifteenth Panzer arrived, with its fifty-six tanks. Rommel had also ordered a reconnaissance battalion to occupy Habata that night to plug this, the "defeated" enemy's only other escape route from the Libyan plateau to the Egyptian coastal plain. But the battalion pleaded lack of gasoline and ammunition and lay low.

Undeterred by these frustrations, Rommel took Gause across the wire into Egypt after dusk. His aide, Alfred Berndt, later described the venture: "His car's steering column snapped. His escort car had been left behind somewhere, and the last trucks of the panzer division were vanishing into the distance. His driver had to get out every 100 yards and kick the front wheels into the correct angle." Then the engine died on them. It was bitter cold, and Rommel and Gause were shivering. At this moment Crüwell, no less, drove by in his Mammut and graciously offered them a lift.

Thus it came to pass that ten German officers and five enlisted men, representing Hitler's Panzergruppe Afrika, were packed into a Mammut on the enemy side of the wire. Nor did the black comedy end there. They could not find the gap through the wire to get back into Libya. Rommel himself took the wheel. After battering the wire fruitlessly, like a demented insect against a windowpane, he switched off the engine and gave up for the night; they went to sleep. In fact they were just north of Fort Maddalena —the British commander's advance headquarters! During the night they could hear enemy dispatch riders and trucks rattling past the stationary Mammut. But the Mammut, which was a captured British vehicle, looked unextraordinary to the passersby and they paid it no attention. At the first light Rommel started up the engine. Soon he found a gap in the wire and slipped gratefully back into Libya.

A thin crescent moon was rising in the morning sky when Rommel rejoined his forces. After a while a lieutenant from a machine gun battalion was brought to Rommel. His name was Borchardt, he said, and he had been sent by his battalion—some way down the wire to the south— to find Stephan's Fifth Panzer Regiment.

"Where is the regiment?" Rommel asked impatiently.

"They must have reached the wire about six miles north of here by now," replied Borchardt.

Rommel set off there at once, past ghostly skeletons of wrecked trucks. He found Stephan and gave him his orders, then returned to Lieutenant Borchardt. "How many cars have you left in your company?" he inquired abruptly.

Borchardt was taken aback; he had expected appreciation. "Uh, three, Herr General!"

"Good," Rommel barked. "If you've any luggage in your car you had better get it out at once. I'm taking your car and driver."

The next day, November 25, was like a nightmare for Westphal, who was at headquarters, seventy miles away. But Rommel enjoyed it. It was like being a company commander all over again, rounding up straggling troops and pointing them toward the enemy. He omitted to issue any orders at all to the Trieste Division, so it moved—on whose volition?—not to the frontier but to El Adem, where Westphal's staff were headquartered. He ordained that a fast raiding force was to be rushed down past Maddalena to Giarabub oasis, 120 miles to the south. But nobody could spare the troops, vehicles, gasoline or ammunition, so nobody went. Rommel obviously believed that the same cowboy tactics he had used at Mechili in April would work again here—that speed and surprise would always triumph over planning and preparation.

He visited Neumann-Silkow's Fifteenth Panzer Division that morning. It had just arrived at the wire. He ordered it to push northward and "seal off the enemy at Sollum from the west." He explained that Ravenstein's Twenty-first Panzer was doing the same from the east. "Kick up dust," he suggested. (He repeated this to Crüwell next day: "We must use every truck and supply convoy we've got to kick up dust; that will deceive the enemy as to our real strength and lead them to surrender." Crüwell expressed "serious reservations.")

The day's fighting was not glorious. One of Neumann-Silkow's panzer regiments beat up a British tank repair workshop of largely derelict and immobile tanks. Meanwhile, Rommel instructed the Fifth Panzer Regiment—now commanded by Major Mildebrath; Stephan had just been mortally wounded—to forget about joining up with Ravenstein and to attack Sidi Omar instead. The regiment had less than twenty tanks and no artillery support. Rommel's order forced them to advance across a minefield he had himself laid, and attack enemy field guns that had been well dug in.

At 800 yards' range the British twenty-five-pounders opened fire. The gunners cheered madly as salvo followed salvo. By dusk the German regiment had ten tanks left, of which only three had guns in working order. Neither gasoline nor ammunition reached them—"because a higher headquarters had directed all our supply trucks to simulate an attack elsewhere," the regiment bitterly reported.

Late that morning the machine gun battalion that had dispatched Lieutenant Borchardt had reached the coast east of the Halfaya Pass—still held by the indomitable

Major Bach, the ex-pastor. "In theory our motor transport should have stopped dead long before," Borchardt later wrote, "because the gasoline we had on paper ran out long ago. But we were driving on the difference between what we reported and what we actually had: our maintenance officers, troop leaders and drivers were always smart enough to have a few jerrycans tucked away. Our real shortage was in water and food." Suddenly Rommel appeared and ordered them to dig in. "For the next forty-eight hours, it turned out, we were the last soldiers to see General Rommel."

It is not easy to follow the Fox's trail after this. Crüwell was not to see him until the next day, November 26. Rommel, a dynamo of energy, appears to have driven from one tired unit to the next. If they had orders from others, he usually revoked or reversed them. The Afrika Korps diary refers scathingly to "misunderstandings and errors" and to Rommel's "interference." Just how acid were the feelings against him is indicated by one enigmatic fact: certain pages of the diary from November 25 onward were removed and retyped (evidently in 1942; one of the retyped pages is even carelessly headed "26.11.1942"). One possible conclusion is that at the time, Crüwell, Westphal and perhaps Ravenstein, too, had started to conspire against Rommel so as to salvage what they could from the wreck of his erratic grand strategy.

The upshot of all this was the entirely unexpected return of Ravenstein's force from Egypt to Libya on November 26. Who ordered it is a mystery. Rommel furiously ordered an inquiry. His battle report, printed months later, tartly observes: "The affair has still not been satisfactorily cleared up." But the sequence of events is clear. Throughout the previous day, Westphal had frantically tried to raise Rommel by radio to tell him that a real crisis was threatening their Tobruk front.

What had happened was greatly alarming. A large force of New Zealanders had come from the Bardia area and captured most of the key points south of Tobruk—including the hard-won Sidi Rezegh airfield and Belhamed hill. Westphal appealed to Crüwell and Rommel to send a panzer division to attack this New Zealand force in the rear.

168

This was the desperate situation when Rommel arrived at Crüwell's Mammut at the frontier at ten-thirty. The sheaf of frantic messages from Westphal made no impression on him; nor did the fact that planes sent to drop the relelvant maps to him had been shot down. He did admit that he had not realized how grim the situation at Tobruk was, but he stubbornly insisted on destroying the enemy here at the frontier first. He again advised Crüwell to "kick up dust" to dupe the defenders. Then he drove north to the coast with Neumann-Silkow's Fifteenth Panzer Division, reaching Bardia at about 1:00 P.M. The panzer division replenished with gasoline and ammunition from Bardia's fortress reserves.

He was still at Bardia that evening when Ravenstein appeared: "Herr General, I am happy to announce that I have arrived with my division."

Rommel was astounded: he had believed the Twenty-first Panzer was on the Egyptian side of the frontier. "What are you doing here?" he demanded. Ravenstein showed him a signal from Westphal, ordering the recall. "A fake!" shouted Rommel. "The British must have our codes."

This was not so. Westphal had indeed sent this bold order—an act of no mean courage for a half colonel of thirty-nine. It is not in the files (evidently willing hands destroyed it later), but Ravenstein's battle report tells us: "In the afternoon [of November 26] my division is ordered to break through to Bardia." He had moved off at five, as dusk was falling, and broke through into Libya. His infantry and machine gunners suffered cruel losses. During the night Westphal had also radioed the Fifteenth Panzer Division—and this signal *has* survived—"C in C cannot be raised at present. Panzer Group headquarters orders you to advance at once to relieve our Tobruk front. Situation very precarious. *Achtung!*"

Rommel must have known that Ravenstein's premature return spelled the end of his desperate foray. He was still furious when he eventually got back to Westphal's bus at El Adem. "He greeted nobody," one of Rommel's personal staff recalled, "but stalked silently into the operations bus and looked at the battle maps. Gause stood behind him. We tried to signal Gause to talk to Rommel to explain Westphal's decision. But it was not necessary. Rommel suddenly announced that he was tired and was going to lie down." When he reappeared from his trailer, he made no further mention of the affair—to everybody's relief.

It was an eloquent silence. In fact, by failing to take an intelligence officer with him, Rommel had contributed to his own defeat. His notion of the enemy's strength and dispositions was completely wrong. A blind man could scarcely have shown less interest than Rommel did in the main supply dumps—six miles square—established by the enemy right under his nose before Crusader. Field Maintenance Centers 62 and 65 were only a dozen miles south of Gabr Saleh. They were clearly marked on documents that were captured by the Fifteenth Panzer Division on November 20 and sent up to Rommel's headquarters. Another dump, FMC 50, lay right across the route taken by Stephan's panzer regiment on the twenty-fourth; the tanks scattered the staff but ignored the stocks, gasoline and a cage of 900 Axis prisoners. *"Gott im Himmel,"* exclaimed Bayerlein after the war. "If we had known about those dumps we could have won the battle."

Yet the last days of November 1941 were still to show Rommel at his best. On paper, his outlook was dim. The Afrika Korps had only forty good battle tanks left (and twenty Panzer IIs); the enemy outnumbered him seven to one in battle tanks. The New Zealand division advancing on Tobruk from Bardia had eighty Valentines and Matildas; the enemy's Seventh Armored Division had had two days to replenish and now fielded 130 tanks. And the Tobruk garrison, which finally established a frail corridor through the siege ring to the New Zealanders on November 26, had seventy tanks as well.

Despite the odds, Rommel again won an astonishing success by December 1.

How did he do it? The factors were perhaps largely psychological. He had established a personal reputation for doing the unexpected—one of the few profits from his dash to the frontier wire. But he also had good tanks, fine commanders and brave men. The cooperation between his tanks and the mobile guns was well drilled, his tactics were flexible. The British commanders were in his view ponderous and orthodox. There was one example of this when his operation began the next day, November 27. The Fifteenth Panzer's fifty tanks made a fast start west toward Tobruk, but after about twenty miles they were blocked by the forty-five tanks of the Twenty-second Armored Brigade; and when the Fourth Armored Brigade also arrived with seventy-seven tanks in Neumann-Silkow's flank at 4:00 P.M., the panzer division was in a really tight corner. Several of his tanks were soon "brewing"—but to his surprise the enemy suddenly called off the action and withdrew to the south. It was dusk and time for the traditional tank night-leaguer. The bewildered panzer division resumed its westward drive.

Another factor was that unlike that of several enemy commanders, Rommel's personal morale was high. He felt that he had regained the lost initiative. "I think we are over the worst," he wrote irrepressibly to Lucie on November 27. "I'm okay myself. I've been in the thick of a running counterattack by us in the desert the last four days, without even a thing to wash with. But our successes have been brilliant. . . . The new operation has already begun." It is easy to understand that this self-deception infuriated more sober generals.

Rommel asked that day for a staff officer from Afrika Korps headquarters to come and brief him—he was now back at Gambut airfield—Crüwell grabbed Bayerlein and a car and drove to Gambut himself, meaning to tell Rommel some home truths about the ugly situation at Tobruk. They arrived and found no sign of Rommel. After much searching they spotted a British truck on the airfield and cautiously approached. "Inside," Bayerlein recalls, "were Rommel and his chief of staff, both unshaven, worn out from lack of sleep and caked with dust. In the truck were a heap of straw as a bed, a can of stale drinking water and a few cans of food. Close by were two radio trucks and a few dispatch riders. Rommel now gave his instructions for the coming operation."

Once again Crüwell ignored Rommel's tactical ideas. Rommel proposed encircling the New Zealanders from their rear. Crüwell wanted to avoid splitting up his panzer divisions for this, and he decided to launch them in one grand slam from the east, toppling the New Zealanders forward into Tobruk. He spent the next day reconnoitering the terrain. At about 9:00 P.M. Rommel sent him a new plan, but Crüwell ignored it as "too late" and summoned both his panzer division commanders, Neumann-Silkow and Ravenstein, to see him at 8:00 A.M. the next day to make sure they followed *his* plan.

General von Ravenstein never arrived. His Mercedes-Benz car was found empty, showing signs of gunplay. "The British have nabbed Ravenstein," Rommel concluded without emotion. He never had liked aristocrats.

On November 29 the desert once again rang to the sound of tank turret hatches clanging shut as the Afrika Korps rolled into action. In mid-morning the Fifteenth Panzer Division again moved off west along the Trigh Capuzzo, followed by the Twenty-first Panzer on its right. The objectives Crüwell had assigned them were the commanding "heights"—in fact barely 150 feet—of El Duda and Belhamed. With only nine battle tanks left, the Twenty-first Panzer was soon halted. But Neumann-Silkow's Fifteenth, with thirty-one battle tanks and twelve Panzer IIs, made good progress. In a curious way, it was in fact Rommel's plan rather than Crüwell's that was being put into effect: Neumann-Silkow had intercepted Rommel's amended plan to Crüwell on the evening before, and decided to follow that. Truly the Afrika Korps was an agglomeration of free spirits.

Rommel went forward just before noon with several Italian generals to watch the battle with Crüwell. "The decision will probably come today," he confidently wrote to Lucie. But it did not. Days of heavy fighting, disappointments, misunderstandings and biting winds, which even the thickest blankets and greatcoats could not keep out, still lay ahead. Even the first day went poorly, and by nightfall he was not at all well pleased. Neumann-Silkow had taken El Duda from the west but lost it again, while the Twenty-first Panzer had barely moved at all from the east.

Crüwell was gloomy when Rommel again visited his headquarters next morning. Rommel afterward scribbled to Lucie, "The outlook's good, but the troops are dog-tired after twelve days of all this. I myself am well, I'm fresh and I feel enormously fit." In the end it was his enormous resilience, and the enemy's corresponding lack of a strong and unified leadership (on which Rommel's own battle report passed comment), that sealed the fate of the New Zealand division. He persisted with his encirclement action, and at ten-thirty opened a five-hour artillery barrage on the enemy stronghold at Sidi Rezegh. The enemy failed to concentrate their armor fast enough to help the hard-pressed New Zealanders. At 1:40 P.M. Rommel again went to Afrika Korps headquarters, to watch the jaws close on the enemy. The large-caliber guns were tearing huge craters in the enemy positions at Sidi Rezegh; the ridge and airfield were obscured by dust and smoke. The enemy's twenty-five-pounders were running out of ammunition, and at 3:40 Neumann-Silkow moved in. It was a hard and violent fight, and it was ten at night before the Fifteenth Panzer could confirm that Sidi Rezegh was once again in German hands.

The final act took place next day, the first of December. Neumann-Silkow's infantry battalions got a foothold on the shallow slope of Belhamed before dawn. Then Colonel Hans Cramer's Eighth Panzer Regiment passed through them; by 8:30 A.M. they had fought their way through to the other side. The encirclement was complete. Only armor could save the New Zealanders now. An armored division did arrive from the south at this time, but in the confusion of battle it mistakenly withdrew the way it had come. Rommel wrote in a letter on the second: "This eases the situation, but if I am any judge of the British they will not give up yet."

His troops were weary beyond measure. One trained enemy eye saw them as practically sleepwalkers, men who certainly did not regard themselves as victorious. The Germans had taken heavy casualties in November—473 dead, 1,680 injured and 962 missing. They had also lost 142 tanks and a large amount of other equipment, and supplies were not getting through to Libya. Rommel, however, still felt on top of the situation. He described December 2 as a "somewhat calmer" day, and hinted to Lucie: "There are certain indications that the enemy is throwing in the sponge."

He wanted to fight one last big battle, to liberate the

Sollum front. But first, he knew, he must restore his soldiers' morale. That evening he ordered a proclamation to be issued to all troops: "The battle . . . has been brought to its first victorious conclusion. In unremitting heavy fighting with a vastly superior enemy we destroyed by December the first 814 tanks and armored cars, 127 aircraft; we captured enormous booty and took over 9,000 prisoners. Soldiers! This great triumph is due to your courage, endurance and perseverance. But the battle is not yet over. Forward, then, to the final knockout blow for the enemy!"

For a third time Rommel and Crüwell dramatically differed on how to deliver this "knockout" blow. Rommel suggested splitting his forces—Neumann-Silkow taking nonpanzer elements of both panzer divisions to relieve the frontier garrisons, while other formations tackled the enemy at El Duda and far to the south. Crüwell hotly protested that first and foremost the Afrika Korps ought to deal with the critical situation southeast of Tobruk. He added caustically, "We must not repeat the error of giving up to the enemy the battlefield on which the Afrika Korps has won repeated victories, and embarking on a new farflung operation before destroying the enemy completely." If, however, Rommel had some good reason, Crüwell said, for making what amounted to yet another foray to the frontier wire, then they should commit the whole Afrika Korps (apart from its tanks, which needed repair). Rommel ignored Crüwell's logic and suffered the corresponding punishment the next day, December 3. Attempting three operations with inadequate forces, he prospered in none.

At last, reality caught up with Rommel. Late that day, he took the first grave decision to abandon all ground east of Tobruk: the Afrika Korps headquarters was evacuated from Gambut, and steps were initiated to salvage Rommel's extensive depots and materiel in that area. In a much darker mood he told all this to Lucie: "The battle continues, but as it is shifting more to the west we have had to regroup during last night. I hope we have pulled it off. The battle is too difficult for words . . ."

Whatever the cause, he had made up his mind on December 3. On the fourth, he claimed to have radio intercepts and air reconnaissance evidence of a strong enemy force approaching from the deep south. He reacted by sending south the whole Afrika Korps, and meanwhile he quietly thinned out and dismantled his siege apparatus east of Tobruk. Tractors hauled the big artillery westward. Depots and half-repaired tanks were blown up. On the fifth, the Afrika infantry division, now renamed the Nine- tieth Light, was first briefed to hold the siege line as long as it could, then informed at 10:15 P.M. that it too would be pulled out.

A discussion earlier that evening had precipitated this final slump in Rommel's hopes. A quiet, objective Italian staff officer, Lieutenant Colonel Giuseppe Montezemolo, had arrived with a message from the Italian High Com- mand in Rome. The message was that Rommel had no hope of getting fresh supplies or reinforcements across the Mediterranean for at least a month. Rommel equally bluntly admitted that the Afrika Korps had only forty of its 250 tanks left, and wholly inadequate ammunition stocks. He proposed abandoning the whole peninsula of Cyrenaica, not just Tobruk. The attempt to hold at the Egyptian frontier was over too. He had already ordered the Italian Savona Division to withdraw into the coastal fortress of Bardia, twenty miles from Sollum, since the ammunition and food in the Sollum line had been used up. Rommel told Colonel Montezemolo that his losses were 4,000, including sixteen commanders. The next day, as if to lend emphasis, word came that Neumann-Silkow him- self had been mortally wounded by a bursting shell.

Bastico was dumbfounded at the colonel's grave report, and he reported in turn to his superior in Rome, General Cavallero. Cavallero reluctantly agreed to forfeit the stranglehold on Tobruk, but directed that Rommel must not throw away the whole of Cyrenaica without good reason—and he must retain Benghazi as a supply port as long as possible.

Bastico sent for Rommel late on December 7.

Rommel had withdrawn his headquarters westward to a ravine near Gazala, some miles west of Tobruk, the interim line that he proposed to defend. He churlishly re- fused Bastico's invitation, claiming he was too busy to get away. So Bastico drove over by car to see him. According to all the diaries it was a stormy meeting. The colorful

Italian record leaves no doubt of that either. Rommel deliberately kept his esteemed Italian superior waiting for fifteen minutes, then called him into the trailer that he was using as his headquarters and, "very excitedly and in an uncontrolled and impetuous manner," put the entire blame for his defeat on the Italian generals—they were inefficient and had not cooperated with him. Bastico angrily interrupted him, whereupon Rommel, "very heatedly, and acting like an overbearing and uncouth boor, yelled that he had struggled for victory for three weeks and had now decided to withdraw his divisions to Tripoli —and to have himself interned in [neutral] Tunisia!" A few moments later he snapped, "We haven't won the battle, so now there is nothing to do but retreat."

# Turning the Tables

FOR the first time in his life, Rommel is on the retreat —a mortifying experience. "How humble one learns to be," he says in a letter to Lucie. His first halt is at the Gazala line, but the slow and panicky Italians, largely unmotorized, are an encumbrance. He does not have the gasoline or ammunition to fight back, and his best men are failing him. Neumann-Silkow lies in a soldier's grave. Sümmermann of the Ninetieth Light Division has also been killed, by an RAF attack. Some of his surviving commanders are succumbing to desert plagues. Even Crüwell is sick, infected by jaundice. And what will become of the 14,000 troops he has left in strongpoints along the Sollum front and in the Bardia fortress, now that the Panzer Group is moving ever farther away from them toward the west? "Don't worry," he writes to Lucie, "I'm feeling okay and hope my lucky star won't leave me."

For one general, the uncertainty of war is over: Ravenstein will soon begin the long journey from Cairo to Canada as a prisoner. He was a good general, but he makes a poor prisoner. He is a gourmet and officer of high breeding, and he misses the captured delicacies that were stowed in the glove compartment of his Mercedes: the Aulsebrook's biscuits, the South African cigarettes, the

Crosse & Blackwell's canned preserves, the Greek brandy and the rum. However, the British look after him well, and their director of military intelligence is even chivalrous enough to invite him over once for tea. The brigadier confides to him that the invitation has aroused a storm of protest, but to Ravenstein it seems a natural courtesy between officers and gentlemen. How is he in his naïveté to know that the only purpose of luring him from his tent is to enable a microphone to be installed in it? (Rommel's generals turn out to be garrulous in captivity. Crüwell and his successor at Afrika Korps headquarters—both of whom are captured in 1942—will tell British microphones, in the civilized comfort of their English country house surroundings, that Hitler is developing a secret long-range rocket to use on England.) In his conversation now with other prisoners, Ravenstein unwittingly reveals much that the British do not know—about the Panzer Group's heavy losses, its mismanagement and, above all, about the widespread "dissatisfaction over Rommel's leadership."

And yet Rommel has by no means shot his bolt. During December 1941 he proves that he is a master of the obstinate retreat. And in January it turns out that he can spring surprises of which a Ravenstein would never have dreamed.

Somehow, Rommel survived the first half of December and thwarted every enemy attempt at outflanking the Gazala line although it was only a dozen miles long and ended in the open, defenseless desert. He was living in a proper house again, with live chickens cackling and scratching the muddy ground outside. By day he toured his fatigued troops. Rain poured down incessantly, and the desert was sometimes a bottomless morass. The bushes were tinged with green—a sign that in the protected valleys of Cyrenaica the African spring would soon arrive. It was good to be out of range of Tobruk's artillery, but at night it was cold and for some weeks he slept in his uniform and greatcoat—unwilling to bathe or change his underwear.

What kept his spirits up even now? First, he knew he still enjoyed Hitler's confidence, even if the Italians had no trust in him at all. As recently as December 11 Hitler had mentioned him by name in an important speech. (In that speech Hitler declared war on the United States—an ominous action that Rommel never referred to in his diaries.) Secondly, Rommel felt on top of the crisis. Ravenstein might have written him off in Cairo, but the Panzer Group was still able to inflict severe losses on the attackers. He had little ammunition or gasoline, but a railroad ferry did reach Benghazi on the nineteenth and unload twenty-two precious tanks for the Afrika Korps. Two days later he cajoled Lucie, "Don't let your head hang down—I'm not doing that here!"

He did not intend to remain long at the Gazala position. He had hinted at this to Bastico on the eighth, and he warned Berlin a few days later that he was planning to withdraw right across Cyrenaica shortly. To the world it looked as though the British had Rommel on the run; in fact he was always one step ahead of them. The Italians felt that he should stand and fight at Gazala, and they suspected that if Rommel pulled back, the largely nonmotorized Italian troops would be left to the mercies of the enemy. That was not the way Rommel was secretly planning it, however. The Italians woud be sent back on the easy coastal road, while the Afrika Korps and the Italian general Gambara's Twentieth Corps would fight a delaying action to keep the enemy from outflanking them across the desert.

His own generals were as perplexed at first as the Italians. When his preparatory withdrawal order hit the Afrika Korps on the afternoon of December 14, Crüwell sharply replied that they had inflicted such losses on the British that it was "totally unnecessary" to withdraw now. Gambara was furious. Bastico flew into a rage because Rommel was not consulting him. The Chief of the Italian High Command, Cavallero, felt that Rommel might be acting overhastily, that he was ignoring the larger implications of the entry of Japan into the war: there were already signs that Britain was having to shift combat units from North Africa to the Far East. When Cavallero flew to Libya on the sixteenth, the Italian commanders poured out their hearts to him.

Gambara wailed, "If you knew how much we have suffered being practically at Rommel's beck and call!"

Bastico chimed in, "He made me wait fifteen minutes!"

Cavallero asked them if they could suggest any alternative, and curtly snapped: "We are all in the same boat. You will just have to grin and bear it."

Then Cavallero called on Rommel himself, and blurted out that the loss of Cyrenaica would be a political bombshell for Italy. Rommel outbid him on that: "The loss of all Tripolitania as well would be an even bigger one!" Later that day Cavallero called on him again. Rommel noted in his diary, "In a voice charged with emotion he demanded that the order for the retreat must be withdrawn." Bastico and Gambara reacted violently but could propose no alternative. The Rommel diary smugly observes, "Their delegation left my headquarters having accomplished nothing." The withdrawal formally began at midnight.

Crossing the uncharted Cyrenaican desert by night was no easier now than during the exhilarating April offensive. Trucks and tanks bogged down and had to be winched clear. By day enemy planes harried and strafed them. Fuel and ammunition were running low. The local Luftwaffe commander Waldau commented on December 20 in his private diary, "Rommel has decided on a further withdrawal, to Agedabia. We cannot judge if he is right. It is all a question of supplies. We are losing a lot of equipment, particularly transport planes—yesterday alone twenty Junkers! (And fourteen of them through bad gasoline.)" On the same day the new commander of the Ninetieth Light Division discussed their plight with his staff: "Nobody can see any escape. The British outnumber us enormously. The puzzle is, why are they following so slowly? Time and again they have enabled us to dodge encirclement. There is only one explanation: their awe of General Rommel, and his capacity to surprise—that's why they're following so hesitantly."

Benghazi, the sprawling, long-suffering capital of Cyrenaica, with its untidy quays, noisy street markets and ever-open brothels, was once more evacuated by the Axis troops and abandoned to the enemy. Before the British marched in, all the Axis supply dumps were thrown open to Rommel's troops. (One German official refused to release warm blankets and clothing from his depot; his orders were to burn them!) After that, the Via Balbia, the highway along the coast, was thronged with army trucks overloaded with crates of canned meat, butter, preserves, fruit, chocolate, beer, cigarettes and even fresh potatoes. Morale in the Panzer Group began to climb, and Rommel said wryly in one letter: "The British were very disappointed not to have cut us off in B[enghazi], and not to have found any gasoline or food there either."

For a time, Rommel hoped to make a stand at Agedabia, south of Benghazi—it was tactically the key to Cyrenaica. "If I give it up, I am giving up all Cyrenaica," he told Crüwell, now fighting obstinately with jaundice. "Because here I've got my hand on the enemy's throat, and I can return and slice clear back to Gazala at any time again." He jolted around the battle lines in his Mammut, checking gun positions and trying to stabilize the Panzer Group's defenses. The Italians were a major headache. Their High Command had little sympathy with his retreat, the generals mistrusted him, the troops showed every sign of imminent disintegration—the looting and gunplay in Benghazi were only one symptom of this. Italian unreliability was the main reason he gave when he requested Mussolini's authorization to withdraw still farther west if need be, and to surrender the distant besieged garrisons at Bardia, Sollum and Halfaya if their food and ammunition ran out. Rommel's language to Mussolini well displays his humanity and moral courage: ". . . I will not be responsible for the useless sacrifice of some 15,000 German and Italian soldiers there" (meaning in the Egyptian frontier garrisons).

Since he had here at Agedabia less than a dozen of the deadly flak eighty-eights—each one could spell death to an entire tank company—he ordered the Italians to manufacture dummy guns and told them to dig in the *real* eighty-eights well and far apart, just as at Halfaya. But a few days later, when he again toured this sector, he found the eighty-eights prominently displayed and attracting heavy shelling. He lost his temper and drove off to find out who was responsible for this "sabotage." He returned rather abashed. "They are dummies," he admitted. "The Italians have knocked them together from telegraph poles. It's the camouflage paint that fooled me." He congratulated the Italian commander: "If and when we fall back farther west, take the decoys with you. There's no need for the enemy to rumble us yet, before we can dream up new dodges."

On December 28 and again two days later Rommel sprang a nasty surprise on the enemy. Crüwell had noticed an inviting gap between the two enemy brigades closest to Agedabia, and threw the Afrika Korps at one of them, the Twenty-second Armored Brigade. In two professional and smoothly executed attacks the Germans destroyed sixty of the tanks that the brigade had painfully brought across the desert—two thirds of its force.

This setback to the British gave Rommel breathing space. He now ordered his forces to disengage surreptitiously and abandon Cyrenaica. He told one division commander on New Year's Day that he was going to rehabilitate and reorganize his forces in a new line running inland from Mersa Brega, and to "train them for an attack in the spring." His commanders all needed rest and recuperation. General Gause had left for Rome and Germany—ostensibly to report to Hitler, but in fact because his nerves were badly tattered. The entire staff of the Twenty-first Panzer Division was undergoing an overhaul, after it apparently suffered a mass nervous breakdown at the end of November. Like Crüwell, Colonel Westphal had now also contracted jaundice. "I'll soon be the only German officer to have fought here from start to finish," said Rommel.

He visited Crüwell on January 2, as the withdrawal stealthily gained momentum. Crüwell's open, boyish face was pallid and tinged an ominous yellow. He was so weak with jaundice that he was bedridden. Rommel told him that he planned to lay 100,000 mines in the new line— they would be brought over by submarine. "I'm going to build a kind of East Wall to protect Tripolitania," he said. A tough force of Luftwaffe paratroopers was coming, and Hitler had finally lifted the embargo on the army's important antitank secret weapon—the Redhead hollowcharge shell (the only answer to the crisis caused by Stalin's T-34 tank and the Russian winter on the eastern front). Hitler had sent Rommel a personal New Year's message, telling of his admiration for the Panzer Group.

"I know I can reply on my Panzer Group in the New Year too," wrote the Führer.

The nights were cold and damp. Rommel lay in bed and looked at the light of the full moon playing through the window. His final retreat was going according to plan. Sadly, the Bardia fortress had had to surrender after a ferocious battle. "Soon the enemy forces that this has released will be another millstone around my neck," he wrote. "I am preparing for them. We are working day and night." Under cover of a raging sandstorm—a gift of Providence that lasted for two days—Rommel pulled his last rear guards out of Agedabia. All his forces, German and Italian, were now in the Mersa Brega line, on the frontier of Tripolitania. "The violent storm," he cheered up Lucie, "seems to be over. The skies are turning blue."

Probably only combat soldiers can appreciate the size of Rommel's achievement in having retreated across nearly 300 miles in one month without serious loss to his force, while still inflicting savage wounds on his tormentors. Yet although he had salvaged the largely nonmotorized Italian troops, Bastico and his comrades did not render appreciation. "Understandably," mocked Rommel in a letter, "these would-be warlords have pulled wry faces. It's easy to criticize."

Praise for Rommel reached him from an unusual quarter. The Afrika Korps diary for December 17 had stated: "According to subsequent dispatches of the U.S. ambassador in Cairo, we had driven straight through the British Twenty-second Armored Brigade. He describes it as a masterpiece."

How did Rommel know what the American ambassador to Egypt was putting in his dispatches? In September, Italian agents had burglarized the U.S. Embassy in Rome and photographed its copy of the "Black Code." For many months thereafter, Italian and German code breakers could eavesdrop on top secret American communications. Of sensational value were the reports sent to the War Department in Washington by the military attaché in Cairo, Colonel Bonner Fellers, because he was a perceptive battlefield observer and kept himself abreast of all the English army's plans against Rommel and its expectations of the Panzer Group's next moves. This was a tremendous advantage to Rommel and helps explain his coming triumph.

Rommel—normally not overly security conscious—kept these "little fellers," as he engagingly termed the American dispatches, close to his chest. There is no mention of them in his diaries (or even his memoirs). Hitler knew about them, however. "Let's hope that the U.S. legation in Cairo keeps us well posted about Britain's military planning, thanks to their poorly encoded telegrams," he wisecracked to Hermann Göring over lunch one day in June 1942. One of Rommel's intelligence staff recalls now: "Rommel used to wait for the dispatches each evening. We just knew them as the 'Good Source.' When Fellers reported to Washington, 'The British are preparing to retreat, they are burning secret papers,' then Rommel would really see red—there was no holding him."

As yet Rommel's preoccupation in January 1942 was survival. But he was growing ever more sanguine. He knew that time was now in his favor. Under Field Marshal Albert Kesselring, a new air force had arrived in the Mediterranean, and squadrons based in Sicily were neutralizing Malta by air raids. U-boats were harassing the British fleet. Rommel wrote approvingly on January 4, "Kesselring's coming to see me again today. We're both now working hand in glove." And the next day: "We're gradually getting more materiel over here. He's really knocking the stuffing out of Malta." That was the day, January 5, 1942, that nine merchant ships—escorted by no less than four Italian battleships—safely docked at Tripoli and unloaded over fifty tanks for Rommel, and 2,000 tons of aviation fuel. This was Hitler's New Year's gift to his favorite commander. "If today's convoy succeeds in getting through," Hitler told General Gause—his guest for lunch in his bunker headquarters—"then the British are going to have to look out!" A few minutes later Gause commented, "It was a relief for us to learn of Japan's entry into the war." Hitler was at that time unperturbed by the fact that he was also at war with the United States, and commented to Gause: "Yes, a relief. But also a turning point in history. It means the loss of a whole continent, India. And that we must regret, because it is the white race that is the loser."

For several days Rommel toured his units, digging in along the line at Mersa Brega. He was now accompanied by his new interpreter, Wilfried Armbruster, a bright young lieutenant with an Italian mother and a talent for mimickry: when Rommel barked insults and orders at the Italian generals, Lieutenant Armbruster barked the translation at them in precisely the same tone of voice.

*Luck is an important weapon in the historian's armory. I had driven to Milan, Italy, to meet Armbruster because he had mentioned to me in a letter that he still had some papers. He was German born, but with the dark round eyes and mobile features of a typical Italian. The "papers" turned out to be press clippings, and I was beginning to regret the journey when, after several hours' discussion, I asked for a certain date. "I'll just check my diaries," he said. Diaries! He had never shown them to anyone before. Eventually he did part with them, but not willingly. They were invaluable in the study of the next phase of Rommel's campaign.*

Rommel's tireless inspections went on. "We drive back and forth across the desert," wrote Armbruster, "at a hellish tempo." On January 15, with Armbruster still in tow, Rommel twice flew up and down the line in his Storch observation plane. He told Colonel Westphal that the terrain did not please him, and he instructed the Afrika Korps to prepare itself to "make forays in every possible direction." He expected the next clash to come soon. The British were still obviously stockpiling for a new offensive, and radio intercepts showed they were experiencing cruel supply difficulties.

These shortages were what Rommel now gambled on. He knew that the British supply line extended over 1,000 miles while he himself was now only 500 miles from Tripoli. And he knew too that the enemy air force would be weak—because the "little fellers" told him so: "The RAF is transferring aircraft to the Far East," Fellers had radioed to Washington, also giving the details of the damage Malta was suffering.

For several nights, Rommel sat up late and brooded over the maps, photos, "little fellers" and quartermaster reports. He demanded that the new tanks coming to him from Tripoli move forward at over 200 miles per day. He estimated that the Panzer Group would now have 150 battle tanks, against the enemy's 360, but this did not deter him. He knew that there comes a point in every retreat when the hunted quarry can round on its pursuers as they filter through some hindering obstacle—like a desert wilderness—and take them on individually and in turn. If he waited any longer, the enemy would regain numerical superiority.

The moment for decision came. He wrote to Lucie on January 17 these graphic words: "Things are going our way—and my head is chock-full of plans: plans I dare not say anything about to the people around me—otherwise they'll think I've gone stark raving mad. But I haven't. It's just that I see farther ahead than they do. You know me," he added. "It's in the small hours that my best new plans are hatched."

What was his new plan? He sent for Heinz Heggenreiner, his liaison officer to the Italians. "I feel," he announced with a grin, "that I've got an *attack* coming on." Heggenreiner was forbidden to say anything to Bastico, however. On the contrary, he was to give the impression that Rommel was planning to retreat still farther.

The next morning he briefed Crüwell—still bedridden with jaundice—and Bayerlein about his "new intention." "The Panzer Group will tackle the enemy buildup southwest of Agedabia," he announced. "At this moment they are fewer in number than we are. We will surprise them —and annihilate them." Armbruster burst with the news and unloaded it into his diary: "Our plans have undergone a radical change. The Tommies are in for the surprise of their lives."

But how to preserve that vital element of surprise? Rommel listed by name the only commanders to be let into the secret. He forbade his artillery to reply with more than desultory shelling. He forbade all truck movements toward the enemy by day—on the contrary, he ostentatiously ran truck convoys westward until dusk, then switched them under cover of darkness toward the enemy.

The tanks and guns were expertly camouflaged. He kept the secret from the German High Command in Berlin and above all from the Italian High Command. (So no Enigma signals went by radio either.) Instead, he arranged for the Panzer Group attack order to be posted on notice boards at roadhouses all along the Via Balbia to the front —*after* zero hour. Zero hour would be 8:30 A.M. on January 21. As that hour approached, the skies lit up with the fires of buildings and ships along the coast deliberately ignited by Rommel to suggest that a major Axis retreat had again begun.

Zero hour. Rommel himself took the lead as he conducted the battle group on the coastal highway through the minefields. On his left was the empty sea; on his right, the barren desert. It was 8:30 A.M. Two hours earlier, he had penned his usual letter home: "I finally believe that God is keeping a protective hand over me and will grant me victory." His men were in fine fettle. Crüwell's Afrika Korps attacked simultaneously, some miles to the right but parallel. He hit heavy going, but Rommel's group jumped the enemy and rolled into Agedabia the next morning. His enemy lacked battle experience. Rommel outwitted, outmaneuvered and outgunned them. "Our opponents have taken to their heels as if stung by a tarantula," he said in triumph. And Armbruster echoed this: "The Tommies don't stand and fight. They have just turned and fled."

The enemy fell back so fast that Rommel's first attempt at encircling them misfired; but not the second. The Afrika Korps totted up its score for the first five days as 299 enemy tanks and AFVs (armored fighting vehicles), 147 guns and 935 prisoners. "Against these our own losses have been very slight: three officers and eleven enlisted men killed . . . three tanks total losses."

Rommel's high-handed behavior infuriated the Italians. On January 23 the chief of their High Command, General Cavallero, flew with Kesselring to see Rommel. Armed with a directive from Mussolini himself, Cavallero admonished Rommel: "Make this no more than a sortie; then you must go straight back to Mersa Brega." Rommel rebelled. He knew he had Hitler's personal backing now, because just a few days before the Führer had awarded him the Swords to his Oak Leaves and Knight's Cross—the first such award to a German army officer. (The Panzer Group had been formally raised to army status, and Rommel himself to Oberbefehlshaber, or commander in chief.) Rommel effectively thumbed his nose at the Italians after that. He told the glowering General Cavallero, "I intend to keep up the attack as long as I can. And only the Führer can stop me, as most of the fighting will be done by German troops." Cavallero departed, growling, according to Rommel's diary.

For a time, his quartermaster staff did give him second thoughts. Major Otto, the Panzer Group quartermaster, flew to Crüwell's headquarters on January 25 with word that Rommel would not be able to continue the offensive since the Duce could not promise the same supply effort in February. Rommel ordered the Afrika Korps not to press its advantage but to limit itself to salvaging booty. But the "little fellers" and radio intercept reports were so alluring—the enemy commanders were rattled and bickering among themselves; there was talk of abandoning even Benghazi—that he saw red again next day. "Now the tables are turned with a vengeance," he wrote to his son. "We've got the British by the short hairs, and I'm going to tear their hair out by the roots."

By noon on January 26 he had decided to throw caution to the winds and continue the attack. He radioed Fritz Bayerlein, Crüwell's chief of staff, to fly to the headquarters of Panzer Army Afrika. There Rommel disclosed that he was going to do just what the enemy did not expect—go straight for Benghazi while the enemy believed he was heading the other way, toward Mechili, as in April 1941. Benghazi would then be looted of all enemy equipment and stores, and then abandoned again: such was Rommel's intention as he set out at the head of a small force from Msus at dusk on January 27. A sandstorm blew up, and then heavy rain. Twenty-four hours of grueling country lay ahead of Rommel. But the prospects were promising. Bayerlein's decoy force feinting toward Mechili had attracted enemy fire, and a radio intercept confirmed that it had been noticed—which was very satisfying for Rommel. His plan was working well.

In London, Winston Churchill lumbered to his feet in

Parliament to answer angry questions about the crisis in North Africa. His own earlier boast that they would soon be in Tripoli rang very hollow now. The hero of the world's press was not Churchill but that accursed panzer general with the Perspex goggles and the Pour le Mérite: "I cannot tell you," said Churchill to the House, "what the position at the present moment is on the western front in Cyrenaica. We have a very daring and skillful opponent against us, and, may I say across the havoc of war, a great general . . ."

"North of Benghazi," said Lieutenant Alfred Berndt in a later broadcast, "there are long columns of an Indian division wending their way along the highway leading out to Derna. They believe that our forces are only slowly moving up from Agedabia. Then, suddenly, like a clap of thunder, General Rommel bursts upon them from the *east*—having approached through those mountains in pouring rain with just a few tanks and armored cars!" He had hit the coastal highway at Coefia at 6:00 P.M. on the twenty-eighth. Here the Via Balbia was elevated, with a ditch on either side. Thus the Indian motor transport attempting to escape Benghazi was trapped. "In less than an hour," continued Berndt, "the Indian division has been smashed. Our troops capture hundreds of trucks: we have done the seemingly impossible—we have overcome every obstacle, driven by our commander's spirit through the marshy wilderness and across the red and slippery mountains of Cyrenaica; and we have struck right into the enemy's flank just as they think that they are safe at last."

Down the road, flames and explosions lit the sky over the port. The British were demolishing and preparing to retreat. Once again Benghazi changed hands. Rommel's booty was immense, including 1,300 urgently needed trucks. That night German radio stations interrupted their programs with the news of his victory. The next day Hitler too heaped praise on him in a speech and promoted him to colonel general. Nobody else had ever made that rank so young. When General Walther Nehring—fresh from the Russian front—saw Hitler a few days later on his way to North Africa, the Führer commanded: "Tell Rommel that I admire him." Rommel was jubilant and privately wrote of his pleasure to have been able to "do my bit for the Führer, the nation and the New Idea." As for the old idea, of falling back after sacking Benghazi, Rommel never mentioned it again.

From Lucie came an ecstatic letter. All she could think of now was that the Lord must have wanted His general to secure this great victory and new honor. "We're all so mighty proud of you, my darling Erwin," she wrote, "and with us the entire German nation, as the storms of applause proved when the Führer mentioned your name yesterday in his big speech and spoke of 'our Colonel General Rommel.' It was so marvelous for us two here to listen to the speech yesterday afternoon and again in the evening." Her house was full of flowers from admirers, her telephone rang itself off the hook, the front door bell kept chiming. Rommel's picture was splashed across all the newspapers. "Today," Lucie wrote him some days later, "they paid special tribute to your name in the evening music broadcast—they played bits of music and the composers' initials spelled out a name backward, 'the name of our popular hero Colonel General Rommel.' You can imagine how my head reels with all this. It's all like some kind of dream, and all my prayers go only to the Lord to be with you and keep helping you toward your goal for the Führer, the nation and the fatherland. This is my waking thought every morning and it's my prayer when I go to sleep at night, my dearest Erwin!"

Now Rommel was making grand plans again. Whereas Hitler had once again prescribed the Panzer Army's mission in terms of merely tying down as many British troops as possible, the Desert Fox had notions of his own. Cyrenaica, thrusting like a balcony into the Mediterranean, with vital airfields dominating Malta and the eastern Mediterranean, must come next. Rommel was going to reconquer all Cyrenaica, capture Tobruk and then advance on Egypt and the Nile.

The Italians, who would have to organize the necessary supplies, were not enthusiastic even about what Rommel had already accomplished. "Rome is putting on the brakes," said Rommel—and added pointedly, "That being so, I think I'm going to have to fly quite soon to the Führer's headquarters." His frustration was again evident in a letter of February 10. "Rome," he wrote, "would like nothing better than to abandon all Cyrenaica again."

But after a triumph like this, his elated troops were willing to go to the ends of the earth with Rommel. Once again he had shown that by his personal presence—by the mere appearance of the Mammut with its waving radio aerial and the familiar stocky figure standing up in its well, bawling orders to other officers with short, characteristic gestures—he could bring punch to just that place in an operation where punch was needed. Here is one voice, Major Carl Cranz, writing in the Nazi newspaper *Völkischer Beobachter* on January 24, 1942: "After we have been driving in scorching heat from four in the morning until dusk, ever onward, getting reports from generals and battery and company commanders, he calls a 'halt for forty winks' in the middle of the desert. And there we sleep, the general and his officers and NCOs and enlisted men, side by side as comfortably as we can in our various vehicles. At the first flush of dawn the column starts moving again."

And here is the war reporter Baron von Esebeck, writing in July 1944: "As we sweep forward to the Egyptian frontier, we find him everywhere, and always there is this strange magic strength that this soldier radiates to his troops, right down to the last rifleman. The privates call him 'Erwin'—just that: 'Erwin,' short and to the point. Not that they intend any disrespect by using his Christian name—it is a mark of profound admiration. Because the guys can understand their commander in chief: when he talks with them he calls a spade a spade; he doesn't sentimentalize with them, but meets them man to man, often uses hard language with them, but also knows how to praise and encourage them and make suggestions, and make complicated subjects easily comprehensible to them. Of course, to start with there were only a few of us— everybody knew everybody else and there was a desert camaraderie: the rifleman saw his general, and for that matter the general his rifleman, eating the same classical Libyan diet of sardines."

Not that the Panzer Army was only "a few" now. Reinforcements were slowly coming. Major General Georg von Bismarck had arrived to take over the Twenty-first

Panzer Division; Lieutenant General Gustav von Vaerst, the Fifteenth Panzer. Both were fine and talented commanders. And 1,300 Luftwaffe paratroopers—veterans of the murderous Crete invasion—flew in, armed to the teeth with the most modern weapons and equipment that Rommel's officers had ever seen. The captured enemy trucks were distributed, the captured tanks and armored fighting vehicles were repainted in Afrika Korps colors, and the palm tree and swastika motif was stenciled on. Rommel drove about the peninsula, chivying and harrying. On February 11 he moved his headquarters to the hub of this desert peninsula. It was still cold, but in Africa spring was coming. His interpreter wrote that day, "It was a wonderful drive. Here in Cyrenaica the almond trees are in blossom, and the entire population flocked to the highways to greet us as we passed."

Then suddenly this dynamo was gone. Rommel, whose super-human energy was the despair of his more mortal staff, drove to the airfield on February 15 and took off for Rome. The tempo slackened, the atmosphere at every level of the Panzer Army eased. The Ninetieth Light Divison probably spoke for everybody in its diary: "C in C has left on furlough, three to four weeks. Everybody breathes a huge sigh of relief, and looks forward to the coming days of calm."

Three evenings later Rommel was in Hitler's secret headquarters in East Prussia. There is no record of their conference, but afterward Martin Bormann's adjutant wrote down Hitler's remarks over dinner—an ungenerous portrait of Winston Churchill. "Churchill is the very archtype of a corrupt journalist," sneered the Führer. "He himself has written that it's incredible how far you can get in war with the help of the common lie. He's an utterly amoral, repulsive creature. I'm convinced he has a refuge prepared for himself across the Atlantic. . . . He'll go to his friends, the Yanks."

Rommel seems to have made no reply.

A month would pass before he returned to North Africa. "Manfred is now as tall as his mother, soon he will overtake me too," he wrote to a relative. But the general was not good company to either Lucie or their son. "I just could not settle down at home," he explained in a letter to a colonel. To know that his army was once again within striking distance of Tobruk, but to have to wait until he had regrouped and stockpiled enough supplies—he was on edge throughout his furlough in Austria.

Back in Libya, he wrote this to a cousin: "The big question is, who will make the first move?" And to an uncle's inquiry as to whether Erwin himself was allowed to decide whether to retreat or launch a counterattack, Rommel made this reply: "I take all such decisions myself, and I'm glad not to have my hands tied in this connection. This war theater is so remote, besides, that it would be quite impossible for any other authority to get involved in the daily conduct of operations."

These letters have survived, because he dictated them to his secretary Corporal Albert Böttcher, and Böttcher dutifully preserved his shorthand pads. The same pads contain the long-lost portion of the Rommel diary. Over the next two months Böttcher filled 140 pages with his tight shorthand, while the Desert Fox drove hectically around Cyrenaica in his swastika-decked Kübel car, exhorting the troops, instructing them in tactics and gun site construction and conferring with their commanders. He found time to inspect the rear areas, too—the quays in bomb-shattered Benghazi, the workshops repairing tanks and decrepit trucks supplied by the Vichy French to help drive the Allies out of Africa. He watched tractor and firing trials with the excellent 76.2-millimeter antitank guns captured in Russia. He organized lines of listening posts to protect the long desert flank against British infiltration.

For one brief month the sandy brown had given way to green, as Cyrenaica succumbed to spring. Lieutenant Armbruster, his accompanying interpreter, wrote: "I have never seen colors like these: the desert is a coast-to-coast carpet of vivid reds, lemon yellows, purples, lilacs, greens, oranges, violets and white." Rommel was to be seen with a movie camera pressed to his sun-blistered face, filming the extraordinary spectacle for Lucie.

His own picture was everywhere that spring. He made the front page of the magazine *Illustrierter Beobachter*, and fan letters cascaded in. At one stage he had just finished reading 150 and another 100 were awaiting his attention. "One secretary is not enough," he told Lucie. And: "Lovelorn letters from all shapes and sizes of females are on the increase." A few days later he sent her a batch to read: "The newsreels have brought the younger females particularly out of their composure."

He had two months to prepare his next move. But his Afrika Korps alone was under strength so there was bound to be some delay. Visiting the Axis air commanders Vittorio Marchese and Otto Hoffmann von Waldau, he announced, "We are going to attack in about two months' time. Our objectives will be first to defeat and destroy the British field arm and prevent its escape into Tobruk, and then to capture Tobruk itself. These are the only forces that the enemy has available for the defense of Egypt. We can follow through into Egypt a suitable time after taking Tobruk."

At the end of March he moved house to a stone building at Umm er Rzem, near Derna. It was not spacious (Armbruster wrote: "A fine Schweinerei there's going to be if the enemy bombers find us!") but it offered protection from the sun and sandstorms. The enemy had also been in residence, because a parting British soldier had chalked on the front door: "Please keep tidy. Back soon." The cheeky words brought a smile to Rommel's face.

A week later he reshuffled his Panzer Army. He was still careful not to reveal to the enemy whether he was merely improving his defenses or preparing a new attack. Rommel knew that the attack on the Gazala line established by the enemy commanders—running down from the coast into the desert, forty miles west of Tobruk—would not be easy. Along that line, from Gazala on the water down to Bir Hacheim, the British had already laid half a million mines—an achievement that astounded and frustrated Rommel. The enemy line cut across all the good desert tracks. The tactical alternative facing him was either a straightforward frontal attack or a long move circling around the desert end at Bir Hacheim. The British would outnumber him (by about 50 percent) in tanks. As he considered, perhaps he remembered General Schmidt's whispered advice to him, while they stood in line waiting for Hitler in February 1940: "Take whichever decision is bolder—it's always best." Rommel took the boldest decision of his life. Alfred Gause, his chief of staff, was to write in 1957: "His decision to send his army's *entire* tank strength on an outflanking move around the southern end was one of exceptional daring, particularly since his supply lines would also have to go around that flank. But if he lost this battle, he stood to lose all Africa."

He had decided on his basic tactics by April 15, when he met General Enea Navarini, commander of the Italian Twenty-first Corps. "We are going to use decoy tactics to cause the enemy to switch the bulk of his forces up to Gazala," he told Navarini. "We'll also be using some elements of the Italian motorized corps for this, but most of the corps will stand by to move down south, around the enemy's flank and rear. The killer blow is going to be dealt to them in the south. We have got to prevent them falling back on Tobruk, therefore fast columns of troops are going to push ahead to Tobruk. . . . The British field army must be destroyed, and Tobruk must fall!"

Intensive training began. The new infantry had to learn how to attack enemy field positions with tanks in support, under smoke screens; officers had to learn how to act as artillery observers in tanks, calling down gunfire from the rear; decoys and dummies had to be built. The Rommel diary finds him inspecting a tank-repair company temporarily busy converting trucks into tank dummies. He visits Luftwaffe workshops and is shown a mysterious vehicle indeed—a truck with an airplane engine and a propeller mounted on it like a giant rear-facing fan. To what purpose? Rommel knew. "C in C is delighted with this design and orders ten such trucks from the Luftwaffe," says the diary. Everywhere there were shortages, from gasoline, ammunition and trucks down to radio sets, panoramic gunsights, sandbags and smoke generators; most of the shortages—except for the swastika flags he needed—Rommel expected to overcome by capturing the rich supply dumps that the British were building up for their own forthcoming offensive. The question was, who would start first—Rommel or the enemy?

His troops' morale was high, despite the atrocious heat, the thirst and the hard work. Their skin was like brown leather caked with the hard gray dust of the desert in which the brave spring flowers had already withered. "The German and Italian soldiers just light up when Rommel comes," wrote Armbruster on April 25. And on the same day Rommel described the "moonscape" around them thus: "Dawn has a fairy-tale beauty in this region of table mountains. Temperatures around freezing point, but it soon gets warm." He added, "I had a couple of lively meetings yesterday with [Admiral Eberhard] Weichold and with General [Curio] Barbasetti [Gambara's successor as chief of staff to the High Command in North Africa]. Apparently Gambara was sent packing because in the presence of some officers he said he only hoped to see the day when he might lead an Italian army against us Germans. The idiot!" The next day Armbruster related: "We went hunting a British reconnaissance unit with the C in C this morning, but the guys beat it. In the afternoon the Führer spoke—we all stopped with Rommel in the middle of the desert and listened to the speech. We got back at 7:30 P.M." (This was the last speech Hitler ever made to the Reichstag—he announced that henceforth he was assuming absolute power.)

At the end of April, Mussolini and Hitler met at Berchtesgaden to discuss Mediterranean operations. At a secret conference on the thirteenth, they ruled that Rommel's attack on the British should come before "Hercules"—a planned German-Italian invasion of Malta, the main thorn in the flesh to Rommel's seaborne supply lines. This fit in with Rommel's own concept. On May 5 he outlined it to his corps commanders at El Cherima and showed them on a map the moves he planned to make: Operation Alpha—the encirclement and destruction of the enemy field army—and Beta, the seizure of Tobruk. They were instructed to brief their division commanders and to have all written orders burned after receipt. A dense sandstorm blew up as they left—Rommel could hardly see even the hood of his car. He longed for his native Swabia. "How beautiful is home, compared with this barren land," he wrote.

Not everybody shared his confidence. Alfred Gause, his chief of staff, had warned him: "You will be risking your entire reputation!" But Siegfried Westphal, his operations officer, argued that on balance they had no option but to attack—to wait any longer on the defensive might put the entire Panzer Army in danger. Once, early that May, Rommel sent for Fritz Bayerlein, the skilled chief of staff of the Afrika Korps: "What would you do if you were the British commander?" he asked, after showing him the battle plan.

Bayerlein did not mince his language. "If I was the British C in C," he said, "I wouldn't be so dumb as to peg all my mechanized forces up here at Gazala and just wait for you to encircle them. The moment I saw what you were up to, I would pull them back down here" —he pointed to a spot southwest of Tobruk. "Then I would fight a running battle with you. I'd strike right into your lengthening flank as you headed up toward the coast!" Bayerlein could see that Rommel was not pleased by his reply.

As the hot, stormy days of May 1942 paraded in languid sequence across the Cyrenaican desert, Rommel sensed the almost palpable nervousness that gripped the army. "The British are expecting us," he commented. "And we are expecting them." With Malta temporarily subdued by the might of Kesselring's bombers, supplies were reaching Rommel on an unprecedented scale. At 9:40 A.M. on May 12, he briefed all his senior commanders. Again Böttcher stenographed a record for the diary: "The enemy army facing us consists of three or four divisions, of which the South African division and elements of the British divisions are in fixed field positions. The enemy is not all that mobile . . . their mobile forces consist of one or two armored divisions, echeloned well to the rear [in fact, tailing back to the area south of Tobruk itself]. Our job is to lure this British field army as far west as possible."

With his short, brisk hand movements he pointed about the map. "We're going to achieve this by creating an impression that we are not going for an outflanking move to the south so much as a frontal breakthrough in the north. This will oblige the enemy to move up his armor. This is why each phase of our attack is staggered—the first feint by our forces will lure them up to the Gazala end of their line. That will begin at about 2:00 P.M. on X day. Our

main force will go in around *here* at dawn the next day"
—and he pointed to the desert end of the enemy line.

"The main force will have begun moving down to its
starting line after dark on X day, starting at 9:00 P.M.
Now, after Afrika Korps's units have reached the start
line I want all armored and mechanized units to get as
much rest as possible. . . . During the night we are then
going to simulate a big panzer buildup opposite the Gazala
end of their front." He then gave the commanders their
separate objectives and jump-off times from the start line.
The real tank force would start rolling at 4:30 A.M. By X
plus 2, the enemy's field army would have been encircled and wiped out—in his reckoning. "You will not stop
to draw breath then, but go straight on to take Tobruk.
You are to reach your start lines for the attack on Tobruk
by X plus 3 at the latest."

Four days later Rommel briefed the commanders of
the infantry. Now he uncovered some more of his planned
tactics. Crüwell would command the two infantry corps
at the northern end of the front. Their feint attack would
begin at 2:00 P.M. on X day—that is, in broad daylight
—and push about ten miles into the enemy positions; a
"major tank attack" would then apparently begin: "A
German panzer battalion and a unit of captured tanks will
attack from Twenty-first Corps's sector, but as soon as
dusk falls the German battalion will withdraw and join up
with our main armored push down *here*"—and he pointed
around the desert flank. Seeing puzzled looks, Rommel explained the purpose of the daylight assault in the
north. "It is *of vital importance* to stimulate a heavy tank
attack here. What we want is for the enemy to abandon
their present armored forces deployment, and move them
up in front of your two infantry corps. That is why we
have scheduled your attack as early as 2:00 P.M."

The calm before the storm. Rommel sat up late, peering
shortsightedly at maps, checking distances with calipers
and talking quietly with his staff. He tackled the rest of
his mail—there were many, many letters to write to
widows whose husbands would never return from Africa.
Hausberg, his own adjutant in 1939–40, had been killed.
Schraepler, his successor, had been run over by the Mam-

mut. And he wrote a belated letter to Hans Keitel, the bespectacled school friend who had helped to build the glider in 1906. "Tell him about the sandstorms here and tell him we're squaring up for the coming march," Rommel instructed his secretary—"the standard reply."

Back in Wiener Neustadt, Lucie's home seemed to have become something of a meeting point for most of the generals' wives. They met for coffee, shared the latest news from North Africa and eagerly scanned news photos for pictures of their men. "How awful for Schraepler to have been killed in such a terrible way," she wrote to Rommel. "Does his widow know how it happened? I'm thinking of inviting her down here . . . because all her thoughts are still in Africa." Frau von Ravenstein, the captured general's wife, also wrote to her, very sad that her husband would not command the Twenty-first Panzer Division in the advance. "She had a greetings telegram from him via Sweden at Christmas," Lucie informed Rommel, "but she's heard nothing from him since then and doesn't even know where he is." General Crüwell had passed through Wiener Neustadt on his way back to Africa from Hitler's headquarters, his features still glazed with shock: his wife of only thirty-four had suddenly died, and he had just buried her. To Lucie it seemed that Crüwell now had only the coming battle to live for, and she wrote down her impressions for Rommel.

Rommel at this time had duties to fulfill as a father. Manfred, now thirteen, had entered adolescence. He had progressed from boyhood Red Indian games to his swearing-in ceremony into the local Hitler Youth troop (Fähnlein), and his letters were full of the excitement of his brand new uniform, the camps, scoutcraft sessions and exploration. He went bicycling by himself around the town and had his first traffic mishap. "There has been a very stupid accident, Papa," he confessed in one letter. "I ran down an old lady at Adolf-Hitler Platz . . ." She broke a leg, and Rommel's insurance had to pay. Worse was to follow—Manfred's next school report. In geography, mathematics and Latin he was barely satisfactory, in physical training and stenography quite inadequate. The teachers' evaluations of Manfred were summed up by Lucie as "hair-raising." " 'This pupil,' " she said, quot-

.ing one report, " 'does not make the slightest attempt to cooperate in the physical exercises. He talks out loud and lacks discipline.' " Rommel noticed that although Manfred had done well at his Hitler Youth sports, swimming and skiing classes, the school gym teacher was spiteful and insulting—the man had said that Manfred would never get anywhere in life except by string-pulling.

"You expect these teachers to have a grain of common sense," Rommel wrote in reply. "I only wish I could get away." At his urging Lucie tackled the teachers about their unfavorable reports and they changed their tune. That satisfied Rommel. "In fact," he observed, "the school ought to be pleased and proud that they can number a son of mine among its pupils. Other schools would scramble for the chance. But this whole institution has now fallen into the hands of priests and clerics. It's not in the least pro-German, let alone National Socialist in outlook."

But Rommel realized that three years of fatherlessness were beginning to affect Manfred, and he sought to remedy the problem with a stern paternal letter. "As you can see, your teachers have had cause to complain about you. You must do your duty in all your subjects and behave properly. That is your main task in this war. I'm particularly pleased to hear that your Hitler Youth duty is to your liking. It will be of great value to you in later life." What else could he say? Manfred too got the standard Africa commentary: "Our supplies have got much better, so my worries are that much less. Soon we shall be squaring up for the coming match."

# The Glittering Prize

ROMMEL fixed X day for May 26, 1942. Everybody was in position at the right time, but after that everything went wrong.

If ever Rommel thought back to this first phase of the new battle for Tobruk—despite the human memory's happy faculty for blotting out what is unpalatable—he probably saw nightmare glimpses like a lantern slide lecture on a battle that is about to be catastrophically lost.

The first flash is of General Rommel waiting for dusk on X day and then—about 8:30 P.M.—announcing: "Operation Venezia!" That is the signal for his entire striking force of 10,000 vehicles to begin its southward move. He moves his car right to the front. Behind him, the two Italian infantry corps have been steadily battering at the Gazala line since 2:00 P.M., and the enemy will have noticed tanks assembling there all afternoon, clattering and roaring and raising an immense pall of dust against the setting sun. Now, however, in the evening, the dust cloud is being churned up by aircraft engines with propellers, mounted on trucks which are slowly circling in the desert. Only one Italian tank battalion is still there now, for the German panzer battalion has already slipped away at 7:00 P.M. to join Rommel's daring advance around the enemy's desert flank.

The next image is of Rommel one hour later, in his car jolting southward across the moonlit desert. Flickering flames from gasoline cans mark the routes. To his left is the Twentieth Corps, with 228 Italian tanks; to his right are the Afrika Korps and the Ninetieth Light Division. Frequently Rommel checks his compass, the car's tachometer, the compass again and his watch. Throughout May he has hammered into his generals the importance of getting the timing right. El Adem, on the Axis bypass road south of Tobruk, is to be reached at 8:30 A.M. "By afternoon at the latest, the ring is to be closed around the enemy," he has ordered.

At 3:00 A.M. he reaches the first stop line for his force, near Bir Hacheim, a desert outpost forty miles below Tobruk. That means they have already successfully outflanked the British line—and there has been no opposition yet. Here the entire force rests. The Afrika Korps is in formation, with Bismarck's Twenty-first Panzer Division on the left and Vaerst's Fifteenth Panzer on the right. Each division is in "area formation"—332 tanks followed by sappers, artillery and signals, with the infantry (in trucks) and antitank units on the flanks. In the center is their "hump," the thousands of trucks of the supply echelons. Everybody takes on extra gasoline, and at 4:30 A.M. the whole monster heads north. Now they are slicing up *behind* the enemy's fortified Gazala line.

What follows is chaos. Rommel's intelligence staff has provided a fatally incomplete account of the enemy's positions and strength. On the maps it prepared for him it has left out one enemy tank brigade and four brigade groups. The enemy has only partly fallen for his decoy tactics. There is enemy resistance, and for hours on end he makes little progress. It is 11:30 A.M. before the Ninetieth Light reaches El Adem, three hours late.

Here is the next image: it is of Rommel, staring through field glasses at an enemy tank silhouette like none he has ever seen before. His intelligence men have not warned him about this new monster either. He barely has time to take in its high structure and the big gun in a side turret, before this tank and its fellows are hurling the first shells into the Twenty-first Panzer Division—at extreme range, and high-explosive shells at that. These are the

American-built Grants, and their seventy-five-millimeter gun packs a bigger punch than any of Rommel's tanks—better even than the nineteen new Panzer III Specials that he has obtained in time for this battle.

Rommel's interpreter scribbles in his diary, "It's a massacre, our squad reels first to the left and then to the right, it's terrible. Tanks are breaking through on our right flank." A rout begins—Afrika Korps headquarters, divisional and regimental staffs hopelessly intermingled with towed guns and trucks. Walther Nehring, commander of the Afrika Korps, is conferring with a flak regiment commander, Alwin Wolz, as this stampede engulfs them. Colonel Wolz describes it: "In the midst of this avalanche I caught sight of some flak eighty-eights. We raced over to them and suddenly found Rommel there, completely hemmed in by panicking troops. He angrily rebuked me that my flak was to blame for all this, because it was not shooting back. I managed to stop three eighty-eights and then the other half of the heavy flak battery of the corps combat group. The armada of enemy tanks was closing in and only 1,500 yards away—twenty, thirty, forty big tanks. Ahead of them were the Afrika Korps's fleeing supply trucks, all quite defenseless to tank attack, and in the midst of this chaos are Rommel, the headquarters of the Afrika Korps, regiments, signals trucks—in short the entire muscle and nerve center of the combat divisions up front." The first eighty-eights open fire; the enemy tanks stop, and this first crisis is barely overcome.

Here is another episode from the first day, May 27, described by the Fifteenth Panzer's commander, Gustav von Vaerst. The northeastward advance of his armor is halted by enemy tanks, so Vaerst sends one of his two panzer battalions circling around to the right to surprise the enemy on their flank. After thirty minutes of give-and-take in which Vaerst loses thirty tanks and the enemy twenty, the enemy detects the flank danger and retires hastily, leaving the route of advance temporarily free again.

Vaerst's leading tank company commander calls to him by megaphone: "Which way ahead now?"

Before Vaerst himself can reply, his adjutant shouts back: "That way! There's Rommel! Follow him!"

And there indeed is Rommel, standing upright in his car as it bounces across the smoking, wreckage-littered battlefield right at the head of his panzer troops.

But by the end of this first day Rommel has advanced only as far as Bir Lefa. He has already lost one third of his tanks. Vaerst's tanks are dry of fuel and low in ammunition. The Panzer Army's supply columns have become detached. In fact, instead of encircling the enemy field army by his bold sweep around the Gazala line, Rommel's own army is now virtually encircled. The cause, in Siegfried Westphal's view, is the total lack of Italian combat effort. The two Italian infantry corps still west of the Gazala line have made no serious effort to assault it frontally, and this has allowed the enemy to move its armored reserve down to meet Rommel's advance. The Italian armored divisions under his command are equally leery. "For two days we lost all contact with them," Westphal recalls, "although we supplied them with German radio trucks. At the time we could not help believing that they were lying very low."

Rommel, careering around the battlefield, seems to have lost control of the fighting. The next day, the Luftwaffe commander General von Waldau begins his diary with the acid observation: "It is difficult to assess the situation owing to the complete absence of reports from Panzer Army's headquarters." Since Waldau does not know where the Axis front lines are, the air force is unable to go to Rommel's help. On the day after that, Waldau repeats his complaint in his diary, but this time he does send in Luftwaffe dive bombers to attack. Often they mistakenly scream down on German tanks and guns and bracket them with bombs. Rommel, temporarily defeated, has to recall his tanks to the west, leaving their supporting infantry to dig in as best they can on the barren battlefield. Radio communication breaks down, and wild rumors sweep about in the vacuum created by the absence of higher command:

"The Afrika Korps has been encircled and is about to capitulate."

"The Tommies have captured all our supplies."

"The British have surrounded us and taken Derna."

"Rommel, Nehring, Crüwell are all dead!"

Not until May 30 does Rommel reestablish radio contact with Waldau. Now Waldau can safely commit his entire air strength. He sends 326 aircraft to sweep the battlefield, and the tide begins to turn in Rommel's favor.

And then the last lantern image. On June 2, 1942, as this first phase ends in victory for Rommel after all, planes fly two heavily bandaged battle casualties back to Waldau's airfield for immediate hospitalization—Alfred Gause and Siegfried Westphal, Rommel's two top staff officers. Waldau regards their comments on Rommel as unprintable. "General Gause and Lieutenant Colonel Westphal came back with severe injuries," says Waldau at the end of that day's diary entry. "Their detailed report on command issues does not lend itself to setting down in this diary . . ."

Rommel's absence on the battlefield may have caused command problems, but there is no doubt that the example he thereby set to his men tilted the balance against the far less flexible enemy. The remarkable events of May 28 and 29, 1942, demonstrated this. On the twenty-eighth —the day Waldau had called "totally obscure"—Rommel ought to have been a very worried man indeed. His army was widely dispersed, his headquarters had been scattered by shellfire and supplies were scant. Once again the ominous instruction had gone out forbidding all troops to wash or shave—water was running low. General Crüwell, now well enough to resume command of the Afrika Korps, was shot down when his Storch flew over an unsuspected British strongpoint, and was taken prisoner.

Uneasy about what was happening to his two panzer divisions, Rommel drove late on the twenty-eighth onto a hill from which he could see the desert battle. Black smoke clouds rolled up into the scorching sky, giving the landscape, in Rommel's eye, a curious, sinister beauty. He decided to concentrate his forces the next day and truck emergency supplies through to them somehow, using the same route that he himself had just taken. There were about 1,500 truckloads waiting south of the battlefield.

After dark a huge convoy of supply trucks was organized. Here is Armbruster's account, in his diary of May 29: "At 4:00 A.M. I drove off with the C in C and we piloted the supply column up behind Ariete's line, heading for the Afrika Korps. . . . Tanks were again attacking us in the flank. Rommel ordered them to be encircled. We found Westphal again and took him along with us. Ariete fell back slightly, and again there was chaos. . . . Shelling began again and Schneider was injured standing next to me. Rommel then led the whole bunch right up to the Afrika Korps. It was a fantastic drive—we were surrounded for a time—but everything came off terrifically."

Thus he had the Afrika Korps back in business.

Rommel set up his Panzer Army headquarters and took stock with Westphal, Gause and Bayerlein. It was obvious that Crüwell's relief attack toward them from the west had not materialized. Rommel decided to abandon his original battle plan: he would screen off the British tanks on the east of his force with antitank guns, and himself smash a wide gap through the minefields to the west to restore a main supply route to his troops.

Operations next morning, May 30, began badly for Rommel. His headquarters came under heavy artillery and air bombardment and three men were killed. His attempt to smash a breach in the enemy line ran slap into a strongly fortified "box"—a pattern of minefields and entanglements heavily defended by infantry and guns —between the two trails Trigh el Abd and Trigh Capuzzo. The local Arabs called this shallow saucerlike depression the Got el Ualeb; Rommel's troops later called it The Cauldron. He had lost eleven tanks before he realized that his intelligence maps were wrong. A desperate battle began with the enemy brigade holding the "box."

It was now that Field Marshal Albert Kesselring dropped in on Rommel. They were very opposite characters. Kesselring was at fifty-six one of the best staff officers and administrators produced by any service. His courage as a Luftwaffe commander was legendary; his optimism was well known—some said it was inborn cheerfulness, others saw it as just an obligatory facade. His permanent toothy grin was his trademark, and he was as popular as Rommel with the troops. He was a soldier's general. He knew ordinary soldiers by name, he was affable and fatherly. Hitler had sent him out to Rome as "Commander in Chief, South," with orders to see that Rommel got his supplies, and he had got the Luftwaffe moving, where Major General Stefan Fröhlich, the lazy Austrian-born commander in North Africa, had failed. By mid-May 1942, however, Rommel suspected Kesselring of adopting the airs of a supreme Wehrmacht commander in the south. "He can run his head against a brick wall for all I care," was Rommel's unhelpful commentary on this. But "Smiling Albert," as he was known, was an officer of integrity and not an intriguer. His attitude toward Rommel was one of admiration, tinged with real concern. He had stepped temporarily into the missing General Crüwell's shoes as commander of the field forces west of the Gazala line, and was astounded at Rommel's loose battlefield control. "From what eyewitnesses told me about the goings-on at Rommel's headquarters on the first day of the tank battle," he later wrote, "they just beggared all description." He now demanded a face-to-face meeting with Rommel, and took off—piloting his own Storch as always—for the southern end of the front.

Rommel drove westward out through the minefield and met Kesselring at Tenth Corps headquarters. Rommel calmly munched a sandwich to express his disrespect for Kesselring. Kesselring's first act was one of characteristic pragmatism and tact: he voluntarily placed himself under Rommel's command, although he was a field marshal himself and six years older than Rommel. In private, out of earshot of the Italians, Kesselring told Rommel to get a grip on his army. Then they discussed tactics. He found Rommel's plan quite good. Basically, it was for the Panzer Army to stay put, behind an antitank gun screen, let the enemy batter itself to pieces on the screen and then counterattack.

On May 31, Rommel renewed the attack on the enemy brigade "box" at The Cauldron. The next day Waldau's bomber squadrons joined in, and Rommel scrambled from platoon to platoon as the main assault force worked its way toward the British positions. The enemy was well dug in, and fought as usual to the last round. Counterfire was intense. Westphal was badly hit by mortar fragments. But after a while Rommel shouted to a panzer-grenadier battalion commander near him, "I think they've had enough, Reissmann! Wave to them with white flags—they'll surrender." Werner Reissmann was skeptical, but his men did as Rommel had suggested—one man pulled off his shirt, others took handkerchiefs or scarves. And the miracle happened. The firing died away, and the enemy wearily crawled out of their foxholes and trenches with their hands in the air. Three thousand troops marched into captivity. More important, a considerable breach—five miles wide—could now be torn in the British line of fortifications from Gazala down to Bir Hacheim. Thus Rommel had his bridgehead.

Later that afternoon heavy artillery fire began to drop around his headquarters. The operations bus was wrecked, and Alfred Gause was severely injured, to Rommel's very real regret—he had begun to find his chief of staff quite irreplaceable. (Even months after, when Gause returned, he still suffered bad headaches and needed repeated furloughs.) Three of Rommel's other officers were killed. "We could have spared ourselves all this if we had only moved off earlier," was Armbruster's diary comment.

Rommel wondered how much Lucie and Manfred knew of this desperate battle. In Lucie's letter of May 28 she had written: "I've got to admit that I listen to the Wehrmacht's news communiqué every day with thumping heart, and I'm always relieved whenever you're having a relatively quiet time." On the thirtieth, the general sent Corporal Böttcher to Wiener Neustadt laden with mysterious parcels and packets for her marked: "Not to be opened until June 6." That was her birthday. The packets contained beautiful Arab bracelets, ear pendants and other trinkets, and the latest battle photographs. "Oh, Erwin," she wrote to him after opening the gifts, "how happy I could be from the bottom of my heart about all this, if only I knew that you were in safety!" The letter took many days to reach the battlefield.

Meanwhile, Rommel's armor reorganized and repaired its wounds, and he planned his next move. Enemy artillery was pounding the breach he had torn through the minefields, trying to halt his supply convoys. "I can hardly put pen to paper," wrote Armbruster on June 2. "Today was appallingly hot, and we had sandstorms too. Men could go crazy in such conditions. Bayerlein is now our chief of staff and Mellenthin is operations officer." Rommel drafted a special announcement to proclaim the fall of the Gazala line, but the next day he had to shelve it —there still seemed to be some fight left in the enemy.

The world speculated. Newspapers debated whether victory was his or the Allies'. On June 2 Moscow declared that Rommel had been captured; no doubt it had confused him with Crüwell. Crüwell had arrived in Cairo, and was shown the famous Shepheard's Hotel. He remarked on its luxury and said: "It will make a grand headquarters for Rommel" His irony pleased Hitler, and the words went around the world.

Rommel decided to deal next with the fort at Bir Hacheim—the strongpoint at the line's southernmost end —and announced that two nonpanzer divisions and dive bomber attacks would do the job. He did not rate the fort as worth much attention. Alfred Berndt later contemptuously referred to its garrison of 4,000 French troops (including a Jewish brigade and many legionnaires) as "Gaullists, swashbucklers and criminals of twenty different nations." But in seven days the battle would still be raging, and the fort's heroic resistance to Rommel and the German air force has gone down in the annals of military history. Many months afterward Rommel was shown the diary of a British prisoner taken at Hacheim; it graphically described the battle:

*May 30.* Light enemy shelling. We've no stretchers and there are 236 injured friends lying all around, Free French troops. Their moaning fills the silence of the night, it's just unbearable to hear. They've given us only ten gallons of water and the French fifty. The heat is oppressive and we're tortured by thirst. . . .

*June 1.* At noon there was a terrible hail of bombs from wave after wave of dive bombers. The trenches and walls of the fort caved in, burying men alive. It's a horrific sight. . . .

*June 2.* Another hail of bombs from twenty airplanes. They come right down low and machine-gun us. We can't hold on. More men are killed, many more. To round off this hellish day the RAF comes and bombs us twice—so much for the help they promised us. . . .

*June 3.* This afternoon we were bombed three times by German and Italian airplanes. We couldn't get any water until evening. There are more injured everywhere. Their screams of agony ring around the ruins of the fort. We just don't know what to do with them. They beg for water, but there's no water to be had.

On June 4, the diary records endless bombing attacks, but still the fort at Bir Hacheim held out. "The air is full of smoke, and in this motionless hot air it just lies in coils around us. I'm dying of thirst, but nobody's got any water to give. . . . At 6:20 P.M. the RAF again flies over and drops some bombs on us." And the next day there were new air attacks. "We don't have any stretchers, we've got no water, we can't even bury our dead. The choking stink of the exploding bombs mingles with the foul smell of rotting bodies—just to see them leaves our nerves in shreds."

Early that day, June 5, 1942, the British launched their only serious attempt to evict Rommel from his bridgehead through the minefields. But thanks to faulty British planning and coordination, fifty-eight of the seventy heavy tanks in the attack were lost to Rommel's guns and an unsuspected minefield. Another force of enemy armor and infantry attacked the eastern rim of Rommel's bridgehead; it fared no better. Rommel counterattacked that afternoon and overran the tactical headquarters of both the attacking enemy divisions in the confusion.

The next day, he repeated the slaughter on the enemy forces that had managed to penetrate The Cauldron. Armbruster wrote: "We knocked out fifty-six tanks yesterday. First class. And on top of that we closed the second pocket during the night and took in 4,000 prisoners and several hundred guns."

The materiel losses that Rommel had inflicted on the British in these two actions were the turning point of the whole offensive. Six months later, when the tide of battle again passed close by the same Cauldron battlefield, a

British artillery officer felt drawn to revisit the scene. "The guns were still in position, surrounded by burned-out vehicles. The gunners lay where they had fallen, the faithful gunlayers still crouched over their sights."

During the Cauldron battle, the fighting at Bir Hacheim had ebbed. The tenacity of the defense astonished and vexed Rommel. There were 4,000 French troops, well protected by a complex system of pill-boxes, bunkers and foxholes; and there were 1,000 volunteers of the Jewish brigade as well. All were commanded by Colonel Pierre Koenig, one of the French army's finest officers. (He later became governor of France's occupation zone in Germany.) Their ferocious defense was raising problems for the whole Mediterranean campaign. Marshal Kesselring watched with mounting impatience—knowing that the battle was using Luftwaffe planes he would soon need for his German-Italian assault on Malta. Rommel, however, still refused to commit his tanks against the fort, because the ground around it was heavily mined.

On June 7 Kesselring flew by Stuka dive bomber to Rommel's headquarters. The heat was unbearable. There was a new, violent argument. By the time he left, Kesselring had extracted a firm timetable from Rommel: he would wipe out Bir Hacheim the next day, thrust through to the coast on the ninth or tenth, pry open the Gazala line, let the infantry divisions pour through to the east and then—the long-sought prize itself: "From June 18 to 22 the attack on Tobruk—in which connection C in C South [Kesselring] rules that *June 25* is the very last date possible for the attack to be concluded."

At 6:21 A.M. the next day the cruel attack on Bir Hacheim began. Stuka dive bombers screamed down on the fort, forty-five of them, supported by three Junker 88s and ten twin-engined Messerschmitt 110s escorted by fifty-four single-engined fighters. But Rommel's men were not ready to attack, so the Luftwaffe effort was wasted. Twice—at noon and again at 5:30 P.M.—Rommel called for fresh dive bomber attacks and each time the infantry failed to follow through. In his diary Waldau raged. "The army still completely misapprehends the air force's capabilities!" he wrote. Waldau himself climbed into a dive bomber and flew over to Rommel's headquarters.

When he landed neither Rommel nor Bayerlein, the new chief of staff, was available—they were on the battlefield commanding an assault group! Armbruster recorded: "Hacheim is still on our menu tomorrow—those guys are damned tough."

Waldau was shocked to receive a fresh demand that evening from Rommel, for a dive bomber attack next day. Just after sunup the bleary fort defenders once again heard the Stuka scream. "There is a thunder like an artillery barrage," wrote Armbruster. "But still we can't smoke them out of their confounded nest." Rommel's infantry were weary, too, and had no desire to die on this hot and barren desert, storming across minefields toward an enemy they could not even see. Rommel now brought up a tank battalion and artillery, and again called for "one last attack" by the dive bombers that evening. Waldau retorted that he had flown 1,030 sorties against the fort already. Kesselring reproached the Panzer Army in a signal: "I am unhappy that the heavy and successful Stuka attacks have not been followed up by panzer/infantry assaults of similar intensity. The Luftwaffe is being prevented from carrying out other important tasks."

He followed this with something of an ultimatum. The next morning, June 11, there would be a dive bomber assault on the fort. "I expect tomorrow's full-scale Luftwaffe attack to be followed by a panzer attack of sufficient strength to deal once and for all with Hacheim."

From the captured British prisoner's diary, Waldau and Rommel later learned that the fort's defenders were by now almost deranged with terror from the air raids. "We're alone and abandoned," wrote this soldier on June 7. "Only God can help. In the eyes of my friends I can see a new gleam—they look like madmen. All of us keep looking involuntarily at the sky. I'd never have believed that air raids could kill so many men." Again the RAF came and bombed them by mistake. Now, on June 10, the man wrote: "Another hellish day. Water, water, water!! That's the scream of the injured, the cry of the survivors. How are we expected to carry on? A bombing raid at 9:00 A.M., another at ten and the rattle of machine gun fire all day long. The stink of corpses is just unbearable and saps all our powers of resistance. The RAF are as good as gone, and it's just as well because they've caused us enough casualties as it is. At 11:30 P.M. we get orders to hand in our heavy trucks and artillery, we're going to see if we can get away. But where to? Nobody bothers about us anymore. We're finished."

The next day, June 11, the diary ends, with these words: "I'm a prisoner, and in good hands."

During the night Colonel Koenig had ordered the garrison to sneak out of the fort under cover of darkness. Trucks were waiting to pick them up. Some 2,700 of the surviving defenders made it to the enemy lines. Thus, three days behind Kesselring's tight schedule, Rommel had finally taken Bir Hacheim. For Rommel, the self-professed master of infantry assaults on defended positions, the stubborn stand at this fort had left a bitter taste.

The fighting of these days produced a nasty revelation. Rommel's troops had captured secret British documents which included instructions on prisoner interrogation. Captured Axis soldiers, said the orders, were to be grilled while still upset and distracted. "They are not to be given food, drink or sleep or other comforts." Rommel's staff sent this text to Berlin on June 5. The next day, Armbruster recorded the repercussion: "On the Führer's orders, British prisoners are to be given no water, meals or sleep until the [British] order is cancelled. So our radio message has caused quite a stir." The British then complied, and Rommel was not faced with an agonizing crisis of conscience.

But the capture of part of the Jewish brigade at Bir Hacheim raised more sinister issues. On June 9, the German High Command sent a secret message to the Panzer Army. There were reports, it said, that "numerous German political refugees" were fighting on the side of the Free French. "The Führer has ordered that they are to be terminated with extreme prejudice. They are to be liquidated mercilessly in combat. Where they are not, they are to be shot afterward, immediately and forthwith, on the orders of the nearest German officer, insofar as they are not temporarily reprieved for the extraction of intelligence. The communication of this order in writing is forbidden. Commanders are to be given oral briefing."

There is no copy of this message in Rommel's files, and none of his staff alive today remembers hearing of it. Given his record of clean fighting, it is possible to assume that he destroyed it and made no mention whatever of it to his commanders.

The belated capture of Bir Hacheim released Rommel's forces to cope with the Gazala line. He had regained the initiative and could counterattack. He still had some 124 battle tanks besides the sixty Italian tanks and twenty-five Panzer IIs, but his infantry strength was low. The enemy had only an ill-assorted mélange of tanks left. And among Rommel's tanks were, in addition to the long-gunned Panzer III Specials, several of the Panzer IV Specials with the vicious, long seventy-five-millimeter main armament.

On June 12 and 13, prior to his main assault on the rear of the enemy Gazala line, Rommel fought two big tank battles. By the end of the second day, the enemy had lost nearly 140 more tanks and Rommel was master of this sector of the battlefield. The British now in fact had only about seventy tanks left, and they could not hope to salvage any of those left lying disabled about the desert. These pawns were swept off the desert board in Rommel's favor. Early the next morning the enemy began to pull their remaining troops out of the Gazala line, and to evacuate the rich forward supply base that they had established at huge expense at Belhamed, southeast of Tobruk.

The Arabs needed no Nazi radio communiqués to know who was winning now. Vagrants clad in fragments of British, German and Italian uniforms—robbed from the bodies lying about the desert—began to appear and led the German commanders to the last hideouts and field stores of the scattered British troops. "Last winter they led the Tommies to our hidden caches," commented a German war diary contemptuously. "They applauded in April 1941 as we drove into Derna, they cheered the British when they began advancing to the west in December, they were hysterical with praise when we returned to Derna again two months ago—and they will be out there cheering again if . . . and who can blame them? Our war is no concern of theirs."

Rommel informed Lucie: "The battle has been won and the enemy are disintegrating." The enemy still held Tobruk and there were garrisons at El Adem and Belhamed, but late on June 16 El Adem fell. By the following evening the much-ravaged Sidi Rezegh battleground was also once again in Rommel's hands. But there had been a desperate fight; the panzers had come under intense shuttle bombing from the nearby Gambut airfield, and Mark IIID Hurricane fighters had appeared, armed with a new and deadly antitank cannon of forty-millimeter caliber. This fearsome weapon had cost General von Bismarck two tanks—four men were killed in one tank outright.

It was now June 17. Rommel's net was tightening around Tobruk. He knew that time was running out—Field Marshal Kesselring would shortly be withdrawing Luftwaffe squadrons for the assault on Malta. That morning Kesselring landed near his headquarters and brought Hitler's congratulations on the big victory won so far. At 3:00 P.M. the tanks of the Afrika Korps and Ariete moved off east, to complete the encirclement. Ariete fell back, and Rommel impatiently radioed to the panzer divisions to press on. At 6:30 P.M., he himself swung the Twenty-first Panzer Division around to the north again. To set the tempo he took his own combat squad right out in front and drove at gathering speed, past bemused British gun tractors and armored cars, toward the coast. It was growing dark, and the Twenty-first Panzer ran into an uncharted minefield—a tank blew up in an ugly ball of flame, killing three men—so Rommel unwillingly called a halt until the first light. But a reconnaissance battalion did reach the Via Balbia at midnight. At 8:05 A.M., June 18, he proudly radioed to the General Staff and Kesselring: "Fortress [of Tobruk] encircled."

Of the RAF there was no trace. It had now had to abandon its forward airfields at Gambut.

Rommel was driving back down the Axis bypass, to establish a new headquarters, when he sighted several empty German trucks. They had run into a belt of mines and their crews had evidently been taken prisoner. Rommel swung nonchalantly out of his car, knelt down and began carefully lifting the mines with his own bare hands.

His personal staff followed his example, and within five minutes they had cleared the mine belt away.

Tobruk! At last he could launch his dramatic panzer and infantry attack on the stronghold that had claimed so many German and Italian lives. He had outlined his basic plan to his commanders weeks before—for instance, to his trusty friend General Navarini on April 15: "The attack on Tobruk will be made from the southeast, probably with the Afrika Korps on the right and the Twentieth Corps on the left." He had assured them then that the fortress was much weaker than in 1941. Gone were the tough Australian troops. Indeed, the minefields and entanglements had been robbed to strengthen the Gazala line. The tank ditch had silted up in desert sandstorms.

This time Rommel was not going to repeat the errors that had wasted so much Luftwaffe effort at Bir Hacheim. On June 18, he called General von Waldau to his new command post, the Hatian strongpoint, just captured from the British, and discussed Luftwaffe tactics for the opening assault. He asked for a maximum dive bombing effort against certain of Tobruk's perimeter strongpoints, the ones designated R49 through R71, at 5:20 A.M. Waldau thought that was too early, but agreed to carry out a trial at that time the next day, the nineteenth. The assault would begin on June 20. Liaison channels were arranged, army and Luftwaffe maps exchanged. Rommel's artillery would fire smoke shells when the Luftwaffe squadrons arrived, to mark out the section of the perimeter defenses to be assaulted. At noon on the nineteenth, Field Marshal Kesselring came and approved all this.

The description of the operation fills twenty pages of the shorthand Rommel diary. It shows him craftily resuming operations toward the Egyptian frontier—even before the attack on Tobruk—that very afternoon. He promptly advanced on Bardia, well down the coast toward Egypt. "C in C accompanies the advance with his combat squad, raising the maximum possible dust in the desert to the left and right of the highway until eighteen miles before Bardia." The two German panzer divisions followed. At four-thirty, however, they were ordered to turn back, while only elements of the Ninetieth Light and other, lesser units continued. Soon it was dusk. Berndt described the scene: "There was a moon, but it was one of those moonlit African nights on which all the silhouettes seemed to shimmer. It was hard to drive; you couldn't tell where the surface ahead rose or dipped. In two columns our tanks and trucks rolled on. Soon our artillery commander reported something quite astounding: our entire heavy artillery sites from 1941, to the south and east of Tobruk, were still intact, and near them had been found thousands of rounds of heavy-caliber shells. We need only drive in and open fire. That would save us a lot of time and gasoline. All night long there were suppressed shouts and grunted commands, and a rumbling and shifting about and now and then a green or red signal from a pocket lamp."

At 2:00 A.M. Rommel reached his own command post in Hatian again. He tried to sleep, but the familiar preattack excitement kept him awake. At about 3:30 A.M. he was told that the panzer divisions had reached their appointed starting lines. Then he slept for a while, shivering slightly, like his troops, because of the intense cold before dawn. At 4:30 A.M. he was already in his car. "Today's the big day," he had just written to Lucie. "Let's hope Lady Luck stays faithful to me. I'm dog-tired, otherwise okay."

At 5:30 A.M., punctual to the minute, the massed German and Italian artillery opened fire. For nearly half an hour there was no sign of the Luftwaffe, but then General Nehring, the Afrika Korps commander, who was standing on the hill next to Rommel, got the news that the squadrons were just coming. The Stukas peeled off and screamed down on their targets. They were unopposed by flak or enemy fighter aircraft, and there were direct hits on all the bunkers. Now it was the turn of Rommel's infantry. Company and platoon leaders stood up and blew the whistle for the attack, and in a chaos of choking dust and smoke, fires and shell bursts, the engineers raced to build a steel bridge across the ditch. At five to eight a bridge was ready, and panzers began to roll into the fortress.

From the Rommel diary: "About 8:00 A.M. C in C drives forward into Fifteenth Panzer's sector, taking his combat squad. Then he drives in an armored troop carrier accompanied by a car (Lieutenant Berndt's) to the mine gap and watches the tanks and a rifle company attacking through the minefields and the bunkers already captured in the rear defense line. The defenders are laying down considerable shellfire on the mine gaps. There are traffic jams in the gaps, and trucks that have run into mines or been shot up."

Rommel could see six British Crusader tanks ablaze. By nine he was confident of victory. He drove to the tank ditch and inspected two captured bunkers. Then he performed an act of calculated bravado: he motioned to a war correspondent to come over, and into his microphone Rommel spoke an announcement for German radio. "Today," he exclaimed, his voice rasping onto the recording disk as the battle still thundered around him, "my troops have crowned their efforts by the capture of Tobruk." With his eyes turned, perhaps, to the sheeted corpses of the riflemen who had only made it this far, he added: "The individual soldier may die, but the victory of our nation is assured." A dispatch rider took the disk to an airfield and it was flown straight to Berlin, for broadcasting that same evening.

His plan was going like clockwork. Everywhere were burning and abandoned trucks and guns, and the geysers of dust thrown up by bursting shells; the air was deadly with flying fragments of razor-sharp rock and shell. By 2:45 P.M. Bismarck's tanks had advanced to an escarpment from which Rommel could see clear down the incline to the port. Columns of enemy prisoners marched past him, their faces sorrowful with defeat. At 7:00 P.M. the German tanks rumbled into the port. An hour later the two big forts, Pilastrino and Solaro, surrendered. Nothing—not even a Rommel—could now save Tobruk.

For months his troops had crouched outside this malicious, hostile parcel of Libyan desert, tortured by flies and plagues, tormented by sub-zero temperatures and baking sun, unable to raise their heads or seek cover between dawn and dusk—and now here he was, standing in the midst of the fortress. He thought of Lucie and Manfred: how proud they were going to be at the next day's news! By candlelight that evening he ate a supper hastily concocted from captured British stores—his eyes betraying that his mind was far away. After the meal he turned to

Colonel Bayerlein, his chief of staff, and blurted out: "You know, it's not just leadership that produces a triumph like this. You've got to have troops who will accept every imposition you put upon them—deprivation, hardship, combat and even death. I owe everything to my soldiers."

Again he was too excited to sleep, yet sleep he must—it was vital if he was to maintain this tempo over the next few days. Midnight saw him slumped in a corner of his car, his head leaning wearily against the window, while his staff lay on the hard ground wrapped in blankets, waiting for the dawn. Rumbling detonations shivered the air as the trapped enemy blew up their big fuel and ammunition dumps. A pall of smoke hung over the port, lit by the fires from below. Against the reflection of the fires in the bay Rommel could see the silhouettes of the funnels and masts of ships partially sunk in the harbor waters.

At sunrise he drove down into the town. Corporal Böttcher stenographed an account in the diary: "After looking around Tobruk, C in C drives west along Via Balbia and meets General von Bismarck. C in C draws particular attention to the coastal wadis where there are still countless prisoners at large. A British army tank brigade offers to surrender. C in C stipulates that its trucks and tanks must be turned over to us intact. The brigade hands over thirty tanks in running order. Left and right of the highway are blazing vehicles and tanks, some set on fire by shelling, others by the enemy themselves. Among the captured South Africans are numbers of drunken blacks. They all look cheerful, and wave and shout, 'The war's over.' "

The capitulation of the rest of the Tobruk garrison followed. "At 9:40 A.M. C in C meets General Klopper—CO of Second South African Division and commandant of Tobruk—on the Via Balbia four miles west of Tobruk. Klopper offers capitulation, says he has ordered all resistance to cease. C in C orders the general's car to fall in behind his own. On the way he passes 8–10,000 prisoners, jamming the highway. At 9:40 A.M. C in C gives staff a signal for OKH [in Berlin]: 'Entire fortress Tobruk surrendered, over 25,000 prisoners including several generals.'" Five minutes later Rommel repeated this to his Panzer Army—and ordered the army to get ready to press straight on toward Egypt.

He set up his headquarters in the Albergo Tobruk, a former hotel, and sent for the enemy generals. H. B. Klopper was a short, wiry South African—the typical staff officer rather than a combat general. Rommel instructed him to see to the repair of the water supply immediately. Again the Rommel diary records an edict that was typical of Rommel: "While the overflowing POW cage on the airfield is being set up, South African officers demand to be segregated from the blacks. This request is turned down by the C in C. He points out that the blacks are South African soldiers too—they wear the same uniform and they have fought side by side with the whites. They are to be housed in the same POW cage."

Back in Germany, the news still had to break. Lucie had heard nothing from Rommel since the tenth, and knew only that the Panzer Army had again formed up around Tobruk. She recalled with a shudder how many lives the fighting there had cost during the year before. "They say you've already taken Sidi Rezegh!" she wrote. "I wonder where you will be now, my darling, at this very moment?" At midday on June 21 she heard the radio announce that there was to be a special communiqué from Hitler's headquarters. Her first thought was that Sevastopol, Stalin's last fortress in the Crimea, had fallen to General von Manstein's siege. But then trumpets sounded the "England Fanfare" (the music always played when there was news of victory over England)— perhaps German U-boats had sunk another 100,000 tons of British shipping? When the announcer proclaimed that Rommel had captured Tobruk, Lucie felt faint with shock. Her first instinct was to ask for congratulations to be radioed to him, but she did not—there must be far more urgent messages for the radio waves to carry.

In Germany the newsreels were already being printed and dubbed—Rommel on a small mound, silhouetted against the sky; Rommel in his command car, after the port's capture; Rommel with Berndt and Bayerlein, driving down into the town in an armored car. "Rommel knows no rest, the battle must go on," the sound track proclaimed. Lucie and Manfred went to a movie theater with continuous performances and watched enthralled. Her next letter to Rommel read almost like an editorial from *Das Reich:* "Full of just pride and admiration, the entire people—and we two in particular—look up to you now that you have pulled off the incredible feat of capturing Tobruk in such a short time. I wonder what you felt like, entering Tobruk with your gallant men."

*In all the surviving 650 handwritten letters from Lucie to Erwin Rommel, there is never any hint of intimacy— nor in his replies. Whether warmer letters existed and were later destroyed by Manfred, or whether the couple hesitated to expose their inner emotions to the Nazi censors, the entire correspondence leaves a curiously cold, clinical impression on those few permitted to have read through it. At any rate, they are the typical letters of a government-issue field marshal's wife.*

Luftwaffe reports on June 21 suggested to Rommel that the British were so dazed by the speed of Tobruk's collapse that they were no longer preparing to make a stand even on the Egyptian frontier. Field Marshal Kesselring realized that Rommel would probably be tantalized by this situation and flew in to Tobruk at midday. According to Friedrich von Mellenthin, of Rommel's staff, the smiling field marshal reminded the Panzer Army commander of the need to throw all their air strength into the Axis invasion of Malta—scheduled for August. Until that island was captured, Rommel's supply lines would always be exposed to air and sea attack. Rommel disagreed emphatically: "Now that we've got the British on the run, there is a unique opportunity for us to push right on to the Suez Canal." Bayerlein, standing in for the injured Gause as chief of staff, later stated that Kesselring came around to Rommel's point of view, adding: "We'll organize supplies for you somehow." Rommel did not really care what Kesselring thought anyway—he had already sent a member of his personal staff to Berlin with a private letter to Hitler seeking permission to invade Egypt. At once.

All afternoon German and Italian troops loaded up the

booty of Tobruk. There was enough gasoline for hundreds of miles of advance. The Panzer Army had captured entire warehouses stacked with pure white flour, cigarettes, tobacco, foodstuffs, jam and clothing. There was beer galore—not the insipid liquid that masqueraded as beer in Britain, but brown, stubby bottles with the familiar blue Munich Löwenbräu labels! The British had bought it in Lisbon.

At 4:00 P.M. Bismarck wedged his Afrika Korps cap firmly onto his close-cropped head, mounted his Panzer IV and signaled the Twenty-first Panzer Division to drive east. As the trucks—now more of British origin than German—fell in behind on the Via Balbia, there was cheering and laughter. Captured radio sets were tuned to music broadcasts and foreign stations. One Axis newscaster quoted yesterday's *Times* of London: "Tobruk's defenses are now stronger than ever before." Another reported a New York radio station's view: "Rommel and the tattered remnants of his defeated army may well be skulking somewhere outside Tobruk. But to talk of any possibility of his capturing the mighty fortress is plain absurd."

To his secretary, Corporal Böttcher, Rommel had dictated an entreaty to his troops to destroy the British army. "During the days to come," he ended, "I shall be calling on you all to make one last great effort to bring us to this final goal."

Toward evening he made one more brief tour of the Tobruk battlefield and enormous captured dumps. Then he returned to the hotel. "After all I've been through," he wrote to Lucie, "I've just got to grab a few hours' sleep." Not since the capture of Longarone, twenty-five years before, had he felt as tired as this.

Mussolini's directive to Rommel in May of 1942 had given him authority to advance only as far as the frontier wire. Before he attempted to invade Egypt, two major problems—in the Italian view—needed tackling first: the Italian navy lacked fuel oil, and Malta was reviving after its ordeal of air attack and blockade. Although supply shipping losses in June were not much greater than in May, the lack of oil meant that Italian warships could escort fewer supply convoys. The disastrous result was that supplies to Libya dropped from 150,000 tons to only 32,000; and these were delivered to distant Tripoli, not the much nearer Benghazi. Marshal Ugo Cavallero, chief of the Italian High Command, drew the Nazis' attention to these two problems in a letter that reached Hitler on June 21. Colonel Walter Scherff, historian for the German High Command, noted Hitler's reaction in his diary: "The Führer's attitude to Operation Herkules (the planned Axis invasion of Malta) is still hostile."

Standing over the map table in the elegant surroundings of the Reich Chancellery in Berlin, as a colonel deftly unrolled the charts of Nazi Germany's spreading dominions, Adolf Hitler saw no need for a pedantic strategy. He had the British on the run, from the Arctic right down to Libya. His army was inflicting annihilating blows on the Soviet forces and advancing on the Caucasus. A letter had just come from Rommel emphasizing his Panzer Army's sparkling morale and reporting the treasure troves of Tobruk, which would enable him to pursue the British deep into Egypt—*provided* Mussolini agreed. Hitler sent a telegram to Mussolini. In it, Hitler described Rommel's victory as a "turning point" in Africa. "The Goddess of Victory approaches commanders in battle only once," he advised. "If they do not clutch her then, she often never again comes within their reach."

It was now June 22. The whole Nazi Reich was intoxicated with the news from Africa. A new bridge was named after Rommel. From gauleiters and generals alike the congratulations poured into Lucie's house at Wiener Neustadt. General Streccius, commandant of nearby Vienna, purloined Hitler's own title by writing to Lucie: "Rommel's name will be ranked among those of the Greatest Warriors of All Time!" Lucie's home was "awash with flowers." She spent that evening with neighbors—the Furstenbergs—and a dozen other friends listening to the special broadcast of recordings flown direct from Tobruk. There was Army Specialist Lutz Koch, Rommel's personal war correspondent, broadcasting his own eyewitness description of the fall of Tobruk; and then Lucie heard the general himself, speaking from the battlefield. She would have preferred to listen alone to his sonorous voice coming from so far away—it was a once-in-a-lifetime moment for her too. Then the program ended and Herr Furstenberg stood up and switched off the radio set, and went downstairs to get champagne.

Hitler too had sat with Goebbels and his personal staff around a radio set that evening. As the program ended, Goebbels commented on the quality of the material: "There's hardly any other general so imbued with the vital importance of combat propaganda as General Rommel. He's a modern general in the best sense of the word." At the word "general" Hitler raised his hand for silence and pointed with a knowing grin to the loudspeaker. Trumpets were sounding a fanfare. There was going to be a special announcement. "From the Führer's headquarters, June twenty-second . . ." began the voice.

In his trailer, 1,500 miles away, Rommel slept. He had been too tired to join his staff as they clustered around the radio in Lieutenant Berndt's car, tuned to the special broadcast from Berlin. At a quarter to ten, Rommel was suddenly wakened by whoops of delight. A fanfare had sounded from the loudspeaker, and the announcer had said: "From the Führer's headquarters, June twenty-second. The Führer has promoted the commander of Panzer Army Afrika, Colonel General Rommel, to the rank of field marshal."

Field Marshal Rommel! "To have become a field marshal is like a dream to me," he confessed to Lucie in his next letter. "All these mighty events of the past weeks trail behind me like a dream."

It was the ultimate honor for a soldier. No one could rise above that rank—unless his name was Hermann Göring, of course. (A special rank had been created to please his vanity.) In Prussia, field marshals could never retire or be dismissed—they remained that rank for life, entitled to a secretary, a horse or car, a driver and other perquisites. It was the traditional tribute to a warrior who had conquered a great fortress or won a great battle. To become a field marshal was to become an immortal.

Rommel was to the manner born. That afternoon, before the conferring of his immortality and without permission from Hitler or Mussolini, he had taken it upon himself to issue marching orders to the Afrika Korps. Both panzer divisions had started rolling at 7:30 P.M., to circle around the frontier defense line to the south. The panzers had seen no sign of the enemy yet—but the night sky above them was frequently pierced by the glare of parachute flares, so the enemy evidently knew what Rommel was up to. His interpreter, Lieutenant Armbruster, caught the excitement in his diary: "June 22. . . . We are moving on again and won't give the Tommies any peace. They believe we are going to need four or six weeks first, but our big attack begins—tomorrow! Let's hope they don't duck out. This is our unique chance. We may even make it to Cairo. . . . Huge supply dump at Capuzzo." Later: "In the evening we tuned in to the special announcement. We're all delighted and Rommel too —like a small boy."

Rommel slept like a log but was up again at six to brief the Ninetieth Light at Bardia for its rapid advance through the wire into Egypt. "Our attack began at 2:00 P.M.," wrote Armbruster. "We drove a long way south, then turned east. The Italians [Twentieth Corps] and Ninetieth Light unfortunately lagged a bit. But at 7:22 P.M. we crossed the wire on the frontier of Egypt and here we spent the night. There are only very few of us." The Rommel diary also recorded that moment: 7:22 P.M.— the moment when the new field marshal began his attempt to conquer Egypt.

The next day, June 24, Rommel heard a sound he had not heard for a week—enemy aircraft engines. The RAF's Desert Air Force had resumed operations, on a terrifying scale. At 6:00 P.M. fifteen Boston bombers attacked in formation. Rommel dived for cover, and most of the bomb load fell around his combat squad. Almost at once, enemy fighter planes streaked in, their machine guns spewing fire. Armbruster, still shaking, jotted in his diary: "A fighter plane has just flown over R.'s car, only twenty feet up. I thought it was curtains." There was no sign of the Luftwaffe—by invading Egypt, Rommel had caught Waldau's squadrons on the wrong foot. His Panzer Army's advance far outpaced the rate at which Waldau could move forward his airfield organization.

Sidi Barrani was occupied without trouble, but the little port was in ruins. The next morning the enemy bombers returned. There were eight separate raids on the Afrika Korps. Over the following days the air raids multiplied. The Italian armored corps commander, General Baldassare, and several of his officers were killed. But Rommel believed he had the British on the run and he refused to be alarmed by this loss of air supremacy. His optimism was infectious. He assured Marshals Cavellero, Kesselring and Bastico when they flew in to see him on June 26, "If my Panzer Army succeeds in breaking through the enemy's line today, by June 30 we'll be in Cairo or Alexandria."

But now there were new factors operating against Rommel. He was venturing into a terrain where no Axis soldiers had yet set foot. And General Sir Claude Auchinleck had taken personal command of the Eighth Army and reversed the plans that had been laid for a last-ditch British stand at Mersa Matruh. Thus when the big port fell into Rommel's hands early on June 29, the haul of prisoners was disappointing—only about 2,000. From a radio intercept, Rommel learned that the British were now slipping away to the east. "Catch them!" he radioed to the Afrika Korps. This was easier said than done. The retreating British had laid all manner of obstacles to trip Rommel's advance. "East of Rahim Duweiry three minefields block the highway," said the Rommel diary. "Ground to left and right of the highway is mined. After several trucks have already hit mines on the road and roadside, C in C and Lieutenant Berndt personally clear the mines away. After 200 mines have been lifted, the road is free again and the advance is rapidly resumed. At dusk C in C halts six miles west of El Daba. In El Daba itself there are gigantic explosions—we can feel the blast wave from six miles away. The sound takes thirty or forty seconds to reach us."

Rommel did not know it, but the Panzer Army had neared its limit. There were signs that day, June 30, that his troops were almost finished. Sometimes his infantry fell asleep in broad daylight and were wakened by the enemy. The Twentieth Corps reported at 8:50 A.M. that it had only fifteen tanks left and was being blocked by eight enemy tanks. Rommel loosened his collar and scribbled a rude reply on a message pad. The air that day

, was hot and full of flying grit, and by afternoon a full sandstorm was howling. Twice Rommel's clutch of trailers, trucks and headquarters cars was bombed and strafed, twice he ordered them moved 1,000 yards—and still the enemy air force came back for more.

He looked beyond the momentary difficulties to the glorious objective: the capture of Cairo. Just 100 more miles to Alexandria, and then . . . "Perhaps I can get away to Italy in July," he wrote longingly to Lucie. "Get passports!!!" He studied his maps. Ahead of his forces the British had withdrawn to a line extending inland from a grubby railroad stop near the coast, El Alamein. Rommel knew it was the enemy's last defensive position of any consequence before the river Nile.

That afternoon, Rommel called his generals to his command post—now concealed among sand dunes. He announced that he was going to attack the enemy before dawn the next day, July 1. The conference was abruptly ended by another bombing raid. "Took cover with C in C in a hole," says the Armbruster diary. "Corporal Günther [Rommel's orderly] injured. Windshield shattered. Terrific sandstorm all evening, and still another air attack on the road. Zero hour is 3:00 A.M. tomorrow." The pendulum of conflict in the desert had now halted. The impetus of Rommel's Panzer Army was almost gone.

# Prelude to El Alamein

ROMMEL is now only 100 miles from the powerful British naval base at Alexandria. To the British it seems quite possible that he will overrun Egypt, and his adversary, General Auchinleck, has drawn up a long list of demolitions in case this should happen: radio stations, telegraph and telephone systems, oil and gasoline installations, transport and power supplies. Defenses are being built near the Pyramids. In the Egyptian capital, a state of emergency has been declared, agents inform Rommel; British troops have taken over Cairo to maintain civil order. Rommel's fame has gone before him. He knows that the Egyptians, tired of British rule, are awaiting his arrival with barely concealed excitement. He hopes that the ensuing riots against the British will seal the Eighth Army's defeat. From his special radio truck, in permanent contact with Ribbentrop's Foreign Ministry, a signal has gone to Berlin: "Field Marshal Rommel requests soonest use of active propaganda in Egypt."

In London, Prime Minister Winston Churchill is fighting for his job. The fiery Welsh Member of Parliament, Aneurin Bevan, has commented once before that Churchill has won one debate after another—but lost one battle after another too. Now members of Churchill's own

Conservative Party have tabled a "motion of censure" against him and his conduct of the war. Sir John Wardlaw-Milne rises and challenges him: "It is surely clear to any civilian that the series of disasters of the past few months—and indeed of the past two years—is due to fundamental defects in the central administration of the war." He is seconded by Admiral Keyes, whose son has died in the futile commando attack on Rommel's headquarters at Beda Littoria. Lord Winterton supports the motion. "Who is the minister who practically controlled the Narvik operation?" he asks Churchill. "It is the present Prime Minister, who was then First Lord of the Admiralty. . . . We never had anything in the last war comparable with this series of disasters. Now see what *this* Government gets away with: because 'the Führer is always right.' "

The next day, July 2, 1942, the parliamentary attack on Churchill mounts in fury. A member blames Britain's defeats on the army's class-ridden mentality. "In this country there is a taunt on everyone's lips that if Rommel had been in the British army he would still have been a sergeant." When Churchill rises, however, he shifts the blame squarely onto his generals—Klopper, Ritchie and even Auchinleck. It is all brilliant oratory. He then describes the defeat in North Africa, sparing no melancholy detail: "If there are any would-be profiteers of disaster who feel able to paint the picture in darker colors, they are certainly at liberty to do so," he observes. Churchill goes on to attribute the Eighth Army's misfortunes directly to Rommel's own ability. Thus Churchill survives the day.

In Germany, his discomfiture has evoked hoots of derision. The *Berliner Börsenzeitung* headlines its report: "Churchill Says—Blame Rommel" In distant East Prussia, Hitler stabs at his unappetizing vegetarian supper and reflects on Churchill's tactical error in boosting an enemy general like that: "People frequently ask how it is that Rommel enjoys so great a worldwide reputation," he says. "Not a little is due to Churchill's speeches in the House of Commons in which the British Prime Minister always portrays Rommel as a military genius." He chuckles. "The mere name suddenly begins to acquire a value. Imagine what would happen if we kept on plugging the Soviet marshal Timoshenko. In the end our own soldiers would come to regard him as some kind of superman."

As the Members of Parliament filed into the voting lobbies, Rommel's troops were deadlocked with Auchinleck's. The Panzer Army had reached El Alamein's defenses with only fifty-five German and thirty Italian tanks. The troops were almost prostrate with fatigue, tortured by sun and thirst. Rommel had allowed himself the luxury of two sea baths, but the water was too warm to be refreshing. When the Ninetieth Light Division pleaded for permission for its riflemen to do the same, Rommel refused and relentlessly pushed them on toward the new battlefield.

Three hours past midnight on July 1, the riflemen, machine gunners and other troops of the Ninetieth Light climbed back into their trucks and moved off in broad formation against El Alamein. Blinded by a sandstorm, Rommel's troops blundered right into the enemy defenses. For the first time the word "panic" figured in a German division's diary. Sections of the Ninetieth Light crumbled away and fled to the rear. Their commanders forced them back onto the battle lines and they dug in. Later Rommel himself drove up to get the attack moving again and promptly felt the lash of the enemy artillery on his own little force of twenty trucks and armored cars.

"It was terrible," wrote Armbruster that evening. "A shell detonated just six feet away from the C in C's car. Under heavy fire we madly dug holes and had to keep our heads down for the next three hours. It was dusk before we could extricate ourselves." To add to their misery, by nightfall it was raining hard and nonstop air attacks had begun.

The Afrika Korps had only thirty-seven tanks left and was still some distance away. The Italians had made no showing. As for the poor Ninetieth Light, it was less than one sixth of its proper strength. Nonetheless, Rommel ordered the division to resume its attack when the moon rose. He was encouraged by news from Luftwaffe headquarters: the British fleet had weighed anchor at Alexandria and was making for the safety of the Suez Canal. Evidently, Rommel felt, Axis morale was better than the enemy's.

"The night was awful," Armbruster wrote. "From midnight to 4:00 A.M. there were six or eight bombers constantly raiding us. I slept in my foxhole." An hour before dawn, the fatigued riflemen of the Ninetieth Light dutifully began a new infantry attack, but without any artillery preparation. After only 2,000 yards their attack petered out in murderous artillery and machine gun fire. Rommel was told at ten in the morning. That afternoon, undeterred, he ordered the Afrika Korps to throw both its panzer divisions into one more attempt to break through to the coast. But at 4:30 P.M. the Ninetieth Light was again stalled, after advancing only 500 more yards. Afrika Korps's two panzer divisions meanwhile clashed with British armored brigades until dark. By then, Nehring had lost eleven more tanks and was down to only twenty-six.

The next day, July 3, Rommel's main thrusts everywhere were blocked. At about noon, his diary finds him under air attack, trying to harry his exhausted tank commanders to yet greater efforts. "C in C is convinced that both panzer divisions are loafing idly around and at 12:50 P.M. orders a forceful advance by the entire Afrika Korps." But Rommel was now addressing only the deaf, or the demoralized, or the dead. Even Ariete, the pluckiest of the Italian divisions, had begun to disintegrate. Fierce New Zealanders had fixed bayonets and charged Ariete that morning, capturing nearly all of Ariete's remaining guns and 380 prisoners; the rest of the Italians had thrown down their weapons and taken to their heels.

The death of one of his best officers—Captain von Hohmeyer, killed by shellfire that evening—seems to have at last brought it home to Rommel that he was fighting a losing battle. "Unfortunately, things aren't going as well as I would have liked," he admitted privately to Lucie. "Resistance is too great and our strength is exhausted . . . I'm rather tired and worn out." Rommel passed his decision to his relieved corps commanders the next morning, July 4. He was going to pull the tattered panzer divisions out of the line and replace them with infantry divisions, primarily Italian. For a while the panzers would rest, replenish and reorganize. Then Rommel would resume the offensive, he assured them.

Mussolini and a collection of Fascist notables had already flown to Libya and were waiting impatiently to stage their grand entry into Cairo. The Duce's white horse was waiting, too. Telegrams were flying back and forth between Rome and Berlin on the appointment of an Italian governor of Egypt and his relation to Rommel and the "Army of Occupation." Meanwhile, enemy propagandists spread concocted rumors that the riches of a conquered Egypt would fall to the German troops alone. The rumor was one of many that caused powerful unrest among Rommel's Italian troops, and in mid-July he told Berlin that "entire battalions" were deserting in battle. Real cracks were now beginning to show in the Axis partnership. From Rommel's headquarters, Alfred Berndt wrote privately to Goebbels that there was much bitterness among the Germans at the undue credit being given to Italian soldiers by the Nazi press. (Goebbels told his staff: "We are going to have to brief Rommel on the reasons why the Führer has deemed it necessary to magnify the Italian effort.")

Rommel himself deplored all such politicking, but chose to disregard it until he had captured Cairo. He was well aware of his awkward situation. His ammunition and gasoline were low, his units under strength. In the month of June, 845 of his men had been killed and 3,318 wounded. His supply lines were long, while those of the enemy were short and well protected. Until now the Germans, although short of arms, had held their own because of the superiority of their weapons; but now the German qualitative superiority was being rapidly whittled away. Recent battles had shown, too, that enemy commanders were benefiting from contact with the Afrika Korps in combat, improving their tactics and procedures.

The line the Italian divisions held extended from the blue waters of the Mediterranean at El Alamein to the impenetrable, sunken, dried salt marshes of the Qattara Depression thirty-eight miles inland. The wilderness of the depression was a spectacle that Rommel never tired of seeing. A dozen times in July 1942 we find him drawn to the high rim looking down on the vast cavity, with its dunes rolling like flat waves into the shimmering distance, out of which rose silent and forbidding flat-topped mountains on which perhaps no human foot had trod. Goebbels's cameramen filmed him gazing down to the floor of the depression, 600 feet below. Was he planning some way of traversing this wilderness to reach the Nile?

Once that July he said to the lieutenant on his intelligence staff who had been an Egyptologist before the war, "Behrendt, I'll be wanting you to seize a bridge intact across the Nile!"

The lieutenant laughed. "Herr Feldmarschall," he said, "you ought to have given me that job in 1939!" Alfred Berndt chimed in: "If you go, I want to go too!" Behrendt shook his head—he knew who would get all the credit in that case.

Rommel planned to throw his panzer divisions through a gap at the southern end of the line on July 11. Two days earlier, he had captured an abandoned enemy strongpoint nearby, at Bab el Qattara. Here in its complex warren of underground galleries, concrete bunkers and well-built slit trenches, Rommel conferred with the Twenty-first Panzer Division's bullet-headed commander, Bismarck, and sketched with his familiar colored pencils the aspects of the coming panzer attack. He set up the Panzer Army's advance headquarters right there in the bunker hospital. But the bunker, he discovered, housed a large flea colony. "The C in C elects to sleep in his car after all," the Rommel diary for July 9 concludes. "The night passes peacefully."

In his sleep he heard thunder. At 4:00 A.M. he heard it again—distant thunder. Not thunder, he realized as his brain cleared, but the mighty roar of field guns in a barrage louder than anything he had heard since World War I. Forty miles to the north of where he now was! The enemy had begun a sudden and wholly unexpected attack on two ridges near the coast, Tell el Eisa and Tell el Makh Khad, defended by Italian infantry. Rommel's main force could hardly have been farther away. "Did we fall into a trap?" asks Armbruster's diary.

Rommel saw the danger that the enemy would break right through and smash his army's supply lines. "We at once drove north with our own combat squad and a battle group from Fifteenth Panzer," said his diary. "C in C personally briefs the two battle groups on the battlefield."

In his absence Mellenthin, acting operations officer, had thrown in every German unit to plug the gap—staff personnel, flak, infantry, signalers, even cooks—because the Italian division Sabratha had just melted away to a depth of 6,000 yards. Waldau's story puts it politely: "There were regrettable symptoms of disintegration in the Italian units. The first real resistance was put up by Seebohm's radio intercept company." Armbruster's diary reflects Rommel's more forceful language: "The Tommies have netted two battalions of the Sabratha shits. Seebohm is missing. It makes you puke."

The death of Captain Seebohm was a terrible blow for Rommel. Seebohm had commanded the brilliant radio intercept company that had so often given Rommel his tactical advantage over the British. Now Seebohm was dead, his irreplaceable trained personnel captured and their collection of code books and enemy orders of battle gone. The loss was bound to hamper Rommel in the months to come, and the captured materials were certain to show the enemy how lax their radio security was. Now the Panzer Army would be fighting blind. To make things even worse—infinitely worse—there would be no more "little fellers" either, the enlightening intercepted messages from the American military attaché in Cairo. The enemy had realized that there was a leak and had recalled Colonel Fellers to Washington. A memo dated June 29 in the files of "Foreign Armies West" in Berlin closes this chapter: "We will not be able to count on these intercepts for a long time to come, which is unfortunate as they told us all we needed to know, immediately, about virtually every enemy action."

The next morning, July 10, the Australians attacked Tell el Eisa and by midday they had captured it. A small column of tanks and infantry scored a further resounding success over the Italians at Deir el Abyad, provoking this outburst from Armbruster at army headquarters: "The Italians ought to be whipped. Six British tanks have just rounded up an entire battalion of the Trento Division and sent them to captivity in their own trucks. This nation of shits deserves to be shot. And we still have to fight for them! Now of all times, just before the finish, these guys turn yellow. It's a crying shame and we feel so sorry that the C in C has to make do with such troops."

These limited enemy attacks had serious tactical consequences for Rommel. They had thrown the Panzer Army off balance and drained gasoline and ammunition reserves that Rommel had planned to use for his own offensive.

On July 13, he launched Bismarck's Twenty-first Panzer Division once more against the enemy line. The plan was to cut off the fortified El Alamein "box," then break in and finish it off. The attack would go in at high noon, when all desert contours shimmer in the heat and melt away—making good gun aiming impossible. Dead on time, Waldau's dive bombers took out the enemy batteries southwest of the "box," and the tanks began rolling until a useful sandstorm swallowed them from view. Rommel went forward to follow the course of the battle, but there was little he could see.

It was not until 5:00 P.M. that he learned that the panzer regiment had halted on a jebel south of Qasaba. Meanwhile the Luftwaffe waited in vain for further orders or requests. Finally, at six-thirty, Waldau sent in a second heavy dive bomber attack and the tanks began rolling again.

After that the battle just fell to pieces. At about 8:00 P.M. Rommel telephoned Waldau. He was in high spirits and announced that the panzer division had exploited the magnificent dive bomber attack to penetrate right through the enemy line—"It's going to try and reach the coast road east of El Alamein tonight." The ugly reality, as described by the war diary of an infantry battalion attached to the Twenty-first Panzer, was different: "We are lying right in front of the enemy barbed wire, and hacking ineffectually away at it with quite useless tools. Only a few sappers have got this far with wire cutters to clear lanes for us. It is almost dusk. The battlefield is lit only by guttering spurts of flame and the wan moonlight. And then our tanks suddenly turn tail. Are they out of ammunition or gas? Captain von Rautenfeld leaps up onto the nearest tank to stop it going back. An antitank shell hits him in the neck and cuts him down. At midnight, Major Schutte leads our battalion back again."

Rommel had returned meanwhile from the battlefield to Panzer Army headquarters. "Toward 10:00 P.M.," his diary reported, "Twenty-first Panzer radios that its attack has finally failed. C in C thereupon orders the division to withdraw to its original start line. Neither the sandstorm nor the well-aimed dive bomber attack nor the powerful support of our artillery was exploited by the division. A unique chance—and they blew it." Just how high were the hopes Rommel had set by this operation is shown by his flustered letter home next morning: "My expectations of the attack were bitterly disappointed. It had no success whatever . . ."

Several of the next rounds in this increasingly confusing fight did go to Rommel. It is no coincidence that those were the days on which he elected to direct the battle from his army command post rather than to dash about the battlefield. Nevertheless, two Italian divisions, Pavia and Brescia, collapsed and the British tactics became only too clear. "The enemy," he wrote to Lucie darkly on the seventeenth, "are rounding up one Italian formation after another. Our German units will be far too weak to stand by themselves. It makes me weep!" Early that day he heard that the Australians had broken through between two more Italian divisions, the Trento and Trieste. Trieste had suffered mass desertions. Rommel was forced to throw in every last reserve he had.

When the Italian High Command—Cavallero, Bastico and Air Force Commander General Rino Fougier—visited him that afternoon, Rommel bleakly told them: "Any more blows like today and I do not anticipate being able to hold the situation." Armbruster, who interpreted their ninety-minute conference, afterward jotted in his own diary: "R. paints the situation pretty black."

To Rommel's relief, the next day, July 18, brought no surprises. The front was quiet. He spent the next two days touring the whole line, directing the laying of minefields and construction of strongpoints. He did not spare the Italians from private criticism. He told the Ninetieth Light's commander, "Through the failure of four Italian divisions that have been virtually wiped out, a temporary crisis has emerged that will last until major German forces arrive here, in eight or ten days' time."

By July 21 he was a bit happier. He had about forty-two fit German tanks in the Afrika Korps, and about fifty Italian tanks. "The front has now calmed down, thank goodness, and I've had a chance to take stock," he wrote privately. "But it's going to be a long crisis yet, because the buildup on the other side is faster than here. Kesselring's going to fly to the Führer's headquarters—a pity I can't do the same." He had started wearing his short trousers again—the heat was too much for full uniform. The dust and flies were terrible, and it was humid, too.

Auchinleck's new attack was a deliberate attempt to destroy Rommel's panzer divisions. A captured enemy soldier confirmed this. It began late that evening with violent air attacks—more spectacular than effective—and an intense artillery bombardment. During the hours of darkness a New Zealand brigade penetrated from the south toward the shallow El Mreir depression—a saucerlike hollow in the middle of the desert. At dawn, tanks were to arrive. However, General Nehring had kept an unflustered watch on these developments and gave his panzer regiments instructions—three hours in advance—to counterattack at 4:15 A.M. Four A.M. found the Germans, including their scanty machine gun and rifle battalions, waiting around the lip of the depression, their watches ticking toward zero hour. The New Zealanders had made themselves comfortable, even setting up tents on the valley floor. At 4:15 A.M. exactly, signal flares arced into the air and tracer fire, high-explosive shells and mortar bombs rained down on the congested mass of invaders. Then the panzers rumbled over the rim and poured into the enemy positions. Of the enemy's armor there was still no sign. This first phase of Auchinleck's attack had cost him 1,000 men and much armament.

The second phase then began. The enemy threw about 100 tanks into the same sector from the east—two virgin tank regiments which had arrived from Britain only two weeks before. At 7:30 A.M. they broke through the minefields and the leading tanks surged far behind Rommel's line. His thin infantry positions were overrun. To Rommel and Nehring it looked like the long-feared end of the army. Then a Colonel Bruer, who was commanding the Twenty-first Panzer in place of Bismarck (who was injured), came to the rescue. He halted the fleeing artillery battalions and turned them to face the enemy. Then his Fifth Panzer Regiment punched into the enemy flank, and the danger was past. In two hours Rommel's commanders, by sheer professionalism and gallantry, had robbed the British of 200 men and eighty-seven tanks.

There was heroism on every level. Nineteen-year-old Günther Halm was a gunlayer manning one of two Russian-built 76.2-millimeter antitank guns that had been positioned so that they would be the last defense before the enemy armor could break through. The gun crew was unable to dig the gun into the rocky ground, so two gunners had to sit on the gun's trails to absorb its recoil. Toward them roared a column of British tanks. In two minutes Halm brewed up four Valentines. The others halted, searched for the barely concealed guns, and opened fire on them. A shell screamed between Halm's legs. A second shell tore off his loader's legs; another gunner took that man's place. Five more British tanks were shot into flames before Halm's gun was disabled by shellfire. By that time the Twenty-first Panzer had arrived and finished off the enemy tanks. One of the captured tank commanders angrily burst out: "Two years of training, a sea journey halfway round the world—and in just half an hour it's all over for us!" One week later Rommel personally decorated Halm with the Knight's Cross. He was the first enlisted man in the German army to win the award.

The next afternoon, July 23, Wilfried Armbruster penciled in his diary: "The tide has turned with a vengeance! The British Twenty-third Armored Brigade has been rubbed out. The Tommies lost 146 tanks and 1,200 men. What an excitement that was, but our C in C directed the whole show from 'the rear' this time, he had every commander on a string and everything just clicked into place. A fine mess he got the British into!"

Rommel toured the battlefield, thanked his troops and handed out medals. "Morale everywhere is sky-high," his diary observed. He had a look at the new British tanks. Some had got within 2,000 yards of the Twenty-first Panzer's command post; they were still there now, their crews captured or buried beside them. "The difficulties we went through the last few days just beggar all description," he confessed in a relieved letter to Lucie. "Of course, we are still nowhere near over the hump. The enemy is vastly superior in numbers. But the 146 tanks that we shot down in and behind our battle lines two days ago will take a lot of replacing: we have now blown them all up. The enemy won't be able to afford many such extravagances."

Now he had time to open his mail. Hitler's chief adjutant, Rudolf Schmundt, had sent the cross-sword badges that Rommel would need as a field marshal. But he read the letters postmarked Wiener Neustadt first. There were new photos of Lucie and Manfred—the boy had been away from home for some weeks at a Hitler Youth camp. With fatherly anxiety Rommel read his son's latest school report—a big improvement on the last one. Lucie wrote that Frau von Bismarck had telephoned from Pomerania, anxious for news of her husband. She had not heard from him for three weeks. Rommel knew how long it took letters to go from Africa, but passed the word to General von Bismarck. (As events turned out, Bismarck had only three more weeks to live.) Lucie also told him of the latest newsreel: it showed Mussolini in Africa, and Kesselring, Cavallero and Bastico touring the El Alamein line with Rommel. Rommel looked far from pleased, in fact very grim-faced indeed. Lucie, better informed of Rommel's problems with supplies and the Italians than the other moviegoers, knew why. One letter from her told of Winston Churchill's recent chastened visit to Stalin in Moscow: "How is the mighty England fallen!" She added, "Today the news said that your adversary Auchinleck has been sacked and replaced by a General Montgomery." The name meant nothing yet to Rommel.

He guessed early in August of 1942 that he still had another four weeks before the British would attempt another move. Meanwhile, Hitler's big push through Russia toward the Caucasus would be bound to affect British dispositions in the Middle East. He knew that the Panzer Army could withstand minor enemy attacks, but he had had to issue the sternest orders to prevent repetitions of the kind of panic that had gripped sections of the line in July. "I demand that every man, at staff level too, hold to his position and not fall back. Abandoning your position means annihilation. By holding our positions in the night battles, we won through with little casualties. Any enemy that breaks through must be mopped up by reserves standing by. . . . Anybody abandoning his position is to be charged with cowardice and stood before a court-martial.—Rommel."

One thing was plain: victory or defeat at El Alamein would rest in the hands of the German troops here. Rommel never forgot that. To other generals, writing to congratulate him on his promotion, he replied: "The credit for this lofty recognition from the Führer is due solely to the courage of my trusty German soldiers."

The gaps were being filled. During July he had received 5,400 replacement troops and the first two regiments of a new division, the 164th Light. That made 13,300 new troops airlifted to North Africa, and more were coming, at the rate of 1,000 every day. By early August one of the Luftwaffe's elite units, the First Paratroop Brigade, was under Rommel's command. Its commander, General Hermann Ramcke, was a lithe, pugnacious veteran of the fighting on Crete. He had a mouthful of metal teeth replacing those he had lost in a parachute accident. His paratroops were well armed and fit, but since they were a Luftwaffe unit and not army, Rommel had little time or sympathy for them. (Like the 164th Light, Ramcke's troops had arrived with no transport of their own. The 164th Light had actually arrived with *bicycles,* which were soon discarded.) However, they were German and disciplined, so they were all fed into Rommel's thickening line of defense between the sea and the great depression. Artillery was arriving, ammunition dumps were building up, dense minefields and mine boxes were being laid out in carefully conceived patterns. New Italian units were also arriving. Rommel omitted them from his calculations. "The stuff that's coming over is virtually useless," he said. On July 29, when he met the new commander of the Bologna infantry division, General Alessandro Gloria, the Italian thumped his chest and proclaimed that Italian troops would *never* desert their posts. "At that the C in C drily enlightened him as to the way things have been around here," observes the

Armbruster diary. (It was later that day that Rommel issued his warning about cowardice.)

The Italians had contributed one first-rate unit, the Folgore Paratroop Division. Their training (by Germans) showed when their commanding officer snapped to attention and swung to a gaping Rommel a salute that would have done a Prussian drill instructor proud. For the rest, Rommel scorned the Italian newcomers. "What I need here," he explained to Alfred Gause in a letter, "are not still more Italian divisions—let alone the Pistoia, with no combat experience at all—but the German soldiers and the German equipment with which alone I am ultimately going to have to carry through my offensive."

There were certain imperatives that cramped his freedom of decision now. Against the advice of his own staff —according to Mellenthin—he had firmly decided to stake his entire Panzer Army on one throw: he was going to break through the enemy line at its southern end, engage the Eighth Army there, and simultaneously mount a lightning attack on the vital bridges across the Nile at Cairo and Alexandria. There is a map in Rommel's papers on which he planned the advance of every corps, division and battalion—half of them surging on from Cairo to the Suez Canal, the other half turning south from Cairo along the Nile toward the heart of Africa. Mysterious visitors arrived at his trailer—Egyptian officers, who assured him that the moment that Rommel's forces hit Cairo and Alexandria they would stage a military uprising against the British. But by September, he knew, the Eighth Army would be too strong for even Rommel to defeat. So it had to be August. And since his daring plan for a night attack would require a full moon, that meant the end of the month. "Then," he wrote to his old adjutant, Ernst Streicher, "I hope we shall succeed in bursting open this last gateway barring our path to Egypt's fertile fields."

Throughout August, Rommel's army dug in. The desert echoed to the staccato blast of pneumatic drills, of demolition charges, of pickaxe and shovel. Tens of thousands of mines were laid, in case the enemy attacked first.

On August 8, the Rommel diary hinted again at his

imaginativeness: "Reconnaissance Battalion Thirty-three is given the job by C in C of finding out whether it is possible to descend to the Qattara Depression with an entire division or even larger formations." Kesselring flew in the next day and approved Rommel's general plans. Armbruster's diary struggled to keep track of the tireless field marshal: "It's stinking hot, but the C in C drives out every day." On the tenth he recorded, "Three camels hit mines here, and we caught five Arabs. They had been trying to cross the minefield by night—you can be dead certain that they were in the pay of the British and trying to spy on us."

Not only did the stupefying furnace temperatures and the unhealthy proximity to the Nile Delta take their toll of the Panzer Army's troops; Rommel fell ill too—at this, of all times. On August 2 he began to feel a general malaise, and by mid-month he was really ill. He was in fact the only officer over forty to have lasted in Africa as long as he had. On August 19 his staff noticed that the field marshal could not get rid of a head cold and was laboring from a sore throat too. They thought it was flu, and he took to his bed while his staff rushed his personal doctor, Professor Horster, to him. Horster reported: "Field Marshal Rommel is suffering from low blood pressure and he has a tendency to dizzy spells. The condition can be attributed to his persistent stomach and enteric disorders, and it has been aggravated by excessive physical and mental efforts over the last weeks and particularly by the unfavorable climate. A *complete* recovery is by no means certain at present, particularly if the demands on him increase; recovery can only be expected from a long stay in Germany under proper medical supervision. *Temporary* treatment here on African soil would appear acceptable."

Rommel radioed this diagnosis to Berlin on August 21 and recommended Heinz Guderian, a panzer general, as a substitute. He sent a telegram to Guderian too. He believed he would have ample time for this "sick leave." Meanwhile Berndt procured a good cook for him and arranged for fresh vegetables and fruit to be flown to him daily—without his being told. "Otherwise, being the man he is, he would refuse to accept the extra rations," Berndt explained in a private letter to Lucie. And he anxiously telegraphed to Goebbels in code, "I suggest sending Professor Brandt [Hitler's personal doctor] out here at once to check field marshal's condition." On August 24, Rommel was well enough to drive briefly to Mersa Matruh for an electrocardiogram.

When he got back to his trailer, there was a radio signal from Keitel, chief of the High Command: Guderian had been turned down, as not healthy enough for the tropics. (The real reason was that Guderian was in disgrace, having disobeyed Hitler during the winter.) So Rommel stayed at his post. He radioed in code to Keitel on the twenty-sixth that in his doctor's opinion he could retain command of the Panzer Army during the coming offensive "while undergoing ambulatory medical treatment." After that he would return to Germany for a cure, and a substitute would stand in for him.

Rommel conducted his last inspections of his entire battle line. As he now prepared his supreme offensive against the assembling forces of the British Empire, however, he was a sick man: sick, but sustained by the hope that with victory in his grasp he could return to Germany —perhaps in mid-September—and spend six weeks alone with Lucie and Manfred, somewhere in the mountains of Austria, where he could sleep in clean sheets, wash in running water and wake without the menacing rumble of the adversary's guns.

# The Ridge

THE British lieutenant general who flies into Cairo on August 12, 1942, to replace Auchinleck has had no combat command since the debacle of Dunkirk, two years before. Small and wiry, Bernard Montogomery has birdlike features and a high, nasal voice that is grating and unfriendly. His knees are white, his face is pink. In many ways, however, he is like Rommel himself: both are lonely men, with more enemies than friends among their fellow generals; both arc high-handed and arrogant, professional soldiers devoid of intellectual qualities; both are awkward and insubordinate officers in harness but become magnificent and original battle commanders in their own right; neither smokes or touches strong drink; both share a passion for winter sports and physical fitness.

Montgomery also has Rommel's flair for public relations. He woos Churchill with a comfortable accommodation near Egypt's bathing beaches, and plies him with brandy and good food—for just the same reasons that Rommel cultivates the admiration of Hitler and the friendship of Goebbels. Both have selected predominantly young and handsome officers for their "military households." They are both publicity conscious. Rather as Rommel wears his famous cap and Perspex goggles, Montgomery flourishes an incongruous Australian bush hat covered with regimental badges. And where as a boy Rommel showed fleeting cruelty toward birds and animals, feeding peppered morsels to swans and guffawing at their agony, Montgomery's career at Sandhurst military academy was marred by his reputation as a particularly nasty type of bully—he was the ringleader, of course.

But here the similarities end. Rommel is now a chivalrous soldier, and honors his enemy whatever the nationality. Montgomery's order to his troops, "Kill the Germans wherever you find them," gives a new accent to the desert war, a ferocity Rommel has scrupulously avoided. Montgomery is an eccentric, while his Nazi adversary is an orthodox military commander distinguished mainly by his flair for improvisation, his tactical insight. Rommel shows battlefield courage, but Montgomery will not be found leading supply trucks up to the front line, personally directing antitank guns onto targets when a breakthrough threatens or scrambling for cover with the leading riflemen during an infantry assault. Rommel relies on his own wits; Montgomery uses the brains of others, and relies on military might to compensate for any planning defects.

One thing must be emphasized: Montgomery's intelligence sources are far superior in August 1942 to Rommel's. It is Montgomery's confident insight into Rommel's mental processes that enables him to last out the main crises, where a less informed commander would have called off the operation. Many of Rommel's top secret radio communications with his High Command are reaching Montgomery as Ultra intercepts only hours later. Thus Cairo learned on November 18, 1941, that Rommel had been so completely deceived about when Operation Crusader would begin that he was still in Rome with Frau Rommel. Thus when Rommel radios the High Command in August 1942 about his illness, Montgomery gets a copy of Professor Horster's diagnosis too. Each time Rommel reports his plan of attack, the Ultra intercepts enable Montgomery to plan an appropriate defense. With great cunning, British intelligence also knows how to conceal its source: planted documents "reveal" to the

Germans that Italian traitors have fed all this information to the enemy—a fabrication that Rommel and history ever after believe.

The Panzer Army was unquestionably weaker than its adversary, but this was nothing new to Rommel. He was 16,000 men below strength, and sickness was reaching epidemic proportions (9,418 of his troops reported sick that month); his establishment was short 210 tanks, 175 troop carriers and armored cars and 1,500 other vehicles. On August 30, the day of his attack, Rommel would field 203 German battle tanks—including 100 of the long-barreled, deadly Specials—but Montgomery would have assembled 767 tanks and he now had hundreds of the new six-pounder antitank gun. Rommel's plan differed only in minor details from all his previous attacks; it was to be the familiar "right hook," out-flanking the enemy's defenses. Perhaps he was wearying or just exhausted by illness, but none of the diaries refers to any new ploys or devices designed to throw the British off balance or off the scent: no truck-mounted airplane engines or carefully planned feint operations.

Unquestionably, his main weakness was going to be his fuel supply. His two veteran panzer divisions had barely enough for 100 miles—provided the going was good. On August 18, Marshal Cavallero had assured him that the 6,000 tons of gasoline that Rommel was demanding would arrive in time for the thirtieth—X day for the attack. But on August 23 the logistics position was "taut," as Rommel put it in a code message radioed to the German naval commander in Italy, Vice Admiral Weichold. Rommel had been promised six ships altogether, loaded with gasoline and ammunition. He appealed to Weichold to see that they arrived by the end of the month, for "without them, execution of the planned operation is impossible." Since all these signals were encoded by Enigma, it is no surprise that four of the six ships were sunk immediately (or that Montgomery was able to deduce the date of Rommel's attack). By August 27, not one of the ships had reached Rommel. When Kesselring's Storch landed at Panzer Army headquarters on the coast, Rommel impatiently told him: "X day depends on whether the gasoline ship scheduled for tomorrow gets in. My final deadline is the thirtieth—the moon's already on the wane." Kesselring slapped him on the back and confidently promised to *airlift* about 700 tons of gasoline to Rommel if all else failed.

By the next morning, Rommel had still not finally decided. He summoned all the generals commanding the armored divisions to his headquarters tent at 8:30 A.M., again went over his plan and warned them: "My deadline for X day is still the thirtieth, but everything still depends on the fuel situation. How far we go on after the end of the Battle of Alamein will depend on our logistic position—on our fuel and ammunition."

On the day after that, Rommel decided he could wait no longer and would initiate the attack next day—the thirtieth, the last date possible—but it could only be of a limited nature now, given the fuel shortage: they could at best hope to disrupt the British forces in the El Alamein line. There would just not be enough fuel to go on to Cairo unless they managed to capture British dumps intact.

The panzer divisions had already begun moving inland down the desert tracks by night, heading for the southern end of the El Alamein line, where Rommel was going to break through. In two night marches this stealthy shift of balance from left to right was accomplished—and Rommel hoped his adversary had not detected it. As he left his sleeping truck early on August 30, he confided to his doctor with a worried frown, "This decision to attack today is the hardest I have ever had to take. Either we manage to reach the Suez Canal, and the army in the USSR succeeds in reaching Grozny [in the Caucasus], or—," and he made a gesture of defeat.

They drove about twenty miles into the desert, and set up advanced army headquarters. Rommel's doctor, Horster, was with them. Waiting for the first news, Rommel began a long letter to Lucie: "Today has dawned at last. How long I've waited for it, worrying whether I was going to get together everything I needed to strike out again. Many things have still not been settled properly at all, and here and there we shall have big shortages. Despite that, I am risking this move because it will be a long time before we get the moonlight, balance of strength, etc., so favorable again. . . . If our blow succeeds, it may help win the war. If it does not, I still hope to have given the enemy a sound thrashing."

It was of course a gamble—a desperate gamble. But the Italians had again assured him in a code message that a shipload of gasoline was arriving next day. In the Gazala fighting in May the odds against Rommel had been the same, but he had won through then; so why not now as well?

"Today," he proclaimed to his troops, "our army sets out once more to attack and destroy the enemy, this time for keeps. I expect every soldier in my army to do his utmost in these decisive days! Long live Fascist Italy! Long live the Greater German Reich! Long live our great leaders!"

Ten P.M., August 30, 1942. A pale moon lights the undulating desert north of the Qattara Depression as Rommel's armor begins moving eastward toward the enemy minefields. To the left of General Nehring's Afrika Korps is the Italian armor—the Littorio and Ariete divisions—and to the left of them the Ninetieth Light. Soldiers waving pocket lamps and shouting instructions guide them toward the gaps in their own minefields, and then they are on their own.

Just before they pass through their own minefields, they hear a long-forgotten sound that brings a lump to the throats of many of the older men: General von Bismarck has sent the band of the Fifth Panzer Regiment to play Rommel's army into battle with old Prussian marches, just as in bygone times. How often a band send-off has been the prelude to disaster—a naval band had played as Hitler's proudest battleship, the ill-fated *Bismarck*, slipped secretly out of its harbor in 1941! It is an eerie sound, and the tank crews and infantry hear only blind snatches above the whine of engines in high gear and the crunch of tank tracks on gravel; but the sound is unforgettable.

Early on August 31, Rommel's mobile headquarters had driven to the Jebel Kalakh, in the wake of his army. He believed that the enemy sector here was only weakly mined and defended. But his intelligence had served him

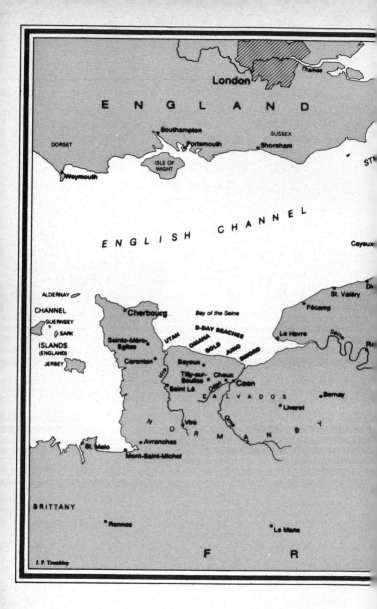

ROMMEL IN FRANCE

0       60 Miles
0       60 Kilometers

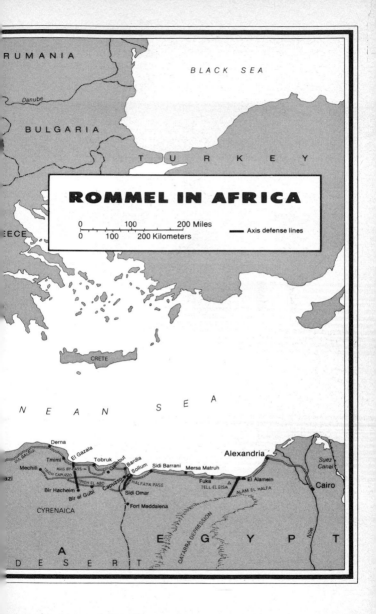

*Rommel's parents. His father was a stern and autocratic schoolmaster who decided his son should have an army career.* (FROM THE ROMMEL FAMILY PAPERS.)

*In 1906 Rommel and a school friend built this glider. It flew, but not far.* (FROM THE ROMMEL FAMILY PAPERS.)

*Erwin fell in love with Lucie Mollin, a dark-eyed beauty who won prizes for dancing. In 1911, when he was twenty, he gave her a photo of himself in the uniform of the Officer Cadet School at Danzig.* (FROM THE ROMMEL FAMILY PAPERS.)

*Marital portraits taken before and after the galvanic achievement of the young Rommel's career: the winning of the Pour le Mérite, Prussia's highest honor.* (FROM THE ROMMEL FAMILY PAPERS.)

*Rommel at the Western Front in 1915. Auspiciously, he had a fox as a pet.* (FROM THE ROMMEL FAMILY PAPERS.)

*The Rommels' only child, Manfred, was born in 1928. When Hitler's war broke out, Rommel hardly had time to see his family.* (FROM THE ROMMEL FAMILY PAPERS.)

*September 30, 1934: the first meeting between Hitler and Rommel. Hitler visits Goslar, and Rommel (helmeted, at right) leads the honor guard.* (FROM THE ROMMEL FAMILY PAPERS.)

In the Polish campaign, Rommel commanded Hitler's headquarters. As officers report here to the Führer at Kielce airfield on September 12, 1939, Rommel finds himself between Hitler and the powerful Nazi party leader Martin Bormann. (U.S. NATIONAL ARCHIVES.)

Rommel's first panzer drive ended at Saint-Valéry, on the English Channel. A British division surrendered to him, and there was bitterness in the face of its commander, Major General Victor Fortune. (FROM THE ROMMEL FAMILY PAPERS.)

*Karl Hanke—a lieutenant in Rommel's panzer division but also one of the most powerful Nazis in the Goebbels propaganda ministry—reports to Hitler during the French campaign.* (U.S. NATIONAL ARCHIVES.)

*Rommel's troops arrive in Africa: on March 31, 1941, he and the Italian field commander, General Gariboldi, inspect the Afrika Korps.* (GERMAN OFFICIAL PHOTO, FROM THE ROMMEL FAMILY PAPERS.)

(RIGHT) *Rommel in Africa.* (ABOVE)
*His chief aide was Lieutenant Alfred
Berndt. He too was a top Nazi, often
dealing with Hitler in Rommel's be-
half.* (FROM FILM CAPTURED BY BRITISH
TROOPS; U.S. NATIONAL ARCHIVES.)

*Rommel's scribes: Interpreter Wilfried Armbruster* (TOP LEFT) *kept a private diary that is revealing about Rommel's operations; Albert Bottcher, Rommel's secretary* (TOP RIGHT) *, took down the Rommel diary in shorthand, now transcribed by the author; Hellmuth Lang* (RIGHT) *kept the Rommel diary in 1944.* (FROM GERMAN NEWSREEL FOOTAGE; ANTONIE BOTTCHER; HELLMUTH LANG.)

*Rommel and Fritz Bayerlein of the Afrika Korps confer between his Mammut command truck (left) and a Panzer III.* (FROM THE ROMMEL FAMILY PAPERS.)

*After the defeat, Christmas 1941: Rommel, General Alfred Gause, Colonel Siegfried Westphal and Major Friedrich Wilhelm von Mellenthin wait outside their headquarters for Italian generals to arrive.* (FROM BARON CONSTANTIN VON NEURATH.)

(LEFT) *Bayerlein with Rommel during the fighting at Kasserine.* (FROM AN ORIGINAL IN THE AUTHOR'S POSSESSION.) (RIGHT) *Major Wilhelm Bach, the ex-pastor who directed the heroic defense of the Halfaya Pass.* (FROM THE ROMMEL FAMILY PAPERS.)

*General von Bismarck, panzer division commander, studies the battle plan prepared by Rommel—whose lips are cracking in the sun.* (FROM THE ROMMEL FAMILY PAPERS.)

(TOP LEFT) *General Johannes Streich, who fell afoul of Rommel and returned to Germany.* (TOP RIGHT) *Lieutenant General Ludwig Crüwell, Rommel's successor as Afrika Korps commander. Captured by the British, he, like Thoma, talked volubly.* (LEFT) *In November 1942 the Afrika Korps commander General Wilhelm von Thoma surrendered to the British at El Alamein; some say he deserted.* (FROM JOHANNES STREICH; U.S. NATIONAL ARCHIVES; BRITISH OFFICIAL PHOTO.)

badly. Almost at once his troops had run into minefields of great density (his sappers later found 181,000 mines in this sector). The minefields were defended by stubborn infantry equipped with heavy machine guns, artillery and mortars. Worse still, at 2:40 A.M. the whole area was illuminated by parachute flares and a nonstop air attack began. The lead elements of the Panzer Army became firmly wedged in the minefields, exposed to the planes, while sappers worked feverishly to clear lanes ahead of them. Trucks, personnel carriers and tanks were hit and began to blaze fiercely. The fires and parachute flares lit the battlefield as bright as day. There were explosions, screams and the rattle of heavy machine guns. Evidently, Montgomery had been expecting the attack—and right here. General von Bismarck was hit by a mortar bomb. Minutes later a British fighter-bomber attacked Nehring's command truck: bomb fragments killed several of his staff, wrecked his radio and riddled Nehring himself. Bayerlein transferred to another vehicle and took temporary command of the Afrika Korps.

Rommel learned of all this only later, at 8:00 A.M., when he drove onto the battlefield. The first report was of the unexpected minefields, which had thrown his whole timetable out of joint. Then Corporal Böttcher registered in the diary: "8:05 A.M., second and third reports come in: Korps commander Nehring has been badly injured. General von Bismarck killed. C in C considers breaking off the battle." Rommel was obviously deeply shocked at this unexpected reverse, but when he met Bayerlein ten minutes later, the colonel announced triumphantly that both panzer divisions had now broken through to the far edge of the minefields—ahead of them lay open desert. Rommel still hesitated. At 8:35 A.M. he radioed to the divisions, "Wait for new orders." Bayerlein argued that to abandon the attack now would make a mockery of the sacrifices made by the men who had breached the enemy minefields. Rommel accepted this argument but introduced a fateful change of plan. Instead of advancing twenty miles due east, with the forbidding ridge of Alam el Halfa on his left, and then wheeling around it to take the enemy's main positions in the rear, the whole force would now turn much sooner and attempt to cross the ridge itself. At 9:16 A.M. the panzer division recorded the new objective: "Alam el Halfa."

When Kesselring flew forward to Bayerlein's command vehicle half an hour later, he was shocked at Rommel's sudden mood of despair. Böttcher recorded, "C in C South [Kesselring] is all for a vigorous continuation of the offensive!!!" The change of axis that Rommel had introduced was precisely the move that Montgomery had expected. Unknown to Rommel, the ridge at Alam el Halfa had been turned into a deathtrap for the Panzer Army. On that ridge Montgomery intended to destroy the Desert Fox's aura of invincibility once and for all.

Between 1:00 and 2:00 P.M., Rommel's tanks began rolling east again. A sandstorm had blown up, giving them a blessed protection from air attack. They made good progress until about four-thirty that afternoon, then wheeled to the north. This new axis took them into soft sand, and everything churned to a standstill at 6:00 P.M., as they faced Point 132—the most dominant feature on the ridge. Thus they had reached the killing ground.

The weather cleared, and the British tanks and artillery massed on the ridge opened fire. After dusk, the bombers came. It was sheer slaughter, but with only thirty miles' fuel supplies left—as the new Afrika Korps commander General von Vaerst bluntly told Rommel—they were stuck. They could not attempt to bypass the ridge to the east, where the going was far better, unless more fuel was brought up during the night.

All night long the slaughter went on. Rommel drove out at dawn, September 1, to watch: the cramped terrain was littered with the wreckage of his tanks; many were still burning. "The idea of continuing with the main offensive has been abandoned because of the grave fuel shortage," Böttcher entered in the diary. Two days before, the Italians had again promised 5,000 tons of gasoline. But now the tanker *Sanandrea* was sunk, with 2,411 tons, right outside Tobruk (and the next day the *Picci Fascio* would follow, with the loss of 1,100 tons). Small wonder that Rommel advised Berlin in a message to play down his new offensive, to avoid any later "setback" in public opinion.

That morning Rommel suffered six bombing attacks.

The air was unbreathable—hot, acrid with smoke and choked with fine sand. Lethal showers of shattered rock fragments added to the blast and shrapnel effects. "An eight-inch bomb fragment punched a hole clean through one of the shovels lying on the rim of his slit trench," wrote Böttcher in the diary. "The red-hot metal fragment landed on the C in C in the trench."

During the night the enemy air attack intensified. Armbruster tells us, "We have never experienced bombing before that was anything like last night. Although we were well dispersed on Hill 92, the bombs came very close. . . . Our combat echelon has had many men killed; three flak eighty-eights were hit and several ammunition trucks." Again bomb fragments fell right at Rommel's feet. Thirty feet away a Volkswagen burst into flames. By 8:25 A.M. he had had enough. He ordered the Panzer Army to retreat to its jump-off positions of August 30, withdrawing stage by stage.

Rommel's troops were speechless and astonished. "This morning," relates the history of the 104th Infantry Regiment, which was clinging to a shallow depression southwest of the ridge, "our drivers bring water forward to us. They tell us that Alam el Halfa has been taken, and that in two hours we'll be marching on. Already we are thinking of the Nile, the Pyramids and the Sphinx, of belly dancers and cheering Egyptians. About 1:00 P.M. our trucks arrive, and we load up. Then we drive off—to the west. To the west? . . . That was an end to our dreams of Cairo, the Pyramids and the Suez Canal!" The battle of Alam el Halfa was over.

At a dinner party in Alexandria, Montgomery announced to his distinguished foreign guests: "Egypt has been saved. It is now mathematically certain that I will eventually destroy Rommel."

When Kesselring arrived at Rommel's command vehicle at 5:30 P.M. that day, September 2, he was grim-faced and left the army commander in no doubt of the damage this setback would do to the Führer's grand strategy. Rommel heatedly explained why he had abandoned the attack, gave a vivid description of the enemy's terrifying air onslaught and demanded a "fundamental improvement of the supply situation." Kesselring privately believed that

Rommel was just using the supply shortage as an excuse to cover his own demoralization. As the armored divisions fought their way back to their starting line over the next few days, he found it hard to understand why the same gasoline could not have been used to prolong their attack—particularly since they would almost certainly have captured some of the enemy fuel dumps in the process. "It was this cast-iron determination to follow through that was lacking," Kesselring said after the war.

For years afterward, postmortems were held into the reasons for Rommel's failure. The main reason was Ultra —that is clear. But scarcely less important was Rommel's illness: he was too weary to see the battle through, even though the cards were stacked against him. "I was convinced at the time," wrote Kesselring, "that this battle would have been no problem for the 'old' Rommel—*he* would never have called it off when it had already succeeded in outflanking the enemy. Today I know that his troops never understood his order to retreat. Just think— he had already outflanked the British 'last hope' line of defense." From Waldau he heard rumors that the enemy's unexpected strength here actually caused Rommel to halt the attack at 8:00 A.M., only to renew it again a few hours later, thus forfeiting the element of surprise. The Rommel diary confirms that this was largely true.

In December of 1942 Hitler showed by his remarks that he was worried by Rommel's change of heart. "There's no doubt," he told General Jodl, "no doubt at all that he was quite wrong to have called off that offensive, probably under the influence of the sinking of the four-thousand-ton tanker. That's Kesselring's view too, and Ramcke shares it. He says, 'It was a mystery to us why he didn't go on with it. We had the British on the run again, we only had to pursue them and knock the daylights out of them.' I really do feel," continued Hitler, "that it's folly to leave a man too long in a position of grave responsibility. It's bound to get him down as time passes."

The victory that Montgomery had scored over Rommel was more psychological than material in nature. Rommel had marginally improved his own defensive line, by retaining the captured British minefields and commanding high ground at Qaret el Himeimat, which gave him a splendid view over Montgomery's southern flank. His casualties were not excessive—536 men killed, of whom 369 were German, and thirty-eight tanks; while the enemy, although well dug in and on the defensive, had lost sixty-eight aircraft, sixty-seven tanks and many more casualties. But the British could afford the losses, while Rommel could not. In particular, the six-day battle cost him 400 trucks—transport that he would sorely miss in November, as events would show. And British morale was now high.

On September 4 he arrived back at his old headquarters, peeled off his boots for the first time in a week and took a bath. He was weary—perhaps weary of war itself. He was impatient for his substitute to arrive, so he could get home and see his wife and son. He had not been with them for six months—young Manfred would soon be as tall as he. At his headquarters there were two letters waiting from Lucie, and a laboriously typed effort from thirteen-year-old Manfred. "Dear Daddy," it read. "Today I learned to type a bit. It isn't easy at all. Don't get mad at me for not writing to you by hand, because it's far harder with a typewriter. It's wonderful that you're coming home on leave. I'm looking forward to it immensely. I was looking at the *Frankfurt Illustrated* just recently and it stresses the way you set your men a good example. It says in the article that when the soldiers of your division in France were asked about the situation, they answered: 'No neighbor division on the right, nobody covering our left flank, nobody behind us—and Rommel out in front!' I sold off eight of my rabbits. I got eight Reichsmarks for them. I'm going to invest the money in fodder for more."

It was September 19 before Rommel's stand-in arrived. General Georg Stumme was a large, good-humored panzer warfare expert who positively relished the new climate here—at first. Kesselring found him more even tempered than Rommel and watched approvingly as Stumme set about repairing the bruised relations between Germans and Italians and between commanders and troops. Rommel briefed him extensively, and showed him the letters he had written appealing for reinforcements and supplies before Montgomery launched his main offensive—probably with the full moon in October.

Before he left for Germany at last on September 23,

Rommel also handed to Stumme the most inflexible instructions for the work still to be done on the El Alamein defenses. Since the line could not be outflanked, Montgomery would have to penetrate it frontally. To minimize the effect of enemy artillery and air bombardment, Rommel designed a defensive system of great depth. The main obstacle to the British troops would be a continuous line of mined boxes, each unoccupied but sown with thousands of mines and booby traps. The front face of this line would be guarded by battle outposts—one company from each infantry battalion. About 2,000 yards behind the boxes were the main infantry defenses. The larger and antitank guns were held well back, and behind them came the armored and mechanized divisions as a mobile reserve.

The mine belts became known as Rommel's "Devil's Garden." Most of the mines were big enough to break a tank track or wreck a truck, but 3 percent of them were of the deadly antipersonnel variety—triggered by trip wires or by being stepped on. Then they sprang into the air like a jack-in-the-box and burst, scattering steel pellets in all directions. Before Montgomery attacked, the Panzer Army laid 249,849 antitank and 14,509 antipersonnel mines. Together with the captured British minefields in the south, there were over 445,000 mines in Rommel's defense line.

Rommel's general tactical plan was to let the enemy attack bog down in his minefields, and then counterattack from the northern and southern ends of the line, trapping Montgomery's elite troops. "If the battle begins," he assured Stumme, "I shall abandon my cure and return to Africa."

*Among Corporal Böttcher's private papers I found a snapshot taken of Rommel leaving his tent on September 23, 1942, on his way back to Germany. He does not look ill —just very tired. That day, the British intercepted German signals revealing Rommel's departure. He saw Mussolini the next day; the Fascist dictator confidentially decided that Rommel's illness was psychological. An Ultra intercept of this estimate was eventually shown to President Frankin D. Roosevelt, who commented: "Rommel must have taken quite a knock. Up to now he has been accustomed to a diet of victories based on intelligence from inside the British camp which, thank God, we have now terminated." [Colonel Fellers had been repatriated from Cairo in July.]*

In Berlin, capital of Hitler's expanding Reich, the marshal was guest of the Goebbels household for several days. There is a full description in the unpublished diary of the propaganda minister. With the beautiful Magda Goebbels bustling around him, Rommel worked up the maps and calculations he would need to sway the Führer. Far into every night the family listened to his spellbinding descriptions of the fighting in Egypt. Gradually they thawed Rommel out of his reserve, until he was telling scornful stories about the Italian nobility and officers—relating one appalling detail after another about their "cowardice," about how they would desert to the first Australian or New Zealand troops they met. He told how he had so often escaped death or captivity himself, evoking squeals of admiring horror from Goebbels and his family. In return Goebbels showed him the newsreel films from North Africa. Before the family's eyes, new life and vitality flowed into Rommel as he relived Tobruk and the pursuit of the Eighth Army to El Alamein.

The Goebbels diary also reveals that he said a word to Hitler on September 29. He had known for some months that Hitler was considering making Rommel commander in chief of the entire German army after the war. Goebbels agreed: "A man like that certainly has what that job would take—laurels won on the field of battle, vitality, clarity of thought and the ability to seize the initiative."

*In Munich, Frau Anneliese Schmundt telephoned my hotel. She is the widow of Rudolf Schmundt, Hitler's chief adjutant, who was killed by the assassins of July 1944. It was ten years since I had first read her diaries and taken tea with her—a quiet, genteel East Prussian who has long put the bitterness of the past behind her. "You're looking into the life of Rommel," she said. "I met him only once—when he came to Berlin in the autumn of 1942. We had given a large dinner party, he phoned Rudolf, and of course Rudolf said he must come around. All the guests waited with excitement for the legendary Rommel to appear—and you know what? My son opened the door, Rommel asked what he had just been given for his birthday, my little boy said a train set, and they both went upstairs and played with it for the rest of the evening. He never came and met our guests at all."*

And so on the last day of September 1942, during one of Berlin's famous early autumn heat waves, Rommel marched smartly into Hitler's study at the Reich Chancellery and was handed the black leather case containing the glittering and bejeweled marshal's baton. Behind Hitler stood Keitel, his adjutant Schmundt and his assembled staff. Behind Rommel stood his own aide, Alfred Berndt, who, for the occasion, had exchanged his army uniform for that of the Nazi Party. At 6:00 P.M. Rommel was the guest of honor at a mass rally at the Berlin Sportpalast stadium. The newsreels showed him marching past the serried ranks of the Party and Wehrmacht to the tribune, being greeted by Hitler, wagging his baton and then raising his arm in something between a wave and the Nazi salute. Every radio station in the Reich carried Hitler's speech of praise for Rommel. He was at the very pinnacle of his achievements.

*Halfway along my research trail, I found the heavy metal baton unexpectedly in my hands, after I had expectantly opened the cardboard box lying at the bottom of the gray metal cupboard in the village in Swabia. It was from this same village that Rommel set out on his last motor journey, I reflected. Such power had once been symbolized by this rod! I remember being puzzled at the stiffly worded letters in army files from his last adjutant, Captain Hermann Aldinger, who was trying to establish what had happened to the cap and baton and demanding their immediate return to Lucie after that last journey. And I recalled the words used by the SS chauffeur that fateful day to describe how he found this very cap and baton lying on the floor of the car and tried to hand them over to his boss in Berlin, Hitler's hunchbacked personal aide, Julius Schaub. "Schaub said, 'I don't know anything about this . . . I want nothing to do with them!' " Schaub had re-*

*coiled from the baton as though it were infected by some plague.*

*But now, in my hands, it was lifeless and inert—like a stick of worn-out batteries—or obsolete, like a device designed to operate a machine that has long since gone out of manufacture. I wrapped the baton up again and returned it to its forgotten cupboard corner.*

Some days later Rommel wrote to Stumme about his meeting with Hitler. "Both the Führer and the Duce have agreed to my intention to hold on to the positions we have won in North Africa at present," he said, "and not to resume the attack until our troops have been thoroughly provisioned and refreshed and more forces have been sent out to us." Rommel added, "The Führer has promised me that he's going to see that the Panzer Army gets every possible reinforcement, and above all the newest and biggest tanks, rocket projectors and antitank guns." Rommel had also demanded huge numbers of rocket projectiles, the 260-millimeter mortar, the big new multiple-rocket projectors called the Nebelwerfer 42 and at least 500 smoke screen generators as well.

Rommel told Hitler of the crippling enemy air superiority, and he delivered a string of complaints about the Italians. Their officers and men were unready, he said, their tanks were too weak, their artillery unable to fire beyond five miles. Italian troops had no field kitchens and were frequently seen begging food and drink from their German comrades. "The Italians are a millstone around my neck," he said. "They're useless except for defense, and even then they're useless if the British infantry attacks with fixed bayonets."

No act of treachery was too mean for Rommel to blame on the Italians. Somehow the enemy had learned that he was ill—"no doubt through Rome." Captured British officers, he said, had told of an Italian who had betrayed Rommel's surprise attack at Alam el Halfa. He explained the sinking of all those ships bringing him gasoline by insisting that traitors in Italy must be signaling the shipping movements to the enemy. "The ordinary Italian soldiers are good," he now told his old friend Kurt Hesse. "Their officers are worthless. Their High Command are traitors."

He made a gesture of frustration. "Give me three shiploads of gasoline for my tanks—and I'll be in Cairo forty-eight hours later!"

The morning of October 3, at Goebbels' request, he attended a press reception for international journalists at the propaganda ministry. As Rommel stepped into the auditorium, all eyes were on him. Deliberately he stopped with his hand on the doorknob. Movie cameras began softly whirring. "Today," he calmly announced, "we stand just fifty miles from Alexandria and Cairo, and we have the door to all Egypt in our hands. And we mean to do something with it, too! We haven't gone all that way just to get thrown back again. You can take that from me. What we have, we hang onto."

At noon his plane left Berlin for Vienna and Semmering mountain, near Wiener Neustadt, where he was to begin his cure. A few hours later he was in the arms of Lucie at last.

# If I Don't Return

**T**WO-FORTY P.M., October 25, 1942. Beneath the low-flying Heinkel 111 bomber, the blue waves of the Mediterranean skim past in an endless blur. This is *DH-YA,* the Heinkel especially converted for Rommel's journeys. Lieutenant Hermann Giesen, the pilot, turns to his passenger and announces, "Landing at Crete in five minutes."

Rommel reflects on the extraordinary events of the last two days. Just twenty-four hours earlier he was convalescing at a mountain villa in Austria, with Lucie—far from the troops desperately fighting street by street for possession of Stalingrad, far from the bomb-torn cities of the Ruhr, far from Egypt. He was lazing, strolling, and reflecting, studying only statistical reports—such as those on the U.S. war effort—and the letters that General Georg Stumme sent him from the El Alamein front. Only yesterday he sent his young aide, Lieutenant Berndt, with letters down to Rome. Berlin and the General Staff were predicting a period of tranquility in Egypt. But at 3:00 P.M. the telephone suddenly rang in his villa. It was Berndt calling from Rome: "Montgomery's offensive has begun—last night! And General Stumme has vanished without a trace!"

All Rommel's lingering suspicions about his enemies in Rome were aroused. Why had they left him in the dark until now? He put through a telephone call to the Wehrmacht High Command. But almost at once they telephoned him instead, and he found Hitler on the line. The Führer's voice was gruff: "Bad news from Africa, Rommel. Nobody seems to know what's happened to Stumme." Rommel offered to fly out to El Alamein at once. "Are you sure you feel up to it?" asked Hitler. Rommel said he did. "Then stand by at Wiener Neustadt airfield," was Hitler's reply. "I'll find out how urgently they need you." Rommel kissed Lucie goodbye and drove to the airfield at once.

After that, silence. He waited at the airfield into the evening for further orders, until it was too dark for his Heinkel to take off. At about 8:30 P.M. the Wehrmacht headquarters in Vienna supplied him with the Panzer Army's latest situation report: Montgomery's main offensive had opened in the north, and it was expected to spread along the entire El Alamein front the next day. "General Stumme drove up front this morning, October 24, and was ambushed. He has been missing since 9:30 A.M., despite an all-out search. He must be presumed wounded and captured. General von Thoma has assumed command of the Panzer Army." Thoma was the new commander of the Afrika Korps—Rommel had yet to meet him.

In fact, Hitler was of two minds: Might it not be better for Germany to reserve Rommel for future employment on the Russian front, rather than rush him prematurely, still an invalid, back to Africa? At 9:00 P.M. he directed General von Rintelen, the senior German general in Rome, to obtain a fresh situation analysis by 3:00 A.M. to help him decide.

Desperate with worry about his "Africans," Rommel waited all night at the airfield for Hitler to telephone again. When he did, he said that the Panzer Army's verdict was that Montgomery's main offensive was about to begin, and that it would be a long, hard battle. Hereupon, according to the Rommel diary, "The Führer gave the C in C the specific order to return to his army immediately and resume command." Rommel's Heinkel took off at

7:50 A.M. and he flew into Rome at ten. Rintelen was waiting on the airfield—Field Marshal Kesselring had already flown down to the battlefield. Rintelen stunned Rommel with the news that the Panzer Army only had enough gasoline left for three days' battle.

Rommel shouted, "But when I left Africa, the army had eight days' gasoline in hand. And it *needed* at least thirty!"

Rintelen coughed apologetically. "You see, I've been on leave until a few days ago. Insufficient attention was paid to the supply situation in my absence."

Rommel raised his voice even more: "Then the Italians must use every possible means, including their submarines and navy, to rush supplies to the Panzer Army. They'll have to start right now." At 10:45 A.M. he was airborne again.

That was this morning. Now the airfield at Herakleion, Crete, is coming into view through the basketlike window frames of Rommel's Heinkel. It is 2:45 P.M. as he steps out, and the refueling tanker moves forward. General von Waldau—now commanding the Luftwaffe's Tenth Air Corps from here—is waiting on the runway. His face is somber as he hands the field marshal the latest messages from El Alamein. There have been heavy tank attacks by the British in both the northern and southern sectors. "In a renewed search of the terrain, the body of General Stumme has been recovered. Cause of death, heart failure."

As Rommel swings around to climb back aboard the Heinkel, Waldau checks him. "I cannot permit you to fly on a Heinkel in broad daylight—it's asking for trouble." Rommel borrows a sleek, modern Dornier 217 bomber instead of the slower plane and takes off for Egypt without further protest. The Dornier lands at the sand-swept airfield of Qasaba at five-thirty, where Rommel's Storch is waiting. He flies on east until the darkness forces him to land, and then he continues along the coast road by car. The horizon ahead is ablaze with the flash of bombs and artillery. Again and again he asks himself: *Has Stumme already lost the battle?* Then he is back at Panzer Army headquarters—the familiar faces, the operations bus, the same barren desert strewn with stones, the same stifling heat, the same scorpions and flies, the same lean, brave troops that he left just thirty-two days before.

At 11:25 P.M. that evening, October 25, his signal goes out to all of them. "I have taken command of the army again.—Rommel."

By the time Montgomery attacked it, Rommel's army was unequal to his in every respect and the British commander knew it. He had told his officers of "Rommell's" sickness, the depleted troop strengths and low food, gasoline and ammunition stocks. "You have all been trained to kill Germans," Montgomery had jotted in his speech notes. "So shoot tanks—and shoot Germans."

Each side had eight infantry divisions and four armored. But Rommel's were far below strength. The Fifteenth Panzer Division had only 3,294 men instead of 9,178, for example. Sickness had disabled 10,000 of Rommel's troops. For weeks his army had been on half rations because of the supply shortage; in the last week before Montgomery's attack, they had had no fats or fresh vegetables. Instead of 46,000 German army troops, the Panzer Army had only just over 29,000 that were combat fit. Montgomery's army numbered 195,000 men, and this crushing superiority was also displayed by his equipment. Rommel had only about 230 German tanks, as well as 320 Italian tanks not really worthy of inclusion in battle calculations. Facing him were Montgomery's 1,029 tanks—including 500 American-built Shermans, superior in armor and gunpower to the Panzer IV.

The revival of Malta and consequent harassment of Rommel's supply routes had devastated the Panzer Army's logistics. In full battle, his Panzer Army needed about 600 tons of gasoline every day; even on quiet days it required 300 tons for routine supply movements to the front. On October 13 Colonel Westphal—standing in as chief of staff for Bayerlein, who had also gone on leave— had written to Rommel that by the end of the month the stockpile would rise to ten "issues" of gasoline, each of them a day's supply. He, Stumme and Kesselring were all sure Montgomery's attack would fail. "While many things have not gone as we would have liked," Westphal's letter said, "you can be certain, *Herr Feldmarschall,* that if the British *do* attack in strength then we'll be ready and waiting for them. We're all itching to give the enemy a real thrashing. We only hope our supply lines don't let us down." And General Stumme had also written, in his spiky and cramped handwriting, "The Tommies are bound to attack—for political reasons they've got no choice. But they are none too happy about it. We're going to wipe the floor with the British."

This cockiness evaporated overnight on October 20. British aircraft and submarines, alerted by Ultra intercepts, had lain in wait for an Italian supply convoy and mauled it. The cruelest loss was the tanker *Panuco* with 1,650 tons of gasoline and cargo for Rommel—sunk by a Wellington bomber. A series of near hysterical radio signals to Rome had followed. Westphal demanded another tanker immediately and insisted on being told when it could put into Tobruk. Back by radio came the obligingly detailed reply, encoded as always on the "leakproof" Enigma machine: "Tanker *Proserpina* sailing evening 21st with 2,500 tons army gasoline, arriving Tobruk early 26th. Tanker *Luisiana* ready to sail with 1,500 tons army gasoline on 25th; if tanker *Proserpina* arrives, tanker *Luisiana* will sail with tanker *Portofino* from Taranto evening of 27th, put into Tobruk approximately 31st. *Portofino* has 2,200 tons army gasoline." When Rommel now arrived back, Westphal told him they were down to their last three issues of gasoline—and one of these was still 500 miles away at Benghazi.

In Berlin, the General Staff did not expect any major enemy attack at El Alamein in the immediate future— so Colonel Ulrich Liss, chief of Foreign Armies West, the intelligence branch concerned, personally assured General von Thoma as they toured the defense line early on October 23.

At nine-fifteen that evening, Montgomery's thunderous artillery bombardment of Rommel's Devil's Garden began.

*Corporal Albert Böttcher's shorthand text for the Rommel diary had ended abruptly on September 7—or so it seemed, as I laid aside the black exercise book in the archives in West Germany. But then during my research I stumbled on an intriguing reference to more shorthand pads, captured by the U.S. Army: "These shorthand notes were, it seems, kept by the adjutant of the German headquarters in North Africa. . . . Writer frequently refers to the OB—Commander in Chief—who is never mentioned by name." I flew to Washington, D.C., went to the Archives building, obtained the microfilm copy, and excitedly threaded it into a film reader. There was no doubt: this was also Böttcher's shorthand! One pad was temptingly headed, "Daily Reports, Pad I"—the title that Rommel had also given his diaries of 1943 and 1944. Until late that night I cranked the photostatic printer, and when I returned to London I had the entire 458 pages in my luggage: three shorthand pads covering El Alamein and Rommel's last months in Africa. The first pad began with October 23, 1942.*

*But what had become of Böttcher himself? His name is only a footnote in the works on Rommel. My search for him came literally to a dead end. A doctor in the little town where, I discovered, Böttcher had worked before the war in a small savings and loan bank, wrote: "A few years ago he committed suicide—he had a drinking problem."*

The Battle of El Alamein had been raging for exactly forty-eight hours when Field Marshal Rommel stepped back into his headquarters truck, late on October 25. The enemy artillery barrage was deafening. Rommel asked why their own guns had not shelled the British as they gathered for the offensive. Both General von Thoma —whom Rommel found to be gaunt, ascetic, pedantic and highly unlikeable—and Westphal explained that the late General Stumme had forbidden any such bombardment as an extravagance. This was a fateful error, in Rommel's view. It had enabled the enemy to overwhelm the outposts and capture German minefields much too cheaply.

Thoma's view was that the enemy were building up their main focus of attack in the north and that the heavy casualties the enemy had taken from the Panzer Army's artillery were forcing them to go cautiously. The enemy's intention was obviously to use infantry to prize open lanes through the minefields, under dense smoke screens, so that tanks could break through. Between the lanes lay an almost featureless patch of elevated ground, Hill 28, high enough to be of value as an artillery observation post. This hill fell to the British during the night.

"During the night there was again intense artillery fire," began the Rommel diary the next morning, October 26. "It merged eventually in one incessant roar of thunder. C in C slept only a few hours, and was already back at his operations truck by 5:00 A.M." He drove forward to watch the enemy's moves through field glasses. He could clearly see the enemy digging in on Hill 28. Over the next days he launched desperate counterattacks on this hill. "Rivers of blood were spilled over miserable strips of land which in normal times even the poorest Arab would never have bothered his head about," he later wrote.

He was convinced too that Montgomery's main breakout attempt was coming here in the north, and his diary shows him during the afternoon of October 26 moving reserves, including the Twenty-first Panzer Division and most of his artillery, from the southern sector—a major gamble, because the Panzer Army's gasoline was already so low that he could never move them back if his conviction should prove wrong. The consequence was that the next day, October 27, Rommel was able to thwart every attempt of the enemy to break through. The Rommel diary noted, "C in C once more ordered . . . the front line *must* be held."

He launched his main panzer and infantry counterattack on Hill 28 at 3:00 P.M. It was unsuccessful, and left the assault troops in coverless terrain where they were subjected to merciless air attack. Rommel returned to his command truck, sick with disappointment. "Nobody can ever know the burden that lies on me," he wrote dolefully to Lucie. "All the cards are stacked against us. Even so, I hope we can pull it off."

One tactical solution would have been to pull back a few miles—out of range of the enemy artillery—and then lure the enemy tanks into a pitched battle, where air power could not intervene to help the enemy either. But Rommel just did not have enough gasoline for that. He had been handed the shocking news that the tanker *Proserpina,* with 2,500 tons of army gasoline, had also just been sunk, followed by the transport ship *Tergestea* with 1,000 tons each of gasoline and ammunition.

Small wonder that he could not sleep that night, but was beset by nightmare images of all that he had watched through his field glasses.

"Dearest Lu," he wrote as soon as he got up the next morning, October 28. "Who knows whether I'll ever manage to write in peace to you, my darling, again. Today there is still this chance. The battle is raging. . . . But the enemy's superiority is crushing and our own resources are pitifully small. It lies in God's hands whether I survive, if this battle ends in our defeat. The lot of the vanquished is difficult to bear. To the best of my belief I have done all I could for victory. Nor have I spared my own person. If I should not return, I want to thank you and our boy for all your love and our happiness, from the bottom of my heart. I came to realize in those few short weeks what you two both mean to me. My last thought will be of you. After I am gone, you must bear the mourning proudly. In a few years Manfred will be a man and I hope he will always be a credit to our family."

After this, he issued a signal—timed 8:50 A.M.—to all his commanders in a scarcely more hopeful vein. He told them this was a battle of life and death, that orders were to be obeyed without question and that every one of them was to fight to the end. "Any soldier who fails or disobeys is to be court-martialed regardless of his rank." The commanders were instructed to memorize the order, then destroy it.

He was certain that Montgomery was about to make his main breakthrough attempt. "C in C decides to transfer still more German units from the southern sector to the north," recorded the Rommel diary, "leaving—apart from Italians—only weak German formations down there." By afternoon, he had seen a captured British map which confirmed that Montgomery's intention was to breach the main defense line near the northern end, then wheel northward to the coast at El Daba. When Rommel drove forward, he could see through his field glasses the enemy massing tightly in the wedge that had been hammered at such cost into the German minefields. At 9:00 P.M. a thunderous artillery barrage began, and at ten the big offensive commenced.

These assault troops north of Hill 28 were General Leslie Morshead's veteran Ninth Australian Division— the force that had cheated Rommel of Tobruk in April 1941. As Rommel had anticipated, this attack was driven farther into the minefields, northward toward the coast. Opposing it was the second battalion of the 125th Panzer-Grenadier Regiment, which fought with unparalleled heroism all night; moreover, here Rommel had installed a powerful screen of antitank guns. By dawn the Australian attack had been halted. Later that morning, October 29, Montgomery was having to rethink his strategy.

What Rommel did not know in his black depression, was that this was also a day of gloom at Montgomery's headquarters. After five days and nearly 10,000 killed and injured, the British frontal assault seemed no nearer the strategic breakthrough than before. In London, Churchill tackled General Alan Brooke, chief of the Imperial General Staff: "Why did Montgomery tell us he would be through in seven days, if all he intended to do was fight a halfhearted battle? Have we not got one single general who can win one single battle?" He announced ominously that he would call a meeting of the Chiefs of Staff at midday. At the meeting, Brooke claimed that Montgomery was really winding up for a new and even bigger attack; but this was pure facade, because Brooke realized that for all he knew Montgomery might in fact be licked. In his office afterward, Brooke paced up and down. "The loneliness of those moments of anxiety," he wrote in his memoirs, "when there is no one one can turn to, have to be lived through to realize their intense bitterness. . . . It was fortunate that on that day I had not yet received a letter from Monty which arrived a few days later telling me what his feelings were at this juncture of the battle . . ."

In Egypt, Rommel is also pacing up and down, silently cursing the Italians and racking his brains for a way of surviving the coming crash. His battle headquarters has been moved some miles to the rear, but he has been on the battlefield all night, watching the heavy air raids, the parachute flares and the fireballs of artillery. At 3:30 A.M.

he goes for a stroll in the darkened desert, to clear his mind: *The British can repeat this display of brute force as often as they wish,* a voice inside him argues. *They can destroy my army battalion by battalion until there is nothing left. However many British tanks and troops I kill, the balance will still tilt each day more against us.* Thirty minutes later, as the first grayness of dawn fingers the horizon, enemy fighter-bombers roar overhead.

One thing is clear to Rommel: If and when the British do break through, his army will be encircled and exterminated if it stays here—because he can never withdraw his heavy equipment and the largely unmotorized Italian infantry at short notice to a new line. At 6:00 A.M., bleary-eyed with lack of sleep, he drives out to a nearby hill. He can distantly make out the wrecks of the enemy tanks knocked out during the night, but the sight does not inspire him. In fact his army has just won a four-day breathing space, but Rommel considers the battle already lost; when Bayerlein reports back from his furlough at 7:00 A.M., the field marshal admits it quite bluntly. Four hours later comes the last straw for Rommel—the tanker *Luisiana*, with 1,459 tons of gasoline, has also been sunk outside Tobruk.

It is significant that Rommel carefully conceals from his Italian superiors his developing plan to retreat to a new line. Indeed, he tells General Barbasetti at noon: "It will be quite impossible for us to disengage from the enemy. There's no gasoline for such a maneuver. We have only one choice, and that is to fight on to the end at Alamein." But Rommel has already red-penciled a new line on his map: it is sixty miles west of the inferno of El Alamein. His diary this day, October 29, proves all this: "2:45 P.M.: C in C enlarges over lunch on his plan to prepare a line for the army at Fuka, to fall back on when the time comes, now that the northern part of the Alamein line is no longer in our hands. 4:00 P.M.: C in C discusses the plan with Colonel Westphal." That same afternoon, Rommel orders all noncombat troops to start moving back to Mersa Matruh—far to the west even of Fuka. Rommel has thereby furtively begun to retreat.

*"Rommel was not devious!"* insisted Siegfried Westphal when I met him in October of 1975, a handsome, ex-four-

*star general living in luxurious retirement in northern Germany. He angrily thumped the polished dining table, so that the crystal glassware and silver rattled. "Of course Rommel had a perfect right to retreat from Alamein, as and when he wished, without informing or consulting the OKW or Hitler!"*

*I disagreed, pointing out that however sound and inevitable Rommel's decision later proved to have been, the consequences were bound to be more than local. It was a strategic decision of the first magnitude, and as such not one to be taken by Rommel alone and concealed from his superiors. It proved impossible to persuade Westphal that Hitler's mistrust of Rommel stemmed from this episode. Westphal is an officer so loyal now to the memory of Rommel that where his present memory conflicts with the diaries of 1942, he unhesitatingly pronounces his version right and the diaries wrong.*

The relative lull in the ground fighting lasted through the last two days of October 1942. Rommel got some sleep, his spirits lifted and he even began to hope he might pull through after all. An Italian ship had arrived safely with 600 tons of gasoline—one day's ration. Field Marshal Kesselring also came on the thirtieth, bringing fresh promises of airlift support—Luftwaffe transport squadrons were beginning to arrive from the Russian front. Rommel expressed his distress to Lucie the next day: "It's a tragedy that this sort of support only starts when things are virtually hopeless."

Late on October 30, the Australian infantry wedged into Rommel's northernmost sector caused a minor flap by thrusting toward the coast again. Thirty enemy tanks duly reached the coast road, but Rommel stopped any further exploitation. His forces took 200 Australians prisoner and destroyed over a score of their tanks. Cavallero radioed to him Mussolini's "deep appreciation" of the local victory, and his confidence that Rommel was going to win the battle too. Rommel was less sure. "The fight is getting on my nerves," he tersely admitted to Lucie.

All this time he was stealthily preparing for the Panzer Army's sudden retreat—he was casting the fatal "backward glances" that no commander should ever allow himself in battle. On October 31 he tipped off those combat units like Ramcke's paratroop brigade that had no motor transport, about the Fuka plan. The next morning his artillery commander General Fritz Krause returned from a secret inspection of the proposed Fuka line: it was ideal —steep declivities at its Qattara end would make it impossible for Montgomery to outflank it. A retreat timetable was worked out, and provisional positions in the line were allocated on the map.

Ironically, now that Rommel had decided on retreat, the Panzer Army had 1,200 tons of gasoline and more was arriving each day. Even ammunition was evidently plentifully on hand in the rear. In March 1943 Kesselring sarcastically told another general, "I still recall how there was a permanent outcry during the Battle of Alamein that they had no ammunition—and when they retreated, *twelve thousand tons* of it had to be blown up!" What Rommel's army lacked now was truck transport, and more than that, it lacked morale.

There could be no doubt that night, November 1–2, that Montgomery's grand slam was beginning. At about 10:00 P.M., 200 guns began a barrage on one narrow sector of Rommel's defenses, while wave after wave of heavy bombers pounded the same sector and targets in the rear. All that long, cold night the field marshal could see parachute flares hanging over the desert. Thoma's Afrika Korps headquarters was hit—all his telephone lines were cut and he himself was slightly injured; the radio waves were jammed and useless. At 5:00 A.M. the next day Rommel drove forward to find out what was happening. The news was that at 1:00 A.M. massed tanks and infantry had broken into the defense system west of Hill 28 on a 1,000-yard-wide front and were pushing remorselessly through the minefields in an attempt to break out. A bloody battle was still raging in the semi-darkness there, but the German and Italian infantry holding that sector were outnumbered and outgunned.

As daylight came, Rommel could see scores of enemy tank hulks in the minefields, but behind them hundreds more were lining up to roll forward into the breach. Scores of enemy armored cars had actually broken right through, like the first spray of water from the fissures that mark the bursting of a dam; they had vanished in the predawn light behind Rommel's lines, where even now they were rampaging around, shooting up soft-skinned supply units. Then the dam burst. At 11:00 A.M. the phone rang, and the long-expected message came to Rommel: "Tank masses have broken through, one or two miles southwest of Hill 28, and are advancing westward." The Rommel diary adds, "Afrika Korps estimates 400 enemy tanks here. Our own panzer strength only meager after counterattacks. According to reports of artillery observers, there are about 4–500 more tanks standing by beyond the mine boxes J and K."

Rommel grabbed a hasty meal—chicken fricassee with rice—then left to fight what was to prove the last great desert tank battle of his career. Lieutenant Armbruster watched him go, and wrote: "Today will probably decide the outcome. Poor Rommel, he has to shoulder too much responsibility and there's so little he can do. Accursed gang in Rome! Pray God we pull it off."

Many times Rommel surveyed the battle from a hill. He snatched a few minutes to write to Lucie: "Things are not going well for us. The enemy is gradually battering us out of our position by sheer brute force. This means the end. You can imagine what kind of mood I'm in. Air raids and still more air raids." Between noon and 1:00 P.M. he counted seven attacks by bomber formations on the remaining defenses west of Hill 28. Despite its Red Cross insignia, the big Field Hospital 288 was bombed, killing three officers. The Rommel diary records that he ordered British officers to be housed there as hostages: "This is to be drawn to the enemy's attention."

At 1:30 P.M. his radio intelligence unit intercepted a signal revealing that Montgomery's directive to his tanks was to turn northeast toward the coast at Ghazal (halfway to El Daba) so as to cut off Rommel's forces north of that thrust. Rommel immediately decided to strip his southern front of his last reserves: he ordered the Italian armored division Ariete and the rest of his artillery to move northward to Tell el Aqqaqir, which was evidently Montgomery's interim objective.

All afternoon the battle continued. The enemy's main tank forces were using American-built tanks, and greatly to the Germans' dismay, there were several hundred of a type not seen before—the Sherman. It was much superior even to the Panzer IV. It was able to open fire at ranges well over 1,000 yards, while its armor seemed impervious even to the flak eighty-eight gun.

By 3:30 P.M. Rommel had seen enough. He had decided to start pulling back his front line that night; he announced his decision to his staff an hour later. "We will hold a combat line on the Rahman Track," his diary quoted. "C in C regards a withdrawal to the Fuka line as inevitable, since the entire northern sector of the Alamein line has been lost, including all our minefields and defense works there."

He reserved his final decision until General von Thoma telephoned him that evening about the battle. "We have done what we can to string together some kind of defense," said Thoma. "The line is intact again, but thin. And tomorrow we'll have only thirty or at most thirty-five tanks fit for action." He added, "There are no more reserves."

Only thirty-five tanks! That clinched it for Rommel. He told Thoma, "My plan is for the whole army to fall back to the west, fighting. The foot units will start their move tonight. Your job in the Afrika Korps will be to stand firm until tomorrow morning, and then fall back fighting, but as slowly as possible to give our infantry a chance to escape." At 7:00 P.M. Rommel asked for the latest ammunition and gasoline positions; both were "bleak." Krause, his artillery commander, warned him, "I don't even have enough gasoline to transport ammunition from El Daba to the battlefront."

Twenty minutes later, Rommel's staff began telephoning advance orders for the retreat. By 9:05 P.M. the last unit of his Panzer Army had the order.

The teletypes that confirmed these telephone messages all began with the same words—"Under superior enemy pressure, the army is preparing to withdraw, step by step, while still fighting." The distance between these clear, brisk signals and the convoluted and verbose signal Rommel sent to Rome for both High Commands at midnight leaves only one conclusion possible: that he intended to conceal his retreat as long as possible from Hitler and

Mussolini. An interim report that he had sent off that afternoon made no mention of his intention at all. As a first stage, during darkness the Tenth Corps infantry would fall back from the Himeimat ridge to the old line occupied before the battle of Alam el Halfa; while the Twenty-first Corps infantry would begin a similar withdrawal in the center. The main retreat the next day would be screened by Rommel's armor—with the Twentieth Corps on the right, the Afrika Korps in the center and the Ninetieth Light Division on the left.

At what time the Italian High Command found out, in Rome, is not certain. Rommel had made thorough arrangements with Barbasetti, in Libya, to lend him truck transport that evening to help evacuate the Italian infantry (Barbasetti let him down). But Cavallero's first information came from Colonel Mancinelli, his liaison officer on Rommel's staff. Cavallero at once radioed him: "Please inform Marshal Rommel that Duce considers it imperative to hold present front at all costs. . . . Supplies are coming by both sea and air, speeded up by every means at our disposal." This signal did not leave Rome until 11:00 A.M. the next day. From his diary it is evident that Cavallero believed Rommel still had over 250 tanks left and all the gasoline and ammunition he needed. "It's his battle!" he had rasped to Kesselring and Rintelen late on November 2.

The unhelpful interim report that Rommel had sent that afternoon reached the High Command in East Prussia some hours later. General Jodl read it out to Hitler. It stated:

Despite today's defensive success, the army's strength is exhausted after ten days of tough combat against immensely superior British ground and air forces. The army will therefore no longer be capable of impeding the strong enemy tank formations expected to repeat their breakthrough attempt tonight or tomorrow. For want of motor transport it will not be possible for the six Italian and two German nonmotorized divisions to withdraw in good order. A large part of these units will probably be overrun by the enemy's mechanized formations. But even our mechanized troops are engaged in such heavy fighting that only part will be able to disengage from the enemy. . . . In this situation the gradual destruction of the army must therefore be assumed to be inevitable despite the heroic resistance and exemplary spirit of the troops. Sgd. Rommel, Field Marshal.

At about the same time, in that quiet country house in England, Rommel's signal was fed into the decoding machine. A teleprinter typed out his cri de coeur. Experts translated and analyzed it—of course, it made no mention of his planned withdrawal—and a few hours later the man called "C," the chief of the British Secret Service, read it out over the scrambler telephone to Churchill and the select few officials allowed to know anything Ultra Secret. A high official at the Foreign Office wrote in his diary: "C. had news, which he phoned to me this morning, which certainly seems to show Rommel is in a fix. I am inclined to think that R. is crying wolf to get more help sent him. But this certainly looks good . . ."

Toward midnight, Hitler himself telephoned one of Jodl's staff officers at the High Command compound: "Is there any further news from Rommel?" The colonel said there was not. "Then telephone Rintelen in Rome," Hitler demanded, "and find out." An hour later the colonel telephoned Hitler back: "Rommel's final daily report has arrived in Rome. It's being decoded now and put on the wire to us. It repeats what he said in the interim report, virtually." Greatly relieved, Hitler went to bed.

At 8:30 A.M. next day, November 3, Field Marshal Keitel galloped into Hitler's bunker and insisted on seeing the Führer. In great agitation he handed over the teleprinter copy of Rommel's midnight report. Near the end of it Rommel had surreptitiously buried his admission that his army had actually begun to retreat: "The infantry divisions are accordingly already being withdrawn during the night of November 2–3," it said. The sentence poleaxed Hitler. Keitel explained that his night duty officers had not noticed this key sentence and had filed the teletype with routine papers. A few minutes later Rommel's routine *morning* report was also in Hitler's hands. It announced that the infantry withdrawal was going "according to plan."

Hitler clutched his head. His frustration and anger at this unexpected turn of events in Egypt were vented at Jodl's administrative deputy, General Walter Warlimont. "At this critical moment, Rommel turned to me and the fatherland," he proclaimed melodramatically. "We should have been a source of inspiration to him. If I had been awakened, I would have taken the full responsibility and ordered him to stand fast. But our Mr. Warlimont is snug asleep, while Rommel is appealing to me." He dictated an immediate message to be radioed to Rommel—one of the most famous signals of the war:

With me the entire German nation is watching your heroic defensive battle in Egypt, with well-placed confidence in your leadership qualities and in the courage of your German and Italian troops. In your situation there can be no thought but to persevere, to yield not one yard, and to hurl every gun and every fighting man available into the battle. Considerable air reinforcements are being transferred over the coming days to C in C South [Kesselring]. The Duce and his High Command will also do their utmost to furnish you with the means to keep up the fight. Superior they may be, but the enemy are surely also at the end of their strength. It would not be the first time in history that willpower has triumphed over the stronger battalions of an enemy. To your troops therefore you can offer only one path —the path that leads to Victory or Death. Sgd. Adolf Hitler.

At 11:05 A.M. Jodl telephoned Hitler's signal personally to Rintelen's adjutant in Rome. At 11:30 A.M. it was on its way from there via Enigma code to Egypt. Shortly, it was being rushed to Churchill in London too—"Hitler has ordered his troops to choose between Victory or Death!"

Again Rommel had not slept. Since 6:30 P.M. on November 2, his troops had been under a terrifying air attack—with over 1,000 bombs per square mile. He lay in his truck, hearing the ceaseless roar of vehicle engines as men and materiel began pulling out of the battle zone. Berndt dictated into the Rommel diary: "By evening countless trucks and tanks of the Littorio Armored Division, packed with troops, are visible on the road as they make their individual ways back. Afrika Korps reports that Littorio is no longer under officer control—it has just burst at the seams. Elements of it are in full flight. There are similar symptoms reported in the infantry of the Trieste Mechanized Division."

"The battle is going heavily against us," Rommel wrote to Lucie in the morning, November 3. "We're just being crushed by the enemy's weight. I've tried to salvage a part of my army—I wonder if I'll succeed. . . . The dead are lucky—for them it's all over. I think of you both constantly with heartfelt love and gratitude. Perhaps fate will be merciful and we can see each other again."

He told his staff that until the new line at Fuka was ready to occupy, he proposed to fight a running battle. He had only just enough gasoline for that. Still more supply ships had been sunk. Then at 9:00 A.M. he drove forward along the coast road to his command post, leaving Colonel Westphal to mind the shop at Panzer Army headquarters. Lieutenant Armbruster sat with Rommel: "Colossal westbound traffic on the road," he penciled in his own diary. "But the battlefront has quieted down. By 11:00 A.M. the Tommies still haven't noticed we're moving out." Indeed, Montgomery's artillery was still pounding the Tenth Corps's Himeimat ridge positions, which had been abandoned several hours before. But at eleven-thirty murderous air attacks began on the coast road—by this time jammed with bumper-to-bumper, hub-to-hub convoys of trucks.

He spent the morning at the artillery command post. The photos show him standing wearily in his open Volkswagen, his tunic creased and paunchy, his head sunk, his face morose. Colonel Bayerlein reported that the Afrika Korps had only thirty-two tanks left, confronting their tormentors in an open semicircle facing east near the Rahman Track. General von Thoma told him by telephone that there were about 100 enemy tanks—including the awesome Shermans—lying wrecked in front of his guns already, so the Afrika Korps was not going out without a struggle.

Rommel drove back to his headquarters bus. He lunched silently with Westphal, inside the bus. At 1:30 P.M. Major Elmar Warning, one of Westphal's staff, climbed into the bus with a paper in his hand and gave it to Rommel. Hitler's famous radio signal had arrived— the signal that ended: "To your troops therefore you can offer only one path—the path that leads to Victory or Death." As Rommel read this signal his mind fused. Something between rage and panic gripped him. Only ninety minutes earlier he had issued still more orders to his troops to retreat; he himself had seen the chaos on the roads, as Italians and Germans jostled to get away from the carnage of El Alamein. But now Hitler had specifically forbidden any withdrawal. What was he to do? Over the next hour he drafted countless replies— Westphal recalls one as saying, for example, "Mein Führer, I will obey as always. But I cannot reconcile blind obedience with my own sense of responsibility . . ." But they were not transmitted. Rommel was trapped between his loyalty to the Führer and the realities of the crisis on the battlefield.

At 2:28 P.M. he telephoned General von Thoma, his Afrika Korps commander. Thoma reported, "I've just been around the battlefield. Fifteenth Panzer's got ten tanks left, Twenty-first Panzer only fourteen and Littorio seventeen."

Rommel tersely replied: "You are to fight on to the very utmost." He read out the Hitler signal, gave Thoma authority to issue direct orders to the tanks of Ariete too, and repeated: "You have got to instill this order into your troops—they are to fight to the very limit."

Thoma saw this as a reliable recipe for complete disaster and suggested withdrawing the tanks to regroup, as he put it.

Rommel shouted into the telephone: "No—the Führer's order is, we are to stand fast to the utmost. There's to be no retreat."

Thoma hesitated. "All right," he agreed, "that is our broad policy. But we must make *minor* withdrawals."

Rommel approved this formula. But the signals that

he issued during the afternoon to the Panzer Army's scattering units still ordered them to hold existing positions on "instructions from the highest level," and that left them no room for maneuver at all.

Rommel's staff, particularly Bayerlein, strongly deprecated this, but the field marshal had not yet learned to disobey a specific order from the Führer. More precious hours were lost while he radioed Hitler a stark account of their plight. "Casualties to German troops in infantry, antitank and engineer units so far run to about 50 percent, and in artillery to about 40 percent. Afrika Korps now down to only twenty-four tanks. Littorio Armored and Trieste Mechanized divisions of Twentieth Corps have been virtually wiped out." To add personal emphasis to this, at 4:30 P.M. he packed off Lieutenant Berndt on the long flight to East Prussia, to persuade Hitler to revoke the disastrous order. Berndt, as a Party official, would be more likely to get a hearing than an army staff officer. Rommel also gave him secret documents to carry to safety in Wiener Neustadt first—his plane would touch down there on its way to Hitler's headquarters.

Apprehensive that his army's inevitable retreat might be construed as open disobedience, at 6:40 P.M. Rommel meanwhile appealed to his commanders: "I demand that you do everything within human powers to bring the present battle to a victorious conclusion by remaining master of the battlefield." When he telephoned Thoma's chief of staff, he rubbed it in: "The Führer's order rules out any kind of fluid defense." He rejected the Korps's proposed new line, and declaimed: "I insist that you hold on where you are—it's vital."

He regarded his army and himself as doomed, as is plain from what he had just written to Lucie. "I can no longer, or scarcely any longer, believe in a successful outcome. What will become of us is in God's hands. Farewell, you and the lad . . ." Into the envelope he tucked all the money he had saved—25,000 Italian lire, or about sixty dollars, and asked Berndt to make sure the letter reached her safely.

*In Munich, I found Elmar Warning, the member of Westphal's staff who handed Hitler's Victory-or-Death*

*message to Rommel. He is now sixty-nine, an interna-
tional banker, a towering man, six and a half feet tall,
with broad shoulders and well-groomed dark hair. In a
sonorous voice that boomed around the oak panels of his
study, he told me about the agony of decision confronting
Rommel that night. "I could see him pacing up and down
in the blackness of the desert near the bus," said Warning. "Westphal called me over: 'Go and keep the field
marshal company. I'm too busy.' So I joined him for two
hours, and we just walked up and down while he battled
with the decision whether or not to resume the retreat.
'If we stay put here,' Rommel said, 'then the army won't
last three days.' And after a while: 'But do I have the
right as C in C, or even as a soldier, to disobey an order?'
And then after more brooding: 'If I do obey the Führer's order, then there's the danger that my own troops
won't obey me.' After that, he exclaimed, 'My men's lives
come first!'*

*"It was on this occasion that he first said: 'The Führer
is crazy . . .' "*

Armbruster had at this point stepped into Berndt's job
and become the writer of the Rommel diary. When he
reached the operations bus at 5:20 A.M., November 4,
Rommel had just arrived too. The irony was that the
battlefront had been quiet for several hours—so had
Rommel ignored Hitler's order, the mass of the Panzer
Army would by now be safely ensconced in the new line
at Fuka. But he had obeyed the order, and fate now
took its course. At 7:25 A.M. Field Marshal Kesselring
arrived—summoned by Rommel's staff from Rome the
afternoon before to give moral support. He had been delayed overnight by engine failure on Crete. ("What I
achieved on November 4 would have been of the greatest,
perhaps even decisive, importance one day earlier,"
Kesselring later said, reproaching himself.) Initially, as
is clear from his remarks to Waldau at Crete, he had intended to insist on obedience to Hitler's order. "The Führer's thinking is naturally governed by the Russian
campaign," he explained to Rommel now, "and his experience in Russia has taught him that clinging obstinately to

existing and well-built positions has always been the best thing to do."

But when Kesselring learned that Rommel was now down to only twenty-two battle tanks, he revised his view at once. (There is a transcript of their discussion among Rommel's papers.) "I would be inclined to regard Hitler's signal as an appeal, rather than a binding order."

Rommel was horrified: "I regard the Führer's directive as absolutely binding."

"You must act as the situation demands," Kesselring argued. "The Führer certainly cannot have intended your army to perish here."

"It came just like a bolt out of the blue," Rommel said bitterly. "And I always thought that the Führer trusted me." He would like most now to stage a fighting withdrawal—"But only if the Führer expressly alters his order to me."

Kesselring advised him to radio Hitler immediately: "Say that with your forces decimated and vastly outnumbered, the line cannot be held and the only chance of retaining at least a part of Africa lies in a fighting retreat." Kesselring promised to send a message to Hitler himself.

Rommel did send such a telegram to Hitler. Meanwhile, for several hours he adhered to the stand-fast order. When he learned at 11:00 A.M. that Trento and Bologna were in full flight, he ordered the Italian officers to force their troops back into battle again. Air reconnaissance detected that the Italian Tenth Corps infantry was also falling back; he repeated the order. Not long after, he had to remind the Twentieth Corps, "Your positions are to be held to the utmost." By this time he had driven forward to the Afrika Korps command post, in a dugout near the twelve-foot-high sand dune called Tell el Mamfsra. From it, he could see enormous dust clouds towering into the autumn sky to the south and southeast, where the tanks of the Ariete Division were in their death throes.

Colonel Bayerlein came to the dugout at 12:55 P.M. He told Rommel that General von Thoma had put on all his medals, denounced the orders to stand fast as "lunacy" and driven off in a tank to the focus of the battle.

Bayerlein had driven after him an hour later and found a cemetery of blazing tanks, corpses and wrecked anti-tank guns. From 200 yards away he had seen the general's tall, gaunt figure standing erect near a flaming tank, his little canvas satchel in his hand, as the British tanks converged on him. From Bayerlein's description, Rommel and Westphal were in no doubt that Thoma had deliberately deserted to the British. Westphal exclaimed, "For God's sake, Bayerlein, keep it to yourself—otherwise Thoma's entire family will have to suffer for it." Soon after, Rommel's radio monitors heard a British unit reporting: "We've captured a German general. He says he is von Thoma." That left no doubt as to the Afrika Korps commander's fate.

*I put all this episode to General Westphal. He revealed to me what the war diaries tactfully do not—that in a later operation Rommel's troops captured British documents, among them an intelligence summary of the British Eighth Army which reported that Thoma had accepted Montgomery's "chivalrous" invitation to dine with him that evening and had made no secret of Rommel's further plans and dispositions in their subsequent conversation. "Rommel never did like that general," reflected Westphal.*

Still Rommel's order to stand fast was obeyed. At three-thirty that afternoon Ariete's last signals were picked up —the plucky Italian armored division had fought to the point of self-immolation. A breach twelve miles wide had now been ripped in the tottering Axis line. The entire Twentieth Corps had virtually ceased to exist. Without waiting for word from Hitler, Rommel now took his fate in both hands. He ordered the retreat.

At 8:50 P.M. Hitler approved it anyway. "In view of the way things have gone," he sourly instructed the field marshal in a signal that reached him only the next day, "I approve your request."

Thus began a harrowing retreat for Rommel's 70,000 men—a 2,000-mile odyssey. How many men would complete it?

# Humiliation

A week passes before Germany officially learns that Rommel's army is in retreat. A week passes before Rommel even writes home. On November 9, 1942, his secretary Corporal Böttcher types a four-word message ("I am all right") for Lucie, and the field marshal scribbles his name beneath it. The next day, Rommel finally writes her a letter: "Since the enemy's breakthrough at Alamein I didn't get around to writing. . . . When an army gets broken through, it gets a raw deal. You've got to fight your way out, and you lose the rest of your fighting power in the process. Things can't go on like this much longer, because we're being pursued by a superior enemy."

Few circumstances gnaw at the marrow of an army so insidiously as retreat. Yet Rommel will now show his great cunning in adversity. Reeling with sickness and bouts of fainting, he carries his 70,000 German and Italian troops across hundreds of miles of North Africa's harsh desert coastline, through the blistering heat of tropical day and the rainstorms and freezing nights. His sixty-mile-long procession of tanks, guns, personnel carriers, trucks and cars is subjected to merciless air attack throughout. For days on end the entire movement is paralyzed by lack of fuel, while Rommel's loyal veterans fight desperate rearguard actions though thirsting for water and starving for food. The weeks become months, but then the green hills and forests of Tunisia come into view, stabbing Rommel with pangs of nostalgia for his native Swabia. "Your retreat has been a masterpiece, Field Marshal!" Mussolini congratulates him.

The Rommel diary is complete for these dramatic months. He makes the same mistakes that he has always made. He overestimates the enemy's strength. He transmits frantic inquiries about shipping movements—never realizing the direct causal link between his own Enigma-coded signals and the sinkings. He clashes violently with the Luftwaffe and the Italian High Command for failing to protect the supply ships. For their part, the Italians accuse him of deliberately abandoning their infantry divisions, and of purloining Italian trucks to rescue German troops from the wreckage of the El Alamein line. They suspect Rommel of plotting to pull out of Africa completely.

The German High Command also mistrusts Rommel. He is seen as disobedient, willful, deceptive and defeatist. He hotly denies these allegations, but his intimate letters and remarks vividly portray that his mind is in commotion. He writes on November 12, for instance, "All our work in this theater has been for nothing. I've made a super-human effort, that's true enough. But for it all to end like this is very bitter." And on the fourteenth: "How far we'll get, I just can't say. . . . How will the war end? I only wish I could rid myself of these terrible thoughts."

By mid-December, Erwin Rommel is writing secretly to Lucie to send him an English-German dictionary by courier. "I think it's going to come in very handy."

Lieutenant Alfred Berndt had reached Lucie's house in Wiener Neustadt on the afternoon of the fourth of November. He handed over Rommel's suitcase of secret papers and his letter. She was still in shock at eleven that evening, when she sat down to write to him. She could not believe what she had heard, it was all like some bad dream. "How can the Lord have deserted us in our hour of need?" she asked him. But she was glad that her husband had somebody solid like Berndt to lean on—loyal and upright, "every inch the kind of National Socialist the Führer wants us all to be." When Berndt returned to her from seeing Hitler, he hinted that the Death-or-Victory signal had been some kind of misunderstanding. Lucie handed him a parcel of fresh-baked cakes to take to her husband, to remind him of his home and family during the coming weeks of travail.

In Germany, everybody waited with her for the news from Africa. Joseph Goebbels reassured his staff at a secret conference on the sixth, "We just have to hope that Field Marshal Rommel will master this situation as he has so many others before."

By that time the Desert Fox had already eluded the first traps set by the fumbling and overapprehensive pursuing enemy. His own headquarters unit had moved off after dusk on November 4. The coastal highway to their right was ablaze with burning trucks and the glare of sky flares, but most of his troops were driving across open desert too. Montgomery tried to outflank him by short, tight turns, but each time the British reached the coastal road they found the bird had already flown and they had encircled nothing. By the early hours of the sixth, Rommel was driving through darkness toward Mersa Matruh, Arab villages looming up and dropping behind in the darkness. But in the morning, when Montgomery closed his main trap—his fourth attempt—just east of Matruh, Rommel had again escaped.

And now torrential rain began to fall, turning the desert into a quagmire stalling every enemy outflanking attempt. Here for two days Rommel took stock. The Panzer Army's fighting strength was negligible. He had only a dozen tanks left. He had lost 1,100 German troops killed, 3,900 wounded and 7,900 missing (comparable figures for the Italians were 1,200 dead, 1,600 wounded and 20,000 missing). The Italian Tenth Corps had been left at the El Alamein line with no trucks, fuel or water; of the Twenty-first Corps, half the Trento Division had been overrun on October 24, the other half and Bologna had suffered the same fate as the Tenth Corps—abandoned to their fate; the Twentieth Corps had been virtually wiped out on November 4. The Afrika Korps was worth only one regiment. The Ninetieth Light Division was down to about one and a half battalions, and only a third of the 164th Light had survived the battle. The only cheering event was the unexpected reappearance of General Ramcke at Rommel's bus on November 7. Ramcke swung him a snappy salute and tartly announced that he and 800 of his Luftwaffe paratroopers—written off by Rommel on the fourth—had ambushed a British truck convoy, stolen its trucks and driven through the enemy army to rejoin Rommel's force. There was malicious delight in Ramcke's metallic smile.

Rommel could not offer them much of a future. His supply position was desperate. Five thousand tons of gasoline had just reached Benghazi, but that was 600 miles ahead of him; there was no extra gasoline on Egyptian soil at all. There were 7,000 tons of ammunition piled up at Tobruk, 100 miles ahead—but between Rommel and Tobruk loomed the mountain passes of Sollum and Halfaya, on the Libyan-Egyptian frontier, and for fifty miles back from the hairpin bends there the only road was chocked solid with the traffic of the retreating army. Twenty-four new tanks were due to reach Benghazi on the eighth; but Rommel's quartermaster warned that nothing could possibly get beyond that point, in order to reach him, for several days.

Every detail of Rommel's plight was known, through the code breakers, to the enemy. On November 7 the official diary kept for General Dwight D. Eisenhower—commander of a new Allied invasion force at that very moment bearing down on the shores of Africa—recorded that Winston Churchill had just sent a very secret signal to him "that a message from Rommel to the German General Staff had been intercepted in which Rommel begged for aid immediately, or his force would be annihilated."

On the eighth, the rains now over, Rommel decided he had to move again. He would have to abandon Mersa Matruh and resume the retreat. He met the panzer division commanders before they moved west again. Armbruster, keeping the Rommel diary in Berndt's absence, noted Rommel's instructions: "Keep the divisions rolling down the highway one behind the other—that way the enemy can't outflank us." Later Rommel told the Luftwaffe commander General Hans Seidemann: "The enemy will probably try to encircle us via Sidi Omar. We won't be able to put up much of a resistance, because we've hardly got any weapons. We salvaged large numbers of men from the 'shipwreck,' but not many weapons."

Early on November 8 Rommel himself headed off for the frontier. Cavallero and Mussolini were continuing to insist that he defend the frontier, and Hitler also expected this. But with his meager forces Rommel saw no prospect whatever of making a new stand there, and he told this to an emissary from Cavallero on the sixth.

At noon a car brought a small, bustling major general to him—Karl Buelowius, the Panzer Army's new engineer officer. Rommel told him to stop at nothing to delay Montgomery's pursuit. He assured him that Lieutenant General Count Theodor von Sponeck's Ninetieth Light Division would fight continuous rearguard actions while the engineers laid mines and demolished roads.

Now the pursuit became a nightmare for the enemy— dummy "minefields" sown with scrap metal alternated with the real thing, arranged with fiendish ingenuity to lull and kill and destroy and maim. Abandoned buildings were booby-trapped with explosives that detonated when lavatory handles were flushed, or when crooked pictures were straightened. Airfields were unusable for weeks after the Germans abandoned them. Buelowius used to deadly effect every day of respite that Montgomery's fumbling gave the Panzer Army.

*Buelowius's name features so often in the Rommel diary that I made a strenuous effort to find him. Like Böttcher's, the trail came to an abrupt end. Said one of his former officers in Düsseldorf, West Germany: "He was always a bit of an eccentric—I got the impression that something had once happened to him, years before. He was interned by the Americans in Tennessee with Count von Sponeck and myself. One evening we were sitting with him and he began screaming: 'They're coming for me!' We calmed him down and he seemed quite normal. The next day he went for a walk with Sponeck. Then that evening he hanged himself—with a luggage strap."*

On the road to the Libyan frontier, Rommel ran into Lieutenant Berndt, who had met Hitler late on the fourth. Berndt quoted Hitler's key message: "The only thing that matters is to reestablish a new front somewhere in Africa. Precisely where is unimportant." The Führer had promised to restore the Panzer Army to its old strength— Rommel would get the entire initial production of the brand new high-velocity version of the deadly eighty-eight gun, the Flak 41, and the first dozen of the mighty new Panzer VI, the Tiger tank, each weighing sixty tons.

Any encouragement that Rommel drew from Berndt's report was short-lived. An hour later Rommel learned from his operations officer, Colonel Westphal, that a huge convoy had just landed over *100,000* American troops in Algeria and Morocco. Thus Rommel would always have this new enemy army advancing on him from the other direction, with virtually no other Axis forces to shield him. Now he felt that a stand was hopeless and it was time to get out of Africa while he could. He radioed urgently to Kesselring to come and see him with Cavallero, "as the position has continued to deteriorate." Neither came. So Rommel decided to send Berndt over their heads—quite literally—by plane to Hitler again. Berndt would put to the Führer the field marshal's startling plan for an immediate "Dunkirk"—not a stand but a holding operation on the coast, to permit the evacuation of the Panzer Army from Africa.

The young lieutenant saw Hitler in Munich on November 12. Rommel's opinions were outlined in his diary of the tenth: "Evidently Rome still believes that Tobruk can be held. In the C in C's view this will lead to our encirclement from the landward, and the annihilation of the army's remnants within a few days. C in C is firmly convinced that with our remaining forces and weapons we cannot even hold Cyrenaica, and that we must prepare for an evacuation of Cyrenaica right now. The Gazala line affords us no support, because we have insufficient troops to man it and we would be quickly outflanked. We must resign ourselves from the start to a withdrawal clear back to the Mersa Brega line, behind which we may possibly find some respite. . . . If it proves impossible to rehabilitate the army on a large scale and to throw out a strong cordon against the enemy forces now advancing from the west as well, then the C in C considers it will be best to withdraw into a defensive position in the mountains of Cyrenaica and to evacuate as many trained soldiers as possible by U-boats, little ships and aircraft at night, and ferry them back to Europe for use elswhere."

Hitler, however, had a much larger political and strategic canvas to consider. To abandon Africa—as Rommel suggested—might result in the overthrow of Mussolini; and an anti-Fascist Italy would have grave consequences for the Reich. So he had no intention of allowing the American troops to exploit their invasion of northwest Africa. On November 10 he had already airlifted the first Axis troops to Tunisia to establish a new bridgehead there under General Walther Nehring, Rommel's former subordinate.

Hitler accordingly gave Berndt this message for Rommel: "Just leave Tunisia out of your considerations. Act on the assumption that we are going to hold on to Tunisia. There is to be no question whatever of your barricading yourself into Cyrenaica and being evacuated from there (Britain's command of the air and sea rules that out anyway). The Führer's headquarters will do everything to rebuild your army via Tripoli with everything you need."

Berndt repeated these words to Rommel. He tried to cheer the field marshal up, but in Hitler's own words Rommel read a veiled rebuke. "I am absolutely convinced that your field marshal and his army did their utmost at Alamein," Hitler had dictated to Berndt, "and that the command of operations there was beyond reproach. And I have persuaded myself that the Panzer Army's withdrawal to the Fuka line *was* only planned after the entire northern sector of the Alamein line was already in enemy hands." Rommel was depressed. On the thirteenth he burst out to Lieutenant Armbruster, "I wish I were just a newspaper vendor in Berlin—then I could sleep nights, without the responsibility I have now."

Berndt resumed the diary, dictating to it on the fourteenth: "In consequence of the many upsets and his interrupted cure, the C in C's health is very poor. Several bouts of fainting." Rommel had abandoned the Halfaya Pass and even Tobruk without a fight: he had neither the troops to garrison nor the ships and aircraft to supply the Tobruk fortress as the enemy had done. He accepted its loss philosophically—after all, nobody could rob him of the fact of his victory there in June. The Italians, however, feared that Rommel was not even planning to halt at El Agheila, where the Mersa Brega line afforded one of the coastline's best defensive positions.

Early on November 15, General Ritter von Pohl, Luftwaffe liaison officer in Rome, arrived in North Africa. It was Rommel's fifty-first birthday. Pohl brought greetings and a big cake from Kesselring, and there was a loving letter from Lucie with a box of the chocolate and almond macaroons that were his favorite. But Pohl also brought a message from Cavallero: "Mussolini wants you to know that massive reinforcements are already flowing into Tunis and Tripoli, but they will take time to reach the front line. The fate of the Axis presence in Africa depends on your holding the new line at Agheila."

Rommel told him the situation. The Panzer Army's Afrika Korps (its panzer divisions) had no gasoline at all and hardly any tanks. Rommel told Pohl that he needed 400 tons of gasoline every day, but on some days he was getting none at all. Yesterday, he said disdainfully, barely forty tons had arrived. "Stop fobbing me off with phony figures," he exclaimed to Pohl. "What I need is gasoline by the *shipload*. If your Luftwaffe offers to airlift certain quantities to me, then I must expect you to keep your word. I need one hundred seventy-five tons to enable my army to move at all. You can't just bring me forty!"

Meanwhile the Italians in Benghazi were indulging in orgies of destruction. The port authorities had fled, and destroyers, submarines and tankers laden with Rommel's gasoline were being diverted to other ports. For days his vehicles thirsted, and his army lay stranded between Benghazi and Agedabia. Waldau of the Luftwaffe, who had come with Pohl, took one look at the "huge convoys of trucks, jammed nose to tail along the highway"—as he scrawled in his diary—and fled back to Crete. Rommel confided to Lucie: "It's enough to make you scream."

The fate of the German merchant ship *Hans Arp*, with 500 tons of Rommel's gasoline, was typical of the grim chaos: It sailed for Benghazi, was diverted to Ras el Ali by the Italians, and redirected by the Germans to Benghazi. From Rome, Rintelen radioed Rommel—in the Enigma code—that the ship would arrive there at dawn on November 17, followed by two destroyers with more gasoline. He also reported that the ships *Algerino, Maraudi, Salon* and *Genari* were bringing fuel from Tripoli, and that the tankers *Giordani* and *Sirio* were each berthing at Tripoli with several thousand tons of gasoline on the seventeenth and eighteenth. With this target list thoughtfully provided to the enemy code breakers, the enemy submarines could hardly miss. The *Hans Arp* was torpedoed at dawn on the seventeenth. The next day Waldau wrote in his diary: "All the tankers have been sunk. How R. is going to keep moving now is a mystery."

The Panzer Army was still 600 miles short of Tripoli. "It's raining and blowing hard," Rommel wrote on November 17. "Our position is all but hopeless because of our lack of supplies. But we must not give up; perhaps we will still manage to get through." His air reconnaissance could see hundreds of enemy vehicles herding near Msus, halfway across the peninsula. But the rain had drenched the desert, and many of them had sunk deep in the soggy morass, while ahead of them the desert had turned into one vast watery lake.

Kesselring managed to airlift eighty tons of gasoline to Rommel, and in the two days' respite granted by the rainstorms, Rommel pulled out of Benghazi and escaped once more.

Down at Agedabia, the fuel crisis began all over again. Rommel ran out of fuel altogether, and Kesselring radioed him: "Gasoline airlift now impossible as you are out of range." Rommel anxiously radioed to his High Command that in all Africa he had only ten tons of gasoline at Buerat, 250 miles farther along the coast, and 500 tons at Tripoli, even farther ahead. He demanded that Hitler be told.

Camping in his little Kübel automobile, with the rain drumming ceaselessly on the metal roof, Rommel brooded on the plight of his proud army. "I dare not hope for a favorable turn in our fortunes," he wrote sorrowfully on the twenty-first. "But miracles do happen." And they did. That morning General Seidemann landed nearby in his

Storch, ran over to the field marshal's car and shouted excitedly that from El Agheila to Mersa Brega the entire coastline was strewn with thousands of crates and oil-drums! It was the cargo of the torpedoed *Hans Arp*, no less, which fate had now spread out at the feet of Rommel's prostrate army. On these last drops of fuel the Desert Fox safely evacuated Agedabia on the twenty-third and carried his Panzer Army to the Mersa Brega line. He had retreated 800 miles from El Alamein—virtually without loss.

Upon reaching the Mersa Brega line, Rommel surveyed it and decided it was a bad place to try and defend. He was anxious to start moving westward again. But Mussolini had ordered him to make his stand here, and Hitler had agreed with him. For the next ten days, Rommel bent all the rules of diplomacy and military usage to persuade them that they were wrong.

Tactically, he was right. The new line was 100 miles long—two and one half times as long as at El Alamein—and he had neither the gasoline nor the mobile forces to counter a determined enemy outflanking attempt. He had only 32,000 mines compared with the 500,000 he had had at El Alamein. His troops had lost most of their heavy weapons and antitank guns. Behind them, as they faced Montgomery, lay a 250-mile desert highway to the port of Buerat; every drop of water and gasoline, every ton of food and ammunition would have to be carried forward across this vast barren tract. Far better in Rommel's view to inflict that 250-mile stretch on Montgomery instead—by retreating to Buerat, or even to Homs, almost on the doorstep of Tripoli, and making a stand there. Armed with these powerful arguments, General Guiseppe De Stefanis, of the Twentieth Corps, was sent by Rommel to Rome on November 20. Cavallero asked the general where Rommel *did* intend to halt his retreat, and De Stefanis shrugged and replied, "Rommel's going to keep withdrawing from one line to another—he even talks of surrendering!" Cavallero was shocked. "If Rommel keeps on like this," he said "he'll end up in Tunisia."

Cavallero flatly refused to allow Rommel such freedom, and this was confirmed, on Hitler's orders, by Keitel. The chief of the High Command promised Rommel reinforcements of tanks and guns, but he once more subordinated Rommel to the little Italian governor of Libya, Marshal Bastico. Rommel repeated all his arguments to "Bombastico," as he had contemptuously dubbed him, on November 22 and even warned him: "North Africa cannot be held." Armbruster's diary notes: "Bastico said he had no authority himself but would ask Cavallero to come over as soon as possible."

A three-hour conference between four field marshals—Rommel, Kesselring, Cavallero and Bastico—took place on November 24. The venue was the Arco dei Fileini—the Marble Arch through which Mussolini's colonial armies had marched into Cyrenaica in the 1930s. Rommel was in a truculent mood. He did not want to hold this line at Mersa Brega, but kept repeating that since Mussolini and Hitler had both now ordered him to do so, it was pointless to debate other possibilities. He just wanted to place it on record that he had only thirty-five tanks and fifty-seven antitank guns, while Montgomery would have over 420 tanks and 300 armored cars. "If this Mersa Brega line is lost," he insisted, "it will not be possible to organize any other resistance before Tripoli."

Kesselring tried flattery. "We're all full of admiration for your retreat from El Alamein," he cajoled Rommel. "To have brought back a major army over eight hundred miles along one highway, without the enemy being able to prevent you, is surely unique in the history of this war!"

Rommel impatiently interrupted. "What am I supposed to do," he asked, "if the enemy ties into my army in the next day or two on this front and then outflanks me with strong forces?" He got no answer.

It was at this time that a poignant episode occurred that annoyed Rommel more than he cared to admit—as Manfred recalled. Armbruster's diary recorded it on November 25: "In the evening there was a movie show at Panzer Army headquarters. We saw *I Don't Know You, but I'm in Love* (old as the hills, but quite nice) and *Roses in the Tyrol*. But the newsreel was a calamity, as it showed Rommel at the Berlin press reception." As Rommel saw the scene with his hand on the doorknob (". . . we have the door to all Egypt in our hands"), the blood rushed to his cheeks; and as hoots of laughter drowned the sound-track, he realized that the same laughter must have sounded in thousands of cinemas throughout the Reich. Was his great name now an object of mockery?

Marshal Bastico radioed to Rommel on November 26 that Mussolini now even expected the Panzer Army to launch limited *counterattacks* on the British advance guards. On no account, said Mussolini, was Rommel to withdraw any farther without his, Bastico's, express permission. Despite this, Rommel briefed Navarini and his own Colonel Müller to prepare the army's further retreat to Buerat.

He put General Gustav Fehn in temporary charge of the Panzer Army—Fehn had arrived in Libya only three days before as Thoma's successor—and then he did something dramatic that was a characteristic Rommel act. Without so much as informing Bastico, he climbed into his Heinkel airplane with Lieutenant Berndt, flew north to Wiener Neustadt—where he said hello to Lucie and put through a telephone call to Hitler's headquarters in East Prussia—and then flew on to land at Hitler's headquarters, 1,500 miles away from Libya, some time after 3:00 P.M. Keitel and Jodl awaited him in person at Rastenburg airfield and darkly asked him what business he had to transact with Hitler. At five he was shown into the conference room of the secret headquarters. The Führer was thunderstruck. His first words to Rommel were, "How dare you leave your theater of command without my permission!"

There was ice in the air for the next hour. (Hitler later ordered only one copy of the stenogram of this special conference S29/42 to be typed; it was eventually destroyed, but two long descriptions survive in Rommel's diary and the Panzer Army papers.) Now Rommel learned that Hitler had far more on his plate than just Libya. On the Russian front, the Sixth Army had just been completely encircled at Stalingrad and there were signs of more trouble farther north at Velikiye Luki. Supplies were being airlifted to the Sixth Army, and Hitler was planning a counterattack under Erich von Manstein's command. Rommel's uninvited appearance from a relatively quiet theater did not please Hitler at all. He paid lip service to

Rommel's "exemplary and unique" retreat, but his temper snapped when Rommel began his carefully prepared speech about his army's weakness, the inconveniences of the new line and the failings of the Italian supply organization.

"How many men do you have?" Hitler interrupted him.

Rommel answered, "Sixty or seventy thousand."

"And how many did you have when the British offensive began?"

"Eighty-two thousand."

"So," Hitler pointed out, "you've hardly lost any."

Rommel persisted, "But we have lost nearly all our weapons. Thousands of the troops do not even have rifles."

Hitler raised his voice: "That is because they threw them away."

Rommel's voice was rising too. "Africa cannot be held," he declared. "The only thing left for us is to try and transport as many Germans out of Africa as we can."

This renewed plea for a Dunkirk put the spark in the powder keg. Hitler shouted: "You are suggesting precisely the same thing my generals did last winter. They wanted to fall back on the German frontier. I refused to allow it, and events proved me right. I am not going to allow it in Africa either. There are sound political reasons why we must retain a big bridgehead in North Africa. If we do not, there will be the gravest repercussions for Italy. So there is to be no talk whatsoever of abandoning Tripolitania. Your army will be given so many weapons that you can put every man possible into the front line. You must cut back your supply echelons to the absolute minimum. Kesselring must use the entire Luftwaffe strength down there to escort supply convoys. I will send an immediate telegram to the Duce—unfortunately he is ill at present—and ask him to receive Göring and yourself."

At 8:00 P.M., with Hitler's earnest promises—of more arms, ammunition and troops, of twenty of the still secret eighty-eight Flak 41s, and of Tiger tanks—Rommel was escorted out of the Führer's headquarters. Shortly after that he found himself in Reich Marshal Göring's opulent state train, *Asia*, rolling down to Rome. For the next forty-two hours he unwillingly witnessed the spectacle of Hermann Göring in the flesh, dismayed at this flabby *six-*

star general in his pearl gray uniform, with bejeweled tie clip and matching rings, fastidiously varnished his fingernails and prattled on endlessly about his growing collection of "liberated" paintings and sculptures. By the time they passed through Munich—where Lucie joined him, her fine features lined with worry—Rommel realized one certainty: the war was lost.

In the shorthand Rommel diary is a tantalizing entry: "November 29, 1942. Journey continued. Frau Rommel came aboard the train in the evening at Munich. See separate transcript of conversation." The document itself is missing, but Rommel evidently considered their confidences highly significant, for a few days later he wrote to her, "I'm glad I was able to talk things over with you, my darling, and about how grave things look for the future." In June 1944, facing defeat in Normandy, Rommel again reminded her, though writing in suitably veiled terms: "You can probably imagine what difficult decisions we shall soon be faced with, and you will remember our conversation in November 1942." What can it have been about? Most probably, he was pondering on how to reconcile his honor and allegiance to Hitler with a formal surrender to the British.

Of that train ride, Lucie later recalled, "My husband was quite shattered. 'They just can't and won't see the danger,' he said. 'But it is coming at us with giant strides. The danger is—defeat.' And in the same breath he added, 'Let's keep our voices down. They may even be bugging our conversation.' " All Rommel's intimates agree that his rowdy meeting with Hitler was a turning point in the development of his attitudes.

In Göring's train, Rommel conceived a new ploy to make the inevitable loss of Libya seem palatable. Why not let the Panzer Army fall back right through Buerat and Tripoli to Tunisia? There it could combine with General Nehring's new force and spring a surprise attack on the raw American invaders. He sent Berndt down the corridor to put the idea to Göring. The Reich Marshal liked it. Rommel amplified: he proposed to fall back on the Mareth line, built by the French on the frontier between Libya and Tunisia before the war. It was well screened to the south and west by salt marshes. And in Tunisia, he pointed out, the main ports—Tunis and Bizerta—were very much closer to Italy. Besides, the country was rich in foodstuffs. Rommel could launch a joint offensive to the west—into Algeria and Morocco!

"The retreat from El Alamein," concluded Berndt's memorandum on the idea, "would suddenly appear in a new light, as a cunning stroke designed to concentrate strength in Tunisia. There would be a world sensation when Rommel suddenly appeared on the offensive in Tunisia."

When the train arrived in Rome, the idea was put to Kesselring, who ridiculed it. He regarded it as one more Rommel ruse to prolong the Panzer Army's "excursion" since El Alamein. He had ceased to regard Rommel as a fitting commander for a Panzer Army. He now accused him of passive resistance, of arbitrary actions like his senseless flight to the Führer's headquarters, of insubordination. Every fresh Rommel retreat, he protested, brought the enemy's airfields closer to Kesselring's bases. The argument raged back and forth at conferences that afternoon with Mussolini and with the assembled Italian generals the next day, December 1. The outcome was a compromise. The Duce ruled that Rommel would be permitted to withdraw yet again, but only to the Buerat line, 200 miles east of Tripoli, and only when he was certain that Montgomery was on the very point of attacking Mersa Brega.

There was a luncheon that day at Rome's lavish Hotel Excelsior. Field Marshal Erhard Milch, whom Göring had summoned from Berlin that morning, wrote in his private papers: "During lunch Göring savagely insulted Rommel, which cut him to the quick. Rommel asked me up to his room afterward, and for several hours I tried to console him. But he was such a nervous wreck deep down inside, that he finally buried his head in my right shoulder and wept for some time. He just couldn't get over Hitler's lack of trust in his leadership."

Göring sent a telegram to Hitler afterward. The Führer read it and turned to Alfred Jodl, chief of his operations staff. "He says Rommel's lost his nerve," Hitler told him.

Thus the curtain went up on the final act in Africa. At 6:30. A.M. on December 2, 1942, Rommel landed back in

Libya. Colonel Westphal met the plane and found Rommel a broken soul. His interpreter quietly observed in his diary: "C in C seems to have been taken down a peg by Führer. We've got to stay where we are for the time being." Rommel himself admitted in a brief letter to Lucie: "I don't feel at all well. My nerves are shot to pieces."

He was weary and apathetic, but immediately began planning for the move across the desert to Buerat that would commence as soon as Bastico gave the word. The next day he got into his Storch and flew to Buerat to survey it from the air. But until more gasoline arrived the Panzer Army had no choice except to remain at its present position.

Somehow, he scraped together enough fuel, and the first of General Enea Navarini's Italian infantry began pulling out of the Mersa Brega line after dark on December 6. Rommel had ordered that one man must precede each truck on foot, guiding it through the darkness, and that any stray lights were to be extinguished by rifle shots if necessary. But soon Afrika Korps headquarters telephoned him that the first Italian division had driven out of the line with headlights blazing, motors roaring and horns honking. All night long the desert road to Buerat was busy with hundreds of army trucks laden with cheering Italians —yet the British noticed nothing. By daybreak the road was again deserted.

Rommel's spirits rose. The rain had stopped and the weather was warmer. He moved into a new and more comfortable trailer built by his engineers. Air reconnaissance told him that 5,000 enemy trucks and tanks were massing to attack his line. But more gasoline arrived and that night—again with headlights lit—the Giovanni Fascisti Division scurried to Buerat. "Apparently the enemy still hasn't realized that we're pulling out," the Rommel diary observed with grim satisfaction on the eighth. "There are now 7,000 vehicles confronting us. C in C is in much better spirits today." Armbruster's diary echoed this: "C in C was in magnificent form—though according to Berndt it's just gallows humor." The next night the Pistoia, the last of the Italian infantry divisions, withdrew without incident as well.

At any moment now Rommel expected the truth to

dawn on Montgomery and an enraged tank onslaught to begin. He spent all day at his headquarters, waiting for the telephone to ring. It was a question of split-second timing. He wanted to zip his remaining forces back just as Montgomery's massed forces wound up for the last punch—there is nothing more satisfying than seeing a bully overreach himself and fall flat on his face. "The countryside is emptying fast," said the Rommel diary. "Now our supply echelons are also pulling out."

Rommel filled the hours of waiting by writing to his son. He made no secret that he might well never see him again, given the enemy's superiority and the Panzer Army's lack of supplies. He and his soldiers, he wrote, were bitter at such a finale to a heroic and often victorious fight. "And now to you, dear Manfred. You know how much I love you and how much your mother and you are in my thoughts. You will soon be fourteen. Soon you will have your school days behind you. Try and see how serious life is, and learn as much as you can at school. You are learning for your own good. You may well soon, dear Manfred, have to stand on your own two feet . . ." It was hard to write like this to a son he hardly knew.

On the morning of December 10, at Afrika Korps headquarters, General Fehn warned him that Montgomery's attack seemed imminent. Enemy fighter-bomber and reconnaissance activity had increased—particularly along the vulnerable southern sector. The next day British forces were seen circling south for a classical outflanking move, just as Rommel had predicted. That evening Rommel watched an entertaining movie appropriately called *Shall We Dance?* Toward midnight the usual methodical artillery bombardment began, as always before a Montgomery attack. German radio intelligence confirmed the intention from intercepts. Rommel issued the code flash "222"—the prearranged signal for the remaining German and Italian armor to withdraw, at least as far as their gasoline would permit them—and then watched another aptly titled movie, *What Happened That Night?*

When daylight came the Mersa Brega line was empty. Montgomery's artillery was still pounding away at it, but again the bird had flown. "Evidently," observed the Rommel diary smugly, "the enemy has not remarked our nocturnal withdrawal. Hundreds of elaborate minefields laid by Buelowius and his experts awaited the probing enemy.

Montgomery's vaunted offensive thus ended in a fiasco. Later that day, December 13, the Rommel diary said: "The British claim to have taken 100 prisoners. An immediate investigation by us has established that the report's untrue—we haven't lost a man."

# The Art of
# Disobedience

FOR the next three days, from December 13 to 15, 1942, the crucial withdrawal of Rommel's panzer divisions from the Mersa Brega line was beset by the fuel crisis. Montgomery must have been aware of it from the Ultra intercepts, but he signally failed to exploit it. Meanwhile relentless air attacks harried Rommel's troops. The one and only highway was scarred and cratered by bombs, the shoulders on either side strewn with blazing hulks of transport. More than once Rommel ran into dive bomber attacks, and had to hit the ditch. The next three gasoline ships were all sunk. Fifteen hundred enemy vehicles were sighted circling warily around his army in the desert, but there was enough gasoline left for only thirty miles. Said the Rommel diary: "It means that the Afrika Korps has already been outflanked." Was this the end, at last?

The two German panzer divisions bringing up the rear of Rommel's retreat, with their fifty-four remaining tanks, never came closer to annihilation than on the afternoon of December 15. But General Fehn, their commander, ordered the tanks of the Twenty-first Panzer Division to empty all their remaining gasoline into the tanks of the Fifteenth Panzer, so that at least one division's tanks could fight on during the night and protect the other until more gasoline could be trucked forward. Thus the Germans managed once more to extricate themselves from the enemy's jaws of encirclement before they fully closed; they scattered Shermans, armored cars and enemy troops in all directions as they burst through to the west again.

That evening the enemy's Radio Cairo and the BBC were heard crowing that Rommel and his army had at last been "bottled up" at Nofilia—a town on the coastal highway that Rommel had in fact slipped through already—and that at that very moment Montgomery was "hammering home the cork." Rommel burst out laughing: "Provided we get some gasoline tonight, they're going to find the bottle empty." Radio Cairo now announced that Nazi troops trapped at Nofilia were "fighting desperately" to break out. The Rommel diary noted with some glee: "In reality, just one platoon of the 115th Regiment got cut off. And they have managed to escape, too, leaving only their transport behind." German aircraft observed that even the road from Mersa Brega to Nofilia was deserted, so evidently Buelowius's lethal handiwork and booby traps were forcing the enemy to make tortuous detours instead. And there was proof that Montgomery was also encountering logistical problems: eight American bombers landed in error at Tamet airfield—still in German hands—and were found to be airlifting gasoline from Tobruk to Montgomery's leading units. The Germans did not let the gasoline go to waste.

Rommel had driven off along the desert road to Buerat early on December 17. The landscape here was very different. "It's already spring where we are now," he wrote home. "The air is spiced with the fragrance of a thousand flowers." His staff were impressed by the Buerat defenses and the deep antitank ditch, but Rommel's eyes were—inevitably—already cast much farther west: to the Mareth line, on Libya's frontier with Tunisia. He claimed that this Buerat line was, like all the others, vulnerable to outflanking in the south. Most of its gun sites were empty, since he had only 160 antitank guns left. He had virtually no mines, ammunition or supplies at Buerat. Most of his troops had only rifles or machine guns—better suited to the defense of a mountain position like Mareth. The more he flew and drove up and down the Buerat line, the less he liked it. Nor did he see any *tactical* reason to defend Tripoli any longer. The big port was already under heavy air attack. And what good was it as a port if no ships could reach it? Of eight more big ships recently bound for Tripoli, all but one had been sunk. So the arguments began all over again.

He made his pessimistic views plain to Marshal Bastico on the first morning of his arrival at Buerat. It all hinged on the gasoline supply. "I have sixty tanks left, with twelve more at Buerat and ten stranded with no fuel at Tripoli," said Rommel. "Many of them are the new long-gunned Panzer Specials. They can pack quite a punch, provided I get the gasoline." Armbruster summarized: "Conference at Buerat with Bastico. He too holds the view that the Buerat line cannot be held, as no ammunition or gasoline has been arriving. We'll need to fall back on the Homs-Garian line [just east of Tripoli]. He also is seemingly for a linkup between the two command theaters"— meaning Libya and Tunisia.

Bastico's report on this to Rome brought an avalanche down upon Rommel. Mussolini himself signaled him: "Resistance to the utmost, I repeat, resistance to the utmost will be offered by all troops of the German-Italian Panzer Army in the Buerat line." The Italian High Command followed this message with an even harsher directive: on no account were the 30,000 Italian infantrymen under Rommel's command to be "sacrificed like the first bunch."

The implied criticism of Rommel's actions after El Alamein infuriated the field marshal. The Rommel diary laid bare his rage. "C in C is absolutely furious at this. He is being ordered to defend the Buerat line 'to the utmost,' though it's by no means clear what the Italians understand by 'utmost.' If he is supposed to evacuate the Italian troops from the front line, then he won't be defending it to the last man but to the last German. It will be all over for the Italian soldiers too, then. And what is he supposed to do if the enemy does not give him the chance to 'defend the Buerat line' but just marches around it, outflanks it?"

There is no doubt that all this pressure was eroding Rommel's mental stability. He clearly considered defeat, and even capitulation to Montgomery, as likely and perhaps inevitable, because on December 21 he again urgently appealed in a secret letter to Lucie: "Haven't you sent off that English dictionary to me yet?"

Not surprisingly, Rommel's attitude aroused fresh distrust in Rome. "When Rommel wants to withdraw," Marshal Cavallero wanly recorded in his private diary, "he just withdraws." Cavallero also detected in Rommel a distinct tendency to exaggerate his own difficulties: "Every day he has a 'desperate battle,' which just is not true." He told Kesselring: "In my opinion, Rommel is just looking for an excuse to retreat. No matter where he was, ever since Sollum/Halfaya Rommel has talked nonstop about withdrawing."

Kesselring had to agree: "Rommel doesn't realize that he still has quite a good hand of cards, if only he would play them."

Rommel refused to listen to Kesselring now. He blamed the Luftwaffe, equally with the Italians, for reducing him to this plight. "Relations with Kesselring are strained," he admitted to Lucie. "He fails to appreciate just how grim our position is." He accused Kesselring of "milking" the supply ships now beginning to dock at Tunis and of giving the new Fifth Panzer Army now being raised in Tunisia the tanks, ammunition and gasoline that rightly belonged to Rommel. There is some evidence that this was so; but it would be wrong to blame Kesselring alone for it. General Hans-Jürgen von Arnim, commanding the new army, was aggressive and optimistic, as Rommel had himself been in February 1941. And what profit was there in trucking the Tiger tanks, high-velocity guns and other supplies all the way down the coast to Libya if Rommel was intent only on retreating?

Rommel's lugubrious radio signals to Rome and Berlin astonished even the enemy, who were regularly intercepting and decoding them. Perplexed, the Joint Intelligence Committee dispatched from London to their Middle East commanders this top secret assessment: "Ever since the battle at El Alamein, Rommel has had the tendency to look over his shoulder. . . . Rommel is again showing signs of nervousness at the danger of a British outflanking movement, and appears to overestimate the British readiness to attack."

Rommel's reluctance to hold on to the Buerat position

brought the conflict with Rome out into the open. His Italian subordinates sided with him, particularly Navarini and General Gervasio Bitossi, the Littorio Division's commander. They pleaded with him to start transporting the 45,000 nonmotorized German and Italian infantry farther westward while there was still time. Still the Italian High Command refused to see things Rommel's way. To Marshal Bastico he complained, "If I'm supposed to accept the responsibility, then they must leave me free to decide just how I tackle the job."

Bastico reported the outburst to Cavallero, and Rommel's plea really stuck in the Italian marshal's craw. "I am against giving Rommel any freedom of action at all," he exclaimed to Kesselring. "Just look how he behaves when he does get it. It's quite clear that all he wants is to get to Tunis as fast as his legs will carry him."

It was now that he first voiced to Kesselring the possibility of repatriating Rommel to Germany and giving the Panzer Army to an Italian general instead. Later that day he took it up with Mussolini too. "We've got to get rid of Rommel," Marshal Cavallero wrote in his diary.

It was nearly Christmas. From all over Germany food parcels and letters poured into Rommel's headquarters. There were crates of oranges, too; he stacked them in his car and drove out to the front to distribute them: "That's what I like the most of all—driving out to the troops," he wrote. "It takes your mind off things, and you can see the fresh young German soldiers." In brilliant sunshine he inspected the best present of all, the first of the deadly eighty-eight-millimeter Flak 41s to arrive from the Reich. Hitler had kept his promise. It was the finest gun of its class in the world.

On Christmas Eve he drove over to Faschia, to inspect the outpost there. "On the way back," wrote Armbruster, "we at last stumbled on a herd of twenty-five gazelles. C in C and I shot one each. Got back at 4:00 P.M., in time for his guard company's Christmas celebration. The C in C even made a speech, and it was filmed by the propaganda men. Father Christmas had something nice to give each of us; the C in C got a giant cake and Bayerlein a leg of mutton. At 8:00 P.M. the C in C's inner circle sat down to dine off the gazelles (there were just the twelve of us, until midnight)." Rommel's own thoughts were in Wiener Neustadt. "Ach," he wrote to Lucie that day, "when will we ever meet again? My worries are as big as ever." Among the presents to Rommel was a miniature gasoline can—filled not with gasoline but a pound or two of coffee.

What Rommel did not know, or refused to believe, was that severe supply problems also plagued Montgomery. In fact, the British could not attack the Buerat line before mid-January 1943. The truth was that Montgomery had such supply troubles that he could only push a small part of his army forward for the attack on Buerat. Which raises the question: would he have risked this thrust if he had not known from the Ultra intercepts that the Nazi field marshal had little intention of making a stand in Tripolitania? Montgomery himself later admitted: "I well knew that if we did not reach Tripoli in ten days I might have to withdraw—for lack of supplies."

Kesselring, more comfortable in Rome than was Rommel in his wet and unsanitary bunker, grew impatient at Rommel's reluctance to hammer Montgomery's probing fingers. He informed Cavallero that the enemy forces "threatening" Rommel were in fact very weak and off-balance. "Something must be done to raise Rommel's confidence in his own capabilities." In the original texts of Rommel's letters there are certainly many hints of his mental anguish. "Slowly our fate here is being sealed," he wrote emotionally on December 28. "It will be a miracle if we can hold on much longer. What happens then will lie in God's hands. We'll fight on as long as we can. I had forebodings about all this when we last met [in Rome], and I told you the salient points. When the fighting here is all over and you get news about my fate, you must act fast—" and he gave Lucie instructions on where she and Manfred ought to live, if he did not return.

By that date Rommel's Panzer Army was safely tucked behind the Buerat line. Now—remarkably, in the circumstances—Rome again bowed before Rommel. On December 31, the last day of a momentous year, Kesselring flew in and drove with Rommel up the coastal highway to see Marshal Bastico. All the accounts—in the diaries of

Cavallero, Rommel and Armbruster and in Rommel's private letters and the records of the Panzer Army—agree that there was a blazing row. Mussolini's new order, in Bastico's words, was that if the Panzer Army's imminent destruction was threatened at Buerat, then it might stage a fighting withdrawal to the next line back: the mountain passes at Homs, to the east of Tripoli. The leaders in Rome had now reconciled themselves to the inevitable loss of Tripoli, but it would take two months to prepare the port for demolition properly; so Rommel's fighting withdrawal must last at least two months.

Rommel was uncharitable. "Your orders are that I am not to allow my army to be wiped out," he snapped. "That alone will be a miracle. Remember the battles we have been fighting recently—each time we only just managed to get our head out of the noose at the last moment." He pointed out that it would take at least eight days to evacuate the infantry to Homs and that Montgomery was unlikely to wait eight days before attacking.

Bastico refused to consider evacuating the infantry prematurely. Rommel retorted: "There's only one choice. Either we get slaughtered here in the Buerat line, or we begin pulling out the infantry immediately. I'm not going to lay myself open to later allegations that I 'sacrificed' them." Bastico challenged him to state his views in writing. Rommel refused: "I must act and act now. I can't possibly submit written proposals and wait for their approval." Bastico undertook to radio all this to Rome.

Two days later, Rommel had his reply. He could start pulling his infantry out of the line, but he was to use his mechanized divisions to prevent Montgomery from reaching the Homs line for three weeks, and to prevent him from reaching Tripoli itself for three more weeks after that. Again Rommel was plunged into despair. "Why attach such senseless deadlines?" he moaned to his staff. "It should be obvious that I will hold out as long as humanly possible."

These words would have rung hollowly in Italian ears, had they heard them, as Rommel's retreat toward Tunisia accelerated over the next two weeks to a gallop. But to understand his frame of mind a wider view must be taken. His actions were dominated by one nightmare—that after the loss of Tripoli, the Americans might attack the remaining lifeline, the road bringing supplies eastward from Tunis. Captured American Air Force officers fed this fear when they revealed to Rommel on January 4 that strong forces were massing for just such an attack.

Now in fertile Tripolitania, Rommel's brave "Africans" were in better health and well fed. The troops had fresh meat, and Rommel's own staff often fed on gazelle. In the evenings they saw movies, read their excellent army newspaper *The Oasis,* drank, played cards, sang to an accordion and read letters from their womenfolk back home.

Several ships with supplies for Rommel docked at Tunis in the first days of 1943—Arnim claimed to be trucking 400 tons of supplies a day down the long road to Rommel at Buerat. But little of this was gasoline, so Rommel had no choice but to begin the evacuation of Buerat. The weather was foul—rain, sandstorms, cold nights. The Afrika Korps remained at Buerat, along with one third of the German and Italian infantry.

On January 6, Cavallero and Kesselring again came to see Rommel and Bastico. Armbruster did a summary: "Four field marshals in conference. Cavallero explains the reasons why they have decided, against their wishes, to abandon Tripolitania. Says Tunisia is more vital for final victory. Kesselring seemed quite hostile toward Rommel. C in C flew into a temper." Kesselring once more urged Rommel to risk a counterattack: "Our air reconnaissance shows that there is only one division of the enemy's first wave present. And the Luftwaffe has local air superiority at present, because the enemy's fighter airfields are still too far back for them to escort bombers." Rommel remained unmoved. He had gotten what he wanted. The only bone of contention between the Italians and himself now would be the rate of his retreat to Tunisia.

There is no doubt that he had, perhaps unconsciously, bent the facts to suit his case. Earlier, he had claimed to be too weak to stage a counterattack; but when Bastico now tentatively proposed that Rommel should advance one division to Tunisia forthwith, to thwart the threatening American attack, he leaped at the idea. In effect it was a way to speed his retreat. The High Command ruled that he should send his 164th Light, but Rommel decided to contribute the powerful Twenty-first Panzer Division instead. This was Erwin Rommel at his most cunning, or most devious. Mussolini fell for the proposal, but not Kesselring. He protested that General von Arnim was quite capable of defending Tunisia without Rommel's assistance. "Rommel is bent only on retreat," warned Kesselring. "He'll use any depletion of his army as a pretext to retreat even faster."

The ultimate irony was that Rommel promptly insisted that the Twenty-first Panzer should turn over all its tanks, guns and equipment to him before leaving Buerat; it could reequip in Tunisia. Hitler agreed, so once again Rommel had gotten his way.

For several days he flew around the countryside in his Storch, getting the feel of the terrain. It was rugged, magnificent country. On January 9 he lunched with the Centauro Armored Division. Armbruster interpreted and put in his diary: "The conversation was very pleasant, as the Centauro's colonel had fought against the C in C during the last world war and was taken prisoner at Longarone. We all had a good laugh."

In Rome there was less good humor. The wheels of jealous intrigue were already whirring. It was openly noised about that Rommel's days in Africa were numbered, and that an Italian would take over the Panzer Army. Cavallero briefed Kesselring in Rome to advise the Führer that in Mussolini's—strictly confidential—view Rommel should be recalled. Rommel apparently got wind of this and took countermeasures. On January 10 Lieutenant Armbruster jotted down: "Colonel B[ayerlein] and the C in C came over to us this morning when we were all still firmly in bed. Berndt has to fly to the Führer's headquarters at once, today."

Rommel's influential aide took off at 5:00 P.M. He did not disappoint the field marshal. Two days later he radioed: "Discussion went very well." When he flew back to Africa he described it all in detail—there is a lengthy record in the Rommel diary. First and foremost, Hitler had assured Lieutenant Berndt: "I intend entrusting to Rommel the supreme command in Tunisia, providing his health is up to it." They had talked in Hitler's bunker in privacy from 10:30 P.M. on January 12 until 2:00 A.M. the next day, although it was the height of the Stalingrad crisis. Hitler had talked of the importance of the Tunis bridgehead. "Only the best will do for Africa. Unlimited quantities of the most up-to-date weapons will be made available. The central issue is unquestionably how to transport them over." Hitler was putting Kesselring in charge of this aspect. "I fully appreciate the difficulties facing your C in C," Hitler said. "But I too have often had to bow to political considerations, and I hope that your field marshal will do so too, however galling it may be. Please assure Rommel that I have particularly deep trust in him."

On January 15, unaware that Rommel's army had all but escaped again, General Montgomery made his next move. "The Tommies are attacking!" wrote Armbruster in his own notebook. "They have 100 tanks in the south and seventy in the north, plus eighty armored cars. Of course we have to fall back with our few tanks. At 1:30 P.M. we shift our headquarters." Rommel ordered the Fifteenth Panzer Division to deploy its few tanks for a rearguard action, and they brewed up thirty-two Shermans for a loss of only two.

"We're on the move again," Rommel wrote home. "The nervous strain is really severe now and I've got to keep a real grip on myself." Correctly expecting Montgomery to follow through with a major night attack, Rommel ordered his forces in the Buerat line to disengage and withdraw forty miles to the first "interim line," fifty miles away. The next night he continued the retreat to the second interim line, another fifty miles distant. On January 17 he ordered this position abandoned too, rightly fearing that the British were developing an outflanking thrust to Tripoli. Montgomery's forces were badly delayed by the minefields and demolitions on the Via Balbia and the difficult country inland. Rommel moved fast—disingenuously blaming the tempo of his retreat on "the considerable depletion of our strength caused by having had to give up the Twenty-first Panzer Division."

Thus, only three days after Montgomery had opened this battle, Rommel's army reached the new line, extending from Tarhuna to Homs on the coast, that Mussolini had not expected him to reach for three weeks. But bigger shocks were in store for Rome.

This was the last defense line before Tripoli itself, but little work had been done on it. Rommel did not expect to stay long. He told Bastico's chief of staff, "We can't really expect to hold off the enemy in the Homs line for more than two days."

Berndt had now arrived back from Hitler's bunker and tried to cheer Rommel up: "The Führer says he's quite satisfied with you." But to all his staff the field marshal's agony was clearly perceptible. They could see the old symptoms of depression returning. They saw to it that Professor Horster, his doctor, was never far away.

"We're outnumbered eight to one," Rommel wearily wrote on January 18. "And supplies, particularly gasoline, are low." The day after that, January 19, was even worse. "The toughest day since we left Buerat," recorded Armbruster. "We drove several times to the Afrika Korps. We stood aloft on a 'warlord's hill,' watching the enemy divisions forgathering for the attack. We had never seen anything like it before. When we were visiting the Twentieth Corps, their heavy artillery—fifteen-centimeter guns —was already shelling the road and us. It stank, and I didn't like it at all. We just got out at the last moment."

Rommel trained his binoculars on the huge dust cloud thrown up by the enemy's advancing tanks. He put their number at 200 or more. A black despair again clutched at him. "As I already told you in November [in Rome], times are getting very, very grim—in the east as well," he gloomily informed Lucie; on the Russian front, an entire German army was facing annihilation at Stalingrad. "Total mobilization of every last German for the war effort is coming, without regard for place of residence, status, wealth or age. Take a look around in good time for something suitable for yourself. Manfred will probably soon also have to work behind a lathe or man an antiaircraft gun. It is a matter of life and death for the German people."

With skillful artillery fire, Rommel halted the tank attack. He instinctively knew that this was only a holding attack, designed to divert him while a greater evil was afoot elsewhere. Sure enough, at 2:00 P.M. an air reconnaissance report reached him about the hill country farther inland, which he had been assured was impassable to tanks. Now the planes had spotted a big enemy force—as many as 1,400 trucks and tanks—sweeping westward across that very terrain. Montgomery's strategy seemed quite clear to Rommel, and at 4:00 P.M. he ordered Tarhuna to be abandoned. Shortly, the Ninetieth Light telephoned him: "Secret documents have been found on a high British officer. They show that the enemy's strategic objective is Zauia." Rommel glanced at a map; Zauia was thirty miles *beyond* Tripoli, on the coast road.

At this, his nerve snapped—the British were driving farther than he thought and threatening to encircle him. He ordered the Tarhuna/Homs line abandoned too. These facts he conveyed to Berlin by Enigma code at 11:35 P.M. that day, January 19. No amount of verbiage could conceal his intention to abandon Tripoli—just *five days* after leaving Buerat.

Montgomery evidently deduced the abandonment, from the Ultra intercept, because the next morning, January 20, he reversed his original strategy and decided to make his main thrust along the coast road, instead of overland.

By having given Montgomery Tripoli—that magnificent port and harbor—on a platter, Rommel saved him from real embarrassment. Montgomery had decided that if he was not in Tripoli within ten days of attacking Buerat, he would have to call off the attempt.

All night long mighty explosions rocked the countryside as the Italians began blowing up their installations in Tripoli. Scarcely less noisy were the rebukes that were flung at Rommel all the next day, January 20, from the commanders in Rome and Marshal Bastico. The latter scolded him in a telegram: "In my view the danger of an outflanking of the right wing of your Panzer Army is neither as imminent nor as serious as you assume. I request you to reconsider the orders you have issued as they threaten to turn the retreat into a rout." Cavallero flew from Rome to Tunis—where Arnim expressed horror at the speed with which Rommel's retreat was bringing the enemy air force, like an attendant epidemic, ever closer—then sent an urgent letter to Rommel by courier: "The

Duce has stated that the orders you issued yesterday evening for a resumption of the retreat to the west are a direct contravention of his directives to you. In the Duce's opinion the situation as known yesterday evening and as shown by today's air reconnaissance does not justify your action."

By this time Rommel had the result of the morning reconnaissance too. It was as the Italians were saying: the British inland force had come to a standstill in the mountainous country. Without doubt, his order for the retreat had been "premature," as Mussolini protested. Rommel evidently recognized the error, and it bothered him for weeks afterward. He appealed to his Italian corps commanders for moral support. Navarini assured him: "I would have acted just the same." But to have acted just like an Italian general should not have commended itself to Field Marshal Rommel.

At 5:00 P.M. he drove to Bianchi—a charming Italian colonial village, typical of those that Mussolini's countrymen had labored for twenty years to build here. Marshals Cavallero, Kesselring and Bastico awaited him, their faces black with thunder. Armbruster interpreted, and penciled later in his notebook: "Violent differences of opinion. The Duce is dissatisfied with C in C's actions, believes we withdrew too soon. But so far our C in C has always had a pretty good nose about the position. The Italians ought not to make such a song and dance—up to now it's always been we who carried the ball and sweated things out." The Rommel diary also admitted that the language used was "forceful." Rommel asked for a firm ruling on whether the Panzer Army was expected to fight to the death here or to arrive as a fighting force in the Mareth line in Tunisia. "You can't have it both ways," he icily told Cavallero. It all sounded very familiar to the Italians —they had been hearing this refrain ever since the collapse at El Alamein.

The next day Marshal Cavallero had a more sober interview with Rommel and handed down another command of Delphic vagueness: "The Duce's directives remain unaltered. The Panzer Army's destruction is still to be prevented—but you are to gain as much time as possible." On this same visit Cavallero confidentially canvassed the

Italian corps commanders about a suitable Italian general to succeed Rommel, in view of the field marshal's repeated disobedience of directives. The hounds were out, and they were baying for Rommel's blood.

Rommel interpreted Cavallero's message his own way. He regrouped his entire army west of Tripoli during the night, and the next morning he ordered the city evacuated of all Axis troops as dusk fell. "He talks of the pain this will cause to the Italians," the Rommel diary related. "But, as he puts it, the pain would be far greater if Tripoli fell into enemy hands on the twenty-fifth *with* the destruction of the army, than on the twenty-third *without* it."

As Tripoli, capital of Libya, transferred into Montgomery's hands—and with it tens of thousands of tons of war materiel that could not be destroyed or moved out in time—Rommel and Bayerlein put the war behind them and drove to Sabratha, site of an ancient and more peaceful civilization that had died two centuries before Christ. The Italian curator showed him around the excavations, and they examined the mosaics in the local museum. Then he drove in silence back to his trailer. He was having unbearable headaches, and Professor Horster prescribed sedatives so that he could sleep.

Were the illnesses that now plagued Rommel once again imaginary, a subconscious refuge from failure and defeat? At his staff's request, Horster had examined the field marshal but found little wrong clinically. But Rommel complained of violent headaches and "nervous exhaustion," which he blamed on blood circulation disorders. On January 22, 1943, the High Command solicitously inquired by radio if his health would permit him to retain command of the Panzer Army once he had conveyed it up the coast to the safety of the Mareth line. Rommel privately wrote to his old friend Schmundt—by now Hitler's chief of army personnel as well as chief adjutant—that in its present form his health would *not* be good enough.

In a long doleful letter on January 22, Rommel prepared Lucie for his early return to Wiener Neustadt. "The way things turned out yesterday has completely vindicated my actions," he claimed. "But, as you can imagine, our dear allies are giving me the sweetest problems. It was only too predictable that they would turn nasty in the end. I don't think they'll be our allies much longer. A country can't change its spots. As for my health, I feel much of a muchness—la, la."

By January 25, the Panzer Army had begun to enter southern Tunisia. Rommel drove along the coast road. As he passed through the port of Zuara, there were ships blazing in the harbor; one blew up in a sheet of flame. He still felt unwell. "I'm so depressed that I can hardly work. Perhaps somebody else will see things in a more favorable light and can make something out of the mess. Take Kesselring, for example—he's always bursting with optimism. He probably sees me as the reason why our army did not put up a longer stand."

Thus Rommel said farewell to Libya, the scene of all his African victories and of the graves of 10,000 German and Italian soldiers. In pouring rain his car crossed the frontier into Tunisia at 5:59 A.M. on January 26. Six hours later, at the new Panzer Army headquarters in Tunisia, Rommel received a signal from the Italian High Command relieving him of duty at such time as he should himself determine. It was the price of disobedience. Rommel petulantly commented, "The sooner the better." But to be replaced by an *Italian* general deeply shocked him, and his heart bled for his poor "Africans." To Lucie he exclaimed, "That really was uncalled for. . . . Surely they could have found a German general to succeed me." All night he lay sleepless in his trailer, listening to the barking and baying of the wild dogs of Tunisia. He was at low ebb.

In the Rommel papers one finds shorthand texts of letters written to Lucie by Alfred Berndt—now promoted on Berlin's orders to full captain—that showed how alarmed his staff was at the field marshal's mental condition. Professor Horster, he said, had advised the High Command that a cure of at least eight weeks, starting on about February 20, was desirable. "The field marshal's condition brings on fits of depression," wrote Berndt, "in which nothing seems as it really is—everything looks blacker and less favorable. . . . He was supposed to take over the whole show here, but medical opinion was against it. The

314

upshot is that he must finish off his cure first, try and forget, and concentrate on getting well again. . . . At present he imagines that everything has a different cause from the real one." Professor Horster's own advice to Lucie was: "Do everything you can to counter his fits of depression."

Then a miraculous transformation took place. In Tunisia's green and fertile hills, a change came over Rommel. He even began planning a new offensive. "The successor they're sending out from Rome is just going to have to wait before he can step into my shoes," he defiantly announced in a letter on February 8. He had chosen a target: the Americans.

# Last Chance for Glory

"THE land," writes Rommel about Tunisia, "is beautiful and fertile, a country of rolling, flowering prairies and cornfields." Here, as far as the eye can see, there are trees, shrubs, orchards, plantations. There are wells with fresh water, well-tended horses, even palm trees. Lieutenant Armbruster, his interpreter, who drives around the area with Rommel, marvels in his diary: "Most of the Arab women here go unveiled, and the people are much friendlier than over in Libya." After they visit Toujane, an Arab settlement clinging high up a mountain face, he writes: "The whole region is magnificent and ruggedly romantic."

Down Tunisia's spine run two mountain ranges. Between them lies a more barren country, and it is here that Rommel will find his main battlefield for February 1943. Half-starved Arabs ride hungry camels across an undulating desert. Here and there are piles of marble fragments, or a splendid arch, or an arrow-straight aqueduct or finely engineered road to mark where Roman civilization passed this way 2,000 years ago. Tides of different races have swept across the plains and swirled around the rocky hills, slaughtering, building, farming, procreating and being slaughtered in turn: Numidians, Berbers, Carthaginians,

Romans, Vandals, Byzantines, Arabs and Turks. There are traces of all these bloods in the people who shyly come out to meet Rommel, from the dusty Arab children to the sheikh and notables of Beni Zelten, Rommel's new headquarters, who come and greet him bearing eggs and other gifts.

On February 2, 1943, the Italian general Giovanni Messe lunched with Rommel. Messe was heir presumptive to the Panzer Army command, but he said he was in no hurry to take over. Rommel gloomily briefed him. "In Africa," he said, "there is no defense line that cannot be outflanked, and that goes for this line at Mareth too."

Messe, a realistic veteran from the Russian front, with a high Nazi medal at his throat, made a good impression on Rommel. He declared, "It is the greatest honor in my life to be the successor of Field Marshal Rommel!"

Rommel had not begun to get his cold feet about the Mareth line until mid-January, when General Krause, his artillery commander, came and drew an unfavorable comparison between Mareth and the far better line possible at Wadi Akarit, farther up the coast. The Rommel diary thereafter contains much evidence of his growing disenchantment with Mareth. It had been built before the war by the French, and its bunkers and pillboxes had deteriorated over the years. Rommel lacked the seasoned combat troops, ammunition and artillery to defend it for very long.

It was an open secret that Hitler and Mussolini were planning eventually to set up an army group headquarters to control all their troops in Tunisia, and that General von Arnim was earmarked for that job. Everyone was waiting impatiently for Rommel to vacate the theater as planned, to take his medical leave. But this he stubbornly refused to do; he was waiting to be ordered out by the German High Command, and they were perversely leaving the choice of a date to him. His continued presence blighted command relations in Tunisia throughout February. "I belong to my soldiers," Rommel told Berndt. "If I myself fix the date for my departure and then something goes wrong a few days later, I'll be accused of not having provided for it, and of having gotten out while the going was good." So Rommel stayed. The whole affair was very awkward for both Arnim and Messe.

Why did Rommel hang on? A clue lay in his intense dislike of General von Arnim. He was everything that Rommel was not—a Silesian aristocrat, son of a general, brush-moustached, respected and quiet-spoken. He was three years older than Rommel but ranked lower. Arnim had been in Africa since December, but there had been no contact whatever between their staffs until January 31, when Lieutenant General Heinz Ziegler, Arnim's deputy, met Rommel to agree on a mutual boundary. Rommel glumly told Ziegler: "As far as our major strategic intentions are concerned, I'm no wiser than you. Given our lack of supplies and our meager forces, I personally consider that any major offensive westward is quite impossible. And in that case it is really rather pointless for us to hold on to the bridgehead in Tunisia in its present form." The decision was left in the air.

This stalemate began to disappear on February 3, though only slowly. That evening the Twenty-first Panzer Division—now under Arnim's control—captured the vital Faid Pass from a small French garrison. This gave to the Germans the chance of striking through the pass at the Americans. On February 4, the Rommel diary shows him visiting the Italian armored division Centauro that already held the only other pass, at Maknassy, and mentioning "the possibility of an operation against Gafsa in the near future." Gafsa was an oasis formerly of 10,000 inhabitants, who lived resplendently in pink buildings among tall palm trees. It was now the center of the powerful American force built up by General Eisenhower for the attack on Rommel's lifeline at Sfax.

The Americans had arrived in northwest Africa with all the swagger that went with parade-ground armies. Captured British and French officers referred to them as "our Italians." By attacking them, Rommel wanted to inflict a stinging blow on American morale—he wanted to show the world that even after a 2,000-mile retreat Hitler's soldiers could still defeat Eisenhower's GIs, however superior their equipment. Right from the start, there was disagreement between Rommel and Arnim on the best way to hurt the Americans. Arnim was not eager to part with any forces for Rommel's plan; while Rommel—still mesmerized by Montgomery's remorseless approach to the Mareth line—refused to disengage his Fifteenth Panzer Division from its rearguard actions there. Arnim had devised a plan to push his Tenth Panzer Division through the recently captured Faid Pass to Sidi Bou Zid, thus consolidating his hold on the mountain range known as the Eastern Dorsale, the "spine" of Tunisia. It would not be possible to execute both plans simultaneously, so Kesselring ruled that Arnim's must come first, followed by Rommel's; Rommel would use both his own and Arnim's panzer forces. Arnim was still reluctant, so Kesselring forced the two commanders to meet on neutral ground—the Luftwaffe command post at Rhennouch—on February 9.

It was eighteen years since Rommel had last met Arnim. Both had been army captains. He had not liked him then, and he disliked him now. Kesselring dictated terms to them: "We are going to go all out for the total destruction of the Americans. They have pulled back most of their troops to Sbeitla and Kasserine. . . . We must exploit the situation, and strike fast."

Arnim proposed to launch his attack on Sidi Bou Zid early on the twelfth. Rommel replied: "I can then start my attack on Gafsa two days later, before the enemy can get away. What counts isn't any ground we gain but the damage we inflict on the enemy."

Kesselring, as usual, was quite excited about their prospects: "I think that after Gafsa we should thrust into Algeria," he said, "to destroy still more American forces." Rommel was not so optimistic. Kesselring suggested that Rommel had only a small-scale attack in mind. He asked Rommel's doctor how soon he ought to be sent on his cure, and Horster replied: "I suggest that he depart on about February twentieth." Kesselring urged Arnim to be patient until then about taking over the promised Army Group command. Kesselring said with a chuckle, "Let's give Rommel this one last chance of glory before he gets out of Africa."

At 8:00 A.M. on February 12 the band of the Eighth Panzer Regiment struck up outside Rommel's trailer. It was two years to the day since Rommel had set foot in Africa. Not many of his "Africans" had survived the two years. Of the 1,000 men who had arrived with the Eighth Machine Gun Battalion, for instance, only four had stayed the entire course. At midday all the officers who had come over with Rommel in February 1941 and were still fighting under his command—nineteen men in all—came for a little reunion. Rommel was lean and sun-tanned, but his face was furrowed with worry, and his eyes were moist as the old memories were refreshed and the band softly played the march that this epic two-year struggle had inspired, "We are the men of the Afrika Korps . . ."

None of them would forget how the rain poured in Tunisia. The rains delayed Arnim's move against Sidi Bou Zid for two days. Meanwhile, on February 13, Rommel drove up to attend a commanders' conference called by General Ziegler on an airfield south of Sfax. Here he met Baron Fritz von Broich, the general commanding the Tenth Panzer Division, and Colonel Hans-Georg Hildebrandt, commander of the Twenty-first Panzer. (Hildebrandt had caustically dismissed Rommel to a Rommel aide with these words: "All he knows is just one word, and he bawls it all the time: *A'greifen* [attack]!"—and he mimicked Rommel's Swabian accent.) Ziegler would be controlling 140 tanks in the attack. Rommel felt very much out of things. "We don't have much to do with it," he commented with noticeable bitterness to Lucie after Ziegler's attack began.

Ziegler's attack on Sidi Bou Zid, code-named "Spring Breeze," began at 6:00 A.M. on February 14, with powerful Luftwaffe support. By 5:00 P.M., the enemy's Combat Command "A" was in rout. Eisenhower was taken completely by surprise by this German attack—in fact, he himself had been in this very village only a few hours before. From the Ultra intercepts of Rommel's and Arnim's code signals the enemy had somehow deduced that this attack was only a feint, to camouflage a much bigger offensive starting farther north. So the enemy were caught on the wrong foot, their reserves miles away and still not released. As the American troops fell back in disorder on Sbeitla, the next township, they left the battlefield strewn with wreckage—forty-four big tanks, fifty-nine half-tracks and twenty-six guns.

Still unconvinced, the American Combat Command

"C" counterattacked the next day with all the subtlety of a goaded bull. For thirteen miles, in a dead straight line across open country, they advanced on Sidi bou Zid. In parade-ground formation, this mass of modern hardware rolled forward, making no attempt to push out forward reconnaissance. As they came within range of the German guns, a tornado of shells swept through them. A pincer attack by Ziegler's Tenth and Twenty-first Panzer divisions completed the ambush. By dusk, the Americans were again in rout, having lost another fifty-four tanks, fifty-seven half-tracks and twenty-nine guns. Eisenhower was furious at the faulty intelligence that had led to this calamity, and demanded his intelligence officer's recall. At a private dinner party in Algiers some days later, he explained to his Allied superiors that he had not sent down reserves because the Ultra intercepts had suggested that this was to be a purely diversionary attack, in advance of a real one elsewhere. "So the Ultra proved to be wrong," noted his aide, Harry C. Butcher, in the diary he kept for Eisenhower. He went on to speculate (incorrectly): "That makes me wonder if we have been listening to something the Germans have purposely been using."

Where was Rommel on that historic day of battle? The diaries show that he was visiting the Mareth line in southern Tunisia. His preoccupation with this position had not receded. When the unexpected news came that afternoon that the panicking Americans had actually pulled out of Gafsa, Rommel's first recorded reaction was open relief that his own scheduled attack on Gafsa was thereby made superfluous.

But then the next day, February 16, a sensational change came over Rommel. He had set out at 7:30 A.M. to see Gafsa himself, and the evocative sight of roads choked with his own advancing tanks, trucks, captured jeeps and wrecked American equipment stirred feelings in him that he had not felt for many months. As his car forced a way through the mobs of grinning Arabs openly hauling away their loot plundered from Gafsa's abandoned villas, Rommel began intently studying his battle maps. Suppose he and Ziegler could keep the Americans on the run, and capture the passes through the western chain of mountains too? Then they could threaten the entire Anglo-American position in Tunisia from the rear! It was a chance of glory indeed.

Arnim had none of Rommel's verve or temperament. He had no intention of promoting a big operation. Rommel proposed to Arnim that Ziegler's two panzer divisions start marching at dusk and capture Sbeitla that same night, but he got no satisfactory reply from Arnim.

Meanwhile he drove on into Gafsa itself. Once more he was in the limelight, and he relished it. The Rommel diary relates, "The Americans have blown up their big ammunition dump without prior warning to the townspeople. Over thirty houses have collapsed; so far the corpses of thirty-four Arab men, women and children have been recovered, eighty more are missing. The Arabs crowd around the C in C's car and celebrate their liberation by the Germans with wild whoops of delight. They shout two names, over and over again: Hitler and Rommel."

Ideas were taking shape in his mind. In a violent hailstorm he drove back, and put through an urgent telephone call to Arnim's headquarters. Arnim's staff assured him they had now decided to start an attack on Sbeitla, which was an ancient Roman settlement at a crossroads on a remote and arid plain. Rommel announced that he had decided to reinforce the Afrika Korps assault group and advance from Gafsa to the next village, Feriana. After that he would have two alternatives, because the road forked: he could strike northwest toward Tebessa, in Algeria; or northeast through Thelepte to Kasserine, where he could join up with Ziegler's panzer divisions arriving from Sbeitla.

The Americans seemed to be in full retreat. Rommel's forces marched through Feriana the afternoon of February 17. Thelepte—the enemy's main air base in the southern sector—fell soon after, with gasoline dumps ablaze and thirty aircraft abandoned on the two airfields. Arab travelers reported that the Americans were blowing up fuel and ammunition dumps as far away as Tebessa. The old Rommel blood was pulsing through his veins again. By 4:00 P.M. he had captured all his objectives on the road to Kasserine, where he hoped to find Ziegler's panzer divisions. But Arnim was moving these panzer divisions —*away* from Rommel.

Rommel was furious. If only he had all three panzer divisions under his command, he would be able to give Eisenhower a real fright. This maddening certainty nagged at him all the next morning. Suddenly his patience snapped. Alfred Berndt, writing to brief Lucie a week later, recalled: "He could see that the successes we had obtained just weren't being exploited fast enough and in the right way. So without standing on ceremony he made a very daring proposal." From the Rommel diary we can pinpoint the precise timing of his decision to inflict a humiliating defeat on Eisenhower. He had lunched, according to Armbruster's notes, with a local sheikh, on mutton and couscous—an Arab dish. Then, sitting in the operations truck, he decided at 12:30 P.M. "to stake everything on one big gamble by throwing all we've got at Tebessa."

"He comments," continued the Rommel diary, "that the situation in this theater of war has always involved some element of risk for him, and he has never before staked the works on one throw of the dice. Even in the most audacious operations hitherto he has always kept enough in reserve to master any sudden twist of fortune, so he has never yet had to fear losing the whole kit and kaboodle. But, he says, the way things now stand we must risk more than we ever would have in the past so as to turn the tables decisively in our favor. If he now pushes through to Tebessa and sends reconnaissance forces north from there, the entire enemy front in Tunisia may well collapse." Rommel radioed this proposal to Rome. "If you agree, I request that the Tenth and Twenty-first Panzer divisions be placed under my command and moved rapidly to assembly area. Thelepte/Feriana.—Rommel." Two hours later, Kesselring replied from Rome with a provisional go-ahead. The same ruling went to Arnim. Now there was no holding Rommel back. He was jubilant.

"That evening," wrote Berndt to Lucie a few days later, "he ordered a bottle of champagne and declared, 'I feel like an old cavalry horse that has suddenly heard the bugle's sound again.' "

In his elation Rommel failed to realize just how obstinate Arnim could be. When he personally telephoned Arnim, from one end of Tunisia to the other, late that evening, the Fifth Panzer Army commander was still hostile. "I am planning my own attack west of Tunis in the next few days and I am going to need my Tenth Panzer Division for that," he informed Rommel. As for Rommel's plan, he maintained that the axis of attack should be farther east, for instance toward Le Kef. Rommel pointed out that that would take the attacking force straight into the enemy reserves, while an attack through Tebessa would put Rommel's axis so far in the enemy's rear that reserves could not possibly intervene in time. Arnim secretly submitted detailed objections to Rome.

Suffice it to say that when the Italian directive arrived from Rome late on the eighteenth it was an irritating compromise. Rommel was assigned control over the Tenth and Twenty-first Panzer divisions as well as his own Afrika Korps assault group, but Le Kef was to be his first objective.

Seven-thirty A.M., February 19. The day dawning under gray and sodden skies was one of the most crucial in Rommel's career. He had barely slept since issuing his final orders three hours before. He was keeping his options open. At Feriana, an Italian armored battle group was standing by to feel northwestward along the main road that led to Tebessa, Algeria. Another group under Buelowius was to force the Kasserine Pass, and the Twenty-first Panzer was going to push northward from Sbeitla to Le Kef. When Rommel saw which force was making most progress, he would take over direct command, and give it the Tenth Panzer Division too. But too much time had been lost through the command conflict with Arnim. At the Kasserine Pass, the Americans had had time to occupy the high ground, and when Buelowius attacked during the morning his infantry were slowed down by heavy and accurate shelling. Rommel drove up to the scrawny little village of Kasserine at 1:00 P.M. to see what was happening. There is an entry in the diary: "Along the road are American trucks with dead men sitting at the wheels, evidently shot up by low-level air strikes." He continued his drive along the road to Sbeitla to check how the Twenty-first Panzer Division's parallel thrust had gone.

He had ordered it to advance north on Ksour, an important crossroads fifty miles farther on. But it had taken Hildebrandt the last four hours to advance only fifteen miles. "The road is deep with slime after days of rain," the Rommel diary continued. "Five miles this side of Sbiba, C in C finds Colonel Hildebrandt and is given a briefing on the progress so far." Hildebrandt's attack had been stalled since noon by mines, and there were excellent British defense forces arriving to stand against him, too. In pouring rain his tanks started rolling again at 4:00 P.M.; they ran into more mines, and Rommel decided to abandon any further thrust along this route. He would resume the offensive the next day elsewhere, through the Kasserine Pass, and he would send the Tenth Panzer Division—when it arrived—to help Buelowius and not the "dawdling" and "inefficient" Hildebrandt.

As dusk fell, he went off to find the Tenth Panzer Division, which had spent the whole afternoon approaching across the darkening prairie from the eastern mountain chain. ("Those fellows are all far too slow," Rommel snapped at Armbruster.) He found the division resting near Sbeitla, the ruins of an ancient Roman settlement. It was only now that Rommel learned that Arnim had interpreted Kesselring's orders very casually: two of the Tenth Panzer Division's battalions were missing; so were the two dozen Tiger tanks. To Rommel, this was a particularly dirty trick. He correctly suspected that Arnim was holding the best units back for a rival show of his own.

*We have little evidence of Rommel's private feelings during this battle. He stops writing to Lucie for several days, but in Böttcher's shorthand pads one finds letters dictated by Alfred Berndt to friends in Germany, and these indicate that at this same time the field marshal is firmly planning to leave Africa forever. Hitler has mentioned either to him or to Berndt that Rommel is to get an army group in Russia after his cure, which is expected to last three months. A villa has already been rented on Semmering mountain in Austria.*

*"Our time is up," says Berndt in one such letter—to the*

*garrison commander at Wiener Neustadt, evidently on February 19. "In a few days' time the field marshal will be free to start his long-needed leave. We're hoping that after two years in Africa he'll get a new command, probably one on the eastern front. . . . He said only yesterday that he feels like an old cavalry horse that has heard the bugle's call again."*

At 7:00 A.M. the next day, February 20, Rommel drove back to Kasserine. He had instructed Buelowius to break through the pass during the night, and then to fork left along a dirt track that led eventually to Tebessa. But none of these objectives had been attained. The enemy were bringing up reinforcements. Rommel felt the initiative slipping out of his grasp. He ordered his driver to take him into the pass's entrance. As he bumped along the asphalt road out of Kasserine village, his eyes focused on the mountain barrier looming ahead—the blue-gray range, rising above the rain-soaked, grassy prairie. Directly ahead the road vanished between two hill masses: the Kasserine Pass, for which a panzer-grenadier regiment had been battling unsuccessfully for over twenty-four hours.

Two miles before the entrance, Rommel found Colonel Menton. The colonel reported that the Americans still commanded the high ground, and thus the road through on the valley floor as well. Rommel was annoyed to find an assault commander directing the battle from the rear, and told Menton to climb into the car with him. He drove forward right to the pass, and set up his mobile headquarters there. A thin rain—half drizzle, half mist—was hanging in the air.

General Fritz von Broich arrived about 10:00 A.M. Rommel curtly asked him where his Tenth Panzer Division's troops were—he wanted a battalion of motorcycle troops sent along the hill route taken by Menton's panzer-grenadiers over the Djebel Semmama, the hill on the right side of the pass. Broich awkwardly explained that he was waiting for an infantry battalion to arrive first. This earned him a savage rebuke from Rommel for disobeying orders. "Now go and fetch the motorcycle battalion yourself, and you are to lead it into action too." He gave Buelowius permission to begin using the new Nebelwerfer rocket launchers. Each six-barreled launcher could lob eighty-pound rocket bombs at targets four miles away. These fragmentation bombs caused sheer panic among the Americans defending the hill positions. The troops on the Djebel Chambi, left of the pass, began to run.

But on the other side of the pass, Menton's panzer-grenadiers reported at 2:00 P.M., there were fifty American half-tracks unloading hundreds of troops, and about thirty big tanks too. Rommel "decided," in the words of his diary, "to *force* a breakthrough."

"C in C then watches," continued the diary, "as the panzer battalion rolls up through the pass, and he watched the exciting spectacle of the tank battle north of the pass as dusk fell that evening. The enemy is evidently badly shaken by our Nebelwerfer bombardment." The panzer battalion destroyed twenty-two tanks and captured thirty half-track armored troop carriers.

Early on Sunday, February 21, Rommel drove into the jaws of the Kasserine Pass and inspected the carnage of the battlefield. Graves were being dug for the dead. Arabs were wandering around, looking for booty. Captured half-tracks clanked past, laden with American prisoners starting their long journey to camps in Germany and Poland. Rommel looked over the knocked-out American tanks and commented on the quality and standardization of the equipment. As for himself, a certain aimlessness—almost apathy, perhaps an "end of term" feeling—seemed to have come upon him. Only yesterday he had bawled out Broich and Buelowius for wasting time; yet not until 2:00 P.M. that day would he resume the offensive from the pass, and the lost hours were used to powerful effect by the enemy.

The wrecks of six enemy tanks littered the hill and road. After a while he drove to the foremost infantry platoons, advancing through a cactus patch east of the road, and watched the progress of the assault. Here the corpses of British soldiers lying by their antitank guns had already been stripped naked by the Arabs.

This was a second "real Rommel day." Armbruster described in his diary the look of adoration on the soldiers' faces as they found Rommel once more among them. And Berndt wrote to Lucie, "You should have seen their eyes light up as he suddenly appeared, just like the old days, among the very foremost infantry and tanks, in the midst of their attack, and had to hit the dirt just like the riflemen when the enemy's artillery opened up! What other commander is there who can call on such respect?" Rommel's leather coat was covered with mud, he was wet and weary, but he was happier than at any time since Longarone: it was like being a platoon leader all over again.

Inexplicably, he now turned and drove back to the Kasserine Pass. Without Rommel on the scene, all the fire and impetus went out of the Tenth Panzer Division's advance. It was not until the next morning that Rommel again concerned himself with Broich. He drove back up the long asphalt road and found that the Tenth Panzer Division, after a confusing battle the night before, had still not captured Thala, the next town to the north.

Had General von Broich pressed on in that direction, he would have found only a weak French detachment in Thala—and beyond that the open road to Le Kef. The Americans were already jittery, evacuating important airfields and destroying stores. The British army commander had also given preliminary authorization for Thala to be abandoned if necessary. The enemy had pulled out of Sbiba during the night—fearing a cross-penetration from Thala—not that the feckless commander of the Twenty-first Panzer Division even noticed that the enemy facing him had gone.

But then, when the Germans failed to press, enemy reinforcements began to trickle forward into Thala again, and the British commander radioed an order to all units: "There is to be *no* further withdrawal under any excuse." Thus the vital moment had passed.

By the time Rommel's intelligence officers brought him that "no withdrawal" intercept, his desire for victory had aready expired and he had all but decided to cancel the offensive. Like the marathon runner who collapses just before the final tape, he was too weary to go on. A real triumph had been in his grasp that morning, February 22,

Hitler bestows the field marshal's baton upon Rommel in September 1942 in his Reich Chancellery in Berlin. His entire staff looks on—Army Adjutant Gerhard Engel, Chief Adjutant Rudolf Schmundt, Navy Adjutant Karl Jesko von Puttkamer, Chief of the High Command Wilhelm Keitel, SS Adjutant Richard Schulze. Rommel, as always, is accompanied by his aide Alfred Berndt (right). (U.S. NATIONAL ARCHIVES.)

The same day, Rommel is the hero of a huge public rally in Berlin. Next to him is Field Marshal Keitel. (FROM THE ROMMEL FAMILY PAPERS.)

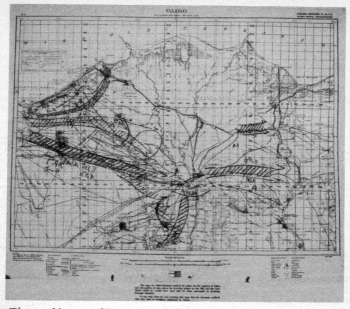

*The markings on this map are Rommel's own sketches of his plan to seize Cairo and the Suez Canal.* (FROM THE ROMMEL FAMILY PAPERS.)

*The rutted desert. Low ridges such as the one at rear were of tactical importance during the battles.* (FROM CAPTURED FILM.)

(OPPOSITE TOP) *A typical empty desert battle scene, with the crew of a German half-track watching an enemy vehicle burning on the horizon. The Panzer III—here in the earlier short-barreled form— was the backbone of Rommel's battle tank force.* (OPPOSITE BOTTOM) *A Panzer IV, with Rommel aloft, advancing through the camelthorn scrub.* (FROM CAPTURED FILM; HANS-ASMUS VON ESEBECK; CAPTURED FILM.)

German infantrymen—in fox-holes burrowed into the desert—wait for an attack. (FROM CAPTURED FILM.)

(BELOW) *The flak eighty-eight was Rommel's best hope against British tanks.* (FROM HANS-ASMUS VON ESEBECK.) (BOTTOM) *Rommel sits in the roof hatch of his Mammut as it rolls eastward along the Via Balbia.* (FROM HANS-ASMUS VON ESEBECK.)

*The Desert Fox. Rommel was renowned for his ability to sense the approach of the enemy.* (FROM HANS-ASMUS VON ESEBECK.

*Ever since his youth, Rommel was fascinated by motor engines.* (FROM HANS-ASMUS VON ESEBECK.)

*After his recall to Germany in March 1943, Rommel feared his career was over. Here, uncomfortable in civilian clothes, he lives again with Lucie (center, with Rommel's sister Helene and Baron von Neurath's wife).* (FROM BARON CONSTANTIN VON NEURATH.)

*Rommel used his spare time that spring to review local Hitler Youth units. He was never happier than when working with young men, he once wrote.* (FROM BARON CONSTANTIN VON NEURATH.)

Rommel moved into new headquarters in March 1944 at this château in La Roche-Guyon, France. The French owners left the splendid original furnishings in the château for Rommel's staff to use. Right, the Hall of Ancestors became the staff's table tennis room. (FROM HELLMUTH LANG.)

Field Marshal von Rundstedt (right), the Commander in Chief West, visited the château in May. Rommel welcomed him in his elegant study with his Chief of Staff Hans Speidel (facing Rundstedt). (FROM HELLMUTH LANG.)

(TOP LEFT AND CENTER) *Speidel had just received this Knight's Cross from Hitler's hands when he joined Rommel in April 1944. After the war, Speidel, who played a role in Rommel's death, appeared with Rommel's widow (left) at a ceremony at Rommel's grave; the year was 1959, and Speidel was by then commander of all NATO land forces in Europe.* (FROM HELLMUTH LANG; ASSOCIATED PRESS.)

(TOP RIGHT) *Rommel inspects the defenses of France against invasion. Next to him in his powerful Horch automobile is his driver Corporal Daniel, later killed, and behind him are aide Hellmuth Lang and operations officer Hans-Georg von Tempelhoff.* (FROM HELLMUTH LANG.)

(RIGHT) *General Feuchtinger shows Rommel his new invention—multiple rocket launchers. But the invasion came before many could be produced.* (FROM THE ROMMEL FAMILY PAPERS.)

(LEFT) *Devices developed by Rommel to thwart the invaders: spikes, steel tetrahedrons and "can openers" to rip out the bottoms of landing craft and mines to blow them up.*

*Poles were planted in fields* (BELOW) *to prevent glider landings, but the gliders landed in Normandy* (BOTTOM), *where Rommel's pole planting had not made much progress.* (FROM HELLMUTH LANG AND U.S. ARMY; GLIDER PHOTO IS BRITISH OFFICIAL PHOTO.)

(OPPOSITE PAGE) *General Wilhelm Meise* (TOP LEFT) *was Rommel's expert in explosives and mines. General Hans von Salmuth* (TOP RIGHT), *commander of the Fifteenth Army, barked at Rommel at first but came to respect him. General Erich Marcks* (BOTTOM LEFT), *the one-legged German corps commander in Normandy, had an ambition: to die in battle. Field Marshal Hans von Kluge* (BOTTOM RIGHT) *replaced Rundstedt, full of an optimism that soon vanished; behind him, in the black panzer uniform, is General Hans Eberbach.* (ALL FROM HELLMUTH LANG.)

*On June 4, 1944, Rommel arrived home from France to celebrate Lucie's fiftieth birthday. Also present were Manfred, Rommel's sister Helene and their house guest, Hildegard Kirchheim (in black). Two days later the phone rang: the invasion had begun.* (FROM THE ROMMEL FAMILY PAPERS.)

*Back in France, on July 17, Rommel called on SS Panzer General Sepp Dietrich to discuss Germany's future. Hours later Rommel's terrible accident occurred.* (FROM HELLMUTH LANG.)

(ABOVE) *Released from the hospital, his skull still dented and one eye shut, he convalesced with Lucie and Manfred at his villa in Herrlingen. This is one of the last photos of Rommel alive.* (PHOTO IN THE AUTHOR'S POSSESSION.)

*Lieutenant Colonel Caesar von Hofacker was sent to enlist Rommel in the anti-Hitler conspiracy. His confession to the Gestapo sealed Rommel's fate.* (PHOTO IN THE AUTHOR'S POSSESSION.)

To this house, the villa at Herrlingen, came emissaries on October 14, 1944, to bring Rommel Hitler's verdict. General Wilhelm Burgdorf, Hitler's chief adjutant, was in charge of the grim mission; he had a cyanide ampule in his briefcase. (PHOTO IN THE AUTHOR'S POSSESSION; U.S. NATIONAL ARCHIVES.)

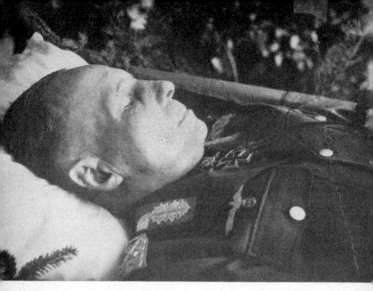

*Rommel on his death bed in the villa's smoking room.* (PHOTO IN THE AUTHOR'S POSSESSION.)

*The state funeral of Field Marshal Erwin Rommel took place as Hitler had promised. The secret of his death was kept until the war was over.* (FROM BARON CONSTANTIN VON NEURATH.)

but he let it slip away. Field Marshal Kesselring and Colonel Westphal—Kesselring's new chief of staff—drove up and found the dejected Rommel sitting listening to the rain pounding on the roof of his operations truck. Nothing they could say would change his mind. They praised him, they cajoled him, they reminded him of the glories of the past, they promised that he had put the Americans in a far tougher jam than he was in. Rommel just sat there, ignoring the ringing of the telephone at his side and shaking his head.

Finally he began to try to rationalize his odd decision to call off the offensive. He referred to Arnim's disobedience in denying him the Tiger tanks and the infantry battalions.

"That may be true," Kesselring retorted, "but you had the authority to overrule Arnim. Why didn't you!"

Rommel gave him a sulky reply. "The offensive toward Tebessa I proposed," he said, "would really have taken the enemy by surprise and been a much bigger success than the one against Le Kef. They just don't understand how to take calculated risks."

Implicitly he also blamed the Italian High Command, suggesting that they had watered down his grand plan. He blamed the conduct of the Twenty-first Panzer Division too, and Kesselring admitted that Hildebrandt's leadership had left a lot to be desired. Rommel also blamed the weather, the mud, the slime, the bad tank terrain and his low combat strengths. But to Kesselring, it was still a mystery. Only last evening Rommel had radioed him the most jubilant report on the battle.

The real truth was most probably that Rommel wanted to get back to the Mareth line as fast as possible. He had no grudge against the Americans, but he had a personal score to settle with Montgomery, the only enemy general to have gotten the better of him. In his discussion with Kesselring, he made no secret of his anxiety to return to the southern sector. He claimed that Montgomery was about to launch a massive attack there (although his army's files show that General Messe—who had been put in command of the "First Italian Army" there when Rommel left for Kasserine—had told him quite the opposite that very morning). Kesselring hotly argued: "We have the initiative now. I strongly dispute your view that the Mareth line is in danger. The Mareth line is a formidable proposition for any attacker, and no commander is going to tackle it without the most thorough preparation."

Rommel again shook his head. His mind was made up. That afternoon he called off the whole attack at Kasserine, and prepared to return to Mareth.

He had inflicted heavy losses on the Americans, of course. Of the 30,000 troops fighting under the U.S. Second Corps, 300 had been killed and over 4,000 taken prisoner. Rommel had also destroyed over 200 enemy tanks, captured sixty and given the Americans a traumatic blow that they would not soon forget. General Eisenhower changed and even sent home top American commanders after Rommel's foray. A new commander came to the U.S. Second Corps, a man closer to Rommel's own stamp, General George S. Patton, Jr.

Eisenhower's naval aide wrote in his official diary this candid admission on February 23: "The outstanding fact to me is that the proud and cocky Americans today stand humiliated by one of the greatest defeats in our history. This is particularly embarrassing to us with the British, who are courteous and understanding, but there is a definite 'hang-headedness.' " Eisenhower now had an Ultra intercept of a German radio report that the American troops had shown poor fighting quality. He wished he could show it to every one of his officers. "Some method of dissociating its source from the fact that it is a breakdown of the Axis cipher might be employed," noted the aide. "The message chagrins any American . . ."

Rommel's own career in Africa was almost over, however.

A week earlier the Italians had recommended that he leave Africa by February 22. On that date a new army group headquarters was due to be set up, to coordinate the fighting of the two panzer armies in Tunisia. Arnim was supposed to become the headquarters' first commander, as soon as Rommel left African soil. In Rudolf Schmundt's war diary as chief of German army personnel there is this entry: "Despite all their own shortcomings, the Italians have remained overbearing and highly sensitive. For political reasons, the Führer has decided that their request [for Rommel's departure] will have to be granted." However, Rommel still gave no sign of stepping down. During Kesselring's visit he talked only of the counterattack on Montgomery that he proposed to mount at Mareth. So Kesselring, somewhat daunted, resorted to a surprising solution. He confidentially asked Rommel if he would accept the army group command himself. Rommel feigned displeasure. "Considering the attitude of the Italian High Command and the fact that Arnim has already been nominated for the job," he said to Kesselring, "I have no real desire to be the army group commander."

Afterward, his aide Alfred Berndt escorted Kesselring back to Kasserine village, and on the way, the Luftwaffe field marshal inquired about Rommel's health. Berndt quoted Horster's words: "There are no clinical objections to Rommel's remaining in Tunisia for about another month, but then he must begin his cure without fail. It should take about eight weeks." Kesselring commented: "I think we shall be doing the field marshal a service if we give him the overall command. We can decide later whether he ought to return to Africa after his treatment is over."

The next day Rommel again sat in his operations truck, mutely listening to the thunderous explosions echoing from the Kasserine Pass a mile away. Members of his staff were playing poker under a nearby railroad bridge. To a battle commander, the dull, deliberate thump of demolitions is a depressing sound, quite different from the exhilarating bark of artillery. Demolitions accompany retreats. At 3:00 P.M. the skies cleared, and the enemy's strategic bombers arrived—over 100, escorted by fighters. When Rommel finally drove off to his new headquarters back at Sbeitla an hour later, a formation of eighteen bombers rolled out its "bomb carpet" only 100 yards ahead of his truck convoy, and he had to hit the dirt.

Awaiting him at Sbeitla was the formal signal from Rome appointing him commander of "Army Group Africa." He viewed his new command with mixed feelings.

# Farewell Africa

ROMMEL took his new job as army group commander very seriously. He canceled the villa on Semmering mountain, and his staff resigned themselves to not seeing Germany for many more weeks. He alone failed to realize that the whole promotion was something of a charade. Without his knowledge, his aide Captain Berndt wrote to Lucie on February 26 to warn her of her husband's complex psychological state. Berndt claimed much of the credit for engineering Rommel's promotion, hoping it would serve as a kind of unorthodox medication. "It was important new proof that the Führer and Duce still trust him," wrote Berndt. "I fixed it to strengthen his belief that—even after our long retreat—people still have absolute faith in him. He himself had begun to believe the opposite."

To Rommel's fury, Kesselring, Arnim and the Italian High Command at first ignored his new authority and dignities. Arnim did not discuss with him his own plan for an offensive toward Béja, code-named "Ochsenkopf" [Blockhead]. Rome dealt directly with Arnim and Messe. So did Kesselring. And when Admiral Wilhelm Canaris, Hitler's intelligence chief, flew down to Tunisia on the twenty-seventh, he made no attempt to visit Rommel. Canaris, of course, was leading a double life—he had been privately plotting Hitler's downfall for several years—and to the anti-Hitler establishment Rommel still counted as a "Nazi," as Hitler's favorite field marshal.

In British government files are the pages of Canaris's diary covering his visit. "Driving into downtown Tunis we pass long columns of American prisoners. They look exhausted and in low spirits, but otherwise well-fed football player types." Arnim sketched a grave picture. "Our current run of local victories mustn't be allowed to distract us," he told Canaris, "from the huge difficulties caused by the supply problem. At present we're getting only a fraction of the supplies we need—25,000 tons a month instead of 80,000. Gasoline can't be brought over except by air and in jerrycans, as the risk to tankers is too great. With a supply situation like ours you can work out with pencil and paper just when the end will come."

Arnim also said: "The command setup is completely obscure even now. Nobody knows who's really in command here in Tunisia. Rommel, who's on the point of going home but is arranging for an attack of his own with two divisions down south first? He's now the army group commander, but he has no staff as such. Or Kesselring, who also interferes in decisions with his army operations officer, Colonel Westphal, from Frascati, outside Rome? Nobody knows!"

That same day Rommel had good cause to telephone Kesselring in a rage about the confused command structure. Westphal had arrived from Rome with an urgent request. Rommel, begged Westphal, should leave the Tenth and Twenty-first Panzer divisions holding the captured passes on the Eastern Dorsale for a few more days—until after Arnim's new attack "toward Béja" had begun. This was the first Rommel had heard of such an attack—Arnim's Operation Blockhead—and he rightly exclaimed: "If there was to be such an attack, it ought to have been sprung on the same day as we attacked toward Le Kef." Furious, he sent for Arnim—now his subordinate. But he learned that Arnim had "been summoned" to Rome that morning. Rommel was speechless with annoyance that one of his generals should be summoned behind his back to Rome, and also that he should go. He decided to spike Arnim's plan, just as Arnim had spiked his. He telephoned the Tenth Panzer Division, learned that it had already begun the withdrawal Arnim did not want to happen, and confirmed that the withdrawal should continue.

Rommel predicted that Arnim's Blockhead assault was too weak to succeed, and by March 3 he smugly told his staff that he had been proved right. "They committed their tanks in a narrow, marshy valley in the north instead of the open terrain farther south," he pointed out. "The second battalion of the Seventh Panzer Regiment has been wiped out, and the Heavy Tank Battalion 501 lost nine of its Tigers." What was more serious for Rommel, however, was that Blockhead had involved a two-day delay to his own attack on Montgomery at Mareth.

Rommel's heart, nerves and rheumatism were again giving him hell, but he was determined to square accounts with Montgomery before leaving Africa. Amid idyllic surroundings he pondered and planned, lay awake at night racking his brains, studied current charts and air photos, measured distances and scribbled calculations. All around the fields were rich with olive groves and corn. "What a colony this would make for us Germans!" he wrote. And a few days later: "The world could be so beautiful for all mankind. There is so much opportunity for contentment and happiness. There's so much that is waiting to be done, especially here in Africa with its wide-open spaces."

His plan had been to spring a savage attack on Montgomery on March 4, before the general himself was ready to attack. "We've got to strike fast," he told his commanders. "We can't limit ourselves to a straight defensive operation. We've got to destroy the enemy's preparations for a general assault. . . . Our first objective will be Medenine." He knew it would not be an easy battle. Montgomery's troops, largely concentrating at Medenine—an important junction of roads and desert tracks—were seasoned desert warriors; and the geography of Rommel's own Mareth line left little scope for a surprise.

On February 28 all the German and Italian generals concerned were called to a battle-planning session at Wadi Akarit. The field marshal had for the first time decided against throwing a standard "right hook" around his own line and the enemy's lines. What he was proposing was a pincer attack, with two divisions (the Tenth and Twenty-first Panzer) striking from the north, near the coast, and one and a half divisions (Fifteenth Panzer and part of 164th Light) working through the mountains to attack Medenine from the south. An attack coming from the north was the last thing Montgomery would expect, argued Rommel.

His plan caused an outcry at the conference. Buelowius pointed out that they had laid thousands of mines in the north. "We've booby-trapped them to prevent their removal. If we blow them up, that will give the enemy advance warning that we're coming."

Messe's counterproposal relied entirely on crossing the Matmata mountain ridge. Rommel disapproved of it, since enemy aircraft could easily block the narrow roads by setting gasoline and ammunition trucks on fire. "A pincer attack is more likely to succeed," he sensibly recommended. "You must throw in all you've got—every tank, every truck, every gun." He asked Messe where Montgomery was siting his guns. The Italian general replied that air photos showed most of them between Medenine and the coast, which seemed another argument against adopting Rommel's plan.

Still Rommel did not give up. He pointed out, "We had a bellyful of fighting the British tanks at long range at El Alamein. But experience here in Tunisia has shown that our tanks are far superior to both the British and the Americans at close range. So our tanks need difficult terrain for their advance." The point was not taken. After five hours, no agreement was reached and Rommel left it to Messe to devise a battle plan himself. Messe adhered to the simple right-hook strategy. Rommel washed his hands of it.

By the time that Operation "Capri"—as it was called—belatedly began, there were disturbing signs that Montgomery had begun switching guns and men from the coast to the southern sector selected by Messe for the breakthrough. Rommel delivered a pep talk to the German commanders on March 5, the eve of Capri, then drove off at 2:00 P.M. along the spectacular and winding mountain roads to Hill 713, the vantage point from which he proposed to watch the battle at a range of fifteen or twenty miles.

Montgomery had in fact been given clear advance notice by the Ultra code breakers of both the direction and the precise timing of the attack. "I made up my mind," he later airily claimed in his memoirs, "that Rommel's attack would be made in a certain way and I planned to receive it on ground of my own choosing." But it was not Rommel's attack, and it failed just as he had anticipated.

For the first hours of Capri, the Battle of Medenine, Rommel saw little of the action from his Hill 713, since the entire battlefield was blanketed by mist. "At 6:00 A.M. precisely," his diary says, "our artillery bombardment begins. The Nebelwerfer rocket launchers open up from the Ninetieth Light's sector. In that predawn twilight, the dazzling flashes of the artillery, seen through the thickening mist, present a battle picture the like of which one seldom sees. The Tenth Panzer Division has moved up through the Hallouf valley, but we cannot see its movements either from Hill 713. By 8:00 A.M. it has cleared enough for us to see the Twenty-first Panzer's movements clearly."

Then the massacre began. Followed by infantry in trucks, the three panzer divisions advanced across the broad, flat plain until they reached a ridge about eight miles from Medenine. Here they ran into the murderous fire of Montgomery's thoughtfully sited antitank gun screen. Montgomery wrote these words: "Rommel attacked me at dawn. It was very foolish of him. I have 500 six-pounder antitank guns dug in on the ground; I have 400 tanks and I have good infantry holding strong pivots, and a great weight of artillery. It is an absolute gift, and the man must be mad." At noon, when Rommel saw General Hans Cramer—who had taken command of the Afrika Korps only the day before—Cramer had to report that his tanks were at a standstill. "The enemy was obviously expecting this attack," Cramer announced. "The ground has been heavily mined, and a defensive gun screen set up facing *southwest*." Enemy prisoners and documents captured by a reconnaissance battalion confirmed that every last detail of Capri was known in advance to Montgomery. It seemed to Rommel that high Italian officers had betrayed the operation, but in truth it was the usual cunning British cover story for Ultra.

At 5:00 P.M. Rommel called off the attack. Altogether he had lost fifty of his 145 tanks, without having effectively delayed Montgomery's own offensive planning by one day. "A pincer attack would have been much more successful," he lamented. "This operation was pointless from the moment it turned out that we had not taken the enemy by surprise."

That evening, General Arnim had a long wait coming before he would step into Rommel's shoes as army group commander. But now, late on March 6, a signal had come from Kesselring, and it was the last straw: "Chief of Wehrmacht operations staff [Alfred Jodl] states that Führer has disapproved your assessment of [Tunis] situation."

The assessment was a graphic balance sheet he had sent up to Hitler after long talks with Arnim and his experts. Arnim had forecast to him: "If supplies don't reach us, it will all be over here in Tunisia by July 1." All told, Rommel's army group now numbered 346,000 Germans and Italians, of whom only 120,000 were combat troops. To keep them fighting, an absolute minimum of 69,000 tons of supplies had to *arrive* each month; to allow stockpiling for future operations, Arnim thought twice that tonnage would be necessary. But in January, despite truly heroic efforts by the Italian merchant marine—who lost twenty-two out of fifty-one supply ships—only 46,000 tons had arrived, and in February about the same.

The meat of Rommel's unashamed proposal to the High Command was this: he should be authorized to retreat yet again, abandoning the Mareth line before Montgomery could even begin his offensive, and withdraw Messe's 200,000 men to the much more easily defended short line running inland from Enfidaville. The two armies—First Italian and Fifth Panzer—would then have to defend a total perimeter of only 100 miles. Rommel admitted that this would mean abandoning all but a small area around the city of Tunis itself, and losing valuable airfieds too. (Kesselring angrily warned in an appendix to Rommel's report that any such further retreat would give the enemy so many airfields that all supply operations into Tunis and Bizerta would become quite impossible. This was undoubtedly correct.) Rommel asked for a "swift decision," since Montgomery would probably attack with the next full moon. Meanwhile he gave the go-ahead for construction work to begin on the new Enfidaville line.

Jodl, the Wehrmacht chief, read out Rommel's letter to Hitler late on March 4. There is a shorthand record of their conversation. Hitler naturally recalled all the fine promises that Rommel had been uttering ever since November 1942, about the advantages of reaching Tunisia. "This is the complete opposite of everything he has been telling us earlier," he raged. "It's quite out of the question for him to retreat to there."

"I'll have a reply drafted at once," said Jodl.

Rommel, still on Hill 713, read the reply early on March 7. He was stunned and dismayed by Hitler's rejection. "Field Marshal Rommel's assessment of the situation," Hitler was quoted as having said, "differs fundamentally from his assessment at the time he was still east of Tripoli, when he regarded all possible crises as being totally abolished if only he could withdraw to the present Mareth line. To withdraw both armies into one cramped bridgehead around Tunis and Bizerta would spell the beginning of the end." The solution that he offered— as stated by Jodl—was that the two panzer armies keep throwing short, sharp punches at the enemy, to keep them off balance. Supplies for Tunisia were going to be "doubled, and later tripled," Hitler assured him. But he did not disclose how.

Suddenly—very suddenly—Rommel felt too sick to go on. He evidently threw away Jodl's reply, because—like many other documents that Rommel found distasteful— it is missing from his files. He abruptly climbed into his car and drove down Hill 713. "During the drive back to headquarters," the Rommel diary relates in a significant passage, "C in C decides to begin his health cure right now—at once." He took leave of his generals that afternoon: Arnim could not come immediately, as he was once again conferring with Kesselring (behind Rommel's back) in Rome; he arrived at 10:00 A.M. the next day. "C in

C makes emotional farewell," wrote Armbruster. "The whole thing stinks."

Arnim begged Rommel to use his influence to save their two panzer armies. "We can't afford a second Stalingrad. There's still time for the Italian navy to get us out of here." Rommel assured him, "I'll try my hardest."' He raised his field marshal's baton in salute, and promised, "If the worst comes to the worst, I shall return." General Arnim believed him.

In fact, he was leaving forever. His personal staff, chauffeurs and cars were already on their way to Semmering mountain, with the typewriters and papers that he would need to write up his campaigns. Lucie would be joining him there. At 7:50 A.M. the next day, March 9, 1943, Rommel climbed aboard a plane at Sfax, with Captain Berndt and Professor Horster, bound for Rome. He was never to set foot in Africa again.

At five past noon he was ushered in to see Benito Mussolini. He had always admired the Fascist dictator, while despising his cronies, whom he considered corrupt and inefficient. The Rommel diary shows that the meeting passed in harmony. In the papers of General Vittorio Ambrosio, new chief of the High Command, there is an Italian text of their twenty-five-minute audience. Mussolini asked in his clear, unhurried German about the failure of Operation Capri:

"Did they know about our attack in advance?"

"Yes."

"What do you think of the Mareth line?"

"We've done all we can to strengthen it. We've laid one hundred and eighty thousand mines. But it's an old French line, which doesn't offer good natural antitank defenses."

"When is Montgomery going to attack?"

"Probably with the next full moon—on about March 15. He's got about eleven thousand trucks and tanks now. His air power may be less than at Alamein, but his artillery will be just as crushing."

With great emphasis Mussolini ground out these words: "We must hang on to Tunisia at all costs. It is Europe's last bastion. If it fails, the balance of world power will perceptibly shift against us."

Rommel did not disagree, but warned that the present 400-mile perimeter of their bridgehead was too long. "It all depends on the supplies," he said.

The Duce ended their audience with these words: "I have always been something of an optimist. We may have our problems, but I know that the British and Americans have their problems too. For us it's basically a question of willpower. Nobody has really lost a battle so long as he refuses to accept that the battle is lost."

At 3:15 P.M. the next afternoon, March 10, Erwin Rommel arrived in Russia. A half colonel drove him from Kalinovka airfield to Werewolf, Hitler's secret headquarters deep in the Ukraine. From this simple hutted encampment, Hitler had masterminded his great summer offensive into southern Russia, only to see it blocked at Stalingrad. A quarter of a million men had been lost there. But already he was on the counterattack.

When Rommel arrived, the Führer was still visiting Manstein's forward headquarters at Zaporozhye. Rommel filled the hours in private conversation with his old friends on Hitler's staff. The Führer's big four-engined Condor returned at 6:00 P.M., and he sent for Rommel. Sipping his pale apple-peel and cinnamon tea, Hitler unobtrusively scrutinized Rommel: the field marshal's face and throat were covered with desert sores—the throat was bandaged. Hans Jeschonnek, chief of the air staff, described Rommel afterward as "very low in spirit—his nerves are shot to pieces." Rommel was also eyeing Hitler. The Führer seemed haggard and unwell, still upset by Stalingrad—but, he remarked, after a defeat people always tended to look on the dark side. "This is a dangerous tendency that often leads people to false conclusions," said Hitler. Rommel knew full well that Hitler was alluding to him. How Rommel hated this "defeatist" label that everybody gave him.

For three days he attended Hitler's big war conferences. He regularly joined the Führer for tea and once he sat talking with him until 1:30 A.M. He was repelled by the jockeying for Hitler's favor. Göring's influence was waning, because the Luftwaffe had failed to prevent the disastrous air raids on Europe's fine cities. There was better news from Admiral Karl Dönitz's U-boat force, and the star of the SS was rising too, because in contrast to the regular army units the elite Waffen SS was performing consistently well in the USSR. Rommel himself reported fully on Tunisia, stressing his difficulties with the Italians. (Goebbels dictated into his diary: "Now we understand why Rommel fell ill!") He again pleaded the case for the far shorter Enfidaville line, but Hitler refused to agree.

On March 11, Hitler unexpectedly sent for him and awarded him the diamonds for his Knight's Cross—Rommel was the first German army officer to get them. Still Rommel refused to relax his demand for the Enfidaville line. "At 11:20 P.M.," states his diary, "the Führer invites Reichsmarshall Göring and the C in C to dine with him. Afterward there is a joint conference."

Rommel stuck to his demand for a reduced line—it was the least he could do for Arnim and his generals. Overnight Hitler pondered that demand, and the next day at noon he sent for him and said he had decided in Rommel's favor—though only partly so. "The infantry elements of the First Panzer Army are to be transferred into the short line [at Wadi Akarit, much farther south than Enfidaville]. The Mareth line is to be defended [by armored units], but abandoned if it is in danger of being breached." This would shorten the Axis front by 160 miles. Moreover, he announced, the navy's commander, Admiral Dönitz, would himself fly to Rome to put pressure on Mussolini to step up the supplies to Tunisia— at least 150,000 tons per month. Now Rommel was content.

Three quarters of an hour later he left Hitler and flew to Wiener Neustadt, where Lucie was waiting. A signal went to Kesselring in Rome: "The Führer has given Field Marshal Rommel leave of absence. . . . This fact is to be kept secret at all costs even from the commanders and troops." Rommel wrote to Arnim about the satisfactory outcome of his bargaining with Hitler, but added: "Unhappily, the Führer has not granted my urgent request to be permitted to return immediately to Africa, but has ordered me to commence my treatment at once. My thoughts and fears will always be for Africa."

Among Mussolini's personal papers is the letter from Hitler that Dönitz carried to Rome two days earlier, a ten-page document typed on the Führer's special large-faced typewriter. "For the time being," explained Hitler, "I have given the field marshal leave of absence to restore his health. This is urgently necessary both in the judgment of the doctors and on the evidence of my own eyes. . . . I must ask you at all costs to keep Rommel's absence on leave and the present change of command in Africa absolutely secret. . . . Whatever posterity may judge of Field Marshal Rommel, to his troops, and particularly to the German soldiers, he was beloved in every command he held. He was always dreaded as an opponent by his enemies, and he still is."

Hitler's use of the past tense leaves a curious taste. Was Rommel now, in March 1943, a has-been? Were those diamonds for his Knight's Cross his final payoff, before he was shelved forever as the penalty for failure in Africa?

# Man in a Gray Homburg

NEARLY nine weeks have elapsed since Rommel climbed into his green and yellow Heinkel and left Africa, flying to Rome and the USSR and then at last landing at Wiener Neustadt and descending the aluminum ladder beneath the fuselage to find Lucie and Manfred waiting for him. The nine weeks have been like a dream, though a haunted one, and now, although he does not know it yet, his rest cure is all but over.

An aide, Lieutenant Schmidt, has been writing Rommel's war diary during these weeks, and Rommel himself has been working on his memoirs of the war. Lucie has done the typing, and Manfred, now fourteen years old, has penciled in the contour lines of the battle maps. The writing has brought back many memories and raised many questions. Ten thousand Germans, including nine generals, have died in Africa since February 1941. Why in God's name has it come to this?

During these nine weeks, Rommel has been chafing at the inactivity, already impatient for a new command. Hopefully he sent a fulsome birthday tribute to Adolf Hitler: "May the new year bring you, *mein Führer*, victory on every front!" On April 28 he flew off to attend a war conference at Hitler's Berghof villa, but apparently made no contribution.

His mind is still fixed upon Africa. He had been staying in close touch with Arnim, who still is technically his deputy. Arnim dutifully was furnishing him with daily situation reports. But then Arnim wrote apologetically to say that Field Marshal Kesselring (who has become openly contemptuous of the departed Rommel) had forbidden Arnim to send him further reports. Rommel was anguished. He was burdened with a sense of failure. He was a field marshal on ice, if not in disrepute. Every day he searched the Nazi press for mention of his letter of commendation from the Führer, and of the award of the diamonds in March. Nothing. "I've fallen from grace," he told Manfred. "I can't expect any important jobs for the time being."

On the other hand, it was clear from the very newspapers that once had proclaimed Rommel's triumphs in Africa that catastrophe was looming at Tunis. Rommel did not need newspapers to tell him that. It had been obvious to him for months, and the fate of his generals—Cramer, Buelowius, even Arnim—had tugged at his mind. He knew that Arnim's position was desperate: he had only seventy tanks left, and he was distilling fuel from low-grade wines and liquors found in the bombed-out city of Tunis. By letter Rommel had been pleading with the High Command to allow the evacuation of at least the most valuable German experts and officers from Africa. But Kesselring, optimistic as ever, told the High Command that holding Tunis would be no problem if supplies were forthcoming. Hitler had chosen to listen to Kesselring. "Tunis," he ordered, "must be held by every means." The army must fight to the last round.

Hitler had sent General Warlimont to Rome, to invite the quivering Italians to use their navy. "Tell them that tanks and divisions are just as nice to look at as warships," he said sarcastically, referring to the reluctance of the Italians to give naval escort to supply ships bound for Africa. "There are no moral reasons for them not to fight. The only moral act is to fight and win this war. What is immoral is to lose, and then scuttle your ships without having fought." Warlimont had returned with reassuring news, but the Führer was not convinced. He told Admiral Dönitz on May 7: "The Duce and the Fascist Party are resolved to stand by us through thick and thin. But there is a section of the Italian officer corps that is already longing for peace. Certain influential circles there are quite capable of treachery."

Hitler now believes that Mussolini can survive the loss of Tunis—but not an invasion of the Italian mainland. This is why, on May 8, a telephone call comes from Berlin to Rommel at Wiener Neustadt: "You are to report to the Führer tomorrow, for further orders."

Rommel flies into Tempelhof airport shortly after noon on the ninth. A half hour later he is with Hitler. Hitler's face is grim. "I should have listened to you before," he says to Rommel. Afterward Rommel writes in his diary: "No particular job yet. Field Marshal Keitel hints at employment in Italy if things get tough for Duce there."

The next day, May 10, Rommel, wearing a long topcoat with his gray homburg pulled well down over his eyes, strolls into Berlin's famous Tiergarten park. A few people pause as they catch sight of him and turn their heads: Can that be Rommel? Hardly, because Rommel is still commanding in Tunisia, if the newspapers are to be believed. They must be believed; Hitler has decreed that every effort be made to make the enemy think that Rommel is still there.

It is just as well for Rommel that he is not. The situation in Tunis is now beyond salvation. This very day the Germans have been surrendering there, and although some pockets will hold on a few more days, it will soon be all over—the whole Axis adventure in Africa. About 250,000 troops will march into Allied captivity, about 150,000 of them Germans.

What Rommel did not know in May of 1943 was that Hitler had calmly assumed that Africa would be lost ever since the field marshal's undisciplined flight to see him in November 1942. Hitler had told Warlimont as much the next day. What mattered, he added, was to win time in order to deny the enemy the straits of Sicily as long as possible. So long as the British and Americans were forced to use the long sea route to Africa around the Cape of Good Hope—instead of the Mediterranean—

they would have a million tons of extra shipping tied up and this would prevent any early seaborne invasion of northern Europe.

The logical extension of these thoughts shows up in Joseph Goebbels's unpublished diary on February 22, 1943: "The Führer will not withdraw from the Italian mainland under any circumstances. He has no intention of retreating north to the river Po, even if Italy itself pulls right out of the war. It is the supreme principle of German overall strategy to keep the fighting as far as possible from our homeland."

Delaying the invasion of Sicily was well worth the sacrifices in Tunisia, in Hitler's view. He boasted in July to his generals on the Russian front: "By hanging on in Tunis we managed to postpone their invasion of southern Europe by over half a year. And moreover, Italy has stayed in the Axis. If we had not hung on, the enemy could have landed in Italy without serious resistance and crossed the Brenner into the Reich at a time when we could not have spared a single soldier because of the Red Army's breakthrough at Stalingrad."

From May 9 on, Rommel saw Hitler frequently. All these war conferences revolved around the same anxious topic: What steps should the Nazis take when Italy was invaded? The invasion might come in the next two or three weeks. Rommel warned Hitler and his staff to expect the worst. As Goebbels wrote after Rommel came for tea in his Berlin garden on May 10, "Rommel has only the lowest opinion of the Italians. He's certain that the moment the British or Americans land in southern Italy the Italians won't make any show of resistance. . . . He describes the Duce as a tired old man."

This was as the battle in Tunis was ending. When Rommel saw Alfred Berndt a couple of days later, his former aide handed him the signal that had just been telephoned through to him for Rommel. It was from Hans Cramer, the last commander of the Afrika Korps, sending farewell greetings to Rommel as the first. And to Hitler, Cramer had radioed: "Ammunition spent. Arms and equipment destroyed. The Afrika Korps has fought until it can fight no more, as ordered. The Afrika Korps must arise again. *Heia Safari!*"

Berndt was now back in his old job as Goebbels's chief assistant. "He's in his element now," Rommel wrote. He sent Berndt a box of cigars as a gift for old times' sake. He owed a lot to Berndt, one way or another.

When Hitler returned to his Wolf's Lair headquarters in East Prussia, Rommel followed. Lacking any army commander in chief—he had sacked Field Marshal von Brauchitsch in December 1941—Hitler was happy to draw on Rommel's combat experience at the war conferences. He showed the field marshal the latest weapons—huge tanks, new assault guns and the portable antitank bazooka called Blowpipe. "The Blowpipe seems very good for close-cover terrain," Rommel noted in his diary. (In the open desert, of course, troops could not get close enough to enemy tanks to use it.)

The growing crisis threatening Italy overshadowed everything. At the end of the war conference on May 15, Hitler delivered a secret two-hour speech analyzing the enemy's likely moves. According to handwritten notes taken by a naval officer, Hitler warned: "In Italy, we can rely only on the Duce. There are strong fears that he may be eliminated or neutralized in some way. The royal family, all leading members of the officer corps, the clergy, the Jews and broad sectors of the civil service are hostile or negative toward us. . . . The Duce is now marshaling his Fascist guard about him. But the real power is in the hands of others." He continued that he had decided to strip the eastern front of eight panzer and four infantry divisions to rush to Italy if an enemy invasion began; he would move these forces into Italy whether or not the Italian government liked it. Rommel would be the ideal commander for such a force. "The next one or two weeks will be crucial," Hitler proclaimed.

Two days later he formally ordered Rommel to assemble a skeleton staff for a new army group headquarters for the task. "I am absolutely delighted with the new job," wrote Rommel. Since it amounted to preparing an armed occupation of Italy (under the code name "Alarich"), his pleasure at being able to settle old scores was genuine. He felt better already—in fact his troublesome sores suddenly disappeared. One by one he briefed his staff and sent them down to Vienna to set up shop. He himself would have to remain in Munich, for security reasons—he must not be identified outside Africa.

On May 21 Hitler returned to his Berghof villa on the Bavarian mountainside; Rommel went with him, and checked into the luxury hotel Berchtesgadener Hof. The next day Hitler signed the secret directions for the new job. Rommel spent the following days drafting plans and timetables for the stealthy infiltration of northern Italy by four divisions, to be followed by at least sixteen more to be under his personal command, when the word was given by Hitler. Hitler meanwhile was laying the foundations for his big strategic counterattack in Russia, Operation Citadel, but he was afraid to trigger it off lest Mussolini's generals suddenly stage a mass defection in Rome, or the enemy launch their invasion. He did not have enough forces to execute both Alarich and Citadel, that was the problem. "We talk about everything under the sun," wrote Rommel on May 30. "We're waiting in suspense to see if the next weeks bring the big battles everybody's talking of. Perhaps nobody wants to make the first move."

Rommel had secured Alfred Gause as his chief of staff once again. It was obvious to both of them that Rommel's job would hinge on keeping open the mountain passes between Italy and the Reich. Even under Mussolini, the Italians had worked steadily at improving their frontier defenses against the Reich. Rommel had noticed this every time he took the train over the Brenner Pass: bunkers were being built, demolition chambers installed in key rail and road bridges. If these mountain passes were blocked by Italians or anybody else, it would seal the doom of any German forces on Italian soil. Hitler ordered that German antiaircraft batteries be supplied to protect the passes. If the Italians rejected them, then "British air raids" were to be faked, using captured bombs. Throughout June, Rommel planned the necessary countermeasures, consulting with German army experts on signals, mountain warfare and paratroop operations.

Every noon he presented himself at the Berghof for Hitler's war conferences. They were held around a long table surfaced with red marble in the tapestried great hall of the villa. The hall had a huge picture window looking out over the valley, a vista Rommel found breathtaking every time he saw it. Two years later he was to reminisce about the conferences: "I was there as an adviser, as a sort of acting commander in chief of the army. That was the idea, but not much came of it because the circle of participants was always much too big to tackle problems squarely." Once, however, Rommel did corner Hitler in private and challenged him about Germany's future, reciting the morbid signs. Italy's collapse seemed inevitable, Rommel said, and Admiral Dönitz had told him privately that they were now losing over thirty U-boats a month; soon they would be facing the entire material strength of the British Empire and the United States, of which the fire raids destroying one German city every night were only a grim foretaste.

"Hitler listened to it all with downcast eyes," Rommel told Lucie and Manfred shortly after. "Suddenly he looked up and said that he, too, was aware that there was very little chance left of winning the war. But the West would never conclude peace with him—at least not the statesmen who were at the helm now. He said that he had never wanted war with the West. But now the West would have its war—have it to the end." It was at about this time that Hitler in his own spidery handwriting amended the draft of a speech due to be delivered by Goebbels on June 5 to the munitions workers—he changed the phrase "when victory is ours" to the significantly different words, "after the struggle is over."

On July 1, 1943, Hitler flew back to East Prussia, for his 2,000-tank attack in Russia, Operation Citadel, would shortly begin. Rommel flew to the Wolf's Lair on the same day and listened to Hitler's speech to his assembled field marshals and generals that evening. In a grave, clear and confident voice Hitler explained the background of the operation. "The blame for our misfortunes must be laid squarely on our allies," he began. "The Italians let us down completely. If, as I repeatedly demanded, they had made timely use of their fleet to escort and transport their troops to Africa, Africa would not have been lost. Now their ships are smashed to pieces in their harbors." What was at stake now? he asked. "Germany needs the conquered territories or it will not exist for long. It must win hegemony over the rest of Europe. Where we are—we stay." And so he went on, until 2:50 A.M.

Frequently during July 1943, Rommel's stocky, alert figure was to be seen standing silently with the other Wehrmacht generals at Hitler's conference table at the Wolf's Lair. The possible reason for his presence was widely discussed in the General Staff. An army captain, Hermann Kaiser, wrote in his diary: "They say Hitler is planning to appoint two chiefs of staff, with Rommel as acting commander in chief of the army." Rommel witnessed the familiar initial euphoria as Operation Citadel began early on the fifth. Huge tank battles raged, far bigger even than El Alamein. Stalin had pitted 3,000 tanks against the 2,000 commanded by Manstein and Kluge, but on the ninth Rommel could note in his own diary after the midday conference: "Attack operations in the east are going well."

Next day came the bombshell: the Allied invasion of Italy—indeed, of Hitler's Europe—had begun. "Noon," wrote Rommel. "War conference with Führer. The British and Americans have invaded Sicily with paratroops and landing craft." From 9:30 P.M. on, he had a four-hour private session with Hitler—evidently urging him to intervene on the Italian mainland now. Hitler hesitated for some days. Kesselring and the diplomats in Rome were reassuring him that Mussolini's position was safe, and Hitler was anxious to avoid any action that might destabilize the situation. On July 15, however, after discussing it with General Jodl, Hitler signed a document appointing Rommel commander of a new headquarters, "Army Group B," with the job of organizing resistance in central Italy. The field marshal interpreted this as being the supreme command in Italy, when the time came.

Meanwhile, Stalin had begun a violent counterattack, just north of Operation Citadel. Rommel listened with fascination as Hitler's other field marshals and generals made their battle reports and dissected their strategy. Kluge and Manstein came, wringing their hands over their tank losses in Stalin's minefields, but claiming to have inflicted crippling losses on the Soviet tanks too. Milch, deputy chief of the Luftwaffe, reported on his plans for revitalizing fighter aircraft production. Admiral Dönitz was frequently there, reporting on his impossible U-boat losses —attributed to some secret enemy radar system (but largely caused by the Enigma leak). In the evenings, Rommel drove back through the barbed wire and sentries to the half-timbered house Hitler had placed at his disposal—it had been Brauchitsch's when he was the army commander in chief—and digested these extraordinary and privileged experiences. He was full of ideas. He felt he had the answers to a lot of Hitler's problems.

On July 17 he enthusiastically poured out his thoughts to his old North Africa comrade Bayerlein, now a general, who had been sent for by Hitler that day. (Rommel had secured the particularly shrewd appointment of a one-armed Stalingrad veteran, General Hans Hube, as German field commander in Sicily; he had now proposed Bayerlein as Hube's chief of staff.) They sat in Rommel's study. The field marshal began: "You know, Bayerlein, we've lost the initiative, there's no doubt about it. We've just learned in Russia that dash and high hopes are not enough. What we need is a completely new approach. For the next few years there can be no thought of resuming the offensive either in the east or in the west. So we'll have to make the most of the advantages that normally accrue to the defense. In the air we must build fighters and still more fighters, and give up all idea of doing any bombing. A few days ago the Führer told me that by the beginning of next year we'll be turning out seven thousand aircraft and two thousand tanks a month. I no longer see things as blackly as I used to in Africa," he concluded, "but total victory is now hardly possible, of course."

Bayerlein inquired how Rommel envisaged his ground defense. Rommel replied, "You remember how difficult we used to find it to attack those British gun screens in Africa? Well, I've been making a thorough study of our experiences in Russia. The Russians just attack head on and try to batter through by sheer weight of numbers. But suppose we give our infantry divisions at first fifty, then one hundred and then two hundred seventy-five millimeter antitank guns each. We'll be able to halt the Russians." This was where Rommel's strategy differed from panzer general Guderian's. Ever since 1942, Guderian had called for more tank production. "We haven't the slightest hope of keeping pace with the enemy's tank production," Rommel pointed out. "But we certainly can with their antitank gun production. Suppose the enemy attacks us in a heavily mined sector and we have built a gun screen, say, six miles deep. They're going to get bogged down in it and have to gnaw their way ahead inch by inch. And meanwhile we'll be installing more and more guns behind the screen at that point, faster than the enemy can gnaw his way through. Once our troops see that we are capable of holding our ground, morale will soar sky-high again."

Three weeks later, Rommel formally asked for 400 antitank guns for each of his infantry divisions; the High Command had to refuse, because of material shortages.

Rommel's constant presence at the Wolf's Lair caused much jealousy, particularly from Göring. Apparently the opposition was effective. On July 18 Rommel noted: "The Führer has been advised not to make me C in C in Italy, since they say I'm anti-Italian. I assume the Luftwaffe's behind this. Thus my employment in Italy recedes into the dim and distant future again." To his great disenchantment, Rommel was informed several days later that his Army Group B—currently setting up its headquarters in a castle in Austria—would move to Salonika, in northern Greece, to direct anti-invasion operations should the enemy land in Greece or Crete. "I am to be Supreme Commander in Greece for the time being," wrote Rommel, "including the islands, so that I can pounce on Italy later." He left Hitler's headquarters on the twenty-third, after a further long private talk with the Führer. Hitler told him details of his own visit to Mussolini in northern Italy a few days earlier. "The Duce's hands are tied," he said at one point. Perhaps Hitler also disclosed what agents in Italy had learned—that there was a plot to overthrow the Duce and replace him with Marshal Pietro Badoglio, a bumbling soldier whose sole job would be to speed Italy's surrender to the enemy.

It was broiling hot when Rommel's plane touched down at Salonika at 11:00 A.M. on July 25. With General Gause, he checked into the roomy Hotel Mediterrane and steeled himself for the dreary task Hitler had given him, the inspection of Greece's defenses. ("The job is not at all to my liking," he complained to Lucie.) Precisely twelve hours after his plane landed, the telephone rang in the hotel. It was General Warlimont, calling from the Wolf's Lair. "The Duce has been arrested!" he exclaimed to Rommel. "You are to report back to the Führer's headquarters at once. Nobody knows what's happening in Italy." At 7:00 A.M. the next day Rommel's plane took off again. That was the last he saw of Greece.

Confusion and uncertainty reigned at the Wolf's Lair as Rommel's plane landed at the airfield at noon, July 26. From all over the Reich the leading lights of the Nazi Party, the Wehrmacht and the state were flying in. Rommel drove through the sentries and minefields to Hitler's conference barracks. Hitler was still shocked and outraged at the treatment meted out to his friend Mussolini. There was little hard news from Rome, but there were reports of anti-Fascist riots. The king and Marshal Badoglio had proclaimed Italy's continued loyalty to the Axis, but Hitler did not believe them. "We can be clear on one score," he declaimed to the thickening crowd around the oak conference table. "Traitors that they are, they will of course proclaim their intention of continuing the fight. Of course! But it will be a betrayal." He smiled contemptuously. "We shall be playing the same game, leading them on, until we suddenly drop like lightning on the whole bag of them and round up the entire gang."

Rommel could guess why Hitler had sent for him. In his private diary he wrote: "We assume that—despite the proclamations of the king and Badoglio—Italy is going to pull out of the war, or at the very least that the British will undertake further major landings in upper Italy." That was the nightmare for Hitler: 1,000 miles of Italy separated 70,000 of Germany's finest troops in Sicily from their home base in the Reich. A leading Fascist who had escaped that day from Rome reported that the new regime would probably announce an armistice with the enemy in eight or ten days, and that the British would probably land as far north as Genoa and Leghorn. That would doom General Hube's troops in Sicily.

Hitler's first instinct was to abandon the battlefield in Sicily at once and evacuate his troops to the mainland as the British had at Dunkirk in 1940. They could leave their tanks and heavy equipment behind. "Their pistols are all they need . . . they can make short work of the Italians with pistols too." He was also strongly tempted to adopt rash expedients—the Third Panzer Division would move to Rome; he would arrest the government, kidnap the king, capture Badoglio, smoke out the Vatican and find out where Mussolini was being held. The situation was not so far lost that an energetic coup by the Nazis could not set things right again, in Hitler's opinion.

Goebbels agreed, but his diary criticizes Rommel for taking a more moderate line. "Rommel as an experienced soldier is more reserved in his estimate of our possibilities. He would prefer our operation to be prepared at greater length, which would make it more likely to succeed. The Führer puts Rommel in charge of the first steps to be taken by the High Command in Italy. Keitel and Jodl fight tooth and nail against giving Rommel command over our troops in Sicily as well: they don't want to see him getting too much power and too many troops—they are envious of him."

Rommel wrote in his own diary, after the argument, "I'm hoping to be sent into Italy soon."

On July 27 Rommel summarized Hitler's noon conference thus: "Although there are two Italian armies in upper Italy and the Italians are obviously planning to betray us, it is not politically possible for us to invade yet. But we're preparing everything, and I have been put in charge of the troop buildup." Hitler still refused to give the word for German troops to roll southward into Italy. At the 8:30 P.M. conference the argument went on. The thick-skinned and rough-tongued Field Marshal Wolfram von Richthofen—commander of the Second Air Force in Italy —had now flown in from Rome. In his own secret diary he wrote: "Everybody is very rude about Kesselring. I counterattack. Some of his dispatches are admittedly psychologically tactless, but by and large they are objective and accurate. I identify myself with them. . . . Rommel knows nothing, thank God says nothing, and is just reveling in feelings of revenge against the Italians, whom he hates. Dönitz is moderate and sensible. Everybody else, especially Ribbentrop, just repeats whatever the Führer says."

The next morning, when Rommel left the Wolf's Lair for Munich, where he was to set up his operations headquarters, he had Hitler's top secret instructions for the invasion of Italy in his pocket. His first task—when the High Command gave the word—would be to secure the mountain passes. If the Italians manned their defenses, they were to be blasted out. Rommel would have two infantry divisions (the Forty-fourth and 305th) and the troops of the mountain warfare school at Mittenwald for the job, and three battle groups of Tiger tanks on loan from training units. To avoid provoking the Italians into reaction, kid glove methods were to be used at first. Rommel was forbidden to show his face even in Austria, let alone in Italy; the same went for Alfred Gause and other famous names on Rommel's staff. Rommel wisecracked that he had been "confined to barracks." His headquarters was camouflaged under the name "High Command Rehabilitation Unit, Munich."

That day Rommel was also proved right in urging caution. In Parliament, Winston Churchill announced that the Italians would have to "stew in their own juice." Hitler relaxed: there would evidently not be an armistice for several days or even weeks. There would be no need for the more drastic expedients that he had prepared. Rommel would have time to infiltrate his troops into northern Italy at a deliberate pace until it would be too late for either the Italians or the British to realize what was happening. He had no sympathy for Italy at all: "Either way, the country's going to become a battlefield. . . . Far better for us to do our fighting in Italy than at home." His own initial intention was to occupy a line across northern Italy from Genoa to Rimini, and then flood all of Italy with reliable German units. He would then fight a long-drawn-out campaign, first in Sicily and then withdrawing northward up the "boot," pausing to defend successive lines drawn across Italy from Cosenza to Taranto, at Salerno, at Cassino and finally along the Apennine mountains. This would give Hitler the respite he needed to restore Nazi Germany's superiority in fighter aircraft and gun production.

On July 29 Hitler obtained from SS intelligence experts the final proof that the new Italian regime was secretly dealing with the enemy. A radiotelephone conversation across the Atlantic, between Churchill and Roosevelt, was intercepted. Churchill talked about the "imminent armistice." So Hitler ordered Alarich, the stealthy Nazi invasion of Italy, to begin the next day. The first of Rommel's units to move in would be the Twenty-sixth Panzer Division. Its secret orders were to occupy positions just north of Rome. Rommel himself briefed the leading battalion commander: "You are to be friendly and amiable toward the Italians. Avoid friction. Tell them we're in good form, that the big battle in Russia is over and that the Reds took heavy losses. Tell them you're in a hurry because you're needed in Sicily!"

The army captain asked, "Suppose they resist?"

"Then negotiate," said Rommel. "If they attack you, then hit back. Do not use Italian telephone lines. Defuse bridges and viaducts—the vibration of marching troops may set them off. Keep well closed up to the rear, so that Italians can't push their own units in between."

It was an unusual feeling for Rommel to send his troops into an operation and be "confined to headquarters" himself, not in the lead. But those were Hitler's orders. He sweltered in his special train in a forest south of Munich, waiting for reports. He was alert and elated. "One way or another," he said triumphantly to Lucie in a letter, "Kesselring has had his last fling in Italy!"

In full combat array, his troops marched along the tortuous heights that formed the Brenner Pass between Austria and Italy, throwing out patrols ahead, with automatic weapons cocked and at the ready. As the thousands of troops and Tiger tanks of the Twenty-sixth Panzer Division approached, consternation seized the Italian officials on the frontier. A phone call went to General Gloria, commanding their Thirty-fifth Corps at Bolzano, thirty-five miles away. Gloria phoned Rome, inquiring whether these German troops had permission to cross or not. Italian railroad officials called up their headquarters in Rome. Italian censors in Venice intercepted the call and phoned the local navy office. The Italian admiralty warned the High Command in Rome—but by the time the news sank in, the panzer division was strung out all along the Brenner Pass and it was too late to react. Rommel's troops began spending their "Occupation Reichsmarks" on Italian soil. At Bolzano, the largely German populace heard the clatter of tank tracks at 1:00 A.M. and turned out in their nightwear to cheer their "liberation" from Italian oppression! General Gloria's reaction was less enthusiastic. Rommel observed in his diary, "We must be on guard for the Italian attitude to change for the worse at any moment."

That day, July 31, Hitler's chief of intelligence, Admiral Canaris, assured Rommel after visiting Italy: "There are no signs whatever that the Italians are plotting to defect. The authorities in Rome have only one desire—to continue the fight with our support." Rommel, wisely, did not believe Canaris. He visited General Valentin Feurstein that evening at the Mittenwald mountain warfare school. Feurstein, a stocky, black-moustached officer personally briefed by Hitler for the mission of opening up or securing the Alpine passes, had spent the day in Bolzano. He had talked to Gloria and the Italian officers. "Their barracks are jam-packed," he exclaimed. "You could raise an entire army corps from those troops. The soldiers' conduct toward German officers is better than toward their own. They'd be happy to fight on our side and end the war. My own view is that we could take them in on a fifty-fifty basis. Their intermediate officers are quite useless."

"Because they've too little understanding of their own men," Rommel interjected.

On August 1 the Bavarian and Austrian troops of the Forty-fourth Infantry Division began crossing the frontier. Known traditionally as the Reich grenadier division "Hoch und Deutschmeister," the Forty-fourth had suppressed the 1848 uprising in Milan. On this new mission, almost a century later, there had been no bloodshed, so far, but now General Gloria violently objected to the unloading of this second German division at Bolzano too. According to Feurstein's war diary, Rommel ordered him to use whatever force necessary to get his way. "Field Marshal Rommel expands on this as follows: Any resistance to German actions is to be broken by force of arms. The Italian officers, and particularly the corps command and his staff, are to be arrested and brought back northward over the frontier." On August 3 the crack SS division, the "Leibstandarte Adolf Hitler," began crossing the Brenner too. Its commander, SS Gruppenführer [lieutenant general] Sepp Dietrich, made a dynamic impression on Rommel—he was full of the special powers bestowed on him by Hitler. Rommel noted with evident approval, "He's fully prepared to play hell with the Italians to make them dance to his tune."

Rommel had now moved into Keitel's little villa at Pullach, outside Munich—the train's stifling heat had been affecting his health. He sent Corporal Böttcher to fetch his field-gray uniform from Wiener Neustadt, so that he would be ready for his personal appearance on Italian soil. "This new job is much more to my liking than the Balkans," he wrote, "but it's not going to be a piece of cake. We can imagine only too well what the Italians have up their sleeve—a quick jump over onto the other side, lock, stock and barrel." On August 4 he added in a mocking tone: "The King of Italy can't seem to find the way out. Evidently the British and Americans haven't given him even the faintest hope of mercy. That leaves him only one choice—either anarchy in his own country or continuing the fight at our side. I expect I'll soon get to know him face to face." Two days later, he hit a note a full octave higher: "Kesselring will probably have to quit soon—I expect he's seething with rage. Mussolini probably won't come back. Evidently the Party was indeed very corrupt; it was swept aside in a matter of hours. Mussolini is said to have been a failure in every respect. On the other hand, it suits us down to the ground to have only one great man leading Europe"—meaning Hitler.

The Italian High Command reacted with increasing firmness to Operation Alarich. They tried to obstruct rail and road movements of Rommel's inflowing divisions. They began moving their own Italian divisions northward —*away* from the Sicilian battlefield!—toward the Alps. Rommel showed great diplomacy. He instructed Feurstein to soothe General Gloria's ruffled feelings, and to talk only of "securing the Alpine passes as a common duty of both the German and the Italian forces." "Try and keep things cool," Rommel said. "Otherwise we'll send the SS." On August 8, however, came the incident that finally convinced him that the new Italian regime was plotting to defect to the Allies. An SS task force sent forward to the naval base at La Spezia was halted and turned back; this could only mean that the Italian navy was being readied for an early escape to the enemy. "It's not a pleasant situation with these shifty, two-faced Italians," he said the next day. "To our faces they utter protestations of eternal loyalty in the common battle, but they trip us up wherever they can, and it looks as though they're making a deal behind our backs."

On Hitler's orders, Rommel flew to the Wolf's Lair again on the eleventh. He arrived in time for the noon conference and found Himmler, Göring, Dönitz and the paratroop general Kurt Student also standing at the table. "Discussing Italy, the Führer turns out to agree with my own views," noted Rommel in his diary. "Führer appears to intend sending me in quite soon. Like me, he doesn't believe in the honesty of the Italians. . . . The Führer says the Italians are playing for time; then they will defect. . . . The Führer evidently wants to adhere to his old plan of restoring Fascism to power, as this is the only way to ensure that Italy will stand unconditionally by us. He has sharp words of condemnation," continued Rommel with pleasure, "for the work of [Ambassador Hans von] Mackensen, Rintelen and Kesselring as they —particularly Kesselring—even today still totally misinterpret the Italian situation and blindly trust the new regime."

At lunch, he sat next to Hitler who gossiped with him with noticeable pleasure. ("Again and again I find that he has complete confidence in me," observed Rommel.) Afterward Rommel outlined his own proposals to General Jodl, chief of the High Command operations staff. "I think I ought to be given command of all Italy," said Rommel, "with two armies, north and south. I could then come under Italian orders, but my army group headquarters would be near Rome so as to exert an influence over the Italian High Command." Jodl raised some levelheaded objections, but Rommel believed he had gotten his own way as usual. At the evening conference, Hitler instructed him to call on the Italian military leaders in person and find out what they were up to. Thus a show-down was inevitable.

An SS guard of honor waited for Field Marshal Rommel as he, along with Jodl, stepped from his plane onto Italian soil at Bologna airfield at 10:00 A.M. on August 15. That was just the start. An entire battalion of motorized SS troops accompanied him and Jodl as they drove to the attractive Italian villa outside the city where they were to meet their "allies." After Italian sentries had taken up positions around and in the villa, the Waffen SS took up positions in a ring around them—the giant, blond Germans standing head and shoulders above the Italians, and occasionally marching up and down outside the main entrance in a thunderous goose step. Rommel, Jodl and all their colleagues carried loaded revolvers in holsters. Seldom can one ally have regarded another with such mistrust—and with such justification: at that very moment emissaries of the Italian High Command were furtively negotiating with the enemy in Madrid.

This did not prevent their spokesman, General Mario Roatta, one of the foxiest members of the Italian General Staff, from protesting: "We cannot permit you to express any doubts as to the propriety of our conduct and orders. To express such doubts is a profound insult to us."

In Rommel's papers in a twenty-page account of the meeting; there is also a twenty-eight page shorthand account in Italian army files. Both make entertaining reading. General Jodl did not mince his language. He asked Roatta right at the start about reports that Italy was withdrawing its army from France: "Is it definite that these divisions are destined for southern Italy—for Sicily—or are they destined for the Brenner?" Roatta first indignantly refused to reply to "such a tendentious question," then denied that the divisions were going to be used to defend the Alpine passes against the Germans. General Jodl persisted, expressing the High Command's amazement that while Germany had loyally rushed forces into Italy for its defense, "to our surprise there has been a simultaneous Italian move in the opposite direction, toward the Alpine passes!"

Roatta answered the rest of Jodl's accusations evasively or diplomatically—he bravely protested and denied, marshaling arguments of increasing complexity. He forthrightly objected to the arrival of the SS division, considering them, as strong Nazis, kin to the overthrown Italian Fascist regime. "We object to their political physiognomy," he said. Jodl replied they were just a mechanized division like any other. According to the Italian note, Roatta retorted: "How would you like it if we sent a Jewish division into Germany, for example?"

Rommel hardly spoke. The Italian protocol on the meeting noted that he smiled only once. Any smiles on Italian faces vanished when Jodl announced: "You will please take note of the fact that the new German troops arriving in Italy are subject to the orders of Field Marshal Rommel." The High Command had decided unilaterally that Rommel should command all German and Italian troops in northern Italy; Kesselring would command in the south. Roatta's plan was very different. Taking a map, he indicated that all Rommel's forces should move from the north to central and southern Italy; only Italians would be left in the north. To the Germans the intention was plain enough—to establish a barrier across the peninsula, one that would cut off the Germans' escape after the forthcoming Italian defection to the enemy. Jodl cabled to the High Command: "Grounds for suspicion remain undiminished." Hitler therefore ordered the rapid evacuation of Sicily to begin, out of concern for German troops there.

Rommel's return to Italy caused uproar in the Italian High Command. General Vittorio Ambrosio wrote a furious letter two days after the Bologna meeting, demanding his withdrawal: "Marshal Rommel may have eminent qualities as a commander, but he is still affected by events in North Africa, Tunisia and particularly El Alamein. Last winter the Italian High Command procured his recall from Tunisia and then ensured that he would not be sent back there. In the circumstances it seems most inappropriate for Rommel to assume command in Italy." The Germans turned a deaf ear on Ambrosio. That afternoon, August 17, Rommel drove to Lake Garda in northern Italy to set up his new headquarters; but the Italians were not helpful—they refused permission for him to lay telephone lines from there back to Munich. The SS division also reported that tank traps had been built on the highway farther south, between Florence and Pisa, that were obviously aligned only against German movements. Rommel wondered how long it would be before the Italian High Command came out in its true colors.

That Lucie and Manfred were still housed in Wiener Neustadt, not far from the Messerschmitt aircraft factories, worried Rommel deeply. He knew from Alfred Berndt —now Goebbels's special expert on air defense—just what had happened a few weeks ago in Hamburg. Forty thousand civilians had been incinerated in one great fire raid. Goebbels had ordered 2 million nonessential civilians to evacuate Berlin, the next likely target. The first big raid hit the Reich capital on August 23, and next morning Gause learned that he had lost his house and everything; Frau Gause had returned home from East Prussia to find only blackened, smoldering ruins.

Rommel telephoned Lucie from Munich, urgently, and told her it was vital to crate up their most precious possessions in good time and remove them to safety. "You see how suddenly it happens!" he wrote next day. "Rather do without the sight of most of our favorite things for the time being, and know them safe in the country, than see them burn." "Even their basement burned out," he added in another letter. "We must get our family papers, carpets, silver, clothing and linen into safety, and fast." To this list he added as afterthoughts their oil paintings, his cameras, the photograph signed by the Führer, a Samurai sword mailed to him by the Japanese embassy—Rommel could not find time to attend the award ceremony—and the hunting guns. When he learned that all Gause's money had been in the bank—also destroyed—Rommel anxiously instructed Lucie: "Take care you don't have too much money in your savings account at Wiener Neustadt. Find out if accounts are automatically transferred to other banks when one is bombed out—I don't expect that the little savings bank at Wiener Neustadt does this." That was real Swabian prudence.

Most of their precious belongings could be taken by truck to the remote farm of an old First World War comrade, Oskar Farny, deep in the Bavarian countryside.

Rommel had already sent him trunks full of diaries and papers. On August 22, he had flown over to see Farny, landing his Storch plane in one of the fields. They lunched on trout, had crab with afternoon tea and reminisced about their times in the Württemberg mountain battalion. After a while Rommel asked Farny point-blank: "What do you think about the war?"

Farny tried to conceal his embarrassment. "If our field marshals start flying into the country and asking the farmers questions like that," he replied, "then the war's not going well."

Rommel nodded agreement, and said: "No doubt about it."

Since early August, Rommel's safe had contained secret orders for Operation "Axis." When Hitler signaled the code word Axis, Rommel was to swoop down on the Italian forces massing in northern Italy, disarm the troops and take over the coastal defenses. It would not be easy. General Feurstein warned him privately that there were nearly 40,000 Italian troops in the Forty-fourth Infantry Division's area alone. Rommel hinted that the code word might be issued very suddenly. "When fighting breaks out with the Italians, you are to strike hard and fast with your heaviest weapons, including the Nebelwerfer"—the rocket missile that had terrorized the Americans at Kasserine. Rommel did not underestimate the seriousness of the German troops' position if, as he expected, the enemy staged a seaborne landing at La Spezia—in the north, right in Italy's "groin"—and the Italian regime simultaneously switched to the enemy side. "Our men would have to fight on two fronts," he explained to Lucie.

The one strategy that Rommel considered most unlikely was the one the enemy subsequently adopted: landing right on the toe of Italy and crawling all the long, exhausting way up the boot. He believed the British would go straight for La Spezia, where the Italian fleet was anchored, thus securing a bridgehead behind the last easily defended "garter" line—the Apennine mountains, from Leghorn across the peninsula to Rimini. In fact, Rommel —as usual—differed strongly from Kesselring, who wanted a concentration of their strength in southern Italy.

Richthofen, the Luftwaffe commander, had visited Rommel on August 17 and argued Kesselring's case: "If we give up southern Italy," he pointed out, "my Luftwaffe will not be able to hold out in the north." (The best airfields were in the south.) In his plane back from Munich, Richthofen wrote in his private diary: "We see eye to eye on how to treat the Italians. But he lacks any overall view. Sees things only from the narrowest possible army standpoint, regardless of the strategic situation. Seems downright pigheaded, thinks just in tactical terms, with a bit of a tic since Africa about his supply problem."

The British Eighth Army landed two divisions right down on Italy's toenail, at Reggio di Calabria, on September 3. Rommel was ordered to report the next morning to Hitler. Rommel's diary noted: "The Führer makes a tranquil, confident impression. He wants to send me to see the King of Italy soon. He agrees to my Italian campaign plan, which envisages a defense along the actual coastline, despite Jodl's objections (which don't hold water in a modern war)." They dined together at eight-thirty. Hitler seriously warned Rommel to be on guard when visiting the King of Italy.

"The Führer has forbidden me to touch any food there," wrote Rommel—adding pointedly, "He's concerned about my health."

Events now came with dramatic swiftness. It was September 8, a hot and airless day all over Europe. Rommel had already sent his luggage down to his new army group headquarters near Lake Garda in northern Italy, but to avoid compromising Operation Axis, he himself was still in Munich. That evening, radio stations all over the world began announcing that Marshal Badoglio had already signed Italy's surrender to the Allies. Badoglio and Roatta denied it for two hours, then admitted it was true. At 7:50 P.M. the German High Command telephoned the code word Axis to Rommel and Kesselring. At 8:20 P.M. it was confirmed in writing: "Marshal Badoglio agrees accuracy of Allied radio broadcasts about Italian surrender. Code word Axis takes immediate effect."

Unfortunately, Rommel's diary is missing for the next weeks, but events can be picked up from his letters, from the war diary of Army Group B and from Italian files.

"Now Italy's treachery is official," he wrote to Lucie on the ninth. "We sure had them figured out right. So far our plans are running smoothly." Rome was seized by German troops, and General Rainer Stahl, a tough Luftwaffe commander, took charge. In Milan and Turin there were Communist-inspired uprisings. Rommel's troops and the SS moved ruthlessly to put them down. In beautiful old Florence there were battles with Italian tanks. The Italian fleet ran to sea from La Spezia and steamed toward enemy-held havens—there was nothing Rommel could have done to prevent their escape. Badoglio, Ambrosio and Roatta fled with their king and crown prince to the mercy of the enemy.

The next day the U.S. Fifth Army launched its seaborne invasion of Salerno, south of Naples. Decoded American radio traffic revealed that the Italians had disclosed the locations of their minefields to the enemy. Kesselring's directive from Hitler was to stage a fighting retreat "if necessary" northward toward Rome—but the American invasion troops put up such a temptingly poor showing against General Hube's defenders that he decided to try and defeat them then and there.

Meanwhile, north of his demarcation line just below Florence—from the island of Elba to Ancona—Rommel set about disarming and rounding up the Italian army. He was not gentle. "In the south," he explained in a letter, "Italian soldiers are already fighting against us side by side with the British. In the north, we're disarming them and packing them off to Germany as prisoners. What an infamous end for an army!" The next day his staff left for the new headquarters near Garda. The diary of General Feurstein's Fifty-first Corps describes an inspection visit by Rommel on the fourteenth. Rommel realized that he had pitifully few troops to defend hundreds of miles of Italian coast, so he laid down a basic rule that was to become a mania for him throughout 1944 as well: "Everything available is to be inserted along the coast itself. *No reserves* are to be held. The enemy must be warded off while still afloat." After dealing with the extraction of military and economic booty from his half of Italy, and the arrival of a railroad gun battery to command the entrances to La Spezia and Leghorn harbors,

Rommel ordered: "If anybody gives shelter to British escapers, they must reckon with the execution of their entire family." Then he flew to his headquarters.

That evening, misfortune befell him. At 9:00 P.M. he was quite well, but ninety minutes later he was writhing in agony. He was violently sick and crippled by abdominal pains all night. He was rushed to the hospital and operated on for appendicitis. A week later they removed the stitches, and on the twenty-seventh he was discharged from the hospital. Of his stomach incision he joked to Lucie: "You'll just have to look the other way."

Many times, as he lay in the hospital, he had heard the air raid sirens sound. All Germany was wondering which city would be the next to suffer Hamburg's fate. Everywhere, painted arrows told the public which way to flee if fire storms broke out again. With a start, the field marshal realized that since Kesselring obviously would soon have to evacuate all southern Italy, the enemy would obtain the magnificent airfields at Foggia. That meant that strategic bomber operations against Austria—including perhaps Wiener Neustadt—would then begin in real earnest. He wrote privately to Lucie begging her to start looking immediately for somewhere else to live. "Best of all would be to move to Württemberg." The longer she waited, the harder would be the house hunting, because soon everyone would be fleeing from the cities of the southern Reich. Lucie, of course, resisted leaving her beloved home.

Kesselring had high hopes of bringing the enemy invasion offensive to a standstill—and even throwing them back into the sea at Salerno. On September 12 he obtained permission for a counterattack. But by September 16 eight enemy divisions had landed and were facing Hube's four divisions. A fighting withdrawal began, northward up the Italian peninsula. Hitler authorized Kesselring to block the enemy's advance by destroying bridges, roads, tunnels and railroad installations all the way. The Italians here had abetted the enemy—now their countryside would pay the price.

This was the situation when Rommel left the hospital on the twenty-seventh. That afternoon, Field Marshal Keitel telephoned from the High Command asking Rommel to fly to the Wolf's Lair for another meeting with Hitler to discuss their autumn strategy. This time Kesselring would also be present. When Rommel walked into Hitler's conference room after noon on September 30, the Führer looked distinctly fatigued—almost ill. He was stooped, and he stammered and barely joined the laughter when General Jodl—discussing whether there was any place for beasts of burden in modern infantry divisions—snapped: "I ought to know: I've had to deal with asses and donkeys nearly all my life!" A lieutenant colonel, present for the first time, whose diary contains the only record of this discussion, wrote: "Only sometimes does the Führer's belief in the correctness of his actions and his faith in victory show passionately through."

Rommel and Kesselring began by reporting the captures they had made in Italy under Operation Axis. They had already disarmed 800,000 Italian troops and transported 268,000 northward to Germany as prison labor. They had taken over 448 tanks, 2,000 guns and half a million rifles. This was not the most astonishing find, however. In three tunnels at La Spezia, Rommel's troops had discovered a hoard of fuel oil for the Italian submarines and warships—38,000 barrels, the equivalent of 1,650,000 gallons of oil, hidden away by the same Italian High Command who had protested all the time that they could not escort supply convoys to Rommel in North Africa because their navy had no fuel! (Much more was found elsewhere in later weeks.)

Göring then chimed in: "We have laid hands on hundreds of first-rate Italian fighter planes too."

Hitler's face showed skepticism, but Kesselring agreed. Hitler exlaimed, "How have these cripples been getting away with it!"

Göring said on impulse, "For years the Italians and the Duce have been quite deliberately tricking us. They just tucked away planes and raw materials. The Duce was so ignorant he ought to be shot."

This remark did not please Hitler, who had just gone to great expense and effort to free Mussolini from the mountain prison in which he had been held. "The real blame lies with the king and his generals," he replied. "They've been planning this treachery for a long time."

Then he turned to Kesselring and Rommel: "Every day, every week, every month that we can hold up the enemy down in the south of Italy is vital to us. We must gain time, we must postpone the final reckoning. Things don't smell rosy for the other side at all. They have just the same problems with manpower and materiel reserves as we do, and the time is going to come when they get fed up with it. There will come a certain point of time when we can no longer win the war by conquering the world, but only by keeping the war dragging on until the other side gives in."

The lieutenant colonel continued his diary account: "Several times the Führer then loudly proclaimed: 'Time, time, time!' "

But time was the one factor that Rommel could not offer. He proposed what at best would be a rapid, safe retreat in good order up the Italian peninsula to the Apennine line, ninety miles north of Rome. Kesselring, however, was doing unexpectedly well against the invaders, and on October 6 he submitted to Hitler a proposal for a final defense of Italy on a line only half as long, ninety miles south of Rome. He was sure he could hold this line at least over the coming winter. As a further bonus, Kesselring's line would deprive the enemy of Rome, and of a springboard into the Balkans. Hitler and Jodl greedily approved.

Rommel felt angry and frustrated that his advice had been ignored. He felt denied of what had been promised him and was rightfully his: the supreme command in Italy. He pointed to the one obvious drawback of Kesselring's plan, namely that the enemy would surely bypass the line at sea and land farther north, on either side of Rome, for example. Kesselring, for his part, said he could not concentrate on the battle with Rommel breathing down his neck from northern Italy and glowering at his every move. These increasingly debilitating squabbles had begun with Salerno, when Rommel had refused to lend Kesselring two first-rate panzer divisions which, in Hube's counterattack, might well have tilted the balance against the enemy. The other commanders watched the infantile backbiting with irritation. On October 13 Field Marshal von Richthofen observed in his diary: "Rommel's take-over of all Italy is now said to be imminent. . . . Let's hope there's then a degree of uniformity in the goings-on down here. With Rommel as pigheaded and worn out as he is, it's not going to be any easier doing business with him and his bunch, but anything's got to be better than the way things are now."

On October 17 Hitler did indeed send for Rommel and confirm that he had decided to honor his promise. Kesselring, he said, was going to be posted to Norway— a backwater, of no military significance whatever in 1943. However, added Hitler, the High Command wanted Rommel to defend the line currently held by Kesselring, from Gaeta to Ortona, throughout the winter; in Jodl's words, the line was "impregnable." Rommel expressed powerful —and highly tactless—reservations. Before taking over as "Supreme Commander, Italy" (the title he proposed), he wanted to inspect Kesselring's theater for himself. And he demanded a clear directive allowing a flexible campaign: "I will then submit to you an unvarnished appraisal of how the battle should be fought—as soon as you have announced my appointment." At all this, Hitler felt a twinge of uneasiness. Speaking some months later, he was to recall: "At that time, Rommel predicted collapse in Italy as being only just around the corner." It was evidently a fractious war conference, because afterward when Hitler's adjutant Schmundt bumped into General Maximilian Hitzfeld—who had been Rommel's adjutant in 1938—Schmundt exclaimed: "It's getting harder every time to see eye to eye with Rommel." Rommel himself cursed out loud about Keitel and Jodl and called them "assholes."

So this was Rommel in October 1943: domineering, obstinate and defeatist by any normal interpretation of those words; outspoken about his own rectitude, no matter how many of his sorrowing friends and admirers he alienated thereby; already worrying about the postwar era, about his personal property and his family's fortunes; but still, instinctively, grasping at the largest, most purple mantle of supreme power that Hitler had to offer.

There are vivid impressions of Rommel at this time. One is by war correspondent Lutz Koch, who accompanied him on his visit to Mussolini on October 12. The Führer had liberated the Duce and reinstated him as the tattered dictator of a shrinking domain being invaded by a relentless enemy from the south and eroded by rapacious Nazi gauleiters from the north. While SS sentries pranced outside, Rommel ranted in German at the Duce, blaming him for the Axis defeat in Africa. At times he shouted so loudly that the puppet Italian ministers cowering in the courtyard could hear.

The other impression is in the penciled diary compiled by General Kurt Dittmar, the German army's widely respected wartime broadcaster. Under "November 8, 1943," Dittmar records his memorable visit to Rommel in Italy. His notes reveal the authentic Rommel:

Expresses contempt for Fascism in Italy. Mussolini's lack of credit. In discussion, Rommel says Mussolini is to blame for the failure of the Italian army. Built fortifications against Germany! The Führer has also begun gradually dissociating himself from Mussolini. He wrote a journal in captivity, pathetic attempts at self-justification, claims he strove his utmost for a satisfactory end.

OKW [German High Command] didn't have the faintest idea about Badoglio's treachery, they took him as a man of his word right to the last moment. . . . Rommel's damning verdicts on OKW operations staff: Jodl, Warlimont and rest are out of place, the whole bunch of them, they've been at their posts far too long. Bitter language about "impregnable defense positions" that exist only in the OKW's fevered imagination. Says of the Führer, he's very farsighted, but the officers around him—and he again lists them, from Keitel through Schmundt (yes, Rommel even includes his friend Schmundt!)—set aside any decision that takes actual situations into account.

Rommel, one of our great historic figures. No defeatist.

Rommel flew back from the Wolf's Lair to his headquarters near Lake Garda two days after seeing Hitler, Oc-

tober 19, 1943. He phoned Jodl, who confirmed that
Hitler's formal order appointing him Supreme Commander
was "on the way." But at 7:30 P.M. the picture suddenly changed. Jodl phoned back, and told Rommel:
"The Führer's order has been set aside for the moment."
What did this mean? Jodl would not say. Rommel met his
new operations officer this day—Colonel Hans-Georg von
Tempelhoff, thirty-six, an urbane, fair-haired veteran of
the Russian front. Rommel showed him the blue chalk
line on the map above Rome that marked his proposed
Apennine line and directed him to write a detailed study
of the best way to fight a flexible campaign of retreat
from Kesselring's present position up to the blue line.

*"It's almost made my hair go gray," wrote Tempelhoff to
a friend in January 1944.*

*Over thirty years later I found Tempelhoff living with
his English-born wife, Marianne, in a villa at the foot of
the Zugspitz mountain in Bavaria. There were many talks
with him—because Tempelhoff was one of the key members of Rommel's staff for the rest of the field marshal's
career and therefore a very important witness. He was
open and pleasant and had an excellent memory, which at
times his shrewd and over-anxious wife tried to stop him
laying too bare. He described how he and Rommel spent
the next weeks preparing the Apennine line, touring the
troops and inspecting the defenses. "I remember one
visit to a big armaments factory in Milan," Tempelhoff
said. "There were big-caliber guns there, all neatly slit
open down the barrel by the Italians so we could not use
them." And he remembered another occasion: "Once at
supper Rommel—heedless of the white-jacketed flunkies
hovering in the background—loudly announced, 'We've
all heard a lot of tales about new secret weapons. Take it
from me, there aren't any. The time is drawing nearer
when we'll have to make up our minds which side to
make a deal with.' One of the officers responded: 'Either
East or West.' To which Rommel replied, 'There's no
question of dealing with the East.'"*

Rommel was the last to discover that he had in fact talked
himself out of a job at the Wolf's Lair on October 17.

Four days later, Richthofen learned it through the Luftwaffe grapevine, and wrote with private relish: "Seems that Rommel isn't going to get the supreme command here in Italy after all. Evidently he put up a poor showing at his conference with the Führer, which doesn't surprise me one bit." Three days after that, the diary of Hitler's manservant describes how he glimpsed Kesselring, Rommel's arch rival, conferring with Hitler, then lunching together with him, Keitel, Jodl and Schmundt. After that, Hitler decided to give the optimist, Kesselring, the supreme command in Italy. It looked to Rommel as though he was headed for his gray homburg hat again. His misery was considerable; his hatred of the High Command became extreme. "Perhaps," he wrote to Lucie a few days later, "I didn't rouse enough hope that our position could be held. Perhaps the reservations I expressed before taking on the command were the cause. Perhaps there were quite different reasons. Anyway—for the time being Kesselring is to remain."

# Think Victory

W E now know that it was Jodl's staff at the High Command who had engineered this abrupt reverse in Rommel's fortunes. One of them wrote six years later that while Rommel's skepticism toward the Italians had been invaluable during the Nazi preparations to occupy Italy, his notorious lack of diplomacy would have made it impossible for him to work harmoniously with the Italians now that a Mussolini "government" had been restored. And, as Schmundt's war diary as chief of army personnel observes, "Unfortunately Field Marshal Rommel is still obsessed by the retreat from Africa. Another job, having nothing to do with Italy, will be better for him."

But what could become of Rommel, and what of his tight-knit staff? The German public would never understand it if Rommel was merely shelved. This was Hitler's dilemma—how to employ the myth-marshal created by his own propaganda machine. As a first awkward solution, Hitler arranged to keep Rommel's army group staff intact: it would stand by to tackle whatever need arose. This should have appealed to Rommel's mathematical mind—because mathematics is a science abounding with "solutions looking for a problem." But to Rommel it was mortifying and humiliating. He felt that he had now finally been put on the shelf.

It was Jodl himself who provided a solution to the Rommel problem. On October 30 he submitted to the Führer a bulky report from the Commander in Chief West, Field Marshal Gerd von Rundstedt—Germany's oldest and senior serving field marshal. The document exposed the horrifying weakness of Hitler's much publicized "Atlantic Wall," under construction since August 1942 along the coastline of Europe facing England. There was virtually nothing to stop a determined enemy invasion comparable with their successful landings at Sicily and Salerno. The coastal fortifications must be overhauled and intensified—and rapidly. Jodl recommended that this would be an ideal job for Rommel and his staff—to take tactical command of the invasion battle, wherever the enemy finally launched it. But Hitler would not go as far as that. He told Jodl to draft a suitable order but to mention only "study assignments" for Rommel, not "tactical command"—that would be going too far.

Hitler gave the news to Rommel at the Wolf's Lair late on November 5. He underlined the job's historic importance for the Reich. "When the enemy invades in the west it will be the moment of decision in this war," he said, "and the moment must turn to our advantage. We must ruthlessly extract every ounce of effort from Germany." Acting on Hitler's direct instructions, Rommel was to study defense plans and devise possible counterattacks if the enemy did get a foothold. Hitler hinted to Rommel that he would be given tactical command when the battle started; but he did not inform Rundstedt of this promise. On the contrary, he had the forethought to send Wilhelm Keitel, the chief of the High Command, secretly to Paris to assure Rundstedt that his position as Commander in Chief West was secure. More than that: "Should the time ever come for your replacement because of failing health," Keitel advised Rundstedt, "the Führer wishes you to know that only Field Marshal von Kluge is in the running to succeed you." The Führer was aware that Rommel was no great strategist, not supreme commander material, continued Keitel; but he was a dynamic soldier. "You'll find Rommel a tiresome person because he doesn't like taking orders from anybody. In Africa, of course, he very much ran his own show. But the Führer believes you are the one man to whom even a Rommel will show due respect." Rundstedt accepted this obvious flattery with an obliging smile, and retired to his luxurious suite upstairs in the Hôtel George V.

Rommel drew enormous energy from his brief, auspicious contact with the Führer. After he flew back to Italy to wind up his affairs, he wrote enthusiastically: "What power he radiates! And what faith and confidence he inspires in his people!"

By selecting Rommel, Hitler had reasoned that alone of the Nazi commanders, Rommel had years of experience of fighting the British and Americans. These enemies knew and feared him. Besides, Hitler wanted to give Rommel a real chance to regain his lost renown.

Rommel, though grateful, was by no means serene. There is a record of his attitude during this time in the diary of his former interpreter, Dr. Ernst Franz. Franz called at Rommel's Lake Garda headquarters on November 15, 1943, to give him birthday greetings—Rommel was then fifty-two. Rommel learned that the new Nazi governor appointed by Hitler for Istria and Dalmatia had issued orders conflicting with his own, and he telephoned Jodl in Franz's presence to protest. "Tell your man," he bellowed into the phone, "that I won't have his little viceroys meddling around with my orders!" His voice still trembling with emotion, Rommel resumed his conversation with his ex-interpreter: "I'm afraid I can't wish you well for the future, dear Franz, because the war is as good as lost and hard times lie ahead. All our propaganda about secret weapons is only bluff." Franz was profoundly shocked by Rommel's pessimism.

On November 21 Rommel bid farewell to Mussolini and Kesselring—separately—then flew out of Italy and went home. Scared that something might happen to Lucie and Manfred at Wiener Neustadt, he had managed at last to move them; he had sent them to live in a village near Ulm, in his native Swabia. They had been quartered at nearby Herrlingen in the summer villa of a Frau Laibinger—widow of an Ulm brewer killed in a British air raid—while the city of Ulm prepared a more fitting domicile for their honored guest. Here in the Laibinger villa Rommel rested in the bosom of his loving family for the rest of November.

Hitler's formal directive instructed Rommel to inspect the defenses of the entire coastline confronting England, starting in the north. On December 1 his staff assembled at the Munich railroad station and boarded his special train. For two weeks they toured the Danish coast. They marveled at the well-stocked food stores and the abundance of luxury goods that were just memories in war-torn Germany. The weather was bleak, the countryside monotonous—not at all like the sleepy valleys and defiles of his native Swabia. He thought it most unlikely that the enemy would invade Denmark, for the simple reason that the balance of air power here was in Germany's favor. Isolated coastal gun batteries were the only defensive strongpoints. His telling comment, dictated to his new young staff officer Lieutenant Hammermann, was: "The main battle line is drawn too far back from the coast." This restated the important principle that he had established in northern Italy: that massive invasion forces were best defeated at the beaches.

On December 14 he took off for southern Germany and a few more days' leave. It was a long flight from Denmark to Bavaria. Rommel watched the unbroken cloud banks glittering beneath his Heinkel in the afternoon sun. Facing him across the folding table was his new engineer expert, the bushy-browed General Wilhelm Meise. After a while, Rommel began to think out loud. "When the invasion begins," he said, "our own supply lines won't be able to bring forward any aircraft, gasoline, rockets, tanks, guns or shells because of the enemy attacks. That alone will rule out any sweeping land battles. Our only possible defense will be at the beaches—that's where the enemy is always weakest."

Meise listened fascinated as Rommel described how he had decided to create an impregnable swathe of minefields and bunkers, six miles wide, along the entire Atlantic wall—like his terrifying El Alamein line, but fifty times as long. "I want antipersonnel mines, antitank mines, antiparatroop mines—I want mines to sink ships and mines to sink landing craft," the field marshal exclaimed above the roar of the Heinkel's engines. He took a sheet of paper. "I want some minefields designed so that our own infantry can cross them, but not the enemy tanks. I want mines that detonate when a wire is tripped; mines that explode when a wire is cut; mines that can be remote-controlled, and mines that will blow up when a beam of light is interrupted. Some of them must be encased in nonferrous metals, so that the enemy's mine detectors won't register them . . ." And with a few deft lines he began drawing just what he had in mind.

Meise later wrote: "Quite apart from Rommel's greatness as a soldier, in my view he was the greatest engineer of the Second World War. There was nothing I could teach him. He was my master."

The new Rommel family home would soon be ready. In 1942 the state had confiscated a villa in Herrlingen which was a Jewish old peoples' home and begun converting it as a night refuge for the mayor of Ulm when the air raids began. But the Party had accused the mayor of "desertion" of his city, so the villa and its spacious grounds were still vacant. The city of Ulm willingly agreed to rent it to the celebrated field marshal. In December 1943 Russian prisoners were still excavating a twenty-foot-deep air raid shelter for the villa, and landscaping work in the gardens was incomplete; so Rommel again spent the two or three days with his family at the villa of the brewer's widow. But one day he did stroll over to see his future home with his ex-adjutant Hermann Aldinger, who was directing the landscaping. He encountered the mayor of Herrlingen and asked two curious questions that the mayor still remembered ten years later. The first was: "Are there many Prussians around here? Don't let so many Prussians come and live here!" And "What do *you* think of the war?" was the second—to which the gasping mayor could think of no safe reply.

On December 18 Rommel arrived back in France for the first time since relinquishing command of the Spook Division in 1940. The balance had shifted grimly for the Germans since then. Now Hitler was facing the British Empire, the United States and the USSR, and Italy had changed to the enemy side. Air raids of 2,000 or 3,000 bombers were a commonplace. Millions of enemy troops were known to be training for the assault on Hitler's "Fortress Europe"—and nobody yet knew where they would land. Rommel's job was to stop them.

He was quartered at Fontainebleau outside Paris, in Madame de Pompadour's elegant château. It was a far cry from the battle trailer and tent of the Libyan desert, and Rommel did not like it. The next day, as he drove into Paris to pay his respects to Field Marshal von Rundstedt, the newspapers were full of his arrival. "Evidently I can't be displayed soon enough to the British and Americans," wrote Rommel—and it pleased him that his name still counted for so much.

It was a long time since he had last seen Rundstedt. At sixty-eight, he was still Germany's most senior soldier; he was the Grand Old Man, respected even by the French. He was loyal to the Reich, but ailing and decrepit. His eyes were circled and puffy; his skin was pale; his thinning hair was plastered to his scalp. He seldom began work before ten each morning, and he wasted hours reading detective novels or Karl May adventure stories, or playing with a big dachshund in the hotel conservatory. His attitude to Hitler was ambivalent. He damned him frequently—"Without Hitler's consent I can't even move my own sentry from my front door around to the back!" —but each time that Hitler sacked him—in 1938, 1941 and again in 1944—Rundstedt meekly accepted the new high office that the Führer subsequently gave him. Rundstedt was too ambitious an old soldier just to fade away.

After lunch he briefed Rommel on the situation here in the west. He concluded, speaking in English (an affectation common among General Staff officers): "To me, things look black." Rommel was frankly appalled by the lethargy of Rundstedt's staff. He recalled only too well how the British had checkmated him in North Africa in early 1942 by laying over 1 million mines in two months; yet in three years only 1,700,000 mines had been laid here in France, and that figure was increasing at the rate of only 40,000 per month. He wrote that day to Lucie,

"I'm going to throw myself into this new job with everything I've got, and I'm going to see it turns out a success."

*In November 1943 the surviving Rommel diary resumes —now evidently kept for him by his much-decorated, one-eyed staff officer Lieutenant Hammermann. Among Rommel's family papers I also found the war diaries of Rommel's Army Group B. And the official files of the armies, corps and divisions in the west also still exist. Together, this material is extremely informative about the coming historic battles.*

*But I chanced upon another source. I called on Lieselotte von Salmuth, a courtly, gray-haired widow then living in a rambling, echoing house in Wiesbaden full of the memories of her late husband. Colonel General Hans von Salmuth commanded one of the German armies in France in 1944, under Rommel. After several hours' polite conversation, she suddenly said: "You know, I still have all my husband's papers and diaries. They're upstairs, in the attic. Nobody is ever going to see them." She must have noticed my ears prick up. She smiled sweetly and said: "Nobody, not even you." I left her an hour later and began a correspondence full of veiled entreaty. When I next set foot in her drawing room, there was a dusty brown leather suitcase on the floor. It contained all her husband's papers.*

Right from the start, Rommel put his money on one hunch: that the most probable coastline to be invaded was the Fifteenth Army's sector, extending from Belgium to the river Somme in France. He set out to tour it, with newsreel teams and war reporters in attendance. On December 20 he drove up to General Hans von Salmuth's army headquarters, a rich, comfortable château near Tourcoing, for lunch. Salmuth was a hard-bitten Prussian-school commander, who had seen tough combat on the eastern front. Condescending toward Hitler's "inspector," Salmuth later admitted an instinctive dislike of generals like Rommel. But Rommel had Hitler's ear, and if this helped inject fresh forces into the western front, then Salmuth was prepared to humor him.

Rommel's notes made it obvious that he had formed a

clear—and, as it turned out, dramatically accurate—image of the enemy's likely invasion tactics. First there would be violent bombing raids; then a seaborne landing on a broad front by hundreds of assault craft and armored landing craft, with fire cover provided by offshore warships and fighter-bombers; there would be simultaneous airborne landings a short distance inland, to prize open the Atlantic wall from the rear and help establish a quick bridgehead.

There is a record of his first talk with Salmuth in the Fifteenth Army files too. It is clear from it that he had already begun to crystallize a defensive strategy. "Field Marshal Rommel's view is that our defense forces must be concentrated much closer to the coast. Our reserves are to be brought up forward and thrown into an immediate counterattack. If the British once get a foothold on dry land, they can't be thrown out again." Rommel told him of his startling plan for a mine belt all along the coast. There were still 600,000 mines waiting to be laid; but even dummy minefields would help obstruct the enemy, as Africa had shown. Salmuth now warmed to the theme: "We'll need above all to have powerful fighter defenses, and fast, once the invasion begins." Rommel reassured him: "I've been promised a thousand fighter planes." Salmuth exclaimed, "With a thousand fighters we can repulse any invasion attempt!"

Rommel and Salmuth toured the Fifteenth Army's sector—the heavily fortified ports, the existing puny minefields only twenty to fifty yards in depth, the pillboxes, the bombproof bunkers for motor torpedo boats at Dunkirk and the much-photographed twelve-inch gun battery on Cap Gris Nez, just twenty miles from the English coast. On Christmas Eve, he was also shown something really secret—the launching sites being built for Hitler's wonder weapons. There were long-range rockets and pilotless flying bombs that would rain down on London when Hitler gave the word. Rommel was astounded to learn that the Nazis did have secret weapons ready after all—here was the evidence of it. At Wizernes was an awesome underground rocket-launching complex, forerunner of the missile silos of today. At nearby Mimoyecques, German engineers and slave laborers were building a subterranean gun battery with 400-foot barrels, permanently aligned on London 100 miles away. These missile sites were reason enough, in Rommel's view, for the enemy to have to invade Europe right here.

Over Christmas he stayed at his desk at Fontainebleau, writing up what he had seen. He was angered by the contrast between the bomb-gutted towns of Germany and the peacefulness of the French and Belgian towns and villages, he wrote Lucie. The hand of war had rested only briefly on them. "Day and night," he went on, "I'm racking my brains on my new job. I've got high hopes that we're going to pull this one off." In fifty letters between now and June 1944, this was the message he kept repeating. It was as though he had consulted a psychiatrist about the bouts of pessimism to which he was prone, and the doctor had advised him to repeat two words over and over again to himself: Think Victory!

When he had last spoken by phone to Lucie, she told him that their son had enlisted for antiaircraft defense—he was just fifteen. "Dear Manfred," he wrote him. "In fourteen days you'll be leaving your parental home and enlisting as a Luftwaffe auxiliary. So life begins in earnest for you. I hope you'll bring us as much joy in uniform as you have up to now. A new way of life is starting for you. You'll have to learn to obey the orders of your superiors without answering back. Often there'll be orders that don't suit you, or that you don't get the point of. Obey without question. A superior can't go into a long palaver with his subordinates. There just isn't the time to give reasons for every order. Remember your moral upbringing and don't fall into bad company. I've talked with you often enough about that. You know the importance I attach particularly to this question of conduct." It brought a lump to the field marshal's throat. It seemed only yesterday that Manfred's rabbits had formed the center of his young life. And yet he hardly knew the boy.

*At his hilltop villa just outside Stuttgart—the city of which he is now mayor—I several times met and talked with Manfred Rommel. He is not much like his father, and in some ways finds the family name something of an encumbrance in his career: he has the talent and evident*

*ability to get to the top without it, and he resents any hint
to the contrary. He has a thick Swabian lisp and, as did
the field marshal, inclines to a certain paunchiness;
Manfred was successfully fighting this tendency over the
two years that I saw him, and at the end of this period his
suits were beginning to hang loosely on his formerly ample frame.*

*"Late in 1943," he told me, "I informed my father that
I wanted to volunteer for the Waffen SS. At the time they
were the elite, they had the best officers and most modern
weapons and their uniform was smartest, too. 'Out of the
question!' snapped my father. 'You'll join the same service I did, thirty years ago.' When I argued, my father
admitted that the Waffen SS had fine fighting qualities
but he did not want me under the command of SS chief
Heinrich Himmler. 'I have reason to believe that Himmler
has been carrying out mass killings,' my father explained.
'I have heard that people like him are trying to burn the
bridges of the German people behind them by actions
like these.' "*

Rommel outlined his defense ideas to Field Marshal von
Rundstedt over tea on December 27. Like Salmuth,
Rundstedt also supported Rommel's basic plan to defeat
the enemy invasion actually on the beaches. But he differed with Rommel on one detail that was to prove important: he would not allow the panzer divisions to be moved
right up to the coast, because, he said, if the enemy invasion then came somewhere else—"And for me too there is
no doubt whatever that the main invasion will most probably come either side of the Somme"—the tanks could not
be moved rapidly across from the sector that Rommel had
committed them to.

The new year, the momentous year of 1944, began.
From January 2 to 5 Rommel inspected the next sector
on his map—the coastlines of Holland and Belgium. He
did not really expect the enemy to risk landing here, because the countryside was broken up by countless waterways and could be easily swamped as well. Again
anger surged within him as he saw how little the tidy
Belgian and Dutch towns and villages had suffered. "Everywhere the deepest peace," he reflected on January 3,

after a 300-mile drive. "They are well paid, they don't have the crippling taxation that we do, and they just can't wait to be liberated from us. Their towns are beautiful and are spared by the enemy. It makes you sick, when you think how hard our people are having to fight to defend our existence against all comers."

A related problem was that this "milk and honey" existence in the west had rubbed off onto the Nazi occupation troops. On paper, Rommel already had 1,300,000 troops here; but many of the coastal divisions were only units that had been sent here to be rehabilitated after fighting on the Russian front. Other divisions had little motor transport, few weapons and hardly any training. In most of the divisions the *average* age was thirty-seven. Seemingly unimportant gaps were being plugged with assortments of Russian troops who had volunteered to fight Stalin—only to find themselves now about to fight Americans, Canadians, Poles and British on French soil.

To Rommel, Paris seemed like a Babel. He had not abandoned his own Puritan life-style—he still did not smoke and rarely touched alcohol. On New Year's Eve his staff had seen him raise only two small glasses of claret to his lips. (Tempelhoff later recalled: "I once had to escort Montgomery in the fifties, and in this respect he reminded me very much of Rommel.") In the Paris of January 1944 there was a thriving black market, and the restaurants, theaters, brothels and cabarets were heavily patronized by the troops. Rommel saw more soldiers in the streets with briefcases and parcels than with weapons and ammunition.

When Hitler sent his trusted and proficient general Alfred Jodl to France early in January, he formed the same distasteful impressions. Jodl's humiliating inspection report to Hitler was widely circulated and Rommel got a copy: "The C in C West," wrote Jodl of Rundstedt, "would do well to exchange his Hôtel George V for a command post where he can see the blue sky, where the sun shines and which smells fresher." Jodl added: "Lower headquarters and officers' accommodations are a danger not only to security but also to inner attitudes and alertness. The bloom of war is completely missing. Deep armchairs and carpets lead to royal household allures. As of

March 1, all staffs are to move into their command posts. Unfortunately," Jodl sneered, "these too have largely been built next door to fine châteaux."

Rommel was equally shocked by the waywardness of the defense planning. His visit to the Luftwaffe commander in France—the 300-pound, sixty-five-year-old, heavy-jowled Field Marshal Hugo Sperrle—was another eye-opener. Sperrle stuck his monocle in his eye, propped up his vast bulk over a map of his airfields and nonchalantly explained that on the first day of the enemy's invasion there would be virtually no Luftwaffe opposition at all. The ground organization had been readied for the squadrons, but these—including pilot-instructors and pupils—would not actually begin arriving from the Reich for some days after the invasion began. Rommel wrote, "The prospects here aren't good at all. From all I had heard previously I've been expecting a lot more from this service."

A few days later he had a visit from his old friend from the Potsdam academy Colonel Kurt Hesse, now a local field commandant based near Paris. Rommel confided to Hesse that he was going to ask for several changes in the lower commanders that he had so far met. They had done virtually nothing for the defense of France. He fixed Hesse with a serious look. "If we don't succeed in driving the enemy back into the sea by the fourth day at the latest," declared Rommel, "then their invasion will have succeeded."

# Death Zone

O N January 15, 1944, Erwin Rommel dictates into his diary these words: "I have instructed that the troops are to ram stakes into the beaches as a barrier against landing craft."

As of this day, Rommel has been given tactical command of all the troops on the coast confronting England. Moreoever, Rundstedt has gone on five weeks' leave, leaving Rommel effectively free of supervision. To Rommel, it is a fine feeling to dictate the destinies of men again. On the tenth, General Warlimont of the High Command has telephoned Hitler's approval of Rommel's basic intention of defeating the enemy on the beaches. Rommel has been given dictatorial powers to this end. He can flood the countryside by damming rivers or, more ruthlessly, letting in the sea. He can uproot and evacuate the French and Belgians living in the six-mile Death Zone he has marked along the coast. He can rip down buildings if they obstruct his artillery's field of fire, and he can cut down entire forests to find the woods he needs. Thus he transforms the coastline of western Europe.

An expert on coastal defense has arrived to help Rommel. He is Vice Admiral Friedrich Ruge, a jovial, cocky Swabian. Ruge had organized the coastal defense forces of France, then become chief naval officer in Italy. Now he is Rommel's naval aide.

*I called on Friedrich Ruge many times at his home in the ancient university town of Tübingen. We would talk for hours over sherry and plates of genteel cakes. My father had fought against him in the great sea battles of the First World War, and it turned out that as an exercise he had translated into German a volume of doggerel,* Ruthless Rhymes for Heartless Homes, *that I had learned to recite as a child. We got on well, and the admiral handed over to me transcripts of his unpublished diaries to explore. He had written them in shorthand, so he had felt it safe to include many of the indiscretions that Rommel uttered over the next climactic months of his life.*

From General Meise, Rommel learned that there were enough captured explosives in France to manufacture about 11 million antipersonnel mines. On January 13, Rommel indicated to the visiting General Jodl that he wanted 2 million mines per month. But even this figure grew. Ruge records a luncheon on January 26 with a visiting general who, discussing mine laying, happened to say: "The fact that there are one million square meters in a square kilometer doesn't occur to most people." That caught Rommel's attention, and he asked Meise: "How many mines can we lay in a square kilometer, then? I make it sixty-five thousand." This gave him, by mid-March, a new target figure. By the time he had mined a one-kilometer strip on the seaward side of the Death Zone, and the strip on the landward side—against airborne landings—and filled in the gap between them, his troops would have laid 200 million mines in France. He did not doubt the feasibility.

His energy appalled his staff and the field commanders. He always left his headquarters before 8:00 A.M. And after the slack months in Italy, he began to jerk his body back into shape. He began hunting and shooting again, to take exercise. He stomped across the muddy fields around Fontainebleau until his limbs ached, gunning down the rabbits, hares and wild boars that were foolish enough to cross his path. It was only the return of his old lumbago trouble that stopped Rommel from indulging his hunting urge still more.

On January 16 he again visited Salmuth's Fifteenth Army on the Channel coast. The superior echelon here was the Eighty-first Corps. The corps had already laid 253,000 mines, mostly on either side of Cayeux-sur-Mer. The general explained that Salmuth was requiring each sapper to lay ten miles a day. "Make that twenty," snapped Rommel.

In private, Salmuth objected to the stiff demands being made by Rommel on his troops. They were getting so exhausted after a day with the pick and shovel that they had no time for real weapons training. "When the battle begins," protested Salmuth, "I want fresh, well-trained soldiers—not physical wrecks."

Rommel decided to show who was now in command. "Evidently you don't intend to carry out my orders," he said in challenge.

Salmuth resorted to Rommel's own tactics—he just scoffed at the field marshal and then patronizingly advised: "Stick around a bit, and you'll soon see that you can't do everything at once. Your program is going to take at least a year to put into effect. If anybody tells you different, then he's either just trying to flatter you or he's a pig idiot."

Rommel waited until his staff had rejoined their cars, then let fly at Salmuth until he was hoarse. Then both lapsed into silence. Very red in the face, Salmuth escorted him to his car. As it started back to Fontainebleau, Rommel cocked a thumb at Salmuth's receding figure and beamed at Ruge: "He's quite a roughneck, that one. That's the only language he understands."

To Lucie the next day the field marshal wrote, "I think we're going to win the battle for the defense of the west for certain—provided we get enough time to set things up." Think victory!

He had circulated all his requirements to his commanders. The document began with the simple statement: "The main battle line is to be the beach itself." Before any enemy landing craft could even reach that beach, he insisted, it must brave mines and murderous arrays of underwater stakes and obstacles. Behind the beaches would be the heavily mined Death Zone, with its infantry and artillery strongpoints; every man capable of pointing a rifle was to be in them, even the bakery companies. Behind the zone would wait—if Rommel got his way—the precious panzer divisions, with their tanks and artillery dug in and waiting to pound the beaches with shellfire.

He had still not gotten his way over the panzer divisions, however. Fighting desperate battles in Russia and southern Italy, Hitler's military reserves were overextended. Moreover, on January 22 the U.S. Fifth Army landed a corps at Anzio, only a bit south of Rome—just as Rommel had predicted. The High Command's only panzer reserves now were those in France, so there was no possibility of letting Rommel embed them permanently in his coastal defense system. Besides, there were long seasons when a major invasion of France was an impossibility. Rundstedt's chief tank expert, General Baron Leo Geyr von Schweppenburg, was schooling the available panzer divisions for sweeping cross-country operations to annihilate the enemy *after* they had landed. Rommel met him on January 8, and saw him at once as the typical red-trousered, blinkered General Staff officer. He discounted Geyr's vast battlefield experience in Russia as irrelevant to the coming campaign. Geyr, for his part, was horrified at what Rommel proposed to do with the panzer divisions —pushing them into the store window, so to speak, as fixed artillery behind a fixed Death Zone. Neither man budged in his views. Both were Swabian, both with a personal pride bordering—as the American interrogators later said of Geyr—"upon the ridiculous," and both obstinate to the point of pigheadedness. From this point on, the files and diaries fulminate with the increasingly explosive controversy.

Eleven weeks after getting the job from Hitler, Rommel went for the first time to look at the more distant coastline, the Brittany peninsula. It was held by the Seventh Army. He started on January 22, and at Le Mans, the Seventh's headquarters, he discussed the possible enemy invasion areas with General Friedrich Dollmann. General Dollmann was sixty-two, unusually tall, imposing—the product not of a long line of soldiers but of a civil service family. He had commanded the Seventh Army for more than four years. Rommel was sure the enemy would invade not Dollmann's area but Salmuth's Fifteenth Army, Dollmann's neighbor on the right. "His main argument," recalled Dollmann's chief of staff, General Max Pemsel, "was the shorter distance the enemy would have to go to reach Germany's vitals, the Ruhr region." Dollmann found the new arrangement which subordinated him to Rommel —a former junior—most distasteful. As the diaries of both Rommel and Army Group B establish, he tried to draw Rommel's attention to the advantage to the enemy of invading Normandy. The countryside of small fields and giant hedgerows positively invited airborne operations, as did the Cherbourg peninsula with the big seaport at its tip. The whole army sector was only weakly fortified. His troops had between them ninety-two different types of guns, 252 different types of shells and only 170 of the excellent seventy-five-millimeter antitank guns and sixty-eight eighty-eights. In Brittany, one division was required to defend a 150-mile front, while another was holding even more, a 180-mile sector.

On January 29 Rommel again set off, this time for Normandy itself. He was crippled by lumbago but carried on for three days, touring the blustery beaches and driving through unsuspecting towns and hamlets with names like Caen and Falaise, Cherbourg and Sainte-Mère-Eglise. At Caen, he called on the 716th Infantry Division, in the green meadow landscapes and the fertile plains of the bocage country. Did he pause for a glimpse at Caen itself—its fine old patrician houses rich with wood carvings, its 900-year-old Abbaye aux Dames and the twin Abbaye aux Hommes which contained the remains of William the Conquerer? What would become of these buildings if the fourteen-inch guns of the British battle fleet opened fire and the enemy's strategic bomber forces arrived overhead?

Then to Saint-Lô, to meet the general commanding the corps defending the Normandy sector, the Eighty-fourth. General Erich Marcks was a tough cookie. A master of military strategy, he had devised the General Staff's original plan for the attack on the USSR—and had paid the price by losing a leg in that campaign. Now he was in Normandy with a wooden leg, grimly determined to wreak revenge on the British for killing half his family in a night air raid. Death on the battlefield was the highest honor to generals like Marcks—and it was an honor the enemy would bestow on him just six days after the battle began. He spoke optimistically but Rommel rebuked him for not packing everything he had into the main battle line. Rommel noted in his diary with some disappointment: "Generally speaking, the troops are not working hard enough on the construction of defenses. They just don't realize how urgent it is. Everywhere there's a tendency to squirrel away reserves, and this will lead to the weakening of the coastal front."

Rommel had made an unforgettable impression on Marcks. The corps commander wrote to his surviving son: "Rommel's the same age as me but looks older—perhaps because Africa and its many trials have left their mark on him. He's very frank and earnest. He's not just a flash in the pan, he's a real warlord. It's a good thing that A[dolf] H[itler] thinks a lot of him, for all his bluntness, and gives him these important jobs."

Rommel's own judgment on the troops in Normandy was harsh: "There's still a lot to do, because many a man here has been living a soft life and hasn't thought enough about the battles that are coming." So he wrote to Lucie. And to Manfred: "In times of peace men grow lazy and self-content."

Like an ugly rash, Rommel's beach obstacles began springing up all along the coast of northwestern Europe. There were concrete and steel tetrahedrons, concrete dragon's teeth, jagged steel "Czech hedgehogs" welded from girders at right angles, and other nameless and indescribable devices, all of them made to rip or pierce the bottoms of Allied landing craft. Rommel lived only for his mission now. No amount of persuasion would get him to stay behind to inspect the fabled Mont-Saint-Michel on his first visit to the broad, sandy bay. He was far more concerned about the huge expanse of sand—ideal for airborne landings. "It needs two flak batteries up on top," he announced, pointing to the abbey's fairy-tale spires. He was not joking. Colonel von Tempelhoff, his new operations officer, wrote in annoyance on January 26, "On our journeys with the field marshal we always drive straight past the monuments and fine architecture. He's so completely wrapped up in his job that he's totally uninterested in anything else except the military needs of the moment. We notice this particularly during the communal meals with him each day." (In Italy it had been the same: they had driven straight through Pisa, despite protests from his staff. "How long has the tower been leaning already?" barked Rommel. "Then drive on, it will still be leaning when the war is over.")

Once at Saint-Malo, lunching in the villa that had belonged to the British industrialist Alfred Mond, Gause showed him lovingly a vase he had just found: it had been produced by the famous porcelain works at Sèvres. Rommel's face lit up. "Porcelain! Meise, why don't we use china for our land mine casings?"

With great ingenuity, he devised new defense techniques. He suggested they try injecting the heavy timber stakes into the beach with the jet of fire hoses. Sure enough, the idea worked: the posts could be embedded to their full depth in the sand in three minutes, compared with the forty-five minutes using conventional pile drivers. Rommel then ordered the troops to clamp mines to the obstacles as well, and to arm the other obstacles with "thorns"—savage iron spikes and jagged steel plates designed to tear open the hulls of landing craft like can openers. To overcome the shortage of mines, Rommel devised ways of using the 1,200,000 obsolete shells at his disposal. The lethal "nutcracker" mine was a shell embedded in a concrete block, with a plank of makeshift trigger to detonate it whichever way a ship brushed past it. He also sketched the tackle and techniques for emplacing these unwieldy artifacts far down the beaches—using floating cranes, or boats, or teams of plow horses. The drawings were printed and distributed to commanders throughout his territory. To overcome other shortages, he established factories for concrete and tetrahedrons, he built power stations, he reopened coal mines. Above all, Rommel's activity created something intangible, here in the west: soldier morale. Gradually the feeling spread that there was a chance of victory after all.

His stocky figure, clad in the new leather topcoat he had bought in Paris, was seen everywhere, advertising his formidable presence. He told the war photographers who accompanied him: "Do what you like with me, if it results in even a one-week postponement of the enemy's invasion." From February 7 to 11 he drove 1,400 miles, inspecting the First and Nineteenth armies on the Biscay and Mediterranean coasts. But this journey was only to deceive the enemy into believing that he was everywhere.

Back at Fontainebleau after that, mounds of paper work awaited him. He still found time to write to Lucie, about his work, his concern about the Russian front—now under heavy Red Army attack in the north and south—and Italy. However, he was convinced that Hitler would master these crises, too. Twenty years later, General Meise recalled that to the very end his chief used language of qualified admiration for the Führer—but not for the other Nazis around him. Once the general tried talking politics with Rommel, but only once. Rommel interrupted, "Meise—you and I can only talk politics if we're in an open field with nobody else in sight for two hundred yards all around." Rommel described Hitler as a fantast, a visionary: "If you see him entirely alone, you can talk quite reasonably with him. But then Martin Bormann and Company come in, and he reverts to his old form."

Old Rundstedt returned from leave on February 21. The next day Rommel left for ten days' well-earned leave himself. He flew home in his Heinkel—although such private flights were now explicitly forbidden because of Germany's urgent gasoline shortage. But he was exhausted. Over the past week he had again inspected the Fifteenth and Seventh army sectors and had observed a major war game organized by panzer expert Geyr in Paris on the seventeenth. Big differences of opinion had been expressed by the army, navy and air force generals. General Marcks had hobbled over to a map, thumped the Normandy coastline and insisted that the invasion would come there, coupled probably with one in Brittany—both aiming at the capture of the big port at Cherbourg. Rommel had replied equally firmly that his naval experts ruled out any invasion operation of Normandy, because of submerged reefs lying across the sea approaches. Geyr had lectured them on his plans for his Panzer Group West to wait in reserve, to fight the landed enemy days later on a killing ground of his own choice. German air power had been virtually nonexistent, in this war game version at least. Salmuth later wrote, "I was deeply shocked by it all."

Lucie had by now moved their household into the big new villa at Herrlingen. When Rommel drove up the short, curving drive, he had a surprise for her—a year-old terrier called Ajax, given him by the Todt Organization. It barked loudly at strangers, so it would make a good watchdog, he told her.

Lucie had something of a surprise for him, too—a visitor: the mayor of Stuttgart, Dr. Karl Strölin, who had won that office because of his early membership in the Nazi Party. He had served briefly in the same unit as Rommel in the First World War. He was a solid and worthy figure, big and upright. Unbeknown to Rommel, he was a member of the anti-Hitler conspiracy. Rommel noticed that he was nervously chain-smoking. From Lucie Rommel's letters, it is clear that Strölin had in fact been putting out definite feelers toward Rommel for several months. When General Gause had flown on leave to Herrlingen earlier in February—where Lucie had kindly offered accommodation for his bombed-out wife—the mayor had come to the villa then and involved Gause and Lucie in long *political* discussions. Gause, ill and depressed after losing everything in that Berlin air raid, had listened readily. Strölin had then flattered Lucie, for all her shrewdness, with theater tickets, free accommodation at a luxury Stuttgart hotel, official cars, wonderful bouquets of flowers—and by the time the field marshal stepped across the threshold of the villa there was also a large painting, donated by Strölin, in which Rommel himself was the central figure.

Rommel had not come to talk politics with strangers. He wanted to be with Lucie and Manfred, he wanted to housebreak Ajax and stroll through the Swabian countryside. Politics interested him as little as Sèvres porcelain. But he politely agreed to see Strölin. The man took some papers out of his case and—in front of Lucie, Manfred and the adjutant Aldinger—launched into a dramatic speech about the criminality of the Hitler regime and the need for Rommel to step in, in person, to "save the Reich." It was a powerful line. One of the papers was a memorandum prepared for the Ministry of the Interior. Others documented actual crimes committed by the Nazis. He spoke of massacres of Jews and other in the east, and concluded: "If Hitler does not die, then we are all lost!" At this Rommel rose to his feet and boomed: "Herr Strölin, I would be grateful if you would refrain from speaking such opinions in the presence of my young son!"

Strölin gathered up his papers and left. His influence on Rommel was nil. The field marshal neither mentioned Strölin—outside of his family—nor saw him again until the last weeks of his life. From all the evidence, it is plain that Rommel was in truth, despite his occasional statements to the contrary, far from accepting that Hitler's defeat was inevitable. When he met General Alexander von Falkenhausen, the aristocratic military governor of Belgium, in Brussels a few days later, he infuriated that elderly gentleman, an anti-Nazi, with his cheery confidence that he was going to inflict a big defeat on the enemy when they hit the beaches. Besides, field marshals whose whole military reputation is staked on forthcoming victory are unlikely to lend their names to a coup d'état.

He got back to Fontainebleau late on March 3 in driving snow. Ruge also noted in his diary that Rommel was "very cheerful." Rommel put a call through to ask Lucie how the terrier was settling down. Afterward she wrote: "You'd have loved to see your Ajax when we went on walks these last two days. He comes to heel fabulously. . . . I don't thing he would ever have learned to obey without your drastic teaching methods."

That was the key to Rommel's character: in his household, as in his work, obedience was the first commandment. He wrote to Manfred now, "I was delighted to see your attitude to duty and everything else in life. Keep it up and do the name of Rommel proud. . . . Only the man who has learned to obey—even against his better instincts and convictions—will make a capable officer, and learn how to master the supreme art of leading other men."

He willingly signed any document proving his own obedience to his Supreme Commander. On March 4, Hitler's adjutant Schmundt brought one such document to Fontainebleau for him to sign. It was a strange story. "The Führer is furious at the treachery of certain generals who have been captured by the enemy, or deserted to them, at Stalingrad," explained Schmundt. The generals have formed themselves into a pro-Soviet committee, Schmundt said, under General Walter von Seydlitz, bearer of one of the most illustrious names in Prussia's military history, and they were smuggling out seditious letters to top German commanders, urging them to stop fighting, since the war was pointless. Dozens of Hitler's top generals had already received such letters. Schmundt told Rommel: "Since the battle of Cherkassy we now have proof that Seydlitz's signature on them is authentic. What matters now is for the Führer to be sure he can trust his field marshals—to know you all stand loyally behind him." Rundstedt's signature already embellished Schmundt's draft manifesto of allegiance to Hitler, dissociating all the field marshals from these traitors. Rommel signed with his usual flourish; after him Kleist, Busch, Manstein and Weichs added their signatures.

Thus we can state with emphasis: at this date, Rommel was still loyal to his Führer. He would play by the rules. There was a small episode the next day, March 5, that showed that. He had gone on a hunt toward Melun, taking Admiral Ruge and General Meise with him. It was sunny, they left their topcoats behind and the thorny bushes dug painfully through their uniforms. After a while they sighted a wild boar, but it vanished before they could shoot; later, they spotted a pig, but that too got away. They stalked through the undergrowth for several hundred yards, and came out into a clearing at about the same time that a big stag strode into the open, majestic and scornful, long enough for them to count the twelve points on its antlers. Meise raised his gun; Ruge had his automatic rifle cocked; but Rommel stood up and waved his Wehrmacht hunting license at them. It ruled quite clearly that stags were not to be shot after February 1. He calmly called out to them, "It's the closed season," and left the fine beast to survive.

# Closed Season

I F Rommel still admired Hitler in early 1944, it was
because the Führer had so often proved right in the
past and confounded his own generals. But in France
Rommel first dared to mistrust Hitler's judgment—on the
crucial issue of precisely where the enemy invasion was to
be expected.

Since mid-February Hitler had several times pronounced that the Anglo-American invasion, when it
came, would be on the Normandy coast and perhaps in
Brittany too, with the strategic objective of capturing
Cherbourg harbor. According to Hitler's Luftwaffe adjutant, Colonel Nicolaus von Below, this fact was established by documents microfilmed by the SS agent
code-named "Cicero," working in the British embassy in
Ankara. "Why on earth should the British have found it
necessary to tell their ambassador in Turkey that?" Hitler
exclaimed. But they had, and from another document he
knew the invasion's code name, too: Operation Overlord.
This fact was also recorded in Jodl's diary—but neither
Hitler nor the High Command trusted field marshals
enough to reveal the source of their knowledge to Rommel.
On March 4 Hitler merely repeated his "hunch" at his
main war conference, setting the High Command's tele-

printer wires humming: "The Führer . . . considers Normandy and Brittany to be particularly threatened by invasion, because they are very suitable for the creation of beachheads." He demanded an immediate review of Normandy's defenses, causing Rommel to set out once again for the bleak and distant Bay of the Seine at 8:00 A.M. on March 6.

To Rommel the long drive seemed a fool's errand. But he picked up General Marcks, the corps commander, and pounced on the two divisions holding the Normandy coast—the 711th and 716th Infantry divisions. "Nice meals afterward," commented Admiral Ruge's diary. "Omelettes, then coffee with whipped cream. After that we toured the coast and gun sites almost as far as the Orne estuary, and then to Trouville. Beach obstacles are now being built everywhere. Pile driving with water jets is working first class." Rommel dined in the officers' mess, kicked up a fuss about an unfortunate unauthorized trial of his beach obstacles made a week earlier during his absence—a captured 120-ton British landing craft had just smashed through his stake obstacles as if they were matchwood!—and retired early to bed in his hotel room, while two sentries stood guard outside.

He rapidly visited the rest of the sector the next day. Southeast of the Vire, large areas of the country were already flooded. At Quineville he saw a five-mile-long barrier of roller-trestle obstacles blocking the beach. Rommel asked Marcks to pass on his congratulations to the troops. Marcks wrote afterward. "These visits are very strenuous because Rommel is a fanatic and it's impossible to do too much on the schemes he's thought up, like the gigantic minefields." On April 5 the general added further impressions: "Rommel is cantankerous and frequently blows his top—he scares the daylights out of his commanders. The first one that reports to him each morning gets eaten for breakfast; the next ones after that get off lighter." As Marcks explained to his mother in another letter, "If there's something he doesn't like, then all his Swabian pigheaded rudeness comes out."

From Normandy, the Cherbourg peninsula and Brittany the field marshal's inspection convoy returned to the permanent command post now built for the Army Group

B at La Roche-Guyon, an inland village picturesquely sited halfway down the Seine, where the river valley loops northward between Mantes and Vernon. Antiaircraft batteries guarded the surrounding slopes and cliffs, which rose from the valley floor "like tall organ pipes," in one writer's vivid descriptive phrase. A tank battalion was exercising in the valley. As the convoy arrived late on March 9, it was still just light enough to make out the château's fine outlines. It was the most opulent of all Rommel's headquarters. It had been built with its back to a cliff face, topped by a half-ruined, 900-year-old Norman round tower. His engineers had blasted extra tunnels into the cliff to house the twenty staff officers and eighty other men who now made up Rommel's army group staff, so that air raids need not disturb them.

That château belonged to the venerable La Rochefoucauld family. Rommel insisted that the family stay— the duchess, a bustling little Danish princess, was alway there as were her daughter Charlotte, an attractive brunette of twenty-one, and her sons. From time to time the duke himself appeared, slightly built, about sixty-five, of unmistakable patrician breeding. Rommel took an instant liking to him. The duke responded (and in consequence suffered a lengthy postwar prison sentence for collaboration). Rommel lived in a small ground-floor apartment opening onto a rose garden. His study was a lofty ducal hall, draped with priceless tapestries and hung with oil paintings; it was redolent of musty books and centuries of wax polishing. Rommel sat at an inlaid Renaissance desk over which three centuries of historic documents had flowed. He found it all most suitable.

Twice during the coming week, Rommel drove over to General Salmuth's Fifteenth Army on the Channel coast—the new headquarters was only eighty miles away. The Seventh Army, in Brittany, had now proposed that, since the wooden stakes alone were not going to sink the landing craft, antitank mines should be strapped to them. Rommel adopted the idea at once and issued the necessary orders to the Fifteenth Army too. Again he told everybody that they must expect the enemy invasion to come here, across the Channel. And this emphasis was expressed not only in the records of the units he visited but in his own conferences at his château as well.

*On the trail of the Fox another rich documentary source on Rommel's private beliefs now appeared by chance. The hunt had led to Captain Hellmuth Lang, who replaced Hammermann as Rommel's personal aide in March 1944. (Rommel had specified to army personnel chief Rudolf Schmundt that the new aide was to be "a major, a panzer officer, highly decorated and a Swabian." Lang filled the bill except for the rank; he had been promoted after he had won the Knight's Cross as a tank commander in Russia.) The mild, bespectacled Lang, now over sixty, greeted me in his four-centuries-old town house in Swabian Gmünd. After a while, Lang took me to see his mother, a lively old lady with as good a memory of events as his, and she displayed her own diary relating to Hellmuth Lang's actions in 1944. The seriousness of the search must have impressed itelf on her, because an hour later she came back into the room carrying an old cardboard box, marked in pencil: "Hellmuth's letters on his life and times with Rommel." It was an invaluable find. But that was only the first find that day. Soon afterward, Hellmuth Lang discovered 100 or more loose sheets of the Rommel diary for 1944—which it had been his job each day to type. I pieced the pages together when I got back to London. Twenty pages were missing. Two months later I found them, 5,000 miles away, in a file box in the archives of The Citadel, a military college in South Carolina.*

Outside, spring was rushing color into the Seine valley. Rommel often strolled with Ruge amid the cowslips or went on "armed promenades"—hunts. There was something about the château that made him think back over his career—as though he sensed that it was nearly over. Ruge's diary is full of the anecdotes the field marshal related, strolling in the romantic gardens or contemplating his favorite view along the valley from a spot beneath two mighty cedars. He talked about Monte Mataiur, about the Maginot Line, and about the sweep forward to El Alamein and the very gates of Alexandria. "Yesterday the Chief again reminisced on his experiences with the Italians," wrote Lang one day that March. "Now I understand why he always refers to them in such drastic language. Incredible, the difficulties he was up against and the way the treacherous clique around Mussolini tried pulling the rug out from under him while he was still in Africa!"

But here, there were no Italians. Rommel fired everybody with his professional enthusiasm for the coming battle. Lang wrote home his first impressions: "There are no cold feet around here when the field marshal's around. Of course things do get tough on individuals, but here in the west we have realized that there must be no second thoughts about the coming showdown—even though it's going to cost a lot of casualties. Even though the war will still be far from won, with the battle in the west the tide is going to turn in our favor."

In three letters to Lucie and Manfred, the field marshal exuded the same confidence. "Provided we get just a few more weeks to reinforce the defenses," he was going to win the battle and thus probably decide the outcome of the war. On March 17 he wrote to Lucie, a few hours before leaving to confer with Hitler at Berchtesgaden: "Here in the west we have every confidence that we can make it—but the east must hold out too."

Hitler had sent a special train to Paris to fetch all the senior generals and admirals from the west to Bavaria. When Rommel reported to the Führer at the Berghof at 2:00 P.M. on March 19, he found the villa's famous silhouette draped in camouflage netting and the mountainside dotted with smoke screen generators to shield Hitler from air raids. There was only a brief ceremony that day: Rundstedt read out the secret manifesto signed by the field marshals and handed it over to Hitler with a flourish. (On Hitler's orders it was eventually read out to every division and fortress commander in the west, so that everybody knew just where the field marshals' loyalties lay; and it was published in the Nazi press on October 18.) They were all Heinrich Himmler's guests for dinner that night.

The next day the scene shifted to a baroque castle a few miles away, at Klessheim. Hitler arrived late, in a driving blizzard, at 3:00 P.M. General von Salmuth was appalled by his appearance: "It was an old, bent man with a pallid, unhealthy complexion who came into the room," he wrote. "He looked weary, exhausted—downright ill." But he still seemed to have his wits about him, because in his one-hour speech—delivered, according to Rommel's diary, "with marvelous clarity and sovereign composure"—Hitler again took the view that the enemy would invade Normandy and Brittany, and not the much closer Channel coast.

"Obviously," Hitler declaimed, "an Anglo-American invasion in the west is going to come. Just how and where nobody knows, and it isn't possible to speculate. You can't take shipping concentrations at face value for some kind of clue that their choice has fallen on any particular sector of our long western front from Norway down to the Bay of Biscay. . . . Such concentrations can always be moved or transferred at any time, under cover of bad visibility, and they will obviously be used to dupe us. The most suitable landing areas, and hence those that are in most danger, are the two west coast peninsulas of Cherbourg and Brest: they offer very tempting possibilities for the creation of bridgeheads, which could thereafter be systematically enlarged by the massive use of air power."

Hitler warmed to his theme. "The enemy's entire invasion operation must not, under any circumstances, be allowed to survive longer than hours, or at most days, taking Dieppe as an ideal example. Once defeated, the enemy will never again try to invade. Quite apart from their heavy losses, they would need months to organize a fresh attempt. And an invasion failure would also deliver a crushing blow to British and American morale. For one thing, it would prevent Roosevelt from being reelected in the United States—with any luck, he'd finish up in jail somewhere! For another, war weariness would grip Britain even faster and Churchill, already a sick old man with his influence waning, wouldn't be able to carry through a new invasion operation."

After that, Hitler showed why defeating the invasion would lead to a total Nazi victory. "The forty-five divisions that we now hold in Europe . . . are vital to the eastern front, and we shall then transfer them there to revolutionize the situation there as soon as we have forced the decision in the west. So the whole outcome of the war depends on each man fighting in the west, and that means the fate of the Reich as well!"

Rommel had not thought of it like that before, and he used this argument several times over the coming weeks. In a way, the entire future of Nazi Germany rested on whether he could win the coming battle. Privately he told Jodl and Hitler that he was confident of destroying the enemy attempt: by the end of April virtually the entire coastline would be saturated with enough obstacles to inflict severe losses on the landing craft. "In my view," stated Rommel, "the enemy's not going to succeed in setting foot on dry ground in these sectors." It was a bold claim, but Rommel backed it with another demand for all the panzer and mechanized forces in the west to be placed under his command; Hitler confidentially agreed to consider it. He also asked Rommel to inspect the coastal defense work of the Nineteenth and First armies on the Mediterranean and Biscay coasts— causing an outburst from Rundstedt that in that case it was pointless for him to remain Commander in Chief West, since Rommel's powers were continually expanding.

Tea was served afterward. Hitler sent the stenographers out and summoned Rundstedt, who had not joined the group. The field marshal arrivel in a sullen mood, emerged five minutes later and stormed down to the train in Berchtesgaden. "What's the point?" he complained to anybody who would listen. "The Führer wouldn't let me open my mouth, so I walked out on him." Rommel got better treatment, and emerged half an hour later with a faint smile on his lips. Outside the door, Hitler's doctor Theo Morell nudged Tempelhoff: "Congratulations! Evidently you're now IA [operations officer] to the new C in C West. Rundstedt lasted only five minutes, and your boss managed thirty." Rundstedt, however, stayed in office, which left the panzer problem unsolved.

For five days after that, Rommel toured the Netherlands and Belgium. The war diary of the Eighty-eighth Corps in Holland records the pith of his instructions at a conference on March 23: "All your forces have got to be committed to the defense of the coastline itself. You won't be able to fight a mobile battle because of the enemy air-ships' gunfire and their air supremacy. You've got to make enemy air-borne landings inside our fortresses and clusters of strongpoints quite impossible. You must pulverize air-landed troops with your artillery. Bring in the local population to help build defense positions and obstacles." He wanted everything ready by the end of April. "On no account," exclaimed Rommel, "must the enemy be allowed to secure a beachhead on the western front."

In Holland the dikes had been opened everywhere, and seawater was still flooding in. It would be ten years before the farmland would recover from the poisoning by salt water. But, Ruge noted, "The people are quite friendly, amazingly enough." Almost paradoxically, these Nazi-occupied countries looked forward to the Liberation but hoped that—thanks to Rommel's efforts—the devastating invasion battle would be shifted elsewhere, into someone else's country. Besides, there was something magical about Rommel's name. One war reporter accompanying him wrote this account: "A cool day. We leave the beach and drive back into the narrow streets of this coastal town, through minefields, tank traps—there is only one narrow lane. On the market square the ruins are a ghostly sight in the pale yellow sunlight. As everywhere else, a crowd of men stand idly around, looking curiously at our two cars. A voice exclaims '*C'est Rommel*,' and you feel excitement suddenly pulse through the crowd. '*C'est Rommel*'—In every town that we pass through on our journeys we hear this shout."

"Much work and worry," the field marshal wrote home on March 27. "Things just aren't going as I would like, and this means I've got to use my elbows, which really takes it out of me." The fight for control of the panzer divisions was heating up. The High Command was refusing to honor Hitler's oral promise of March 20—on the contrary, it constantly drew on the panzer divisions in France as a strategic reserve for the war in the east. Authoritative voices disputed the wisdom of Rommel's plan to locate his tanks right behind the coastline—

among them, General Guderian, now Hitler's chief tank adviser, and the Seventh Army's General Dollmann. The loudest in opposition to Rommel was Rundstedt's expert on tanks, General Geyr von Schweppenburg. Small wonder, then, that when this tall, elegant, red-trousered panzer officer first appeared at La Roche-Guyon on March 29, the field marshal lost his temper after a very few minutes and snapped at Geyr in frustration: "Listen, I am an experienced tank commander. You and I do not see eye to eye on anything. I refuse to work with you anymore. I propose to draw the appropriate conclusions." Geyr, every inch a cavalier, swung a smart salute at him, turned on his heel and marched out—determined never to expose himself to such rudeness from Rommel again. Rommel dictated to Lang a summary for the diary, ending: "Strong difference of opinion, with no positive result."

That was an understatement of no small consequence.

# The Silent Swabian

**M**ID-APRIL, 1944. After weeks of dry weather the rains have come to France. Rommel stands at the windows of his château room and wonders how many more weeks he has left to prepare for the biggest battle of his life. All Germany depends on him. Hitler has said so.

Late on the fifteenth, an army car drives through the tall wrought iron gates and squelches to a halt at the main door. An unfamiliar officer climbs out into the rain. His bags are carried inside the château to the turret room that is to be his quarters, and he reports to the field marshal. He is Lieutenant General Speidel, his new chief of staff. Rommel had made the difficult decision a month earlier to release Alfred Gause, who has shared so much of his destiny since July 1941. He values and trusts Gause, but during their furlough at Herrlingen the general and his wife fell out with Lucie in the blameless way that houseguests often do—Gause had once rebuked Hermann Aldinger for arriving late for work in the garden, and Lucie had found Frau Gause getting on her nerves. Eventually Lucie actually demanded that Rommel replace Gause as his chief of staff, and the field marshal meekly complied, writing her on March 17: "Let's draw a line underneath it all . . . I am going to. Perhaps G. will find another post. Of course, it's a tough decision for me to have to change my chief at a time like this." Rommel had now written privately to Schmundt asking him to give Gause the next available panzer division to command.

Gause's successor is no ordinary general. At Hans Speidel's throat Rommel glimpses the Knight's Cross that Hitler has just personally given him for the Eighth Army's heroic fighting retreat on the Russian front. He probably remembers Speidel as the silent fellow Swabian he met in 1915 in the Argonnes forest, and again between the wars in the Thirteenth Württemberg Infantry Regiment. Speidel was one of two replacements offered to him by the General Staff, with the highest recommendations. Rommel has, as usual, picked the Swabian.

At forty-six, the newcomer is six years younger than Rommel. The field marshal finds this owlish, bespectacled general, with his excellent history degree and polished manners, a congenial change—and a useful complement to his own one-track mind. He is academic, prudent, aesthetic and music loving. Rommel writes to his wife on April 16, "He makes a good, fresh impression. I think I'm going to get on well with him."

Indirectly, Erwin and Lucie Rommel had between them signed the field marshal's own death warrant in replacing Gause with Speidel. By April 1944, Spiedel was a general with a secret and with something of a "past" as well. He had been involved ever since Stalingrad in the plans of the opponents to Hitler. It is a fair guess that the anti-Hitler members of the General Staff had assigned him to Rommel only for this reason. Only one day before his arrival here, he discussed with Strölin, the mayor of Stuttgart, the need to lure Rommel into the plot. Rommel suspected none of this. As he himself wrote in a remarkable private letter months later to Hitler, he trusted Speidel implicitly, frequently leaving him at the château to "mind the store" while he went forward to tour the coastal sectors.

Jodl had pleaded with Speidel at the Berghof to boost Rommel's morale. "Do what you can to cure him of his bouts of pessimism. He's suffered from them ever since

Africa." There is more than enough evidence—both in his own writings and in Rommel's letters home—to prove that Speidel did quite the reverse. He brought immediate dark tidings about the disastrous situation on the Russian front, where the two southern army groups were in full retreat and the Crimea had been lost. The mood in Rommel's diary changed from the very day of the general's arrival: "What will later historians have to say about these retreats? And what will history say in passing its verdict on *me*? If I am successful here, then everybody else will claim all the glory—just as they are already claiming the credit for the defenses and the beach obstacles that *I* have erected. But if I fail here, then everybody will be after my blood."

*At his forest home, south of Munich, Eberhard Wolfram, major on Rommel's personal staff, graphically described to me Speidel's gloomy influence on the field marshal's communal mealtimes. "In Rommel's absence, Speidel took over the table, and his whole conversation revolved only around 'that asshole at the Berghof,' meaning Hitler. When I arrived the mood of these table discussions was one of abject defeatism . . . except when Rommel came in. Then the tenor of the discussion changed; nobody dared go so far with their defeatist remarks."*

During these short months of their association, Speidel gained an intellectual grip on the simple, plain-speaking soldier. Rommel stood in obvious awe of him. Once he sent Hellmuth Lang to fetch Speidel, and the general told Lang, "I'll come when I'm ready" (an attitude that Gause would never have dared adopt.) Speidel became known at the château for his phlegm and tranquility. In a private letter Lang described a further incident on June 18, 1944: "I had the radio on in my anteroom, playing Beethoven's Ninth rather loud. The door was flung open, and Rommel asked me to switch off 'that awful noise.' I switched off—only to hear the same music coming even louder from Speidel's room. Rommel shrugged and went back to his study, to suffer Beethoven without further protest."

A second factor, as unknown to Rommel as the disastrous Enigma leak had been, also dominated his fortunes from now on. An intricate and ingenious Allied deception plan, code-named "Fortitude," had begun. Its objects were to suggest that the invasion was due as early as May, and that it would hit the Strait of Dover, in the Fifteenth Army's sector. Even without Speidel, Rommel would have had little chance of seeing through the deception, for Hitler's intelligence services were well infiltrated with anti-Hitler men. Rommel's own intelligence officer was an honest, mild-mannered army colonel, Anton Staubwasser, assigned to Rommel because he was an intelligence expert on Britain. Staubwasser had some clerks and two interpreters, but no intelligence sources of his own. He had to rely on data furnished by the General Staff's Foreign Armies West branch—whose chief was later hanged by the Nazis as a member of the anti-Hitler conspiracy—and by Rundstedt's much bigger staff. There was virtually no air reconnaissance over England because of the Luftwaffe's weakness.

Thus the Fortitude planners had a pushover. They fed false reports to Hitler's intelligence networks that the invasion was imminent. Long before necessary, the British government began stopping or censoring mail, and prohibited even foreign diplomats from leaving (although one, a Swede, was allowed to "slip through"). Civilian travel was restricted. Public buildings were requisitioned as hospitals. A premature bombing offensive began against the German railroads. Non-existent American forces were "moved" into southeastern England—facing Salmuth's Fifteenth Army—by faking radio traffic and reports to German agents.

Only Adolf Hitler, "that asshole at the Berghof," smelled a rat.

On April 6 he said to Jodl: "The whole way that the British are serving all this up to us, it looks phony. This latest news about the restrictions they are ordering, their security clampdown and so on now—you don't normally go in for all that if you're really up to something. . . . I can't help feeling that the whole thing's going to turn out to be a shameless charade." When Hitler was informed of the "troop movements" detected toward southeast England, he grunted: "Now what I ask myself is this: why make such a song and dance about it? We wouldn't, I guarantee you! And they don't need to either, do they? They could perfectly well marshal their forces over here [in the southeast], then load them on board and ship them over to here [Normandy]. We've no real way of finding out what they're really up to over there." A few minutes later, Hitler announced: "I'm in favor of pushing all our forces into *here*," and he pointed to the Normandy coastline.

Rommel's next inspection trip, however, from April 17 to 19, went not to Normandy but again to the Fifteenth Army. This time he took Speidel. Two other cars were filled with his staff, war reporters, and accordions to be handed out to the hardest workers. He liked to drop in on the lower echelons unawares—one sentry was so flustered by the field marshal's appearance that he stuttered, "*Jawohl,* Herr Major" to him. Everywhere the very landscape was changing shape according to Rommel's orders. The fields were heaped with stone cairns, or bristled with stakes and poles to keep gliders from landing. The beaches were jungles of barbed wire, wooden beams, concrete artifacts and mines. Everywhere were the skull and crossbone signs warning of minefields—whether fake or real even Rommel could not tell. Of course, there were still infuriating errors: junior officers had seen fit to countermand some of Rommel's orders; cows were still permitted to graze in some of the dummy minefields; secret fortifications built in a green meadow were camouflaged with old black netting. Rommel drafted a twenty-two-page manual for all his commanders summarizing all his practical hints. He sent a copy to Hitler, too, and Schmundt wrote back with the Führer's congratulations—he too was "a practical man," Schmundt said.

Because he paid them good money, French men and women also joined the labors, volunteering by the thousand to dig, lay bricks, pour concrete or weave rush matting needed to stop the beach obstacles from silting up. "Get the French countryfolk to help erect the obstacles," he said in a speech to one division, near Le Havre. "Pay them well and promptly for it. Point out that the enemy is least likely to invade where the most obstacles have been erected! The French farmers will be only too glad to line their purses. Have them march out to work singing like the BDM [the League of German Maidens]! Convince them it's in their own interests. The enemy is already going to have his work cut out to get out of the sea—so the time will come when he tries attacking us from the rear." On his return he wrote to Lucie: "People here don't think the enemy's going to attack much before May. I want it to be as late as possible, because I've still got so much that's of importance in the pipeline." He was more confident than ever of victory now.

There was still one big flaw. The panzer controversy was still unresolved, and General Geyr's views as commander of Panzer Group West still prevailed. From the commander of the paratroop corps Rommel had recently learned that the enemy had the capability to set down three divisions of airborne troops in a space of only ten minutes, probably with large numbers of antitank guns. Geyr predicted that the enemy would attempt a paratroop landing deep inside France, and wanted to hold back all panzer forces to counterattack there. At a heated discussion in Paris on April 10, Rommel heaped scorn on him. "In my view," he wrote to Jodl, "any strategic airborne landing by the enemy is doomed to disaster sooner or later, *provided* we succeed in sealing the coast." He said the same to Schmundt, adding: "This is going to be the war's most vital battle; the fate of the whole Reich is at stake." If the panzer divisions reached the coast too late, a second Anzio-like battle of attrition would result: "the worst possible situation for us." He asked Schmundt to arrange a new meeting for him with the Führer—but much would have happened before Rommel next saw Hitler.

Throughout April he lobbied to have General Geyr's panzer divisions moved up toward the coast. The Twelfth SS Panzer Division ("Hitler Jugend") lay widely dispersed inland and would take at least two days to reach even Caen in the face of heavy air attack, he argued. The Second Panzer Division was over fifty miles from the Somme sector of the coast. In each case, Rommel feared the enemy would set down antitank gun screens by air in the empty space between the panzer divisions and his Atlantic wall. "Things haven't turned out the way I thought had been agreed on March 20," he bitterly wrote to Lucie after the Paris meeting, referring to the promise of control over all forces. Rundstedt chuckled over Rommel's discomfiture and told his chief of staff, Günther Blumentritt: "Rommel's like an unlicked cub—not a fox at all. He's too ambitious. In Africa things didn't turn out too well for him, and now he dearly wants to be somebody here."

Rommel continued pushing for his own strategy. "Provided we succeed in bringing our mechanized divisions into action in the very first few hours," he wrote to Jodl on April 23, "then I'm convinced that the enemy assault on our coast will be completely defeated on the very first day. . . . Contrary to what was agreed on March 20, however, they have still not been put under my control and they're lying too far back from the coast, widely dispersed." He added candidly, "I've had some hard words with Geyr about all this, and I can only get my own way if he is put under my orders in good time." Prophetically, Rommel concluded: "If I have to wait for the enemy invasion actually to *occur* before I'm allowed to submit through routine channels an application for the panzer divisions to come under my orders and move forward, then they'll probably arrive too late."

The Second Panzer Division was a case in point. Rommel wanted it on the Somme, north of Amiens, so that its leading battle group actually stood on the coast at Abbeville. Geyr wanted it far inland. Rundstedt diplomatically thought that somewhere in between might be best. On April 25, Rommel ordered the division pushed forward to touch Abbeville. Returning from the movies the next day, he found that it had not been advanced and he sharply attacked all the "obstructionists." Ruge quoted him as stating quite bluntly: "The panzer divisions are going to be moved forward, whether they like it or not!"

The result was an angry visit by General Geyr to the château on the afternoon of the twenty-eighth, accompanied this time by General Guderian, Hitler's own panzer expert, who was on a fact-finding tour of France. Guderian's staff officer Baron Konrad von Woellwarth later wrote that it was a "decidedly tempestuous conference," particularly when Geyr and Guderian learned that Rommel now proposed to dig in all the tanks on the coastline: "The very strength of panzer formations," Woellwarth noted, "lay in their combination of firepower and mobility." Guderian insisted that all the tanks must be held well out of range of the enemy's warship artillery— all the landings in Italy had shown that. (He reported to Hitler: "We'll have to lay down a precise stop line, forward of which no panzer divisions may be moved.") Rommel was speechless at this lack of comprehension of the coming battle: "If you leave the panzer divisions in the rear, they will never get forward. Once the invasion begins, enemy air power will stop everything from moving." Geyr insisted that his tanks could roll by night, or even by day if they kept to 150-yard spacings. Rommel educated him about the enemy's parachute flares, that lit the night sky as bright as day.

In retrospect, the arguments were evenly balanced. Given the enemy's overwhelming air power, we can accept that both the Geyr and the Rommel strategies, if adopted wholeheartedly, would have amounted to the same thing. Hitler refused to accept Guderian's advice favoring Geyr. The upshot was a feeble compromise. By a High Command order dated May 7, three—and only three—panzer divisions were turned over to Rommel: the very good Second Panzer, the reborn Twenty-first Panzer, with a strange complement of captured tanks, and the excellent 116th Panzer. The remaining four panzer divisions were left far inland as a High Command reserve. "The enemy's intentions are at present so obscure," General Jodl wrote to Rommel that day, "that some capability for strategic command must be maintained by means of keeping a separate, if modest, reserve. These High Command reserves will be released for operations—without further application by yourself—the moment we can be certain about the enemy's intentions and focus of attack." That sounded reasonable enough.

Roughness of tongue no longer came easily to Rommel. He was mellowing to the timeless allures of France. He was putting on weight—the food was too good, and an afternoon's hunt sometimes provided four wild boars for the château's mess table. Once he went horseback riding, for the first time since 1939, on a tiresome and placid gray. He told Ruge that the horse would have been just the thing for a seventy-year-old country parson, and as he dismounted he sighed. "That was so tedious that now I'm itching with impatience all over," he said. "I can't stand tedious people either—I expected you've noticed that already!"

Relations with the Rochefoucauld family deepened. The duchess had sent over four bottles of the château's finest 1900 claret to celebrate the Führer's birthday. Rommel's younger staff officers took turns escorting the beautiful Countess Charlotte. In this part of France the upper classes were decidedly pro-German, fearing the consequences of communism for Europe, and the populace largely followed their lead. And of course there was the ancient antagonism, in these parts, to Britain. Rommel traveled freely, without a bodyguard.

Strolling in the woods with Hellmuth Lang on a glorious spring afternoon, April 23, he ruefully contrasted all this beauty with the ugliness of war. And again he shuddered at the responsibility he had accepted for the survival of the Nazi Reich. "History," he said, "takes account only of those who know victory. There is no art in being a warlord for a wealthy country, richly endowed with all the materials for war. But I—I have to be satisfied with what little I've got, and try to defeat the enemy with only the most modest means. And defeated they must be, if Bolshevism is not to triumph over us. Even then, when we have defeated Britain and the United States, the war with Russia won't be over because it has enormous resources of men and raw materials. Perhaps," he predicted, "perhaps then a united Europe will come forward to fight this enemy." Lang carefully recorded these somber words in the Rommel diary.

Agents were now reporting that the enemy invasion was slated to begin in the first or third week of May 1944. Again Rommel turned his attention to the Fifteenth Army's defenses. He wrote to Manfred on his return, "In Britain morale is very low. There's one strike after another, and the screams of 'Down with Churchill and the Jews' and 'We Want Peace' are growing louder—bad omens for such a risky offensive." (He evidently still believed everything that Goebbels told him.) Still his ever restless brain grappled with the tactical problems. Brainstorm after brainstorm issued from the château. He suddenly ordered the erection of powerful floodlights and flares on masts along the beaches, pointing seaward, to dazzle and dismay the invasion craft at the very last moment before they hit the barriers: "Landing against the glare of floodlights will be extraordinarily difficult for the enemy," he announced. He personally briefed commanders on unorthodox ways of destroying both gliders and paratroops—there were to be booby traps and grenades on the antiglider obstacles strung across the fields. "You've got to visualize them fluttering in by moonlight like swarms of locusts!"

In five heavy Wehrmacht automobiles he and his staff set out on April 29 for another look at the Biscay and Mediterranean defenses. There was little for his posse of war reporters to record, but on the drive through the Pyrenees mountains he did stop beneath a prominent rocky overhang near Perpignan, climb out onto the road and strike a familiar pose for the photographers: "The British are bound to recognize that rock formation," he explained. "Now they'll see I've been down here too."

He arrived back at his château late on May 3, eager to phone Herrlingen. One of his terriers, Elbo, sighted the familiar leather topcoat and marshal's baton, yelped with joy and shot out toward him from under the desk—skidding and splaying so comically that Rommel shook with laughter. He was in good form. The call to Lucie was put through. She told him that their puppy Ajax had just been run over outside the villa. Rommel consoled her. Before putting the phone down, he asked, "Can you send me a sketch of your shoe size? I'm going to buy you a pair in Paris for June sixth." June the sixth—that was Lucie's fiftieth birthday.

Hitler had still not fallen for the Allies' Fortitude deception. He was now more certain than ever that the invasion would come in Normandy, and a phone call went to General Speidel—in Rommel's absence—late on May 1 to say that the Führer impatiently wanted information on the prospects of Marcks's corps being able to defend Normandy. At a war conference the next day, without waiting for Speidel's answer, Hitler decided to inject even stronger forces into the Normandy and Brittany peninsulas—a paratroop corps and airborne troops as well. In-

terestingly, the war diary of Naval Group West shows that Admiral Theodore Krancke had also deduced— from the pattern of the enemy's bombing and mine laying efforts, and from such Luftwaffe reconnaissance photos of southern England as there were, that the big ports of Le Havre and Cherbourg were likely to be the enemy's main invasion objectives. But for months there had been an ugly personal feud between Rommel's naval aide, Admiral Ruge, and Admiral Krancke, and Krancke's views either did not reach the château or were disregarded. Rommel's eyes remained on the Channel coast.

When General Dollmann proposed, on May 5, shifting the whole of the Seventy-fourth Corps from Brittany to Normandy if there were to be a large-scale invasion there, Rommel rejected the idea. And when Lieutenant General von Schwerin—who was now commanding the 116th Panzer Division—reported to him the same day, Rommel briefed him: "We expect the invasion on either side of the Somme estuary." He dictated to Hellmuth Lang: "I'm more confident than ever before. If the British give us just two more weeks, then I won't have any more doubts about it." And to Lucie on May 6, "I'm looking forward with the utmost confidence to the battle—it may be on May 15, it may not be until the end of the month." He did curiously telephone the High Command that day to inquire just why they had ordered the reinforcement of Normandy. Jodl replied that the Führer had "certain information" that Cherbourg was the first strategic objective. "Furthermore," he disclosed, "we have intelligence reports that British experiments at penetrating your types of beach obstacles have been successful." This evidently jolted Rommel: he telephoned General Marcks to expect a visit from him in Normandy in three days' time.

He set out early on May 9 toward Normandy, grumbling with skepticism. The first thing he noticed was that there was much less enemy air activity in the Seventh Army's sector than in the Fifteenth Army's, which reinforced that skepticism. But everywhere he could see the results of his efforts. Veritable forests of stakes and fiendish obstacles darkened every beach. Miles of the countryside across the root of the Cherbourg peninsula had been flooded on his orders. Roads were mined and

barricaded. There were troops and guns everywhere. He dined with Marcks at Saint-Lô ("We get on well together," wrote Marcks, "although we're two very different types") and finished his two-day tour with a visit to General Edgar Feuchtinger's Twenty-first Panzer Division at Falaise.

Feuchtinger was a Nazi Party favorite—he had organized each annual Nuremberg Rally—but he still evidently lacked military discipline, because at 8:00 A.M. there was nobody at the panzer regiment's headquarters. When the colonel, von Oppeln-Bronikowski, eventually arrived, trailing alcohol fumes, Rommel snorted: "You're lazy stinkers! What happens if the enemy invasion begins before eight-thirty?" The colonel gasped, "Catastrophe!" and slumped into a chair. Amazingly, the field marshal took no action. Ruge explained in his diary, "Rommel saw at once that he was a good fellow, and he didn't hold this lapse against him."

Most of Feuchtinger's officers had never had anything to do with tanks before—Feuchtinger had resourcefully mechanized the division with an extraordinary array of captured Czech, French and Russian tanks. If the enemy invaded Normandy, Feuchtinger's would be the only panzer division on the spot.

Afterward, Marcks, the corps commander in Normandy, wrote a half-serious letter home: "Opinion at present is that the Tommies have decided to tackle *me*. . . . I've been given a lot of fine new soldiers, and I've been busy unpacking them from their cardboard boxes and setting them up. This brings the number [in the Eighty-fourth Corps] up to more than 100,000. It's highly gratifying to see the number and the quality of divisions that we can still turn out in this, the fifth war year! The latest to arrive here (the Ninety-first Airborne Division) is a real elite: we had nothing remotely like it left by 1918. So I'm looking into the future in good heart, whatever they choose to throw at me. I've got this hunch that things won't start heating up until about my birthday." Like Lucie Rommel, General Marcks had his birthday on June the sixth.

Hans Speidel's arrival brought to the château a casualness that Rommel soon learned to copy. Although the

tension was slowly building to a climax, Rommel went on long strolls with his terriers, or hunting with the French landowners, while Speidel stayed behind to take care of things.

On May 12, they threw a sumptuous banquet for General Eduard Wagner, the army's powerful quartermaster general. Rommel knew that Wagner took a delight in food and hoped to bribe him in this way to give the Atlantic wall more weapons, like bazookas, that were in short supply. It never occurred to the plain-minded field marshal that Speidel had other aims: that the real motive for Wagner's visit was to confer with Speidel on Hitler's overthrow —indeed, his assassination. (Speidel admitted this motive in his earliest postwar manuscripts, then later denied it.) By this time, the Berlin conspirators had given Speidel the go-ahead to try to enlist the field marshal. They needed Rommel's name to make their deeds palatable to the broad mass of the army after Hitler's assassination. Early in May, the ex-chief of the General Staff, General Ludwig Beck—one of the key conspirators—had sent an intermediary to Paris to urge the military governor, General Carl-Heinrich von Stülpnagel, to prepare a putsch there to be coordinated with the assassination attempt. The intermediary, code-named "Baron von Teichmann," then went to Zurich and filed a report on May 17 for the Swiss secret service. "Beck also asked me," he wrote, "to get Stülpnagel to approach Rommel as soon as possible and inform him that Hitler was to be assassinated."

Stülpnagel decided to work through Speidel and had no difficulty approaching him, since Speidel had been his chief of staff in 1940. Moreover, Dr. Max Horst—Speidel's brother-in-law—was on Stülpnagel's Paris staff and himself one of the plotters there. Horst briefed Speidel on his mission, at the Hôtel Raphael in Paris. "Speidel promised to proceed with the utmost caution and cunning," wrote another eyewitness of the meeting. Speidel warned it would not be easy to convert Rommel into the kingpin of a coup d'état.

Of all these activities Rommel remained happily unaware. He still trusted Speidel. Years later, Meise recalled in a letter, "They were both Swabians. You used to see them talking in Swabian dialect to each other—they *un-*

*derstood* each other." But they did not, because Speidel had now started his endeavor. New faces began to appear at the château—people invited into the plot by Speidel. They invariably visited him during Rommel's absence at the front—the diaries establish this. For instance, there was a well-known author, Ernst Jünger, now an army captain on Stülpnagel's staff; he was drafting a peace manifesto for the plotters. He came late on May 13, just after Rommel had left to inspect the Fifteenth Army. "We ate together," wrote Jünger in a diary, "strolled in the park and then downed a bottle of wine high up in the oldest portion of the château, under the Norman battlements. . . . It does you good to see that Speidel doesn't suffer the malady of those other chiefs of staff you see withdrawing late at night to their rooms, laden with bulging piles of urgent papers. About him there is the aura of calm that reminds you of the steadiness of the axle of a big wheel, or the eye of a cyclone." Jünger watched Speidel as he gazed at a flower and remarked on the beauty of the Seine valley unfolding beneath them with its meadows and trees in full blossom. Together they ambled through the village. The wisteria was blooming, the white stars of the clematis, the lilac and laburnum, an intoxicating mixture of color and fragrance. "The war in Europe," said Speidel after a while, "will be all over by this autumn."

That was not Rommel's view, of course. He was getting ready for a long battle. He had driven off from the château that morning, May 13, for a last look at the Fifteenth Army. "I'm glad it was I who landed this job," he had dictated to Lang for the diary that same day, "because before it, people were writing me off as a sick man. But the Führer trusts me, and that's good enough for me." He was boisterous and cheerful. Seeing the Second Panzer Division still practicing mobile warfare, he yelled, "When they come, don't start maneuvering—just keep shooting!" Another division complained it lacked machine guns. Rommel retorted, "Then take the guns off the enemy when they drop in on you!"

General von Salmuth beamed at Rommel's praise of his fortifications along the Channel coast. After lunch—in the subterranean bowels of an immense V weapon bunker being built near Le Châtel—he delivered a speech of congratulations for Rommel. Division commanders proudly announced their totals: one had emplaced 98,000 stakes, another 96,000. Rommel himself distributed accordions as prizes for the biggest totals. Altogether by this date 517,000 beach obstacles had also been dragged, rammed, pile-driven or water-jetted into position along the coast; over 30,000 were already loaded with Teller mines. Over 4 million mines had been laid in the Death Zone. Only in Normandy was the result more threadbare; bombing had disrupted rail and road transports of the necessary cement and materials. Here the antiairborne-landing obstacles had only just been begun, and beach obstacles had been completed only along the high-water mark. But now Admiral Krancke was warning loudly that the enemy would probaby change their invasion tactics and land at low tide instead—intelligence observation of British invasion trials earlier in May, and decoded signals, had established this.

As far as the Fifteenth Army's sector was concerned, however, Rommel was 100 percent confident. As newsreel cameras whirred, he spoke to batteries of microphones and troops of the Wehrmacht and Todt Organizations assembled in front of the big guns of Strongpoint Atlantic, south of Le Touquet on the Channel coast. He talked of his confidence—"the confidence I have with regard to the coming historic battle here in the west." Throughout Germany, Rommel's presence in France had inspired a wave of optimism. The secret Gestapo morale reports disclosed the remarkable fact that nearly everybody was looking forward to the invasion: "People see it as our last chance to turn the tide. There is virtually no fear of the invasion discernible."

"Mid-May already," wrote the field marshal in mild puzzlement to Lucie on the fifteenth. "And still nothing doing. . . . I think it's going to be a few more weeks yet." That afternoon he drove to a country house outside Paris for the christening of a colonel's daughter—normally he detested christenings, but Speidel had begged him to make an exception. (In fact, Speidel wanted the excuse to meet Stülpnagel.) Rommel was photographed briefly with the infant, and with Stülpnagel and Bayerlein, the other godfathers, under the flowering chestnut trees, then returned to his château.

Bayerlein was now commander of the crack Panzer Lehr Division, which had been specially established, down to the last armored personnel carrier, for anti-invasion operations. Rommel knew him, of course, from Africa and confided to him, "I'm afraid that things may go here as they did in North Africa—I'm afraid of our supply routes being bombed to pieces until finally nothing more is even crossing the Rhine, just as in Africa nothing was getting to me across the Mediterranean."

Because he could not get away, Rommel telephoned Hitler at noon the next day, May 16, to report progress. He described the multiple rocket launchers developed by General Feuchtinger: "I can well imagine that these could be fired from bunkers in broadsides of forty-eight at a time. They travel five thousand yards. Feuchtinger tells me he's quite capable of procuring the rocket ammunition." Hitler approved the idea. Rommel proudly added, "The morale here of commanders and troops alike is magnificent. One corps has already planted nine hundred thousand stakes against airborne landings, and its' gotten hold of a million grenades to arm them with explosives over the next weeks." It was the first time in his life that he had phoned Hitler. Afterward, he wrote home: "He was in the best of spirits and didn't spare his congratulations on our work here in the west. I hope to make faster progress than ever now." Ruge, who had listened in on an earpiece, was fascinated by Hitler's remarks. Speidel—who had also listened in—was less pleased: the prospect of enlisting the field marshal for his anti-Hitler conspiracy must have seemed more distant than ever.

After that, Rommel drove briefly back to Normandy to check that General Marcks was bringing all his reserves into the front line, as Rommel had dictated. "I can't venture too far afield right now," he explained to Lucie. "One never knows when the balloon will go up." Later that day, May 17, he drove on into Brittany. The sun shone, the country was dazzling with apple blossoms. At Le Val-André, where mile upon mile of empty beaches had stretched before him on his last visit, there was now an impenetrable thicket of Rommel obstacles—barbed wire, tetrahedrons, concrete dragon's teeth, Czech hedgehogs and timber stakes topped with Teller mines or steel "can openers." He dined with the local commanders and reminisced nostalgically about the booty of Tobruk two years before—the pineapples, English beer, crab's legs and other delicacies—and he told them about the captured New Zealander, Brigadier G. H. Clifton, who four times escaped and was four times recaptured in the desert. Long after dark, Rommel was drawn back to the beach again, and he strolled with Admiral Ruge deep into his manmade forest of deadly obstacles. "Let the enemy invade us now," he told a division commander the next day, "but with trembling knees."

He drove back to La Roche-Guyon, content. He himself would have liked to go to Herrlingen, but he wrote to Lucie there could be no thought of that. However, when General Speidel asked if he might take a few days of home leave again over Pentecost, Rommel indulgently agreed. Speidel left on May 24. In fact, he was going to consult with other anti-Hitler conspirators in Württemberg.

It was on the twentieth that the two British commandos, sent as part of the Fortitude deception, were driven to Rommel's headquarters for interrogation. Their capture near the Somme estuary seemed another indication as to where the invasion was likely to come, although Lieutenant Lane said he thought the Somme-Dieppe coastline was too heavily fortified to be invaded. He was asked, "Are such commando spy missions really necessary, if the invasion is imminent?" Lane answered: "The invasion is not imminent at all—you overestimate our enterprising spirit!"

There was nothing more that Rommel could do but wait. He went on rabbit hunts or strolled with Ruge and Meise in the woods. The terriers went with them—young Treff bouncing excitedly about the fields like a rubber ball. When the rabbits went to ground, Rommel borrowed ferrets from the French farmers to fetch them out. From Germany there were alarming reports of new air raids, including some on Stuttgart, capital of Swabia. He wondered how Manfred's antiaircraft battery had made out. Once he was forced into the tunnels of the château as enemy bomber squadrons glittered past thousands of feet overhead. "The French are suffering badly," he informed Lucie on May 29. "Three thousand dead among their population in the last forty-eight hours alone." It was the preinvasion bombardment beginning.

On Whitsunday, the twenty-eighth, he drove to the forest of Choisy. He chatted with Lang about Göring and the Luftwaffe: "While the others were building up their air power, we were fast asleep. Now we're paying the penalty. My impression is that the people around the Führer often didn't tell him their real opinions about the situation." At the edge of the forest, they climbed back into their car and drove over to see the Marquis de Choisy, whose friendship Rommel had made in 1940. The marquis was an imposing person, though rather frail now. His son had been fighting for three years with the Wehrmacht in Russia. The mother was pert and lively, without a kind word for the British. Rommel already knew their daughter, a fresh-faced young girl who had often visited her relatives, the Rochefoucaulds, at the château. "These people," wrote Lang that day, "are staking everything on Germany and this is what the Chief wants. Because then, when the invasion comes, they'll have to side with us because they've already compromised themselves too far. The Chief's view is that Germans and French—and all Europe—must stand united if our crusade against Bolshevism is to be won." (The marquis was hanged later by De Gaulle.)

Back at La Roche-Guyon, Rommel and Lang sat up late with the Rochefoucaulds. Rommel thought the duke rather a lifeless old gentleman, but his heart was evidently in the right place because when they left for their own quarters he raised his family to their feet to drink a toast: "To Germany's victory." A few days later, Rommel could not help noticing that the four beautiful tapestries that had hung for centuries in his vast study had quietly been removed and put in storage—so evidently the family believed the invasion was about to begin.

There is no contemporary evidence that Rommel's views on the target and prospects of the invasion had changed. All the evidence still pointed to the Fifteenth Army's sector, closest to the English coast: it was attracting two enemy reconnaissance flights for every one over the Seventh Army. In this last week there were 246 enemy air raids on targets north of the Seine, and only thirty-three south of the river. (Rommel's weekly reports spoke of the mounting French public anger at the enemy over these raids.) Provided the enemy invaded here, Rommel knew he could defeat them. He appealed to Jodl in a letter on May 23 for Hitler to begin his missile attack on London as soon as possible, to throw another wrench in the enemy's works and provide them with another urgent reason to capture the Fifteenth Army's sector—the secret missile-launching sites. Unexpected confirmation was brought from England by none other than Hans Cramer, the last commander of the Afrika Korps, somewhat improbably repatriated to Nazi Germany because of his bad asthma! He called on Rommel, and tipped him off that the enemy invasion would be on either side of the Somme.

Rommel checked the moon and tide tables: there were no good invasion tides until after June 20. He spent June 2 hunting with his marquis, and went to Paris the next day to see Rundstedt and pick up the shoes for Lucie. Rundstedt's written appreciation was, "There is still no sign that the invasion is imminent." That day, however, Rommel did send out a significant instruction to his commanders, without *fully* realizing what he was saying: "The enemy has conducted repeated invasion maneuvers at *low* tide, which means we may have to take such an invasion seriously into account." All Rommel's beach obstacles had, of course, been built on the assumption of a high-tide invasion. A rush program would have to begin now to push the obstacles down to the low-tide line as well. "You are to try to complete this by June 20," his order concluded. The next morning, June 4, Rommel drove to Germany on leave. He took Colonel von Tempelhoff, his operations officer, with him, and left Speidel at the château to mind the store. Lucie would get her shoes.

At Hitler's headquarters, a less sanguine mood prevailed. Jodl's High Command staff—correctly expecting the invasion target to be the Cherbourg peninsula—checked their tide tables and warned Hitler on June 2, "Favorable invasion dates occur between June 5 and 13." In France, such warnings went unheeded. Some people there even began to doubt there *would* be an enemy invasion, such was the triumph of Fortitude. That was certainly the view of Field Marshal Hugo Sperrle's Luftwaffe superiors. It was the view of General Blumentritt ("I'm beginning to think it's all been one big British hoax"). And in the diary of Luftwaffe major Werner Beumelberg on July 23 is the startling similar remark that Cramer said he had heard from Rommel before his departure: "There's not going to *be* an invasion. And if there is, then they won't even get off the beaches!"

Only the one-legged General Erich Marcks was still uneasy, as he surveyed the two divisions in the Calvados area of the Normandy coastline, the 716th and 352nd: each had a thirty-mile sector, to defend. "It's the weakest sector of my whole corps," he had conceded to Salmuth on May 30, when Rommel brought all his senior commanders to Caen for a weapons display. A couple of days later Marcks again stood there, on a hill at Arromanches-les-Bains, gazing out to sea as though he expected to see warships come up over the horizon. He told an army captain at his side, "If I know the British, they'll go to church next Sunday for one last time, and sail Monday [June 5]. Army Group B says they're not going to come yet, and that when they do come it'll be at Calais. So I think we'll be welcoming them on Monday, right *here*."

# With Their Pants Down

**N**EAR a ruined city in France, Rommel stands with a tattered little notebook in his hands, curiously turning the pages and examining the smudged ink inscriptions. It is not his notebook—General Feuchtinger has just handed it to him. Feuchtinger's Twenty-first Panzer Division has captured it during the battle still raging between the Germans and the Allied invaders around this city in June 1944. It turns out to be the private diary of an English officer, a Captain Alistair Bannerman, and it is written in the form of a long letter to Elizabeth, the young wife he left in a Dorset farmhouse when he went off to lead an antitank platoon against the Germans. From it Rommel, with the help of an interpreter, learns something of the souls of the men he is fighting, and of their last days in England as they prepared for the biggest invasion in history.

The diary begins on Sunday, May 28, 1944—the day that Rommel spent with the Marquis de Choisy. At the unnamed army camp in Sussex, in southeastern England, total security has just been imposed and all movements in and out are strictly controlled. For the first time Captain Bannerman feels trapped. He realizes he may never see his young family again, and the diary begins to meander between the idyllic past, the tedious present and the horrible events to come. "We don't feel majestic at all at the moment," he writes. "There are too many little pinpricks in this life. The eternal drill, the being pushed around, hobnailed boots and sweaty socks, and now the caged existence too—these are all petty irritations that erect something of a wall between us and life as the journalists and politicians care to portray it from their exalted viewpoints. I have tried explaining to my own platoon that we're about to make history and that one day their children will read of our deeds in the history books, but all I get are faint smiles. . . ."

And so the diary goes on—one moment reflecting that tank landing craft are more comfortable vessels than the infantry assault boats in which the soldiers were vomiting all over each other during a rehearsal for invasion, the next moment indulging in nostalgia for boat trips in May in Dorset, picnics, his wife's soft dress and tender moments with her in spring. "Then I think of you, my family, in October when the apples are already in the storehouses and the autumn flowers are running riot through the gardens with their copper red and blue colors. The mornings are cool and moist with dew, making the lawn shimmer with jewels, but it's still warm enough to lie full length in the open air as I did last October, watching Andrew learn to walk. . . ."

Thus Bannerman prepares for the coming battle. "We're perspiring in clumsy boots and disinfected uniforms," he writes, "kitting out and loading our iron monsters, to destroy Nature on the other side of the Channel." He has commanded this antitank platoon for eighteen months and had only a few weeks' leave with Elizabeth. "I know which of my men are happily married, and which have kids and I know some of their names. I know the shirkers and the know-it-alls." At times he is annoyed with the jaunty proclamations by Churchill, Montgomery and Eisenhower. "It's monstrous to speak of this coming blood sacrifice of men as though it were a day at the races or a game. It is not. War is an evil business, it impinges on human liberty, dignity and peace with a kind of dullness, greed and apathy and turns all men into crawling animals lusting to get at each other's throats, to destroy each other's noble and beautiful cities and values that have taken 2,000 years to create. . . . To soldiers sitting in Nissen huts Churchill's radio rhetoric sounds a bit embarrassing. They have no great faith in the new world, they have no belief in any great liberating mission. They know it's going to be a charnel house. All they want us to put an end to it all, and get back to civvy street, to their homes, their private lives, their wives and loved ones."

The diary returns to Sunday, May 28:

We've just eaten and then listened to a speech by our commander. He repeated some of the things that Montgomery's just said to the battalion commanders. . . . He says the first four days are going to be vital, and we're going to have to take risks. We've got to go hell for leather to gain ground. Our commander says that the time for our own big risk will be the first six hours, when we have to thrust inland with as much force as possible to reach our main objective—a city they've code-named "Poland." I don't know what that is. It's a well-kept secret; thank God our security seems to be up to scratch in this respect. What a moment that's going to be, when we open our maps on board ship and find out the real name of the place we're going to attack. . . . The commander says the patch of ground we're going to invade was recently inspected by Rommel, and it's been reinforced even more, as have the rest of the coastal defenses. They've planted some most unpleasant stakes and spikes in the water and no doubt they've laid on a lot more surprises for us. But Monty says we can't overcome their surprises just by sitting back and waiting. They say the Xth Panzer Division has already moved closer to our area. It's got about twenty Tigers, ninety Panthers and over 100 Panzer IVs, so it's clear that my six little guns are going to have their work cut out if they attack our battalion.

Now it is May 31. In France, Rommel is checking the tide tables and deciding he can safely leave soon for Germany. In Sussex, the invasion troops are getting their last letters from home. "Now it is only war," Bannerman writes in his diary:

> I long for you so much, for your understanding, your quiet love and your tenderness, and today I want so much to smother your mouth with a flood of wild and reckless kisses, to lie by your side and feel the unbearable sweetness of your naked body in a cool room, with the summer breeze like a zephyr on your skin. Oh the torture of it all, to feel this summer desire in my blood, this rightful longing for you, you darling and desirable woman. And yet to know that duty and barbed wire, destiny and human folly are putting thousands of miles between us! . . . What a gigantic effort each man now has to make, to face up to something like this. Men who may have had only little of life, men with little education and little knowledge and with no philosophical supports, men with ailing, estranged or poor or needy families, men who have never been loved, men who had never had high ambitions or wanted a new world order. Yet we're all here, we're all going, as ordered, willingly into battle. I hope the country recognizes these men for what they now have to do. . . .

Bannerman's mind keeps going back to Dorset's warm and gentle landscape, to country walks, to love and laughter:

> *Winnie the Pooh!* I've got it in my assault library—that and my New Testament. Soon the roses will be out, pink roses would look exquisite on your blue-and-white striped dress. If you were here, I'd undo your dress button by button, then kiss first the nape of your neck, and then the little hollow in your throat, and then the gentle dip between your breasts. And that's where I'd put the roses, a perfect decoration for such a pretty place. . . . Tomorrow's June the first, and we're going one step closer. We're moving forward to the embarkation area. Today we were given the passwords for the first few days.

We've topped up our fuel tanks and taken on rations and ammunition.

June 1. At the embarkation area they wait, and speculate on what city "Poland" will be. They stroll, drink beer, strum the piano in the mess and sing songs like "We Must Never Say Goodbye" and "Moonlight Becomes You" and "As Time Goes By." He hears alarming news: that panzer division has now sniffed forward to "Poland" itself and been practicing counterattacks.

June 2. Rommel is again shooting with the Marquis de Choisy. Bannerman is writing: "This morning we heard that we move off tomorrow at the crack of dawn to embark. So the game's beginning."

June 3. Rommel is in Paris, buying shoes for Lucie. Bannerman's diary says: "Up early, after waking at 4:30. Dressed by hurricane lamp, had just enough time for Communion at five before we drive off at six." The day is spent winching the heavy guns and gear aboard the landing craft. "D day is Monday, so we've only got tomorrow, Sunday, left."

June 4. In the morning, as Rommel leaves France for his home in Herrlingen, Bannerman writes:

I have written a letter to you, but I don't know if anybody's coming to collect them. We're riding at anchor, and there's a strong wind and the sea's quite rough. . . . We've got these monster trailers on board, and the deck is packed with tractors, jeeps, personnel carriers, guns and tanks, and the men have been sleeping on duckboards or in their vehicles, with three blankets apiece. I turned in shortly after nine, in the wheelhouse, and slept quite well on a stretcher. I believe D day's going to be tomorrow, so I haven't much time left. . . . I pray for courage, though I know I'm no hero. . . .

On Sergeant Matthews's personnel carrier, in which I'm supposed to go on land, the entire section has chalked the names of their girls and a cupid's heart. So in order not be left out, I've added your name to the gallery too. You're in between Lance Corporal Baker's Doris and Sergeant Matthews's

Vera. The harbor's overflowing with ships, barrage balloons are up and the men are eating their meals in little groups. I wonder what dress you're wearing? It's 1:00 P.M., I suppose you're just taking Andrew down for Sunday lunch. Your sunburned arms are preparing his food, and he's clamoring for it from his high chair. If I was with you now, I'd interrupt you just long enough for a kiss, and see the laughter in your eyes as you turn around and offer me your soft lips, before you turn back like a good mother to the job at hand. How I love to see Andrew's half-shy surprise when he sees us embrace. . . . We've been in the harbor all day. The invasion's been postponed because of bad weather, the harbor's full of ships.

Bannerman goes ashore to stretch his legs. Rommel is doing the same, in Germany, with Lucie.

June 5. Bannerman writes:

There's still a strong wind blowing, but soon after breakfast we weighed anchor and sailed. The chalk cliffs lit up in the sun like white curtains along the shallow green coastline. The white fleet of tank landing and support craft with their large silver barrage balloons and the motorboats throwing up white plumes of spray make a lovely picture of blue and white and silver. Part of Britain's armada: it looks more like a regatta.

The signal's been given: "Open sealed orders at 0700 hours." Another order from a motor boat: "Sailing time 1230 hours." So tomorrow must be D day. We sailed at 12:45 P.M. I mustered all the men and told them this is it. It wasn't easy to speak, as I had to grip the railing with one hand, the papers in the other, and prevent the wind from tearing the megaphone out of my hands as well. I had to shout to make myself heard above the wind, the sea and the engines. I told them, with a great feeling for the drama of the moment, that tomorrow is D day and that our first assault waves hit the beaches at 7:25 A.M. Our objective is the city of Caen. Normandy and Brittany are to receive our invasion forces.

That night, Bannerman does not sleep well.
June 6:

> I think we all can't help feeling from time to time
> we must be dreaming. My friend James spoke for us
> all when he said, "I keep feeling that my wife's go-
> ing to give me a wallop on the backside and tell me
> I've overslept and I'm half an hour late for break-
> fast." It's now 3:00 A.M., and I've been up on the
> bridge. The moon's shining and it's quite bright but
> a bit overcast. I can see the columns and rows of
> little ships and dark balloons, silhouetted fore and
> aft of us against the gray sea. . . . And so we sail on
> toward Caen. And you, my angel, are sleeping, I
> hope, fast asleep in the nursery. Your thoughts have
> been such a help to me. I've drawn a lot of strength
> from them. I can imagine you listening to the nine
> o'clock news each day, and thinking lovingly of me.
> I hope that Andrew is fast asleep with his golden
> head on his little pillow, and that Richard is lying
> snug in his tiny cot.

The hours pass, as the invasion fleet slowly approaches
Normandy. Bannerman can see antiaircraft fire to the right
of him—that must be the Cherbourg defenses. "I expect
that you've heard the news by now, my darling. My eyes
grow quite moist, as I realize that you may at this very
moment be listening to the news. . . ."

His diary comes to an abrupt halt soon after.

Bannerman's landing craft had been part of an immense
invasion fleet—6,483 ships, including six battleships,
twenty-three cruisers and 104 destroyers. All day long it
had sailed from England toward the Normandy coastline,
as conspicuous a movement as there has ever been, especially in this the age of the reconnaissance plane, radio,
radar and secret agents. Yet nobody on the German side
had detected the fleet's approach. If just one Nazi patrol
boat had been stationed in the English Channel, it could
have given Hitler ten hours' warning—but the German
navy had declared the seas too rough for their own patrol
boats to put to sea. The German defenders received no

warning until the first enemy shots were fired at them. Paratroops landed right in their midst and caught them unawares. Thus the British radio commentators could claim, "The Germans were caught with their pants down."

The astonished and angry German High Command on June 9 ordered Rommel's headquarters to investigate in full whether this insinuation was true—that the German forces had been surprised. Backward and forward went the teleprinter messages concerning what General Speidel's staff came to dismiss with guilty levity as the "underwear inquiry." Rommel evidently guessed where the dirty linen was and squelched all further action, to protect his own and Rundstedt's officers. On July 4 Tempelhoff, Rommel's operations officer, advised the Seventh Army: "The commission of inquiry into the events of June 5–6 is a dead duck."

If ever a situation warranted such an inquiry, it was this one. On the eve of the invasion, the entire German command structure in France was in disarray. Rommel, who had always stressed the need to thwart the enemy invasion in its first few hours, was on leave in Germany. At Rommel's château, La Roche-Guyon, Speidel was standing in for him, and Staubwasser, the intelligence officer, for Tempelhoff, who, like Rommel, had gone to Germany. Speidel was serenity itself, but for all his staff experience in Russia he had "never actually commanded anything larger than an old-fashioned infantry company," as the jealous General Geyr later acidly observed. He was not a man of action. There were other gaps as well. General Salmuth of the Fifteenth Army had only just returned from two days' hunting in the Ardennes, where he had been completely out of touch. General Dollmann had left the Seventh Army's headquarters for Rennes, in Brittany, to which he had called all his commanders for a planning conference the next day. Worse, the Twenty-first Panzer Division's General Feuchtinger had absented himself to Paris to amuse himself, taking his very capable operations officer with him—and Rommel had no other panzer division within immediate striking distance of Caen and the Normandy beaches. Only General Marcks, the commander in Normandy, was at his post. That evening he had hobbled with his corps staff into his command bunker at Saint-

Lô for the first time, as if he sensed that his time had come.

How was it possible that the German commanders could have been oblivious to the fate about to befall them? The answer to this reveals a deeper puzzle yet: German intelligence had given General Speidel strong evidence that the invasion would take place on June 6, but he had declined to alert the Seventh Army.

*The historian searches Speidel's records in vain for the truth behind this inexplicable lapse. Hans Speidel himself frankly admitted to me, "There were quite deliberate omissions from Army Group B's war diary, resulting from instructions either by Rommel, by Tempelhoff or by myself." Tantalizingly, the telephone log kept by Rundstedt's intelligence staff during these days is missing until the dawn of D day itself. But fortunately the records of the High Command, the Seventh and Fifteenth armies, the navy and the SS survive in sufficient volume to enable us to reconstruct the story—a story that seemed almost incredible to me when I first heard it in January 1969 from Colonel Oskar Reile, the chief of German counterespionage in France at the time of the invasion. I found Reile to be a man of medium height, slight physique, and dark-haired. He could easily have been mistaken for a Frenchman, for he spoke fluent French with an educated accent. His German, too, was elegant: his phrases unhurried, his conversation beautifully ordered, his thoughts flowing obediently in the sequence that he needed them. I listened intently as he told his astonishing tale.*

The facts were these: the enemy were known to have assigned to certain cells of the French underground important sabotage operations to coincide with D day. Particular bridges were to be blown, roads mined and railroads sabotaged. How to tip off these cells as to the date, without telling the Nazis? Each cell had been told to listen for its own secret code phrase to be broadcast by the BBC in two halves. The first half would signify that there were no more than two weeks to go before D day. And if the second half was thereafter broadcast, D day would follow within forty-eight hours. It was a precise, and new, system.

But since late 1943 Colonel Reile's agents had infiltrated a significant fraction of these French underground cells, and by February 1944 he knew precisely which code phrases to instruct his numerous radio monitors, quartered in the Hôtel Lutetia in Paris, to listen for.

The monotonous vigil had continued through March, April and May. Then, on June 1, his monitors rushed into his office at the Lutetia. The BBC had just transmitted 125 of the half phrases—so D day would occur in the next two weeks! Very significantly, those cells which the enemy suspected of having been infiltrated—and Reile knew which they were—did not get the dramatic messages: so this must be the real thing. Equally significantly, those cells that did get the messages were located in Brittany and Normandy, and in the Lille-Amiens area (across the German supply route).

Tremendously excited, Reile informed Rundstedt in Paris and the Gestapo in Berlin. The Gestapo informed the High Command and—the records show—clearly spelled it out to them: an invasion would occur before the fifteenth, and reception of the second half phrase would be the final clue as to the actual day. It was the scoop of the Second World War.

Hitler was informed on June 2, and the High Command passed the extraordinary information on to the General Staff's experts in Foreign Armies West—the agency responsible for briefing the lower army echelons on intelligence matters. This agency did nothing.

The chief of this agency was Colonel Alexis von Roenne. A General Staff colonel, a baron born in the Baltic states, Roenne was distant, suave and fluent in French and Russian. It can surely be said that he was among those responsible for Rommel's defeat in France. Together with the chief of his English section, Major Roger Michael, an ambiguous figure—his mother was British; he was seen after the war wearing a U.S. Army uniform, then he vanished behind the Iron Curtain—Roenne consistently fed to Army Group B data on the enemy's strength and intentions that was so thoroughly false that it is impossible to believe it was by accident. It had to be part of the anti-Hitler plan. Colonel Paul Brendel, Roenne's operations officer from April 1944 until the end, later remembered

Roenne as "an intellectual but aloof person, impossible to make friends with. That countless German soldiers would pay for his actions with their lives, left him stone cold." Roenne undoubtedly felt, along with the other conspirators, that by expediting the inevitable defeat the plotters were actually saving German lives in far greater number. Roenne was executed later as a traitor to Hitler.

Runstedt's staff was told about the half phrases directly by Colonel Reile. Why it also did nothing is controversial. It seems that Rundstedt's intelligence officer, Colonel Wilhelm Meyer-Detring, had originally instructed lower echelons late in 1943 to ignore BBC "alerts." When word came from Reile, Meyer-Detring was on leave, and his deputy ignored the announcement. In any case, Rundstedt's staff probably felt that since Rommel had, five months before, taken direct command of the coastal armies, it was up to him to alert those armies.

Rommel's intelligence officer, Colonel Staubwasser, maintains he was not even told about the *new* two-part phrase system. At any rate, he wet-blanketed the first storm beacon lit by Reile—regarding it as merely more of the same old stuff—and drafted these words on June 3: "The increased transmissions of alarm phrases by enemy radio since June 1 for the French underground cells is not, on previous experience, to be interpreted as an indication that the beginning of the invasion is imminent." Speidel countersigned this report. Early the next day, June 4, Rommel left for home, taking the parcel of shoes for Lucie. The formal pretext for his journey was an interview —as yet unarranged—with Hitler.

This brings us to the events that occurred at the château on the fifth, the day before the invasion. That morning, Speidel telephoned his colleagues in the Paris section of the anti-Hitler resistance and invited them to come to the château for drinks in the evening. One of them, a senior war reporter attached to Rundstedt's staff, remembers that Speidel prefaced the unexpected invitation with the words "The Old Man's gone away." (At 5:45 P.M. Speidel was heard telephoning one of the main anti-Hitler plotters in Berlin, General Wagner, and saying that Rommel would probably be away for some time since he was not going to see Hitler until the eighth or ninth.) It seemed to Speidel that the coast was clear—in both senses. The enemy invasion was probably going to come at the Strait of Dover—that was what Colonel von Roenne, whose Foreign Armies West was giving Rommel so much misinformation, had *ordered* all his staff to predict. But the tides there would not be favorable for many days. So it was with an easy mind that Speidel settled down for a rewarding evening.

Soon Speidel's guests arrived. They dined, ambled about the gardens, then split into two groups in his room in the château's Norman turret. In one group, a count and a consul general listened to the anecdotes of a colonel. In the other, Speidel talked with Ernst Jünger and other conspirators and discussed the peace manifesto drafted by Jünger, to be proclaimed after the overthrow of Hitler. The bulky document lay on the table.

Outside, the moon had risen. The cognac flowed in warming, golden rivulets through the conversation. Some time after ten o'clock, the subdued voices in Speidel's group were interrupted by the shrill ringing of the telephone. It was Colonel Staubwasser, calling from Tempelhoff's desk. The Fifteenth Army intelligence officer had just telephoned from Tourcoing, said Staubwasser, to report that at 9:15 P.M. one of their radio monitors had picked up the second code phrase being broadcast by the BBC to the French underground. There was no doubt about it. As the Fifteenth Army intelligence officer had just pointed out to Staubwasser, this meant that D day might be the next morning, June the sixth. "General Salmuth," Staubwasser told Speidel, "has already alerted the whole Fifteenth Army!" This confronted Speidel with a decision: should Dollmann's Seventh Army, in Normandy, also be alerted?

General Speidel put down the phone. Retaining his nonchalance, he went to Staubwasser and advised him to telephone Rundstedt's headquarters for advice. Then he returned to his guests. Staubwasser made the call, and after a while one of Rundstedt's aides telephoned Staubwasser back from Paris with the desired ruling. According to Staubwasser, it was that the Seventh Army was not to be alerted. So it was not. There is no record of any of these conversations in the war diary of Army Group B.

Toward midnight, Speidel's guests began to leave.

Their drive back to Paris would be much longer than usual, now that the Seine bridges had been bombed. Speidel chatted with the late-goers for a while. At 1:00 A.M. he went to bed. It was now June the sixth.

Who can say how much of this story Rommel was ever told? His reputation had seemed bedeviled by slipshod intelligence and careless staff work ever since Operation Crusader in Libya in November 1941.

It is only now that the events at Rundstedt's headquarters in Paris that night can be patched together.

Reile had also again intercepted the BBC messages and he telephoned Rundstedt's staff. Then he personally took a written summary of their importance to Major Reinhard Brink, Rundstedt's counterespionage liaison officer. Brink took the document in to Rundstedt's operation officer, Colonel Bodo Zimmermann. The colonel was a generation older than Rundstedt's other staff officers, arrogant and old-fashioned, with a wooden antipathy toward all intelligence sources. He refused to take the warning seriously. However, Rundstedt's staff did issue this immediate signal to all stations: "Several phrases known to us since the autumn of 1943 to give brief notice of the start of the invasion, were broadcast for the first time today by the British radio. While we cannot expect that the invasion itself will be announced in advance by radio, it is to be anticipated that the sabotage acts prepared against our transport and communications networks in connection with the invasion, and perhaps armed uprisings as well, are to be set off by these messages." Among the commanders sent this message was Speidel at Army Group B.

This, then, was the situation at 1:00 A.M. Speidel and most of his staff had gone to bed. The Fifteenth Army was at maximum alert, the Seventh Army was not; its guard was down. And Rommel was 500 miles away, at Herrlingen. About this time the first six soldiers of the invasion parachuted onto the base of the Cherbourg peninsula; around them descended hundreds of shadowy shapes—straw dummies, designed to convince the Nazis that this was only a spoof invasion, while the "real" one would be far away. The six men concealed themselves well, then let fly with flare pistols and loudly played phonograph records of small arms fire and soldiers' oaths. It was a further twist of Fortitude, designed to perplex and confuse.

After that the real airborne landings, by parachute and glider, began in the Normandy area. The 716th Infantry Division sounded the alert at 1:10 A.M. Marcks alerted his corps one minute later. The Seventh Army finally went on alert at 1:35. As it did, its chief of staff, General Max Pemsel, telephoned Rommel's château. Speidel was awakened, spoke to Pemsel, and then called Rundstedt's staff in Paris. But at 1:40 A.M. Speidel got reports of other airborne landings well up the coast, in the Fifteenth Army's sector, and soon he learned that straw dummies had been found in Normandy. These revelations made it possible for him to assert that the big action was elsewhere. For the rest of the night he was to hesitate. Repeatedly he told the Seventh Army, which was in the path of the gigantic assault, that the enemy must be staging only a "local attack" in Normandy. He even reassured Rundstedt's staff at 3:00 A.M. that he was taking it all "very calmly." "It's possible," he said, "that people are taking bailed-out air crews for paratroops!"

Again Max Pemsel, from the Seventh Army, phoned the château to try to correct Speidel's blithe attitude. "It is a major operation," he insisted vehemently. Speidel, however, was transfixed by new reports from the Fifteenth Army's area, miles away. Two prisoners from the British First Airborne Division (whose plane had in fact lost its way and landed them there in error) had revealed under interrogation that still more landings were to follow. Speidel took this to mean the landings would come in that same area. Reluctant to commit his panzer division's wrongly, Speidel refused to commit them at all.

As the hours wore on, the reports multiplied. Heavy bombers had been heard passing over the Channel Islands, flying slowly—obviously towing gliders. By three-thirty there were hundreds of gliders landing around Caen, to the rear of Rommel's Death Zone. Naval radar detected massed ships approaching the coast of Normandy. At 3:42 A.M. the dogged Pemsel phoned the château and screamed that the depth of the airborne landings proved that this was obviously a huge operation.

At 3:50 A.M. General Blumentritt, Rundstedt's chief of staff back in Paris, also shifted to Pemsel's view. "The width of the sector under attack shows this is no operation of purely local significance," he said.

At 4:30 A.M. Pemsel reported that his army's artillery was already shelling warships.

At 5:15 A.M. a map of Caen was found in one of the crashed gliders—certainly a clear indication of the extensiveness of the invaders' intentions; getting to Caen would be no small effort. Again the nervous Seventh Army chief of staff insisted to Speidel's headquarters that all the facts pointed to "a major enemy assault." Still Speidel kept his nerve.

Outside the château, Speidel could see the gray of dawn in the eastern sky. In other Allied invasions, the enemy had always landed before dawn. At 5:40 A.M., twenty minutes after dawn, he telephoned Pemsel. "Have any troops actually *landed* from the sea?" he asked. Pemsel had to admit that they had not. Only the day before, in fact, the German naval staff had suggested that the landings might come *after* dawn; decoded enemy radio signals had revealed that the Allies' big invasion rehearsal of May 4 had begun two hours after low tide, and in broad daylight.

At 6:15 A.M. Pemsel's anxious voice again came on the telephone from Normandy. At 5:30 A.M., he said, colossal naval bombardment of Rommel's Death Zone and beach obstacles had begun.

Speidel once again resisted Pemsel's inference. Indeed, he put his own arguments to Pemsel with such persuasiveness that Pemsel, worn down, wrote into the Seventh Army diary a new assessment completely reversing his earlier alarmist view. "The purpose of this naval bombardment," wrote Pemsel, "is not yet apparent. All in all, these appear to be just diversionary operations mounted in connection with later assaults planned for elsewhere."

After this, beginning at 6:40 A.M. there is a two-and-a-half-hour gap in the war diary kept by Speidel's operations staff. We know that Speidel did telephone Tempelhoff to begin the long drive back from Germany, but why the gap from 6:40 A.M. until 9:05 A.M.? There is one clue in the Fifteenth Army's war diary. It says that at 6:45 A.M. the Fifteenth got a phone call from Max Pemsel, reporting the latest news. "A naval bombardment has begun from offshore, but there has been no invasion attempt so far. We at Seventh Army expect to be able to cope with the situation with our own means." That was splendid news. On hearing it, General von Salmuth commented to his own chief of staff, "So—the enemy invasion has failed already," and went to bed. This was clearly the belief at Château La Roche-Guyon as well. Speidel later admitted, faced with the evidence of these war diaries, "Yes, it is quite possible that we all went back to bed as well."

# Normandy

AT Herrlingen, Rommel usually gets up early enough to catch the seven o'clock news. Then he bathes, shaves, dresses and breakfasts at nine or ten on a clear soup prepared by Lucie. Then he goes out for a stroll. But today, June 6, 1944, is different. It is Lucie's birthday. The villa is full of flowers—the finest bouquet is from the field marshal himself—and there are the presents to be arranged on the drawing room table. In his red striped dressing gown and slippers, Rommel contentedly busies himself with the gifts, helped by one of Lucie's houseguests—Hildegard Kirchheim. (She is the wife of General Heinrich Kirchheim, who was one of Erwin's earliest officers in Africa.) The Paris shoes take pride of place.

There is a knock at the door, and the housemaid, Karolina, comes in. "Herr Feldmarschall Rommel is wanted on the telephone!" Rommel assumes it is General Schmundt, Hitler's adjutant, calling from Berchtesgaden—he had telephoned yesterday to say that the Führer would probably find time to see Rommel today. Rommel walks through the sliding door into the smoking room and picks up the phone. It is Speidel, calling from La Roche-Guyon: the enemy invasion has begun.

The blood drains from Rommel's face. For a moment he says nothing, then: "I'll return at once!" His hand crashes down on the telephone hook. He jerks it up and down until the operator replies. "A Führungsblitz call to the Führer's headquarters, at once!" he barks. The girl hesitates to clear the lines for him. "Dammit, girl," snaps the field marshal, "this is Rommel speaking. Give me a line at once!" When the call goes through, he tersely reports the situation and his intention to return to France, then hangs up and vanishes to change into his uniform. "Get my Daniel up here with the car at once," he shouts at his manservant, Private Rudolf Loistl. "And get Lang to meet me at Freudenstadt."

*We cannot state with certainty what time this was. Speidel's version is that he called Rommel at 6.00 A.M., which indeed would have been tardy enough. But the only such call to Rommel is fixed in the war diary of Army Group B more than four hours later, at 10.15 A.M. According to the diary kept by Hellmuth Lang's mother, Lang left at ten-thirty to rendezvous with Rommel. Rommel certainly left Herrlingen no earlier than that. Hildegard Kirchheim recalls, "I waited about thirty minutes after the call came, until Lucie came into the room and told me in great agitation that Erwin had already left for France." She also remembers that Lucie then tried on the shoes; they did not fit.*

If Rommel had been tuned to the enemy's radio stations, he would have heard the formal enemy proclamation of the momentous news, an hour sooner. "Under the command of General Eisenhower," said the broadcast, "Allied naval forces supported by strong air forces began landing Allied armies this morning on the coast of France." After El Alamein, this was the second time that Rommel would arrive back at his headquarters too late to save a battle.

What had jolted Speidel's staff out of their slumber? Probably it was the alarmed telephone call that General Pemsel of the Seventh Army suddenly put through to the château soon after 9:00 A.M., reporting that enemy troops and even tanks were swarming ashore in Normandy. "The enemy ships lay hove to, offshore, for a long time," Pemsel explained. "They only began the invasion after the tide turned." Rommel's beach obstacles had been demolished at the first light by enemy commandos and sappers who had slipped in with small craft. Within five minutes of the first infantry hitting the beaches, the first tanks were rolling up the shallow slopes. Shock troops had attacked the surviving bunkers with flamethrowers and explosives. Where there were cliffs, they were scaled by rope ladders projected by rockets from the approaching landing craft. The violent bombing and naval bombardment had torn great gaps in Rommel's minefields and Death Zone. As Rundstedt observed with more than a trace of malicious pleasure in 1949, the enemy had foiled all Rommel's gadgets: "The invasion began at low tide, not high tide as our navy had presupposed; their tanks merely drove through the flooded terrain, and the stakes did not prevent the airborne landings."

No counterattack had begun. Three panzer divisions were within striking distance, but none was moving to the invasion beaches. The Twenty-first Panzer—still minus General Feuchtinger, who was off in Paris—could have moved up from Caen in less than two hours; it had begun to stir restlessly at 4:00 A.M., but Speidel had refused to commit it despite Marcks's frantic pleas. Thus hours were lost.

Nor were Rundstedt or the High Command's General Jodl in any position to intervene. Nobody—least of all Speidel's staff—was prepared to swear that this was the only invasion, and not a feint. Colonel von Roenne, of Rundstedt's Foreign Armies West, still spreading misinformation, several times telephoned Speidel's intelligence officer. "This is not the main invasion yet—that's going to hit the Fifteenth Army later," he said on one occasion, and much the same on the others. Jodl accordingly vetoed any release of the High Command's panzer reserves toward Normandy: the fanatical Twelfth SS Panzer ("Hitler Jugend") and the hard-hitting Panzer Lehr Division were the closest. For the Germans this was the tragedy, that Rommel was not there; he would have used his famous tongue and temperament to cut through the Gordian knots restricting the panzer reserves. "If people had listened to me," he wrote to Lucie afterward, "we would have counterattacked with three panzer divisions on the first evening and we would probably have defeated the attack."

At midday he picked up his aide's car at Freudenstadt—to meet him Lang had driven through Stuttgart at sixty miles an hour with his horn blaring—and they raced on into France. Rommel was sick with anxiety and halted briefly at Rheims at 4:55 P.M. to telephone the château for the latest news. As Speidel replied, it sounded hopeless. The enemy had torn a twenty-mile breach in the Atlantic wall and had already poured seven divisions into the bridgehead; they had set down two British airborne divisions around Caen and two U.S. airborne divisions onto the Cherbourg peninsula. After a ten-hour delay, the High Command had at last lifted its veto on the Twelfth SS and Panzer Lehr divisions for a counterattack; but the Hitler Jugend would not arrive until the next morning and the Panzer Lehr not until June 8.

"It's a major operation here," reported Speidel. "But it still doesn't rule out the possibility of a further major enemy invasion somewhere else!"

Rommel impatiently inquired: "How far has our own counterattack progressed?" Speidel informed him that the Twenty-first Panzer was awaiting further reinforcements. Rommel rasped: "Get the division moving into the attack right now! Don't await further reinforcements—attack at once!"

From the northwest of Caen, General Marcks himself soon led the Twenty-first Panzer's striking force into battle, standing up in his own open BMW car. Six tanks punched a narrow corridor through the invading British forces and reached the coast at Luc-sur-Mer: a two-mile stretch of Rommel's Death Zone was still intact and fighting. But the tank force lacked cohesion, and when hundreds of enemy aircraft flew low overhead at 7:20 P.M., releasing thousands of parachutes in the rear of the panzer division, Feuchtinger—by now back from his jaunt to Paris—lost his nerve and abruptly called off the attack. In fact, the parachutes were only a supply drop that had gone off course. Colonel Zimmermann of Rundstedt's staff, asked confidentially by Meyer-Detring the next morning what countermeasures had been begun, replied graphically, "So far, a load of shit. Feuchtinger took to his heels."

At 10:00 P.M. on D day, June 6, Rommel's car finally screeched to a halt at the château's main steps. His artillery chief, Colonel Hans Lattmann, wrote: "This evening Rommel got back from his wife's birthday: that was a short trip. He didn't even make it as far as the Chief," meaning Hitler. "He's very calm and collected. Grimfaced, as is to be expected." By this hour, Eisenhower had put 155,000 troops ashore in a series of Normandy bridgeheads totaling eighty square miles. Rommel's troops had inflicted over 10,000 casualties on them, but, as Marcks told his staff—and even by the field marshal's own earlier definition—the invasion had obviously succeeded. Moreover, Rommel was now told: "A further major invasion operation is to be expected on the Channel coast, as Dover is now completely hidden behind a smoke screen."

This waiting for the "second enemy invasion" was to befuddle Rommel's strategy for the next five weeks.

Rommel spent most of that night, June 6–7, trying to find out what was happening in Normandy. The Allies were jamming the Germans' radio and many telephone lines were down, but once Rommel managed to get through on the phone to the Seventh Army, and he barked at General Max Pemsel: "You've got to stop the enemy from getting a foothold, whatever happens!" He also managed to order the Twenty-first Panzer Division and the Hitler Jugend to stage a counterattack the first thing next morning—starting at about eight o'clock. Sepp Dietrich's First SS Panzer Corps would take overall command of the attack. But Feuchtinger of the Twenty-first had only about seventy tanks still running, and it was 9:30 A.M. before the Hitler Jugend began to arrive, having suffered heavily from enemy air attack on the way. Dietrich fumbled, kept postponing the counterattack—despite a visit from Rommel during the day—and then halted operations for the night.

Shortly before noon that day, June 7, Rommel telephoned General Jodl—now at the Berghof with Hitler—and formally complained about the total lack of German air force and navy intervention. Significantly, he warned Jodl: "My general impression is that we must assume that the enemy is going to make another invasion focal point elsewhere." Despite this, Hitler's staff were optimistic. General Geyr von Schweppenburg—commander of Panzer Group West—had now assumed overall direction of the five panzer divisions in or approaching Normandy, and Hitler believed they would launch their decisive counterattack the next day. That evening a naval officer reported from Hitler's war conference at the Berghof: "Like Field Marshal Rommel, the Führer sees the situation as wholly favorable, and is in confident anticipation of the success of our countermeasures."

The entire German public was hypnotized by the news from France. Gestapo reports on morale in Breslau, Berlin, Kiel and Koblenz showed that everybody trusted Rommel's ability implicitly. Now people recalled Hitler's confident prophecy on June 5, explaining why he had abandoned Rome that day without a fight: "The invasion this year is going to result in an annihilating defeat for the enemy at the one place where it really counts." Now too the public understood why their Führer had economized everywhere else—so as to concentrate everything on victory in the west. Voices in Kiel, Stettin and Hamburg were heard by Gestapo agents greeting the enemy invasion with enthusiasm: "At last we know what's what!" "This is the moment of decision." "Now we know that it all hasn't been in vain, and we're not finished yet." The Gestapo summary concluded: "With one stroke the mood has completely changed."

Initially, this complacency was also reflected by Speidel's staff (though not by Rommel). Hellmuth Lang wrote home, "There's a marvelous tranquility shown by all concerned, particularly our chief of staff Speidel." At night they now all slept in the air raid shelters tunneled into the cliff, in paneled rooms with central heating, air conditioning and, above them, 100 feet of rock. They took things very calmly. As soon as Rommel left for the battlefield each morning, his staff retired to the table tennis room, Speidel and Ruge taking on artillery chief Lattmann and the Luftwaffe colonel Queissner or, less strenuously, the beginner General Meise, their engineer chief. Sometimes Speidel was called to the telephone, but otherwise they could forget the invasion battle.

Not Rommel. There is in him the same restless urge as

in Africa, which drives him out to the battlefield again and again "to keep an eye on things," to keep his finger on his army's pulse, to find out how much more each grenadier in his foxhole can take, where artillery support is needed, where to rush the reinforcements and supplies. One war correspondent, watching him confer with his battle commanders, writes afterward: "Where knowledge and ability have their own human limitations and *intuition* begins— that extrasensory instinct, a child born of inspiration and perception—that is where the true leadership qualities of a warlord are to be seen. Rommel has them." There are photographs showing him in these days, confidently striding the battlefields—walking past the wreckage of a crashed Flying Fortress B-17 bomber, inspecting the enemy troop-carrying gliders that have crashed into the tall earth dikes topped with tangled, thorny hedges some ten or fifteen feet high that characterize the tight little fields and apple orchards of Normandy. And here he is with the Panzer Group commander Geyr, and with SS General Sepp Dietrich—a former sergeant major in the Bavarian cavalry who played a murky role in the Nazi misdeeds after Hitler's rise to power.

The enemy troops that Rommel sees are all young— they average twenty-two or twenty-three. His own infantry divisions often average thirty-five or thirty-seven; only the good panzer divisions like the Hitler Jugend or the Panzer Lehr are as young as these Allied troops. As at El Alamein, the enemy has poured equipment and ammunition into the fighting on a scale that the Nazis cannot match. To beat the flooded terrain, they have amphibious tanks. To thwart the mined Death Zone, they have special tanks with rotating drums in front flailing the ground with chains. Or, more crudely, the enemy just drive herds of "liberated" French cattle through the minefields ahead of them. They have better maps of the defenses than Rommel has himself. Above all, they have warships hurling broadsides far into the bridgehead at the dictate of spotter planes, and they have the weight of many air forces. As Rommel drives out once more to visit General Geyr on June 8, he sees thousands of enemy planes roaming the skies. Nothing bigger than a company dare move by day within sixty miles of the bridgehead. One immediate consequence of the air attack is a complete breakdown of radio communication: General Geyr has lost three quarters of his radio trucks already; Dietrich has only four sets left working out of twenty. Hellmuth Lang writes on the tenth: "So far Rommel has driven forward to one command post or another every day to exert personal control. But driving isn't the unalloyed pleasure that it used to be."

The German command structure was anything but simple. Each panzer division commander had to make sense of a mass of conflicting orders emanating from the High Command, from Rundstedt, Rommel, Dollmann (at the Seventh Army), Geyr (at Panzer Group West), and Dietrich (First SS Panzer Corps). The Panzer Lehr Division had now arrived from Chartres, but it had lost eighty-five armored vehicles, five tanks, and 123 trucks, including eighty gasoline tenders, in air attacks on the 100-mile approach. The division was now licking its wounds near Tilly-sur-Seilles, a village ten miles west of Caen. With nearly three intact panzer divisions a determined commander could have blasted a big gap in the enemy bridgehead. But when Rommel phoned the Seventh Army at 8:10 A.M., they told him that Dietrich was still hesitating to counterattack until later in the morning. "Bayeux's already been overrun by the enemy, but Carentan is still in our hands." Carentan was vital for the defense of the Cherbourg peninsula. Dietrich was planning to strike north to the coast. Rommel snapped: "The First SS Panzer Corps is to move off as soon as possible, with all three divisions, with its main weight on the left."

That sounded simple, but when Rommel arrived at Dietrich's command post that afternoon, things weren't going well. A thousand enemy gliders had landed right in the path of the Twenty-first Panzer's attack, disgorging thousands of paratroopers who had virtually wiped out Feuchtinger's infantry support; he had only fifty-five tanks left by dusk. Dietrich told Rommel that the enemy had tanks that could open fire at ranges of over 3,500 yards. Rommel sent a battle group—half of the Twenty-first Panzer and half of the Twelfth SS—northwestward to try to recapture Bayeux, but here they came well within range of the enemy battleships' big guns. The regrouping for this attack had wasted many hours.

Geyr was critical of the dispersal of the panzer divisions. "Thus the fist was unclenched just as it was ready to strike," he said later. At 4:40 P.M. Colonel Bodo Zimmermann, back in Paris, put the battlefield position like this to Rundstedt's intelligence officer, Meyer-Detring: "At present we are stuck. What isn't very pleasant is that the enemy is making ground. . . . In my view we've thrown a whole day away. Our tanks are locked in battles where they ought not to be, and we can only hope that the Panzer Lehr Division manages to slice through at Bayeux fast. Every minute counts. The trouble is, we're short of truck space. I'm afraid of a race for Saint-Lô. If there is one, things are going to turn very nasty." Ten minutes later, Zimmermann learned that the big British and American bridgeheads in Normandy were about to link. "Rommel's absence on the first day is to blame for all this," said Zimmermann.

By the evening of June 8, both Rommel's and Rundstedt's staffs were wide awake to the strategic danger facing them. Two vital U.S. secret documents had fallen into Nazi hands. The First U.S. Division landing on "Omaha" beach, northwest of Bayeux, had suffered heavily from heavy seas and powerful German defenses—the enemy had evidently known nothing of the extra German infantry division which Rommel had inserted at this point. Many of the American amphibious tanks had foundered, and landing boats had been devastated by German machine gun fire. In one crippled boat that had drifted ashore was found the field order of the entire U.S. Seventh Corps. This scoop was followed by another: A German engineer battalion had recaptured a coastal village, killing a young American officer in a shoot-out; in his briefcase the 100-page operation orders for the U.S. Fifth Corps had been found. *Close* scrutiny of these American documents would have told the Nazi experts a lot about Eisenhower's plans: for example, that forces were being committed to this invasion on such a scale that none could possibly remain back in England for any second invasion. But General Max Pemsel, chief of staff of the Seventh Army, perhaps discouraged by his earlier attempts to spread the word, sat on the documents for several days and telephoned only brief and incoherent extracts through to Rommel's staff.

"It's all very vague," complained Staubwasser at the château.

What was quite clear, even without captured documents, was Eisenhower's intention of taking Cherbourg immediately—and that if Cherbourg fell to the Allies it would be disastrous for the Germans. With Cherbourg, the Allies would no longer need to land men and machines on beaches—a slow and tricky business—but could unload them quickly and in great quantity through a major deepsea port. The Continent would soon be flooded with Allied might. So Hitler issued a string of instructions over the next days to prepare Cherbourg for a long siege.

Meanwhile the High Command was anxious about the lack of decisive action in Normandy. It was high time, they thought, to begin rolling the Fifteenth Army's surplus strength down into the battle. On the evening of June 8, Colonel Zimmermann in Paris telephoned Speidel. "Rommel," he said, "has got to decide whether he's going to get a big success tonight with the forces he already has. Rundstedt does not think he will, he thinks we're going to have to strip other fronts ruthlessly to provide further strength." When Speidel relayed this message to Rommel later that evening—just after his arrival back at the château—Rommel was annoyed at this fresh interference from the High Command. He phoned Jodl. "My intention is to split the two big enemy concentrations in two," he said, "with most weight on the left. We can't attack before tomorrow. The enemy's trying to breach through toward Cherbourg. . . . We've got to prevent their two major bridgeheads from linking up."

From the Berghof end of the telephone line came sounds of disagreement. Jodl also insisted, "I do not think we have to fear any second invasion in the west." Rommel was indignant at the general's naïveté: "May I point out that the enemy has so far committed only one of their two army groups, and this is precisely why we cannot afford to pull any forces out of the Fifteenth Army's area, and certainly not from Calais." Jodl calmly repeated: "There's not going to be any second invasion." (The conversation is recorded in the army group's war diary.) Rommel hung up on him.

There is something tragic about the way Rommel in June 1944 blindly adheres to what his intelligence experts tell him. Rommel, who in the past has burned his fingers on every occasion when he ignored intelligence, has now learned to listen—not realizing that the data the intelligence experts are feeding him are partly faked by members of the German anti-Hitler conspiracy for their own secret purposes and partly concocted by the enemy. As part of the Fortitude deception, the enemy has devised an entire fictitious army group, the "First U.S.," purportedly under General Patton's command. On June 2 an agent reports this to Berlin. Data on its strength follows. All along Colonel von Roenne had been overestimating the enemy's forces, but now the perplexed enemy chiefs of staff, as they read the Ultra intercepts, can see Roenne inventing British, Canadian and American divisions which even they have not conjured forth! Even more surprising: Speidel's staff are regularly adding even more divisions onto Roenne's figures, for good measure. Thus, on June 6— D day evening—Colonel von Roenne issues a secret summary: "Of approximately sixty major formations in southern England, at most only ten or twelve divisions, including airborne troops, are so far involved in this operation." He concludes that the Allies must be planning further invasions, because so far none of the twenty-five divisions "known" to be in the First U.S. Army Group has appeared.

Such fighting as there is in these days is confused and ill-concerted. In the tangled and obstructive hedgerow country, the tank battles are short, swift and fought at point-blank range. On June 9 Bayerlein's confident young tank crews, barely older than schoolboys, are sent rolling toward Bayeux beneath the lustrous golden evening skies of Normandy. They are quite fearless and sure of victory. There is the corporal who pauses to run his hands along the white hedgerow flowers, oblivious of the deafening shell bursts, then swings lithely up into the Tiger that is to become his blazing coffin only minutes later. There is the young lieutenant, poking his blond curly head out of his turret, punching an imaginary hole in the air and shouting: "Like that—we can do it"—the gesture only half finished as a shell fragment cleaves his forehead and his tank bursts into flames. The survivors fight on, elbow to elbow in their shirt sleeves and black uniform trousers, with days of stubble on their chins, sweating in the furnace temperatures inside their tanks.

British armor is known to have reached the woods north of the next village, Lingèvres. Bayerlein orders the attack to continue. Engines bellow and caterpillar tracks clatter horrendously as the Panthers and Tigers grind through the narrow village streets, past a wrecked Goliath, a German remote-control tank, and into the wood 300 yards away: the wood is nothing but dense, tangled shrubbery with a few tall trees. "Battle stations!" is called. Then "Hatches shut!" The tank commanders can see only ahead, through a small, fist-sized, armored glass aperture, and all sounds from outside are deadened except the crack of exploding shells. As they burst through into the open again, they are only fifty yards from the nearest enemy tanks. Their earphones are suddenly alive with orders and commands from a dozen Panther commanders. A Churchill is hit and belches smoke. At point-blank range each side hurls armor-piercing shells at the other. Right and left of them, the German crews see still more enemy silhouettes crawling through the gardens, meadows and orchards.

Once a Panther is crippled and calls for help. Another tank roars over to it, and a crewman climbs out into the melee of battle and hooks up towing chains to the Panther; it is dragged back to safety. The British put up a smoke screen and slip out of sight. The battle ebbs. A German gunner stumbles down from a burning armored vehicle, both eyes gouged out by a bullet, murmuring incoherently, and he dies soon after. Phosphor shells hit three Panthers in rapid succession; their crews feel the excruciating heat of the flash and flame; some do not get out but cook in place; others escape, but they are on fire. Crews from nearby vehicles try to beat out the flames or to tear off their burning clothes. But it is impossible to do this fast enough. A naked man staggers past, his body horribly blistered and swollen. "I'm Schmielewski, I'm Schmielewski," is all he can say. He and the other injured are pulled up onto an army truck. Schmielewski lies on the floor of the truck, with big open eyes. He will make

no sound of pain until death relieves him from his agony.
The village of Lingèvres has to be given up.

Rommel spent the whole afternoon of June 9 at the
Seventh Army's headquarters at Le Mans. He was now a
very worried man. Some of the worries were imaginary—
for instance, Hitler and the High Command had suddenly
warned that Belgium was due to be invaded the next
morning (there had been fresh BBC messages). But the
imaginary danger had a serious result for Rommel: Hitler
ordered the powerful First SS Panzer Division, with no
less than 21,000 troops, held back to meet the putative
threat to Belgium instead of sending it to help Rommel in
Normandy.

Another worry of Rommel's was very real. The Americans were about to break out of their bridgehead at
Sainte-Mère-Eglise and stream westward across the Cherbourg peninsula. Rommel told Dollmann: "We've got to
stop the enemy from reaching Cherbourg, whatever happens."

To meet the threat to the Cherbourg peninsula, Rommel
was trying to bring up some elite troops, but this movement was badly delayed by the lack of truck space and
fuel and by air attacks. In consequence, he ruled on the
afternoon of June 9: "We'll have to remain on the defensive at first . . . and not counterattack until all our forces
are completely ready." Thus another day had passed without decision.

The next morning, Rommel again drove forward to
Normandy. There was still intense enemy air activity—
thirty times he had to jump out of his car and dive for
cover. He could not reach Sepp Dietrich at all. To discuss
the proposed attack that seemed so urgently necessary,
Rommel called at Geyr's Panzer Group headquarters in
the afternoon, in an orchard at La Caine, twenty miles
south of Caen; at least the ships' guns could not reach
them there. Together they studied the maps spread out on
the table in Geyr's headquarters bus. Sepp Dietrich's panzers were due to attack northward in the afternoon. But
the enemy's own attacks had been building up steadily all
day, said Geyr, and he was being thrown onto the defensive. Geyr told Rommel that he lacked gasoline and am-

munition, and he complained that the Nebelwerfer brigade
—the rocket launchers—and the antiaircraft corps promised by Göring had still not arrived. The enemy air force
was destroying villages, he went on, blasting bridges and
strafing roads regardless of the French civilians. There
was no sign of the German air force. Geyr's war diary
states the result of their conference thus: "The attack will
not take place."

This same day, June 10, in Berlin, Admiral Dönitz
secretly admitted to his staff: "The invasion has succeeded. The Second Front is now a fact."

That evening, when Rommel arrived back at his
château, he phoned Jodl at the Berghof about the disaster
looming. "I suggest you send some gentlemen from the
OKW to come and have a look for themselves," he concluded. Afterward he poured his heart out in a letter to
Lucie: "The enemy's air superiority has a grave effect on
our movements." And: "The invasion is quite likely to
start at other places too, soon. There's simply no answer
to it." Thus, just four days after D day, Field Marshal
Rommel appeared to have already given up the fight—
although in fact he still outnumbered the enemy by nearly
four to one in divisions in France and he had not even
committed his most powerful panzer divisions to the battle.

If ever he needed a lively and dynamic chief of staff at
his side it was now. But he had only Hans Speidel, and
Speidel had his own fish to fry. While Rommel was away
visiting Geyr that afternoon, Speidel had dropped his mask
fractionally and revealed to his staff at the château, as
they all sipped tea, that he was plotting against Hitler.
Admiral Ruge noncommittally recorded the admission in
his secret diary: "He [Speidel] told us of his journey
over Pentecost—and hinted it was not just family affairs."
We now know that Speidel had conferred at his Black
Forest home in Freudenstadt two weeks earlier with
Mayor Karl Strölin and ex-foreign minister Konstantin von
Neurath on ways of forcibly replacing Hitler with Rommel.

So far, Speidel had not mentioned this plan to Rommel
himself. One of Speidel's co-plotters, Walter Bargatzky,
wrote in 1945: "Speidel proceeded very cautiously, pre-

paring Rommel for the possibility of a revolution and—when he believed he had caught Rommel's fancy— engineered a visit by Hofacker to Rommel's headquarters." Lieutenant Colonel Caesar von Hofacker, forty-eight, was General von Stülpnagel's adjutant in Paris; Rommel had known his father, Lieutenant General Eberhard von Hofacker, commander of a Württemberg infantry division. Another plotter, Speidel's brother-in-law Max Horst, witnessed their first polite interview during June: Hofacker did not venture out of his reserve, nor did Rommel. Major Reinhard Brink, Rundstedt's counterespionage adviser, wrote in 1945: "Rommel kept aloof from these first attempts to communicate with him on this matter."

Rommel had always adhered religiously to his oath of allegiance to Hitler. And unlike Speidel he had recently signed that manifesto formally reasserting it. But he found himself in a distinct dilemma now. Things were clearly getting out of control. Early on June 11 he knew that Geyr's attack near Caen had come to nothing. Then a telephone message came saying that an American fighter-bomber had blasted Geyr's headquarters bus an hour after he and Rommel stepped out of it, killing the entire Panzer Group staff.

Shortly after getting this shocking message, Rommel and Speidel made the hour-and-one-half trip from La Roche-Guyon to Paris to see Field Marshal von Rundstedt at his headquarters. The upshot was a lugubrious telegram from Rundstedt to Hitler, warning that if they could not establish a stable front line soon the situation might "force fundamental decisions." Rommel also drafted—and the next day dispatched—a vehement telegram to Keitel, chief of the High Command, on the worsening situation. He specifically called Keitel to bring this telegram to Hitler's attention. One thought kept recurring to him: this is El Alamein happening all over again.

After the meeting with Rundstedt, Speidel stopped by the office of General Blumentritt, Rundstedt's chief of staff. They talked in whispers about the folly of holding a rigid line in Normandy—as Hitler had ordered—and the need to make some kind of deal with the enemy. Blumentritt was to write confidentially in January 1946, "This was the first time that Speidel told me that a circle of men was forming in the Reich to make representations to the Führer. Speidel named [Field Marshal Erwin] von Witzleben. [General Ludwig] Beck, [Mayor Karl] Goerdeler. He added that if necessary they were going to force Hitler to toe their line. He said nothing about any assassination, there was just going to be a formal approach to Hitler. Speidel also told me that Field Marshal Rommel had sent him on leave to Württemberg for a few days, and that he had talked with the mayor of Stuttgart [Karl Strölin] there."

Speidel must have put some of these ideas to Rommel on this fateful day, June 11, perhaps as they were driving back from Paris, and he seems to have talked about the Nazi mass extermination atrocities as a powerful argument against Hitler. Later that day, agitatedly pacing the château grounds with Admiral Ruge, Rommel said he thought that unilateral surrender in the west was "the best solution in the present situation," but he ruled it out. After a while, he tried to look on the bright side: "The strength of our position still lies in the rivalry there is between the Russians and the Anglo-Americans. Hitler has also frequently said that he doesn't know either what will become of us—but he is absolutely convinced that everything will turn out all right in the end." Rommel then hinted to the admiral that the Nazi leaders did not have clean hands. He spoke of "massacres" and commented: "I have always deliberately fought clean."

Ruge responded, "You are the best man that Germany has." Rommel probably did not grasp what the admiral was getting at.

The news from the bridgeheads was that German troops had just abandoned the city of Carentan—although it was the key to the whole Cherbourg peninsula. Marcks, bitterly disappointed at this setback, drove forward to the Carentan battlefield the next morning. An hour later he was a shattered corpse in a ditch—his wooden leg had kept him from scrambling out of his car fast enough to avoid an enemy air attack. Sick with worry, Rommel wrote to Lucie: "The battle's not going at all well for us, mainly because of the enemy's air superiority and the big naval guns. In the air we can only put up 300 to 500 sorties against their 27,000." (This was an exaggeration.) "I reported to the Führer yesterday. Rundstedt is doing the same. *It's time for politics to come into play.* We are expecting the next, perhaps even heavier invasion blow to fall on us somewhere else in a few days' time. The long-husbanded strength of two world powers is now taking effect against us. It will all be over very quickly."

On June 12, the day that General Marcks died, Geyr lunched at the château—still ashen-faced from his narrow escape. (Rommel was at the front, visiting General Gerhard von Schwerin's 116th Panzer Division to warn it to expect a possible new invasion east of Dieppe on the Channel coast.) Geyr asked for a new command posting. Speidel waved the request aside: "I've got a special job lined up for you."

*It was not until 1947 that the former General Baron Leo Geyr von Schweppenburg deduced what Speidel had had in mind in June of 1944. By then Geyr was in American captivity and was directing a historical project on the Normandy fighting. One day the Americans brought him together with Speidel—who was by then long free again—at Oberursel, near Frankfurt. Speidel admitted to him, said Geyr, that he had caused two good panzer divisions, the Second and the 116th, to be deliberately withheld from the Normandy fighting on a pretext, in order to use them for the plot against Hitler. In 1947, that accomplishment spoke highly for Speidel and strengthened his credentials as an anti-Nazi. He repeated the boast in his various manuscripts—which I found in drafts in archives at The Citadel, in Charleston, South Carolina, Washington, D. C., and Swabian Gmünd—and in his 1949 memoirs,* Invasion 1944. *But astonished fellow generals began to query the cryptic claim in the book, and Speidel was beginning to climb rapidly up through the NATO military command. These circumstances altered the value of the old claim of inspired disobedience, and Speidel adjusted them accordingly, first playing them down, then denying them. One newspaper editor, however, was indelicate enough to quote Speidel's earlier claim, whereupon Speidel's friend Admiral Ruge wrote to the editor: "Speidel is now chief representative of the former Ger-*

*man Wehrmacht, dealing with the issue of German rearmament. If he is perpetually accused—unjustly—of having been a saboteur to the battle on which the fate of his country depended, his influence and usefulness will suffer considerably."*

Count Gerhard von Schwerin, the commander of the 116th Panzer Division, was, like Speidel, an admirer of General Beck, the main anti-Hitler plotter in Berlin. Schwerin had been in Africa with Rommel from the beginning, until he had defied him and been sent packing. When the enemy invasion of Normandy occurred, Schwerin and his panzer staff were relieved not to be transferred there—on D day, puzzlingly enough, they shifted instead away from Normandy, to the Channel coast. On their way, as they drove past Rommel's château, Schwerin halted in a forest nearby and dictated to his secretary, Master Sergeant Gerhard Lademann, a memorandum on Germany's situation. He considered it hopeless and suggested a change of regime, and he hinted that his own 116th Panzer Division was loyal only to him. Then he had his intelligence officer, Major Arthur Holtermann, take the one-page typed document—of which he had ordered that no copy be made—over to the château and deliver it to Speidel. From then on Holtermann acted as secret courier between Speidel and Schwerin. Speidel informed Schwerin that the division was being held back as a reserve for use in the planned overthrow of the Hitler regime. Thus, while Rommel was desperately pulling in reinforcements from as far afield as the Russian front and southern France, Schwerin's 116th Panzer Division remained idle until July 19. (No use could be made of the other anti-Hitler panzer division, the Second; on June 12 the High Command intervened and moved it to the Normandy front.)

*There seems little doubt as to the authenticity of this account of the 116th, and historians may well care to speculate how far Rommel could have tilted the battle in his favor had he had use of its panzers in Normandy from the start. Quite apart from Speidel's own earliest writings, the facts are testified to by Schwerin himself, by Geyr, by*

*Holtermann—who kept a pocket diary—and by Lade-
mann. All are unanimous on one significant point: they
dealt only with Speidel, never with Rommel, on the secret
reason for holding the division back. Among the files
of the anti-Hitler resistance I also found this note by
Baron Friedrich von Teuchert, a top civil servant on
Stülpnagel's staff, describing a discussion between Speidel
and another plotter, Lieutenant Colonel von Hofacker, of
what should happen in Paris during an anti-Hitler putsch:
"A particular worry was the presence of powerful Waffen
SS units. It was arranged that these should be committed
to such an extent on the big day that they could not disengage from battle. One reliable division (Schwerin's panzer division) was being held back, ready to mask Paris."*

*Today Count von Schwerin is an old man living in a
large farmhouse on the shores of a Bavarian lake. Like
Speidel, he did well for himself after the war—he became the architect of the new German army. What vexes
him, he told me, is that Speidel will no longer admit
that he had withheld the 116th. "No doubt he has his
reasons," said Schwerin darkly.*

At 10:00 A.M. on June 12, Rommel telephoned Field
Marshal Keitel at the Berghof, referred to Rundstedt's
gloomy telegram of the day before and warned that his
own views were equally grave. Keitel quieted him: "I've
already briefed the Führer about it. You're going to get
two panzer divisions from the eastern front." They were
to be the high-grade Ninth and Tenth SS Panzer divisions.

Meanwhile, Hitler ordered Rommel to counterattack
the Normandy bridgehead's eastern end and destroy the
British forces there piecemeal. Rommel had to comply,
although privately he saw the greater tactical risks developing at the western end, and he would have preferred
to throw his panzer divisions at the ill-experienced American troops there before they could overrun the Cherbourg
peninsula. But on June 13 German forces were unable to
recapture the town of Carentan, the key to the peninsula,
and thus Rommel was faced with a difficult choice:
Should he commit his available forces at the western end
of the Normandy front to defending the "Fortress
Cherbourg," or to preventing a major American break-

through southward into France itself? He himself was in no doubt that the latter task was more urgent. When he spoke to General Blumentritt the next afternoon, June 15, Rommel argued that while a dramatic fighting retreat northward up the peninsula might well delay the enemy's advance on Cherbourg, it would erode the German forces to a point where not enough would be left to hold the port very long. Speidel telephoned Max Pemsel at the Seventh Army the next morning, June 16, and told him to begin a partial withdrawal northward. Said Rommel: "It's time for somebody to take a bold decision. If we try hanging on to everything, we are going to lose the lot."

Some time later Speidel telephoned Pemsel again: Hitler had forbidden any retrograde movement up the peninsula. Speidel had sat on this news for an hour, and by this time the retreat had already begun. The change of policy caused an unholy chaos at the Seventh Army's headquarters. Rommel, on his own authority, allowed General Dollmann to pull some forces out of the peninsula to help block the resulting American breakthrough at Saint-Saveur to the west. "If we interpret the Führer's order literally," he told Rundstedt over the telephone, "and all our forces in the peninsula stay just where they are, then the enemy will roll northward along completely open roads behind our own troops and reach Cherbourg before the day is out. Our mobile troops must be given freedom of movement."

To Rommel the crisis seemed to be coming to a head. "It appears dubious whether the gravity of the situation is realized up above," he wrote to Lucie on June 14, "and whether the proper conclusions are being drawn." He repeated his demand for the High Command to send somebody to Normandy to see the situation for himself. After a nerve-racking visit to the battlefield that day, he observed: "Was up front again, the situation's not getting any better. We must be prepared for the worst. The troops—SS and army alike—are fighting with extreme courage but the balance of strength is remorselessly tilting against us every day."

That night at the château, Ruge could see how depressed and thoughtful Rommel was. The admiral went for a stroll in the grounds with him, and repeated some of the things that Speidel had whispered to him during their table tennis game after dinner. A few hours later, Rommel wrote to Lucie a candid admission of defeat: "You can probably imagine the kind of difficult decisions we shall soon be facing—and you'll recall what I told you in November 1942." That was when he had hinted to her in Rome that he might have to approach the British for an armistice.

How easy the decisions would have been for Rommel and Rundstedt if they did not have to fear at any moment the imminent invasion of the Channel coast by "General Patton's army group." The Fifteenth Army could have been stripped of its infantry and those troops sent to the Normandy bridgehead. The panzer divisions could be pulled out of their purely defensive role and redeployed for a massive counter-attack. But in Berlin Colonel von Roenne still refused to abandon the view that a killer left hook was about to be launched by Patton directly across the English Channel. The Luftwaffe strongly challenged this view, pointing out that the enemy were packing all their available tactical air force units into Normandy. Rundstedt's intelligence officer, Meyer-Detring, also called Roenne's attention to the fact that the enemy's best combat divisions had all already turned up there. But Roenne remained adamant. On June 15 he assessed Patton's force at twenty-five divisions.

Rundstedt's operations officer, Bodo Zimmermann, phoned his intelligence officer and said anxiously, "We've got to face up to this question squarely and, if need be, pull out even more forces from sectors farther up."

This brought a loud protest from the château. Staubwasser, Speidel's intelligence man, phoned Meyer-Detring. "I hear that the view now gaining ground," he said, "is that we must start ruthlessly bringing in all available forces as there's unlikely to be a second invasion before August. Who says so?"

Meyer-Detring explained the logic: "The enemy have already committed their most experienced units. We've got to take our courage in both hands. We can't keep on being led up the garden path by a theoretical risk until August!"

The next day, June 16, the skies over the château were obscured by low clouds and drizzle. Admiral Friedrich Ruge, Rommel's naval aide, darkly reflected in his diary: "Every day one asks: how long can this go on?"

Hitler correctly guessed that Rommel was now in much the same mood as had prompted his retreat from El Alamein, and he decided to intervene in person. Rommel wanted someone from the High Command to come to see for himself? Hitler announced to his astounded staff that he would fly to France in person. Nine o'clock the next morning, June 17, therefore, found him awaiting Rundstedt, Rommel and their two chiefs of staff at the reserve Führer's headquarters built near Soissons, 300 miles from Normandy. The cluster of carefully camouflaged bunkers had well-furnished and carpeted workrooms, in one of which the dramatic conference took place. The field marshals politely stood while Hitler sat on a low wooden stool, absently fingering his metal-rimmed spectacles or marking symbols on the map with a colored pencil selected from the bunch held in his left hand.

Rommel briefed Hitler first, concealing nothing. The infantry divisions were melting away like snow in a desert sun. Supplies and reinforcements were not getting through. He cited the debilitating effect of the enemy air attacks and naval bombardment, but insisted that every man who survived was fighting "like the devil"; his seventeen- and eighteen-year-olds were acting like veterans—"like young tigers." But Montgomery, said Rommel, was using the same brute force in Normandy as he had in North Africa: saturation bombardments were followed up by a relentless onslaught of sophisticated weapons and armored vehicles.

Then Rundstedt spoke. He asked Hitler outright to abandon the costly rigid defense of the whole Cherbourg peninsula, and to allow an orderly withdrawal into the port and fortress instead. Hitler was in a mood to take realistic decisions, and agreed without further argument —knowing this would inevitably allow the Americans to sever the peninsula complete. But he ordered the northern battle group to fight for every inch as it fell back slowly northward into the fortress, and he directed Rommel to nominate a "particularly capable" commandant for Cherbourg. "The fortress is to hold out as long as possible—if possible until about mid-July."

These few hours with Hitler cast a powerful new spell on Rommel. (Lang shrewdly observed in a letter home that the field marshal "cannot escape the Führer's influence.") It was no coincidence that Hitler had also invited the commander of the V weapon corps to report to him in the field marshals' presence at Soissons. For weeks Rommel had been demanding an early opening of the V weapon attack on London. Now he learned that *1,000* of the pilotless V-1 flying bombs, each with a devastating one-ton warhead, had been launched at London over the last few days. With a smirk, Hitler showed Rommel reports on the destruction from German agents in England. To cheer up General Dollmann back in Normandy, Rommel telephoned him from the bunker. "The effects of the V-1 bombardment," he said, "are very considerable after all."

Yet there was one brief remark by Rommel that showed that his nagging doubts persisted. After claxons sounded an air raid warning, the officers had trooped into Hitler's air raid shelter, and when Rommel noticed that the stenographers were temporarily missing, he ventured to put his cards on the table and hinted to Hitler—as Blumentritt, a neutral and reliable witness, recalled in January 1946—"that politics would soon have to come into play, otherwise the situation in the west would soon deteriorate too far for salvaging." (Jodl and Speidel also remembered some such phrase.)

Hitler made a frosty retort: "That is a matter which is no concern of yours. You must leave that to me." Rommel's words must have nettled Hitler deeply, because he quoted them to the two generals who replaced Blumentritt and Speidel many weeks later. Hitler told them that his reply had been: *"The time isn't ripe for a political decision yet."* (In August 1944, he amplified this remark: "I believe that I've shown adequately enough in my time that I'm capable of making political capital too. But to hope for a favorable political opportunity to arise at a time of grave military setbacks is obviously infantile and naïve. Such opportunities may indeed occur—but not until you have achieved some renewed victory.")

By the time the all clear sounded, the worst Normandy crisis had passed in any case. When Rommel phoned Dollmann again to instruct him to begin the fighting withdrawal into Cherbourg, the Seventh Army commander proudly announced that the Americans' three-day attempt at smashing through to the road junction at Saint-Lô had been thwarted. They had been routed and had taken heavy casualties—the body count in one sector alone was 1,000 Americans, and there were hundreds of prisoners. Rommel instructed that the corpses at Saint-Lô were to be thoroughly searched for documents useful for propaganda purposes. On this battlefield, Rommel learned, American troops had begged the Nazis for doctors to tend their injured. The Germans had sent over medics, under white flags, and the Americans had released German prisoners out of gratitude.

It was a new Rommel, buoyant and confident, who returned to the château. Speidel was grimly silent at his side. To Lucie, Rommel wrote: "I'm looking forward to the future with much less anxiety than one week ago. The V weapon offensive has brought us a lot of relief. . . . A quick enemy breakthrough toward Paris is now barely possible. We've a lot of stuff coming up. The Führer was very cordial and in a good humor. He realizes the seriousness of the situation." In short, Rommel was in the familiar state of post-Hitler hypnosis. Admiral Ruge wrote in his secret diary: "Rommel is back again. Went for a stroll with me afterward. The 'underwear' inquiry has not been mentioned, there have been no reproaches, Rommel visibly relieved. Stacks of bonbons on account of our counteroffensive. Führer very optimistic, calm, sees situation differently from us. He must have downright magnetism."

General Speidel was frustrated and bitter at the change in the field marshal, fearing that Rommel's optimism would make him resistant to his overtures. To his plotter colleagues Speidel mockingly described the Fürher at Soissons as "aging, stooping and increasingly incoherent" —a dictator whose lunch consisted of a huge mound of rice, three liqueur glasses of multicolored medicines, and a variety of pills. Speidel had noted down certain solecisms of Hitler's, and read them out to his staff amid loud guffaws that evening. "Don't speak of Normandy as 'the enemy's bridgehead,'" mimicked Speidel, "but as 'the last piece of enemy-occupied France'!" And, "The enemy won't last out the summer!"

Rommel's situation report to the High Command on June 19 reflected his new buoyancy. He crowed that the enemy had achieved no successes either at Caen or at Saint-Lô, and at Caumont they had even lost ground. They had fallen weeks behind their timetable and were having to throw more strength into Normandy than intended. So far they had lost over 500 tanks and 1,000 planes. And—an important point—the whole population in Rommel's command area sympathized with him, he said, particularly since the enemy bombing had begun; since D day, resistance and sabotage incidents had been negligible.

Of course, there was still the war of nerves. Rommel was determined that the Fifteenth Army, up the coast from Normandy, should not get caught "with its pants down" like the Seventh. He was actually hoping for the second invasion—for there he would fight his biggest victory. Late on June 16 Luftwaffe radar operators had reported the same kind of electronic jamming and "radar spoofs" as had preceded the Normandy landings, but this time these phenomena were focused on the Channel coast, and here over the next days the tides would be particularly favorable for landings. Many times Rommel now journeyed over to the Fifteenth Army sector and wondered exactly where "Patton's army group" was going to invade.

Hitler was skeptical. At Soissons he had echoed Meyer-Detring's argument—his words are in the protocol for the meeting—that "the enemy have already committed all their battle-experienced divisions to Normandy, which suggests they now have their hands full." Rommel disagreed, and June 19 found him once again checking the defenses between the river Somme and Le Havre. He informed the panzer commander Schwerin that day that this was where he expected the new enemy invasion. He ordered Salmuth's main reserves here moved even closer to the coast. "I've learned a lot from Normandy," he explained. "It'll be impossible to move them forward once the new invasion begins because of the enemy's air superiority."

On June 22 Rommel and Hellmuth Lang drove forward to visit the Fifteenth Army again. All day long the air above them vibrated to the deep-throated organ note of the pulse-jet powering the V-1 flying bombs as they hurtled toward London. Rommel was thrilled by the spectacle of the little stubby aircraft streaking low across the sky, trailing a jet of flame behind them. "Fantastic," wrote Lang. The V sites gave the enemy more than enough motive to invade here. Patton's "army group," according to new reports from Colonel von Roenne, was evidently as large as Montgomery's. Rommel was waiting for Patton—waiting, waiting, totally disoriented by Fortitude, so obsessed by a potential threat from a purely theoretical army group that he underestimated the very real and present threat to France in Normandy.

While Rommel was fussing over the Channel coast, events were moving with dramatic speed in the Cherbourg peninsula. By June 18 the Americans had sliced right across the foot of the peninsula, thus isolating the German troops—and anti-Soviet Russian mercenary troops—to the north. These defenders were to stage a fighting retreat, out to the tip of the peninsula, to fall back into the fortified city of Cherbourg and to deny the enemy access to this vital port as long as possible. The navy confirmed to the High Command that the port was stocked with enough food for at least eight weeks' siege. By June 22, however, the garrison's position was desperate. The American commander had pursued the defenders with a vigor that astonished all the German generals with any previous experience of this enemy. This was Major General Lawton "Joe" Collins, handsome, active and hard-hitting—the mirror image of the Erwin Rommel who had battled northward along these same roads in 1940.

Rommel had virtually written off Cherbourg some days earlier, when he secretly ordered the Seventy-seventh Infantry Division out of the peninsula before it was cut off there by the enemy. The fortress commandant named by Rommel, the aristocratic and haughty Lieutenant General von Schlieben, had only the tattered remnants of three divisions under his command. Hitler had ordered

Schlieben to conduct the battle for Cherbourg "just as Gneisenau fought to defend Kolberg" [in the Napoleonic Wars]. But now he learned that somebody—defying his own orders—had removed the powerful Seventy-seventh Infantry Division from the peninsula. The High Command furiously ordered an inquiry. Rommel kept his own part in weakening the peninsula a guilty secret—severely embarrassing Rundstedt's staff. "Army Group B's not telling the whole truth," Colonel Zimmermann said on the telephone to Meyer-Detring. "They have not . . . breathed a word about the break-out of the Seventy-seventh Division. We didn't give the order for that from here. But somebody must have . . . and when we asked for copies of Rommel's orders, I was told 'Rommel only gives orders orally.' "

The uneasiness in Paris was shared by Hitler's staff. General Schmundt telephoned the château from the Berghof. "I'm worried about Schlieben," he said. "I don't get the impression that he's an iron personality. The honor and reputation of the entire German officer corps rest on how long we hang on to Cherbourg. If there's the slightest doubt, then you must fly the roughest, toughest man into the fortress instead. The whole world is looking at Cherbourg." At this Rommel himself phoned Schmundt and assured him that General von Schlieben had his full confidence.

Rommel's June 23 letter to Lucie indicates that Hitler's spell on him had begun to wear off. "Militarily, things aren't at all good," he wrote, adding, "We must be prepared for grave events." The major new Soviet offensive in Poland, steamrolling toward Berlin, deeply worried him.

The field marshal spent all the following day in Normandy again. Everywhere, Rommel's heavy automobile passed blazing supply trucks and destroyed weapons. Because of the danger of air attack, his young driver, Corporal Daniel, had to keep off the fast main highways and use the lesser roads instead, roads that curved more and were bordered by tall trees or hedges. Rommel could not afford to take chances—he had already lost too many valued commanders here since D day: Marcks; Geyr's entire staff; the seriously injured SS brigadier Ostendorff;

General Heinz Hellmich of the 243rd Infantry, killed by a fighter-bomber on June 17; the Seventy-seventh Infantry's General Stegmann, mortally wounded the next day. Rommel, more cautious than ever before in his life, did not want to be the next. It was 11:00 P.M. before he got back to the château after a 400-mile drive. Ruge met him and observed that Rommel was shaken by the casualties his infantry was suffering. That night the field marshal wrote to Lucie: "Given a sufficient weight of bombs and heavy shells, the enemy can make any place they want ripe for assault."

Upon his return to La Roche-Guyon, Rommel had found an order from the High Command awaiting him. He was to investigate the feasibility of launching a counterattack in the rear of the American forces besieging Cherbourg. Rommel heaped scorn on the proposal. "We've barely managed to patch our defensive line together in western Normandy," he said. "The front is not at all suited for an attack."

On June 25 the end was fast approaching in Cherbourg. Rommel had issued to General von Schlieben the carefully worded decree: "On the Führer's orders you are to fight to the last bullet." (Both he and Rundstedt had refused to order any unit to "fight to the last man.") Rommel stayed at the château all day, depressed and lonely, waiting for the inevitable. Schlieben was urgently appealing for Luftwaffe support, and the air force had prepared a major operation; but Rommel forbade it— Cherbourg was a lost cause—and ordered the sorties elsewhere. "I have reported [the situation] perfectly clearly to the top level," he said to Ruge. "But up there they refuse to draw the consequences. They refuse to see that their war is coming unstuck."

Listening to Rommel, Ruge remembered the two British commandos who had been brought to the château in May. Only yesterday, at a meeting of plotters that Speidel had held at the château in Rommel's absence, Ruge had said: "One of them wanted dreadfully to know exactly where he was so he could come back here after the war. He said he was going to turn France upside down to find the place. He told the field marshal to his face that he was the man Germany needed for its postwar reconstruction." So Rommel was dissatisfied with Germany's leaders, and even the enemy saw Rommel as Germany's natural new leader. Gradually all the pieces were clicking into place.

That afternoon, while Cherbourg went through its death throes, Rommel and Ruge climbed up to the cliff-top and sat on the field marshal's favorite bench. Beneath them was a breathtaking view of the river, along which barges were now at last beginning to carry war supplies toward Normandy. Ruge had had a lot of shrubbery cut away just yesterday to improve the vista. After a silence Rommel began to talk. (Afterward Ruge jotted his words down in his shorthand diary.) "Fancy ordering me to attack Cherbourg!" he said. "I was glad enough to have managed to piece together even a semblance of a defensive front!"

Again they expressed their exasperation with the High Command, and Ruge spoke of shooting—shooting the people who were running the war, if that was the only way out. Rommel emitted an ironic laugh: "You're a rough 'un, Ruge!"

Ruge persisted. "They've got to see things as they are," he said. "That's what we've been missing for years, at the top level."

Rommel nodded. "They're trying to pass the buck on to me," he said, probably referring to Keitel and Jodl. "The Führer has a kind of magnetic effect on everybody around him—they're always in a kind of trance. Soon he'll have to take the consequences, but he always evades the issue. He just keeps ordering: 'Fight to the last man.'" The field marshal sighed. "This is the third time I've had to watch a catastrophe approaching," he said. As they stood up to go back down to the château, Rommel remarked, "I'm curious to see what the next few weeks will bring."

Late that evening, the last radio messages were picked up from Schlieben's headquarters in Cherbourg. A few hours later the High Command ordered a thorough inquiry into the Seventh Army's affairs—somebody must be to blame for the ignominiously swift collapse of Cherbourg's resistance. Either General Dollmann or his chief of staff, Max Pemsel—or both—would have to go.

As if the capture of Cherbourg weren't bad enough, Rommel now received indications that the second major invasion was imminent. A captured RAF officer was overhead whispering to a cellmate, "We're going to invade the coast between Le Havre and Dunkirk at the end of July." Two days later, Speidel's staff again warned Rommel that huge forces were standing by in southern England: "There are still sixty-seven divisions in Britain, of which at least fifty-seven can be utilized for a major enterprise." How were Hitler or Rommel to know that the RAF man was a "plant"? And that only *twelve* enemy divisions were actually left in Britain—and destined only for Normandy?

In Normandy it was a race against time now for those two old adversaries, Rommel and Montgomery. The Allies had established themselves on the soil of Europe, but had not yet thrust out from their position; the Germans had established new defensive lines. The question became: Which army would attack first?

Rommel had installed his finest divisions at the Caen end of the front, expecting the real threat to develop there. He had said as much to Pemsel of the Seventh Army on June 15: "The enemy's push toward Paris is far more dangerous for us than one into Brittany." Thus he again underestimated the Americans, a vestige of his experiences in Tunisia. He tended to disregard the reports coming from his own interrogation center at Châlons, which described the young West Point-trained American army officers as tougher, tauter and altogether "more Prussian" than their British allies. So far there was little evidence of American strategic intentions; but radio intelligence and Montgomery's own dispositions indicated that the British intended to capture Caen—the "Poland" in Bannerman's diary—and then push southeast across the good tank country toward Falaise and Paris, the heart of France. "A major invasion between the Somme and Le Havre may well be coupled with such a thrust," Rommel said on June 26.

Rommel's orders were for the Ninth and Tenth SS Panzer divisions, now arriving from the real Poland, to prepare to slice through the enemy bridgehead toward

Bayeux, cutting the coastline near Arromanches. This would wrench the British forces away from their supply lines—they would choke like a deep-sea diver with a severed air pipe.

Montgomery, however, spoiled this plan and got in his offensive first. Two hours after dawn on June 26, after a day of shelling, bombing and tank and infantry attacks, he threw a heavy attack at Rommel on the western side of Caen, under a lowering sky. This sector was held by Sepp Dietrich's First SS Panzer Corps. Like a solitary bulwark the Twelfth SS Panzer (Hitler Jugend) Division slowed this attack to a momentary standstill, south of Cheux. It took appalling losses but destroyed sixty of Montgomery's tanks, often at point-blank range. To General Dollmann it was clear that the enemy were on the point of breaching his Seventh Army and enveloping Caen. Sepp Dietrich begged for infantry and tanks. At 9:00 P.M., as heavy rain began to fall on the day's battlefield, Dollmann appealed to Rommel: could Rommel use his own panzer forces assembling for the Bayeux attack to help Dietrich defend Caen? Rommel crisply ordered the Seventh Army commander: "Tell SS General Hausser to scrape together everything he can." Paul Hausser commanded the Second SS Panzer Corps; but so far only the Ninth SS Panzer Division had come this far forward, and the Tenth SS Panzer Division was still way back.

Dollmann, never a man of action, began to lose his nerve. Bayerlein of Panzer Lehr later commented that the easy life led by Dollmann and Pemsel at their remote and luxurious château headquarters—well back, at Le Mans —had turned them soft. "Dollmann was a zero," said Bayerlein. According to Ruge's diary, Pemsel's nerves were also wearing under the strain. Both men probably knew from the grapevine that their days were numbered. But Rommel, characteristically, supported all his commanders now that they were under criticism from the hated High Command. When the High Command now sarcastically inquired just where Dollmann's headquarters was, Rommel replied: "That is irrelevant in the present situation," and "I am not going to criticize them for it." That Rommel had begun to tolerate the incompetent was a sign of his decline.

Twice Dollmann picked up the phone and ordered Hausser to send his SS corps to help Dietrich defend Caen, and twice he changed his mind. At first Dietrich actually seemed to have fended off the British attack, but early on June 28 it was resumed and the enemy seized an intact bridge across the Odon—the last river obstacle before the Orne, the main river on which Caen stood. At this Dollmann really panicked and diverted Hausser's entire Second SS Panzer Corps against this penetration. Hausser requested a tactical delay to enable him to prepare a proper attack, designed to pinch on the slender British finger from both sides. At this juncture—8:10 A.M.— the war diary of Dollmann's Seventh Army headquarters has been tampered with, but he appears to have overridden Hausser's request and ruled that the attack should begin immediately. Dollmann was past caring about the outcome, anyway. Two hours later Dollmann was dead.

*Hitherto it has been believed that Dollmann suffered a heart attack. But his chief of staff, Max Pemsel, related to me one evening, in the Munich apartment of General Jodl's widow, that Dollmann stepped into Pemsel's bathroom at the château at ten o'clock that fateful morning and swallowed poison. For two hours Pemsel kept the general's death a secret, then reported it to La Roche-Guyon as "death from heart failure."*

*A year after first revealing the truth about Dollmann's death to me, Max Pemsel decided to make it a matter of public record and quietly mentioned the suicide in a military annual. "General Dollmann's burden of anxiety grew worse and worse. His protests to his superiors were ignored, and he learned that his army would not be getting any outside assistance during its desperate defensive actions." Pemsel continued, "When Hitler blamed General Dollmann during the night of June 28–29 for the premature loss of Cherbourg, Dollmann was able to disprove it in a telegram in which he referred to faulty intervention by others in his own command affairs. After dispatching this telegram he bade me farewell at 3 A.M., and committed suicide at his command post."*

No doubt the truth about Dollmann's death did cross Rommel's mind. Probably he was glad that Dollmann at least had been spared the High Command's threatened inquisition. It may be that this was an indication that Erwin Rommel thoroughly approved a general's preference for suicide with honor to the uncertain outcome of a formal inquiry. He ordered a full-dress military funeral for Dollmann in Paris.

Half an hour after he had received word of Dollmann's sudden death, his telephone rang again. It was General Blumentritt, Rundstedt's chief of staff. Both field marshals, Rundstedt and Rommel, he said gravely, had been ordered to report to the Führer in person the next day.

# A Colonel Calls
# on Rommel

JUNE 28, 1944, late afternoon. In a big Mercedes flying a field marshal's pennant, Rommel speeds eastward through France toward the German frontier. Hitler has summoned all senior commanders from the west to the Berghof, his mountain villa above Berchtesgaden, for a meeting the next day. Germany's fortunes have reached a desperate pass. On the Russian front, an entire army group has caved in, and onrushing Soviet armored divisions are bearing down on Germany's own frontier. In Normandy, the Anglo-American bridgehead is threatening to burst. Rundstedt, the Commander in Chief West, has asked for "directives for the future fighting." Hitler knows what that means. Rundstedt wants permissions to retreat —permission to slink lamely out of range of the enemy naval guns at first, then out of range of the enemy bombers—and then to the West Wall, on the frontiers of Germany.

That is what embitters Hitler. His commanders can never see beyond their own immediate theater of war. They clamor for a "war of movement" although most of the infantry have no motor transport and will be overrun. Hitler's strategy is to fight his battles at extreme range from Germany's cities—in the Balkans, in Russia, Italy and France. He is trying to buy time, so that he can bring his new weapons into action, the rockets, electric submarines and jet aircraft that only Nazi Germany has yet developed. His commanders seem to know only ways of staving off defeat, of prolonging the agony. Hitler is asking for a chance to fight on to ultimate victory. This is why he has ordered a new counterattack in Normandy. This is why, on Hitler's personal orders, 600 British and American prisoners are herded now through streets of spitting, jeering, fist-shaking Parisians from the Gare du Nord to the Gare de l'Est—so that the French can see Germany's enemy in defeat.

Somewhere north of Paris, on the main highway to the frontier, Rommel's car halts near another car, out of which Rundstedt himself wearily climbs. Rommel's staff officer, Major Eberhard Wolfram, overhears snatches of their whispered conversation. "Herr Rundstedt," says Rommel, "you and I both believe that this war must be stopped now. I intend to make no bones about it when we see the Führer." After more whispered remarks, Rommel climbs back into his car and they drive on. The glass partition is up, so his driver cannot hear. The field marshal begins thinking aloud, then abruptly turns to Major Wolfram. "Listen, this is what I'm going to tell the Führer tomorrow. As I stand here, I regard myself as responsible to the whole German people. I have a lot to answer for, not just as a military commander, and that tells me how I have to act. The political situation is crystal clear: we have the whole world ranged against us, and not the slightest chance of winning. Despite everything, the enemy have won a foothold in the west." And so Rommel goes on, until they reach Ulm, where they part for the night.

*When I visited Wolfram in his home in Bavaria, he told me what happened that night. "I stayed with my wife at the Deutscher Hof Hotel in Ulm," he said. "I had the maps for the Führer conference with me, and I spread them on the bed, swore my wife to secrecy and told her what I had overheard. She was shocked and burst out: 'But that's mutiny!' Of course she was quite right, and it rather took me aback because I of course was so totally immersed in the defeatist 'breakfast mood' at Speidel's table."*

*I had brought with me a copy of Wolfram's lengthy report, written at the time, on Rommel's meeting with Hitler, which is in the official records of Army Group B. Wolfram and I went over it, and he told me things he had not thought appropriate to include in that document.*

Rommel spent the few night hours at Herrlingen with Lucie and Manfred, whom he had had released from his antiaircraft battery for the day. They all drove down to Ulm to collect Wolfram in the early morning. Then Rommel bid his family a formal farewell—just in case his coming confrontation led to his arrest. "You may never see me again," he told Manfred.

Lucie gripped Major Wolfram's arm as she pleaded, "Herr Wolfram, make sure you bring back my husband safely."

On the drive down to Berchtesgaden, Rommel said to Wolfram: "I think I ought to have a word first with Goebbels and Himmler." When they arrived, he did in fact see Goebbels first. He told Goebbels his intentions and said, "I shall urgently need your support." Goebbels listened shrewdly, nodded once or twice, but said nothing. Rommel was optimistic after that: "I think we've won a powerful ally," he told Wolfram. The major was less sure.

Exactly the same happened with Himmler, the chief of the SS. Rommel was able to quote the harrowing reports and predictions of Himmler's own SS generals in Normandy—Sepp Dietrich and Paul Hausser. Again Rommel was pleased with the outcome.

The main conference with Hitler began at 6:00 P.M. in the great hall of the villa. Hitler, Rommel, Rundstedt and the other military commanders stood on one side of the long table surfaced with red marble; it was covered with war maps. Facing them across the table were the Reich ministers, some diplomats and other officials. The Führer began by passing around air photographs of the damage being inflicted on London by the V-1 flying bombs. Thousands of buildings were being wrecked there every day. He then introduced two young officers from the V-1 catapult regiment in France and had them report to him, a typical theatrical master move—their eagerness could not fail to impress the audience. Rommel and Rundstedt were puzzled to find Field Marshal von Kluge present; he had had an automobile accident many months before and had not held an active command since that time.

Then the drama began. Hitler invited Rommel to speak.

The field marshal cleared his throat. "Mein Führer, I am here as commander of Army Group B. I think it is high time that I—on behalf of the German people to whom I am also answerable—tell you the situation in the west. I should like to begin with our political situation. The entire world is arrayed now against Germany, and this balance of strength—"

Hitler slammed his hand down on the map and interrupted. "Field Marshal, please stick to the military situation."

Rommel stubbornly continued: "Mein Führer, history demands of me that I should deal first with our *overall* situation."

Again Hitler sharply stopped him: "You will deal with your military situation, and nothing else." Not even Rommel could ignore that, and he complied.

Hitler expressed his disappointment that Rommel and Rundstedt had not been able to counterattack the Americans in the Cherbourg peninsula. As Jodl noted in his private diary, "The Führer explained just what the advantages of such an attack on the Americans would have been. The Führer said it was very painful for him to have to forego that attack on Cherbourg. Now there's nothing to do but absorb the present British offensive [at Caen] and prepare our own counterattack there." Hitler reminded them that victory on the ground would go to whichever army could sustain the highest rate of buildup. Montgomery's seaborne supplies were far more vulnerable than Rommel's; so the proper strategy would be to contain the enemy in Normandy, forcing them to waste gasoline and ammunition while at the same time strangling their supply lines.

Hitler turned to Rommel again. This time the field

marshal appealed to the others present to state their own views, and looked particularly at Goebbels and Himmler. Both avoided his glance, and an icy silence followed. "Mein Führer," said Rommel, "I must speak bluntly: I can't leave here without speaking on the subject of Germany."

At that Hitler's voice rang out: "Field Marshal, be so good as to leave the room. I think it would be better that way."

The conference continued without him. Hitler called in Admiral Dönitz and Reich Marshal Göring. He ordered Göring to use air mines, torpedoes and remote-controlled bombs against Montgomery's supply routes. "We've got to lay mines and still more mines in the Seine bay, with the tenacity of a bulldog. It's incomparably more effective to sink a ship's whole cargo than to have to fight the unloaded personnel and materiel separately on land at a later date." Dönitz was given similar orders. He was to use midget submarines, too, against the invasion fleet. Hitler ordered the Third Air Force commander Hugo Sperrle to sweep the enemy out of France's skies as soon as his fighter squadrons had been replenished. In fact, Hitler ordered 1,000 brand new fighters sent to France immediately.

"We can nourish the battle only if we manage to get our own supplies through," he continued. "And that means that the navy, air force and our own domestic economy must turn over every modern truck they have to the army transport convoys." He also proposed a way of exorcising the scourge of the enemy strafing planes. From Paris all the way forward to Normandy, the roads must be turned into deathtraps for the enemy planes by concealed nests of antiaircraft guns. He concluded, "Then, if everything goes well, perhaps we can launch a counterattack on the Americans after all."

Rommel left the Berghof at 9:15 that evening, June 29, 1944. He had seen his Führer for the last time.

It was late the next day before Rommel was back at the château—determined once more to execute Hitler's will whatever the consequences. On his arrival the news was of bloody fighting for possession of Caen. Rommel had no intention of relinquishing the city yet. The next day he was to explain to General Geyr, once more in command of Panzer Group West, that the Führer's instructions at the Berghof had been these: "The enemy has been forced to move because of our V weapon operations. What matters now is to wear them down by gunfire and by slinging rapid punches at every opportunity. Caen will be the main pivot of the enemy thrust toward Paris. So we've got to pack more and more forces into the line there."

Sepp Dietrich's panzer divisions had taken terrible punishment in Montgomery's attack of June 29; meanwhile, the crucial counterattack had been delayed by enemy fighter-bombers and by artillery and naval gunfire. General Geyr ordered the attack continued during the night. "This is our one big chance," he explained. By noon the next day the tanks were again taking an incredible punishment from the artillery and ships' guns, and a depressed General Geyr indicated to the Seventh Army, his superiors, that "in the interests of the troops and of our cause" he intended to submit a candid report on the situation that evening. In the evening he revived the tank assault, but by midnight it had ground to its final halt, well short of its tactical objective. It was the last Nazi counteroffensive in Normandy.

Geyr's report to his headquarters, when it came, was repeated to Speidel and Rundstedt. It recommended the immediate evacuation of the Caen bridgehead, to enable the Germans to hold a new front line out of range of the enemy ships' lethal guns. By the time Rommel's Mercedes drove up to the château steps, Speidel had already approved Geyr's recommendation. "You are authorized herewith to begin systematic evacuation of Caen North and the bridgehead," Speidel said, "as the situation demands."

Rommel dramatically dissented—he was still unwilling to give up the city—and just after midnight on July 1, Speidel had to telephone Geyr that any evacuation of Caen was conditional on the approval of the High Command. When Rommel drove forward to Geyr's command post at noon, he insisted that the panzer divisions stay where they were, close to the battlefront. The protocol in the Panzer Group's files shows that the field marshal lectured the unhappy Geyr at some length, conveying to him everything the Führer had told him. In any event, Caen was held for a long time after this.

Runstedt, to Geyr's dismay, had forwarded Geyr's report with his own endorsement to the Berghof. Hitler was enraged. When Rommel got back to the château that evening, July 1, Günther Blumentritt, Runstedt's chief of staff, came on the line from Paris almost at once, telling Speidel, in great agitation: "The Führer has flatly forbidden any withdrawal from Caen. The present lines are to be held. All further enemy penetrations are to be stopped by determined defense, or by limited counterattacks." Despite this admonition, Speidel still instructed Geyr to go ahead with his preparations for the panzer divisions' withdrawal. From the Berghof, Jodl called Blumentritt and said Geyr's report lacked the "ice-cold logic" and clarity of thought that the crisis called for. Obviously Geyr had become "infected"—as Jodl put it—by Field Marshals Rommel and von Rundstedt.

Rommel, however, had held firm on the matter of keeping Caen. At 10:00 P.M. he repeated Hitler's ruling to Geyr—that the line at Caen was to be held. Thus he survived the axe that now fell on the mutineers. At 11:30 P.M. Blumentritt telephoned: "The Führer has ordered the dismissal of General Geyr." (Fearing that Geyr might defect to the British, Hitler also instructed that he was not to be told until his successor—Hans Eberbach, a Swabian like Rommel—actually took over the Panzer Group.) And later that troubled night Rommel's fluttering staff learned that a Hitler messenger was already on the way to Paris with a high medal for Rundstedt, and a sealed letter in which the Führer expressed concern about the field marshal's health. The elderly Rundstedt took the hint and resigned his command in France the next day.

The torrid, stupefying heat of the French summer had momentarily broken, and a light drizzle fell after the evening meal on July 2. From the château's Hall of Ancestors came the sound of Speidel's staff playing table tennis. Rommel stood at the tall window of his room, talking in subdued tones with Admiral Ruge about the day's events. The army's supply situation was catastrophic. Rommel's artillery expert had just returned with bad news about the ammunition shortages. He needed a minimum of 3,500 tons of supplies each day, but was not getting even one tenth of this. Rundstedt's old quartermaster general had been sacked, but the newcomer—Colonel Eberhard Finckh—was quite incompetent at supply (in fact, Finckh had gotten the job only because he was a member of the anti-Hitler conspiracy, but Rommel could not suspect that). Rommel himself had no control over the other services in France, so although the Luftwaffe had 19,000 tons of truck space and the navy well over 10,000 tons, he was powerless to order them to make some available to the starving ground forces.

To cap it all, Rommel complained to Ruge, Hitler did not trust him. Hitler doubted that ships' guns could have sufficed to halt the counteroffensive, and he had asked the German navy to report on the range and ammunition stocks of the enemy ships' guns in question; the Führer had even ordered Rommel's generals to count the shell bursts in their vicinities. "We are supposed to believe what the High Command tells us," Rommel told Ruge, "but they refuse to believe us."

He had spent the morning in Paris with Rundstedt attending the funeral of General Dollmann. (On Rommel's orders, the French newspapers described the general's death as having been "in action.") Rommel had expected to replace Rundstedt, but Hitler had sprung on him an unpalatable surprise: Field Marshal von Kluge, and not Rommel, would step into Rundstedt's shoes. Rommel discussed this with Ruge, and after their conversation the admiral wrote in his secret diary: "Rommel is taking the pressure and the mistrust badly." With Ruge, Rommel had evidently revived his old theme, of the urgent need for an armistice on at least one front. "Settlement with either the USSR or the Anglo-Americans," Ruge's notes read. "Rommel in favor of settling with the West. But it's high time for our politicians to act while we have any trump cards at all left in our hands." He added, "The field marshal says he only wishes the next four weeks were over."

Soon after Rommel arrived back at the château from Normandy the next afternoon, July 3, Kluge visited him. Nine years older than Rommel and senior to him in rank,

Hans von Kluge was a veteran of the Russian front—hard-bitten and uncompromising. He was Prussian, alert and of renowned sagacity. The rumor was that when enemy fighters strafed *his* car he stayed in it to prove he was no coward. And he was no coward. He was robust and aggressive, and his face radiated the confidence he had soaked up over the last week as Hitler's guest at the Berghof. He had come to Normandy with a zealous determination to execute Hitler's instructions to "hold fast at any price." From Kluge's smooth, iron-gray hair to his gleaming boots, Rommel took an immediate dislike to him.

Kluge's first words did not help. "The first thing is, you must get accustomed to obeying orders like the rest," he snapped. Rommel saw a squall blowing up and sent Speidel and Tempelhoff out of the room. In an interrogating manner, Kluge demanded to see the pessimistic reports Rommel claimed to have had from his generals.

Rommel's jaw sagged. "You seem to forget you are speaking to a field marshal," he said.

"I'm perfectly well aware of it," Kluge retorted. "But you have taken very independent positions up to now, and you always got your own way in defiance of your immediate superiors by going over their heads to the Führer."

"My job is quite clearly defined," replied Rommel. "I have to defend the coast, and I demand that Commander in Chief West place all the necessary forces and means at my disposal to that end." He added that on the supplies and logistics side, Kluge had a rich field for endeavor: "Just look at the bungling of your quartermaster!"

Kluge's response was: "Up to now you haven't ever really commanded any unit bigger than a division!"

Smarting under this insult, Rommel shouted back: "And you still have to meet the British in battle!"

Kluge told his staff afterward that he had scored more heavily than Rommel in this slandering match. He had certainly made clear to Rommel that he was not to bypass him and deal directly with the Führer. But the Fox still found ways of making his voice heard to Hitler. That same day he dictated a ten-page critique on the Normandy battle so far—claiming in detail that each of his demands both before and after D day had been turned down by

Jodl and the High Command: demands for reinforcements in Normandy, for antiaircraft guns and for extensive sea mining along the coast. (It was a specious document, because the actual records of April and May show that he had placed a very different emphasis on these "demands.") Rommel obviously saw it as a defense brief, should a court-martial ever be held into these catastrophic events. He addressed one copy to Rudolf Schmundt, Hitler's adjutant. "I've sent it to 'John the Apostle,'" he told Admiral Ruge, chuckling. "He always hands on everything to his boss." And he sent a copy to Kluge, too, with a covering letter: "The rebuke you made at the beginning of your visit, 'Now you too will have to learn to carry out orders,' deeply hurt me. I request you to inform me of your reasons for this rebuke." Kluge did not deign to reply.

Rundstedt's unexpected replacement by Kluge had revived the Paris conspirator's hopes of exploiting Rommel's name in their coming revolution against Hitler. Kluge was believed to have expressed sympathy with their aims some time after Stalingrad. Speidel at once informed General von Stülpnagel, linchpin of the conspiracy in Paris, of Rommel's rough treatment at Hitler's hands and his awakening interest in a separate peace with the Western powers.

Speidel had conceived a technical method of surreptitiously contacting the Americans. The Americans had startled the Nazis by releasing eight German Red Cross nurses captured in Cherbourg and allowing them back through the lines. Perhaps, thought Speidel, one or more could return carrying a letter from Rommel? Speidel's staff telephoned Paris: "Are we permitted to radio thanks to the Americans for treating the nurses so decently?"

Kluge's staff flatly forbade it: "Just because they observe international law for once, that's no reason to go thanking them for it!"

Still, Speidel evidently discussed his ideas with Rommel because after supper on that day, July 3, the field marshal cryptically said to Admiral Ruge, "I'm going to have to lend them my name. But my name alone isn't going to be enough to see things through."

The next morning he set off early in drizzling rain for Rouen—where he was expecting "Patton's army group" to start its invasion any day now. On the way he spoke in a low voice to Ruge about the need to make an armistice offer to the British and Americans. The question was, how would they react if Rommel made such an offer? "All the efforts of my troops have been for naught!" he said, and groaned. Ruge softly contradicted him. In 1918, too, everything had seemed helpless, but it was precisely the world's vast respect for the qualities of the German soldier that had speeded Germany's rebirth. "The same respect is there today, Herr Feldmarschall. And they particularly respect *you*."

Over the next days, Rommel very cautiously sounded out his commanders, while ostensibly discussing the Normandy operations. On July 5 he conferred with Geyr's successor, General Hans Eberbach—a cheerful, plucky Swabian, whose Panzer Group West was the main defense force at Caen. Rommel admitted to Eberbach that there were a lot of factors still in their favor. Montgomery was proceeding with excessive caution, and his divisions still did not actually outnumber Rommel's; moreover the new German tanks like the Panther and Tiger were much better than the enemy's. "And," said Rommel, "I've seen a lot of strange missile-launching sites that show we have more than just the V-1 up our sleeve." But Montgomery had a huge materiel and air superiority, Rommel went on, that outweighed all these factors. So in Rommel's view they could only keep fighting now "to obtain peace terms that are not too harsh."

In all his private talks, Rommel lavished blame for the plight of his forces upon the High Command and General Jodl. But ironically his own staff deserved far more blame, for they continued to lead him to expect a second invasion. All his decisions were hamstrung by this fear. "You've got to hold two panzer divisions to be switched north if there's a new invasion, or to the Seventh Army if there's a big break-through there," he told Eberbach. Would Rommel have regarded a Nazi defeat in France as so inevitable if Speidel's staff were not still exaggerating the enemy's waiting divisions in England *fivefold* at this time? To Rommel, everything depended on smashing "Patton's army group" when it landed.

Meanwhile, across the foot of the Cherbourg peninsula American pressure had suddenly built up against Rommel's troops, starting early on July 3. But the difficult terrain of valleys, alluvial swamps and thickly wooded hills, coupled with Hitler's order to yield not an inch, made the going for the enemy very tough, and after a few days their offensive bogged down. Rommel sent Bayerlein's Panzer Lehr Division across to a new position northwest of Saint-Lô on July 7—this time heeding Seventh Army warnings that the American commanders were proving much more adept at mobile warfare than the British.

Rommel still held the strong bridgehead west of the river Orne at Caen: one month after D day, the British had still not captured their "Poland." But on the seventh they began a savage new attempt, opening with a heavy bombardment on the defensive positions. Ships' guns and field artillery poured 80,000 shells into Rommel's troops that night, and in a forty-minute raid starting at 9:50 P.M., at Montgomery's personal request, the RAF's strategic bombers thundered 2,560 tons of explosives into the medieval city. The Sixteenth Luftwaffe Field Division, holding the northern suburbs of Caen, was badly shaken and suffered severe officer casualties when the British ground assault began at 4:20 A.M. But Kurt Meyer's young Twelfth SS Panzer Division—average age only eighteen and a half years—crawled out of the ruins, salvaged what guns and tanks it could, and fought a spectacular defensive battle in which no less than 103 British tanks were destroyed. They told Rommel that with their handful of Tigers they had sent the enemy "running for their lives."

The proud French city itself had been wiped out. Eberbach later described the scene: "Caen was just a heap of rubble and virtually impassable after that, with the citizens laboring to recover their dead and injured with admirable courage." The craters and wreckage barred the British tanks for a whole day, and when they finally pushed on through to the river, the enemy found that Rommel's troops had blown the bridges and were already reestablished in depth along the other bank.

Rommel rightly claimed this as a tactical victory, but to repeat it he knew he would need far more ammunition transported to the front. As General Alfred Gause, Rommel's old colleague from Africa and now Eberbach's chief of staff at Panzer Group West, pointed out on July 10,

"By a great effort we just managed to shoot off 4,500 shells. Our troops' morale is high, but courage alone won't be enough against the enemy's sheer weight of metal. Even our First World War veterans say they've never known anything like it. The enemy make up for their own poor morale by shelling and bombing." Rommel had the ammunition—but it was back in Germany. The railroads were crippled by bombing. The navy and Luftwaffe refused to lend him their trucks. He had ordered France's neglected inland waterways restored at top speed, and barges were now chugging forward to Normandy with big loads of gasoline and ammunition; miraculously the enemy had still not spotted Rommel's ruse. But the new Quartermaster West, Colonel Finckh, lacked any kind of initiative —he had just twiddled his thumbs for the last ten days, according to Ruge's diary.

A black comedy—which incidentally proves Rommel's ignorance of Speidel's plotting—ensued. On the eighth he had sent the veteran general Friedrich Dihm to find out what was snagging the new waterways system. When he heard Dihm's pungent criticism of Finckh's bungling and lethargy, Rommel "hit the roof" and, noted Ruge, the agitated Hans Speidel on July 11 "had his work cut out persuading Rommel not to take the whole matter up with Kluge," Finckh's superior. Speidel, of course, knew what Rommel did not—that the colonel had been sent to Paris only as a prop for the anti-Hitler plot. The assassin-elect, Stauffenberg, had briefed Finckh on June 23 before Finckh left for France. Stauffenberg had scathingly told him: "You know, Finckh, we don't have any real field marshals left. Whatever the Führer orders, they all shit in their pants and nobody dares speak up against him." (Finckh later admitted this to the Gestapo under interrogation.)

Rommel had spent the Saturday evening of July 8 at the Caen battlefront. Twice he visited the Panzer Group's headquarters, arranging with Gause and then Eberbach to haul out their heavy guns and regroup them in depth to choke off any enemy penetration. He drove back to the château, dead tired, toward midnight. Speidel had spent the day in Paris, plotting with the military governor of France, Stülpnagel. Together, Speidel and Stülpnagel decided that Rommel had to be won over—now or never. They therefore arranged a meeting for Rommel at the château the next day with Stülpnagel's adjutant Caesar von Hofacker, the eloquent and debonair dynamo of the conspiracy in Paris. It was to prove a milestone in the field marshal's life—or rather, a tombstone.

The mood at the château the next morning, Sunday, was grim. The breakfast table talk revolved around a new High Command request to Army Group B to suggest an operation capable of wiping out the enemy bridgehead in Normandy. Speidel, who in his latest report to the High Command still insisted that "over sixty" enemy divisions were standing by in Britain—against even Roenne's fictitious estimate of forty-five and a true figure of only twelve —guffawed. "Let's draw up a brilliant plan with lots of arrows," he said, "making them as pointed as possible. No need for it to be feasible!" He now openly dared to make such remarks in Rommel's presence.

The field marshal gloomily echoed this sarcasm. "If we plan to attack the British at the eastern end, then we'll only be told to attack the Americans instead," he said. "And as soon as we finish regrouping for that, they'll change their minds all over again." (Ruge wrote these remarks down in his shorthand diary.)

The telephone calls logged that day, July 9, at the château spelled out the crisis at Caen. Rommel told General Blumentritt, Kluge's chief of staff: "Leave the High Command in no doubt whatsoever that we won't be able to hold the present lines if the enemy attack again in the same strength as yesterday." At 11:40 A.M. Gause came on the line from the battlefield: "At this moment our positions are under saturation shelling." At 3:15 P.M. he again telephoned: "The enemy are already claiming to have reached Caen city center." At 7:35 P.M. Speidel phoned Gause back: "To prevent any enemy breakthrough across the Orne at Caen, you are to move forward the First SS Panzer Division [the Leibstandarte Adolf Hitler] and commit it immediately." (This also suited his political plan, namely to tie up all the loyal SS troops inextricably before the anti-Hitler coup.) Rommel took the phone, and spoke to General Eberbach in person: "We've got to stop the enemy breaking through at Caen at all costs. Use the First SS Panzer Division for this."

All this meant one thing: Rommel's mind was elsewhere when Speidel ushered in a tall, handsome lieutenant colonel in Luftwaffe uniform, Caesar von Hofacker. Speidel tactfully left them alone. The field marshal brusquely inquired, "Now, what is it that you have to tell me?" and the fateful interview with Stülpnagel's adjutant began.

*No one knows definitely what was said. Reconstructing their discussion is difficult, since the Gestapo interrogations of Hofacker are missing. Perhaps they were destroyed on Hitler's orders, to preserve Rommel's reputation; alternatively, they may have been removed as a part of a postwar American initiative to sanitize the Nazi files of key documents relating to senior NATO generals like Speidel before the files were given back to West Germany. A National Archives official in Washington indicated to me that certain collections of files were laundered like this in the 1950s. Also, unlike other People's Court records, the trial of Hofacker in late August 1944 is not in the East German archives. In short, I have drawn blanks everywhere.*

*Some conclusions, however, can be drawn from secondary sources. Hofacker did the talking while Rommel merely listened. The colonel made no reference to a specific opposition movement—let alone any assassination. They discussed the war's progress in general terms.*

*The secondary sources are these: Speidel related much of this to the Gestapo. His interrogations, like Hofacker's, have vanished from the files, but the Gestapo's chief inquisitor, Dr. Georg Kiessel, wrote about them when he himself was in a prison cell: "Hofacker spoke about half an hour with Rommel, explained that the situation called for swift action and that if the Führer refused to act then he must be coerced. There was no talk of an assassination." Afterward, wrote Kiessel—who can have learned this only from Speidel—the field marshal took Speidel for a walk in the château grounds and dismissed any idea of coercing Hitler as quite out of the question. "I'll go and see the Führer quite soon," suggested Rommel, "and ask his permission for a meeting with Field Marshal Montgomery. I'm certain that Montgomery won't deny me that*

*—as one old rival to another. And then I'll persuade him to agitate in Britain for a joint campaign with us against Russia."*

The interview left Rommel unchanged and unimpressed —just as after Mayor Strölin's approach in February 1944. He never saw the colonel again, and all the indications are that he forgot him. But Hofacker did not forget. He drove back to Paris, fast, dashed triumphantly into his rooms at the Hôtel Royal Monceau and said to his fellow conspirator Baron Gotthard von Falkenhausen, "I've just spent the most interesting hour of my life. I put all my cards on the table—I told the field marshal everything!"

Hofacker was a romantic, an impetuous dreamer. Over the next hours, his recountings of the interview multiplied the scale of his achievement every time he described it. He told Baron Friedrich von Teuchert, another civil servant on Stülpnagel's staff, "I was far more successful than I hoped. Rommel can scarcely be restrained, he wants to lash out at once. Even if the plot in the Reich fails!" And he told Stülpnagel: "Rommel has placed himself completely at our disposal." Unwittingly, the field marshal was the toast of the Paris plotters that night. (Teuchert and Falkenhausen survived to write their recollections of all this after the war ended.) Hofacker asked Teuchert that same night to draft a letter for Rommel to smuggle somehow through to Montgomery, offering surrender. Teuchert delegated the job to Stülpnagel's legal adviser, Walter Bargatzky (who also wrote his recollections). Bargatzky had the letter ready before dawn. Rommel never saw it.

The next morning Hofacker hurried off to Berlin. Dr. Elmar Michel, another of Stülpnagel's legion of conspirators, has described how he drove the colonel from Paris to the railroad at Metz. Hofacker talked all the time about the plan to assassinate Hitler, Göring and Himmler at a war conference. "Stülpnagel has sent me to Berlin to ask them to act immediately," Hofacker said in a furtive whisper—although they were quite alone in the car. "I've briefed Rommel. He's placed himself wholly at our disposal and says he's willing to lead the armistice talks with the Western powers."

Michel nodded vigorously, without taking his eyes off

the road, and replied: "We need a personality like Rommel if our revolution is to succeed without splitting the whole nation!"

These were significant utterances indeed. Hofacker had also spoken with Field Marshal von Kluge—and Kluge asked two days later for a word with one or another of the German nurses who had been in contact with the Americans in Cherbourg. (Blumentritt phoned Meyer-Detring to ask where the nurses were.) Obviously Kluge was exploring possible postal channels to the enemy.

In Berlin, Hofacker met his cousin, Colonel Klaus von Stauffenberg, on the eleventh and told him of his triumph at the château. Stauffenberg, a dashing man in his forties, had been chosen as the assassin, although he was scarcely agile; he had been severely maimed by a mine in Tunisia. Hofacker claimed that the western front would collapse within six weeks. He then saw Mayor Carl Goerdeler, the civilian head of the plot, and advised him that Rommel had been won. On July 16, Stauffenberg told his assembled conspirators that they now had the western commanders with them. "They will cease hostilities on their own initiative," he said, "withdraw our troops to the West Wall, and take steps to launch a joint offensive by both the Western powers and Germany against the Soviet Union." (The Gestapo learned all this from their inquiries.)

Hofacker also sent a Luftwaffe general, Karl Barsewisch, to inform General Heinz Guderian in East Prussia that the "field marshals in the west" were planning to surrender and that a coup against Hitler was imminent. Guderian stayed well clear—he hated Kluge and was undecided about Rommel. In fact, he left discreetly for the country estate that the Führer had just given him, and waited to see what happened.

Haunted by the specter of defeat, over the next few days Rommel remained undecided on how to act. He had his hands full with the continuing battle. He drove to the battlefields and met his commanders, but he hesitated to speak bluntly about the future.

Now the Americans resumed their offensive southward out of the Cherbourg peninsula. On July 11 their artillery delivered an unprecedented weight of fire on the German paratroops defending the vital Saint-Lô crossroads, and this was followed by a big infantry attack. The Germans fought well but took heavy casualties—in some sectors all the defenders were either dead or injured. After supper that night Admiral Ruge wrote, "The field marshal came and joined us. After Speidel left, he spoke very gravely about our situation. There's a breakthrough threatening on our left flank—our divisions are just burning out."

At breakfast the next day Rommel said absently: "You can't keep basing your actions on wishful thinking. Only on sober, harsh reality." The reality that day was that the paratroops were down to only quarter strength, and the Americans had set up loudspeakers announcing that the attack on Saint-Lô was about to resume, inviting the paratroops to desert.

Rommel could see no way out, conscious as he was of his oath of allegiance to the Führer. Since D day, he had lost 97,000 men, including 2,360 officers, but he had received only 6,000 replacements. He had lost 225 tanks, and had been given only seventeen. The raw infantry divisions now arriving were no match for the mass enemy attacks launched after hours of air and artillery bombardment. The enemy's air attack on the transport system had reduced the supply of ammunition to a trickle. He dared not weaken the Fifteenth Army's sector to transfer significant forces into Normandy; but the Seventh Army now holding off the American offensive urgently needed at least two fresh infantry divisions. Admiral Ruge challenged Rommel early on the twelfth as to when General Jodl of the High Command would actually come and see things for himself. Rommel replied, "I've been forbidden to telephone anybody anymore. Kluge will have to do it."

Kluge, Commander in Chief West and still Rommel's superior, came to the château later that day. Gone was his dominating and arrogant manner. A bleak, hangdog air replaced the cheerful confidence he had brought from Hitler's Berghof a week before. He had deteriorated visibly. Rommel pointed to the breakout now threatening hourly at Saint-Lô. The Seventh Army had to get reinforcements from somewhere. Kluge evidently asked Rommel to furnish him with a written estimate of their prospects. After leaving the château, he telephoned Jodl:

"I want to stress once again that I'm no pessimist—but in my view the situation couldn't be grimmer." Templehoff commented to the admiral, as they watched Kluge take leave of Rommel: "On the main points they now see eye to eye." And strolling on the cliff above the château the next morning, Rommel said to the admiral in quiet triumph: "The way I snarled at him on his first day here has worked wonders. When he arrived his instructions were very different, but now he has seen for himself that there's nothing to be done."

Rommel went off that day to continue fighting the enemy. Speidel renewed his clandestine contacts with the anti-Hitler plotters. Under cover of a routine visit to Kluge and Blumentritt, he went on to Paris to see Stülpnagel and learned the details of the planned simultaneous coup d'état there. Later he also dropped a hint to General Hans von Salmuth, commanding the Fifteenth Army. Salmuth privately wrote, "I gave my blessing to Speidel's intentions." These intentions were, in Speidel's own words, that the two field marshals should open secret negotiations with the enemy, offering to withdraw German troops from France, Belgium and Holland in return for the immediate cessation of the bombing of German civilians. That a shrewd general like Speidel should seriously expect the British and Americans to abandon their war aims, let alone the doctrine of unconditional surrender, while leaving Hitler's conquests in the east intact, shows the land of illusions in which the conspirators were living.

There can be no doubt of Rommel's personal loyalty toward Hitler at this time, whatever his loathing of Jodl and the High Command. "The tragedy of our position is this," Ruge recorded him as saying on July 13. "We are obliged to fight on to the very end, but all the time we're convinced that it's far more vital to stop the Russians than the Anglo-Americans from breaking into Germany." He thought the collapse would come in four weeks, so any political decision would have to come very soon. Ruge himself wrote in his diary, "We've got to exploit the differences between our enemies. Best of all would be if the Führer himself would take the requisite steps. But to judge from all his utterances, it's not likely that he will.

On the other hand, says Rommel, the Führer is a great man and a man of sound political instinct, so he ought to be able to hit on the right solution by himself."

The next day Rommel again watched the desperate fighting at Saint-Lô. The front line could collapse at any time, he concluded. On Rommel's return, Speidel drafted a vivid report to Kluge on the crisis for Rommel to sign; it was ready the next day, July 15. Its language was uncompromising: "In the circumstances," it concluded, "it is to be anticipated that in the near future the enemy will succeed in breaking through our thin front line, particularly in the Seventh Army's sector, and thrusting on into the wide open spaces of France. . . . Apart from the local reserves which are presently tied down by the fighting in Panzer Group West's sector"—at Caen—"and which can move only at night owing to the enemy's air superiority, we have no mobile reserves available to prevent any such breakthrough on the Seventh Army's sector." Rommel took his pen and added a final paragraph that was blunt and brave: "Everywhere our troops are fighting heroically," he wrote, "but the unequal struggle is drawing to its close. In my view the political consequences of this have just got to be drawn. As commander in chief of the army group, I feel obliged to make myself quite plain."

He stepped out of his study, found Speidel and Templehoff waiting for him, and announced: "Here— here's the signature you wanted!" The others were taken aback at his postscript, and persuaded Rommel to strike out the word "political." The report was retyped and forwarded to Kluge the next day with a brief covering note: "With reference to our verbal discussion on July 12 I am sending you the enclosed observations as my contribution to a situation assessment. Signed: Rommel." Thus Rommel had acted. He had put his own name and reputation on the line. He had issued an ultimatum—or so he saw it—for Kluge to send up with his own added authority to the Führer. "I'm curious to see what becomes of it all," he admitted to Admiral Ruge. "It's all the same to me whether they give me the boot or the chop—not that I believe they'll actually do that. But commanders in responsible positions must be permitted to speak their minds."

July 15, 1944: 3:30 P.M. Rommel set off to inspect the Caen battlefront—slaughterhouse of both Montgomery's and his own troops. He crossed the Seine in an assault craft, then raced to Normandy in his big open Horch, with young Corporal Daniel at the wheel. It occurred to him that enemy guerrillas had recently ambushed several cars in this area, so he ordered a detour by less active roads. There were hundreds of trucks rolling westward now, thanks to his use of the inland waterways; at last supplies were reaching the battlefield. As he drove the last ten miles to Caen, he could see the depth of the defensive system already constructed by Eberbach and Gause: line upon line of tanks, guns and infantry. He spent some time with the gory survivors of the Sixteenth Luftwaffe Field Division, still holding the main line. The troops had lost all their antitanks guns in the murderous RAF bombing raid, but now they were ready and waiting with Panzerfaust bazookas.

The villages of inland Normandy were idyllic and oblivious of war. "Here a small farm cart," noted Ruge, "packed with our infantrymen. There our troops strolling with the local girls. Apparently the villagers are all still here." Rommel had indeed packed these villages with infantry. Montgomery was going to have the battle of his life, if ever he got this far. Rommel moved on to see General Feuchtinger's Twenty-first Panzer Division—bivouacked in an orchard. A few hundred yards away the French country life continued undistracted. "A father was cutting his young boy's hair. A real Saturday afternoon atmosphere."

On the way back to the château that evening, Rommel took the same road he always took—rather recklessly, Admiral Ruge thought. The field marshal reminisced nostalgically about his school years. Then, jolted back to reality by the blackened skeletons of burned-out trucks, he again talked about the war. "War is so senseless, nobody profits by it. The farmers go on farming, the workers go on working just the same." To the astounded admiral, the field marshal ventured his own wild dream that one day Germany might be a British dominion, like Canada. "When will there be a decision?" asks Ruge in his diary.

Rommel waited impatiently for a reply to his "observations." He was in dead earnest. On July 16—the day he sent the document to Kluge—he again drove up to the Fifteenth Army's sector, this time to inspect the Seventeenth Luftwaffe Field Division near Le Havre. The day was hot and humid; sometimes the sun broke through the clouds. The division's command post was in a limestone cave in a hill covered with beech trees near Fécamp. After the conference the division's operations officer, Lieutenant Colonel Elmar Warning, escorted the field marshal back to where the cars had been parked under cover against air attack. Colonel Warning had served on Rommel's staff at El Alamein, and he asked Rommel about the true situation—"because," he said, "we can count the days off on our tunic buttons before the breakthrough comes."

Rommel regarded Warning's Afrika Korps shirt and replied with startling candor: "I'm going to tell you this much: Field Marshal von Kluge and I have sent the Führer an ultimatum, telling him the war can't be won militarily and asking him to draw the consequences."

"What if the Führer refuses?" asked Warning.

"Then I'm going to open up the western front," answered Rommel. "Because there's only one thing that matters now—the British and Americans must get to Berlin before the Russians do!"

# Kill Rommel!

CURSING softly under his breath, burly Captain Raymond Lee, of the British Special Air Service, gathers up his parachute in the darkness. His men are safe, but some equipment has been broken in the landing and a vital item is missing. All night is spent looking for it. At 8:50 A.M. he sends a pigeon fluttering back to England with a message for the War Office: "Landing okay, but fifteen miles southeast of target. Can't find white box, possibly not dropped. Three leg bags smashed, no radio left. Civilians scared stiff and not helpful. Will do our best. Boche plentiful in area, they say, but still hold out."

For months the British have been searching for Rommel's secret headquarters. Back in May it was reported variously as at "Gaillon" and at La Roche-Guyon. On May 26 a British agent stated that Rommel was at the château of the Marquis de Rochefoucauld, sited "at the foot of a rock." Not until July 14 was final confirmation received, from Major William Fraser of the Gordon Highlanders. He had been parachuted into central France, 200 miles away, to establish a guerrilla base codenamed "Houndsworth," into which a large Special Air Service force would later be dropped to harass the German routes from the Mediterranean to Normandy.

Fraser's radio signal to London read: "From Hounds-worth 102. Very reliable source states Rommel's head-quarters at Château de la Roche-Guyon. . . . Rommel there May 25, staff permanently there. Rommel arrives left bank Seine, crosses by motor launch. Walks and shoots in Forêt de Moisson. Send maps from this area to area [of] Mantes, also three snipers' rifles. Would prefer you not send another party for this job as [I] consider it is my pigeon."

At SAS headquarters outside London, the maps were scrutinized: Fraser was too far away to reach the château safely carrying three snipers' rifles; and he had a specific task already. His commander, Brigadier R. W. McLeod, radioed to him: "Regret must forbid your personal attack on Rommel. Appreciate you consider him your pigeon, but your task [is] to remain in command [of] present area. This pigeon will be attacked by a special party . . ." Not easily fobbed off, Fraser signaled back the next day: "Have here Monsieur Defors who owns the estates all around Rommel headquarters. All the keepers, etc., have been in his family service for years. His relations live all around and he has contacts all the way en route." The brigadier's reply was the same: "Regret decision must stand."

After this, Brigadier McLeod acted with accustomed speed. He sent for air photos of the château. Routine cover of the village had been flown on May 13, and now the eight-by-sixes were pulled from the files and sub-jected to stereoscopic examination by experts. They dis-covered that the whole area had been surrounded by barbed wire. On July 20, the brigadier assigned Operation Instruction Number 32 for the mission: "Intention: to kill, or kidnap and remove to England, Field Marshal Rommel, or any senior members of his staff." It was a death warrant for Rommel, because while snatching him and flying him back to Britain would obviously be a sen-sational coup, the odds against flying him out safely were probably insuperable: killing him would be easier. Mc-Leod admitted that retaliation would be "inevitable" against the local villagers, just as the Nazis massacred the village of Lidice after the killing of Reinhard Heydrich, and more recently the French village of Oradour-sur-

Glane. Nevertheless he ordered the dropping of an SAS squad into France near the city of Chartres, with orders to kill Rommel.

It is Raymond Lee who leads the five-man team, a professional assassin with half a dozen notches already on his rifle butt. How is he to know, as he leaps out into the darkness over France on July 25, that another fate has already overtaken his chosen victim? Lee will spend his next weeks futilely searching for Rommel, and then ambushing German transport behind the lines.

*Colonel Hans Lattmann, Rommel's artillery officer, has described an incident that again revealed Rommel's secret intentions. "We were driving to the Eighty-sixth Corps," Lattmann told me. "On the way we had a puncture. We got out, and the field marshal took me on one side and we walked up and down while Daniel the driver and Lang changed the wheel. He asked me, 'How do you think the war's going to end, Lattmann?' I replied, 'Herr Feldmarschall, it's pretty obvious we're not going to win but I hope we've got the strength to get a fair settlement.' And then he said: 'I'm going to try and use my good name with the enemy to make a deal with the West, against Hitler's will—but only on condition they agree to fight side by side with us against Russia.' "*

Every day now Rommel was covering 250 miles or more in his Horch, meeting his battle commanders. The military records reveal nothing of the agonies of conscience that he was suffering. They only show Rommel methodically and single-mindedly preparing to defeat Montgomery's coming offensive. Any day now Montgomery would attempt to smash his way out of the frustrating Caen bridgehead toward Falaise and Paris. But postwar documents clearly indicate that each such conference between Rommel and his generals also contained an unrecorded, secret portion in which he hinted at his armistice plans. There is, for example, this off-the-record talk with General Eberbach, the Panzer Group commander. "We can't go on like this," Rommel told him.

Eberbach was noncommittal. "Can you imagine the

enemy even starting preliminary talks with us," he asked, "so long as Adolf Hitler is in power?"

Rommel shook his head. "I'm relying on your support. We've got to cooperate, if only for the sake of the German public who have been so decent throughout all this."

Eberbach expressed powerful misgivings that what Rommel was planning would unleash a civil war in Germany—and Rommel knew he was right. He wondered what Hitler's reply would be to his ultimatum.

Another such talk took place on July 17, when he visited the First SS Panzer Corps. Sepp Dietrich's operations officer indicated that Montgomery's preparations were all but complete. Then Dietrich himself arrived, a stocky peasant type with a lined and weather-beaten face. He had been one of Hitler's most loyal followers. Rommel tackled him in Hellmuth Lang's presence with the words: "Would you always execute my orders, even if they contradicted the Führer's orders?"

The SS general stuck out his bony hand for Rommel to shake: "You're the boss, Herr Feldmarschall. I obey only you—whatever it is you're planning."

More private talk followed, which Lang could not hear. After that, Rommel climbed into the Horch and told Corporal Daniel to drive back to the château. The late afternoon air was heavy and hot. Rommel was silent, then told Lang: "I've won Dietrich over."

As usual the long straight roads were strewn with burning trucks and automobiles caught by enemy fighter-bombers. But today the roads were also cluttered with refugees from Normandy: somehow the French had smelled the aroma of approaching death. Their horse- or ox-drawn carts were laden with household goods and decked out with white cloths in the hope of escaping the aircraft cannon fire. As Rommel's command car roared past, raising clouds of dust, the Frenchmen who recognized him waved and doffed their hats. Lang wrote that day, "We find very little hatred from the French on these trips. They have far less love for the Tommies and Americans."

On his knees Rommel had a road map. In the back, next to Lang, was a corporal acting as aircraft lookout. After two hours the number of recently wrecked trucks multiplied—in some there were still dead and injured, so there must still be enemy planes about. Approaching Livarot, the lookout spotted eight enemy planes. Rommel shouted to Daniel to take a covered, leafy lane that ran parallel to the main road, but after some miles the lane converged on the main road again. They took Route N179 out of Livarot toward Vimoutiers. Almost at once the lookout saw two more aircraft, and these were diving in toward them. Rommel yelled to pull off into a narrow side road about 300 yards ahead—but before the Horch made it, the first Spitfire was already thundering in at treetop height behind them. At 500 yards' range it started pumping machine gun and cannon fire out of its wings— Rommel could see the flashes, as he looked back, his hand on the door handle. Cannon shell exploded in the road behind, then all along the left side of the Horch. Hot fragments of metal and glass tore into his face. Daniel's left shoulder was shattered by a cannon shell. He fought to control the car but it careened down the long hill at high speed and crashed into a tree on the other side of the road, spewing its occupants out across the pavement and then richocheting empty across the road again into a ditch. Rommel's head struck something and his skull caved in. Blackness engulfed him as the second Spitfire swooped in and opened fire.

The attack had been at about 6:00 P.M. Three hours later Speidel found out about the "road accident" and phoned Kluge at once. Kluge traced the hospital. The surgeon in charge phoned him back—Rommel was still in a coma. "He won't be fit again before 1945," the surgeon said. To Kluge, it seemed like an act of God. Now he blessed his own prudence—because whatever the reason, he had not yet, in fact, sent Rommel's grim ultimatum on to Hitler. Now he, Kluge, would have complete tactical control in Normandy after all, without interference from a headstrong Rommel. Perhaps his hand would bring victory for the Nazis where Rommel had only been preparing to retreat. He put through a Führungsblitz call to the High Command in East Prussia and announced that until a replacement could be found for Rommel, he had decided to assume control in Normandy himself. "I must have a tough man here," he said. "There's no question of anything else." Later he said to Schmundt, Hitler's chief adjutant, "I need men here who are resolute and tough." These remarks reveal Kluge's assessment of Rommel's command qualities.

Hitler took the unsubtle hint and placed Kluge himself in formal command of Army Group B, while retaining him as Commander in Chief West. Kluge moved his desk to the château, leaving Blumentritt to mind the store in Paris. Characteristically, he declined to eat with Rommel's staff: they were banished to the mess below the château, with their juniors. Only Speidel was invited to share Kluge's table. He loftily promised his colleagues to come down and join them on days that Kluge was away. Amid hoots of laughter, one officer replied: "We'll put that to a vote." The old camaraderie was evaporating fast, now that Rommel had gone.

To Rommel, the blackness seemed to last an eternity. He felt only pain, jolting and heat. He was lying on a stretcher, covered with rough bandages. He could not see, but he could feel blood trickling out of his mouth and ears. Soon, half conscious, half dead, he was lifted off the stretcher and bedded down on cushions in a Mercedes with the back of its front seat tilted flat. Somebody, a medical orderly, was holding his bandaged head on his lap. Rommel drifted in and out of consciousness, heard the engine start, felt the car move, caught bits of sentences like "Luftwaffe hospital at Bernay" and "thirty miles yet." He heard the engine note whine higher and Lang screaming again and again, "Spitfires coming in left!" "Dive bomber coming in right!" Again and again the driver braked and swerved off the highway—was it still Corporal Daniel? Rommel lifted his head each time he heard Lang shout and he tried to get up, while the orderly gently held him down. The head pain stabbed him with sudden spasms, his legs kicked at the instrument panel, but then the car halted and urgent hands lifted him onto a stretcher to carry him to the operating room.

Several times he groaned out loud, "My head, my head." He was being X-rayed, he could feel the cold table and hear hospital sounds. He heard Corporal Daniel's voice, soft and young, as scissors cut away his bloodsoaked tunic: "I must know how my field marshal is. What happened to my car? Don't cut my clothes. . . . Make sure you don't cut up my money." Daniel's voice trailed into silence, into a coma from which he would never awake.

When Rommel himself recovered consciousness the next day, July 18, he was in a second-floor room of the Luftwaffe hospital at Bernay and Lang was sitting patiently at his master's bedside. Lang told him that local Frenchmen had swathed his gashed and battered head in strips of cloth, and that Monsieur Marcel Lescene, the pharmacist at Livarot, had injected two ampules of camphorated oil which had probably saved Rommel's life: it was an old-fashioned but workable way of preventing sudden heart failure.

That same day Rommel won another battle too. His troops defeated Montgomery's last attempt to stage a strategic breakout from Caen. In the red light of dawn 2,000 British and American bombers had come in from the sea, spread out in a great fan and hurled nearly 8,000 tons of bombs at the French city, including deadly fragmentation devices designed to kill or maim anyone in their blast radius. Two thousand French civilians had died and 1,300 more had been injured, and their city had sunk in ruins. The Sixteenth Luftwaffe and 272nd Infantry divisions had been blotted out in Rommel's first line, and at 7:45 A.M. Allied tanks had begun to plunge southward into the smoke and settling dust clouds left by the bombardment. These were the vanguard of over 700 tanks assembled by Montgomery to pour through the breach that he was confident of tearing in Rommel's battle lines.

But this was no ordinary front line. After the first there were a second, a third, a fourth and a fifth line. In the second, some eighty-eights and several of the formidable Tiger tanks had survived. The bombing had not eliminated the third line—infantry-held villages—either. It was late afternoon before the enemy's boldest tank crews even came near the fourth line—massed guns, high up on Bourguébus ridge south of the shattered city. Here Rommel had emplaced nearly eighty 88s, a dozen even bigger antiaircraft guns, 194 field guns and 272 of the

terrifying Nebelwerfer six-barreled rocket launchers—
making a total of 1,632 barrels—commanding the battlefield. Montgomery's intelligence officers had told him
nothing about these lines. Behind the ridge the villages
were also strongly held by SS infantry. In reserve five
miles farther back Rommel had stationed forty-five
Panzer Vs and the remnants of the Hitler Jugend Division
in two strong battle groups, each with forty tanks.

By evening, with 126 enemy tanks destroyed, the offensive had been halted—far short of its objective at Falaise,
short even of the Bourguébus ridge. As the offensive began, Montgomery had issued an exultant announcement to
the world's press; now he had to face the chagrin of withdrawing the Eleventh Armored Division to the river and
calling off the attack. Advised by General Omar Bradley
to grin and bear it, the British commander snapped: "I'm
finding it increasingly difficult to grin." Since D day, the
British had now lost 6,010 killed and the Americans 10,
641, and they had fallen weeks behind their battle planning.

Thus, despite the enemy's crushing use of strategic
bombing forces and despite the damaging Enigma leak,
Rommel had gained a real victory. It was his last, and it
was fitting that it was over his nemesis, Montgomery. At
the time, admittedly, the victory was unrecognized. Kluge
expected the attack at Caen to be renewed immediately
and—without consulting General Speidel—he telephoned
the High Command at midnight to insist on the transfer of
Schwerin's 116th Panzer Division to Caen. It had lain
fallow on the Channel coast since the spring, preserved
by the anti-Hitler plotters for their forthcoming coup d'état.
But Kluge refused to be blinded by Speidel's warnings that
despite the enemy reinforcements sent to Normandy there
were still "fifty-six divisions" waiting in England to launch
a second invasion. Thus the sprectre of "Patton's army
group" had finally been laid. General Jodl approved
Kluge's request a few minutes later, and the Fifteenth
Army's reserves began rolling toward Normandy.

*I had been worried during my research about a certain
puzzle—the omission of important telephone conversations from Rommel's army group diary. Speidel himself*

*warned me to use the diary cautiously—he recalled the field marshal regularly saying of an evening, "Well, Speidel, what lies shall we tell the war diary this time?" So I tracked down the lieutenant whose job it had been to compile it—Hans Dümmler. I interviewed him in his large, paneled boardroom in Munich, where he is now president of one of Germany's most imposing insurance conglomerates. Suave, his face tanned to a leathery brown, and looking twenty years younger than he is, Dümmler at first denied hotly that the diary had been doctored in any way. Then a twinkle came into his eye. "I'll tell you one phone conversation that I did take down in shorthand, and then tore up. It was the shortest conversation I had ever listened in to. It was on the afternoon of July 20, 1944. Somebody telephoned Speidel from Paris. 'Hello, Speidel,' he says. And then just one word: 'Dead.' 'Goodbye,' says Speidel, and put the phone down."*

On July 18, the day of Montgomery's failure to breach the Caen line, Colonel Caesar von Hofacker left Berlin for France. In Paris the next day he told his fellow plotters that the assassin Stauffenberg was about to act. Early on the twentieth, the plotters learned that Hitler was going to be killed at about noon. Colonel Finckh, the Quartermaster West, advised against tipping off Kluge, the Commander in Chief West, in case nothing happened; but Speidel evidently *was* warned, as his later remarks showed. Shortly after 12:30 P.M. Stauffenberg duly planted a suitcase bomb in Hitler's war conference hut in East Prussia. He then escaped and flew back to Berlin. From there he telephoned his associates in Paris. Finckh told Kluge's chief of staff, Blumentritt, "Herr General, there's been a Gestapo coup in Berlin, and the Führer has been assassinated." About three-thirty, Blumentritt tried to reach Kluge at the château, but Speidel told him that Kluge was on the battlefield and would not return until evening. Speidel asked Blumentritt to come to the château at once. Hofacker and Stülpnagel also hurried to La Roche-Guyon.

In Kluge's absence, Speidel refused to take decisions. He withdrew into his office, and when his operations officer, Tempelhoff, inquired what he proposed to do now that Hitler was dead, he pleaded that he was too tied up with the Normandy fighting just now. Speidel's instinct served him well.

The field marshal returned at 6:15 P.M. Speidel told him the news. Kluge too wavered, uncertain whether or not to stop the battle—as the conspirators were urging him to do—in order to do an about-face to fight the Russians. Now he remembered approaches made to him a year before by emissaries from Field Marshal von Witzleben and General Beck. He had sent them packing. "Gentlemen," he had said, "I want you to leave me out of your little game." Twice now the phone rang for him at the château—anonymous calls from Berlin: "Herr Feldmarschall, you've got to make up your mind now." Each time Kluge put the instrument down without speaking. Like Rommel, he had signed that manifesto of allegiance to Hitler in March 1944—he could hardly join a conspiracy now.

At 6:28 P.M. the German radio was interrupted with news of the assassination attempt and the announcement that Hitler had survived: "Apart from minor burns and bruises, the Führer was uninjured." Staubwasser, the intelligence officer, innocently rushed word of the radio bulletin to Colonel von Tempelhoff. The colonel waved it aside. "The Führer is dead," he insisted. "The field marshal, Speidel and I are in the know. It's been in the cards for some time."

Several conflicting telegrams and telephone messages now reached Kluge and Speidel. Some insisted that Hitler was alive, others claimed that he was dead. Hofacker and Stülpnagel implored the field marshal to force Hitler's hand by capitulating in France. Kluge rebuffed them: "If the swine is still alive, my hands are tied. I must obey orders."

At 8:40 P.M. Jodl's deputy, General Walter Warlimont, himself telephoned Kluge from Hitler's headquarters: "This morning a wretched attempt was made on the Führer's life. The Führer is completely unscathed." Kluge hung up, turned to his staff and said unemotionally: *"Ja, an assassination attempt that failed."* Hofacker asked permission now to brief the field marshal more fully on the conspiracy. Kluge nodded, listened quietly, then stood up and absolutely dissociated himself from it. A cold shudder ran down Stülpnagel's spine as it dawned on him that

Hofacker's claim to have won over both Rommel and Kluge was false. "Herr Feldmarschall," he exclaimed, "I was under the impression that you were in the picture!"

Kluge shook his head firmly. *"Nein,"* he replied. "Not an inkling of it."

Speidel was a passive observer of the tragicomedy. There was nothing else he could do.

A formal dinner was then served to all present. Hofacker left the table after a while and went to Tempelhoff, whom he begged to phone Berlin. "Nobody's sure what's happening," said Hofacker. "You know Stauffenberg personally. Can't you phone him and find out?"

Surprisingly, Tempelhoff managed to get a line to the War Office. He spoke with his old war academy comrade Colonel Merz von Quirnheim for a few seconds; then the telephone at the other end went dead. Moments later the door into Tempelhoff's room burst open, and Hans Dümmler, who had been listening in, writing the war diary, snatched the telephone from Templehoff's hand. "Herr Colonel!" he exclaimed. "Don't get involved! It's dynamite!"

After midnight, Hitler himself made a broadcast. His voice was unmistakable, and it was quivering with anger at the outrage. Now there was no doubt at all that the plot had failed. Not long after, Tempelhoff, listening on his phone extension, overheard Kluge call up his son-in-law, an army doctor in a Paris hospital. "I recently asked you about a certain item," said Kluge cryptically. "Can you bring me one at once? . . . I'll have you picked up by a launch from across the river." Kluge had decided that, like General Dollmann, he might need cyanide.

# Who Killed Rommel?

D URING these anxious events at the château, Rommel is far away—still at the Luftwaffe hospital at Bernay, thirty miles from the blood-stained and shell-scarred patch of asphalt where his Horch was shot up. The Luftwaffe's neurosurgical consultant, Professor A. Esch, is treating him. The X rays show that Rommel has sustained a quadruple skull fracture. His survival astonishes the surgeons. One says, "They're going to have to rewrite all the textbooks after this case."

The field marshal is a restless, obstinate and disobedient patient. Esch sedates him with morphine, chloral hydrate and barbiturates, and performs lumbar punctures. He records in his treatment notes that the punctures produce a clear fluid with no blood—a good sign. The field marshal suffers no "major motor deficit" and responds satisfactorily to strong sensory stimuli. But a "complete left oculomotor lesion" makes it impossible for him to open or move his left eye, and he is deaf in his left ear.

In his darkened room, however, Rommel can hear the incessant rumble of army trucks on the highway and the wooden clatter of refugee carts. This is enough to tell him that the battle is not going well. He broods ceaselessly on the danger to his troops if the dam finally bursts in Normandy. When Tempelhoff visits him, Rommel cries out:

"Bicycles! The troops must get as many bicycles as they can, so they don't get cut off."

On July 22 Speidel and Ruge call to pay their respects. As soon as the doctors leave them alone, Rommel swings out of bed and sits up to show how "fit" he now is. Speidel brings him up to date on the battle in the bridgehead. At Caen the British have been checked, although at an appalling cost in German infantry. The Americans captured Saint-Lô on the eighteenth, but so far they have been prevented from gaining a breakthrough there either. Since D day the enemy have lost 2,117 tanks. But Rommel's forces have lost 2,722 officers and over 110,000 men are killed, missing or injured. Incredibly, Speidel still insists that a second invasion is imminent. "In Great Britain there are fifty-two divisions still standing by," he says, "of which about forty-two can be transported to the Continent." His head swimming with pain, Rommel lies down again, and the visitors are ushered out.

One topic was barely mentioned by Speidel to his chief —the fiasco of the attempt on Hitler's life two days before. And Rommel's only comment was: "It's going to have undreamed-of repercussions." But when earlier visitors had brought him the first sensational news of the assassination attempt, Hellmuth Lang had seen how Rommel had blanched and expressed his disgust in forceful terms. He had pressed for details with such urgency that the aide was convinced Rommel had known nothing. Never once, even to his most intimate friends, did the field marshal condone what Stauffenberg had attempted. For Rommel had always been Hitler's man. As Blumentritt later pointed out to Hans Eberbach, "Though Rommel never extolled the Führer, he never strongly condemned him." When Kluge called on him a few evenings later, Rommel kept on repeating, "Madness. Incredible. Against the Führer! Nobody wanted *that*." To Lucie, the field marshal exclaimed as soon as he could dictate a letter, "Coming on top of my accident, the attempt on the Führer's life has given me a terrific shock. We can thank God that things turned out as well as they did."

The conspirators had evidently misunderstood Rommel and Kluge. And Sepp Dietrich, who had earlier told Rommel he would put Rommel's orders ahead of Hitler's, now spoke his fury at the plot. He angrily commented to Admiral Ruge on July 22 that they could thank the sabotage efforts of the conspirators for the failure of the war machine in Germany. ("I hadn't thought of that," Ruge admitted in his diary.) Rommel's other staff took a similar line. His engineer general, Wilhelm Meise, wrote to him, "Today we can see things in quite a different light, Herr Feldmarschall—particularly the constant undercutting of your plans by the inadequate supplies provided by the Quartermaster General." That quartermaster general was Eduard Wagner; he put a bullet through his head after the assassination attempt failed. "The swine!" shouted Hitler, learning of Wagner's treachery. "He did well to shoot himself, otherwise I would have hanged him. In the open countryside of the Ukraine, we have bazookas in abundance where they can't be used. And in the hedgerows of Normandy where our troops can ward off the enemy's superabundance of tanks only with such bazookas, we have none!"

At 5:00 A.M. on July 23, a specially modified automobile gently transported Rommel on a stretcher even farther away from Normandy, to the thousand-bed hospital at Le Vésinet just outside Paris. He was put in a small, brightly furnished private room. "I'm in the hospital now and being well looked after," he dictated to Lucie the next day. "Of course I've got to keep quiet until I can be moved home, and that won't be for another two weeks yet. My left eye's still gummed up and swollen, but the doctors say it will get better. My head's still giving me a lot of trouble at night, but I feel very much better in the daytime."

He continued to be an undisciplined patient, and refused to recognize how serious his injuries in fact were. He repeatedly climbed out of bed, until a surgeon finally brought him a human skull from the pathology department and deliberately battered it in with a hammer: "That's how bad your skull has been crushed. We know that from the X rays." For some days after that the field marshal did as he was told.

Every day Admiral Ruge sat at his bedside and read books to him. Rommel whispered to him that he urgently needed to see Hitler, to discuss Germany's future. "As I see it, our only hope will be to make peace on one front, so that we can commit our entire strength to holding the other," he told the admiral on July 24. And the next day Ruge stenographed this: "Rommel is determined to see the Führer and tell him his views about the situation—and about making a separate peace on one front. Someone's got to tell him."

Every day the doctors had the same battle with him. Rommel wanted to get out and see Hitler, he wanted to resume command in Normandy before it was too late. But every night he was in extreme pain. Lang wrote on the twenty-sixth: "Last night he had an appalling headache, probably because of the hot and oppressive weather." By day Rommel sat impatiently on the edge of his bed, swiping at passing flies with a slipper—but it was difficult to hit them, with only the one eye working. One thing nagged at the back of his mind. The Nazi press had made no announcement of his injury—the whole world still believed he was directing the fighting in France. "Apparently," Lang suggested in a letter, "Rommel's name is still being counted on as a military factor." Rommel himself was less sure—the silence seemed to indicate that the blame for the inevitable collapse was going to be pinned on him. He had received a brief telegram from the Führer: "Accept my best wishes for your further speedy recovery." But after that, nothing.

At first, Speidel's battlefield reports were distinctly encouraging. "So far as they concern the American offensive at Saint-Lô," wrote Lang on July 28, "General Speidel seems very confident. And a line of fortifications appears to be under construction on the eastern front as well." But terrible air raids were now falling on Germany, and Stuttgart—the beautiful capital city of Rommel's native Swabia —suffered cruelly, with nearly 1,000 people killed in the last week of July. Speidel brought stark descriptions of the damage to Rommel, and they deeply affected the field marshal.

The British announced that Rommel had been injured and might even now be dead. Rommel seized the opportunity for a press conference in Paris on August 1, 1944; he struggled to pull a uniform jacket over his hospital pajamas, and he turned his relatively intact profile toward the press photographers. "The British have written me off," he announced to his own staff correspondent, Baron von Esebeck. "But it's not the first time they've pronounced me dead. And I'm not gone yet—not by a long shot."

At approximately the same moment, 900 miles away in his bunker in East Prussia, Adolf Hitler sighed, took off his metal-rimmed eyeglasses, and sent for General Jodl. He still had the document he had been reading in his hand when Jodl stepped into the bunker. It was disturbing proof against Kluge and Rommel, from Gestapo chief Ernst Kaltenbrunner. In his unpublished diary, Jodl noted: "Five P.M.: the Führer asks me to read a report from Kaltenbrunner on the testimony of Lieutenant Colonel von Hofacker about his talks with K. and R. The Führer is now looking for a new Commander in Chief West. He plans to question R. after his recovery, and then to retire him without any further fuss."

What had happened was this. After the macabre supper party at the château on July 20, Kluge had sacked General von Stülpnagel from his staff and privately recommended that he try to escape. Stülpnagel and Hofacker had driven back to Paris in low spirits. Stülpnagel—for whom Rommel had always had a close affection—summoned to Germany by Keitel the next day, attempted suicide. It failed, and in the resulting delirium he was heard murmuring Rommel's name. Hofacker, meanwhile, had been given 4,000 francs by his friend Baron von Falkenhausen and also advised to flee. Far better for Rommel had he done so, but instead Hofacker decided to stay and brazen things out.

Kluge felt compelled to set up a formal commission of inquiry, and all Stüpnagel's staff were questioned, including Hofacker. Just what his motives were for revealing so much, first to Kluge's commission and then to the Gestapo, we shall never know; but there is a powerful clue in Hofacker's remark to his co-conspirator Falkenhausen on July 22: "Why don't I go to Kluge and demand his protection? I can threaten to expose his own ambivalent actions before the assassination attempt."

The temptation for the expendable small fry to shelter behind the names of two popular and powerful field marshals was very strong. Hofacker did not resist it. In a

British prison camp—bugged by hidden microphones—General Blumentritt later described to General Eberbach the curious behavior of Hofacker, which he himself had witnessed. Blumentritt had been telephoned by the Gestapo chief in Paris, SS General Carl-Albrecht Oberg, and invited to sit in on Hofacker's next session at the Hôtel Raphael, Stülpnagel's former headquarters. "Names are being mentioned," Oberg warned Blumentritt in obvious embarrassment as they went in. "And among them that of your boss Kluge! I can't believe it—I'm sure there's been some kind of misunderstanding. Rommel's name has been mentioned too." "Picture the scene," said Blumentritt in 1945. "Here is Hofacker, sitting on a sofa, smoking a cigarette. Everybody's very pleasant. The conversation with Hofacker is nice and friendly. It lasts from about four to eleven P.M. He tells them *everything*, explaining, 'I know my own life is forfeit now.' "

But "everything" is not what Hofacker told the Gestapo. He never once betrayed the real conspirators, his close friends like Speidel, Falkenhausen, Teuchert, Horst and Michel; he put the finger only on the two field marshals—evidently a desperate attempt to escape the firing squad himself.

By July 30, the Gestapo had also interrogated Colonel Georg Hansen, Hitler's new chief of intelligence. Hansen admitted that in Berlin on the sixteenth Stauffenberg, the assassin, and Hofacker had quoted Kluge and Rommel to their fellow plotters as believing that the western front would cave in under the sheer weight of Allied troops and materiel within two weeks.

All these reports went to Hitler.

On August 12, the fugitive Mayor Carl Goerdeler, one of the principal conspirators, was also picked up. Like Hofacker, Goerdeler baffled the Gestapo by inundating them—in Goerdeler's case with documents, statements and lists of alleged fellow plotters. By the fourteenth, this report was also ready. Himmler's liaison officer, the odious Hermann Fegelein, put it to Hitler. On that day a Luftwaffe general attending the noon war conference noted in his diary, "Strained atmosphere. Fegelein hints that even more generals and field marshals are implicated in the Twentieth of July." A few hours later SS chief Heinrich Himmler arrived to see his Führer—and in his brief-case was a note pad with these words as Item 5: "West. Kluge—Rommel." What he told Hitler was the last straw.

Kluge evidently got word of this indictment. All the next day, August 15, he was mysteriously absent from his headquarters. Hitler suspected that the field marshal had been out trying to contact the enemy, so he sacked him immediately and without notice and recalled him to Germany. Kluge swallowed that cyanide pill rather than face the music.

Hofacker was removed to the Gestapo headquarters in Berlin, still singing like a canary. Somebody—probably Finckh—now testified that General Hans Speidel had also known of the assassination plot. By August 25 Hitler was clamoring for that general's arrest. "The interrogations prove that he was in it up to his neck," Hitler insisted. Field Marshal Walter Model, whom Hitler himself had rushed to France as Kluge's successor, flatly refused to part with Speidel—the allegations sounded to him like a monstrous Gestapo fabrication. But Hitler himself was adamant. He selected General Hans Krebs, a hard-nosed officer from the eastern front, to replace Speidel, and he ordered Krebs to clean out Speidel's "thoroughly infected" army group staff first.

Now Hitler learned that Tempelhoff, Rommel's operations officer, was married to an English woman. Also that Hans Lattmann, Rommel's artillery officer, was a brother of Martin Lattmann, a general who had deserted to the Russians at Stalingrad and was now regularly broadcasting from Moscow. To Hitler's suspicious mind, these alien influences probably lay at the root of Rommel's incurable pessimism. Perhaps, thought Hitler, they explained the extraordinary report that Rommel had signed on July 15. Before sending General Krebs out to France, Hitler lectured him. "What he [Rommel] did was the worst possible thing a soldier can do in the circumstances," said Hitler. "He tried to find some other way out than the purely military. At one time, you know, he was also predicting imminent collapse in Italy; yet it still hasn't happened. Events proved him wrong there and justified my decision to leave Field Marshal Kesselring in charge. . . . I regard Rommel, within certain limitations, as being an exceptionally bold and clever commander. But I don't regard him as a stayer, and everybody shares that view."

By this time, therefore, as the shorthand record reveals, Hitler's feeling toward Rommel was one of benign disappointment, rather than malevolence or a sense of betrayal. But this would change when further interrogation reports reached him.

Rommel knew nothing of all these suspicions against him. He was concerned for a time with nothing more momentous than establishing that his recent injuries entitled him to a sixth wound stripe and thus the coveted Golden Wound badge; his personnel file shows that he got it on August 7, 1944. He was mending well at the Paris hospital, but he was pale, his left eye was still closed and there was a thumb-sized dent in his forehead. Hans Lattmann spent thirty minutes alone with him on the sixth and wrote the next day: "It does a soldier good to see how this man's heart beats only for his people and the fatherland, and how conscious he is of his responsibility toward the Führer and his troops. . . . He has only one thought, to get well as soon as possible and return to us."

To this colonel, too, Rommel whispered, "As soon as I'm well again I must see the Führer and tell him bluntly it's time to call a halt—the Germans have suffered too much." And he said much the same to his old friend Colonel Hesse the day after. He told him of the accident, and of his ultimatum of July 15, and of the battle for Normandy. Twice Professor Esch came in to end the visit, and twice Rommel sent him away. "There's only one solution in France," he told Hesse. "We've got to retreat. But the Führer just refuses to see it that way—he's learned nothing from the loss of Stalingrad, he always wants to fight for every square inch of ground. That's going to lose us the war." When Hesse finally rose to leave, wishing Rommel a rapid return to his headquarters, Rommel looked meaningfully at him and commented: "I think that this knock on the head was the best thing that could have happened to me."

That same day Rommel was pronounced well enough to be transported back to Germany, and General Speidel came to take leave of him. At Speidel's request Rommel gave him a photograph, and he scrawled a generous dedication on the back.

On August 8 Erwin Rommel was driven home from Paris to his native Swabia. As he walked unsteadily into the villa at Herrlingen, Lucie and the manservant Rudolf Loistl met him. Rommel saw their horror at his head injuries, and forced a grin: "So long as I don't have to carry my head under one arm, things can't be all that bad." The best brain and eye surgeons were only a few miles away at the University of Tübingen. They were pleased with his progress but warned it would be at least eight weeks before he could return to duty. To his brother Karl he wrote on the twenty-third, "I've got to have absolute rest until all the bits and pieces are properly set again. The first walks outside the house have caused some pretty awful headaches." The neighbors saw him strolling in the garden, unsteadily leaning on Manfred's arm, with the new gold wound badge sewn on his uniform. Occasionally he talked about the assassination attempt—painfully shaking his head in disbelief that anybody would have obeyed the orders that emanated from the plotters in Berlin, let alone from a discredited colonel general like Beck. "Hitler would be much more dangerous dead than alive," he told Manfred. "What I wanted all along was to act independently in the west, and get an armistice."

He was still kept informed daily on his army group's operations, but few officers could come and see him. General Meise wrote on the twenty-sixth, "Your staff pines for you, Feldmarschall, and we hope you will soon recover enough for the Führer to call on you to save the German Reich. And then we shall all want to serve under you again, Feldmarschall." As for the trials of the plotters, Rommel knew little more than what the press reported. Every army officer involved was first being tried by an army Court of Honor; if a prima facie case was made out against him, Hitler discharged him from the army and he was at the mercy of the People's Court. On August 29, this court condemned to death Stülpnagel, Hofacker and their fellow plotters from Paris. All except Colonel von Hofacker were hanged the same day. Hofacker, still talking volubly, was to survive for four more months.

It was in these summer months of 1944 that Rommel first really came to know his son Manfred, now fifteen, and talked to him man to man. Sometimes he spoke of the first years of his marriage: "There's not much to show for all my triumphs," he said, chuckling, "but I can claim one success: I did prevent your mother from bringing a piano into our household." (How Rommel hated piano music!) Manfred had been given leave from his flak unit so that he could read official papers aloud to his father. In France, General Patton had at last appeared in the flesh —but in Normandy, and in command only of an army, not an army group. It had achieved a breakthrough at Avranches, on the coast, and Rommel knew that nothing could now save the German Seventh Army. "How I wish I had just been a shepherd on some Swabian hillside," Rommel said with a sigh.

Once Lucie's brother-in-law Hans Seitz called, wearing his uniform as a Nazi propaganda official. Seitz, a boyhood friend of Rommel's, found himself asking him outright about his attitude to their Führer. Rommel answered that his conscience was clear. "But," he added, "there may be microphones behind the wallpaper," and he led Seitz out into the garden. "For me," he thereupon amplified, "Adolf Hitler is the Supreme Commander and my duty as an officer is to obey. But I've spoken my mind quite plainly to him." Then his face clouded with anxiety: "I hear they've found a briefcase belonging to Goerdeler, and do you know, there was a note in it saying that since I am the only soldier whom the enemy respects, I must take power after the revolution. That may cost me my neck," he observed. Just before Seitz left, Rommel pulled himself upright on the garden seat, covered his good eye and strained his facial muscles to raise the closed eyelid slightly. "You know, I must be getting better, Hans. I think I can see you."

There were odd happenings at the house in Herrlingen. Once Rommel's manservant Rudolf heard something scratching at the front door—and when he jumped up to the window he saw someone flitting into the darkness. The local mayor reported that Frau Wolfel, a neighbor, had seen suspicious characters shadowing Rommel, evidently the Gestapo. After that Rommel obtained an army sentry from the Ulm garrison, and he never went out without a pistol in his pocket. He told Manfred to do the same, since he could not guarantee that he himself could shoot straight. Soon they saw the shadowers themselves, when they strolled in the local woods or went collecting mushrooms around the Upper Herrlingen chapel. One night his sentry opened fire on an intruder. Was the Gestapo really watching him, Rommel must have wondered, and if so, why?

He decided to watch his step more carefully. He had heard of Kluge's sudden death and probably put two and two together. When Colonel Hans Lattmann's crippled seventy-five-year-old mother was arrested by the Gestapo in August as a reprisal for her other son's defection to the Russians, the colonel wrote Rommel asking him to intervene. Rommel wrote back on September 1, politely declining. But, he assured the colonel, "In a few weeks I hope to get back to you all again." That was not to be. Just two days later Erwin Rommel was formally retired from the position of army group commander. His aide Hellmuth Lang confidently predicted, "There's probably some new job lined up already for him to take over as soon as he is well again."

A severe shock awaited Rommel. General Speidel arrived at Herrlingen. He complained to Rommel that his successor, Hans Krebs, had arrived out of the blue with a letter dismissing him and ordering him back to Germany; no reason whatever had been given. Worse was to follow. The next evening Ruth Speidel telephoned him from the Speidel home in Freudenstadt—the Gestapo had arrested her husband and taken him to Berlin. Rommel, ignorant even now of Hans Speidel's involvement in the Stauffenberg assassination plot, could only assume that a witch-hunt was beginning against the western front commanders "responsible" for the collapse in France. From this moment on, he always carried around with him neatly folded copies of the "defense exhibits" he felt he was going to need to justify his decisions at the château, such as the prophetic letters of July 3 and 15 to the High Command.

Speidel's brother-in-law Max Horst, Baron von Falkenhausen and other plotters had been arrested at the same time, and taken to the Gestapo headquarters in Berlin, a building still bearing the enamel plate of the YMCA—the previous Gestapo headquarters had been blitzed. Their guilt was beyond doubt, but since all have survived the war, one gathers that they outwitted their ponderous Gestapo interrogators in one way or another. Falkenhausen, for instance, was confronted on September 6 by a tall, angular plain clothes detective with blond hair and cold fisheyes: "Did you ever discuss with Hofacker the possibility of making a separate peace deal with the West or the East?" After a time, the detective said: "Why not admit that you knew perfectly well about Hofacker's part in the affair? Everybody else has already confessed." And then, as a written statement was drawn up for the baron to sign: "Admit that on July 24, if not earlier, Hofacker told you everything. He has said as much himself"—and he flourished a document with a red top secret stamp. Falkenhausen lied convincingly, and the People's Court eventually acquitted him.

Speidel's turn came some days later. Hitler was convinced that Speidel was guilty—but the general's superior intellect rescued him time and time again. All he would at first admit to the Gestapo, who interrogated him on September 11 and 12, was the stroll in the château grounds with Rommel after Hofacker's visit on July 9, and Rommel's plan to obtain Hitler's permission to meet Montgomery. He admitted visiting Rommel in the hospital on July 22. "Rommel told him," wrote the Gestapo inquisitor Georg Kiessel, "that since the assassination attempt he now felt bound to view that conversation with Hofacker in a very different light."

However, Hofacker's story was significantly different. He claimed to have discussed the actual assassination plot with Speidel, before going in to see the field marshal. The Gestapo hammered away at Speidel to know whether or not he had reported this to Rommel (so evidently Hofacker himself did not claim to have discussed it with Rommel). Either way, Speidel was in a jam. Unless he were to put all the blame on Rommel, he could only accuse Hofacker of lying. Unfortunately, the actual Gestapo interrogation records on Speidel are missing. He himself wrote in an unpublished 1945 manuscript: "The series of interrogations ended with a face-to-face confrontation with Hofacker, lasting several hours. Hofacker had complete control of himself, although showing signs of physical ill treatment. He shielded me magnificently. When his earlier testimony was put to him, he withdrew what he had said about my having been an accessory to the assassination plot, saying, 'My memory must be at fault.'" It must be said that there are reasons to doubt *Speidel's* memory of events, however.

Eventually, Speidel and Hofacker did set their signatures to at least one joint statement of some sort for the Gestapo, because the Gestapo then showed it to Max Horst—so Horst recalled.

*I had walked in heavy rain up the steep hill to Max Horst's villa in an exclusive suburb of Bonn one morning in 1976. His wife, who was Frau Speidel's sister, tactfully withdrew while Horst described his Gestapo imprisonment and interrogations to me. It was Horst, a jovial Central European of medium build and light blue eyes, who had driven Hofacker to the château for the first, innocuous meeting with Rommel in 1944. "The Gestapo didn't use violence or torture us," Horst told me. "They preferred more refined psychological techniques. For instance, I was suddenly awakened at three or four A.M. in Moabit prison, driven across Berlin to the Gestapo and interrogated by intimidating plain clothes officials. They screamed at me, 'You're lying!' but I didn't react to that. Once the official opened a folder, took out a document and covered it so I could see only one line. 'Do you recognize these two signatures?' he shouted. And of course I did—there was Hans Speidel's on the left and Hofacker's on the right. The man shouted at me, 'Either these two are lying, or you are.' After that I was taken back to Moabit prison."*

The weeks of sleeplessness made Rommel moody and incautious. He wrote to Hans Lattmann on September 27, "I'm very dissatisfied with the slow progress my recovery is making. I'm suffering badly from insomnia and constant headaches, and I'm not up to very much at all. You can imagine how hard it is for me to have to remain idle at times like these." He made no secret of his criticism of the direction the war was taking. He heard rumors of Hitler's plan for a mighty winter counteroffensive against the British and Americans in Belgium, and growled at Manfred, "Every shell we fire at them in the west is a shot fired against ourselves." He had no sympathy for the Nazi regime, if it could hound innocent generals like Speidel. When the local Nazi big-wig, Eugén Maier of Ulm, treated him to a sanctimonious lecture—"If we couldn't have faith in our Führer, then whom could we trust?"—Rommel angrily retorted: "You can't have any faith in him at all. Since I saw the Führer in November 1942 I have come to realize that his mental faculties have steadily declined."

There was still no word of poor Speidel's fate—it made the field marshal's blood boil. Ruth Speidel wrote on September 26, and Rommel replied sympathetically on October 1, again mentioning his insomnia and headaches. On the same date he penciled a long letter to Hitler. He began it by regretting that his health was still not good enough for him to accept any fresh burden. "The quadruple skull fracture," he wrote, "the unfavorable turn of events in the west since my injury and not least the dismissal and arrest of my own former chief of staff, Lieutenant General Speidel, of which I learned only by chance, have all placed an intolerable burden on my nerves." He did not stint his praise of the general, and reminded Hitler that he himself had awarded Speidel the Knight's Cross. "In the west Speidel proved in his very first weeks to be an outstandingly efficient and capable chief of staff," Rommel said. "He ran a tight ship, showed a great understanding for the troops and loyally helped me complete the defensive capability of the Atlantic wall as rapidly as possible with the means available. When I drove to the front—which was almost every day—I could rely on Speidel to transmit my orders to the armies as arranged between us beforehand, and to deal with superior and equivalent echelons as I would have myself."

Then followed perhaps the most significant sentence in the letter. "I cannot imagine," wrote the honest and forthright field marshal, "what can possibly have resulted in Lieutenant General Speidel's dismissal and arrest. . . .

Unfortunately," he continued, "it proved impossible to fight the defense of Normandy so that the enemy could be destroyed while still afloat or at the latest while setting foot on land. I set out the reasons for this in the attached letter of July 3, which General Schmundt no doubt showed you at the time." He described his acrimonious relations with Field Marshal von Kluge and concluded the long letter with these words: "You, mein Führer, know how I have done everything in my power and capabilities, be it in the western campaign of 1940 or in Africa 1941/43 or in Italy in 1943 or again in the west in 1944. Just one thought possessed me, constantly—to fight and win for your New Germany. Heil mein Führer!—E. Rommel."

Hellmuth Lang has the pencil draft of this letter. There is a carbon copy in Rommel's personal papers, so it appears to have been forwarded to Hitler. But by this time the field marshal's name was hopelessly contaminated. On September 28 Martin Bormann, Hitler's secretary, had submitted to the Führer a report from a Nazi functionary —evidently Eugen Maier of Ulm, to whom Rommel had spoken so bluntly about Hitler's decline—laying bare Rommel's undiminished hostility to the regime. Five years earlier, during the Polish campaign, Bormann had been publicly snubbed by Rommel; now he could get even. Bormann scribbled this comment on the report: "This confirms other, even worse facts that have already reached me."

The Gestapo interrogations of General Speidel were also complete, and on October 4, 1944, the army's Court of Honor was specially reconvened to hear the evidence. Speidel was not present. As chief of the High Command, Field Marshal Keitel himself presided, with five generals —including, ironically, the cautious Guderian—as the panel of judges. One of the five, however, was killed in a road accident, and Lieutenant General Heinrich Kirchheim, an Afrika Korps veteran whom Rommel had insulted after the failure of the last unsuccessful attack on Tubruk in 1941, found himself ordered to attend. Kirchheim and Guderian both swore affidavits later describing the hearing.

In a sense, not only Speidel but Rommel too was on

trial now—and by the most unfavorable of juries, his fellow generals. The judges had to decide, as it turned out, whom to hang—Speidel or Rommel. According to Kirchheim's testimony, Gestapo chief Ernst Kaltenbrunner (for whom Speidel had developed quite a liking) himself stated the prosecution case. "Speidel," said Kaltenbrunner, "has admitted under interrogation that he was informed of the assassination plot by an emissary from Stülpnagel," no doubt indicating Hofacker. "But Speidel claims to have duly reported this to his immediate superior, Field Marshal Rommel, and he says it is not his fault if the field marshal did not pass his warning on. In fact—this is Speidel's case —he did not realize that Rommel kept the warning to himself."

Kaltenbrunner argued in response to this that Speidel's excuse was not good enough. "If we assume," he continued, "that what Speidel claims did in fact happen, would Rommel really have kept it secret from his own chief of staff that he intended to sit on the warning? The fact remains that if Speidel had himself reported the plot to the High Command, then the assassination attempt could have been nipped in the bud." Thus, Kaltenbrunner argued, Speidel was at the very least an accessory to murder. (Four men had died as a result of the bomb blast, including Rudolf Schmundt—Rommel's friend—who had just succumbed to his injuries after ten weeks of agony.)

"At this," wrote Kirchheim afterward, "there was an uneasy silence. Probably the same thought occurred to the other judges that occurred to me—that the case as set out incriminated not only Speidel but also Rommel, and to a far graver degree." Kirchheim, of course, had had a rough deal from Rommel in 1941; Guderian lost no love for the field marshal either. Both knew that a "thumbs down" for Speidel would clear Rommel. Both opted the other way. When Keitel announced, ominously, "The Führer has expressed the view that there can be no doubt that Speidel is guilty," Kirchheim boldly pointed out that the burden of proof was on the prosecution, and that if General Speidel *said* he had reported the plot to Rommel, it was for the prosecution to prove the contrary. Guderian supported this argument.

Kirchheim described the hearing in a private letter to

Speidel on August 18, 1945. "I spoke out for your acquittal," he wrote, "but your close relationship with Rommel was adduced as being particularly damning, since it appeared to be out of the question for Rommel to have kept from you something as important as this—as not having forwarded your report. Guderian defended you at length, with great force and skill." Thus the ball was put back in the Gestapo's court. Speidel was not thrown out of the army—the People's Court could not get hold of him. And the witch-hunt against Rommel accelerated.

*Distinctly uncomfortable, I had to raise directly with General Hans Speidel the curious question of how he had passed through the jaws of the Gestapo and survived, while Rommel had had to die. Speidel, after all, became one of NATO's top commanders and one of West Germany's most venerated figures. News photographs bear testimony to his solicitude for the Rommel family—Lucie leans heavily on his arm as they attend Bundeswehr military parades to mark the field marshal's anniversaries. Speidel looked me squarely in the eye, and emphatically denied making any statements to the Gestapo. "If Kaltenbrunner produced any," he asserted, "then they were forgeries." I argued that the Gestapo would not have dared to produce forged documents to the six shrewd army officers of the Court of Honor, thereby risking subsequent exposures. Besides, why had Speidel not denied them in his reply to Kirchheim's 1945 letter? I quoted to him one of my favorite ironic lines from the philosopher Friedrich Nietzsche: "My memory says this did happen. But my conscience says 't were better it had not happened. Gradually memory yields to the dictates of conscience."*

*Speidel's family sat in a tense half circle around us, eager for his reply. My pencil waited. He heaved his bulk into an easier sitting position. "Herr Irving," he said finally, "my conscience is clear."*

Three days after the court met, on October 7, 1944, Keitel phoned Rommel's villa to ask him to come to Berlin. "We'll be sending a special train to Ulm to fetch him," he told Rommel's aide. He also stipulated a firm date, October the tenth. Rommel discussed it with his family. "I'm not going to make it easy for these gentlemen," he said. Then he phoned Keitel back, but he was put through instead to General Wilhelm Burgdorf, who had stepped into the dead Rudolf Schmundt's shoes as chief of army personnel and Hitler's chief adjutant.

"What's this meeting going to be about?" inquired Rommel.

Burgdorf's gruff voice replied, "The Führer has instructed Field Marshal Keitel to discuss your future with you." Burgdorf and Rommel were old comrades from the Dresden infantry school days, but the field marshal was still uneasy. "I'm afraid I can't come," he explained. "I've an appointment with my specialists on the tenth, and they say I mustn't make long journeys in my condition."

It seems that he had lost interest now in a new job. He appeared more concerned with small matters. For example, though as a field marshal he was entitled to a car for life, Keitel's office had recently given notice that Rommel's big Horch was going to be taken away from him in mid-October, leaving him with a little BMW that had been converted to wood-gas operation. Rommel was also distracted by premonitions. When Carl Schwenk, an industrialist in nearby Ulm, visited the villa, Rommel remarked: "You won't see me again, they're coming for me." And he quietly told his elderly adjutant, Hermann Aldinger—veteran of the heroic battle for Monte Mataiur—that in the event of his death he wanted to be buried in one of three places, Heidelberg, Heidenheim (his birthplace) or here in Herrlingen—but somewhere small and solitary, not majestic at all. He had always been something of a small and solitary figure.

On the eleventh Admiral Ruge, now retired, came through and for a couple of days they reminisced. Ruge recorded in his diary: "We dined pleasantly on roast venison and a country soup, then went down the road for some champagne. Chatted until well after midnight. The field marshal isn't as fresh as I had expected. He complains about constant headaches and a lack of vitality. For the time being he has turned down Keitel's offer of another job. He's very angry that his car is being taken away from him and that they won't let him keep his sentry at the house. But otherwise he's in good spirits. His eyelid is working again, but the eye doesn't see as well as it did before."

Together Rommel and Ruge drove fifty miles the next morning to Augsburg, with Rommel himself at the wheel. Perhaps this display of vigor was an error, because it contradicted his professed reluctance to go to Berlin because of poor health. This and the other information flowing from Gestapo agents still shadowing him was bound to revive suspicions at Hitler's headquarters. One agent said that the conspirator Karl Strölin, major of Ulm, had visited him, and the agent listed the exact times. Another described Rommel's walks "leaning on his son's arm." Yet another agent had rifled the hotel room of one of Rommel's former officers, at Bad Gastein, and kept watch on the officer from behind a newspaper; the officer's wife had inserted a note in her diary for the agent: "To the snooper. Mind your own business!" But, most damaging, there was the flow of reports from the Gestapo interrogators and from the People's Court. Hofacker had now signed a lengthy statement alleging that Rommel had actually guaranteed the plotters his active support if the assassination succeeded.

After a war conference on October 12, Hitler briefed Keitel—a tall, moustached and distinguished-looking figure who had shared so many other crises with him—to make Hofacker's testimony available to Rommel. Hitler also dictated to Keitel a letter to be handed to Rommel, setting out two alternatives. If Rommel still claimed to be innocent of Hofacker's allegations, then he must report to the Führer. If not, his arrest and trial would be inevitable—and as an officer and gentleman Rommel ought to avoid that by taking the appropriate action. How many times in Prussia's long history had one officer carried a pistol to a fellow officer who had besmirched his profession, and placed it on the table before him!

Keitel, the very personification of a Prussian officer and gentleman, handed the letter and the interrogation reports to General Burgdorf to carry down to Herrlingen in person. He indicated to Burgdorf that it would be better, if Rommel did choose the second alternative, to offer him poison rather than a pistol. His death could then be hushed up as "by natural causes." Burgdorf in turn ordered Major General Ernst Maisel, head of the legal section of the army personnel branch, to accompany him as an official witness.

Hitler had thereby accorded his pet field marshal one last favor, something he had granted to none of the conspirators he had strung up on piano wire. The nation should never learn that Erwin Rommel had gone over to the traitors. Not even Lucie was to be told. Hitler also kept the truth from top Nazis such as Göring and Dönitz. Rommel's personnel files were to contain no hint of this "blemish" on his career.

Early on October 13 Gestapo agents saw Rommel, Lucie and Aldinger drive off in the Horch for one last time—to see Rommel's long-time friend Oskar Farny. About 11:00 A.M., Hitler's headquarters phoned the empty villa. The manservant Rudolf Loistl took the call and answered that the field marshal was out. When General Burgdorf himself phoned, he got the same reply. Burgdorf told Rudolf, "Please be so good as to inform the field marshal that he will be receiving another general and myself tomorrow between noon and one P.M." Before Burgdorf and Maisel set out from Berlin, in a small Opel provided by the Reich Chancellery's motor pool, Maisel phoned his principal aide, Major Anton Ehrnsperger, to meet them on the autobahn near Leipzig at three.

Later that day a message reached the Wehrmacht garrison at Ulm to send an officer to the railroad station to meet the express from Berlin next morning—to pick up a large wreath. The Germans always had known how to plan in fine detail. For several days, in fact, a "Study Group F"—under Burgdorf's Lieutenant Colonel Fressen —had been drafting a program entitled "Sequence for a State Funeral (R.)." Only the date and place still had to be filled in.

When Rommel returns to the villa that evening, he is weary from the long drive, but content: still fearing air attack—or worse—he has deposited with Farny the last of his treasures—his valuables, Leica camera and Lucie's jewelry. When the manservant repeats General Burgdorf's telephone message, Rommel never suspects the real purpose of the generals' coming visit. The optimist in him hopes that he is to be given a new command, perhaps the defense of East Prussia, for the Soviet army is already storming the very frontiers of Germany. He jots down on a blotter the points he is going to raise with Burgdorf first: "Need car for driving to treatment in Tübingen. Motorcycle for staff officer. Secretary. Staff officer." (These are all perquisites to which a German field marshal is traditionally entitled for life.) But then the pessimist in him speaks. Suppose he is, after all, going to be tackled about the reasons for the military collapse in France? The next morning, October 14, wearing his favorite brown jacket, the field marshal walks with young Manfred, who is in the gray-blue uniform of a Luftwaffe auxiliary. Rommel muses out loud: "There are two probabilities today. Either nothing happens at all—or this evening I won't be here."

At the Ulm railroad station, the wreath has already arrived.

On the autobahn not many miles away, Burgdorf's Opel stops briefly near a powerful eight-seater police limousine, packed with plain clothes men. From the snatches of conversation he overhears, Major Ehrnsperger realizes that their commander in chief is in charge of the surveillance of Rommel's movements.

At the villa Rommel changes into his open-collared Afrika Korps tunic. Then he puts on his Pour le Mérite—its blue enamel chipped and dented from the car crash. He sends for Rudolf and says: "Open the garden gate—the two gentlemen will be coming from Berlin."

Promptly at noon the bell jangles. Rudolf opens the front door, and the final act of the drama begins.

Wilhelm Burdorf steps in. He is a large and florid man. His deputy, Ernst Maisel, is somewhat shorter, with a long pointed nose, foxy ears and twinkling eyes. Both are at pains to act courteously and correctly. Everyone salutes. Lucie invites the two to stay for lunch, but Burgdorf declines: "This is official business." He asks if they can talk privately with Herr Feldmarschall. For no reason at all, a feeling of relief floods over Rommel—the generals note the expression on his face—but all the same, as he takes his visitors through into his ground floor study, he turns to his adjutant and says: "Have that Normandy dossier ready, Aldinger!"

Meanwhile, Major Ehrnsperger waits in the garden. He is joined there after a while by Aldinger, and they chat about the Dresden infantry school, where Rommel was the major's instructor, and about the battle of Monte Kuk in 1917.

Rudolf walks out to the little Opel and invites the driver to bring it in through the gate. The driver shakes his head. "That doesn't make sense," sniffs Rudolf.

The driver coldly retorts, *"Kamerad,* you do what you're told and I do what I'm told."

Farther down the lane Rudolf can see another, larger car waiting.

In the study Burgdorf looks gravely at his old friend and then speaks. His first words cruelly destroy all Rommel's expectations. "You have been accused of complicity in the plot on the Führer's life," he declares, and hands over the letter from Keitel. Burgdorf reads out the written testimonies of the army officers under Gestapo arrest—Hofacker, Speidel, Stülpnagel. They are damning indictments, particularly Hofacker's. He hands the testimonies to Rommel: the doomed colonel has described from his death cell how Stülpnagel sent him to see the field marshal with various proposals, and how "after some thought" Rommel agreed to them. The colonel now even claims that as he was leaving the château Rommel called after him, "Tell your gentlemen in Berlin that when the time comes they can count on me."

Burgdorf sees an agonized expression flicker across Rommel's features. How can Rommel explain that he had no part whatever in the assassination plot—never even knew about it? That "all" he was contemplating was a possible separate armistice with Montgomery, with or without the Führer's consent? Even to admit that will put him on the scaffold now. His life is forfeit—but perhaps he can at least save Speidel's. He hesitates and then announces, according to General Maisel's recollection: *"Jawohl.* I will take the consequences. *Ich habe mich vergessen* [I forgot myself]."

After this candid admission there can be no going back.

He quickly asks Burgdorf, "Does the Führer know about this?" Burgdorf nods. Rommel's eyes mist over, and Burgdorf asks Maisel to leave them alone for a few minutes. He now states what is not in the letter—the Führer's promise that if Rommel will commit suicide, then the secret of his treason will be kept from the German people, a fine monument will be erected in his memory and there will be a state funeral. The usual steps, moreover, will not be taken against his next of kin; on the contrary, Lucie will draw a full field marshal's pension. "This is in recognition of your past services to the Reich."

Still stunned by the unexpectedness of it all, Rommel asks for a few minutes to think things over. He is tired and unsteady. How ironic that he, Erwin Rommel, who has survived bombs, aircraft cannon fire, tank shells and rifle bullets in two world wars, should have to die now because of a failed conspiracy to which he has never been a party, organized by a General Staff to which he did not belong!

"Can I take your car and drive off quietly somewhere?" he asks Burgdorf. "But I'm not sure I can trust myself to handle a pistol properly."

"We have brought a preparation with us," Burgdorf softly replies. "It works in three seconds." He joins Maisel and Ehrnsperger in the garden while Rommel goes upstairs to Lucie's bedroom.

Rommel's face is an expressionless mask. "In fifteen minutes I will be dead," he tells Lucie in a distant voice. "On the Führer's instructions I've been given a choice between taking poison or facing the People's Court. Stülpnagel, Speidel and Hofacker have implicated me in the July twentieth conspiracy. And it seems I was nominated as the new Reich President on the list of Mayor Goerdeler." He bids Lucie his last farewell. She does not weep—the tears come only later, when she is alone. Neither of them has expected this sudden twist in his fortunes. She feels faint, but bravely returns his last embrace.

Afterward he tells Rudolf to fetch his son, and announces with a steady voice what is about to happen. Then he sends Manfred to get Aldinger. Captain Aldinger bounds up the stairs carrying the Normandy dossier.

Rommel waves it aside: "I won't be needing it—they came about something quite different." Downstairs, the generals are waiting.

It has turned into a fine autumn day. By the time he walks down the steps, Rommel has recovered his poise. Rudolf helps him into his topcoat and hands him his cap and field marshal's baton. Rommel shakes hands with his staff and strides out of the villa for the last time, Manfred loping silently at his side. In his pocket Rommel finds his house keys. He hands them with his wallet to Manfred. "Speidel has told them I was one of the leading men in the July twentieth conspiracy," he tells his son. "He says that only my injury prevented me from taking a direct part. Stülpnagel said much the same."

They have reached the Opel now. Burgdorf salutes and murmurs: "Herr Feldmarschall!" Manfred marvels at his father's composure. Rommel puts his foot on the running board, then turns around and says, "Manfred, I think Speidel's probably had it, too. Take care of Frau Speidel, won't you?"

He climbs into the back of the car with Burgdorf. The driver, an SS master sergeant, lets in the clutch, and the Opel vanishes down the road toward the next village.

The driver was thirty-two-year-old Heinrich Doose. He later told what followed. After 200 yards Burgdorf ordered him to pull over. "I had to get out," he said, "and General Maisel walked on with me up the road for some distance. After a while, about five or ten minutes, Burgdorf called us back to the car. I saw Rommel sitting in the back, obviously dying. He was unconscious, slumped down and sobbing—not a death rattle or groaning, but *sobbing*. His cap had fallen off. I sat him upright and put his cap back on again."

## WHO KILLED ROMMEL?

Plötzlich und unerwartet verschied nach seiner schweren Verwundung vom 17. 7. 1944 im 53. Lebensjahr mein geliebter Mann und der treueste Freund seines Sohnes, unser lieber Bruder, Schwager und Onkel

**Generalfeldmarschall Erwin Rommel**

Ritter des Ordens Pour le Mérite
Inhaber des Ritterkreuzes mit Eichenlaub, Schwertern und Brillanten, des goldenen Verwundetenabzeichens und anderer hohen Auszeichnungen.

Sein Leben war Dienst am Vaterland.

In tiefer Trauer im Namen aller Angehörigen
Frau **Lucie-Maria Rommel**
**Manfred Rommel**, z. Zt. Luftwaffenhelfer.

Herrlingen b. Ulm, am 14. 10. 1944.

Von Beileidsbesuchen wird gebeten, Abstand zu nehmen.

# Inquest

ONE episode captures the essence of Erwin Rommel. It took place in 1944, during the last fatiguing weeks before the Normandy landings. Rommel, during his excursions, often paused for lunch or afternoon tea at the hostels run for his troops by German women's units. Pretty air force girls and nurses used to besiege him for autographs, and some were so bedazzled by this famous and virile soldier that they embarrassed him with gifts, favors and affectionate offers. On this day their avidity and the scent of their French perfumes roused even the dour field marshal. As he stepped out of one such home to his waiting Horch, he turned to General Wilhelm Meise, his chief engineer. "You know, Meise," he said with a wry grin, "some of those girls are so darned attractive I could almost be a rat!"

But Rommel knew he never would. If there was one quality that was supremely his, it was instinctive fidelity.

As soon as the war was over, Rommel began to be linked with the plotters around the assassin Stauffenberg. It was probably inevitable. In April 1945 young Manfred revealed that his father had committed suicide after Generals Burgdorf and Maisel had visited the house in Herrlingen—only that, but it was enough to allow people to draw conclusions. So many other high-ranking officers, after all, had been tied to the plot and then killed themselves. But to the Rommel family, who still believed the anti-Hitler plot dastardly, and loyalty to Hitler a field marshal's only proper course, the link with Stauffenberg was a smear. On September 9, 1945, Lucie issued a statement. "In order to keep the name of Rommel clean," she said, "and to uphold the field marshal's honor as a son of Württemberg, I want it made quite clear that my husband had no part whatever in the preparations for, or the execution of, the July 20 plot. My husband always stated his opinions, intentions and plans quite candidly to the very highest authorities, even if they did not like it."

That was certainly the truth. But the plotter label clung to Rommel. The Americans, for example, still in the grip of the Rommel myth and ready to conclude that their favorite Nazi, Rommel, must surely have been part of the plot against their arch-foe, Hitler, treated Rommel like a hero of the German resistance and hunted down every general felt to have had a hand in his Socratic death. Keitel was accused at the Nuremberg trials of having "murdered" Rommel. On June 6, 1945, the homestead of his friend General Meise was officially turned over to looters by the American commandant of Berchtesgaden —they had confused Meise with General Ernst Maisel, who had accompanied Burgdorf to Herrlingen with the poison.

But the genesis of the myth of Rommel the plotter went back, of course, to Colonel von Hofacker and General Speidel. Hofacker, through wishful thinking or calculation, had left his meetings with Rommel at the château telling all and sundry that Rommel had been won over. And in his first Gestapo interrogations, on July 22, 1944, he stated it as a fact. Speidel had been more subtle, both before and after July 20, but the effect was similar.

Speidel's reasons for implicating Rommel, however, went beyond the conspiratorial, in the first instance, and self-justification, in the second. During the postwar years, for quite another purpose, he set out to build up the "plotter" Rommel legend. By 1946 it was plain to even the dullest German that in postwar Germany only those with a proven connection to the Stauffenberg plotters would be considered reliably anti-Nazi and be given power. Speidel had been Rommel's chief of staff. If Rommel could be cast in the role of honorable conspirator and maintained as such, then Speidel's credentials as a plotter would gain legitimacy. If Rommel could be made into a figure eligible for exaltation in postwar Germany, then Speidel, by association, would be exalted too. He admitted quite frankly to another German general in an American prison camp in 1946: "I intend making Rommel into the hero of the entire German people."

In a book which Speidel published upon his release from captivity, he proceeded to construct the myth. It was a book that was to blind and bedevil history ever after. Briefly summarized, his argument held that beginning with April 1944—the time of his arrival as Rommel's new chief of staff—a stream of plotters marched in columns of four through the portals of the château, where Rommel warmly greeted them and assured them that he supported their plans and devices and was willing to assume power after Hitler's overthrow. There is no evidence in support of Speidel's account. On the contrary, Rommel's own private letters and his remarks as recorded at the time by his staff officers and Friedrich Ruge and Hellmuth Lang disclose his continued, though eventually strained, loyalty to Hitler throughout the entire period. Speidel's general historical accuracy can be judged from his contention that Rommel had always expected the invasion to hit Normandy (Speidel's "hero" had to be prescient), and that it was Hitler and the foolish generals of the High Command who had obliged him to tie his reserves down to the Fifteenth Army's sector until mid-July of 1944.

Apparently, Speidel's gambit worked. Rommel became indelibly the myth-marshal and Speidel, aglow with reflected glory, rose from prisoner of war to become the new commander of the army of the Federal Republic of West Germany and, later, a top general of the North Atlantic Treaty Organization. Ruge, by a like process, came to command Germany's new navy.

What is the truth? There is no doubt that by mid-June of 1944 Rommel had become aware of the basic criminality of the Hitler regime. From Ruge's shorthand diary we know that Rommel had begun talking of his troubled feelings, mentioning the rumors of "big massacres" by the Nazis and of the killing of fifty escaped British airmen at Sagan prison camp, and his suspicion that Hitler's hands were "not clean." As the battle in Normandy tilted ever more against him, Rommel began to indulge in daydreams. He began flirting with the idea of acting against Adolf Hitler's commands and dealing directly with the enemy. But he probably knew that he never would. He was like the faithful husband who occasionally finds satisfaction in fantasies of infidelity, but never actually commits adultery. "I could almost be a rat!" he had said to Meise. Almost, but not quite.

Yet he was brave enough to go much farther than most generals in stating his views to Hitler. Twice in June 1944 he orally told the Führer that it was time to draw conclusions; in July he had sent his grave and outspoken ultimatum, designed for Hitler's eyes; and he had tried to enlist Field Marshal von Kluge in a joint approach to Hitler. The rest—the "letter to Montgomery," the idea of voluntarily opening the Normandy front to the enemy, the naïve idea of a joint German/British/American drive against the Red Army—these projects just lurched around Rommel's brain and surfaced occasionally in conversation with his most trusted intimates. Not, of course, that he could volunteer this subtle point in his own mitigation when Burgdorf and Maisel called at the house in Herrlingen in October 1944.

Like the marriage vow he had sworn to Lucie in Danzig in 1917, the oath of allegiance he and every officer had sworn to the Führer in 1934 was inhibiting enough to prevent a man of Rommel's convictions from actually "cheating." Besides, he and the active field marshals had personally signed a second testimony of allegiance to Hitler in March 1944. Non-Germans may find it difficult to accept that upstanding generals could become tyrannized by their own oath of allegiance. But they were—their entire military careers had been dominated by it and by the ethos that superior orders have to be obeyed. Victories had flowed from it, defeats had been impeded. Rommel demanded instant obedience from his juniors, and he liked to believe he was an obedient man himself. Had he not written in July 1941 to his commander in chief, Brauchitsch: "Above all I must demand from my officers that they set an example and obey"? Had he not sternly advised his own son in December 1943: "Obey without question"?

And how Hitler's generals had obeyed! In the First World War, when Germany had lost 2 million men in battle, only ten of those casualties were generals. In Hitler's war every combat general right up to army group level went onto the battlefield himself, flying by Storch, driving in tanks or armored cars or crawling on hands and knees. Literally hundreds of them were killed in action, in blind obedience to their oath, however hopeless the situation seemed. The agony, the conflict within Rommel between the dictates of his conscience and his allegiance to Hitler, can be seen mirrored in the strength of feeling on this issue for years after the war. General Blumentritt—Rundstedt's chief of staff—wrote down his own reactions in 1947 on learning from Speidel for the first time that he had been one of the Stauffenberg plotters. "I still cannot change my own opinion," wrote Blumentritt. "An oath is an oath and remains an oath, particularly in 'impossible' or 'hopeless' situations—that's when the oath is needed most. . . . Troops fighting for their lives have a basic right to expect their commanders to be loyal, even when the going gets too rough."

What can we say about Rommel the man?

Born, like any other child, without adjectives, he had accumulated few that were out of the ordinary in his infancy and youth. As a schoolboy he was frail but diligent, as a young man he became disciplined, tough and inventive. As a husband and father he was affectionate, devoted and imaginative.

It was in the army that he first began the ascent to distinction. He was fearless, brave, resourceful, reckless, self-confident. He was ambitious: though conscious of his humble origins as a schoolmaster's son, he aspired to the highest goals and was impatient for the power and responsibility of high rank. In the last weeks of his life he admitted to Manfred, "You know, even as an army captain I already knew how to command an army!" In all his life there was never one instance of his showing personal fear, and he went to his rendezvous with death with the same unflinching tread as he had gone into battle all his life.

Age, maturity and rank did add less enviable qualities, it is true. He became dogmatic, reluctant to heed professional and superior advice, brash, immodest and oversensitive to rebuke.

As Hitler said of him in August 1944, "He is not a real stayer." General Ferdinand von Senger und Etterlin, himself a fine panzer commander, recognized in Rommel a common type of officer defect: during any run of victories he was a real source of inspiration to his men; but he was all too rapidly discouraged by defeats.

As a strategist, Rommel was shortsighted. He saw only the immediate welfare of his own troops as an issue, while blindly refusing to accept that political or strategic considerations might demand a course of action that seemed tactically unacceptable. For instance, he allowed his ignorance of Hitler's grand strategy in 1941—the forthcoming attack on Russia—to lead him to a fateful overextension of his own forces in Libya. In 1943, Rommel could not see any profit at all in playing for time—but from Allied files now released to scrutiny, we perceive how inconvenienced Churchill and Roosevelt were by Hitler's stonewalling tactics in Italy and the Balkans. At times, in fact, Rommel seems to have been guided only by one thought—to retreat into Germany as fast as his troops could travel. It did not noticeably perturb him that his accelerated retreat from Libya into Tunisia, and later from southern Italy toward the Alps, was exposing the Balkans to enemy invasion or the southern Reich to Allied strategic bombing. When the danger of the Italy-based strategic bombers dawned on him, in the summer of 1943, he concerned himself only with trivia—like the safety of his bank account in Wiener Neustadt.

When, as often happened, events went against him, self-pity swamped Rommel's writings. His letters home to Lucie appealed for her compassion and sympathy. He blamed everybody else for his predicament, and never once himself—as well he might have, for having in 1941 thumbed his nose at Franz Halder's dark warnings about the likely supply difficulties, or for overreaching the stop lines dictated to him by Berlin and Rome. His hostility toward men like Halder and especially General Alfred Jodl, one of Germany's most perceptive strategic thinkers, revealed Rommel's poor judgment of character; so did his praise for generals like the weak Cherbourg commandant General von Schlieben.

Yet for all these shortcomings, Rommel's ability was undeniable. As Hesse said, "He was extremely hard, not only with others but with himself as well. There was a dynamo within him that never stopped humming, and because he was capable of great feats he expected a lot from his subordinates as well, and didn't recognize that normal human beings do have their physical and mental limits." We can remember Rommel's genius for the unexpected, his mechanical gifts, his original tactical devices. Combat troopers are not fools; they can sift the charlatans from the great commanders. Without exception, Rommel's troops—of whatever nationality—adored him.

History will not forget that for two years he withstood the weight of the entire British Empire on the only battlefield where it was then engaged, with only two panzer divisions and a handful of other ill-armed and undernourished forces under his command. He was a twentieth-century Hannibal—there is no doubt of it. Hannibal too was clean, upright, beloved by his troops. He too triumphed by cunning, and by his deadly and accurate assessment of the numerically superior enemy's intentions; he too fought on distant battlefields, bereft of adequate support from home. Just as Hannibal had used the ancient Gauls to hold the center at Cannae, and his African cavalry to encircle the Romans, Rommel stationed his long-suffering Italian allies in the front line, while his mechanized panzer elite outflanked the enemy. Both warriors fought their last great battles on almost the same ground—Hannibal at Zama, Rommel at Kasserine. And Hannibal too was forced to swallow poison by his enraged compatriots.

What monuments now stand to Rommel? There is a bare wooden cross above the grave that holds his ashes. And there is a stone memorial at Kilometer 31 before

Tobruk on the Via Balbia, commanding the graves of all his fallen soldiers, the "Africans" of whom he was so proud—Prittwitz, Ponath, Sümmermann, Neumann-Silkow, Bismarck and so many more. Once a year survivors come to greet them in his name, and that is his other monument: he lives on in their memory. And when the hot storm blows, and the skies cloud over with red, flying sand, and the *ghibi* begins to howl, perhaps they hear once more a Swabian voice rasping in their ears: *"Angreifen!"* "Attack!" And then a fainter cry: "Mount up!" And then the thunder of the panzer columns starting their engines and rolling off eastward against the enemy.

# Acknowledgments

ERWIN Rommel would be approaching his ninetieth year if he were still alive today. So even if he had been a man of many friends—which he was not—their number would be dwindling. Any biographer of Rommel is forced, therefore, to rely more heavily on the documents and less on the human memory; and the documents are deposited in towns no less widely dispersed than the surviving few who with justifiable pride call themselves his friends. Without exception, however, the archives' staffs have made my repeated visits really enjoyable. I will mention first the West German Bundesarchiv-Militärarchiv at Freiburg—where the Rommel Papers are deposited in duplicate, under severe access limitations imposed by the family—and the Bundesarchiv-Zentralnachweisstelle at Cornelimünster and the Bundesarchiv itself at Koblenz. The Cabinet Office Historical Section in London provided me with German papers on Rommel not seen before, and I am thankful to Clifton Child and Mrs. Nan Taylor for them. Equally, Lieutenant Commander Mal J. Collet, USNR, provided great hospitality and assistance at the archives of The Citadel, the famous military academy at Charleston, South Carolina. The staffs of the National Archives in Washington and the Imperial War Museum in London bore my several visits with much fortitude, and I have reason to be grateful to Professor Messerschmidt of the West German defense ministry's Militärgeschichtliches Forschungsamt as well. Finally, the later chapters of this book rely heavily on materials disclosed to me by the Institut für Zeitgeschichte in Munich, where the Sammlung Irving—as they are generous enough to call the section of their vaults housing my documents collection— has accordingly been enhanced by approximately six cubic feet of the documents and diaries I assembled for the writing of this book.

So much for archives. Many of the fine photographs come from negative originals supplied by Hans Asmus Baron von Esebeck, whose father was the famous war reporter on Rommel's staff; most of the rest—and much of the documentation—comes from Manfred Rommel, Lord Mayor of Stuttgart and son of the field marshal. He himself plans one day to write about his father, and I know what qualms he must have overcome before letting me use his precious documents and photographs before he does. I am happy to place on record my indebtedness to Manfred Rommel's generosity and Frau Lilo Rommel's hospitality. I spoke twice with Lucie Rommel before she died; it is to her that I owe my good fortune in obtaining access to the Rommel correspondence, which otherwise remains sealed for many decades to come.

Hellmuth Lang donated to me large portions of the 1944 Rommel diary and other papers, and many of the photographs are from his collection. Vice Admiral Friedrich Ruge lent me his transcripts of his own shorthand diaries—and allowed me to check them where necessary against the Gabelsberg stenography of the original —and Lieutenant Colonel Adalbert von Taysen allowed me to read his own official history of *Tobruk 1941* in manuscript form before publication. Lastly, I must thank Wilfried Armbruster, of Milan, for lending me his entire diaries, written while he was Rommel's interpreter from 1941 to 1943, although he, like Manfred Rommel, was originally thinking of publishing something himself one day.

Of those who rendered personal recollections or assistance I will single out only these: Alistair Bannerman, for permission to quote his extraordinary D day diary; K. H. von Barsewisch; Hans-Otto Behrendt; Antonie Böttcher; Peter von Bredow (Guderian's adjutant in 1944); Anthony Cave-Brown, for the papers on the 1944 attempt on Rommel's life; Ernst H. Dahlke; the Deutsches Zentralarchiv, Potsdam, East Germany, for information on Hofacker's trial; Hans Dümmler; Anton Ehrnsperger; Gotthard Baron von Falkenhausen; Oskar Farny; Fridolin Fröhlich, for the hunting license valid in occupied France in 1944; Heinz-Günther Guderian, son of the famous panzer general and a leading Bundeswehr tank commander in his own right; Wolfgang Hagemann; Kurt Heilmann; the late Professor Kurt Hesse, for access to the papers he had collected for his own biography of Rommel before a dispute with Lucie stifled the project. Also Eberhard von Hofacker; Arthur Holtermann; Anton Hoch; W. M. James, of North Carolina, another would-be Rommel biographer who found the subject one of such sheer immensity that he was glad to make his own invaluable collection available to me instead; Ernst Jünger, for permission to quote from his diaries; David Kahn, for material on Colonel Bonner Fellers; Hildegard Kirchheim, for excerpts from her husband's papers; Gerhard Lademann; Hans Lattmann; Ronald Lewin—himself author of accomplished books on Rommel and the Afrika Korps—for casting a professional eye over early drafts of this book. Also Rudolf Loistl; Ernst Maisel; Johanna Martin —who gave me the fine autographed Rommel portrait that forms the frontispiece; Fritz Memminger; Wilhelm Meyer-Detring; Egon Morasch; Constantin Baron von Neurath; Winston G. Ramsey, editor of *After the Battle* magazine; Hellmuth Reinhardt; Hans Roschmann; Fabian von Schlabrendorff; Gerhard Count von Schwerin; Hans Seitz; Hans Speidel, for extracts from a still unpublished 1945 manuscript he wrote about his period of Gestapo interrogation and subsequent fortress arrest. Also Anton Staubwasser, for patiently explaining again and again how Army Group B arrived at its intelligence estimates in 1944; Johannes Streich; Ernst Streicher, Rommel's adjutant, for photographs and combat reports dated 1917; Hans-Georg von Tempelhoff; Elmar Warning;

# ACKNOWLEDGMENTS

Siegfried Westphal; Konrad Baron von Woellwarth—one of Guderian's 1944 staff—and Eberhard Wolfram.

Finally, I am grateful to Carla Venchiarutti for her work in the archives and interpretation of the Italian documents; and all historians, not just I myself, owe a debt to Jutta Thomas for her patient deciphering of the shorthand Rommel diaries.

DAVID IRVING

*London*
*June 1977*

# The Sources

BA-MA    Bundesarchiv-Militärarchiv, the West German military archives at Freiburg.

CO    Cabinet Office file, now in Imperial War Museum, London.

CSDIC    Combined Services Detailed Interrogation Center.

IFZ    Institut für Zeitgeschichte (Institute of Contemporary History), Munich.

MGFA    Militär-Geschichtliches Forschungsamt, the research branch for military history of the West German defense ministry, Freiburg.

*MR*    *Marine Rundschau,* journal.

NA    National Archives, Washington, D.C.

OCMH    Office of Chief of Military History. Its files of German military studies (MS) are now in the NA.

SI    Sammlung Irving, the collection of David Irving's research documents archived at the IFZ, open to all researchers (occasionally subject to donor restrictions).

T-    NA microfilm serial number.

*VFZ*    *Vierteljahrshefte für Zeitgeschichte,* quarterly published by IFZ.

*WR*    *Wehrwissenchaftlicher Rundschau,* journal.

ZS    Document series at IFZ.

# BASIC DOCUMENTS

The very earliest records are in Rommel's personnel files. Two folders exist, CO, AL.451; and BA-MA. Pers.6/5 (also an OCMH photocopy in NA, X-672/3). These contain summaries of his combat experience. From Ernst Streicher I obtained carbon copies of Major Theodor Sproesser's battalion action reports for the period of October 24 to December 9, 1917. They can be compared with Rommel's own manuscript history (T84/277, /278), the official history published years later by the Reichsarchiv, volumes 12a and 12b, and the supplement that Rommel obliged them to print, *Nachtrag zu den Bänden 12a und b.* Additionally, there exist a number of letters written between the war years by Rommel to his family and friends.

Apart from his letters, the main source on his period as commandant of the Führer's headquarters is its war diary (T77/858). I also drew on the diary and letters of Colonel Nikolaus von Vormann, one of Hitler's liaison officers at that time. Extensive records on the French campaign in 1940, exist; I used particularly Rommel's own manuscripts (T84/275 to /277) (later published in part by Basil Liddell Hart as *The Rommel Papers*), the war diary of the Seventh Panzer Division and the manuscripts of one of his panzer battalion officers, Lieutenant Ulrich Schroeder (BA-MA, N 20/2). Rommel's exploits in this campaign also generated, of course, countless articles in the Nazi newspapers—*Das Reich, Völkischer Beobachter, Signal* and *Die Wehrmacht,* to list only four.

Any historian writing on the North African fighting between February 1941 and March 1943 is confronted by an embarrassing mountain of documentation. Again, Rommel's own papers (T84/276 and /277) serve as a starting point, as well as his own letters. At the highest level are the files of the OKW (German High Command). I also used Helmuth Greiner's pencil draft of its war diary, items on microfilm T77/780 and General Staff files (T78/324 to /326). I referred extensively to the Naval High Command's war diary and its special appendixes on the Mediterranean, supply problems, coalition warfare and Italy

(BA-MA, files PG/31780, 31747, 32212, 32446, 32447, 33102, 33316, 39971, 45044, 45056, 45098, 45133, 45134, 45137). The German army records also exist in abundance: the war diaries of the Afrika Korps (T314/2, /15, /16, /18, /21, /23 and BA-MA, RH 24—200/77); of Panzer Group Afrika (T313/423 and /430); of Panzer Army Afrika (T313/423, /430 and /467, /471 to /475 and /480), with many duplicates—the OCMH files X-714 to X-729 at the NA, and CO files AL.743, AL.866 and AL.500 at the Imperial War Museum, and in Rommel's own papers (T84/279). The war diary of Army Group Afrika exists only in Rommel's papers (T84/273, /276 and /282). For the last stages of the campaign, material was also derived from the war diary of Arnim's Fifth Panzer Army (T313/416).

Extensive documentation survives from the German divisions under Rommel's command in Africa: the war diaries of the Ninetieth Light (T315/1155 to /1159), the Fifteenth Panzer (T315/664 to /667) and the Twenty-first Panzer (T315/767 to /769). The war diary of the Fifth Light Division (early 1941) was also recently retrieved and is now in BA-MA (file RH 27—21/52.) Some records of the Italian units fell into German—and subsequently into American—hands, and will be found on NA microcopy T821; they include the records of the Ariete Armored Division at El Alamein, General Messe's account of the Battle of Mareth and similar items. I also used the records of the Italian High Command (Comando Supremo) on microfilms T821/125 and /252, and General Ambrosio's diary (T821/144). The messages sent by the liaison officer, Constantin von Neurath, to Berlin will be found in German foreign ministry files (the files of the Secretary of State and the Undersecretary of State relating to the war in Africa).

Interestingly, Rommel kept a special record of signals relating to his 1942 illness (T84/277). Finally, I made some use of the Canaris/Lahousen "fragments" (CO, AL.1933), the war diary of the German army personnel branch (T78/39) and the unpublished diaries of Joseph Goebbels, Erhard Milch, Hoffmann von Waldau, Walther Hewel and Wolfram von Richthofen. My exclusive transcript of the Rommel diaries—dictation taken by Corporal

Albert Böttcher between November 1941 and March 1943 —is now deposited at the BA-MA. Other items in the same file include hastily written notes of meetings between Rommel and Italian commanders during the summer of 1941.

The main source on Rommel's command of Army Group B during its preparations for the military occupation of Italy (code names Alarich and Axis) is the Rommel diary, May 9 to September 6, 1943. Kept in the first person, the diary exists in virtually illegible photostats in London and Washington (e.g., on T84/283). I have deposited a clean retranscript of the diary in the IFZ, SI. From September 1943 onward, the war diary of Army Group B is intact, in the Rommel Papers (T84/280 et seq.); see too its appendixes, T311/276. I also used the war diary of Gruppe Feurstein, later known as the Fifty-first Corps (T314/1263, /1264 and /1270) and the Forty-fourth Infantry Division (T315/2371)—both of which were heavily involved with the military infiltration of northern Italy in the summer of 1943. I drew also on the records of the Italian High Command and army units confronting the Germans there (T821/21, /248 and /353). The German High Command records of Axis and Alarich are on NA microfilms T77/792 and /893; German naval files on this episode are in the BA-MA, PG/32216 and /32217. Records of Rommel's several heated conferences with his Italian counterparts will be found in his diary (see above) and in the Italian files (T821/249 and /252).

While the war diary of Army group B continues throughout Rommel's last campaign in France in 1944 (T84/280 to /282) and there are many volumes of important appendixes (T311/1, /3, /4, /24 and /278), there is a gap in the Rommel diary after September 1943. From November 21, 1943 to February 22, 1944, it was kept for him by Lieutenant Hammermann, his one-eyed aide (OCMH file X-501) and from March 5, 1944, by Captain Hellmuth Lang. I found carbon copies of Lang's text—written daily in Rommel's own language and submitted to him for approval—at Lang's home in Schwäbisch Gmünd and in Charleston, South Carolina; I have deposited them in IFZ, SI. The last entry is June 8, 1944.

Further appendixes of the Army Group B diary are in CO files AL.1532/7 and AL.1697/3. I also drew on Heinz Guderian's records (T78/622), and the files of Fremde Heere West [Foreign Armies West] (T78/451), and particularly its daily brief situation reports (BA-MA, H2/266a).

Above Rommel was General von Rundstedt as C in C West. The C in C West files that I relied on include BA-MA, RH 19-IV/8, /9, /10, /11, /27, /31, /33, /35, /39, /88 and /89. Of greatest value are the intelligence records of Meyer-Detring—his invasion summaries filed in /132 and /133, and his records of telephone conversations from June 6, 1944 (/134) and during July 1944 (/142).

Below Rommel were the armies and army corps. I used the war diary of the Fifteenth Army (T312/524) and its appendixes (T312/509, /514 and /516), the war diary of the Seventh Army (T312/1564) and its telephone logs during June 1944 (CO, AL.528/1) and July (AL.973/1) and the war diary of the Fifth Panzer Army, formerly Panzer Group West (AL.1901/1) and its appendixes (T313/420). For the preinvasion period I found useful information in the war diaries and files of these German corps: the Sixty-seventh (T314/1533), the Eighty-first (T314/1589), the Eighty-second (T314/1601) and the Eighty-eighth (T314/1620). Manfred Rommel lent me several files of "Chefsachen"—special top secret items—from his father's papers: original drafts, correspondence with Jodl, Hitler, Schmundt and Keitel. I also read the navy's "Invasion 1944" files (BA-MA, PG/33398, /33399), and made use of the diaries of Vice Admiral Friedrich Ruge, Alfred Jodl, Hans von Salmuth, Karl Koller and lesser officers (I have deposited all in the IFZ).

Rommel's strafing injury on July 17, 1944, led to the final phase of his life. I have listed below the manuscripts among which I investigated his alleged involvement in the plots against Hitler. He is barely mentioned in the Gestapo interrogation reports (T84/19, /20 and /21). I used one entry in the Luftwaffe general Werner Kreipe's diary of August 1944. I was fortunate to obtain from Major Anton Ehrnsperger a folder of notes and statements going back to November 1947, generated by the various postwar attempts to prosecute the—clearly wholly innocent—General Ernst Maisel for the "manslaughter" of Rommel. Maisel was finally acquitted in 1961 (Ehrnsperger accompanied Burgdorf and Maisel to the Rommel home in Herrlingen). Burgdorf committed suicide in May 1945. In his official files is a folder on the preparations for Rommel's funeral (T78/41) and the funeral program (T84/277).

## MANUSCRIPTS AND ARTICLES

ALDINGER, HERRMANN. *"Mit General der Panzertruppen Rommel unterwegs." Der Gebirgler,* July 1941.

ARNIM, HANS-JÜRGEN. Papers. BA-MA, N61/4, parts I, II, III; N61/5, parts IV, V, VI.

————. Answers to questionnaire, 1951. OCMH, MS C-094.

ASSMANN, HEINZ. Telexes from Führer's war conferences. BA-MA, PG/32121.

BARGATZKY, WALTER. "Memoirs of 20 July 1944 in France." October 20, 1945. Hoover Library, Palo Alto.

BARSEWISCH, K. H. "My Political Attitude." July 15, 1945. IFZ, SI.

BAYERLEIN, FRITZ. Interrogation, February 8, 1946. OI-IIR 29.

————. "Panzer Lehr Division." OCMH, MS ETHINT 66.

————. Answers to questionnaire, October 18, 1947. OCMH, MS T-3.

BERNDT, ALFRED. *"27 Monate Kampf in Afrika."* Broadcast script, May 22, 1943. Rommel Papers.

BLUMENTRITT, GÜNTHER. "German Soldier Morale." OCMH, MS B-338.

————. Remarks to a British army officer, June 7, 1945. CSDIC report SRGG 129 C.

————. Manuscript, England, January 1946. IFZ, ZS 208/I.

————. "Chain of Command in the West." OCMH, MS C-069a.

————. "OB West and the Normandy Campaign."

OCMH, MS ETHINT 73.

―――. U.S. Fifth Corps Operations Plan. OCMH, MS B-637.

BÖTTCHER, ALBERT. Shorthand pad. BA-MA H 48/3.

―――. Shorthand pad. NA, Microfilm T84/259.

BRINK, REINHARD. Statement, July 20, 1944. September 4, 1945. IFZ, SI.

BUTTLAR, HORST VON. Answers to questionnaire. OCMH, MS C-069c.

CARACCIOLO, MARIO. Memoirs of general commanding Fifth Italian Army, summer 1943. NA film T84/187.

CORDIER, SHERWOOD S. "Erwin Rommel As Military Commander: The Decisive Years, 1940–42." Ph.D. dissertation, University of Minnesota, 1963.

―――. "Panzers in the Desert: The Afrika Korps Wins the First Battle of Sidi Rezegh." *Armor,* July-August 1962.

―――. "Rommel's Greatest Triumph–The Gazala Campaign, 1942." *Armor,* May-June 1963.

CREVELD, M. VAN. "Rommel's Supply Problem, 1941–42." *Royal United Services Institution Journal,* September 1974.

D'AGOSTINI, BRUNO. "With General Rommel at the Tobruk Front." *Il Messagero,* May 25, 1941.

DAVIS, RICHARD A. "On a Road in Normandy, 17 July 1944." *Surgery, Gynecology & Obstetrics,* 1961, pp. 242–54.

DIETRICH, SEPP. Interrogations, June 1, 1945, June 11, 1945, and June 14, 1945. PW 13/SAIC/11, SAIC/43, SAIC/46.

EBERBACH, HANS. Manuscripts. IFZ, ZS 30.

―――. Remarks to Blumentritt, August 19, 1945. CSDIC report GRGG 1347.

―――. Letter to Dr. E. Klink. MGFA, April 11, 1967.

ESCH, UDO VON. Interrogation by OCMH, October 28, 1945.

ESEBECK, HANNS-GERT VON. *"Der Marschall."* Essay, July 17, 1944. BA-MA, N 105/1.

FALKENHAUSEN, ALEXANDER VON. "Memoirs 1922–1945." OCMH, MS B-289.

―――. Letter to General Geyr, January 14, 1961. IFZ, ED.91/12.

FALKENHAUSEN, GOTTHARD VON. Manuscript. IFZ, ZS-225.

FEUCHTINGER, EDGAR. "Twenty-first Panzer Division." OCMH, MS B-441.

FRANZ, ERNEST. *"An Rommels Seite: Nach Tagebuchnotizen." Der Frontsoldat erzählt*, 1954, pp. 25ff.

GAUSE, ALFRED. *"Die Führungsmethoden Rommels in Afrika."* June 1957. IFZ, SI.

———. Article in *Armor*, July–August 1958.

———. *"Der Feldzug in Nordafrika im Jahre 1941." WR*, 1962, pp. 594–618.

———. *"Der Feldzug in Nordafrika im Jahre 1942." WR*, 1962, pp. 652–73.

———. *"Der Feldzug in Nordafrika im Jahre 1943." WR*, 1962, pp. 720–28.

GERSDORFF, RUDOLF VON. "Anti-invasion Preparations." OCMH, MS B-122.

———. Confidential manuscript on attempts to win Rommel for the conspiracy. IFZ, ZS-47/II.

GEYR, LEO VON. "Panzer Tactics in Normandy." OCMH, MS ETHINT 13.

———. "Panzer Group West." OCMH, MS B-466.

———. Papers. IFZ, ED 91.

———. Letter in *Süddeutsche Zeitung*, September 4, 1960.

———. *"Zu Problemen der Invasion von 1944." Die Welt als Geschichte*, 1962, pp. 79–87.

———. *"Vor 20 Jahren begann die Invasion." Rundschau am Sonntag*, June 7, 1964.

GUDERIAN, HEINZ. "Panzer Employment, Western Front." OCMH, MS ETHINT 39.

HALDER, FRANZ. Letter to W. James, April 30, 1963. The Citadel.

HAMMERSTEIN, KUNRAT VON. Extract from memoirs. IFZ, ED 91/16.

HENNES, LUDWIG. *"Wettfahrt mit dem Tode um Rommels Leben zu retten."* Typescript. IFZ, SI.

HESSE, KURT. Papers. BA-MA, N 558.

———. *"Wandlung eines Mannes und eines Typus, Feldmarschall Erwin Rommel."* IFZ, SI.

———. *"Die Niederlage in Frankreich, 1944."* BA-MA, N558/77.

HEYDTE, BARON VON DER. Letter in *Süddeutsche Zeitung,* June 19, 1960.

HOLTZENDORFF, HANS-HENNING VON. "Reasons for Rommel's Successes in Africa, 1941–42." OCMH, MS D-024.

JAMES, W. Papers. The Citadel.

JODL, ALFRED. "U.S. Operations." July 31, 1945. OCMH, ETHINT 52.

———. Nuremberg pretrial interrogation, October 2, 1945.

KAISER, HERMANN. Diary, 1943. OCMH, MS B 285. With interpolations by Guderian. IFZ, SI.

KEITEL, WILHELM. Interrogation by U.S. Strategic Bombing Survey, June 27, 1945.

———. Nuremberg pretrial interrogations, August 30 and September 28, 1945.

———. Papers. BA-MA, N54/70.

KESSELRING, ALBERT. "Special Report on Events in Italy, July-September 1943." OCMH, MS C-013.

———. Interrogation, September 8, 1945. OCMH.

———. *"Ereignisse um den 22.2.1943 in Tunesien, 10 September 1949."* OCMH, MS C-066.

KIESSEL, GEORG. Manuscript, August 6, 1946. IFZ, SI.

KIRCHHEIM, HEINRICH. Letter to Hans Speidel, August 18, 1945; affidavit for Guderian, September 16, 1947; letter to Heinz-Günther Guderian, October 23, 1965. IFZ, SI.

KOCH, LUTZ. *"Rommel, wie er wirklich war."* Deutsche Soldatenzeitung, September 11, 1952.

KRAUSE, FRITZ. *"The Mareth Line."* April 5, 1947. OCMH, MS D-012.

KRAUSNICK, HELMUT. *"Erwin Rommel und der deutsche Widerstand gegen Hitler."* VFZ, 1953, pp. 65–70.

KRIEBEL, RAINER. *"Feldzug in Nordafrika 1941/43."* OCMH, MS T-3.

LANG, HELMUTH. "Report on Rommel's injury, July 17, 1944." IFZ, SI.

———. Affidavit for Sepp Dietrich, May 27, 1950. IFZ, SI.

LEBRAM, HANS. *"Kritische Analyse der Artillerie des Atlantikwalles."* MR, 1955, pp. 29–38.

MEISE, WILHELM. Letter to W. James, March 21, 1964. The Citadel.

MELLENTHIN, FRIEDRICH VON. "Reasons for Rommel's Success in Africa 1941/42." OCMH, MS D-084.

————. "Panzer Army Africa's Pursuit to El Alamein." OCMH, MS D-171.

MEYER, HUBERT. "*12.SS Panzer Division Hitler Jugend Juni bis September 1944.*" OCMH, MS P-164.

MICHAELIS, KLAUS. "*Dr. Karl Strölin, Oberbergürmeister der Stadt Stuttgart von 1933–1945.*" IFZ, MS 128.

MICHEL, ELMAR. Manuscript. IFZ, ZS-272.

MONTGOMERY, THE VISCOUNT OF ALAMEIN. "Operations in North-West Europe from 6th June 1944 to 5th May 1945 (Despatch of June 1st, 1946)." *London Gazette,* September 3, 1946.

MÜLLER-GEBHARD, PHILIP. "*Afrika Korps.*" OCMH, MS D-006.

MUTH, HEINRICH. "*Bemerkungen zum Rommelfilm.*" *Geschichte in Wissenschaft und Unterricht,* 1952, pp. 671/75.

*Observer, The.* "Rommel." Profile. July 5, 1942.

PATTON, GEORGE S. "Operation Crusader." *Armor,* May-June 1958.

PEMSEL, MAX. "Preparations for Invasion." OCMH, MS B-234.

————. "U.S. Fifth Corps Operations Plan." OCMH, MS B-656.

————. Letter to W. James, January 9, 1968. The Citadel.

————. Article in *Die Gebirgstruppe,* No. 4, 1974.

————. "Generaloberst Friedrich Dollmann. Zu seinem 30. Todestage." Article in *Deutsches Soldatenjahrbuch,* 1974.

REISSMANN, WERNER. "*Krise und Gegenstoss in der Wüste.*" OCMH, MS B 149/51.

RINTELEN, ENNO VON. "The German-Italian Cooperation during World War II." OCMH, MS B 495.

ROHWER, JÜRGEN. "*Der Nachschubverkehr zwischen Italien und Libyen vom Juni 1940 bis Januar 1943.*" *MR,* 1959, 105.

ROMMEL, ERWIN. Letter to General Otto Hitzfeld, May 27, 1944. BA-MA, N558/77.

————. Letter to Adolf Hitler, October 1, 1944. Pencil draft in possession of Hellmuth Lang.

ROMMEL, LUCIE. Statements, Stuttgart, September 9, 1945, about General Hans Speidel and American looting of Rommel possessions. BA-MA, N558/77.

————. Letter to Karl Strölin, August 10, 1947. IFZ, ZS 588.

————. Letters to Erwin Rommel. Restricted. NA, T84/R273.

ROMMEL, MANFRED. Declaration, Riedlingen, April 27, 1945.

————. Letter to General Ulrich de Maizière, December 2, 1971.

————. Foreword to Warren Tute, *North African War*. London, 1975.

RUGE, FRIEDRICH. *"Küstenverteidigung und Invasion."* Written 1946/47. MGFA.

RUNDSTEDT, GERD VON. Answers to questionnaire. OCMH, MS C-069f.

SCHROEDER, ULRICH. Papers, 1939–40. BA-MA, N 20/2.

SCHWERIN, GERHARD VON. "116th Panzer Division in Normandy." OCMH, MS ETHINT 17.

SPEIDEL, HANS. *"Zur Vorgeschichte des 20. Juli 1944."* 1947. OCMH, MS B-721.

————. *"Generalfeldmarschall Rommels Führung, Vorbereitungen zur Rettung des Reiches und Ende 1944."* Undated draft typescript. IFZ, SI.

————. Earlier draft of above typescript, ca. 1946. IFZ, SI.

————. *"Gedanken Rommels über die Abwehr und die Operationen im Westen 1944 und Betrachtungen."* March 31, 1947. OCMH, MS B-720.

————. *"Beurteilung der Westlage vor der Invasion."* 1948. OCMH, MS C-017.

————. Note on conversation with General Geyr. April 5, 1952. The Citadel.

————. Letter to Lutz Koch, October 21, 1946. IFZ, SI.

————. Affidavit for Dr. Karl Strölin, 1948. IFZ, ZS 579/I.

STAUBWASSER, ANTON. Affidavit for Dr. Laternser, July 1946. IFZ, SI.

————. *"Die Feindbeurteilung durch Heeresgruppe B vor der Invasion."* October 1, 1947. OCMH, MS B-675.

————. *"Die Alarm-Frage in der Invasions-Nacht (5./6. Juni 1944)."* December 1947.

STREICH, JOHANNES. *"Erinnerungen an Afrika."* Unpublished lecture notes. IFZ, SI.

"TEICHMANN, BARON VON." *"Bericht über eine Besprechung mit den Generälen Beck und Stülpnagel."* Zurich, May 17, 1944. IFZ, F 86.

TEMPLEHOFF, HANS-GEORG VON. Operations file, 1944. CO, AL 510.

————. Papers. BA-MA, N 105/1.

TEUCHERT, FRIEDRICH VON. Manuscript. IFZ, ZS-309.

VAERST, GUSTAV VON. *"Vormarsch und Angriff eines Panzer-Regiments in der Wüste, 26./27. Mai 1942."* OCMH, P-149.

————. "Fifteenth Panzer Division." OCMH, MS D-083.

VOIGTSBERGER, HEINRICH. "116th Panzer Division (6 June–12 August 1944)." OCMH, MS B-O17.

WARLIMONT, WALTER. Answers to questionnaire. OCMH, MS C-069e.

————. *"Die Stellung des deutschen Offizier-Corps zur politischen Führung nach 1933."* July 27, 1945. OCMH.

————. *"Die Insel Malta in der Mittelmeer-Strategie des Zweiten Weltkriegs."* WR, 1958, pp. 421–36.

WEICHOLD, EBERHARD. *"Die deutsche Führung und das Mittelmeer unter dem Blickwinkel der Seestrategie."* WR, 1959, pp. 164–76.

————. Letter to Kurt Hesse. BA-MA, N 558/133.

*Welt, Die.* News item dated November 23, 1948.

WERNER, THEODOR. *"Der General."* Schwäbische Zeitung, April 5, 1941.

WESTPHAL, SIEGFRIED. Interrogation, August 29, 1945. PIR AIC 1828.

————. Interrogated by Walter Rapp, June 9, 1947. NA, Record Group 238.

————. Answers to questionnaire. October 15, 1947. OCMH, MS T-3.

YOUNG, DESMOND. Letter to *Picture Post* magazine, April 8, 1950.

ZIEGELMANN, FRITZ. "Capture of U.S. Fifth Corps Operations Plan on 7 June 1944." OCMH, MS B-636.

ZIMMERMANN, BODO. Answers to questionnaire. OCMH, MS C-069d.

# BOOKS

ABERGER, HEINZ-DIETRICH, and TAYSEN, ADALBERT VON. *Nur ein Bataillon.* Essen, 1972.

ABETZ, OTTO. *Das offene Problem.* Cologne, 1951.

AGAR-HAMILTON, J. A., TURNER, L. C. F. *The Sidi Rezegh Battles, 1941.* London and New York, 1957.

ALEXANDER, THE EARL. *The Alexander Memoirs, 1940–1945.* London, 1962.

AUCHINLECK, SIR CLAUDE. *Despatch: Operations in the Middle East,* London, 1948.

BARNETT, CORRELLI. *The Desert Generals.* London, 1960.

BAUM, WALTER, and WEICHOLD, EBERHARD. *Der Krieg der Achsenmächte im Mittelmeer-Raum.* Göttingen, 1973.

BENDER, ROGER JAMES, and LAW, RICHARD D. *Uniforms, Organization and History of the Afrika Korps.* Mountain View, Calif., 1973.

BERGOT, ERWAN. *The Afrika Korps: The Corps d'Elite.* Paris, 1976.

BERNOTTI, R. *Storia della guerra nel Mediterraneo.* Rome, 1960.

BHARUCHA, P. C. *The North African Campaign 1941–43.* London, 1956.

BLUMENSON, MARTIN. *Rommel's Last Victory.* London, 1968.

BLUMENTRITT, GÜNTHER. *Von Rundstedt.* London, 1952.

BRAGADIN, M. A. *The Italian Navy in World War II.* Annapolis, 1957.

BRYANT, SIR ARTHUR. *The Turn of the Tide,* 2 vols. London, 1957–59.

BUTCHER, HARRY C. *My Three Years with Eisenhower.* New York, 1946.

CACCIA-DOMINIONI, PAOLO. *Alamein, 1933–1962.* London, 1966.

CARVER, SIR MICHAEL. *El Alamein*. London, 1962.

————. *Tobruk*. London, 1964.

CAVALLERO, UGO. *Comando Supremo. Diario 1940–43 del Capo di S. M. G.* Rocca Casciano, 1948.

CHURCHILL, SIR WINSTON. *The Second World War*. 6 vols. London, 1948–54.

CIANO, COUNT GALEAZZO. *Diary, 1939–1943*. London, 1946.

CLIFFORD, ALEXANDER. *Three against Rommel*. London, 1943.

CLIFTON, GEORGE. *The Happy Hunted*. London, 1952.

COCCHIA, ALDO. *La Guerra nel Mediterraneo–La Difesa del Traffico coll' Africa Settentrionale*. Rome, 1958.

CONNELL, JOHN. *Auchinleck*. London, 1959.

————. *Wavell*. London, 1964.

DE GUINGAND, SIR FRANCIS. *Operation Victory*. London, 1963.

EHRMAN, JOHN. *Grand Strategy*. Vols. V–VI. London, 1956–58.

EISENHOWER, DWIGHT D. *Report by the Supreme Commander of the Combined Chiefs of Staff on the Operations in Europe of the Allied Expeditionary Force 6 June 1944 to 8 May 1945*. London, 1946.

————. *Crusade in Europe*. New York and London, 1949.

ESEBECK, HANNS-GERT VON. *Afrikanische Schicksalsjahre: Geschichte des deutschen Afrika Korps unter Rommel*. Wiesbaden, 1949.

GOEBBELS, JOSEPH. *The Goebbels Diaries*. London, 1946.

GUDERIAN, HEINZ. *Panzer Leader*. London, 1952.

————. *Erinnerungen eines Soldaten*. Neckargemünd, 1960.

HALDER, FRANZ. *Kriegstagebuch*. 3 vols. Stuttgart, 1963–64.

HAUSSER, PAUL. *Waffen-SS im Einsatz*. Göttingen, 1953.

HAYN, FRIEDRICH. *Die Invasion: Von Cotentin bis Falaise*. Heidelberg, 1954.

HECKMANN, WOLF. *Rommels Krieg in Afrika*. Bergisch Gladbach, 1976.

HEIBER, HELMUT, ed. *Hitlers Lagebesprechungen*. Stuttgart, 1962.

HOFFMANN, PETER. *Widerstand, Staatsstreich, Attentat*. Munich, 1970.

HOWARD, MICHAEL. *The Mediterranean Strategy in the Second World War*. London, 1968.

HOWE, GEORGE F. *U.S. Army in World War II*. *Washington, passim*.

HUBATSCH, WALTHER, ed. *Hitlers Weisungen für die Kriegführung 1939–1945*. Frankfurt, 1962.

IRVING, DAVID. *The Rise and Fall of the Luftwaffe*. London and New York, 1973.

———. *Hitler's War*. London and New York, 1977.

JÄCKEL, EBERHARD. *Frankreich in Hitlers Europa*. Stuttgart, 1966.

JACOBSEN, OTTO. *Erich Marcks, Soldat und Gelehrter*. Göttingen, 1971.

JÜNGER, ERNST. *Strahlungen*. Tübingen, 1949.

KAY, ROBIN. *Chronology: New Zealand in the War 1939–1946*. Wellington, 1968.

KESSELRING, ALBERT. *Soldat bis zum letzten Tag*. Bonn, 1953.

KIPPENBERGER, SIR HOWARD. *Infantry Brigadier*. Oxford, 1949.

KOCH, LUTZ. *Erwin Rommel: Die Wandlung eines grossen Soldaten*. Stuttgart, 1950.

LEWIN, RONALD. *Rommel As Military Commander*. London, 1968.

———. *The Life and Death of the Afrika Korps*. London, 1977.

LICHEM, HEINZ VON. *Rommel 1917*. Munich, 1976.

LIDDELL HART, SIR BASIL. *The Other Side of the Hill*. London, 1951.

———. *The Tanks*. 2 vols. London, 1959.

LONG, GAVIN. *To Benghazi*. Canberra, 1952.

MACDONALD, J. F. *The War History of Southern Rhodesia 1939–1945*. Vol. I. Salisbury, 1947.

MAJDALANY, FRED. *The Battle of El Alamein*. London, 1965.

MANZETTI, FERRUCCIO. *Seconda Offensiva Britannica in Africa Settentrionale e ripiegamento Italo-Tedesco nella Sirtica Orientale, 18 Novembre 1941–17 Gennaio 1942*. Rome, 1949.

MARAVIGNA, PIETRO. *Come abbiamo perduto la Guerra in Africa*. Rome, 1949.

MAUGHAN, BARTON. *Tobruk and El Alamein*. Adelaide, 1966.

MELLENTHIN, FRIEDRICH WILHELM VON. *Panzer Battles, 1939–1945*. London, 1955.

MOLL, OTTO E. *Die deutschen Generalfeldmarschälle 1935–1945*. Baden, 1951.

MÖLLER, HANNS. *Geschichte der Ritter des Ordens "pour le mérite" im Weltkrieg*. Berlin, 1935.

MONTGOMERY, THE VISCOUNT OF ALAMEIN. *Memoirs*. London, 1958.

MURPHY, W. E. *The Relief of Tobruk*. Wellington, 1961.

PLAYFAIR, I. S. O. *The Mediterranean and the Middle East*. 4 vols. London, 1956–1966.

REILE, OSKAR. *Geheime Westfront*. Munich, 1962.

RINTELEN, ENNO VON. *Mussolini als Bundesgenosse*. Tübingen and Stuttgart, 1951.

ROMMEL, ERWIN. *Krieg ohne Hass*. Heidenheim, 1950.

———. *The Rommel Papers*. Edited by B. H. Liddell Hart. London, 1953.

RUGE, FRIEDRICH. *Rommel und die Invasion*. Stuttgart, 1959.

SCHMIDT, HEINZ WERNER. *With Rommel in the Desert*. Durban, 1950.

SCHRAMM, WILHELM VON. *Rommel–Schicksal eines Deutschen*. Munich, 1949.

———. *Der 20.Juli in Paris*. Bad Wörishofen, 1953.

SIEBERT, FERDINAND. *Italiens Weg in den Zweiten Weltkrieg*. Frankfurt, 1962.

SPEIDEL, HANS. *Invasion 1944*. Tübingen and Stuttgart, 1949.

STRÖLIN, KARL. *Verräter oder Patrioten? Der 20.Juli 1944 und das Recht auf Widerstand*. Stuttgart, 1952.

TAYSEN, ADALBERT VON. *Tobruk 1941: Der Kampf in Nordafrika*. Freiburg, 1976.

VERNEY, G. L. *The Desert Rats*. London, 1954.

WAVELL, SIR ARCHIBALD P. *Despatch: Operations in the Middle East from 7th February 1941 to 15th July 1941*. London, 1946.

WESTPHAL, SIEGFRIED. *Heer in Fesseln*. Bonn, 1950.

———. *Erinnerungen*. Mainz, 1975.

WILMOT, CHESTER. *Tobruk 1941*. Sydney, 1945.

———. *The Struggle for Europe*. London, 1952.

WINTERBOTHAM, FREDERICK. *The Ultra Secret*. London, 1974.

YOUNG, DESMOND. *Rommel*. London, 1950.

ZANUSSI, GIACOMO. *Guerra e catastrofe d'Italia*. Rome, 1948.

# Index

# INDEX

Army Group B (*continued*)
  Rommel as commander of,
    350
  war diary of, 364, 377, 390,
    442, 475
  war diary omissions of, 433,
    436, 439-40, 503-504
Arnim, Hans-Jürgen von, 303,
  307, 308, 311, 320-44 *passim*
Arras, 60, 62, 67
"Atlantic Wall," 374, 520
  *see also* English Channel coast
  defenses
Auchinleck, Claude, 7, 226, 228,
  229, 230, 237, 239
Augustin, Colonel, 149
Australian forces:
  in Egypt, 234, 237, 267, 270
  in Libya, 88, 97, 105, 112,
    122, 216
Austria:
  annexation of, 39
  in World War I, 17-18
Avesnes, 56-57
Avranchees, U.S breakthrough
  at, 516
Axis Operation, 363-64, 367

Bab el Qattara, 233
Bach, Wilhelm, 126-28, 166
Badoglio, Pietro, 352-53, 354,
  364, 365, 370
Bad Polzin, 41-42
Balbo, Italo, 79
Baldassare, General, 226
Balkans, 368, 537
  German invasion of, 89
Bannerman, Alistair, diary of,
  425-31, 470
Barbarossa, 111, 131, 134
  *see also* Soviet Union
Barbasetti, Curio, 196, 268, 273
Bardia, 76, 101, 109, 117, 163,
  168-70, 175, 177, 181, 183,
  216, 225
Bargatsky, Walter, 454, 489
Barsewisch, Karl, 490
Barthel, Major, 138
Bastico, Ettore, 134-36, 138, 143-
  44, 148-49, 175-76, 179-80,
  183, 186, 226, 236, 239,
  292-312 *passim*
Battleaxe operation, 125
Bayer, Lieutenant, 15
Bayerlein, Fritz, 141, 151, 157,
  160, 170, 171, 186, 188,
  197, 206, 209, 212, 220,
  221, 249, 250, 262, 268,

276, 278, 280-81, 304, 308,
  313, 351, 419, 452, 471, 485
Bayeux, 448-49, 451, 470-71
bazookas, 494, 509
BBC, 157, 301, 453
  secret codes transmitted by,
    433-35, 436-37
BDM (League of German
  Maidens), 409-10
Beck, Ludwig, 417, 456, 458,
  505, 515
Beda Littori, 137-39, 141, 150
Behrendt, Hans-Otto, 79, 93, 96,
  233
Béja, 332, 333-34
Belgium:
  anticipated invasion of
    (1944), 379-80, 382-83, 385,
    402, 453
  invasion of (1940), 46-47, 52-
    54, 67
Belhamed hill, 157-58, 168, 173,
  215
Below, Nicolaus von, 18, 19, 20,
  396
Ben Gania, 88, 91, 92
Benghazi, 88-89, 97, 110, 112,
  146, 175, 188, 189, 193, 223,
  285, 289-90
  British occupation of (1941),
    181
  German recapture of, 189-90
Beni Zelten, 317
Beresford-Peirse, Noel, 125, 128
Berlin, fire raids on, 362
*Berliner Börsenzeitung*, 229
Berndt, Alfred, 121, 122, 130,
  165, 189, 209, 216-17, 220,
  226, 232, 233, 242-43, 256,
  259, 276, 278, 279, 283-84,
  287, 288, 293, 295, 296,
  308, 310, 314-15, 317, 323,
  325, 331, 339, 346-47, 362
Beta Operation, 196, 217-20
Beumelberg, Werner, 424
Bevan, Aneurin, 228
Bir el Gubi, 88, 156, 160, 161
Bir Hacheim, 88, 194, 202, 208
  German attack on, 209-14
Bir Lefa, 204
Bir Tengeder, 88
Biscay coast, German defenses
  on, 392, 402, 414
Bismarck, Georg von, 191-92,
  202, 215, 218, 219, 222,
  233, 235, 237-38, 248, 249
*Bismarck*, 248
Bitossi, Gervasio, 304
Bizerta, 134, 135, 296, 338

562

# INDEX

# INDEX

# THE INTERNATIONAL BESTSELLER!

# KG 200

## J. D. GILMAN
## AND
## JOHN CLIVE

A Luftwaffe squadron that spoke perfect English.
If they'd succeeded, we'd all be speaking perfect German.

"This novel of aerial assassination, inspired
by actual historical events, booms right along to
an explosive finale."
*Publishers Weekly*

"Masterful ... the implications are spine-chilling."
*The Denver Post*

### Selected by 2 Book Clubs

Avon    39115/$2.25

**KG 9-78**